Effective Criminal Defence in Europe

Ed Cape
Zaza Namoradze
Roger Smith
Taru Spronken

Effective Criminal Defence in Europe

Criminal Justice 2007

With financial support from Criminal Justice Programme
European Commission – Directorate-General Justice,
Freedom and Security

With financial support from Open Society
Institute

Ius Commune Europaeum

Ed Cape
Zaza Namoradze
Roger Smith
Taru Spronken

Effective Criminal Defence in Europe

ISBN 978-94-000-0093-3
D/2010/7849/85
NUR 824

© 2010 Intersentia
Antwerp – Oxford – Portland
www.intersentia.com

Cover photograph © Peter Kirillov - © Tom_u - Dreamstime.com

PREFACE AND ACKNOWLEDGEMENTS

This book is based on a research project, 'Effective defence rights in the EU and access to justice: investigating and promoting best practice', which was conducted over a three year period commencing in September 2007. The research was funded by an action grant from the EU Justice, Freedom and Security Directorate[1] and by the Open Society Institute. The project could not have been conducted without this generous financial support, for which we are very grateful.

The overall aim of the research project was to explore access to effective defence in criminal proceedings across nine European jurisdictions, but the project team also set out to contribute to effective implementation of the right of suspects and defendants, especially those who lack the means to pay for legal assistance themselves, to real and effective defence. Whilst the European Convention on Human Rights embodies fair trial rights, which include the right to legal assistance in criminal proceedings, the jurisprudence of the European Court of Human Rights demonstrates that many people who are suspected or accused of crime do not, in practice, enjoy such rights. Since the turn of the century a number of attempts have been made within the context of the European Union to establish minimum procedural rights for suspects and defendants but, although receiving widespread support, they met with little success. Ratification of the Lisbon Treaty and the introduction of the Stockholm Programme may, as we explore in this book, signal a change of fortune.

The project was co-ordinated by Professor Taru Spronken of Maastricht University, the Netherlands, working with: Professor Ed Cape of the University of the West of England, Bristol, United Kingdom; Zaza Namoradze, Director of the Open Society Justice Initiative's Budapest office in Hungary; and Roger Smith, Director of JUSTICE, a human rights NGO based in London, United Kingdom. All have current or previous experience as practising lawyers, and have wide knowledge and experience of criminal justice systems in a range of jurisdictions. Ed Cape and Taru Spronken collaborated, together with others, on a previous project funded by the EU under its AGIS programme, concerning the rights of suspects at

---

[1]   Reference No. JLS/2007/JPEN/215.

V

the investigative stage of the criminal process.[2] Taru Spronken has also carried out a number of projects concerned with defence rights and the criminal process in the EU, including studies on procedural rights (Spronken and Attinger 2005, Spronken et al. 2009) and on best practice in relation to an EU-wide letter of rights in criminal proceedings.[3] Zaza Namoradze has directed a large number of projects concerning legal aid reforms, including national legal aid reform initiatives in Lithuania and Bulgaria and was involved in designing and implementing a study on access to justice in nine EU accession countries (Public Interest Law Initiative 2003).[4] Roger Smith has extensive experience of researching and writing on legal aid and methods of delivery of legal services, and the organisation of which he is Director has published extensively on criminal justice and the EU.

A project of this nature inevitably relies on a large number of people. The project team were given considerable assistance by a number of people, including Anna Ogorodova and Morgane Landel (Justice Initiative), Hayley Smith and Rachel Fleetwood (Justice), and Liesbeth Baetens (Maastricht University). All of them played a key role. Steven Freeland (Professor of International Law at the University of Western Sydney, Australia) brought his considerable knowledge, skills and experience to the task of editing the country reports which are set out as chapters in Part II. The in-country researchers, of course, played a crucial role and their names are set out in the respective chapters in Part II. The in-country reviewers also played an important role in providing a critique of, and validating, the data provided by the in-country researchers. The reviewers were: Gert Vermeulen (Belgium), Michael Zander (England and Wales), Jussi Tapani (Finland), Jacqueline Hodgson (France), Thomas Weigend (Germany), Karoly Bard (Hungary), Giulio Illuminati (Italy), Malgarzota Wasek-Wiaderek (Poland) and Asuman Aytekin Inceoglu (Turkey).

In addition, the project advisory team provided valuable guidance, particularly in the early stages of the research. The advisory team included: Marelle Attinger, Karoly Bard, Lee Bridges, Yonko Grozev, Nadejda Hriptievschi, Han Jahae, András Kádár, Valentina Stoeva and Katalin Szarvas.

We thank Yleen Simonis at METRO, the Institute for Transnational Legal Research, at the University of Maastricht, for editing the final text, and extend our gratitude to all of those, both named and unnamed, who have contributed to the research project and the book.

We hope that this book, and the research reported in it, will contribute to a deeper knowledge and understanding of the factors that influence effective criminal defence, and will be a source of inspiration for a more constructive and effective programme of policies and actions within the EU designed to make access to effective criminal defence available to all who need it. The research is to be

---

[2]   Cape, E., Hodgson, J., Prakken, T. & Spronken, T., *Suspects in Europe*, Antwerp: Intersentia, 2007.

[3]   The project, 'EU-wide Letter of Rights in Criminal Proceedings: Towards Best Practice', also funded by the European Union, JLS/2008/JPEN/032, is expected to be finalised in June 2010.

[4]   Public Interest Law Initiative, Forum Report: Access to Justice in Central and Eastern Europe, Budapest: Public Interest Law Initiative, 2003, available at <http://www.pili.org/images/forum_report.pdf>.

presented, and the book launched, at a conference in Brussels on 24 and 25 June 2010, to which are invited many of those who will have responsibility for implementation of defence rights. We trust that this book will provide them with a valuable source of information and analysis. The millions of people who, every year in the EU, are arrested, detained or prosecuted have a right to be dealt with fairly and justly.

May 2010

Ed Cape
Zaza Namoradze
Roger Smith
Taru Spronken

TABLE OF CONTENTS

BIOGRAPHIES

1. Authors

1.1. *Ed Cape*

Ed Cape is Professor Criminal Law and Practice at the University of the West of England, Bristol, UK, where he is Director of the Centre for Legal Research. A former criminal defence lawyer, he has a special interest in criminal justice, criminal procedure, police powers, defence lawyers and access to justice. He is the author of a leading practitioner text, *Defending Suspects at Police Stations* (5th edition, 2006), and is a contributing author of the standard practitioner text, *Blackstone's Criminal Practice* (2010, published annually). He has conducted research both in the UK and elsewhere, and his research publications include *Demand Induced Supply? Identifying Cost Drivers in Criminal Defence Work* (2005), *Evaluation of the Public Defender Service in England and Wales* (2007), and *Suspects in Europe: Procedural rights at the Investigative Stage of the Criminal Process in the European Union* (2007). He is also the co-editor of *Regulating Policing: The Police and Criminal Evidence Act 1984 Past, Present and Future* (2008).

1.2. *Zaza Namoradze*

Zaza Namoradze, Director of the Budapest office of the Open Society Justice Initiative, oversees programs on legal aid reform, access to justice and legal capacity development. He has been engaged with legal aid reforms in several countries, including Lithuania, Georgia, Ukraine, Moldova, Bulgaria, Mongolia, Sierra Leone and Nigeria. He previously served as staff attorney and, later, Deputy Director of OSI's Constitutional and Legal Policy Institute (COLPI), where he designed and oversaw projects in constitutional and judicial reforms, clinical legal education and human rights litigation capacity building throughout the former Soviet Union and Eastern Europe. He has worked for the legal department of the Central Electoral Commission in Georgia and was a member of the State Constitutional Commission. He graduated from Law Faculty of Tbilisi State University, studied in the comparative constitutionalism program of the Central European University and earned an LL.M from the University of Chicago Law School.

1.3.   Roger Smith

Roger Smith is the Director of JUSTICE. His previous appointments include Director of Legal Education and Training at the Law Society (1998-2001); Director of the Legal Action Group (1986-98); Solicitor to the Child Poverty Action Group (1980-86); Director of the West Hampstead Law Centre (1975-79); Solicitor to the Camden Law Centre (1973-75); and Articled Clerk to Allen and Overy (1971-73). He is an Honorary Professor with the University of Kent and a visiting professor at London South Bank University. He is author of various publications, particularly on publicly funded legal services. In June 2008 he was awarded an OBE for services to human rights.

1.4.   Taru Spronken

Taru Spronken is Professor of Criminal Law and Criminal Procedure at Maastricht University and defence lawyer at the *Advocatenpraktijk Universiteit Maastricht*. As both practitioner (since 1979) and academic (since 1987) she is specialised in proceedings before the European Court of Human Rights in Strasbourg. She has a special interest in the role and professional responsibility of defence counsel and has published extensively on defence rights and human rights in criminal proceedings. She is co-editor and author of a leading companion to criminal defence, *Handboek Verdediging* (second edition 2009) that contains many practical, legal and ethical aspects of criminal defence in the Netherlands, as well as international European aspects. In her current research she focuses on the implications of EU cooperation in criminal matters for procedural safeguards in criminal proceedings and the right to fair trial. Her research publications in this field include: *A place of greater safety* (2003); *Procedural Rights in criminal proceedings: Existing Level of Safeguards in the European Union* (2005); *Suspects in Europe: Procedural rights at the Investigative Stage of the Criminal Process in the European Union* (2007); *EU Procedural Rights in Criminal Proceedings* (2009).

2.   Project Team Members

2.1.   Liesbeth Baetens

Liesbeth Baetens is Junior Researcher at the Department of Criminal Law and Criminology of the Law Faculty of the Maastricht University. From May 2009 onwards she assists Professor Taru Spronken in two projects, 'Effective Criminal Defence Rights in Europe' and 'EU-wide: Letter of Rights – Towards Best Practice'. Her research interests include: criminal law, human rights law and humanitarian law. In 2008 – 2009 she was enrolled in the Master's Programme Globalisation and Law at the Maastricht University and graduated cum laude. During her studies she participated in extracurricular activities such as the European Law Moot Court and the International Women's Human Rights Clinic. In 2008, she obtained her Master in Law cum laude from the Catholic University Leuven, Belgium. She also went on exchange to the University of Sydney, Australia.

2.2. Steven Freeland

Steven Freeland is Professor International Law at the University of Western Sydney, Visiting Professor International Law at the University of Copenhagen and Visiting Professional within the Appeals Chamber at the International Criminal Court.

He sits on the Editorial Board of both the *Australian Journal of Human Rights* and the *Australian International Law Journal*, as well as a series of books entitled *Studies in Space Law*. He is also actively involved in the publication of a series of casebooks annotating the jurisprudence of the International Criminal Court, the International Criminal Tribunals for the former Yugoslavia and for Rwanda, the International Criminal Court, the Special Court for Sierra Leone and the Special Panels for Serious Crimes in East Timor.

He has published extensively on various aspects of International Law and has been invited to present conference papers and keynote speeches in Australia, Austria, Belgium, Bulgaria, Canada, China, Denmark, France, Germany, India, Italy, Japan, The Netherlands, New Zealand, Singapore, Spain, Sweden, Turkey, United Kingdom and United States.

2.3. Morgane Landel

Morgane Landel is currently Associate Legal officer for Legal Aid at the Open Society Justice Initiative. She worked for 4 years as a criminal defence lawyer in London where she represented legal aid clients exclusively. She has also worked on war crimes investigations in the Prosecutor's office of Bosnia Herzegovina. She carried out a three months investigation in Colombia and produced a report on abuses linked to the criminal justice system, in particular violations of defendant's rights and failure of the state to investigate allegations of violence and crimes committed by the police and army. She did her undergraduate degree in International Relations at LSE, her professional legal training at the College of Law in London and her LLM at Columbia Law School.

2.4. Anna Ogorodova

Anna Ogorodova is PhD researcher at the Maastricht University, Maastricht, Netherlands. Previously she worked as Associate Legal Officer at Open Society Justice Initiative, law reform program of the Open Society Institute (international private foundation). She was responsible for national criminal justice reform and legal aid projects. Anna holds a law degree from Tomsk State University in Russia and LLM in Human Rights from Central European University in Budapest.

2.5. Hayley Smith

Hayley Smith is research assistant at JUSTICE. Before joining the organisation in 2009, she completed a masters specialising in human rights and international law at University College London. Hayley also holds an undergraduate law degree from the University of Oxford and has worked pro bono to represent individuals in social security tribunals in the UK. Her research areas at JUSTICE have included judicial diversity and human rights. She has assisted the Director of JUSTICE, Roger Smith, in the project 'Effective Criminal Defence Rights in Europe'.

3. Authors and Reviewers Country Reports

3.1. Belgium

3.1.1. Laurens van Puyenbroeck

Laurens van Puyenbroeck studied law at the University of Ghent. He holds a master in European Criminology and European Criminal Justice Systems (Ghent University).

Since 2004 he is defence lawyer at the bar of Ghent. In 2005 he joined the Institute for International Research on Criminal Policy (IRCP) of Ghent University and has in that capacity contributed to various research projects and publications in the field of EU judicial and police cooperation, trafficking in persons, drug policy and procedural rights in criminal proceedings. Since 2006 he is a part-time academic assistant at the Department Criminal Law and Criminology of Ghent University.

3.1.2. Gert Vermeulen

Gert Vermeulen (° 1968, Master of Laws, PhD in Law) is professor criminal law and head of the department criminal law and criminology at Ghent University (Belgium). He is also director of the Institute for International Research on Criminal Policy (IRCP), established within the latter department, and co-director of the Governance of Security (GofS) association research group. He teaches *inter alia* international criminal law, European criminal policy, EU justice and home affairs and European and international institutions and organisations. He has been involved in many dozens research projects, *inter alia* in the field of (international and European) criminal law and policy, in particular police and judicial cooperation in criminal matters, organised crime, terrorism, drug policy, trafficking in human beings, sexual exploitation of children, prostitution, witness protection, human rights, rights of the child, data protection and procedural guarantees. He has widely published in these and other areas (<https://biblio.ugent.be/person/ 801000853051>) and has conducted research or acted as an expert or consultant for the Council of Europe (Pompidou Group, Greco, Expert Group Sexual Exploitation Children, CARDS), the European Commission (Phare/Tacis, Taiex, Stop, Falcone, Hippokrates, Daphne, Agis, Criminal Justice, Prevention of Crime), the Belgian (2001), Dutch (2004), Austrian (2006), Slovenian (2008) and Belgian (2010)

Presidencies of the EU, and the UN (expert group on THB, global report on involvement of transnational organised crime in trafficking in human beings and smuggling of persons).

3.2. *England and Wales*

3.2.1. Michael Zander

Michael Zander, Emeritus Professor, London School of Economics. Author of many books including *The Police and Criminal Evidence Act 1984* (5th ed., 2005) A member of the Royal Commission on Criminal Justice (1991-93) and author of the Royal Commission's main piece of research, *The Crown Court Study*, 1993. Currently a member of the Home Office PACE Strategy Board. Legal Correspondent of The Guardian (1963-88). A frequent broadcaster on radio and television.

3.3. *Finland*

3.3.1. Jussi Tapani

Jussi Tapani is professor criminal law at the university of Turku. He is one of the leading scholars on economic crimes in Scandinavia. In his earlier studies, including the dissertation from 2004, he has studied economic crimes and business activities from various perspectives.

3.3.2. Matti Tolvanen

Matti Tolvanen, professor in Criminal Law and Procedure Law at the University of Eastern Finland. Tolvanen obtained his LL.D. at the University of Turku. Tolvanen has published books, articles and research reports in criminal law, criminal procedure and criminal policy, which are also his main competence areas. He has also frequently given lectures in several domestic and foreign universities and institutes.

3.4. *France*

3.4.1. Pascal Décarpes

Pascal Décarpes, born 1977 in France. Master of Politics & Master of Law. Criminologist at the criminological unit of the Ministry of Justice of Hessen (Germany). PhD student under the direction of Prof. Dünkel, Department of Criminology (Greifswald) & former research assistant and lecturer at the University of Greifswald (Germany). Independent expert by the Directorate General Justice, Freedom and Security (European Commission). Board member of the French Society of Criminology.

3.4.2. Jackie Hodgson

Jackie Hodgson, professor of law at the University of Warwick, has conducted extensive empirical research into the criminal justice systems of France and of England and Wales, looking at the investigation and prosecution of crime (including in terrorist cases) as well as defence issues and the suspect's right to silence. The results of these studies have been published in a number of monographs and articles. She has gone on to extend this comparative work into the EU context, considering the provision of defence rights and the consequences of EU police and judicial co-operation. She has provided expert witness reports in a number of European Arrest Warrant and extradition cases. She currently holds a British Academy/Leverhulme Senior Research Fellowship for her project 'The Metamorphosis of Criminal Procedure in the 21st Century: A Comparative Analysis'.

3.5. *Germany*

3.5.1. Dominik Brodowski

Dominik Brodowski is a senior research assistant at the chair of German, European and international criminal justice, Professor Dr Joachim Vogel, Eberhard Karls Universität Tübingen, Germany. He is a graduate in law of the Eberhard Karls Universität Tübingen, Germany, and of the University of Pennsylvania Law School, USA.

3.5.2. Christoph Burchard

Christoph Burchard is a lecturer (*Akademischer Rat a.Z.*) of German and international criminal justice at the Eberhard Karls Universität Tübingen, Germany. He holds a doctorate in law from the University of Passau, Germany, and a LL.M. from the New York University School of Law, USA.

3.5.3. Nathalie Kotzurek

Nathalie Kotzurek works as research assistant for criminal defence lawyers Professor Dr Gunter Widmaier and Dr Ali B. Norouzi in Karlsruhe, Germany. She is a graduate in law of the Eberhard Karls Universität Tübingen, Germany, and of the Université Paul Cezanne, Aix-en-Provence, France.

3.5.4. Jochen Rauber

Jochen Rauber is research assistant at the chair of German, European and international criminal justice, Professor Dr Joachim Vogel, Eberhard Karls Universität Tübingen.

3.5.5. Joachim Vogel

Joachim Vogel holds the chair for German, European and international criminal justice at Eberhard Karls Universität Tübingen, Germany. He is also a judge at the Higher Regional Court (*Oberlandesgericht*) Stuttgart, Germany.

3.5.6. Thomas Weigend

Thomas Weigend is professor of criminal law and criminal procedure at the University of Köln (Cologne, Germany). He has published several books, including *Anklagepflicht und Ermessen* (1978) and *Deliktsopfer und Strafverfahren* (1989) as well as more than 100 articles in Germany and abroad, mostly on problems of (comparative) criminal procedure and international criminal law. He has been co-editor of *Zeitschrift für die gesamte Strafrechtwissenschaft* since 1988 and a member of the Board of Editors of *Journal of International Criminal Justice* since 2008.

3.6. *Hungary*

3.6.1. Károly Bárd

Károly Bárd is chair of the Human Rights Program of the Central European University (Budapest). He started his career at the Faculty of Law of Eötvös Loránd University Budapest. Between 1990 and 1997 he served as vice-minister and later as deputy state secretary in the Ministry of Justice of the Republic of Hungary. Professor Bárd is a member of the Board of Directors of the European Institute for Crime Prevention and Crime Control affiliated with the United Nations (HEUNI). Currently he serves as Pro-rector for Hungarian and European Union Affairs of the Central European University.

3.6.2. András Kádár

András Kádár is a 37-year old attorney at law. He is the co-chair of the Hungarian Helsinki Committee (HHC), a human rights NGO focusing on – among others – access to justice and defendants' rights. Besides providing representation before domestic and international forums, including the European Court of Human Rights, he has been responsible for the HHC's various projects aimed at reforming Hungary's criminal legal aid system. He was actively involved in the drafting process of Hungary's legal aid law in 2003. He has participated in several conferences and seminars dealing with the issue of defence rights and legal aid, and published a number of articles on the topic.

3.7. Italy

3.7.1. Michele Caianiello

Michele Caianiello (Bologna, 1970), is associate professor in Criminal Procedure, and European & International Criminal Procedure at the University of Bologna, Faculty of Law. He graduated *cum laude* in 1994, with a thesis on the detention pending the proceedings. From 2000, he is *Doctor Juris* in Criminal Procedure, with a thesis on the International Criminal Tribunals. He also lectures in European Criminal Procedure at the LUISS University of Rome. In his academic career he studied the subject of the decision to charge a suspect with a crime, especially the powers recognised by the law to the victims and to the private citizens on this issue. He also conducted a research in the field of Evidence Law in the International Criminal Justice Systems. He is the author of 2 books (*Poteri dei privati nell'esercizio dell'azione penale*, Giappichelli, 2003; *Ammissione della prova e contraddittorio nelle giurisdizioni penali internazionali*, Giappichelli, Torino, 2008). He is a lawyer since 1998, and practiced until 2006, in the field of Criminal Law.

3.7.2. Giulio Illuminati

Giulio Illuminati (Ancona, 1946) is Professor Criminal Procedure at the Faculty of Law of the University of Bologna. He is head of the Department of Law of the University of Bologna, and chief and coordinator of the PhD course in Criminal Law and Procedure. At present he also lectures in Criminal Procedure at the L.U.I.S.S. University *Guido Carli* in Rome. He is member of the Editorial Board of the review *Cassazione penale*. He is member of the Board of the Directors of the series of essays and comments *Procedura penale* published by Giappichelli, Turin. Between 1987 and 1989 he was appointed as member of the Committee, established by the Minister of Justice, for the drafting of the New Code of Criminal Procedure; in 2000, he was member of the Committee for the drafting of the Rules of Procedure and Evidence before the justice of the peace. From July 2006 to December 2008 he has been member of the Ministerial Committee that drafted a Bill of Delegation for the reform of the Code of Criminal Procedure. In June 2009 he taught a course at the National Prosecutors College of the People Republic of China, organized by the China-EU School of Law.

3.8. Poland

3.8.1. Dorris de Vocht

Dorris de Vocht is assistant professor of criminal law and criminal procedure at Maastricht University. She coordinates and teaches courses on criminal (procedure) law at bachelor's and master's level. In 2009 she successfully defended her doctoral dissertation on the right to legal assistance in Polish criminal procedure. Her current research mainly focuses on procedural rights of suspects in criminal proceedings within the European Union.

3.8.2. Małgorzata Wasek-Wiaderek

Małgorzata Wąsek-Wiaderek, (Ph.D. in law from Catholic University of Lublin; LL.M. in European Law at the *Katholieke Universiteit Leuven*), since 2002 associate professor at the John Paul II Catholic University of Lublin (Department of Criminal Procedure, Criminal Executive Law and Forensic Sciences); since 2004 member of the Research and Analyses Office of the Polish Supreme Court.

3.9. Turkey

3.9.1. Asuman Aytekin İnceoğlu

Asuman Aytekin İnceoğlu has studied law at İstanbul University Faculty of Law where she obtained her Bachelor of Laws (LL.B.) degree in 1996. Upon graduation, she has worked at Yarsuvat Law Firm as a trainee. She attended Marmara University Faculty of Law to complete her masters degree in law (LL.M.) in 2000 where she specifically focused on 'presumption of innocence and the right to remain silent'. She subsequently enrolled to the PhD program at Marmara University and obtained her doctorate degree in law in 2006. During her PhD studies, she focused on economic crimes and banking crimes in particular. Dr. İnceoğlu is currently an Assistant Professor at İstanbul Bilgi University Faculty of Law, where she teaches criminal law general and special provisions, criminal law and human rights, banking crimes and introduction to moot court competition. Dr. İnceoğlu is also working on mediation, hate crimes/hate speech and crimes against women on which she is giving seminars and doing international projects, some in collaboration with UN and the Turkish Ministry of Justice.

3.9.2. Idil Elveris

Idil Elveris graduated from Istanbul University School of Law in 1996. She obtained her LLM degree from Tulane University in 1998 and practiced as a lawyer and legal consultant in New York, Kosovo, UK and Istanbul. She joined Istanbul Bilgi University School of Law in 2003 and has pioneered legal clinics in Turkey. Her areas of interest include access to justice, poverty and law, judiciary, justice system and courts. She is currently writing her PHD thesis in the Istanbul Bilgi University Political Science program.

PART I

EFFECTIVE CRIMINAL DEFENCE
IN A EUROPEAN CONTEXT

Ed Cape
Zaza Namoradze
Roger Smith
Taru Spronken

CHAPTER 1 EFFECTIVE CRIMINAL DEFENCE AND FAIR TRIAL

1.   Introduction

Each year millions of people in Europe are arrested or detained by the police or other law enforcement agents. The majority will be citizens of the countries in which they are arrested, but a significant number will be foreign nationals, and a small but growing number will have been arrested under a European Arrest Warrant.[1] For a variety of reasons,[2] no further action will be taken against many of them and their arrest and detention at a police station will comprise their full experience of the criminal justice system. Many other people will be the subject of criminal investigations without being arrested or detained. For those who are prosecuted, a significant proportion will be dealt with by one of the increasingly popular forms of guilty plea or expedited trial procedures, which will often mean that there will be no judicial, or independent, consideration of the strength of the evidence of their guilt or the legality of the procedure. Some will have been enticed to co-operate with such procedures, which have significant economic and other benefits for the state but not necessarily for victims, by the offer or prospect of a swift process, less time in pre-trial detention or a reduced sentence. Many will experience custody, not only at a police station, but also in the form of pre-trial detention or imprisonment which may range from days to years.

The aim of this book, and the project which forms the basis of it, is to contribute to effective implementation of the right of suspects and defendants, especially those who are indigent, to real and effective defence, as part of a process of advancing observance of, and respect for, the rule of law and human rights. More specifically, the aim of the research project is to explore access to effective defence in criminal proceedings across nine European jurisdictions, and to provide empirical information on the extent to which the procedural rights that we identify as being

---

[1]   In 2007, 9,413 European Arrest Warrants (EAW) were issued, and 3,368 people were arrested under an EAW. See Council of the European Union Information Note 10330/08 dated 11 June 2008 on 'Replies to questionnaire on quantitative information on the practical operation of the European Arrest Warrant' – Year 2007.

[2]   For example, because they are innocent or there is insufficient evidence to prosecute them, or because they are subjected to some form of diversion from prosecution.

indispensable for effective criminal defence are provided for in practice. A further aim is to produce a set of monitoring indicators that are relatively simple to use, which may be used to assess effective criminal defence in a range of jurisdictions.[3]

Our approach places the suspect and accused at the centre of our enquiry. In the European context they, of course, have the rights guaranteed by the European Convention on Human Rights (ECHR) and, in particular, the right to liberty under article 5 and the right to fair trial under article 6. Both sets of rights may be understood as being essential to the doing of justice. It is commonplace, after all, to speak of criminal *justice* systems. Justice does not simply involve outcomes, but also processes; it is, or should be, systemic, as the term 'criminal justice system' implies. A person may receive a just outcome but nevertheless feel rightly aggrieved if they have not been dealt with justly. An ultimately successful appeal against conviction, secured on the basis that the absence of legal advice meant that a confession made to a police officer was unreliable, which is determined following months, if not years, in pre-trial detention, is likely to leave the accused resentful and distrustful not just of the police, but of the whole criminal justice apparatus.[4] The importance of regarding justice as being systemic has, in effect, been recognised by the European Court of Human Rights (ECtHR) in its jurisprudence on fair trial. As we explore further, particularly in Chapter 2, the court has held that a trial that, prima facie, is fair in terms of what goes on in the court room may, nevertheless, not be fair as a result of the way in which the investigation has been conducted or the accused treated.[5]

We are not, however, simply concerned with justice or, indeed, fair trial. Our focus is more specific – effective criminal defence as a precondition for effective enjoyment of fair trial guarantees. We take as our starting point article 6 of the ECHR paragraph one of which provides that in the determination of any criminal charge everyone is entitled to a fair and public hearing. This is underpinned by the presumption of innocence in paragraph two, and the article then sets out in paragraph three a number of minimum rights that must be accorded to anyone who is charged with a criminal offence.

Everyone charged with a criminal offence has the following minimum rights:

> a) to be informed promptly, in a language which he understands and in detail, of the nature and cause of the accusation again him;
> b) to have adequate time and facilities for the preparation of his defence;
> c) to defend himself in person or through legal assistance of his own choosing or, if he has not sufficient means to pay for legal assistance, to be given it free when the interests of justice so require;
> d) to examine or have examined witnesses against him and to obtain the attendance and examination of witnesses on his behalf under the same conditions as witnesses against him;

---

[3] It should be noted that we have not sought to deal with the specific issues raised by the regulation and treatment of those suspected or accused of terrorist offences. Most, if not all, of the jurisdictions examined have special rules regulating the investigation and prosecution of terrorist offences, but these take a variety of forms and taking them into account would have significantly increased the complexity of our study.

[4] For the integrative effects of justice, see Tyler 2006.

[5] See, in particular, p. 38-40.

e) to have the free assistance of an interpreter if he cannot understand or speak the language used in court.

We argue that these rights are not only essential to fair trial as an outcome, but are also essential to fair trial when considered in terms of process. This approach derives support from the ECtHR which, in *Al-Khawaja and Tahery* v. *UK*, stated that

> '[a]s minimum rights, the provisions of article 6 § 3 constitute express guarantees and cannot be read… [merely] as illustrations of matters to be taken into account when considering whether a fair trial has been held'.[6]

Furthermore, as the ECtHR stated in *Pishchalnikov* v. *Russia*,

> 'even if the primary purpose of article 6, as far as criminal proceedings are concerned, is to ensure a fair trial by a "tribunal" competent to determine "any criminal charge", it does not follow that article 6 has no application to pre-trial proceedings. Thus, article 6 – especially paragraph 3 – may be relevant before a case is sent for trial if and so far as the fairness of the trial is likely to be seriously prejudiced by an initial failure to comply with its provisions'.[7]

The ECtHR in *Pishchalnikov*, following previous jurisprudence, further reiterated that 'although not absolute, the right of everyone charged with a criminal offence to be effectively defended by a lawyer, assigned officially if need be, is one of the fundamental features of fair trial'.[8] The court was referring to the right to legal assistance under article 6(3)(c), and it accepted that for the right to fair trial to be 'practical and effective' rather than 'theoretical and illusory' article 6 requires that legal assistance should normally be available at the investigative stage. Furthermore, it repeated the long-standing view of the ECtHR that the right to silence and the right not to incriminate oneself reflect international standards that are integral to the right to fair trial.

We develop this approach a stage further. We argue that effective criminal defence is an integral aspect of the right to fair trial, and that it requires not only a right to competent legal assistance but also a legislative and procedural context, and organisational structures, that enable and facilitate effective defence as a crucial element of the right to fair trial. The argument is based on the premise that however good legal assistance is, it will not guarantee fair trial if the other essential elements of fair trial are missing. Thus effective criminal defence has a wider meaning than simply competent legal assistance. It is therefore necessary to approach the assessment of access to effective criminal defence in any particular jurisdiction at three levels:

(a)   Whether there exists a constitutional and legislative structure that adequately provides for criminal defence rights taking ECtHR

---

[6]   ECtHR 20 January 2009, Nos. 26766/05 and 22228/06, § 34.
[7]   ECtHR 24 September 2009, No. 7025/04, § 65.
[8]   At § 66.

jurisprudence, where it is available, as establishing a minimum standard.

(b)   Whether regulations and practices are in place that enable those rights to be 'practical and effective'.

(c)   Whether there exists a consistent level of competence amongst criminal defence lawyers, underpinned by a professional culture that recognises that effective defence is concerned with processes as well as outcomes, and in respect of which the perceptions and experiences of suspects and defendants are central.

In order to provide a baseline for our examination, and assessment, of access to effective criminal defence we explore in Chapter 2 the ECtHR jurisprudence on the rights set out in article 6 ECHR, and also the jurisprudence on articles 5, 8 and 10 ECHR where this concerns the right to release during the pre-trial phase, confidential lawyer/client communication, and freedom of speech in the context of criminal procedure. We examine the extensive jurisprudence on the presumption of innocence, the rights to silence, equality of arms, adversarial trial and pre-trial release as elements that have an overall impact on the position of the accused. We continue with an examination of the right to information and the right to defence and to legal assistance. In addition, we examine the rights that promote effective participation, such as the rights to investigate and to seek exculpatory evidence, to have adequate time and facilities to prepare a defence, to be present at hearings and to question witnesses. We also consider the rights to interpretation and translation, which are essential to effective participation for suspects who do not understand or speak the relevant language. Finally, jurisprudence on the rights to reasoned decisions and to appeal is explored.

We analyse each of the countries in the study by reference to ECtHR jurisprudence and standards in Chapter 12. We recognise, however, that the various rights and standards cannot be considered in isolation from each other. Each has a dynamic relationship with some or all of the other rights. For example, the ability of a defence lawyer to effectively advise his or her client, whether at the investigative or trial stage, will be dependant on the information that is made available to them by the investigating or prosecuting authorities, and the timing of such disclosure. In order to identify the ways in which the rights we have explored relate to each other we have developed an analytical model, the effective criminal defence triangle, which we use to analyse the data relating to the countries in our study. In using this method of analysis we seek to gain insights into the range of factors that either strengthen or weaken access to effective criminal defence, and develop a better understanding of the relationships between them. Our 'triangle analysis' is set out in Chapter 13.

In placing the suspected or accused person at the centre of our enquiries we have been concerned to examine the question of access to effective criminal defence from their perspective. We do so for a number of reasons. First, the focus of the ECtHR on rights being 'real and effective' is an acknowledgement of the fact that although rights may be provided for constitutionally, or in codes or legislation, this does not necessarily mean that such rights are given effect so that they are experienced as rights by those most affected by them. Second, there is a danger that the concerns of those institutions and professionals that have power or 'voice' are heard above those who are the subjects of criminal investigations and proceedings, who have neither organisations to speak on their behalf nor legitimacy in the eyes of either governments or the public. In many jurisdictions the predominant political concern in recent years has been efficient and effective management of the criminal justice process, and the interests of victims of crime. This is exemplified by a motif of criminal justice policy in England and Wales, which describes the purpose of criminal justice policies as being to 'rebalance the system in favour of victims, witnesses and communities'.[9] Third, in those jurisdictions where there are developed systems of legal aid, even when debate moves beyond the issue of whether remuneration rates for lawyers are adequate, attention is rarely paid to the concerns of 'consumers' of legal services.

2. The human rights context

Although we are examining effective criminal defence in a European context, and principally look to the ECtHR as providing a basis for establishing minimum standards for effective criminal defence, normative standards may also be gleaned from a range of international conventions and agreements. Furthermore, developments within Europe and especially in the European Union (EU) have significant implications for criminal defence standards and, as explained below, with the coming into force of the Lisbon Treaty the influence of the EU in this area is set to grow further.

2.1. The global context

The right to fair trial of those accused of a criminal offence is guaranteed by the constitutions, criminal codes or common law in almost every country in the world.[10] As both a consequence and a cause, the right is safeguarded in all major human rights treaties and conventions.[11] Whilst for those European countries which are signatories to the ECHR the convention provides the major source of international fair trial rights, the ECtHR itself frequently makes reference to international standards in particularising fair trial rights.[12] Often cited in the context of criminal defence rights is the Havana Declaration on the Role of Lawyers ('the Havana Declaration'). This was agreed at the 8th UN Congress on the Prevention of Crime

---

[9]   See the government White Paper *Justice for All*, CM 5563, July 2002 (Home Office 2002). Similar phrases have been widely employed in a range of UK government documents throughout this century.

[10] See Cape et al. 2007, p. 10, and Spronken & Attinger 2005, and for a recent affirmation of common law rights in England and Wales see *R* v. *Davis* [2008] UKHL 36.

[11] Art. 14 International Covenant on Civil and Political Rights; Arts. 10 and 11 Universal Declaration of Human Rights; Art. 8 § 2c-e American Convention on Human Rights; Art. 7 § 1c African Charter on Human Rights and Peoples Rights.

[12] See for instance ECtHR 27 November 2008, *Salduz* v. *Turkey*, No. 36391/02, § 32-44 under the heading Relevant International Law Materials.

and the Treatment of Offenders, Havana, Cuba in 1990. It expands the entitlement of a suspect to a lawyer, which is set out in article 14 of the International Covenant on Civil and Political Rights (the equivalent of article 6 of the ECHR), by indicating what states must do to make that entitlement a reality. One of these requirements is that governments must ensure the provision of sufficient funding and other resources for the poor and, as necessary, to other disadvantaged persons.[13]

The international criminal courts that have been established to try, and punish, serious violations of human rights and humanitarian law, such as the International Criminal Court for the former Yugoslavia (ICTY), the Rwanda Tribunal (ICTR) and the International Criminal Court (ICC), apply standards for effective defence that have been developed by the ECtHR and by the UN Human Rights Committee (HRC).[14] The ICC Statute specifically provides that the ICC should apply and interpret the law in accordance with internationally recognized human rights, and develop standards for effective criminal defence that are in accordance with those of the ECtHR and the HRC. A right to be informed 'prior to questioning' of the grounds for suspicion that a person has committed an offence within the jurisdiction of the ICC, and the right of a person to have their lawyer present when they are being questioned when there are grounds to suspect that they have committed a crime within the jurisdiction of the court, is provided for in the ICC Statute.[15] It also acknowledges the right to have a lawyer present during interrogation,[16] and provides that if the right is violated evidence obtained should be excluded at trial.[17] Further, according to the European Committee for the Prevention of Torture and Inhuman or Degrading Treatment or Punishment (CPT), the right to have a lawyer present during police interrogation is one of the fundamental safeguards against ill-treatment of detained persons.[18]

## 2.2.	The EU and procedural rights in criminal proceedings

A relatively new player in the field of procedural rights is the European Union (EU). Since the Maastricht Treaty of 1992, the Amsterdam Treaty of 1997 and the subsequent Conclusions of the Council of Ministers meeting in Tampere, Finland in 1999 (generally known as the Tampere Conclusions[19]), there has been increasing concern for procedural rights in criminal proceedings because the 'area of freedom, security and justice', on the basis of 'judicial co-operation' and 'mutual recognition' of judicial decisions, requires mutual trust and confidence between the Member States of the EU. Divergent standards for suspects' procedural rights in the EU have

---

[13]	Art. 1.3.
[14]	See Tuinstra 2009.
[15]	Art. 55.
[16]	Statute of the International Tribunal for the former Yugoslavia, art. 18 § 3.
[17]	Decision on the Defence Motion to Exclude Evidence ICTY in Zdravko Mucic, 2 September 1997, Case No. IT-96-21-T, Trial Chamber II.
[18]	See Committee for the Prevention of Torture 1992, § 36-38.
[19]	Commission of the European Communities, Presidency Conclusions, Tampere European Council 15 and 16 October 1999, SI (1999).

hitherto hindered the full acceptance of the principle of mutual recognition.[20] Proposals from the European Commission (the Commission) for procedural safeguards for suspects and defendants in criminal proceedings throughout the EU, which passed through various stages (from the green paper ('Green Paper') issued in 2003[21] to draft proposals in 2004[22] ('draft framework decision')), and a German Presidency draft in 2007 ('German Presidency draft'), ultimately failed to obtain consensus.[23]

The proposals aimed to provide a balance between the need to facilitate 'co-operation between authorities and the judicial protection of human rights'.[24] Of prime concern to the Commission were two rights that are also at the centre of the concerns of this project. As the Commission put it in its Green Paper:

> 'Some rights are so fundamental that they should be given priority at this stage. First of all among them is the right to legal advice and assistance. If an accused person has no lawyer, they are less likely to be aware of their rights and therefore to have those rights accepted. The Commission sees this right as the foundation of all other rights. Next, the suspect or defendant must understand what he is accused of and the nature of the proceedings so it is vital for those who do not understand the language of the proceedings to be provided with interpretation of what is said and translation of essential documents.'

In addition to the rights to legal assistance, to translation and interpretation, and to information, the Commission added a right to consular assistance and special protection for vulnerable suspects. Other fair trial rights, specifically those concerning bail and fair procedures for handling evidence, were reserved for separate treatment, the former because it was already the subject-matter of a measure in the mutual recognition programme, and the latter because the subject-matter was so large that it should be covered by a separate programme.[25]

In evidence to a United Kingdom Parliamentary enquiry, the Commission confirmed that the aim of the draft framework decision was 'not to fix new standards but to make the standards of the European Convention on Human Rights more efficient, more concrete, making them more transparent and providing the tools for them to be effectively protected'.[26] The Commission had said in its draft framework decision that its intention was 'not to duplicate what is in the ECHR but rather to promote compliance at a consistent standard'.[27] Eurojust[28] agreed that the issue was not the standards themselves but 'compliance'.[29]

---

[20] See Vernimmen-Van Tiggelen & Surano 2008, and Vernimmen-Van Tiggelen, Surano & Weyembergh 2009.
[21] COM (2003) 75 final.
[22] COM/2004/0328 final.
[23] Of 5th June 2007 10287/07.
[24] See Green Paper § 1.5.
[25] *Ibidem*, § 2.6.
[26] House of Lords 2005, § 16.
[27] Draft Council Framework Decision, COM/2004/0328 final, Explanatory Memorandum, § 9.
[28] A judicial body established by Council Decision 2002/187/JHA to improve the fight against serious crime by facilitating the optimal co-ordination of action for investigations and

→

Ultimately, there was insufficient consensus between member states for these proposals to proceed. However, the issue on which they failed was not their relevance or need but, as the press release for the relevant meeting of the Justice and Home Affairs Council put it, '[t]he dividing line was the question whether the Union was competent to legislate on purely domestic proceedings (at least 21 member states share this view) or whether the legislation should be devoted solely to cross-border cases'.[30]

2.3.   The Lisbon Treaty

The scene has changed considerably since the Treaty of Lisbon entered into force on 1 December 2009.[31] In the field of judicial co-operation in criminal matters the Treaty abolished the pillar structure and the requirement for unanimity that was found in the Third Pillar, and provides for the sharing of decision-making power between the European Parliament and national governments in the Council.[32] The need for unanimity had meant that a small minority of member states were able to prevent the adoption of minimum procedural safeguards for suspects and defendants, and the abolition of the national veto is likely to break the deadlock. In the area of criminal law the Treaty underlines the principle of mutual recognition, requiring a court in one EU country to recognise and enforce a criminal conviction from another.[33] It provides for police cooperation involving all police and specialised law enforcement agencies.[34] This cooperation is to include the collection,

---

prosecutions covering the territory of more than one Member State with full respect for fundamental rights and freedoms.

29 House of Lords 2005, § 17.

30 Press Notice, Justice and Home Affairs Council, 12-13 June 2007.

31 Treaty of Lisbon amending the Treaty on European Union and the Treaty establishing the European Community, signed at Lisbon, 13 December 20072007/C 306/01. For the consolidated versions of the treaties as amended by the Treaty of Lisbon see the Treaty on European Union (TEU) and the Treaty on the Functioning of the European Union (TFEU), No. 2008/C 115/01, Official Journal of the European Union, C 115, Volume 51, 9 May 2008. For Judicial Cooperation in Criminal Matters see Chapter 4 of the Treaty of the Functioning of the European Union (TFEU).

32 There are, however, negotiated exceptions to these general principles. Under the Treaty the presumption is that no new or amending provision in the area of justice and home affairs will apply to UK or Ireland. When a new measure is proposed these countries will have three months to decide whether to opt in to the process. If their opt out from and amending measure would result in the measure becoming inoperable for other member states, the existing measure would no longer be binding or applicable to them. In addition, an EU member state can apply an emergency brake if it feels that the measures proposed will affect fundamental aspects of its criminal justice system. This provision applies both to mutual recognition and to substantive law reform. Once applied, the emergency brake will halt the legislative process whilst the matter is referred to the European Council. The European Council has four months to refer the draft back to the Council of Ministers, thus terminating the suspension. If there is no agreement on referral back then, within the same time frame, if at least nine EU sates want to go ahead with the proposal, they can do so under a procedure called 'enhanced co-operation'.

33 Art. 82 TFEU.

34 Art. 87 TFEU.

storage, processing, analysis and exchange of relevant information. This is likely to impact on the conditions for the availability and admissibility of evidence in cross-border cases. Finally the Treaty allows for the creation of a European Public Prosecutor if all national governments agree to create such an office.[35]

On the eve of the coming into force of the Lisbon Treaty the Swedish Presidency again took up the issue of procedural safeguards by presenting a roadmap for strengthening the procedural rights of suspected and accused persons in criminal proceedings which provides for a step-by-step approach.[36] The first step is to adopt a directive on the right to interpretation and to translation in criminal proceedings, followed by a directive on information on rights (the letter of rights), and a directive on the right to legal advice for both suspects and accused persons.[37] Together with rights to communication, for vulnerable persons and to review of pre-trial detention, these measures are regarded as fundamental, with action on them identified as being a priority. The roadmap was incorporated into the Stockholm Programme for the period 2010-2014,[38] which was adopted by the European Council on 10/11 December 2009. An Action Plan for implementation will be drawn up under the Spanish Presidency, the adoption of which is expected in June 2010.[39] Thus procedural rights are on the EU agenda again, but it is still uncertain how the legislative process will develop and whether the proposed instruments will provide added value in making defence rights standards more concrete and effective.

2.4. The Court of Justice of the European Union and the ECHR

The Lisbon Treaty will also enhance the role of the European Court of Justice (ECJ) in relation to procedural rights. Even before the coming into force of the Lisbon Treaty the ECJ has ruled on defence rights in criminal proceedings,[40] and whilst doing so has often referred to case law of the ECtHR.[41] Following ratification of the Lisbon Treaty the ECJ will play a part, in parallel to the ECtHR, in developing case

---

[35]   Art. 86 TFEU.

[36]   Roadmap with a view to fostering protection of suspected and accused persons in criminal proceedings, 1 July 2009, 11457/09 DROIPEN 53 COPEN 120.

[37]   Proposal for a Directive of the European Parliament and of the Council on the right to interpretation and to translation in criminal proceedings, 9 March 2010 COM(2010) 82 final, 2010/0050 (COD).

[38]   See the Annex to the Presidency note of the Council of the EU 2 December 2009, The Stockholm Programme- an open and secure Europe serving and protecting the citizens, 17024/09, § 2.4. which is scheduled to be presented in June 2010.

[39]   European Council 10/11 December 2009, Conclusions EUCO 6/09.

[40]   See Klip 2009, Part II § 2.2, which contains extensive reference to case law of the ECJ with regard to fair trial and the rights of the defence, the right to be informed of the charge, access to the file, the right to remain silent, the right to privacy and the inviolability of the home, the right to be present and to be represented, free choice of counsel, the lawyer-client privilege, the right to be tried within a reasonable time, the right to an effective remedy, to an independent and impartial tribunal and to a reasoned decision.

[41]   See, for instance, ECJ 26 June 2007, C-305/05, *Ordre des barreaux francophones et germanophone*, *Ordre francais des avocats du barreau de Bruxelles* v. *Conseil des Ministres*, ECR 2007 I-535, § 31, and the *Pupino* case, ECJ 16 June 2005, C-105/03 ECR 2005 I-5285, § 59-60.

law on 'the rights of the individual in criminal proceedings', on which the EU may adopt Directives in accordance with article 82 § 2 of the Treaty on the Functioning of the European Union (TFEU).[42]

Furthermore, the Lisbon Treaty amends article 6 of the TEU to provide for recognition of the Charter of Fundamental Rights, which was originally proclaimed by EU institutions at the Nice Inter-Governmental Conference in December 2000.[43] In the area of civil rights, the Charter expressly sets out the right to a fair trial, the presumption of innocence until proved guilty, and the right not to be punished twice for the same offence. The Charter will thus become legally binding, with the result that the fundamental rights that it contains become operational in respect of EU legislation and in relation to the implementation of EU law in national law. This means that, for the first time, the EU has set out in one place fundamental rights from which every EU citizen can benefit. In addition, article 6 § 3 of the TEU now expressly states that fundamental rights, as guaranteed by the ECHR as they result from the constitutional traditions common to the Member States, shall constitute general principles of the Union's law. Finally, the Lisbon Treaty opens the way to accession of the EU to the ECHR. This will mean that the EU and its institutions will be accountable to the ECtHR in respect of matters governed by the ECHR in the same way that EU Member States are currently bound in respect of domestic matters. As a consequence, EU institutions will be directly subject to the ECHR, and the ECJ will be able to directly apply the ECHR as part of EU law and EU law will have to be interpreted in the light of the ECHR.[44]

2.5. New perspectives on enforcement mechanisms

The inclusion of the area of freedom, security and justice in the legal order of the EU will provide a new perspective on the possibilities for EU citizens, including suspects and defendants in criminal proceedings, to protect their rights because it can be argued that the enforcement obligations of EU Member States, and the EU itself, will also be applicable to the rights that are embodied in the ECHR.

Most important for the purposes of our research is that the TFEU allows for minimum rules to be adopted in relation to the mutual admissibility of evidence, rights of individuals, and victims of crime in criminal matters.[45] Although the

---

[42] See footnote 31. For the text of art. 82 § 2 see footnote 45.

[43] Art. 6 § 1 TEU states 'The Union recognises the rights, freedoms and principles set out in the Charter of Fundamental Rights of the European Union of 7 December 2000, as adapted at Strasbourg, on 12 December 2007, which shall have the same legal value as the Treaties'.

[44] It should be noted that the jurisdiction of the ECJ, with respect to acts adopted before the Lisbon Treaty came into force, does not extend to Justice and Home Affairs for five years (Protocol 36 Article 10) and then, if the UK notifies the Council six months before the end of the period that it does not accept the increased powers, those acts will cease to apply to the UK.

[45] Art. 82 § 2 TFEU that provides: '2. To the extent necessary to facilitate mutual recognition of judgments and judicial decisions and police and judicial cooperation in criminal matters having a cross-border dimension, the European Parliament and the Council may, by means of directives adopted in accordance with the ordinary legislative procedure, establish minimum rules. Such rules shall take into account the differences between the legal traditions

→

competence of the Union to make regulations in this area appears, according to the text of article 82 § 2, b TFEU, to be limited to mutual recognition issues and cross-border cases, the consequences for criminal procedure at the national level should not be underestimated. For example, regulations concerning the rights of individuals in relation to the gathering of evidence for the purposes of the European Evidence Warrant (EAW) can hardly be expected to have an impact only on cross-border cases. Since, in particular, it may not be known at the time that evidence is being gathered that the case will involve the issuing of an EAW, evidence gathering in all cases will have to comply with relevant EU requirements or there will be a risk of non-compliance if an EAW is, in fact, issued in a particular case. Moreover, the ECJ jurisdiction is not bound by article 82 TFEU, which establishes the competence of the EU to issue regulations. Article 6 § 3 of the TEU now expressly states that fundamental rights, as guaranteed by the ECHR as they result from the constitutional traditions common to the Member States, shall constitute general principles of the Union's law. As a result, these principles may also be invoked in domestic proceedings that have no direct cross-border component.

This opens the way to the enforcement mechanisms of the TFEU, which have a different character and impact than the *ex post* complaint procedure of article 34 of the ECHR, and which could be of complementary significance to the Strasbourg enforcement mechanisms. Although the ECHR has brought into being the most effective international system of human rights protection ever developed[46] it is commonly accepted that the ECtHR faces major challenges, especially as regards its case-load[47] but also because of the weakness of the enforcement mechanisms once violations of the convention have been established. Sixty per cent of the cases in which the ECtHR finds violations originate in failures to comply with the ECHR that have already been identified by the court.[48] The EU enforcement mechanisms operate in a different way. Article 267 TFEU provides for the general competence of the ECJ concerning questions of interpretation of the Treaty.[49] In national criminal proceedings every court or tribunal may request the ECJ to give a preliminary ruling on a relevant issue. Where such a question is raised with regard to a person in custody, the ECJ has created a procedure for hearing applications on an urgent

---

and systems of the Member States. They shall concern: (a) mutual admissibility of evidence between Member States; (b) the rights of individuals in criminal procedure; (c) the rights of victims of crime; (d) any other specific aspects of criminal procedure which the Council has identified in advance by a decision; for the adoption of such a decision, the Council shall act unanimously after obtaining the consent of the European Parliament. Adoption of the minimum rules referred to in this § shall not prevent Member States from maintaining or introducing a higher level of protection for individuals.'

[46] See the speech of Mr. Wildhaber, President of the European Court on Human Rights, on the occasion of the opening of the Judicial Year in 2006.

[47] On 1 December 2009 the total number of pending applications was 117,850. See <www.echr.coe.int>.

[48] In 2008 the ECtHR delivered 1,543 judgments of which 23% were classed as importance level 1 or 2. See Annual Report 2008 European Court of Human Rights, p. 67, available at <www.echr.coe.int>.

[49] Before the Lisbon Treaty the ECJ had jurisdiction to make preliminary rulings on the interpretation of Third Pillar legal instruments based on art. 35 TEU. The most notable example is the *Pupino* ruling ECJ 16 June 2005, C-105/03 ECR 2005 I-5285.

basis.[50] Given the changes brought about by the Lisbon Treaty, the ECJ will be required to rule on a preliminary question taking into account both the relevant case law of the ECtHR and the general principles of criminal procedure that the ECJ has independently developed.[51]

In addition, the Commission has the power to bring a case against a member state that it considers has failed to fulfil an obligation under the TEU or TFEU.[52] This will be especially relevant when directives on procedural safeguards have been adopted. A finding that a member state has not fulfilled its obligations under the Treaties requires that state to bring its national legislation into compliance. In addition the Commission may request the ECJ to impose financial penalties if the member state does not comply with Court's judgment.

The Lisbon Treaty came into force towards the end of the research project described in this book. As will be seen in the following chapters, there is significant non-compliance with the fair trial provisions of the ECHR across European jurisdictions, and one of the major conclusions of our study is that it is necessary for the EU to establish minimum rights for suspects and defendants in order to ensure access to effective criminal defence and, ultimately, fair trial. However, as has been sketched out here, the advent of the Lisbon Treaty is likely, even without the adoption of such measures, to have an impact on procedural rights in member states. It will be interesting to see how the ECJ will deal with the challenge to establish the 'rights' component of the area of Freedom, Security and Justice and how its case law will relate to the ever-developing jurisprudence of the ECtHR.[53] It would be much more satisfactory for such developments to take place within the context of a clear, detailed and rational set of safeguards established by the EU.

3.   The research project

The overall aim of the project, as set out earlier, is to contribute to effective implementation of the right of suspects and defendants, especially those who are indigent, to real and effective defence, as part of a process of advancing observance of, and respect for, the rule of law and human rights. The specific research objectives are –

- To define the content and scope of the right to effective criminal defence, and the corresponding state obligations to ensure the 'practical and effective' implementation of this right for suspects and defendants in general, and for those who are indigent in particular.
- To produce a set of monitoring indicators against which national practices can be assessed in order to determine the level of implementation of the

---

[50]   Art. 33-42 Court of Justice Information Note on references from national courts for a preliminary ruling (2009/C 297/01), Journal of the European Union 5 December 2009, C 297/1.

[51]   See Klip 2009, Part II § 2, and Part IV § 10.

[52]   Art. 258 TFEU.

[53]   For two examples of the 'tuning' process of the two European Courts and the process of cross-fertilization see ECtHR 10 February 2009, *Sergey Zolotukhin* v. *Russia* (GC), No. 14939/03 and ECtHR 17 September 2009, *Scoppola* v. *Italy* (GC), No. 10249/03.

right to an effective defence, and as it applies to indigent defendants in particular.

- To develop a methodology for monitoring the implementation of the right to effective defence of criminal suspects and defendants based on the indicators identified which can be used in other jurisdictions to evaluate the extent to which effective defence rights are available in such jurisdictions.

- To conduct a study of effective criminal defence in nine European jurisdictions.

- To disseminate the results of the research, and the monitoring indicators developed in the research, in order to: (a) raise awareness of the level of implementation of suspects' and defendants' rights to effective criminal defence and essential procedural guarantees among government and EU officials, as well as legal professionals and civil society groups, using the example of the monitored states; (b) raise the interest of other groups to take similar initiatives in other countries not covered by the project; (c) raise Governments' and legal professions' interest in engaging in the field; and (d) identify further practical steps for the effective implementation of the right to effective criminal defence of indigent defendants throughout Europe.

The project team conducted an initial study in three EU jurisdictions; Belgium, England and Wales, and Hungary; followed by studies in Italy, France, Germany, Poland, Turkey and Finland. The reason for choosing these jurisdictions was that they constitute examples of the three major legal traditions in Europe; inquisitorial, adversarial and post-state socialist. There is some disagreement amongst comparative lawyers as to whether socialist legal systems constitute a discrete legal tradition.[54] However, Hungary and Poland, in common with other accession states that had formerly been part of the 'Eastern bloc' of nations, had been required to make significant adjustments to their legal systems as a condition of membership of the EU,[55] and we hypothesised that there were likely to be significant differences in terms of access to effective criminal defence as between such jurisdictions and those jurisdictions with an inquisitorial tradition that had not been part of the Eastern bloc. All of the nine jurisdictions in the project, with the exception of Turkey, are members of the EU and include inquisitorial jurisdictions with a Napoleonic tradition (e.g., France and Belgium) and those that have significantly departed from that tradition (e.g., Germany and Italy). Turkey was included as a potential member state of the EU, and which was worthy of study in its own right.

Whatever the legal tradition, many elements of the right to effective defence are not contingent upon the financial resources of the accused. For example, the absence of a right to legal assistance during police interviews affects wealthy and indigent suspects alike. On the other hand, if there is a right to legal assistance, inadequate mechanisms for ensuring that indigent suspects can have access to legal

---

[54] See the discussion and references in Cape et al. 2007, p. 6. Summers has argued that there is one European legal tradition, although Field convincingly disputes this. See Summers 2007, and Field 2009.

[55] See, for example, Open Society Institute 2001, and Open Society Institute 2002.

assistance will result in them being specifically disadvantaged as compared to suspects who can afford to pay for legal assistance. Thus an important focus of the research was the right to effective criminal defence for those suspects and defendants who cannot afford to pay privately for legal services and who are therefore dependent on some form of financial assistance (which may take a variety of forms including state funding or subsidy, pro bono assistance, etc.). The range of jurisdictions chosen for the study was, therefore, also intended to reflect a range of provision of state-funded legal assistance for those suspected or accused of crime.

It is generally accepted that conducting cross-jurisdictional research presents many challenges, and this is particularly so in the case of research that seeks to examine and understand how criminal processes work in practice.[56] Beyond the hurdles of language, different terms may be used to signify similar processes but, more importantly in terms of impeding understanding, similar terms may be used to signify different processes or stages. The terms 'arrest' and 'charge', or even 'criminal offence' must, for example, be treated with care. The ECtHR, of course, has had to develop its own 'autonomous' meanings for many such expressions in order to enable it to apply the ECHR to specific jurisdictional contexts in a way that is consistent.[57] Perhaps more important than terminology, however, is the fact that perceptions of the way in which countries deal with criminals, and those suspected or accused of crime, are often closely linked to perceptions of, and attitudes towards, national identity and concepts of nationhood. Criminal justice systems and processes are pre-eminently a dynamic product of histories and cultures that are highly specific to nations or jurisdictions.[58] One consequence of this is that criminal procedures in foreign jurisdictions are often perceived as being 'strange', if not 'unfair'.[59] Conversely, from within a jurisdiction they are often viewed as 'natural' and in accordance with longstanding norms and values that reflect notions of national character. In many countries, including most that we have examined in this research, this familiarity appears to result in a lack of critical thinking, and critical research. Most criminal processes and procedures in most of the jurisdictions in the study have simply not been explored by empirical research, so that with few exceptions, the primary form of information about how criminal justice processes 'work' is anecdote or supposition.[60] This is exacerbated by the fact that in most of these jurisdictions reliable statistical data concerning many aspects of the criminal justice system, such as numbers of people prosecuted, the proportion of those prosecuted who are kept in pre-trial detention, average length of pre-trial detention, the number of people arrested and/or detained by the police, spending on criminal legal aid, etc., is often not routinely collected or not publicly available.

---

[56]   The complexities of the enterprise are well exemplified in Jackson, Langer & Tillers 2008.

[57]   See the discussion in Cape et al. 2007, p. 15 and 16.

[58]   There is an extensive literature in this regard but see, for example, Delmas-Marty & Spencer 2002, especially ch. 1, and Hodgson 2005.

[59]   See, in particular, Field 2006, p. 525.

[60]   The principal exception to this pattern is England and Wales where a large number of empirical studies have been conducted, although mostly in the 1980s and 1990s. In relation to France, see Field 2006, p. 525.

The research team, and the in-country researchers, have largely had to work with what data and information is available. As is explained in the next section, most of the in-country researchers were able to interview various professionals involved in criminal processes, such as defence lawyers, prosecutors and judges, but this was essentially small-scale empirical research designed to provide insights rather than to provide statistically valid research data. Although the project was generously funded by the European Commission and the Open Society Institute, conducting large-scale empirical research across nine jurisdictions was well beyond the available budget. Even less possible was the kind of in-depth comparative research that would have enabled us to understand the complex historical and cultural factors that influence criminal procedures, of the kind explored by a limited number of academic researchers such as Hodgson and Field.[61] We have, of course, employed mechanisms designed to ensure the validity of our data, and of our analysis, which we explain further in the next section. However, it is important to note that the complexity of criminal justice systems and procedures, the value-laden nature of the context, and the fast-changing nature of the subject matter,[62] means that some of our findings may be contested and contestable. We believe that this is a positive attribute of the research, and we hope that one of the outcomes of our work is that it generates lively debate that contributes to a deeper understanding of criminal justice processes, both within and between jurisdictions.

4.   Research methodology

We explained earlier our approach to the relationship between effective criminal defence and the right to fair trial, to identifying the constituent elements of the right to effective criminal defence, and to the dynamic relationship between those elements. This resulted from early discussions of the project team the members of which were aware of the need to adopt an approach that, in the context of developing EU involvement in criminal procedure, would command widespread approval. The team then developed a detailed set of research questions, designed to elicit information about the constituent elements identified, which would provide the foundation for the research instruments subsequently employed. It was initially hoped that resources and time would permit the use of a number of fieldwork-based data collection methods, including interviews, observations and the examination of case files (for example, files held by courts, prosecutors and defence lawyers). However, it rapidly became apparent that to use such methods across a significant number of jurisdictions would not be feasible, particularly if the aim was to obtain statistically valid data. For this reason, it was decided to primarily use existing data supplemented, where possible, by interviews and to concentrate on

---

[61]   See, for example, Field & West 2003, and Hodgson 2005.

[62]   For example, in a number of jurisdictions, such as the Netherlands, Belgium and France, legislative changes are in progress in order to comply with the *Salduz* decision (ECtHR 27 November 2008, *Salduz* v. *Turkey*, No. 36391/02). In other jurisdictions, such as Scotland, such changes are being resisted (see *HM Advocate* v. *McLean* 2009 Scot (D) 11/12) but the resistance is the subject of challenge.

adopting measures that would support and enhance the validity and credibility of such data.

The research method, which was refined following use of the research instruments in the first three pilot jurisdictions was as follows. An in-country researcher with knowledge and experience of the criminal justice system and processes was appointed for each of the jurisdictions. In the first stage of the process, the in-country researcher collected 'desk review' data using a detailed pro-forma designed to elicit information about the criminal justice system in general, and the constituent elements of effective criminal defence in particular.[63] In addition, they prepared a 'critical account' of the criminal justice system using a structured approach determined by the project team. This information was then reviewed by the project team which provided feedback to the in-country researcher on (a) whether the information adequately covered the questions and issues raised in the pro-formas, (b) whether any of the information provided required clarification, and (c) what empirical research (in particular, interviews) could usefully be conducted.

In the second stage the in-country researcher conducted interviews with a range of professionals (where this had been recommended by the project team) and sought any further information identified in the review of the first stage. Using this information, and the data obtained in the first stage, the in-country researcher prepared a country report according to a detailed structure determined by the project team. The country report was then reviewed by the project team and by an in-country reviewer. The in-country reviewers were appointed by the project team, and were all noted legal academics and/or professionals from that jurisdiction. The in-country researcher was then asked to revise their country report in accordance with the feedback from both the project team and the in-country reviewer. The product, the country reports, provided the basis for the analysis conducted by the project team, and they constitute the chapters in Part II of this book.

As noted above, the project team was concerned that the research method and data obtained should be both valid and credible. Thus a number of mechanisms were adopted in order to achieve this. A project advisory group, drawn from noted professional and academic lawyers from a number of European jurisdictions, met in November 2007. The function of this group was to provide critical comment on both the research strategy adopted and on the project team's approach to defining effective criminal defence. A conference, attended by approximately 70 delegates from the jurisdictions covered by the research (and other European jurisdictions), was held at Maastricht University, the Netherlands, in November 2008 to discuss the findings from the first three jurisdictions, the approach to analysing the data and the preliminary conclusions that might be drawn from that data. A key aspect of the validation of the data was the role played by the in-country reviewers. Their role was to correct any factual errors, to make suggestions regarding the clarity of the country reports, to consider the validity of any conclusions drawn from the available evidence, and to make appropriate suggestions as to what further data might usefully be obtained.

---

[63]   The various research instruments are set out in the appendices.

The final phase of the research involved the analysis of the data in respect of all nine jurisdictions in the study, and to draw conclusions and recommendations from that analysis. Our analysis is fully set out in Chapters 12 and 13. A summary of our findings, and our recommendations, are set out in the Executive Summary and Recommendations in Section III.

5.   How to read the book

The book is designed to serve as a full, and final, report of the 'Effective defence rights in the EU and access to justice: investigating and promoting best practice' project. It therefore includes not only the country reports of the nine jurisdictions in the study, but also an account of the research methodology, an extended account and analysis of ECtHR jurisprudence on what we identified as the essential elements of effective criminal defence, a description of our approach to analysis of the data, and our analysis, conclusions and recommendations. The account and analysis of ECtHR jurisprudence can be found in Chapter 2. The country reports in Part II serve as a database of the criminal justice systems and processes as they relate to effective criminal defence for the jurisdictions that were included in the project. Our analysis by reference to ECHR standards is set out in Chapter 12, and our 'triangle analysis' of the data and the conclusions drawn from it can be found in Chapter 13. A summary of the findings and recommendations in respect of each jurisdiction can be found in the Executive Summary and Recommendations.

6.   Bibliography

Books

Cape et al. 2007
Cape, E., Hodgson, J., Prakken, T. & Spronken, T., *Suspects in Europe*, Antwerp: Intersentia, 2007.

Delmas-Marty & Spencer 2002
Delmas-Marty, M. & Spencer, J., *European Criminal Procedures*, Cambridge: Cambridge University Press, 2002.

Hodgson 2005
Hodgson, J., *French Criminal Justice*, Oxford: Hart, 2005.

Jackson, Langer & Tillers 2008
Jackson, J., Langer, M. & Tillers, P. (eds.), *Crime, Procedure and Evidence in a Comparative and International Context: Essays in honour of Professor Mirjan Damaska*, Oxford: Hart, 2008.

Klip 2009
Klip, A., *Criminal Law in the European Union*, Antwerp: Intersentia, 2009.

Spronken & Attinger 2005

Spronken, T. & Attinger, M., *Procedural Rights in Criminal Proceedings: existing levels of safeguards in the European Union, Brussels: DG Justice and Home Affairs*, 2005, available at <http://arno.unimaas.nl/show.cgi?fid=3891>.

Summers 2007

Summers, S., *Fair Trials: The European Criminal Procedural Tradition and the European Court of Human Rights*, Oxford: Hart, 2007.

Tuinstra 2009

Tuinstra, J., *Defence Counsel in International Criminal Law*, The Hague: T.M.C. Asser Press, 2009.

Tyler 2006

Tyler, T., *Why People Obey the Law*, Princeton: Princeton University Press, 2006.

Vernimmen-Van Tiggelen & Surano 2008

Vernimmen-Van Tiggelen, G. & Surano, L., *Analysis of the future of mutual recognition in criminal matters in the European Union, Brussels: DG Justice and Home Affairs*, 2008, available at <http://ec.europa.eu/justice_home/doc_centre/criminal/recognition/docs/mutual_recognition_en.pdf>.

Vernimmen-Van Tiggelen, Surano & Weyembergh 2009

Vernimmen-Van Tiggelen, G., Surano, L. & Weyembergh, A., *The future of mutual recognition of criminal matters in the European Union*, Brussels: University of Brussels, 2009.

Articles in Journals

Field 2006

Field, F., 'State, Citizen, and Character in French Criminal Process', 33 *Journal of Law and Society*, 4 2006, p. 522-546.

Field 2009

Field, S., 'Fair Trials and Procedural Tradition in Europe', 29 *Oxford Journal of Legal Studies*, 2 2009, p. 365-387.

Field & West 2005

Field, S. & West, A., 'Dialogue and the inquisitorial tradition: French defence lawyers in the pre-trial criminal process', 14 *Criminal Law Forum*, 2003, p. 261-316.

Official Sources

Committee for the Prevention of Torture 1992

Committee for the Prevention of Torture, *2nd General Report*, CPT/Inf (92) 3, available at <http://www.cpt.coe.int/EN/annual/rep-02.htm>.

Home Office 2002

Home Office, *Justice for All*, CM 5563, London: The Stationery Office, 2002.

House of Lords 2005

House of Lords European Union Committee, *Procedural Rights in Criminal Proceedings HL Paper 28*, 1st Report of Session 2004-5, London: The Stationery Office, 2005.

Open Society Institute 2001

Open Society Institute, *Monitoring the EU Access Process: Judicial Independence*, Budapest: Open Society Institute, 2001.

Open Society Institute 2002

Open Society Institute, *Monitoring the EU Access Process: Judicial Capacity*, Budapest: Open Society Initiative, 2002.

Ed Cape
Zaza Namoradze
Roger Smith
Taru Spronken

CHAPTER 2 THE EUROPEAN CONVENTION ON HUMAN RIGHTS AND THE RIGHT TO EFFECTIVE DEFENCE

1.   Introduction

At the heart of our examination in this chapter are the requirements that, according to the ECHR case law, states must meet in order to provide suspects and defendants with effective defence rights. The ECHR contains two explicit references to criminal procedure.[1] The principal provision is article 6 ECHR, the text of which we set out in Chapter 1 § 1. The second is article 5 concerning pre-trial detention and bail, which provides that arrest and detention must be lawful and in accordance with a procedure prescribed by law, that there must be a reasonable suspicion that the person committed an offence (art. 5 § 1), and that the person must be informed promptly of the reasons for his arrest and of any charge against him (art. 5 § 2). Habeas corpus applies (art. 5 § 4) and there is a conditional entitlement to release pending trial (art. 5 § 3). Other articles are also relevant to particular aspects of effective criminal defence. Article 3 ECHR, which bans torture and ill treatment, is relevant to the conditions under which a detainee is held or interviewed. Article 8 ECHR, which protects privacy, is relevant to safeguards such as the confidentiality of lawyer/client communications, free access to legal advice and to safeguards concerning the investigative powers of the police.[2] However, in this chapter we concentrate on article 6 and on the pre-trial release provisions of article 5.

The rights encompassed by article 6 have been expanded upon by principles developed in the jurisprudence of the ECtHR, such as those concerning the equality of arms between the prosecution and the defence,[3] the privilege against self-incrimination and the right to silence,[4] the right to adversarial trial, and the immediacy principle (meaning that all evidence should normally be produced at

[1]   Art. 7 ECHR, the legality principle, is not considered here because it is principally concerned with substantive criminal law, as opposed to criminal procedure.
[2]   Such as telephone tapping, secret surveillance, the taking of DNA samples etc.
[3]   ECtHR 15 May 2005, *Öcalan* v. *Turkey*, No. 46221/99, § 140.
[4]   ECtHR 25 February 1993, *Funke* v. *France*, No. 10828/84 and ECtHR 19 March 2009, *Bykov* v. *Russia* No. 4378/02.

trial in the context of adversarial argument).[5] The provision of legal representation should be 'real', or 'practical' and 'effective', not 'theoretical and illusory',[6] and the accused should be able to exercise 'effective participation' in criminal procedure.[7] With regard to article 5 the ECtHR has held that proceedings conducted under article 5 § 4 (pre-trial detention) should in principle also meet, to the greatest extent possible in the circumstances of an ongoing investigation, the basic requirements of a fair trial, such as the right to an adversarial procedure,[8] and that the safeguards of article 6, especially paragraph 3, are also applicable in the pre-trial proceedings.[9]

Although the major principles are clear, it is often difficult or impossible to draw detailed, generalised, conclusions from the case law because the ECtHR assesses whether proceedings were fair as a whole on the particular facts of an individual case.[10] For example, it was unclear for a long time at what moment the right to legal assistance arises. For years the ECtHR held that the right to have a lawyer present during police interrogation could not be derived from article 6 § 3 ECHR.[11] Recently, however, the ECtHR has underlined the importance of the investigative stage of criminal proceedings and has indicated that access to a lawyer should be provided as from the first interrogation of a suspect by the police.[12] Nevertheless in countries where this right does not exist, such as Belgium,[13] France,[14] and the Netherlands[15] it is still disputed what the term 'access' means, and

---

[5]   ECtHR 28 August 1991, *Brandstetter* v. *Austria*, Nos. 11170/84, 12876/87, 13468/87, § 67; ECtHR 6 December 1988, *Barberà, Messegué and Jabardo* v. *Spain*, Nos. 10588/83, 10589/83, 10590/83, § 78.

[6]   ECtHR 13 May 1980, *Artico* v. *Italy*, No. 6694/74; ECtHR 9 October 1979, *Airey* v. *Ireland* No. 6289/73; ECtHR 9 October 2008, *Moiseyev* v. *Russia*, No. 62936/00, § 209 and ECtHR 24 September 2009, *Pishchalnikov* v. *Russia*, No. 7025/04, § 66.

[7]   ECtHR 26 May 1988, *Ekbatani* v. *Sweden*, No. 10563/83; ECtHR 23 February 1994, *Stanford* v. *the United Kingdom*, No. 16757/90.

[8]   ECtHR 13 February 2001, *Garcia Alva* v. *Germany, Lietzow* v. *Germany* and *Schöps* v. *Germany*, Nos. 23541/94, 24479/94, 25116/94 and ECtHR 9 July 2009, *Mooren* v. *Germany*, No. 11364/03, § 124-125.

[9]   ECtHR 24 November 1993, *Imbrioscia* v. *Switzerland*, No. 13972/88, § 38; ECtHR, Grand Chamber, 27 November 2008, *Salduz* v. *Turkey*, No. 36391/02, § 50 and ECtHR 11 December 2008, *Panovits* v. *Cyprus*, No. 4268/04 § 64.

[10]   ECtHR 20 November 1989, *Kostovski* v. *the Netherlands*, No. 11454/85, § 39; ECtHR 6 December 1988, *Barberà, Messegué and Jabardo* v. *Spain*, Nos. 10588/83, 10589/83, 10590/83.

[11]   ECtHR 6 October 2001, *Brennan* v. *the United Kingdom*, No. 39846/98; ECtHR 14 December 1999, *Dougan* v. *the United Kingdom*, No. 44738/98.

[12]   ECtHR, Grand Chamber, 27 November 2008, *Salduz* v. *Turkey*, No. 36391/02; ECtHR 11 December 2008, *Panovits* v. *Cyprus*, No. 4268/04; ECtHR 24 September 2009, *Pishchalnikov* v. *Russia*, No. 7025/04 and ECtHR 13 October 2009, *Dayanan* v. *Turkey*, No. 7377/03.

[13]   In Cour de Cassation 11 March 2009, No. P. 090304 F/1, the Belgian Court of Cassation ruled that it can not be derived from the *Salduz* case that the suspect has a right to have his lawyer present during the interrogation. The Court of Appeal in Antwerp ruled otherwise on 24 December 2009, No. C/2105/09, and excluded the evidence that had been obtained during an interrogation without the presence of a lawyer (appeal in cassation has been lodged by the prosecution).

[14]   In France there are signs of a change. On 29 January 2010 the Paris Court nullified a 'garde a vue' because the 30 minutes of contact that a lawyer can have with his client are not sufficient to prepare a defence according to the requirements of the ECtHR.

whether it applies where the prosecution has not relied on something said by the accused in the absence of a lawyer.[16]

What we endeavour to do in this chapter is not only to identify minimum standards that can be derived from the ECtHR jurisprudence with regard to a selected range of defence rights, but also to identify the gaps and uncertainties that still remain with regard to these rights. It is not our intention to deal with the voluminous case law exhaustively, which has already been done very well elsewhere.[17] Rather, we want to distil the basic outlines and provide a manageable overview in order to provide the basis of a normative framework for the assessment of the country reports in chapters 12 and 13.

1.1. The defence rights addressed in this study

The fair trial requirements enshrined in the ECHR encompass many principles and procedural rules that, of course, all contribute to a fair trial. However, in this analysis we concentrate on those elements that we argue are paramount in ensuring access to effective criminal defence.[18] They are as follows.

1.1.1. Presumption of innocence, right to silence, equality of arms and adversarial trial

In § 2 we analyse those rights and principles that have an overall impact on how criminal proceedings are conducted and how other defence rights are regulated: the right to be presumed innocent, the right to silence, the principle of equality of arms and adversarial trial. We also examine the safeguards relating to pre-trial detention because the deprivation of liberty is intimately linked with the presumption of innocence, and may in practice influence reliance on the right to silence.

The right to information

The right to information is analysed in § 3. For our purposes there are three aspects to this right: the right to be informed of the nature and cause of the accusation, as stipulated in article 6 § 3a ECHR; the right to be informed of other defence rights such as the right to legal assistance, and the right to call witnesses; and the right to be informed of information obtained in the (ongoing) criminal investigation and to have access to the file.

---

[15]   In the Netherlands the Supreme Court ruled that the *Salduz* Judgment of the ECtHR does not imply a right to have a lawyer present during police interrogation, HR 30 June 2009, NbSr 2009, 249.

[16]   *HM Advocate* v. *McLean* 2009 Scot (D) 11/12. See also Spronken et al. 2009, p. 43 and 50.

[17]   See, for instance, van Dijk & van Hoof 2006, Harris et al. 2009, and Trechsel 2005.

[18]   See Chapter 1 § 1.

Right to defence and legal assistance

The right to defend oneself and the right to legal advice and representation, including the right to legal aid, is dealt with in § 4. In this section we also deal with the right to choose a lawyer and to communicate with the lawyer in private.

Rights that promote effective participation

In § 5 we examine procedural rights that are relevant, instrumentally, in ensuring effective participation in the truth-seeking and guilt-determination process. They can be divided into four categories: the right to investigate facts, or to seek exculpatory evidence; the right to participate in the proceedings, for example, by being present at during investigative acts and at hearings, which is closely related to the equality of arms requirement; the right to adequate time and facilities for preparation of the defence; and the right to examine witnesses and experts.

Right to free interpretation and translation

The right to free interpretation and translation, of the accusation, the evidence, and lawyer/client consultations, is assessed in § 6.

Right to reasoned decisions and appeal

Finally the right to reasoned decisions and the right to appeal are addressed in § 7.

2. Procedural rights relating to fair trial in general

There are rights and principles that have an overall impact on the way in which criminal proceedings should be conducted, that set standards for rules of evidence and that regulate the fundamental roles and positions of the participants in the criminal investigation and trial. We refer to the right to be presumed innocent that is laid down in article 6 § 2 ECHR and the right to silence, including the prohibition on self-incrimination which, surprisingly, is not specifically mentioned in the ECHR, but which is confirmed in ECtHR case law. Entwined with these rights and principles is the right to liberty and security as guaranteed by article 5 ECHR. In addition, the principle of equality of arms and the right to an adversarial hearing, which not specifically mentioned in article 6 ECHR, are seen by the ECtHR as fundamental aspects of the right to a fair trial. The ECtHR has consistently held that criminal proceedings, including procedural elements, should be adversarial and that there should be equality of arms between the prosecution and defence. We will examine in this section what the scope and implications of these general principles are.

2.1. The right to be presumed innocent

The presumption of innocence laid down in article 6 § 2 ECHR entails, according to the Court, three requirements.[19] First, judicial authorities must not presume that the accused has committed the offence he is charged with. In the Court's judgment, the presumption of innocence is violated if, without the accused having previously been proved guilty according to law and, notably, without his having had the opportunity of exercising his rights of defence, a judicial decision concerning him reflects an assumption that he is guilty. This may be so even in the absence of any formal finding; it suffices that there is some reasoning suggesting that the court regards the accused as guilty if this has not been proven according to law.[20] Article 6 § 2 governs criminal proceedings in their entirety 'irrespective of the outcome of the prosecution'.[21] However, once an accused has been found guilty the presumption, in principle, ceases to apply in respect of any allegations made during the subsequent sentencing procedure.[22] The presumption of innocence also affects public officials and can be violated if a statement of a public official concerning a person charged with a criminal offence reflects an assumption that he is guilty before this has been proved according to law.[23] In this regard the Court emphasises the importance of the choice of words by public officials in their statements before a person has been tried and found guilty of an offence.[24]

Second, the presumption of innocence has fundamental implications for evidential rules: the burden of proof is on the prosecution and any doubt should benefit the accused (in dubio pro reo).[25] Furthermore it implies that a court's judgment must be based on evidence as put before it and not on mere allegations or assumptions.[26] In Telfner, the question was whether the national courts could base a conviction for causing injury by negligence in a car accident solely on a report of the local police that the applicant was the main user of the car and had not been home on the night of the accident. The ECtHR reasoned that these elements of evidence, which were not corroborated by evidence given at the trial in an adversarial manner, were not sufficient to constitute a case against Telfner and that the burden

---

[19] ECtHR 6 December 1988, *Barberà, Messegué and Jabardo v. Spain*, Nos. 10588/83, 10589/83, 10590/83, § 77.
[20] ECtHR 21 February 1983, *Minelli v. Switzerland*, No. 8660/79, § 37. This reasoning also applies to proceedings that concern the confiscation of assets: ECtHR 1 March 2007, *Geerings v. the Netherlands*, No. 30810/03, § 41-51; or compensation of damages after an acquittal or stay of criminal proceedings: ECtHR 25 August 1993, *Sekanina v. Austria*, No. 13126/87, § 30; ECtHR 13 January 2005, *Capeau v. Belgium*, No. 42914/98, § 21-26; ECtHR 15 May 2008, *Orr v. Norway*, No. 31283/04, § 50-55.
[21] ECtHR 21 February 1983, *Minelli v. Switzerland*, No. 8660/79, § 30.
[22] ECtHR 5 July 2001, *Phillips v. the United Kingdom*, No. 41087/98, § 28-36.
[23] ECtHR 10 October 2000, *Daktaras v. Lithuania*, No. 42095/98, § 41; ECtHR 26 March 2002, *Butkevičius v. Lithuania*, No. 48297/99, § 46-54; accordingly the principle of the presumption of innocence may be infringed not only by a judge or court but also by other public authorities including prosecutors.
[24] ECtHR 10 February 1995, *Allenet de Ribemont v. France*, No. 15175/89, § 35.
[25] ECtHR 6 December 1988, *Barberà, Messegué and Jabardo v. Spain*, Nos. 10588/83, 10589/83, 10590/83, § 77.
[26] ECtHR 20 March 2001, *Telfner v. Austria*, No. 33501/96, § 19.

of proof was shifted unjustly from the prosecution to the defence.[27] The presumption of innocence is, however, not absolute and may be restricted as long as the authorities are able to strike a fair balance between the importance of what is at stake and defence rights.[28] Accordingly, presumptions of fact or of law are in principle not prohibited under the Convention as long as they respect defence rights, implying that the presumption must be rebuttable by the suspect.[29] As a consequence the suspect might have to bear a part of the burden of proof.

Third, the prosecution must inform the accused of the accusation so that he may prepare and present his defence accordingly.[30] The latter illustrates the connection between the presumption of innocence and the need for effective and practical defence rights.[31]

2.2. The right to silence including the prohibition of self-incrimination

In contrast to the right to be presumed innocent, the right to remain silent is not explicitly mentioned in article 6 ECHR, although they are closely linked.[32] It is, however, settled case law of the ECtHR that the right to silence and the right not to incriminate oneself are fundamental features of the concept of fair trial as they are 'generally recognised international standards which lie at the heart of the notion of a fair procedure' under article 6 ECHR.[33] Their rationale lies, inter alia, in the protection of the accused against improper compulsion by the authorities, thereby contributing to the avoidance of miscarriages of justice and to the fulfilment of the aims of article 6.[34] The right not to incriminate oneself, in particular, presupposes that the prosecution in a criminal case must seek to prove their case against the accused without resort to evidence obtained through methods of coercion or oppression in defiance of the will of the accused.[35]

It is important to note that according to the Court's case law, article 6 ECHR and the privilege against self-incrimination, come into play as soon as a person is

---

[27] ECtHR 20 March 2001, *Telfner* v. *Austria*, No. 33501/96, § 15-20.

[28] ECtHR 19 October 2004, *Falk* v. *the Netherlands*, No. 66273/01.

[29] ECtHR 7 October 1988, *Salabiaku* v. *France*, No. 10519/83, § 28.

[30] ECtHR 6 December 1988, *Barberà, Messegué and Jabardo* v. *Spain*, Nos. 10588/83, 10589/83, 10590/83, § 77.

[31] See for instance with the right to be informed, § 3.1 below.

[32] ECtHR 17 December 1996, *Saunders* v. *the United Kingdom*, No. 19187/91, § 68; ECtHR 21 December 2000, *Heany and McGuinness* v. *Ireland*, No. 34720/97, § 40; ECtHR 21 April 2009, *Marttinen* v. *Finland*, No. 19235/03, § 60.

[33] In *Funke* the Court held for the first time that the right to silence and the *nemo tenetur* principle are part of the fair trial concept of art. 6 § 1 ECHR; ECtHR 25 February 1993, *Funke* v. *France*, No. 10828/84, § 41-44. See also ECtHR 17 December 1996, *Saunders* v. *the United Kingdom*, No. 19187/91, § 68; ECtHR 8 February 1996, *John Murray* v. *the United Kingdom*, No. 18731/91 § 45; ECtHR 21 December 2000, *Heany and McGuinness* v. *Ireland*, No. 34720/97, § 40, recently confirmed in ECtHR 22 July 2008, *Getiren* v. *Turkey*, No. 10301/03, § 123.

[34] ECtHR, Grand Chamber, 27 November 2008, *Salduz* v. *Turkey*, No. 36391/02, § 54-55.

[35] See *inter alia* ECtHR 17 December 1996, *Saunders* v. *the United Kingdom*, No. 19187/91,§ 68; ECtHR 21 December 2000, *Heaney and McGuinness* v. *Ireland*, No. 34720/97, § 40; ECtHR 6 April 2000, *Decision on the admissibility of J.B.* v. *Switzerland*, No. 31827/96, § 64; ECtHR 5 November 2002, *Allan* v. *the United Kingdom*, No. 48539/99, § 44.

'charged' with a criminal offence which it taken to mean when 'the situation of the [person] has been substantially affected'.[36] In *Zaichenko* the Court considered that, on the facts of the case, police suspicion of theft should have been aroused at the time that the applicant was stopped at a road check and was not able to produce proof that he had purchase the diesel found in his car. Although he was not accused at that moment, the Court found that it was incumbent on the police to inform the applicant of the privilege against self-incrimination and the right to remain silent before asking him for further 'explanation'. By subsequently using the statement then given to the police, without him being informed of those rights, as evidence for a conviction constituted a violation of article 6.[37]

The Court has also held that the privilege is linked with the right to have access to a lawyer, and has explicitly stated that 'early access to a lawyer is part of the procedural safeguards to which the court will have particular regard when examining whether a procedure has extinguished the very essence of the privilege against self-incrimination'.[38] Despite its fundamental nature, the right to remain silent can be restricted provided that the authorities can invoke good cause.[39] The Court adopts a rather strict attitude towards accepting justifications. If the very essence of the right to remain silent is destroyed, there will be a violation.[40]

It follows from the jurisprudence that a distinction can be made between an attempt to compel the defendant to give certain evidence[41] and the drawing of inferences from a person's silence.[42] In both situations all the circumstances of the case must be taken into account in order to determine whether the right to remain silent has been breached.[43] Factors to which the Court will have regard in determining whether there has been a violation include the nature and degree of compulsion, the existence of any relevant safeguards, and the use of the material so obtained in subsequent proceedings.[44]

With regard to the application of the right to remain silent and the prohibition of self-incrimination, it is not necessary that the allegedly incriminating evidence obtained by coercion or in violation of the right to silence or self-incrimination is actually used in criminal proceedings, before the right not to incriminate oneself applies. A violation of the right not to incriminate oneself can be found even though

---

[36]   ECtHR 17 December 1996, *Saunders* v. *the United Kingdom*, No. 19187/91 § 67 and 74 and ECtHR 19 February 2009, *Shabelnik* v. *Ukraine*, No. 16404/03, § 57.

[37]   ECtHR 18 February 2010, *Zaichenko* v. *Russia*, No. 39660/02, § 42 and § 52-60.

[38]   ECtHR 24 September 2009, *Pishchalnikov* v. *Russia*, No. 7025/04, § 69.

[39]   ECtHR 8 February 1996, *John Murray* v. *the United Kingdom*, No. 18731/91, § 47; ECtHR 21 December 2000, *Heany and McGuinness* v. *Ireland*, No. 34720/97, § 47.

[40]   ECtHR 21 December 2000, *Heany and McGuinness* v. *Ireland*, No. 34720/97, § 57-58; ECtHR 10 March 2009, *Bykov* v. *Russia*, No. 4378/02, § 93.

[41]   ECtHR 25 February 1993, *Funke* v. *France*, No. 10828/84, § 41-44.

[42]   ECtHR 8 February 1996, *John Murray* v. *the United Kingdom*, No. 18731/91, § 45; see also ECtHR 29 June 2007, *O'Halloran and Francis* v. *the United Kingdom*, Nos. 15809/02 and 25624/02, § 45-46.

[43]   ECtHR 29 June 2007, *O'Halloran and Francis* v. *the United Kingdom*, Nos. 15809/02 and 25624/02, § 53; ECtHR 2 May 2000, *Condron* v. *the United Kingdom*, No. 35718/97, § 59-63.

[44]   ECtHR 5 November 2002, *Allan* v. *the United Kingdom*, No. 48539/99, § 44. See also ECtHR 21 December 2000, *Heany and McGuinness* v. *Ireland*, No. 34720/97, § 55; ECtHR 11 July 2006, *Jalloh* v. *Germany*, No. 54810/00, § 112-123.

no proceedings were subsequently brought or where the person is subsequently acquitted.[45]

2.3. Bail or the right to be released pending trial

Closely related to the presumption of innocence and the right to silence are the safeguards relating to the right to liberty and security under article 5 ECHR, since there is a clear tension between these rights and the use of pre-trial detention.

Article 5 § 3 of the Convention provides:

> 'Everyone arrested or detained in accordance with the provisions of paragraph 1 (c) of this article shall be … entitled to trial within a reasonable time or to release pending trial. Release may be conditioned by guarantees to appear for trial.'

The principles established by case law of the ECtHR with regard to this provision are that national judicial authorities must ensure that, in a given case, the pre-trial detention of an accused person does not exceed a reasonable time.[46] To this end they must examine all facts for or against the existence of a genuine requirement of public interest justifying deprivation of liberty. A departure from the rule of respect for individual liberty can only be justified with due regard to the principle of the presumption of innocence and courts have to set this out in their decision when refusing an application for release. The persistence of reasonable suspicion that the person arrested has committed an offence is a condition *sine qua non* for the validity of continued detention but, after a certain lapse of time, it no longer suffices.[47] After that, continued deprivation of liberty must be justified by other grounds, which may include the risk of absconding or re-offending, the risk of collusion, or the fear that the evidence will be destroyed.[48]

The Court has underlined the need for convincing and consistent justifications,[49] and that an assessment must always be made *in concreto*.[50] Moreover, the grounds for continued detention and the existence of the specific facts outweighing the rule of respect for individual liberty must be convincingly demonstrated and be reconciled with the presumption of innocence.[51] Continued detention can be justified only if there are specific indications of a genuine requirement of public interest which, notwithstanding the presumption of

---

[45]   ECtHR 21 April 2009, *Marttinen v. Finland*, No. 19235/03, § 64.
[46]   Pre-trial detention that exceeds two years is, according to the Court, too lengthy, and requires adequate justification.
[47]   ECtHR 5 April 2005, *Nevmerzhitsky v. Ukraine*, No. 54825/00, § 135.
[48]   ECtHR 24 April 2003, *Smirnova v. Russia*, Nos. 46133/99 and 48183/99, § 59.
[49]   ECtHR 23 September 1998, *I.A. v. France*, No. 28213/95, § 108, 110 and 111.
[50]   ECtHR 12 March 2009, *Aleksandr Makarov v. Russia*, No. 15217/07, § 116; ECtHR 12 June 2008, *Vlasov v. Russia*, No. 78146/01, § 103.
[51]   ECtHR 26 October 2000, *Kudla v. Poland*, No. 30210/96, § 110-117; ECtHR 12 March 2009, *Aleksandr Makarov v. Russia*, No. 15217/07, § 117-118 and ECtHR 12 June 2008, *Vlasov v. Russia*, No. 78146/01, § 104.

innocence, outweighs the rule of respect for individual liberty.[52] The gravity of the charge cannot, in itself, justify a long period of detention.[53] The presumption should always be in favour of release, and there must be a regular review of whether grounds for detention continue to exist.[54] For example, the danger of perverting the course of justice ceases to be a justification after the evidence has been collected.[55] Where the grounds are 'relevant' and 'sufficient', it must also be ascertained whether the competent national authorities displayed 'special diligence' in the conduct of the proceedings.[56]

When determining an application for pre-trial detention alternative measures, such as the deposit of a bail surety or other conditions designed, for example, to ensure the applicant's appearance at trial or to prevent them from interfering with evidence, must be considered by the determining authority.[57] The second limb of article 5 § 3 ECHR does not give judicial authorities a choice between either bringing an accused to trial within a reasonable time or granting him provisional release pending trial. Until conviction, the suspect must be presumed innocent, and the purpose of the provisions of article 5 § 3 ECHR is essentially to require the suspect's provisional release once his continuing detention ceases to be reasonable.[58]

2.4. Equality of arms and adversarial hearing

The ECtHR has frequently held that equality of arms between prosecution and defence, and an adversarial hearing, are fundamental aspects of the right to fair trial, including the elements of such proceedings that relate to procedure. The Court considers the principle of equality of arms as one of the features of the wider concept of a fair trial, meaning that each party must be afforded a reasonable opportunity to present his case under conditions that do not place him at a disadvantage vis-à-vis his opponent.[59] Moreover, any difficulties caused to the defence by limitations on his rights must be sufficiently counterbalanced by procedures followed by the judicial authorities.[60]

A closer examination of the jurisprudence reveals that the cases that the Court has dealt with in terms of equality of arms and adversarial hearing concern access to the case file or the disclosure of documents, the questioning of witnesses and

---

[52] ECtHR 26 October 2000, *Kudla* v. *Poland*, No. 30210/96, § 110-117.
[53] ECtHR 23 September 1998, *I.A.* v. *France*, No. 28213/95, § 104.
[54] Well established case law since ECtHR 27 June 1968, *Neumeister* v. *Austria*, No. 1936/63, § 4.
[55] ECtHR 26 October 2000, *Kudla* v. *Poland*, No. 30210/96, § 114; ECtHR 12 March 2009, *Aleksandr Makarov* v. *Russia*, No. 15217/07, § 117 and ECtHR 15 September 2009, *Jamrozy* v. *Poland*, No. 6093/04, § 36-41.
[56] ECtHR 23 September 1998, *I.A.* v. *France*, No. 28213/95, § 102.
[57] ECtHR 21 December 2000, *Jablonski* v. *Poland*, No. 33492/96, § 83; ECtHR 5 April 2005, *Nevmerzhitsky* v. *Ukraine*, No. 54825/00, § 137; ECtHR 28 July 2005, *Czarnecki* v. *Poland*, No. 75112/01, § 37-44.
[58] ECtHR 6 February 2007, *Garycki* v. *Poland*, No. 14348/02, § 39.
[59] ECtHR 15 May 2005, *Öcalan* v. *Turkey*, No. 46221/99, § 140.
[60] ECtHR 26 March 1996, *Doorson* v. *the Netherlands*, No. 20524/92, § 72 and ECtHR 23 April 1997, *Van Mechelen and others* v. *the Netherlands*, Nos. 21363/93, 21364/93, 21427/93, 22056/93, § 54.

experts, or the possibility of responding to, or challenging, depositions or observations made by the prosecution.[61] To avoid overlap this case law will be discussed in the sections that deal with these topics below.[62] What can be said here is that most of the case law addresses the equality of arms requirements during the trial phase, including appeal and cassation proceedings. There is much less case law regarding the equality of arms requirement at the investigation or pre-trial phase. In its recent case law the ECtHR has, however, acknowledged that the pre-trial phase is becoming increasingly important. National laws may attach consequences to the attitude of an accused at the investigation stage that are decisive for the prospects of the defence in any subsequent criminal proceedings as the evidence obtained during this stage determines the framework within which the offence charged will be considered at the trial.[63] Therefore, the Court has ruled in *Salduz* that the accused be allowed to benefit from the assistance of a lawyer at the initial stages of police interrogation, *inter alia* because this will contribute to 'the fulfilment of the aims of article 6, notably equality of arms between the investigating or prosecuting authorities and the accused'.[64] In *Dayanan* the Court, for the first time, gave a clear account of what equality of arms at the investigation stage actually means. The Court stressed that the principle of equality of arms requires that a suspect, at the police interrogation stage, must be afforded the complete range of interventions that are inherent to legal advice, such as discussion with and instructions to the lawyer, the investigation of facts, the search for exculpatory evidence, preparation for interrogation, support of the suspect and control of the conditions under which the suspect is detained.[65]

3.   The right to information

The right to information is a crucial aspect of the overall right to defend oneself. Three dimensions can be distinguished. First, the right of anyone charged with a criminal offence to be informed of the nature and cause of the accusations against him.[66] Second, the right to information in the sense of being informed of the defence

---

[61]   See for instance ECtHR 31 October 1991, *Borgers* v. *Belgium*, No. 12005/86, § 24-28; and ECtHR 12 April 2006, *Martinie* v. *France*, No. 58675/00, § 45.

[62]   § 3.3 Information concerning material evidence available to the police or prosecutor, and § 5.4 Right to call and question witnesses.

[63]   ECtHR, Grand Chamber, 27 November 2008, *Salduz* v. *Turkey*, No. 36391/02, § 54-55.

[64]   ECtHR 24 September 2009, *Pishchalnikov* v. *Russia*, No. 7025/04 § 68, and see also the case law discussed in § 4.2 of this chapter.

[65]   ECtHR 13 October 2009, *Dayanan* v. *Turkey*, No. 7377/03, § 32: 'En effet, l'équité de la procédure requiert que l'accusé puisse obtenir toute la vaste gamme d'interventions qui sont propres au conseil. A cet égard, la discussion de l'affaire, l'organisation de la défense, la recherche des preuves favorables à l'accusé, la préparation des interrogatoires, le soutien de l'accusé en détresse et le contrôle des conditions de détention sont des éléments fondamentaux de la défense que l'avocat doit librement exercer.'

[66]   Art. 6 § 3 ECHR.

rights provide for in the ECHR, which is not covered as such by the ECHR. Third, to have access to the evidence on which these accusations are based.[67]

3.1.   The right to information about the nature and cause of the accusation

The rationale of articles 6 § 3a and 5 § 2 ECHR, that impose obligations on the authorities to inform a suspect of the nature and cause of the accusation, is to enable the suspect to fully understand the allegations with a view to preparing a defence[68] or to challenging the lawfulness of his detention.[69] Even though both articles are fairly specific in the information they require, they are limited to factual information concerning the reasons for the arrest, the nature and cause of the accusation, and the legal basis for both.[70] The level of information that has to be communicated to the suspect or accused is strongly dependant on the nature and complexity of the case, which is always assessed by the ECtHR in the light of the right to prepare a defence (art. 6 § 3b)[71] and, more generally, the right to a fair trial (art. 6 § 1).[72] It follows that the authorities can be required to take additional steps in order to ensure that the suspect effectively understands the information.[73] The jurisprudence implies that most problems of compliance arise with regard to the positive measures that should be taken to secure the effective benefit of a fair trial. It is not sufficient to make the information available, in the sense that the suspect could have asked for it. The duty to inform the suspect of the nature and cause of the accusation rests entirely on the prosecuting authority's shoulders and cannot be complied with passively by making information available without bringing it to the attention of the defence.[74]

The ECHR does not give any indication as to the means to be used to provide the required information. Although in *Kamasinski* the ECtHR decided that a suspect should in principle be provided with a written explanation of the indictment in case he does not understand the language, the Court accepted that oral explanations were sufficient in order to comply with article 6 § 3a.[75]

In conclusion, the extent of the duty to provide information is, to a certain degree, at the discretion of the judicial authorities and article 6 § 3a does not, in itself, guarantee that a suspect will receive sufficient information to enable him to fully prepare his defence. Recent research shows that there appears to be no

---

[67]   According to case law on arts. 5 and 6 ECHR.
[68]   ECtHR 25 July 2000, *Mattoccia* v. *Italy*, No. 23969/94, § 60.
[69]   ECtHR 30 August 1990, *Fox, Campbell and Hartley* v. *the United Kingdom,* Nos. 12244/86, 12245/86, 12383/86, § 40.
[70]   ECtHR 16 December 1992, *Edwards* v. *the United Kingdom*, No. 13071/87, § 35-38.
[71]   See § 5.3 of this chapter.
[72]   ECtHR 25 March 1999, *Pélissier and Sassi* v. *France*, No. 25444/94, § 54 and ECtHR 25 July 2000, *Mattoccia* v. *Italy*, No. 23969/94, § 60 and 71.
[73]   ECtHR 19 December 1989, *Brozicek* v. *Italy*, No. 10964/84,§ 41; ECtHR 25 July 2000, *Mattoccia* v. *Italy*, No. 23969/94, § 65 and ECtHR 30 January 2001, *Vaudelle* v. *France*, No. 35683/97, § 59.
[74]   ECtHR 25 July 2000, *Mattoccia* v. *Italy*, No. 23969/94, § 65.
[75]   ECtHR 19 December 1989, *Kamasinsksi* v. *Austria*, No. 9783/82, § 79; ECtHR 25 March 1999, *Pélissier;* and *Sassi* v. *France*, No. 25444/94, § 53.

consensus between EU jurisdictions as to when the right to information arises, and that different rules are applied in relation to persons who have not been arrested.[76]

3.2. *Information on defence rights*

The second aspect of the right to information deals with the way in which a suspect is to be informed of his rights. In contrast to the first aspect, this is not explicitly mentioned in the ECHR implying that there is no right, as such, to be so informed. However, there is ECtHR case law that requires judicial authorities to take positive measures in order to ensure effective compliance with article 6.[77] This is specifically reflected in the decisions in *Padalov* and *Talat Tunc*, in which the Court required the authorities to adopt an active attitude in order to inform suspects of their right to legal aid.[78] In *Panovits* it was held that the authorities have a positive obligation to provide suspect with information on the right to legal assistance and legal aid if the conditions relating to them are fulfilled.[79] It is not sufficient for this information to be given in writing, for instance by a Letter of Rights. The Court stressed that authorities must take all reasonable steps to ensure that the suspect is fully aware of his rights of defence and understands, as far as possible, the implications of his conduct under questioning.[80]

Existing research shows that the way that suspects are informed of their rights varies widely across EU jurisdictions, and that in a majority of them information on procedural rights is provided only orally, decreasing the effectiveness of the information and making it more difficult to monitor.[81]

3.3. *Information concerning material evidence available to the police or prosecutor, and access to the case file*

It is established case law of the ECtHR that the prosecution authorities should disclose to the defence all material evidence for or against the accused,[82] and that both parties must be given the opportunity to have disclosed and comment upon the observations and evidence of the other party.[83] In *Natunen* the Court ruled that disclosure obligations must include the opportunity for the suspect to acquaint

---

[76] See Spronken et al. 2009, p. 107.
[77] ECtHR 13 May 1980, *Artico v. Italy*, No. 6694/74, § 36 and ECtHR 30 January 2001, *Vaudelle v. France*, No. 35683/97, § 52, 59 and 60.
[78] ECtHR 10 August 2006, *Padalov v. Bulgaria*, No. 54784/00 and ECtHR 27 March 2007, *Talat Tunc v. Turkey*, No. 32432/96.
[79] ECtHR 11 December 2008, *Panovits v. Cyprus*, No. 4268/04 § 72-73.
[80] ECtHR 11 December 2008, *Panovits v. Cyprus*, No.4268/04, § 67-68. See also ECtHR 31 March 2009, *Plonka v. Poland*, No. 20310/02, § 37-38 and ECtHR 24 September 2009, *Pishchalnikov v. Russia*, No. 7025/04, § 79-80.
[81] See Spronken et al. 2009, p. 92-98.
[82] ECtHR 16 December 1992, *Edwards v. the United Kingdom*, No. 13071/87, § 36.
[83] ECtHR 28 August 1991, *Brandstetter v. Austria*, Nos. 11170/84, 12876/87, 13468/87, § 66; ECtHR 16 February 2000, *Jasper v. the United Kingdom*, No. 27052/95, § 51 and ECtHR 6 September 2005, *Salov v. Ukraine*, No. 65518/01, § 87.

himself, for the purposes of preparing his defence, with the results of investigations carried out throughout the proceedings.[84]

The right to full disclosure is, however, not absolute and can be restricted for a legitimate purpose such as the protection of national security or sources of information, to protect witnesses at risk of reprisals, or to keep police methods of crime investigation secret.[85] Any such restriction must be strictly necessary and be remedied in the subsequent proceedings.[86] For example, non-disclosure of certain material should be counterbalanced by making the information accessible at the appeal stage and giving the defence ample time to respond to it.[87] The ECtHR also requires that the (non-) disclosure of information should always be scrutinised by the trial judge since he is in the best position to make an assessment of the need for disclosure. On the other hand, the ECtHR has held that the person requesting that specific documents be disclosed is required to give specific reasons for the request.[88]

There is no specific case law under article 6 ECHR clarifying at what point in proceedings material evidence should be disclosed. In the context of article 5 § 4 ECHR the ECtHR has, however, given some indication of both the stage at which material should be disclosed and the extent of that disclosure. In cases relating to pre-trial detention hearings the Court has ruled that the principle of equality of arms requires defence access to those documents in the investigation file which are essential in order to effectively challenge the lawfulness of pre-trial detention.[89] According to the Court this means that the accused be given a sufficient opportunity to take account of statements and evidence underlying them, such as the results of police and other investigations, irrespective of whether the accused is able demonstrate the relevance to his defence of such information. Although the Court acknowledges the need for criminal investigations to be conducted efficiently, which may imply that some information should be kept secret in order to prevent suspects from tampering with evidence or undermining the course of justice, this legitimate goal cannot be pursued at the expense of substantial restrictions on the defence. Therefore, information which is essential for the assessment of the lawfulness of a detention should be made available in an appropriate manner to the suspect's lawyer.[90] In addition the Court has ruled that abstracts of the case file do not suffice, nor does an oral account of facts and evidence. Authorities should

[84] ECtHR 31 March 2009, *Natunen* v. *Finland*, No. 21022/04, § 42 and ECtHR 15 November 2007, *Galstyan* v. *Armenia*, No. 26986/03, § 84.
[85] ECtHR 16 February 2000, *Jasper* v. *the United Kingdom*, No. 27052/95, § 43 and ECtHR 24 June 2003, *Dowsett* v. *the United Kingdom*, No. 39482/98, § 42.
[86] ECtHR 16 February 2000, *Jasper* v. *the United Kingdom*, No. 27052/95, § 43 and ECtHR 16 December 1992, *Edwards* v. *United Kingdom*, No. 13071/87, § 39.
[87] ECtHR 16 December 1992, *Edwards* v. *the United Kingdom*, No. 13071/87, § 35-37 and ECtHR 18 March 1997, *Foucher* v. *France*, No. 22209/93, § 35-38.
[88] ECtHR 24 February 1992, *Bendenoun* v. *France*, No. 12547/86, § 52.
[89] ECtHR, 13 February 2001, *Garcia Alva* v. *Germany*, *Lietzow* v. *Germany* and *Schöps* v. *Germany*, Nos. 23541/94, 24479/94 and 25116/94 and ECtHR 9 July 2009, *Mooren* v. *Germany*, No. 11364/03, § 124-125.
[90] ECtHR 13 February 2001, *Garcia Alva* v. *Germany*, No. 23541/94, § 41-42 and ECtHR 9 July 2009, *Mooren* v. *Germany*, No. 11364/03, § 121-124.

facilitate the consultation of files at times when this is essential for the defence, and should not be over-formalistic in doing so.[91]

Again, existing research reveals that practice varies widely across member states. In particular, in most states neither defence lawyers nor their clients have a right to information concerning the evidence relating to the alleged offence during the investigative stage. However, most member states do give a right to information about the evidence to the accused (or their lawyer) at the trial or trial preparation stage, although the precise formulation of the right varies enormously and, in particular, depends upon whether the jurisdiction has an inquisitorial or adversarial tradition.[92]

4. The right to defence

It is important to stress that article 6 ECHR grants the suspect both the right to defend himself in person and the right to be assisted by counsel. These are not equivalent alternatives. Both forms of defence have their own procedural function: the suspect contributes his personality and his knowledge of facts and circumstances, and the lawyer his legal knowledge and professional experience.

4.1. Right to self-representation

The right of self-representation is paramount, and the suspect or accused can waive his right to be assisted by counsel.[93] According to the ECtHR a person charged with a criminal offence is entitled to be present at his own trial and to participate in the proceedings.[94] The right of a suspect to choose to defend himself rather than be assisted or represented by a lawyer is a complex issue and raises questions as to whether a suspect can always decide to defend himself and whether a lawyer can be assigned to him against his will. This issue, which has been frequently raised before the International Criminal Tribunals,[95] has been also addressed by the ECtHR which has ruled that the right to self-representation is not absolute;[96] member states enjoy a wide margin of appreciation and may require compulsory appointment of a lawyer if the interests of justice so require.[97] The Court accepted in *Croissant* that

---

[91] ECtHR 13 February 2001, *Schöps* v. *Germany*, No. 25116/94, § 47-55; ECtHR 9 July 2009, *Mooren* v. *Germany*, No. 11364/03 § 121-125.

[92] Spronken et al. 2009, p. 94.

[93] ECtHR 24 September 2009, *Pishchalnikov* v. *Russia*, No. 7025/04, § 77.

[94] ECtHR 12 February 1985, *Colozza* v. *Italy*, No. 9024/80, § 27 and ECtHR 16 December 1999, *T.* v. *the United Kingdom*, No. 24724/94, § 88-89.

[95] Very recently the ICTY appointed counsel in the *Karadzic* case in the interests of justice, arguing that the right to self-representation can be restricted when the accused substantially and persistently obstructs the proper and expeditious conduct of his trial, thereby confirming previous case law: ICTY 5 November 2009, *Prosecutor* v. *Radovan Karadzic*, No. IT-95/18-T. See Tuinstra 2009, ch. VII.

[96] EComHR 5 July 1977, *Decision on the admissibility of X.* v. *Austria*, No. 7138/75 and ECtHR 25 September 1992, *Croissant* v. *Germany*, No. 13611/88, § 29.

[97] EComHR 5 July 1977, *Decision on the admissibility of X.* v. *Austria*, No. 7138/75; ECtHR 25 September 1992, *Croissant* v. *Germany*, No. 13611/88, § 27; ECtHR 15 November 2001, *Decision*
→

these circumstances can include the subject matter of the case, the complexity of the factual and legal issues, and the personality of the accused,[98] or when an appeal is lodged.[99] This implies that in certain circumstances it is considered to be in the accused's best interests to have the assistance of a lawyer so as to be better informed of his rights and in order to prepare a good defence. It remains questionable, however, whether forcing a lawyer upon an unwilling client can be considered in compliance with a right to a fair trial. The International Criminal Tribunal for the former Yugoslavia (ICTY) argued in the *Seselj* case that the phrase 'in the interests of justice' potentially has a broad scope:

> 'It includes the right to a fair trial, which is not only a fundamental right of the Accused, but also a fundamental interest of the Tribunal related to its own legitimacy. In the context of the right to a fair trial, the length of the case, its size and complexity need to be taken into account. The complex legal, evidential and procedural issues that arise in a case of this magnitude may fall outside the competence even of a legally qualified accused, especially where that accused is in detention without access to all the facilities he may need. Moreover, the Tribunal has a legitimate interest in ensuring that the trial proceeds in a timely manner without interruptions, adjournments or disruptions.' [100]

It is clear from this that 'imposed' legal assistance in such cases is justified by reference to the interests of the tribunal, to assure an expeditious trial, rather than in the interests of the accused. It has proved extremely difficult in cases of compulsory defence for counsel, in the absence of instructions from the client and without the client's assertions as to what he believes to be the truth and his understanding of events, to effectively represent the accused, who does not want to be his client. As the US Supreme Court stated in *Faretta* v. *California*:

> '[t]his Court's past recognition of the right of self-representation, the federal-court authority holding the right to be of constitutional dimension, and the state constitutions pointing to the right's fundamental nature form a consensus not easily ignored. [...] We confront here a nearly universal conviction, on the part of our people as well as our courts, that forcing a lawyer upon an unwilling defendant is contrary to his basic right to defend himself if he truly wants to do so.'

The Court found that:

> '[t]he language and spirit of the Sixth Amendment contemplate that counsel, like the other defence tools guaranteed by the Amendment, shall be an aid to a willing defendant – not an organ of the State interposed between an unwilling defendant and his right to defend himself personally. To thrust counsel upon the accused, against his considered wish, thus violates the logic of the Amendment. In such a case, counsel is

---

on the admissibility of Correia de Matos v. *Portugal*, No. 48188/99; ECtHR 14 January 2003, *Lagerblom* v. *Sweden*, No. 26891/95.

[98]   ECtHR 25 September 1992, *Croissant* v. *Germany*, No. 13611/88, § 30.

[99]   ECtHR 24 November 1986, *Gillow* v. *United Kingdom*, No. 9063/80, § 69.

[100]   ICTY 9 may 2003, Decision on Prosecution's Motion for Order Appointing Counsel to Assist Vojislav Seselj with his defence, *Prosecutor* v. *Vojislav Seselj*, Case No. IT-03-67-PT, § 21.

not an assistant, but a master, and the right to make a defence is stripped of the personal character upon which the Amendment insists.' [101]

4.2. The right to legal advice and representation

The right to legal advice is a key issue in procedural rights for suspects. A suspect who is assisted by an effective lawyer is in a far better position with regards to the enforcement of all of his other rights, partly because he is better informed of those rights and partly because a lawyer is able to assist him in ensuring that his rights are respected.[102]

One of the basic obligations of a lawyer is to assist his client, not only in the preparation for the trial itself, but also in ensuring the legality of any measures taken in the course of the proceedings.[103] According to the ECtHR, legal assistance must be effective and the State is under an obligation to ensure that the lawyer has the information necessary to conduct a proper defence.[104] If the particular lawyer is ineffective the State is obliged to provide the suspect with another lawyer.[105]

4.3. The point at which the right to legal assistance arises

For many years the ECtHR has held that the right to legal assistance arises immediately upon arrest.[106] Where the suspect has to make decisions during police interrogation that may be decisive for the future course of the proceedings he has the right to consult a lawyer prior to the interrogation.[107] Although the ECtHR acknowledged that the physical presence of a lawyer could provide the necessary counterbalance to pressure used by the police during interviews,[108] it stated that a right to have a lawyer present during police interrogation could not be derived from article 6 § 3 c ECHR.[109] This approach was in contradiction to that of both the

---

[101]   *Faretta* v. *California*, 422 U.S. 806 (1975), at 807.

[102]   Green Paper, section 4.1.

[103]   EComHR 14 December 1983, *Can* v. *Austria*, No. 9300/81 and ECtHR 4 March 2003, *Öcalan* v. *Turkey*, No. 63486/00.

[104]   ECtHR 9 April 1984, *Goddi* v. *Italy*, No. 8966/80 and ECtHR 4 March 2003, *Öcalan* v. *Turkey*, No. 63486/00.

[105]   ECtHR 13 May 1980, *Artico* v. *Italy*, No. 6694/74.

[106]   ECtHR 8 February 1996, *John Murray* v. *the United Kingdom*, No. 18731/91; ECtHR 6 June 2000 *Magee* v. *the United Kingdom*, No. 28135/95.

[107]   ECtHR 6 June 2000, *Averill* v. *the United Kingdom*, No. 36408/97.

[108]   ECtHR 6 June 2000, *Magee* v. *the United Kingdom*, No. 28135/95 and ECtHR 2 May 2000, *Condron* v. *the United Kingdom*, No. 35718/97: 'The fact that an accused person who is questioned under caution is assured access to legal advice, and in the applicants' case the physical presence of a solicitor during police interview must be considered a particularly important safeguard for dispelling any compulsion to speak which may be inherent in the terms of the caution. For the court, particular caution is required when a domestic court seeks to attach weight to the fact that a person who is arrested in connection with a criminal offence and who has not been given access to a lawyer does not provide detailed responses when confronted with questions the answers to which may be incriminating.' (§ 60).

[109]   ECtHR 6 October 2001, *Brennan* v. *the United Kingdom*, No. 39846/98; ECtHR 14 December 1999, *Dougan* v. *the United Kingdom*, No. 44738/98.

ICTY[110] and the European Committee for the Prevention of Torture and Inhuman or Degrading Treatment or Punishment (CPT),[111] both of which acknowledged that the right to have a lawyer present during police interrogation is one of the fundamental safeguards against ill-treatment of detained persons.

More recent judgements of the ECtHR have underlined the importance of the investigation stage for the preparation of the criminal proceedings, and have referred to the recommendations of the CPT:

> 'The Court finds that in order for the right to a fair trial to remain sufficiently 'practical and effective' Art. 6 § 1 requires that, as a rule, access to a lawyer should be provided as from the first interrogation of a suspect by the police, unless it is demonstrated in the light of the particular circumstances of each case that there are compelling reasons to restrict this right.'

The ECtHR has further indicated that even where compelling reasons may exceptionally justify denial of access to a lawyer, such restriction must not unduly prejudice the rights of the accused. As a consequence, the ECtHR considers that the lack of legal assistance during a suspect's interrogation would constitute a restriction of his defence rights, and that these rights will in principle be irretrievably prejudiced when incriminating statements, made during police interrogation without access to a lawyer, are used to secure a conviction.[112]

This new interpretation of article 6 § 3c of the Convention, also referred to as the 'Salduz doctrine', has been confirmed in several judgments. In the (post-Salduz) case law the ECtHR has convicted the defending States (in many cases Turkey) by merely referring to the Salduz principle and adding that no exceptional circumstances were present that could justify an exception to this jurisprudence.[113] Moreover, in the case of Shabelnik v. Ukraine the ECtHR made a clear stance as regards the interpretation that should be given to its new jurisprudence:

> '...the applicant, having been warned about criminal liability for refusal to testify and at the same time having been informed about his right not to testify against himself, could have been confused, as he alleged, about his liability for refusal to testify, especially in the absence of legal advice during that interview'.[114]

The conclusion can be drawn that the right to legal assistance arises as soon as a person is made aware by the authorities that he is suspected of having committed a

---

[110]   Art. 18 § 3 Statute of the International Tribunal for the former Yugoslavia (ICTY). Decision on the Defence Motion to Exclude Evidence from ICTY in Zdravko Mucic, 2 September 1997, Case No. IT-96-21-T, Trial Chamber II.

[111]   2nd General report (CPT/Inf (92) 3), sections 36-38,to be found at the website of the CPT: <http://www.cpt.coe.int>.

[112]   ECtHR, Grand Chamber, 27 November 2008, Salduz, No. 36391/02, § 54-55 and ECtHR 11 December 2008, Panovits v. Cyprus, No. 4268/04, § 66 and 70-73.

[113]   ECtHR 10 March 2009, Böke and Kandemir v. Turkey, Nos. 71912/01, 26968/02 and 36397/03; ECtHR 3 March 2009, Aba v. Turkey, Nos. 7638/02 and 24146/04; ECtHR 17 February 2009, Aslan and Demir v. Turkey, Nos. 38940/02 and 5197/03; ECtHR 17 February 2009, Oztürk v. Turkey, No. 16500/04.

[114]   ECtHR 19 February 2009, Shabelnik v. Ukraine, No. 16404/03.

criminal offence, and that the suspect should be made aware of the suspicion by being cautioned as to his right to silence.[115] The Court has held several times that the task of the lawyer in this situation, amongst other things, is to help to ensure respect for the right of an accused not to incriminate himself.[116]

The right to legal assistance may be waived, but the ECtHR emphasised in *Pishchalnikov* that such a waiver 'must not only be voluntary, but must also constitute a knowing and intelligent relinquishment of a right. Before an accused can be said to have implicitly, through his conduct, waived an important right under article 6, it must be shown that he could reasonably have foreseen what the consequences of his conduct would be'.[117] In the Court's view a valid waiver cannot be established by showing only that a suspect responded to further police-initiated interrogation even if he has been advised of his rights. An accused who has expressed his desire to participate in investigative steps only through counsel should, according to the ECtHR, not be subject to further interrogation by the authorities until counsel has been made available to him, unless the accused himself initiates further communication, exchanges, or conversations with the police or prosecution.[118]

In *Dayanan* the ECtHR underlined the importance of a suspect being assisted by a lawyer during police interrogations and found a violation of article 6 ECHR even though Dayanan had referred to his right to silence during police interrogation and had not given any evidence to the police. As already stated in § 2.4, the Court stressed in this case that the principle of equality of arms requires that a suspect, already at the stage of police interrogations, must be afforded the complete range of interventions that are inherent to legal advice, such as discussion of the case, instructions by the accused, the investigation of facts and search for favourable evidence, preparation for interrogations, the support of the suspect and the control of the conditions under which the suspect is detained.[119]

4.4. The choice, and free provision, of a lawyer for indigent suspects

Art. 6 § 3c makes clear that suspects have a right to choose their lawyer if they are paying for the lawyer's services privately, but is ambiguous when legal assistance is to be provided free of charge. The provision stipulates that a suspect has the right to

---

[115]   See § 2.2 above and ECtHR 18 February 2010, *Zaichenko* v. *Russia*, No. 39660/02, § 42 and § 52-60.

[116]   Established case law, which may be termed the *Salduz* doctrine, and recently confirmed in ECtHR 1 April 2010, *Pavlenko* v. *Russia*, No. 42371/02, § 101.

[117]   ECtHR 24 September 2009, *Pishchalnikov* v. *Russia*, No. 7025/04 § 76. See also ECtHR 31 March 2009, *Plonka* v. *Poland*, No. 20310/02 and ECtHR 1 April 2010, *Pavlenko* v. *Russia*, No. 42371/02, § 102.

[118]   ECtHR 24 September 2009, *Pishchalnikov* v. *Russia*, No. 7025/04 § 79.

[119]   ECtHR 13 October 2009, *Dayanan* v. *Turkey*, No. 7377/03, § 32: 'En effet, l'équité de la procédure requiert que l'accusé puisse obtenir toute la vaste gamme d'interventions qui sont propres au conseil. A cet égard, la discussion de l'affaire, l'organisation de la défense, la recherche des preuves favorables à l'accusé, la préparation des interrogatoires, le soutien de l'accusé en détresse et le contrôle des conditions de détention sont des éléments fondamentaux de la défense que l'avocat doit librement exercer.'

free legal aid on two conditions, first if he does not have sufficient means to pay for legal assistance, and second when the interests of justice so require. The ECtHR holds that the suspect does not have to prove 'beyond all doubt' that he lacks the means to pay for his defence,[120] and indicates three factors that should be taken into account in determining eligibility:[121]

- The seriousness of the offence and the severity of the potential sentence,
- The complexity of the case, and
- The social and personal situation of the defendant.

The case law shows that the right to legal aid applies whenever deprivation of liberty is at stake,[122] a narrowing of the definition of 'interests of justice'. Denying legal aid during periods in which procedural acts, including questioning of the applicants and their medical examinations, are carried out is unacceptable according to the ECtHR.[123] The Court has, however, confirmed that the right to choose a lawyer can be subject to limitations, in particular in cases where the state pays for the legal assistance.[124] Although the Convention does not explicitly include a requirement to inform suspects and defendants about the right to legal assistance, it follows from *Padolov* and *Panovits* that the judicial authorities must actively and adequately inform suspects thereof enabling them to receive legal representation.[125]

The ECHR allows Member States a certain margin of appreciation in choosing a system to make free legal advice available. There is, however, no specific jurisprudence on a number of issues that are of major importance for the effectiveness of the right to free legal advice. Existing research shows that the provision of legal aid is the Achilles heel in many criminal law systems of the EU. Only a bare majority of EU states have a legal aid merits test, and there is a considerable variation as to the content and meaning of means tests. In many states a means test does not exist in a standardised form. Application procedures are often vague and it is frequently not clear how the determining authorities come to their decisions. In fifty per cent of EU states the law does not impose a time limit for determining legal aid applications, and many states do not allow for choice where a lawyer is provided under legal aid.[126]

Remuneration for defence lawyers providing legal aid services varies widely among EU states, and information provided by member governments on criminal legal aid expenditure indicates that in practice there must be problems in compliance with the requirement of article 6 § 3c.[127] However, this is not apparent

---

[120] ECtHR 25 April 1983, *Pakelli* v. *Germany*, No. 8398/78, § 34.
[121] ECtHR 24 May 1991, *Quaranta* v. *Switzerland*, No. 12744/87, § 35.
[122] ECtHR 10 June 1996, *Benham* v. *the United Kingdom*, No. 19380/92.
[123] ECtHR 20 June 2002, *Berlinski* v. *Poland*, No. 27715/95 and 30209/96.
[124] ECtHR 14 January 2003, *Lagerblom* v. *Sweden*, No. 26891/95, § 54.
[125] ECtHR 10 August 2006, *Padolov* v. *Bulgaria*, No. 54784/00, § 53-55 and ECtHR 11 December 2008, *Panovits* v. *Cyprus*, No. 4268/04 § 64.
[126] Spronken et al., § 3.2. See also Bowles & Perry 2009.
[127] See the Report of the European Commission for the Efficiency of Justice (CEPEJ) European Judicial Systems – 2008, Council of Europe September 2008, fig. 18 on p. 46, and Spronken et al. 2009, p. 71.

from ECtHR case law, probably because suspects who do not receive legal aid (in time) are not willing or able to exhaust domestic remedies in order to file a complaint with the ECtHR.

4.5. The right to private consultation with a lawyer

An essential condition for effective legal assistance is the confidentiality of the lawyer/client relationship, which includes the right to confidential communication and unrestricted access. This means that there is a need for guarantees that lawyers are able to visit and speak with their clients in confidence, without surveillance by third parties.[128] The ECtHR has dealt with the protection of professional privilege under both article 6 and article 8 ECHR. The landmark decision is *Niemietz* v. *Germany* in which the ECtHR stated in general terms that 'where a lawyer is involved, an encroachment on professional secrecy may have repercussions on the proper administration of justice and hence on the rights guaranteed by art. 6 of the Convention'.[129] In other decisions the Court refers to rights as guaranteed by article 6, such as the right to seek advice pending criminal proceedings. In *Schönenberger and Durmaz* correspondence sent by the lawyer to his detained client was stopped because the authorities had learned from its contents that Mr. Durmaz had given his client advice to make use of his right to silence. The Court found a violation, reaffirming the right to remain silent as being a right enshrined in article 6, and that therefore the interference was not in accordance with article 8 § 2 ECHR because it was not necessary in a democratic society.[130] The ECtHR held in *S.* v. *Switzerland*[131] that article 6 § 3c should be interpreted so as to guarantee that lawyer/client communications are confidential. Intercepting such communications violates 'one of the basic requirements of a fair trial in a democratic society'.[132] In a recent case the Court confirmed that correspondence with lawyers, whatever its purpose, is always privileged and that intercepting mail is only permissible in exceptional circumstances such as where there is a reasonable belief that privilege is being abused; meaning that the correspondence would endanger prison security or the safety of others or otherwise be of a criminal nature.[133] Accordingly, the surveillance of contacts based on the risk of collusion cannot serve as a justification as this was the very reason for detention.[134]

Another guarantee related to unrestricted access is professional privilege enjoyed by lawyers. They cannot be compelled to disclose what has come to their knowledge in the context of the defence. This means not only that defence lawyers cannot be forced to disclose confidential information, but also that sufficient measures must be taken to prevent confidential information from coming to the

---

[128]   ECtHR 27 November 2007, *Zagaria* v. *Italy*, No. 58295/00, § 30.
[129]   ECtHR 16 December 1992, *Niemietz* v. *Germany*, No. 13710/88, § 37.
[130]   ECtHR 20 June 1988, *Schönenberger and Durmaz* v. *Switzerland*, No. 11368/85.
[131]   ECtHR 28 November 1991, *S.* v. *Switzerland*, No. 12629/87, 13965/88.
[132]   ECtHR 12 May 2005, *Öcalan* v. *Turkey*, No. 46221/99.
[133]   ECtHR 9 October 2008, *Moiseyev* v. *Russia*, No. 62936/00, § 210. See also, ECtHR 25 March 1992, *Campbell* v. *United Kingdom*, No. 13590/88, § 48.
[134]   ECtHR 31 January 2002, *Lanz* v. *Austria*, No. 24430/94, § 52.

knowledge of the judicial authorities through the application of investigative methods such as interception of telecommunications.

Some member states have provisions enabling lawyer/client consultations to be intercepted or listened to and the case law of the ECtHR in this respect shows that safeguards to protect lawyer client privilege are left to variable local or national customs and often are not in accordance with the requirements of article 8 of the Convention.[135]

4.6. The standards, role and independence of lawyers

The ECHR does not contain any explicit provision regarding the role, or standards, of criminal defence lawyers. The Havana Declaration[136] does provide that governments must ensure that lawyers are able to perform their professional functions without intimidation, hindrance, harassment or improper interference (art. 16) and also provides that lawyers must not be identified with their clients or their clients' causes (art. 18). However, there is nothing that equates with this in the ECHR. In *Nikula*[137] the ECtHR held that 'the threat of an *ex post facto* review of counsel's criticism of another party to criminal procedure [the prosecutor] is difficult to reconcile with defence counsel's duty to defend their clients' interests zealously'. The freedom of a lawyer to defend his client as he sees fit has been also assessed by the Court under the freedom of speech provision of article 10 ECHR. In *Nikula* the Court held that it would not exclude the possibility that, in certain circumstances, an interference with counsel's freedom of expression in the course of a trial could also raise an issue under article 6 ECHR with regard to the right of an accused client to receive a fair trial. Equality of arms and other considerations of fairness militate in favour of a free and even forceful exchange of argument between the parties. The basic approach of the ECtHR in this respect is that lawyers are certainly entitled to comment in public on the administration of justice, but their criticism must not overstep certain bounds. In that connection, account must be taken of the need to strike the right balance between the various interests involved, which include the public's right to receive information about questions arising from judicial decisions, the requirements of the proper administration of justice and the dignity of the legal profession. The national authorities have a certain margin of appreciation in assessing the necessity of interference, but this margin is subject to European supervision as regards both the relevant rules and the decisions applying them. Where criticism of a judge or prosecutor by lawyers is confined to the

---

[135]   See ECtHR 25 March 1998, *Kopp* v. *Switzerland*, No. 23224/94; ECtHR 25 November 2004, *Decision on the admissibility of Aalmoes and 112 others* v. *The Netherlands*, No. 16269/02; ECtHR 27 September 2005, *Petri Sallinen and others* v. *Finland*, No. 50882/99; ECtHR 7 June 2007, *Smirnov* v. *Russia*, No. 71362/01; ECtHR 28 June 2007, *The Association for European Integration and Human Rights and Ekimdzhiev* v. *Bulgaria*, No. 62540/00. See also Spronken & Fermon 2008.

[136]   The Havana Declaration on the Role of Lawyers, agreed at the 8th UN Congress on the Prevention of Crime and the Treatment of Offenders, Havana, Cuba, 1990.

[137]   ECtHR 21 March 2002, *Nikula* v. *Finland*, No. 31611/96.

courtroom the margin of appreciation narrower than where that criticism is voiced, for example, in the media.[138]

As regards the quality of the work of defence lawyers, the ECtHR has been reluctant to hold states liable for the failures of lawyers who, as members of independent liberal professions, should regulate themselves. The ECtHR has frequently held that:

> 'A state cannot be held responsible for every shortcoming on the part of a lawyer appointed for legal aid purposes … [States are] required to intervene only if a failure by counsel to provide effective representation is manifest or sufficiently brought to their attention.'[139]

However, in relation to legal assistance during police interrogation, the ECtHR has recently critically assessed the effectiveness of the assistance given by a lawyer acting under legal aid to his client in police custody in preventing breach of the privilege against self-incrimination and facilitating the effective exercise of the right to remain silent, and held that the police had a responsibility for keeping a close eye on the (in) effectiveness of the lawyer.[140]

5.   Rights that promote effective participation

The rights we address in this section all relate to the means available to suspects and defendants to participate in proceedings and to effectively conduct their defence.

5.1.   *The right to investigate the case*

Article 6 ECHR does not contain any explicit provision giving the defence the right to seek evidence, investigate facts, interview prospective witnesses[141] or obtain expert evidence. The possibilities to conduct these kind of activities during the preliminary investigations depend highly on the nature of the criminal procedure and vary significantly within the EU. Existing research[142] shows that inquisitorially-based criminal justice systems often prohibit active defence at the pre-trial phase

---

[138]   See ECtHR 21 March 2002, *Nikula v. Finland*, No. 31611/96, § 46; ECtHR 20 May 1998, *Schöpfer v. Switzerland*, No. 25405/94 § 33 and ECtHR 17 July 2008, *Schmidt v. Austria*, No. 513/05.

[139]   ECtHR 24 November 1993, *Imbriosca v. Switzerland*, No. 13972/88. See also ECtHR 19 December 1989, *Kamasinksi v. Austria*, No. 9783/82; ECtHR 10 October 2002, *Czekalla v. Portugal*, No. 38830/97, § 65; ECtHR 7 October 2008, *Bogumil v. Portugal*, No. 35228/0317/168; ECtHR 21 April 1998, *Daud v. Portugal*, § 38; ECtHR 14 January 2003, *Lagerblom v. Sweden*, No. 26891/95, § 56 and ECtHR 26 January 2010, *Ebanks v. the United Kingdom*, No. 36822/06, § 73 and 84-82.

[140]   ECtHR 1 April 2010, *Pavlenko v. Russia*, No. 42371/0, § 108-114. It should be noted that this was in the context of the applicant having specifically rejected the lawyer appoint to assist him, and that the police had carried out informal 'talks' with the applicant in the absence of the lawyer.

[141]   What is meant here are facilities to enable the defence to make decisions such as whether or not to call witnesses. The calling and questioning of witnesses itself is provided for in art. 6 § 3d ECHR.

[142]   See Cape et al. 2007, and Spronken et al. 2009.

and merely allow reactive defence: only when the results of the official (pre-trial) investigation are made known to the accused is he in a position to propose further investigations such as the questioning of (additional) witnesses or counter-investigation by an expert. In most systems the accused lacks powers and financial resources, for instance, to interview unwilling prospective witnesses or to conduct their own investigation of the facts. In some jurisdictions investigation by the accused or his lawyer is even regarded as obstructing the course of the official investigations. If the suspect or accused wishes to investigate, he has to ask the police, prosecutor or the investigating judge for permission and for help, and defence is thus dependant on their willingness to act. The only relevant ECtHR case is *Dayanan*,[143] in which the ECtHR stressed that as from the police interrogation stage, the accused must be afforded the possibility of investigating facts and, in particular, potentially favourable evidence. However, there is no case law (yet) which elaborates this.

5.2. The right of a defendant to be tried in their presence and to participate in the process

In principle the accused has the right to be present at hearings and to participate actively in the process.[144] This presupposes that the accused has a broad understanding of the nature of the trial process and of what is at stake for him or her, including the significance of any penalty which may be imposed. The defendant should be able, *inter alia*, to explain his version of events and indicate any statements with which he disagrees. This can be done by his lawyer, with whom the suspect must be able to discuss those facts which should be put forward in his defence,[145] but the presence of the lawyer cannot compensate for the absence of the accused.[146]

A suspect is, however, not required to actively co-operate with the judicial authorities.[147] A trial in absentia is not in itself incompatible with article 6 ECHR as long as the accused may subsequently obtain, from a court which has heard him, a fresh determination of the merits of the charge where it has not been established that he has waived his right to appear and to defend himself.[148] If the suspect has received a summons and deliberately does not attend trial, a retrial may be refused.[149] Although the Court has stressed the prime importance of the accused

---

[143] ECtHR 13 October 2009, *Dayanan v. Turkey*, No. 7377/03, § 32.
[144] ECtHR 12 February 1985, *Colozza v. Italy*, No. 9024/80, § 27-33. ECtHR 16 December 1999, *T. v. the United Kingdom*, No. 24724/94, § 88-89; ECtHR 18 October 2006, *Hermi v. Italy*, No. 18114/02, § 58-67.
[145] An overview of the case law in this respect can be found in ECtHR 14 October 2008, *Timergaliyev v. Russia*, No. 40631/02, § 51-56.
[146] ECtHR 16 December 1999, *T. v. the United Kingdom*, No. 24724/94, § 88; and ECtHR 25 November 1997, *Zana v. Turkey*, No. 18954/91, § 67-72.
[147] ECtHR 10 December 1982, *Corigliano v. Italy*, No. 8304/78, § 42 and ECtHR 15 July 1982, *Eckle v. Germany*, No. 8130/78, § 82.
[148] ECtHR 12 February 1985, *Colozza v. Italy*, No. 9024/80, § 27-33; ECtHR 1 March 2006, *Sejdovic v. Italy*, No. 56581/00, § 82-84.
[149] ECtHR 14 June 2001, *Medenica v. Switzerland*, No. 20491/92, § 59.

appearing at his trial, the absence of the suspect should not be punished by depriving him of the right to legal assistance.[150] A lawyer who attends a trial for the apparent purpose of defending the accused in his absence must be given the opportunity to do so.[151]

In appeal or cassation proceedings the right to be present can be restricted if the proceedings are limited to questions of law and do not review the facts.[152] A relevant factor is whether the presence of the suspect would add value to the trial. Thus whether there is a need for a public hearing in the presence of the suspect depends on the nature of the appeal system, the scope of the court of appeal's powers, and the manner in which the applicant's interests are presented and protected.[153]

5.3. Adequate time and facilities for preparation of a defence

The right to adequate time and facilities in order to prepare a defence is closely linked with the other defence rights that are stipulated in article 6 ECHR, especially the right to information,[154] and can be seen as a general provision to 'guarantee not rights that are theoretical or illusory but rights that are practical and effective'.[155] The first requirement is that the defendant must be informed properly and promptly of the accusation, be allowed timely access to the file, and be afforded sufficient time to comprehend the information and subsequently to prepare a proper defence.[156] Access to the prosecution file has to be offered in due time, but does not release the prosecution from its obligation to inform the accused promptly and in detail of the full accusation against him. That duty rests entirely on the prosecuting authority's shoulders and cannot be complied with passively by merely making the information available without bringing it to the attention of the accused.[157]

In *Natunen* the Court ruled that the guarantee of 'adequate time and facilities for the preparation of his defence' implies that the substantive defence activity may comprise everything which is 'necessary' to prepare for the main trial, and that the accused must have the opportunity to organise his defence in an appropriate way and without restriction as to the possibility of putting all relevant arguments before the trial court. Furthermore, the facilities which should be enjoyed by everyone charged with a criminal offence include the opportunity for the accused to acquaint himself, for the purposes of preparing his defence, with the results of investigations carried out throughout the proceedings. Failure to disclose to the defence material evidence, which contains such particulars that could enable the accused to

---

[150]   ECtHR 23 November 1993, *Poitrimol* v. *France*, No. 14032/88, § 35.
[151]   ECtHR 22 September 1994, *Lala* v. *the Netherlands*, No. 14861/89 § 30-34; ECtHR 21 January 1999, *Van Geyseghem* v. *Belgium*, No. 26103/95, § 33-34.
[152]   ECtHR 10 February 1996, *Botten* v. *Norway*, No. 16206/90 § 39.
[153]   ECtHR 29 October 1991, *Fejde* v. *Sweden*, No. 12631/87, § 27.
[154]   See § 3 of this chapter.
[155]   ECtHR 21 April 1998, *Daud* v. *Portugal*, No. 22600/93, § 36-43; ECtHR 7 October 2008, *Bogumil* v. *Portugal*, No. 35228/03, § 46-49.
[156]   See also § 3; ECtHR 21 December 2006, *Borisova* v. *Bulgaria*, No. 56891/00, § 41-45.
[157]   ECtHR 25 July 2000, *Mattoccia* v. *Italy*, No. 23969/94, § 65.

exonerate himself or have his sentence reduced, would constitute a denial of facilities and, therefore, a violation of the right guaranteed in article 6 § 3b ECHR.[158]

The time necessary for preparation will depend on the circumstances, such as the complexity of the case, the severity of the (possible) sentence and the assistance of a lawyer.[159] If the nature of the accusation changes during the proceedings, the defendant must be allowed the time to react to it, and accordingly a court should make allowances for difficulties caused to the defence if suddenly confronted with another version of the events.[160]

The requirement of adequate time and facilities also implies that authorities should exercise diligence in order to ensure that the rights guaranteed by article 6 are enjoyed in an effective manner. This means that an active attitude is required from the authorities, for example, in order to enable the suspect to receive legal assistance,[161] to enable the lawyer to come to the police station to visit the suspect before an interview,[162] and to enable the suspect to call and question witnesses.[163]

5.4. *Right to call and question witnesses, including experts*

The right of the accused to examine or to have examined witnesses against him, and to obtain the attendance and examination of witnesses *a décharge* under the same conditions as witnesses *a charge*, as laid down in article 6 § 3d ECHR, constitutes an essential element of a fair trial and is closely linked with the principle of equality of arms and the right to adversarial proceedings.[164] Consequently, it implies that, as a rule, all evidence must be 'produced in the presence of the accused at the public hearing with a view to adversarial argument'[165] and that the defence must have an equal opportunity as for the prosecution to summon witnesses. However, since this right can be subject to exceptions,[166] it is in principle for national courts to assess whether it is appropriate to call a witness.[167] A defendant requesting a witness to be heard should explain why it is important to hear that witness and why it is necessary to establish the truth.[168] Even though the regulation of evidence is primarily a matter for national law, the ECtHR will examine whether the proceedings as a whole, including the way in which the evidence was submitted,

---

[158]   ECtHR 31 March 2009, *Natunen* v. *Finland*, No. 21022/04, § 42-43.

[159]   ECtHR 7 October 2008, *Bogumil* v. *Portugal*, No. 35228/03, § 48-49.

[160]   ECtHR 25 July 2000, *Mattoccia* v. *Italy*, No. 23969/94, § 67.

[161]   ECtHR 10 August 2006, *Padalov* v. *Bulgarie*, No. 54784/00, § 53-55; ECtHR 27 March 2007, *Talat Tunc* v. *Turkey*, No. 32432/96, § 61-62.

[162]   ECtHR 24 September 2009, *Pishchalnikov* v. *Russia*, No. 7025/04, § 79 and ECtHR 11 December 2008, *Panovits* v. *Cyprus*, No. 4268/04, § 70-71.

[163]   ECtHR 17 July 2001, *Sadak and others* v. *Turkey*, Nos. 29900/96, 29901/96, 29902/96, 29903/96, § 67.

[164]   ECtHR 6 December 1988, *Barberà, Messegué and Jabardo* v. *Spain*, Nos. 10588/83, 10589/83, 10590/83, § 78.

[165]   ECtHR 15 June 1992, *Lüdi* v. *Switzerland*, No. 12433/86, § 47; ECtHR 28 February 2006, *Krasniki* v. *Czech Republic*, No. 51277/99, § 75 and ECtHR 20 January 2009, *Al-Khawaja and Tahery* v. *the United Kingdom*, Nos. 26766/05 and 22228/06, § 34.

[166]   Recently confirmed in ECtHR 29 April 2009, *Polyakov* v. *Russia*, No. 77018/01, § 31.

[167]   ECtHR 6 May 2004, *Perna* v. *Italy*, No. 48898/99, § 29.

[168]   ECtHR 6 May 2004, *Perna* v. *Italy*, No. 48898/99, § 29.

were fair.[169] In addition, a decision to refuse to hear a witness should adequately state the reasons for the decision.[170]

The fact that statements produced during a police or judicial investigation are used at trial is not, in itself, inconsistent with paragraphs 1 and 3 (d) of article 6 provided that defence rights are respected.[171] It is settled case law that the defendant be given an adequate and proper opportunity to challenge and question a witness against him, either when he makes his statements or at a later stage.[172] Consequently, the lack of any opportunity for a confrontation with a witness will result in a violation of the fair trial principle.[173] It is also implied that a conviction must not be based solely or to a decisive extent on statements of a witness who the accused has had no possibility to challenge.[174] In *Al-Khawaja* v. *UK* the Court clearly recalled that, while handicaps encountered by the defence arising from the use of untested statements as evidence can be counterbalanced by procedures followed by the judicial authorities,[175] when untested statements are the sole or decisive basis for conviction, article 6 ECHR will be violated.[176]

Special difficulties occur with regard to anonymous witnesses. The Court has highlighted the dangers of keeping the identity of a witness from the accused and has adopted a prudent and strict attitude towards this.[177] Reliance on anonymous informants at the pre-trial stage is, in itself, not incompatible with article 6 ECtHR, but the subsequent use thereof by a court to support a conviction raises problems under the Convention. In *Doorson* the Court established three criteria in order to check whether an anonymous statement could be relied upon: first, whether there are sufficient reasons for maintaining the anonymity of the witness; second, whether the handicaps encountered by the defence are sufficiently counterbalanced by the procedures followed by the judicial authorities; and third, whether the anonymous evidence was not the sole or decisive basis for the conviction.[178]

Although article 6 § 3d ECHR relates to witnesses and not experts, the Court accepts that the guarantees contained in article 6 § 3 are constituent elements,

169 ECtHR 6 May 2004, *Perna* v. *Italy*, No. 48898/99, § 29; ECtHR 23 April 1997, *Van Mechelen and others* v. *the Netherlands*, Nos. 21363/93, 21364/93, 21427/93, 22056/93, § 50; ECtHR 15 June 1992, *Lüdi* v. *Switzerland*, No. 12433/86, § 43; ECtHR 26 March 1996, *Doorson* v. *the Netherlands*, § 67 and ECtHR 14 December 1999, *A.M.* v. *Italy*, No. 37019/97, § 24.
170 ECtHR 22 April 2000, *Vidal* v. *Belgium*, No. 12351/86, § 34.
171 ECtHR 24 November 1986, *Unterpertinger* v. *Austria*, No. 9120/80, § 31.
172 ECtHR 15 June 1992, *Lüdi* v. *Switzerland*, No. 12433/86, § 49; ECtHR 20 September 1993, *Saïdi* v. *France*, No. 14647/89, § 43; ECtHR 23 April 1997, *Van Mechelen and others* v. *the Netherlands*, Nos. 21363/93, 21364/93, 21427/93, 22056/93, § 51; ECtHR 14 December 1999, *A.M.* v. *Italy*, No. 37019/97, § 25.
173 ECtHR 20 September 1993, *Saïdi* v. *France*, No. 14647/89, § 44.
174 ECtHR 27 February 2001, *Luca* v. *Italy*, No. 33354/96, § 40.
175 Counterbalancing factors include: the possibility for the defence to ask questions, the existence of other supporting evidence, the possibility for the defence to verify the reliability of the witness and the accuracy of his statements.
176 ECtHR 20 January 2009, *Al-Khawaja and Tahery* v. *the United Kingdom*, Nos. 26766/05 and 22228/06, § 37 and 38. This judgement further clarified the principles expressed in the case ECtHR 26 March 1996, *Doorson* v. *the Netherlands*, No. 20524/92 § 72-76.
177 ECtHR 20 November 1989, *Kostovski* v. *the Netherlands*, No. 11454/85, § 42.
178 ECtHR 26 March 1996, *Doorson* v. *the Netherlands*, No. 20524/92, § 70-76.

amongst others, of the concept of a fair trial set forth in article 6 § 1 ECHR. As a consequence the Court applies to the hearing of experts the same criteria as to the hearing of witnesses. If the suspect was not given the opportunity to question experts, in order to subject their credibility to scrutiny or to cast any doubt on their conclusions, either at the pre-trial stage or during trial, article 6 § 1 may be violated.[179] In *Bönisch* the Court ruled that experts that are called by the defence should receive equal treatment to court-appointed experts.[180] Where an expert has been appointed by a court, the parties must in all instances be able to attend the interviews held by him or be shown the documents he has taken into account. What is essential is that the parties should be able to participate properly in the proceedings before the trial court.[181]

6. Free interpretation and translation

A defendant who does not speak or understand the language of the proceedings is clearly at a disadvantage.[182] In order to remedy this vulnerable situation, article 6 § 3e provides for the right to free interpretation.[183] In *Luedicke, Belkacem and Koç v. Germany* the Court made clear that the term 'free' implies a 'once and for all exemption or exoneration'.[184] Consequently, defendants may not being ordered to pay the costs of an interpreter.[185] Article 5 § 2 and 6 § 3a ECHR require, in more general terms, that everyone who is arrested or charged with a criminal offence shall be informed promptly, *in a language which he understands*, of the reasons for arrest and of the nature and cause of the charge against him.[186] The interpretation must enable the defendant to understand the case against him and to defend himself, in particular by being able to put his version of events before the court.[187] Therefore, the scope of this right is not limited to oral statements made at the trial hearing but also covers documentary material, and pre-trial proceedings.[188] Accordingly, the right to interpretation implies a right to translation of necessary documents. In *Kamasinski* the Court specified that not every document requires to be translated in written form. Oral interpretation provided by an interpreter or by the defence lawyer will be sufficient as long as the defendant understand the

---

[179] ECtHR 4 November 2008, *Balsyte-Lideikiene* v. *Lithuania*, No. 72596/01, § 63-66.

[180] ECtHR 6 May 1985, *Bönisch* v. *Austria*, No. 8658/79, § 32-33.

[181] ECtHR 18 March 1997, *Mantovanelli* v. *France*, No. 21497/93, § 33 and ECtHR 2 June 2005, *Cottin* v. *Belgium*, No. 48386/99, § 32.

[182] ECtHR 19 December 1989, *Kamasinski* v. *Austria*, No. 9783/82, § 79 and ECtHR 18 October 2006, *Hermi* v. *Italy*, No.18114/02, § 68.

[183] This is also expressed in art. 14.3.a & f ICCPR and in art. 55.1.c and 67.1.f of the Rome Statute.

[184] ECtHR 28 November 1978, *Luedicke, Belkacem and Koç* v. *Germany*, Nos. 6210/73, 6877/75, 7132/75, § 40.

[185] ECtHR 28 November 1978, *Luedicke, Belkacem and Koç* v. *Germany*, Nos. 6210/73, 6877/75, 7132/75, § 46.

[186] See also art. 67.1.a of the Rome Statute.

[187] ECtHR 18 October 2006, *Hermi* v. *Italy*, No.18114/02, § 70.

[188] ECtHR 28 November 1978, *Luedicke, Belkacem and Koç* v. *Germany*, Nos. 6210/73, 6877/75, 7132/75, § 48, ECtHR 19 December 1989, *Kamasinski* v. *Austria*, No. 9783/82, § 74 and ECtHR 18 October 2006, *Hermi* v. *Italy*, No. 18114/02, § 69.

relevant document and their consequences. For example, the fact that the verdict is not translated is not in itself incompatible with article 6 as long as the defendant sufficiently understands the verdict and the reasoning thereof.[189]

Following from the decision in *Cuscani* an active attitude is required from the judicial authorities since they should verify the accused's need for interpretation, even though the conduct of the defence is essentially a matter between the defendant and his lawyer, and even though the defendant did not explicitly request interpretation.[190]

The mere appointment of an interpreter is, according to the ECtHR, although necessary, is not sufficient. Member States are required to exercise a degree of control over the adequacy of the interpretation.[191] Furthermore, the Court has highlighted the importance of judges since they are the ultimate guardian of the fairness of the proceedings.[192]

It should be noted that existing research reveals that national rules on what documents are to be translated vary considerably among the Member States, as does the right to interpretation. In some member states there is no provision for interpretation during lawyer/client consultations.[193]

7. The right to reasoned decisions and appeal

From the perspective of the defence there is a clear link between the right to reasoned decisions and the right to appeal. The rationale for having a requirement that decisions be reasoned is manifold. It provides for the possibility that decisions may be reviewed by an appellate body, it allows a defendant to prepare for an appeal, and it demonstrates to the parties that they have been heard in a fair and equitable way.[194] Moreover it permits public scrutiny of the proper administration of justice.[195]

7.1. *Reasoned decisions*

According to the ECtHR it follows from the fair trial requirement that national courts must indicate with sufficient clarity the grounds on which they base their decisions.[196] Most cases that the Court has dealt with concern situations where national courts did not give reasons for rejecting a defence argument, for refusing to allow documents to be added to the case file, or for rejecting evidence. The

---

[189]   ECtHR 19 December 1989, *Kamasinski v. Austria*, No. 9783/82, § 85.
[190]   ECtHR 24 September 2002, *Cuscani v. the United Kingdom*, No. 32771, § 38 and 39. In this case, the defendant suffered from a hearing impairment.
[191]   ECtHR 19 December 1989, *Kamasinksi v. Austria*, No. 9783/82, § 74 and ECtHR 18 October 2006, *Hermi v. Italy*, No. 18114/02, § 70.
[192]   ECtHR 18 October 2006, *Hermi v. Italy*, No. 18114/02, § 72 and ECtHR 24 September 2002, *Cuscani v. the United Kingdom*, No. 32771, § 39.
[193]   See Spronken et al. 2009, p. 84.
[194]   ECtHR 1 July 2003, *Suominen v. Finland*, No. 37801/97, § 37 and ECtHR 11 January 2007, *Kuznetsov and Others v. Russia*, No. 184/02, § 85.
[195]   ECtHR 27 September 2001, *Hirvisaari v. Finland*, No. 49684/99, § 30.
[196]   ECtHR 16 December 1992, *Hadjianastassiou v. Greece*, No. 12945/87, § 33.

obligation to provide adequate reasons does not imply that courts must provide detailed answers to every argument.[197] The extent of the obligation will vary according to the nature of the decision and a possible violation thereof, and is consequently always to be considered in light of the circumstance of the case.[198]

Even though courts enjoy a certain margin of appreciation in choosing between arguments in a particular case and in admitting evidence, the authorities are obliged to justify their activities by giving reasons for their decisions.[199] The notion of fair trial requires courts at least to address the essential issues that have been submitted to them, and findings reached by a lower court should not simply be endorsed without further explanation.[200] Where an appellate court dismisses an appeal on the basis of reasons given in the lower court, it must be verified whether the reasons given by the lower court enabled the parties to make effective use of their right of appeal.[201] National courts may not avoid the essence of complaints and should always undertake an examination of the merits of those complaints.[202]

Since case law of the ECtHR on reasoned decisions remain somewhat vague, and highly dependent on the circumstances of the case, and example provided the case of *Gradinar* may help to clarifying the way the Court assesses whether sufficient reasons have been given:[203]

> '111. The Court notes that a number of findings of the Chişinău Regional Court were not contradicted by the findings of the higher courts and that, accordingly, they must be considered as established facts [...] These included the fact that G. [*Gradinar*] and the other accused were arrested and detained on the basis of a fabricated administrative offence, during which period of detention they were questioned and made self-incriminating statements in the absence of any procedural safeguards [....]. There was no response to the finding that G. had unlawfully been shown the video recording of D.C.'s statement at the crime scene [...] in order to obtain consistent statements by all the accused.
>
> 112. The Court further notes that the higher courts did not deal with the finding of the lower court that G. and the other co-accused had an alibi for the presumed time of the crime [...], and that a number of serious procedural violations made unreliable most of the expert reports [..].
>
> 113. The higher courts also relied on the many witness statements in G.'s case. However, the Court observes that no comment was made on the finding by the lower court that some of those statements were fabricated by the police [....].

---

197 ECtHR 19 April 1994, *Van de Hurk* v. *the Netherlands*, No. 16034/90, § 61; ECtHR 8 April 2008, *Gradinar* v. *Moldova*, No. 7170/02, § 107.

198 ECtHR 9 December 1994, *Ruiz Torija* v. *Spain*, No. 18390/91, § 29; ECtHR 9 December 1994, *Hiro Balani* v. *Spain*, No. 18064/91, § 27 and ECtHR 21 May 2002, *Jokela* v. *Finland*, No. 28856/95, § 72.

199 ECtHR 1 July 2003, *Suominen* v. *Finland*, No. 37801/97, § 36.

200 ECtHR 21 May 2002, *Jokela* v. *Finland*, No. 28856/95, § 73.

201 ECtHR 21 May 2002, *Jokela* v. *Finland*, No. 28856/95, § 73.

202 ECtHR 11 January 2007, *Kuznetsov and Others* v. *Russia*, No. 184/02, § 84.

203 ECtHR 8 April 2008, *Gradinar* v. *Moldova*, No. 7170/02, § 111-116.

114. The Court concludes that while accepting as "decisive evidence" […] the self-incriminating statements made by the accused, the domestic courts chose simply to remain silent with regard to a number of serious violations of the law noted by the lower court and to certain fundamental issues, such as the fact that the accused had an alibi for the presumed time of the murder. The Court could not find any explanation for such omission in the courts' decisions and neither did the Government provide any clarification in this respect.

115. In the light of the above observations and taking into account the proceedings as a whole, the Court considers that the domestic courts failed to give sufficient reasons for convicting G. and thus did not satisfy the requirements of fairness as required by article 6 of the Convention.'

7.2. The right to appeal

The right to review of a conviction by a higher tribunal is not contained in the ECHR itself, but can be found in article 2 of the Seventh Protocol thereto.[204] All Council of Europe Member States, except for Belgium, Germany, the Netherlands, Turkey and the United Kingdom, have ratified this Protocol. State Parties enjoy a considerable margin of appreciation in relation to the implementation of this right within their jurisdiction. Article 2 § 2 of the Protocol contains several possible restrictions, for example, with regard to offences of a minor character. It is also accepted case law that a review by a higher court may be confined to questions of law, leaving out factual questions.[205] Limitations must, however, pursue a legitimate aim and must not infringe the very essence of the right to review.[206]

Where appeal procedures are provided for, the ECtHR has ruled that they must comply with the guarantees of article 6 ECHR.[207] The Court has emphasised that a fair balance should be struck between, on the one hand, a legitimate concern to ensure the enforcement of judicial decisions and, on the other, the right of access to the courts and the rights of the defence.[208] In this respect the Court has ruled in a number of similar cases that have been brought against France that it is contrary to the fundamental guarantees contained in article 6 ECHR to declare an appeal on a point of law inadmissible solely because of a refusal by the appellant to surrender to custody. Such a ruling compels the appellant to subject himself in advance to the deprivation of liberty resulting from the impugned decision, although that decision

---

[204] Protocol No. 7 to the Convention for the Protection of Human Rights and Fundamental Freedoms, adopted on 22 November 1984, entered into force on 1st November 1988. Art. 2 reads: 1 Everyone convicted of a criminal offence by a tribunal shall have the right to have his conviction or sentence reviewed by a higher tribunal. The exercise of this right, including the grounds on which it may be exercised, shall be governed by law. 2 This right may be subject to exceptions in regard to offences of a minor character, as prescribed by law, or in cases in which the person concerned was tried in the first instance by the highest tribunal or was convicted following an appeal against acquittal.

[205] ECtHR 28 May 1985, *Ashingdane* v. *the United Kingdom*, No. 8225/78, § 57.

[206] ECtHR 13 February 2001, *Krombach* v. *France*, No. 29731/96, § 96 and ECtHR 25 July 2002, *Papon* v. *France*, No. 54210/00, § 90.

[207] ECtHR 14 December 1999, *Khalfaoui* v. *France*, No. 34791/97, § 37.

[208] ECtHR 29 July 1998, *Omar* v. *France*, No. 24767/94 and ECtHR 29 July 1998, *Guérin* v. *France*, No. 25201/94 § 40.

cannot be considered final until the appeal has been decided or the time-limit for lodging an appeal has expired. This, according to the Court, impairs the very essence of the right to appeal by imposing a disproportionate burden on the appellant, thus upsetting the fair balance that must be struck between the legitimate concern to ensure that judicial decisions are enforced, and the right of access to the Court of Cassation and exercise of the rights of the defence on the other.[209] However, the ECtHR has not provided detailed guidelines regarding implementation of the right to appeal.

8.   Conclusions

8.1.   The challenge of defining minimum standards

Drawing conclusions as to minimum standards established by ECtHR case law is a precarious undertaking since the Court always assesses whether proceedings in an individual case were fair as a whole. The fact that certain requirements are not met in a preliminary stage of the proceedings does not necessarily lead to a violation of Convention rights provided that the shortcomings are compensated for or repaired at a subsequent stage. In addition most rights are not absolute in the sense that they may be weighed against other legitimate interests such as the proper course of criminal proceedings or the interests of witnesses. Furthermore, our analysis demonstrates that the various elements that can be found in the fair trial requirements are very much interwoven. Principles, such as the equality of arms, the presumption of innocence, adversarial proceedings and the prohibition on self-incrimination, function as general normative standards in themselves that have an impact on other requirements such as the right to have access to the case file or the right to call and question witnesses. Therefore, as the Court has often stated, the guarantees in article 6 § 2 and § 3 are specific aspects of the right to a fair trial set forth in article 6 § 1, and complaints are considered from the angle of both paragraphs taken together. In addition, the Court has the advantage of hindsight that parties and courts at the national level do not have during the course of ongoing proceedings. For example, the question of whether the requirement that a conviction must not be based solely or to a decisive extent on statements of witnesses the defence could not test nor challenge, can only be answered after the national court has reached its final verdict. The constituent element of the right to call and question witnesses cannot, therefore, easily be converted into a regulation at the national level that would be helpful in regulating the right of the defence to call witnesses in the course of the proceedings. At most one can deduce from the case law an evidentiary rule that courts must respect when deliberating upon a case.

We must also bear in mind that many provisions allow member states a margin of appreciation as to how the fair trial requirements are implemented. It is,

---

[209]   ECtHR 23 November 1993, *Poitrimol* v. *France*, No. 14032/88, § 38; ECtHR 29 July 1998, *Omar* v. *France*, No. 24767/94 and ECtHR 29 July 1998, *Guérin* v. *France*, No. 25201/94, § 40; ECtHR 25 July 2002, *Papon* v. *France*, No. 54210/00, § 90; ECtHR 14 December 1999, *Khalfaoui* v. *France*, No. 34791/97, § 37.

therefore, not always possible to define and articulate detailed standards that are operational and/or applicable to all criminal law systems or to particular stages of the criminal process. There is, however, a development within the jurisprudence of the court that facilitates the drawing of conclusions for the implementation of elementary procedural rights at the national level. The ECtHR now usually includes in its judgments a paragraph in which it expresses its general views on the issue under scrutiny. Sometimes the Court gives very detailed directions on how national proceedings should be regulated or conducted and what sanctions should apply if the requirements are not met. A very clear example can be found in the *Salduz* doctrine with regard to the right of access to a lawyer at the investigative stage.[210] Furthermore, the ECHR is a so called 'living instrument' with the consequence that the way in which its provisions are interpreted and applied may be revised as criminal justice systems themselves evolve in order to deal with the changing character of criminal activity or policy. This also means that interpretations might be formulated in a more exacting manner as the European consensus as to what is required evolves.

Finally, it is important to remember that the case law of the ECtHR is 'complaint driven'. As a result, elements that we identify as important to effective criminal defence and that in principle are provided for in the ECHR, may not have been the subject of a Court decision because the issue has not been brought before it.

With due regard to these reservations we here seek to identify minimum standards that are applicable to the selected range of rights that we address in our study, and attempt to clarify the gaps that still exist in the ECHR provisions or in the Strasbourg case law. It is not our intention to repeat what has already been covered in this chapter, although some repetition is inevitable, but to summarise the main findings and highlight points that are of particular importance to our analysis of effective criminal defence in the jurisdictions in our study. The issues raised also directly contribute to our analysis, conclusions and recommendations in Chapters 12, 13 and the Executive Summary and Recommendations.

8.2. Procedural rights relating to fair trial in general

In § 2 we identified the main characteristics of the right to be presumed innocent, the right to silence, the principle of equality of arms and adversarial trial, and for the reasons stated we included pre-trial detention in the analysis.

8.2.1. Presumption of innocence

According to ECtHR jurisprudence, the right to be presumed innocent has three dimensions: authorities, including public officials, should not voice opinions about the guilt of the accused before guilt has been established according to law; the burden of proof is on the prosecution; and in order to allow the suspect to prepare and present his defence the prosecution has a duty to inform the suspect of the accusation.

---

[210] See § 4.3 of this chapter.

8.2.2. The right to remain silent

The right to silence is regarded as a fundamental feature of the concept of fair trial. It protects the accused against improper compulsion, and contributes to the avoidance of miscarriages of justice and to the fulfilment of the aims of article 6 ECHR in general. The right to silence is closely related to the right not to incriminate oneself, which underlies the basic requirement that the burden of proof is on the prosecution. However, the right to remain silent is not considered absolute by the ECtHR and can be restricted. This is problematic from the viewpoint of effective criminal defence in situations where there is a duty on the suspect or accused to disclose information that could be incriminating, and when inferences can be drawn from silence such as is the case in England and Wales.[211] Although the ECtHR scrutinises situations where the privilege against self-incrimination or the right to silence have been under pressure, this is an assessment made with hindsight. The mere existence of mechanisms that restrict the right to silence are detrimental to the effectiveness of the right itself because at the time these restrictions are applied (during the course of the criminal investigation), it is hard to foresee whether, in the end, the right balance will have been struck. In particular, the person under investigation cannot know whether their silence will be treated as incriminating, or in some other way detrimental, whether this results from application of the law or, indeed, from the *de facto* attitudes of the police, prosecutors, judges or juries.

8.2.3. The right to be released pending trial

There is a large amount of ECtHR case law regarding article 5 § 4 ECHR that gives clear guidance on the use of pre-trial detention. Pre-trial detention should not exceed a reasonable time and justifications for it should be demonstrated by courts in their decisions. The *conditio sine qua non* for detention is a reasonable suspicion that the arrested person has committed an offence. After a certain period of time, however, other justifications are required, which must always be made *in concreto* and must outweigh the right to individual liberty and the presumption of innocence. Alternative measures or conditional release pending trial must always be considered.

What is striking about the case law is that general references to the seriousness of the alleged offence do not suffice. Grounds must always be concrete, relevant and sufficient and be weighed against genuine requirements of public interest that must be convincingly demonstrated. Therefore, domestic legislation should provide for pre-trial release as being, at least, a prima facie right which may only by denied if one or more of the conditions regarded as valid by the ECtHR is satisfied, and where alternative measures such as conditional release are not adequate to deal with the concerns. Furthermore, procedural mechanisms should exist to ensure that those who make decisions concerning pre-trial release take in account the particular circumstances of the case and do not simply make the decision in a formulaic way.

---

[211]   See Chapter 4 § 2.3.4.

8.2.4. Equality of arms and adversarial hearing

With regard to the principles of equality of arms and adversarial hearing, the main rule established by the ECtHR is very general: all elements of criminal proceedings should be adversarial and there should be equality of arms between the defence and the prosecution. With regard to these principles it is notable that the case law mostly deals with complaints that are related to the trial phase (access to the case file, disclosure of material, questioning of witnesses and the possibility to react to arguments that have been brought forward by the prosecuting authorities). Only recently has the ECtHR acknowledged that the pre-trial phase is becoming increasingly important for the outcome of criminal proceedings. As a result the court has ruled that the suspect should have the benefit of legal assistance no later than the commencement of police interrogation. There is however no jurisprudence (yet) as to what the impact of the equality of arms principle and the principle of adversariality are on pre-trial investigations, or to what extent the criteria that have been formulated for the trial phase are also applicable to the investigative phase; for instance, with regard to the disclosure of material, attendance at investigative acts, and preliminary questioning of witnesses by the police.

8.3. The right to information

We have divided the right to information into three distinctive parts:

- the right to information as to the nature and cause of the accusation (that is laid down in article 6 § 3a ECHR);
- the right to information on defence rights, which is not provided for under articles 5 or 6 ECHR;
- the right to information on material evidence gathered by the police and access to the case file, which is not explicitly mentioned in articles 5 or 6 ECHR.

8.3.1. Information on the nature and cause of the accusation

The Court has ruled that there is a positive obligation on the authorities to inform the suspect of the nature and cause of the accusation and, if necessary, take additional steps in order to ensure that the suspect has understood the information. Articles 5 and 6 ECHR do not give any indication as to the means to be used to provide this information. The ECtHR has ruled that, in principle, it should be done in writing but that oral information suffices. The extent of the duty to provide information is, to a certain degree, at the discretion of the authorities and there is no clear case law at what precise moment the right to be informed on the accusation arises.

8.3.2. Information on defence rights

With regard to information on defence rights there is case law indicating that the authorities are required to inform the suspect about the right to legal aid and the right to a lawyer. Implicit in this case law is also the requirement that the suspect should be informed of his right to silence before questioning. Again there is no case law on when this information should be given, the means that should be used (for instance, by a 'letter of rights'), or how the information should be given, orally and/or in writing. The Court merely assesses whether the information in the individual case was practical and effective.

8.3.3. The right to disclosure of material evidence and access to the file

The prosecution is obliged to disclose to the accused all material evidence for or against them, and the accused should have the opportunity to comment on the material. The disclosure obligation includes the opportunity for the suspect to acquaint himself, throughout the proceedings, with the material for the purpose of preparing his defence. The right to disclosure is, however, not absolute and can be restricted for good cause but non-disclosure must be remedied in the subsequent proceedings and always be under the supervision of the trial judge.

There is no case law specifying the moment at which the material evidence should be disclosed, although it can be derived from the case law under article 5 § 4 ECHR (review of pre-trial detention) that documents in the investigation file that are essential in order for the accused to effectively challenge the lawfulness of pre-trial detention should be disclosed during the investigation stage.

8.4. The right to defence and legal assistance

8.4.1. The right to self-representation

We have distinguished in our analysis between the right to self-representation and the right to legal assistance, and that they are not functional alternatives. The principle that the suspect has the right to defend himself in person, and can waive his right to be assisted by a lawyer, is paramount. Nevertheless the ECtHR has ruled that the right to self-representation is not absolute and compulsory representation by a lawyer can be acceptable where the case is complex, the personality of the suspect requires representation, or in case of appeal procedures.

Although the assistance of a lawyer can be considered to be in the interests of the accused, we have expressed our doubt that forcing a lawyer upon an unwilling client can be considered to be in compliance with a right to fair trial.

8.4.2. The right to legal advice and representation

We have identified the right to legal assistance as a key issue for effective criminal defence. Since the *Salduz* judgment[212] there is more clarity as to the moment that the right arises, namely, as from the first interrogation of a suspect by the police. Previous case law had already indicated that there should be an opportunity to consult a lawyer *before* the first police interrogation. What makes the *Salduz* case law exceptional is that the ECtHR, which normally does not interfere with the assessment of evidence at the national level, clearly states that incriminating statements made in absence of a lawyer may in principle not be used to secure a conviction. The ECtHR is also very strict in assessing whether the right to legal assistance was waived. A waiver is not accepted if it cannot be established that it was a knowing and intelligent relinquishment, and an accused who has expressed his desire to speak to a lawyer may not be interrogated, even if he has been advised of his rights, before the authorities have given the accused the opportunity to consult with his lawyer. Even if the suspect keeps silent during his interrogations and has made no incriminating statements, article 6 ECHR will be violated if he has not had access to a lawyer. The principle of equality of arms requires that from the time that interrogation commences the suspect has had access to the full range of interventions that are inherent to legal advice.

This development in the jurisprudence of the ECtHR will probably significantly contribute to the practical effectiveness of legal assistance during the early stages of police interrogation, in particular because the Court has precisely defined the moment at which the right arises, under what conditions it can be waived, what the right constitutes and what the sanctions should be if the right is violated, namely exclusion of evidence. However, there is still a lack of clarity as to whether the right to legal assistance includes a right to have a lawyer present *during* police interrogations.

8.4.3. The choice and free provision of a lawyer for indigent suspects

Those who can pay for legal assistance are free to choose a lawyer, but choice can be subject to limitations where the state pays for legal assistance. Legal assistance free of charge should be provided for indigent suspects when the interests of justice so require. This test is always satisfied when deprivation of liberty is at stake. Other relevant factors are the seriousness of the alleged offence, the severity of the potential sentence, the complexity of the case, and the personal situation of the defendant.

There is no case law on the procedural rules required to ensure that free legal assistance is available other than that judicial authorities must actively and adequately inform suspects in order to enable them to receive legal assistance. Reliance on judicial authorities is, in practice, particularly problematic for legal aid at the investigative stage since this is a time when there is normally no judicial involvement, and when decisions have to be made very quickly.

---

[212]   See § 4.3.

8.4.4. Private consultation with a lawyer

The right to confidential communication with a lawyer is regarded as a basic requirement of a fair trial and follows from article 8 ECHR as well as from article 6 ECHR. Correspondence with lawyers, whatever its purpose, is always privileged and may only be intercepted if there are grounds for suspecting that privilege is being abused. Risk of collusion may never serve as reason for limiting contacts with a lawyer. States are also required to prevent disclosure of confidential information, such as through the interception of telephone conversations.

8.4.5. Lawyer's standards, roles and independence

The ECHR has held that lawyers, as members of an independent and liberal profession, should regulate themselves, and does not interfere with the role, standards or quality of legal assistance, except in situations when a failure to provide effective representation is manifest and sufficiently brought to the attention of the authorities. In that case authorities should intervene. The case law, however, protects freedom of expression in favour of a free and even forceful exchange of argument between parties in the courtroom in accordance with the requirements of the principle of the equality of arms. Criticism in public or the media is allowed, although this criticism must not overstep certain boundaries. In this respect a balance should be struck between various interests such as the public's right to receive information, requirements of the proper administration of justice, and the dignity of the profession. The cautious approach of the ECtHR to the quality of legal assistance is understandable. However, from the suspect or defendant's perspective the result is that they may be left without redress if they were legally represented, but the quality of that representation was deficient. Recent case law does show, however, that the ECtHR is willing to scrutinize the effectiveness of defence counsel during police interrogation, when the right to silence and the privilege against self incrimination are under pressure.[213]

8.5. Rights that promote effective participation

8.5.1. The right to seek evidence and to investigate facts

Article 6 ECHR does not provide for any explicit safeguards regarding the ability of the defence to seek evidence, investigate facts, or interview (prospective) witnesses, in particular at the investigative stage. This can be considered a significant gap in the ECHR protection of fair trial and one that operates to the detriment of effective participation by the accused. The ECtHR has acknowledged the increasing importance of the investigation phase in criminal proceedings as the evidence obtained during this stage determines the framework in which the offence charged will be considered at the trial. In *Dayanan* the Court stressed that the defence should be afforded, as from the initial police investigation, the facilities to investigate facts

---

[213]   See § 4.6 of this chapter.

and search for favourable evidence, but there is no case law (yet) in which this has been further elaborated.[214] The lack of guidelines for the pre-trial phase is also relevant to the other rights that concern active participation, addressed below.

8.5.2. Presence at hearings

The right of the accused to be present at hearings is essential for effective participation. Again this right has been elaborated merely in relation to the main trial, and not to the investigation phase. The Court has held that in principle the defendant has the right to be present at hearings and should be put in a position that enables them to actively participate. This right can, however, be waived and trials in absentia are not *per se* in violation of article 6 ECHR. The right to be present can only be restricted if the proceedings are limited to questions of law and do not review the facts.

8.5.3. Adequate time and facilities

The right to adequate time and facilities to prepare the defence includes the right to be informed of the accusation, the right of access to the file, and the facilities that should be offered to the defence. The main characteristic of the Court's case law in this respect is the emphasis on positive obligations on the authorities to ensure that rights guaranteed by article 6 ECHR are practical and effective. This requires an active attitude and diligence on the part of the authorities. However, the ECtHR has not particularised what is meant by *adequate* time and *adequate* facilities.

8.5.4. Question witnesses and experts

As a rule all evidence should be presented in the presence of the accused at a public hearing with a view to adversarial argument. This is especially the case with regard to the examination of witnesses. The right to call and question witnesses at the main trial is, however, not absolute and it is for the national courts to assess whether it is appropriate to call a witness. The same rules apply to the testimony of experts. It can be considered a general rule that the use of untested statements must be counter-balanced by measures that do not put the defence in a disproportionately adverse position, and that untested statements may never be the sole or decisive evidence in securing a conviction. Here again the assessment of the ECtHR is made in hindsight, which makes it difficult to formulate more specific and detailed rules for the right to call and question witnesses on the basis of the jurisprudence.

8.6. Right to free interpretation and translation

Interpretation and translation must enable the suspect to understand the case against him and to defend himself by being able to put his version of the events before the court. The scope of this right is not limited to oral statements made at

---

[214] See § 2.4.

trial but covers documentary material and pre-trial proceedings. The ECtHR is clear that defendants may not being ordered to pay the costs of an interpreter and that the authorities must control the adequacy of the interpretation. Other issues are, however, less clear. It has not yet been decided whether free interpretation also applies to lawyer/client communications, and with regard to the translation of documents the Court has ruled that not every document requires translation and that oral interpretation can often be regarded as sufficient.

8.7.   Right to reasoned decisions

It follows from the principle of fair trial that national courts must indicate with sufficient clarity the grounds on which they base their decisions. The extent of this obligation is highly dependant on the nature of the decision and the circumstances of the case. The minimum level is that courts should at least address essential issues that have been submitted to them in order to enable the accused to effectively use his rights and remedies.

8.8.   Right to appeal

The right to appeal is not contained in the ECHR itself but in article 2 of the Seventh Protocol, which not all member states have ratified.[215] The ECtHR has ruled that where appeal proceedings are provided for the guarantees of article 6 ECHR are applicable. The Court has dealt with a number of cases concerning the French practice of declaring an appeal inadmissible if the applicant has not surrendered to custody. This is, according to the ECtHR, contrary to the fundamental guarantees contained in article 6 and impairs the very essence of the right of appeal.

---

[215]   See § 7.2.

9.   Bibliography

Books

Bowles & Perry 2009
Bowles, R. & Perry, A., *International comparison of publicly funded legal services and Justice systems*, Research Series 14/09, London: Ministry of Justice, 2009.

Cape et al. 2007
Cape, E., Hodgson, J., Prakken, T. & Spronken, T., *Suspects in Europe*, Antwerp: Intersentia, 2007.

Harris et al. 2009
Harris, D.J., O'Boyle, M. & Warbrick, C., *Law of the European Convention on Human Rights*, 2nd ed., Oxford: Oxford University Press, 2009.

Spronken et al. 2009
Spronken, T., Vermeulen, G., de Vocht, D. & van Puyenbroek, L., *EU Procedural Rights in Criminal Proceedings*, Antwerp: Maklu, 2009.

Trechsel 2005
Trechsel, S., *Human Rights in Criminal Proceedings*, Oxford: Oxford University Press, 2005.

Tuinstra 2009
Tuinstra, J., *Defence Counsel in International Criminal Law*, The Hague: T.M.C. Asser Press, 2009.

van Dijk & van Hoof 2006
van Dijk, P. & van Hoof, G.J.H., *Theory and Practice of the European Convention on Human Rights*, 4th ed., The Hague: Kluwer Law International, 2006.

Articles in Journals

Spronken & Fermon 2008

Spronken, T. & Fermon, J., 'Protection of Attorney-Client Privilege in Europe', *Penn State International Law Review*, 27(2), 2008, p. 439-463.

PART II

NATIONAL APPROACHES TO EFFECTIVE CRIMINAL DEFENCE

Laurens van
Puyenbroeck

CHAPTER 3 BELGIUM[*]

1. Introduction

1.1. *Political context and background of the criminal justice system*

Belgium has a population of approximately 10.7 million. It is divided into three regions, each having a separate official language system: the Dutch speaking Flemish region, the French (and partly German) speaking Walloon region and the bilingual (Dutch and French) Brussels Capital region. Belgian history has been dominated for decades by the political quarrel between the Flemish and the Walloon regions. Besides their respective economic, cultural and social identity, the language issue is crucial for an understanding of the sensitive nature of the struggle between the Dutch and French speaking communities. One example of this differentiation is the creation, in the late 1990s, of the Wallonian and Flemish bar associations out of the national bar association. This separation has often resulted in a different approach to various issues, for instance in relation to deontological matters.

The Belgian criminal justice system is primarily based on the French (Napoleonic) Penal and Criminal Procedure Codes. In 1967, a new Penal Code was introduced in Belgium. The Criminal Procedure Code (CPC) is still the same as the old Napoleonic Code of 1808. Although it no longer appears in its pure form, the Belgian criminal procedure still has many inquisitorial characteristics. Since 1998, a number of important reforms have been made. A first reform in 1998 concerned the organisation of the pre-trial investigation, and was aimed at strengthening the position of the suspect and victim and creating greater transparency.

A second reform followed after the so-called 'Octopus-consultation':[1] a new institution was created, the High Judicial Council, which intended to 'depolitise' the

---

[*] This country report has been reviewed by Gert Vermeulen, professor criminal law at Ghent University.

[1] Named after the eight political parties that negotiated the Octopus agreement. On 28 May 1998, the Octopus agreement was approved by both the majority parties as well as the (democratic) opposition parties. The agreement incorporated a major reform of the police force and specific reforms of judicial organisation.

judiciary and to improve the service towards citizens. In addition, the organisation of the Prosecutor's Office was changed *inter alia* by introducing a federal prosecutor.[2] Finally, the police landscape was drastically changed by reforming the various (fragmented) police services into an integrated police service, structured at two levels, a federal level and a local level.[3]

In 2002, a proposal for a new CPC was presented by a specially appointed commission. Generally speaking, the proposal does not introduce radical change. It nevertheless incorporates a number of innovative elements, which have both been welcomed and criticized.[4] The improved legal position of both suspects/defendants and victims (for example, for requesting additional inquiries or for viewing the file) could be seen as one of the threads throughout the proposal. The proposal was approved by the Senate on 1 December 2005 and sent to the Chamber of Representatives, where it is still pending. The new CPC is not likely to be adopted in the short term, the lack of political enthusiasm and insufficient financial resources probably being the main reasons.

As will be illustrated further throughout this report, the European Convention on Human Rights and Fundamental freedoms (ECHR) plays an important role in the Belgian judicial system, since its provisions are directly applicable before the Belgian courts. Particularly in the field of criminal procedure legislation, the ECHR has proven a useful mechanism to modernise outdated criminal procedures, by shifting it into a direction that entails more respect for the rights of the defence. Belgium has already had several decisions made against it for violations of the rights contained in article 6 ECHR. The recent *Salduz* and *Panovits* judgments of the European Court of Human Rights (ECtHR) are expected to have a considerable impact, by introducing a right to legal assistance at the initial phase of police interrogation, since such a right is at present not legally recognised.

1.2. Main characteristics of criminal proceedings

1.2.1. The investigation stage

The Belgian criminal justice system consists of two main stages. The pre-trial or investigation stage is non-adversarial. Its proceedings are written and in secret. The investigation is not executed autonomously by the police, but is always led by a magistrate, the public prosecutor. In about 10% of criminal cases, the investigation is led by a competent magistrate, the investigating judge (who is, at the same time, a judge and an examining magistrate). These investigations are referred to as 'judicial investigations'. When enforcement orders (for such measures as an arrest warrant, a telephone tap or a house search) have to be issued, the intervention of the investigating judge is obligatory. The public prosecutor is (except under some legally defined circumstances) not competent to issue such orders.[5] When the investigating judge issues an enforcement order for which he is exclusively

2 Law of 22 December 1998 (S.B. 10 February 1999).
3 Law of 7 December 1998 (S.B. 5 January 1999).
4 See *inter alia* Traest & De Tandt 2004, p. 6-24; Schuermans 2005, p. 39-54.
5 Art. 28*bis* § 3 CPC.

competent (such as an arrest warrant),[6] the investigation *automatically* becomes a judicial investigation.[7]

The prosecutor led investigation is entirely non-adversarial: all inquiries are made without the presence of the suspect, who is not in any way allowed to view the file. The judicial investigation is partially adversarial, particularly since the 1998 reform, which allowed formally accused suspects and civil parties to request access to the file and to make additional inquiries. This legislative change has increased the difference between both types of investigation. The distinction between these is often criticised, because the circumstances differentiating between both forms of investigation are not (sufficiently) determined by objective criteria.

In the investigation, the suspect is not expected to actively participate in the evidence gathering. Using private detectives for tasks that are normally assigned (exclusively) to the police is forbidden.[8] The outcome of the investigating proceedings is put in writing and is included in a criminal file that will serve as the basis for the second (trial) stage.

1.2.2. The trial stage

The distinction between the two types of investigations is important in terms of the way trial proceedings are initiated. At the end of a prosecutor led investigation, the prosecutor decides autonomously what should be done with the results of the investigation and whether the case should be brought before a trial judge. If the prosecutor decides to proceed, the case will be brought before a police court or correctional court by means of a 'direct summons'.[9] A direct summons can also be instituted by a civil party, which automatically brings the case before a trial court.

In the case of a judicial investigation, the pre-trial stage can only be closed by an investigating court, which can refer the defendant to the trial court by a referral order, if there are serious indications of guilt regarding a certain offence. The most serious offences (*de facto* those where a murder or an attempted murder is involved) will always be investigated by an investigating judge and are brought before a jury (the Assize court).

The trial stage is adversarial. Its proceedings are (mainly) oral and public. The equality of arms is guaranteed to a large extent. Nevertheless, trial proceedings still

---

[6]   The same applies when the investigating judge is requested to issue a warrant for a house search or for searches in certain other private places, a warrant for an observation using technical means, a warrant for a telephone tap or a warrant for granting a witness full anonymity.

[7]   The Prosecutor has the possibility, according to art. 28*septies* CPC, to request the investigating judge to order another investigating measure (other than these six), for which the judge is exclusively competent without initiating a judicial investigation. After the investigating measure has been executed, the investigating judge decides freely whether to send the file back to the prosecutor or to continue the investigation himself/herself (in that case it becomes a judicial investigation).

[8]   Law of 19 July 1991 regulating the profession of private detectives (S.B. 2 October 1991).

[9]   In some cases, persons can also be called to appear before a police court or correctional court through a 'notification by minutes' (art. 216*quater* CPC), or a notification for immediate appearance (art. 216*quinquies* CPC).

have considerable non-adversarial characteristics. The trial stage is mainly based on the results of the investigation (included in the criminal file). Prior to the initial hearing, the trial judge will usually have prepared the case using the criminal file: the judge will then lead the trial on this basis. As a result, the information gathered during the pre-trial stage is of crucial importance and will weigh considerably (often exclusively) in the trial stage. A Belgian trial judge will be more active during the trial stage than his/her common law colleague. The judge will usually lead the (trial) investigation him/herself and can order additional inquiries *ex officio*. The defence does not have an absolute right to call and interrogate witnesses: it is the judge who determines the necessity of hearing a witness at trial and who leads the interrogation. Belgium law does not involve a genuine cross-examination in the Anglo-Saxon meaning.

The Belgian criminal procedure respects, *at least in theory*, the immediacy principle: all the evidence must be produced at trial.[10] In practice, however, this principle has little application, since the trial stage is often restricted to a verification of the evidence procured during the pre-trial investigation.[11]

Belgium does not have a guilty plea system or expedited proceedings as exists in common law countries. Even if the defendant pleads guilty, the court still has the duty to review *ex officio* the regularity of the evidence, the possible prescription of the prosecution and, in case of a confession, whether the facts confessed is indeed punishable by law.[12]

1.3. Significant data

The gathering and analysing of data on the criminal justice system in Belgium is, when compared to some other European countries, not well developed. Although there is data on the total number of new cases (and pending cases) before the police and correctional courts in a specific year, there is no way of calculating the proportion of those arrested who are then proceeded against. There is, at present, no linking between, for example, the data of the trial courts and those of the investigating judges. This makes it impossible to assess the evolution of a case (from arrest to referral and trial).

Prison overcrowding is one of the most prominent problems in the Belgian criminal justice system.[13] On 1 September 2006, for example, there was an occupancy level of 117.9%. The Belgian imprisonment rate in March 2007 was 95 per

[10]   Art. 190 CPC.
[11]   De Smet 1996, p. 65-76.
[12]   Recently, support for the introduction of such simplified proceedings has increased. The Antwerp Public Prosecution Office, together with the Antwerp bar, have been consulting for some time on a plea bargaining procedure. This would involve a simplified procedure for suspects who confess to facts, in exchange for which – with their consent – the trial stage would be limited to a debate on the sentence. Informal negotiations on the sentence would then be possible. Although this initiative has gained much support among practitioners, it has also been criticized, particularly among politicians (who do not agree with a legal framework for 'negotiating with criminals').
[13]   See *inter alia* Beyens, Snacken & Eliaerts 1993; Daems 2007, p. 41-57.

100,000 citizens,[14] which puts it in the middle compared to the European countries. This rate has risen gradually over the last 15 years (from 71 in 1992, to 81 in 1998, and 88 in 2004). A remarkably high percentage of the prison population consists of foreigners (41.6% on 1 September 2006).[15] One of the causes for the prison overcrowding is the high number of pre-trial detainees (44.3% on 1 March 2007). Despite various efforts, the extent of recidivism has remained relatively unchanged (around 42%), while for some offences such as drug-related crimes, it is at worryingly high proportions.

1.4. Legal aid system

In 1998, the legal aid system was divided into first-line and second-line legal aid.[16] Apart from these two, a third category of legal aid has to be distinguished: those persons who cannot afford the costs involved in (criminal) proceedings (for example, for taking a copy of the criminal file) can submit a request for 'free legal aid'.

The first-line legal aid falls under the competence of the Commission for Legal Aid and aims to provide a first advice to citizens seeking justice. These citizens can go to the 'house of justice', where they are assisted by lawyers. When a detailed legal advice is required, or when a legal procedure is unavoidable, citizens are referred to the Legal Aid Bureau (LAB), which is the competent body to provided second-line legal aid.[17] Every lawyer-trainee is obliged to cooperate with these bureaus during their (three year) traineeship. Since 1 September 1997, lawyers who are listed on the roll of lawyers can continue to cooperate with the bureau if they are registered.

Data on legal aid at the national level is only available for second-line legal aid. This data is general (both for civil and criminal cases). It has been estimated that criminal matters account for nearly 25% of all cases where (second-line) legal aid is sought. The data shows a significant increase in the annual budget for (second-line) legal aid: from 18,790,329.18 Euro in 1998-99, to 36,129,000 Euro in 2003-04, and 52,641,000 Euro in 2006-07 (representing an increase of 13.03% compared to 1998-99).

The decision regarding a person's entitlement to free or subsidised legal advice is made by the local LAB. When legal aid is refused, the applicant can appeal against this decision before the labour court within a month after notification of the decision. When legal aid is granted, the applicant receives a document with the

---

[14]   Based on an estimated national population of 10.59 million at the beginning of March 2007.

[15]   See <http://www.prisonstudies.org> ('world prison brief').

[16]   The legal framework consists of arts. 508/1 to 508/23 of the Judicial Code.

[17]   The legal basis for these bureaux is art. 508/7 Judicial Code, which states that, in order to provide assistance to indigents, the council of the local bar organizes such a bureau. Each lawyer has an obligation to inform poor persons that they are entitled to legal aid (fully or partially free of charge) and to refer them to the LAB or, if the lawyer is registered on the roll of lawyers, to take the necessary steps to get appointed under the second-line legal assistance regime.

name and address of the appointed lawyer, the category under which the appointment is made (fully or partially free of costs), and also a brief outline of the rights and duties of the applicant and, in case of legal aid partially free of costs, the amount that should be paid to the lawyer. The appointed lawyer is informed in writing (or, in case of extreme urgency, by telephone).

The availability of free or subsidised legal advice is subject to both a means test (insufficient income) and a merits test (which does not differ according to the stage of the proceedings). Citizens who apply for legal aid on the basis of insufficient financial resources have to prove their (net) income and their exceptional debts (which are effectively discharged on a monthly basis). The application has to be accompanied by an official document indicating the family composition. The specific income criteria are determined by Royal Decree.[18]

The second category involves a limited number of circumstances, in which citizens can automatically receive free legal aid. These circumstances are also determined by Royal Decree[19] and include persons who are in custody, receive social assistance, persons who have a disabled child, persons who rent a government low cost house, minors, certain foreigners (for procedures related to their status) or mentally disabled persons.

The specific tasks covered by (second-line) legal aid are defined in a list defined by Ministerial Decree. Each task is linked to a number of points (each point representing a certain sum of money). With regard to criminal proceedings, this includes almost every possible procedure. The list of tasks that are remunerated is added in the *Annex* to this report. The average remuneration per case (i.e. amounts paid to lawyers) can be calculated by multiplying the average number of points per case by the average value per point. In 2006-07 the average number of points per case was 15.11 for the Flemish bar association and 16.53 for the French (and German) bar association. The average value per point for 2006-07 was 24.28 Euro (this value has been steady over the past three years). This gives an average remuneration per case of 367 Euro (Flemish bar) and 401 Euro (Walloon bar).

---

[18] Royal Decree of 18 December 2003. The income criteria are changed annually, taking account of the evolution of the consumer price index. As of 1 September 2008, the criteria are: (1) to be entitled to fully free legal aid, a monthly net income of 865 Euro for single persons; a monthly net (family) income of 1,112 Euro for single persons who live together with a dependent person, or for the cohabitant with his spouse or any other person with whom a natural family is formed; (2) to be entitled to partially free legal aid a monthly net income between 865 and 1,112 Euro; a monthly net (family) income between 1,112 and 1,357 Euro for single persons who live together with a dependent person, or for the cohabitant with his spouse or any other person with whom a natural family is formed.

[19] Royal Decree of 18 December 2003.

2.   Legal rights and their implementation

2.1.   *The right to information*

2.1.1. The right to be informed of the nature and cause of the accusation

Suspects[20]

Interrogations of suspects in the pre-trial stage (whether it concerns a prosecutor led investigation or a judicial investigation) are done by the police. The only exception is the situation where a suspect is brought before the investigating judge with the aim of placing him/her in pre-trial custody. In those cases the investigating judge will personally be obliged to interrogate the suspect regarding the facts forming the basis of the accusation, and for which an arrest warrant can be issued, unless the suspect is a fugitive or is hiding.[21]

The interrogation of persons – irrespective of the capacity in which they are interrogated – is subject to certain minimum requirements contained in the CPC.[22] If the person is interrogated in the capacity of a suspect, *he/she does not have to be informed of the nature and cause of the accusation.* Moreover, the police are not obliged to tell a suspect that they are interviewing that he/she is a suspect.[23] The right contained in article 6.3.a ECHR has been deemed the Supreme Court as not apply to interrogations conducted by the police during a criminal investigation.[24]

Since 1998, however, the CPC has contained an important exception to this principle: when, in the course of a judicial investigation, the investigating judge considers that there exist *serious indications of guilt*, the investigating judge is obliged to officially inform that person of the nature and cause of the accusation.[25] This

---

[20]   A suspect is defined as a person who is the target of a criminal investigation (irrespective of whether it is led by the prosecutor or the investigating magistrate) and who has not yet been indicted to appear before a trial court. A defendant, on the contrary, is a person who has been officially indicted as a result of a criminal investigation to appear before a trial court (police court, correctional court or Assize court).

[21]   Art. 16 § 2 of the Law of 20 July 1990. Art. 145 of the proposal for a new CPC foresees that the investigating judge should interrogate each suspect personally; a violation of this obligation would lead to the nullity of the investigation. The implementation of such an obligation in practice would require a substantial increase of the number of investigating judges.

[22]   Art. 47*bis* CPC. These minimum requirements also apply to judicial investigations (art. 70*bis* CPC).

[23]   The proposal for a new CPC (art. 123) stipulates that 'each person who has been interrogated several times during the last year about the same fact by the prosecutor or the police, can ask the Public Prosecutor's Office by means of a petition if he is suspected of having committed an offence punishable with a sentence of one year imprisonment or more'.

[24]   Cass. 14 December 1999, *Arr. Cass.* 1999, No. 678.

[25]   Art. 61*bis*, 1° CPC. The obligation exists for each fact for which there are serious indications of guilt. This is mainly a theoretical principle. In practice, few investigating judges will inform a person that the investigation has uncovered serious indications of guilt regarding another (new) fact. This will usually be covered by notification at the end of the investigation, at which point the person will be informed of any new fact, in relation to which he/she is officially accused.

formal act of accusation is called the *inverdenkingstelling*. The aim is to avoid a situation where suspects are not aware that they are the subject of a judicial investigation until the moment they are invited to the hearing before the investigating court that can refer them to the trial court.

The CPC does not stipulate, however, that the obligation *immediately* arises from the moment that there exist serious indications of guilt. The necessities of the investigation (for example, a planned house search or telephone tap) can require that the person concerned is *temporarily* not informed. If, however, the subject is left unknowing without this being necessary for the investigation, the right of defence may be violated. Although the freedom of the investigating judge to determine the moment at which he/she informs the person is thus not absolute,[26] there is no legally prescribed sanction if the judge does not issue such a formal accusation. The absence or irregularity of the accusation as such does not lead to the nullity of the procedure.[27] Only when the investigating judge has (flagrantly) sought to violate the rights of the defendant (for example, by denying him the legally foreseen rights without this being necessary for the investigation), will any absence or irregularity be sanctioned.

According to the CPC *each person who is the target of prosecution in the framework of a judicial investigation has the same rights as the person who is formally accused.*[28] This means that a person who is targeted in a request by the prosecutor for a judicial investigation, or in a complaint by a civil party before the investigating judge (which automatically initiates a judicial investigation), is no longer treated as a mere suspect. This person will have the same rights as those who have been officially accused by the investigating judge. This provision aims to avoid a situation where the investigating judge would postpone the official notification so as to deny that person the right to ask permission to view the file, or to the right to make additional inquiries. This principle is sometimes referred to as the *implicit or virtual accusation.*[29]

It is, however, remarkable that, although these persons have the same rights as those who are officially accused, the investigating judge is *not* obliged to inform

---

[26] It should be noted in this respect that every person against whom there exist serious indications of guilt, or who has been targeted by a request from the prosecutor or a civil party's complaint, must appear at the end of the investigation before the investigating court when it will make a decision about how the case is to proceed (the 'arrangement of proceedings' decision) (art. 127 CPC). This means that, even if the person is unaware during the investigation, a notification of this appearance will be sent. Due to the fact that this notification initiates a new (binding) period during which the file can be viewed, and additional inquiries can be made, the rights of defence are to be respected at that time.

[27] Cass. 2 October 2002, *R.D.P.* 2003, 125. Whether the right of defence has been flagrantly breached is judged in the light of the whole procedure

[28] Art. 61*bis*, 2° CPC.

[29] The virtual accusation can follow, for example, from an investigating measure from which it could appear that there are serious indications of guilt and that the subject is possibly targeted by a judicial investigation (telephone tap, house search). This is, however, not necessarily the case: these measures can also be ordered with the aim of gathering evidence regarding a third party. In those circumstances, the secrecy of the investigation on the one hand does not allow for an explanation to the subject of the investigative measure. On the other hand, this person cannot be formally accused, because he/she is, at that point, not (yet) a target of the investigation.

them of the fact that they are the subject of a judicial investigation and, *a fortiori*, to inform them of nature and cause of the accusation (and this regardless of the fact of whether the investigating judge does or does not consider that there exist serious indications of guilt).

The official act of accusation by an investigating judge can be done in different ways. If it is done verbally (following an interrogation by the judge), this will be contained in the official report of the interrogation. In the other cases, the information will have to be supplied in writing (this can be done by mail or fax). The investigating judge is not obliged to interrogate the person before he makes the official accusation. The act of accusation cannot be delegated to the police or prosecutor. If the suspect is unreachable, the accusation can be done *in absentia*.

The formal act of accusation is limited to judicial investigations led by the investigating magistrate. Due to the fact that about 90% of all investigations are prosecutor-led, it can be concluded that, in the great majority of criminal investigations, there is no legal obligation to inform persons about the fact that they are the target of an investigation (even when interrogated by the police), and that they are informed of the accusation only when presented with an indictment (and thus become a defendant).

Defendants

Defendants must always be informed of the nature and cause of the accusation for which they have to stand trial. The way in which they are informed depends on how the case is brought before the court. This is usually done by a direct summons, or a referral order.[30]

If the case is instituted before the police court or correctional court by a *direct summons*, the writ of summons will indicate the nature and cause of the accusation. The CPC does not determine precisely how the writ should describe the charges and does not contain a nullity provision. According to the Supreme Court, a summons can only be declared null if an *essential component* of the writ is missing, or if it is proven that the irregularity violates the right of defence.[31] A fundamental requirement arising from the Supreme Court's case law on the content of the writ is that the charge should describe the underlying facts clearly enough to allow the defendant to defend him/herself.[32] In order to be sufficiently clear, the writ should specify the place, the date, the offence and its essential factual components.

If the case has involved a judicial investigation, the trial proceedings are initiated by a *referral order* of an investigating court. The procedure before the investigating court is a key moment. At this point, suspects are notified of the

[30] Defendants can also be called to appear before a police court or correctional court by a notification by minutes (art. 216*quater* CPC), or a notification for immediate appearance (art. 216*quinqies* CPC). An exceptional situation is where a defendant commits an offence in the courtroom (for example, insulting the judge, the King). According to art. 181 CPC, the President will immediately make an official report thereof, will hear the defendant and the witnesses and will immediately impose the sentences foreseen by law.

[31] Cass. 12 November 2002, *Arr. Cass.* 2002, 2449.

[32] Cass. 4 February 2003, *Arr. Cass.* 2003, 322; Cass. 12 November 2002, *NjW* 2003, 130.

offences for which they can be referred to the trial court. If the formalities of this procedure are not respected (for example, if there is an irregular notification), every further step in the criminal proceedings will be nullified. After referral by an investigating court, the defendant is notified of the date on which the proceedings are initiated. In that case, the notification does not initiate the trial, but only counts as a fixation of the date.

2.1.2. The right of access to the file

Suspects

Because of the principally non-adversarial character of the pre-trial stage, suspects do not have the right to view the criminal file during investigation. Although each person has *the right to ask* the prosecutor for permission to view (and take a copy of) the file,[33] this request is usually denied until the investigation is closed.[34] At present, there are three important exceptions to this general principal of secrecy.

The first exception relates to persons who have been officially accused by an investigating judge. Since 1998, these suspects have the right to file a request to the investigating judge to view the file. If this request is denied – which, in practice, often occurs – the suspect can appeal against this decision before the investigating court.[35] It was pointed out by several judges that, at present, many lawyers do not use the possibilities already offered by the law to request permission to view the file.

The second exception concerns those suspects who have been placed in pre-trial custody following an arrest warrant. These suspects appear before an investigating court regularly (within five days following the arrest and after that, in principle, each month). Before any hearing in which it is decided whether to extend their arrest, these suspects have the right to view the criminal file for a limited and legally defined period (in principle one day before the first appearance and two days before subsequent appearances).

The third exception is the situation where a judicial investigation is closed and the investigating court decides on how the case is to proceed (the 'arrangement of proceedings' decision). All suspects who have the status of an accused (those who have been officially informed by the investigating judge, or who are the target of prosecution in the framework of a judicial investigation) have the right to view the file before the hearing for a period of at least 15 days (or three days when one of the

---

33   Art. 96 Royal Decree of 27 April 2007.

34   The proposal for a new CPC (art. 124) foresees the possibility that each person suspected of having committed an offence punishable with a sentence of one year imprisonment or higher, can ask the Prosecutor to view the file (the same right exists for the person injured by such an offence). The decision of the Prosecutor regarding this request would not be subject to any appeal.

35   A similar right exists for those persons who are the target of prosecution in the framework of a judicial investigation and who have not been officially accused (art. 61*bis*, 2° CPC), as well as for victims who have officially filed a complaint before the investigating judge in the course of a judicial investigation (civil party).

suspects is in pre-trial custody). This is also the first moment in the pre-trial stage at which suspects have the right to take a *copy* of the file.

On the basis of these exceptions, some point to the fact that there is discrimination between those suspects against whom there exist serious indications of guilt, but who are not arrested, and those suspects who are arrested. The first category will not automatically have the right to access the file, but will have to request permission from the investigating judge, while the latter will have the opportunity to view the file regularly.

Defendants

From the moment at which they are summoned, defendants (and/or their lawyer) have the right to view (or take a copy of) the criminal file. The request for a copy of the file implies the payment of a certain amount of money for each copied page, with a maximum of 2,500 Euro. Indigent defendants can submit a request for exemption from these costs. For persons who have to appear before the Assize court, this right exists from the moment of referral. Each party in an Assize case has a right to a *free* copy of the entire file.

2.1.3. Information on rights (letter of rights)

According to the minimum requirements applicable to interrogations of persons (irrespective of their capacity) in the course of a criminal investigation, *each interrogated person is told at the start of the interrogation that (a) he can ask that all questions which are asked and all answers that he gives, are noted in the exact wordings; (b) he can ask that a specific inquiry is made or a specific interrogation is done; and (c) his declarations can be used as legal evidence.*

Belgian criminal procedure does not include a *letter of rights*. Moreover, there is no obligation for police officers or investigating judges who interrogate suspects to inform them on the right to remain silent.

The fact that suspects who are arrested are not expressly informed about their (procedural) rights means that they depend entirely on the assistance of a lawyer. This can have a discriminating effect on those groups who cannot afford a private lawyer. Lawyers appointed under legal aid do not always have a habit of visiting their clients (regularly) in prison, or are themselves not always aware of the defence rights to which their clients are entitled.

Although most questioned professionals[36] favoured the introduction of a letter of rights, there was no consensus. Some suggested instead that the minimum requirements on interrogations should be extended (for example, with an obligation to mention the right to remain silent), and that it should be made clear from the interrogation reports that the suspect has not only been informed of his rights but also effectively understands the content of these rights.

---

[36] For the purpose of writing this report, several interviews were conducted between August and October 2008 in two cities, including Brussels. Among the interviewees were four judges, one investigating magistrate, three prosecutors, 11 defence lawyers and one interpreter.

2.2. The right to defend oneself

2.2.1. The right of a suspect/defendant to defend themselves

Although suspects and defendants are in principal allowed to defend themselves, there is no legal provision expressly recognising this in criminal matters, nor is there a legal obligation to inform suspects/defendants of this right.

According to the Judicial Code,[37] the parties in a *civil* procedure can submit their conclusions and arguments themselves, unless the law prohibits this. The Code further stipulates that, in those cases where the law does not oblige the assistance of a lawyer, the judge who determines that a party is incapable to discuss his case with the necessary *decency* or with the necessary *clarity*, due to *anger or lack of skills*, can deny that party from submitting its conclusions and arguments itself. The Supreme Court has ruled that this provision also applies to criminal cases. It does, however, not allow the judge to deny a defendant the right to submit written conclusions.[38] The judge should solve this by ordering the defendant to seek the assistance of a lawyer.

The sole exception to the right to defend oneself is in cases before the Supreme Court. In these proceedings, the parties submit their arguments through a written memorandum, which must be signed by a lawyer.

2.2.2. The right to legal advice and/or representation

The Constitution[39] guarantees the right to legal assistance. Although this right in criminal proceedings arises even before the moment of arrest, namely when a person is notified of a possible involvement in criminal proceedings (for example, an invitation from the police for an interrogation), there is no legal obligation to inform persons of this right.[40]

Legal assistance during police interrogation

At present, the right to legal assistance in criminal proceedings does not imply the *right to a lawyer during interrogation* by the police or an investigating judge.[41] The

---

37   Art. 758, 1°.
38   Cass. 18 September 1979, *Arr. Cass.* 1979-80, 63.
39   Art. 23, 3°.
40   Art. 144 of the proposal for a new CPC contains an obligation for the investigating judge, when he officially accuses a suspect (i.e. informs him/her that there exist serious indications of guilt), to inform this suspect that he/she has the right to choose a lawyer. At present, investigating judges in practice already inform suspects of this right during interrogation (this is expressly mentioned in the minutes of the interrogation).
41   The proposal for a new CPC does foresee such a right: art. 86, 5° (on the police interrogation) stipulates that 'on the request of the interrogated person, after his first interrogation, he/she can be assisted by a lawyer during the interrogation. The lawyer assists the interrogated person on the compliance with the rules of interrogation. The interrogation is suspended until the lawyer is present.' Art. 147 of the Proposal contains a similar provision for

→

only exception is the so-called summary interrogation,[42] which, although not used frequently, gives the right to a suspect in pre-trial custody to request an interrogation by the investigating judge within ten days prior to each appearance before the investigating court of first instance. The lawyer and the prosecutor can be present during this interrogation.

As a result of recent case law of the ECtHR, Belgian legislation on this point will have to be changed. In the *Salduz* judgment of 27 November 2008,[43] the ECtHR stated that, in principle, access to a lawyer should be provided as from the first interrogation of a suspect by the police, unless it is demonstrated in the light of the particular circumstances of each case that there are compelling reasons to restrict this right. According to the ECtHR, the rights of the defence will, in principle, be irretrievably prejudiced if incriminating statements made during police interrogation without access to a lawyer are used for a conviction.

In the *Panovits* judgment of 11 December 2008,[44] the ECtHR followed a similar approach and expressly indicated the positive obligation of the authorities to 'furnish the applicant with the necessary information enabling him to access legal representation'. Although these judgments do not expressly state that a suspect has a right to the presence of a lawyer during interrogation, (the Court only speaks of 'access' and 'assistance'), it is clear that both rulings will inevitably lead to a considerable change in Belgian practice.[45]

Some of the questioned professionals proposed to compensate the fact that lawyers are not present during investigative actions such as interrogations or confrontations, by making audio recordings of all interrogations. At present, interrogations are, as a rule, not audio recorded. It could be questioned, however, whether this would in any event be sufficient, in the light of the new requirements specified by the ECtHR.

Closely related to the aspect of legal assistance at the stage of police interrogation is the debate on the extension of the arrest period from 24 hours to (at least) 48 hours. Many interviewees were in favour of such an extension. In their view, the current 24 hour period is too short to take all the necessary steps,[46] Moreover, the 48 hour period would allow a brief psychological examination of the suspect (in order to assess at this stage whether the suspect is possibly mentally impaired and to allow a better assessment of the danger he/she may pose).

Finally, it is said that the 48 hour period would lower the number of pre-trial detentions, since many cases seem to 'solve themselves' within a few days. Not all

---

interrogations of suspects by the investigating judge, with the exception of the words '...after his first interrogation...' (the first interrogation of a person will always be done by the police).

42   Art. 22, 3° of the Law on pre-trial Custody.

43   ECtHR 27 November 2008, *Salduz* v. *Turkey*, No. 36391/02.

44   ECtHR 11 December 2008, *Panovits* v. *Cyprus*, No. 4268/04.

45   For an analysis of the consequences for Belgian practice, see Van Puyenbroeck & Vermeulen 2009.

46   These may include deprivation of liberty; initial interrogation by the police (possibly requiring the use of an interpreter); notification of the prosecutor who then, if an arrest warrant is deemed necessary, has to request the intervention of the investigating judge; possible additional inquiries; the interrogation by the investigating judge; and the issuing of the arrest warrant.

of the questioned professionals agreed with these arguments. The question was raised whether the problems could not be solved simply by a more efficient judicial apparatus during the first 24 hours.

Legal assistance of suspects in pre-trial custody

Suspects in pre-trial custody can never be restricted from seeing their lawyer in private. In practice, however, Belgium does not have a formal system that guarantees access to a lawyer 24 hours a day. At present it is impossible for a person who is arrested to consult a lawyer during the arrest period of 24 hours (meaning the first 24 hours after the person has been deprived of his liberty by the police).[47] Moreover, after this first 24 hour period, and during the whole detention, the restrictions on access to prisons should be taken into account.[48]

The effect of the right to legal assistance can differ according to the financial resources of the suspect in pre-trial custody. Those suspects who have to request the appointment of a lawyer under legal aid will usually have to wait longer to talk to the lawyer than those who can contact their (private) lawyer immediately after they enter prison.

Legal assistance of minors and mentally vulnerable persons

When a juvenile[49] has committed an act described as an offence, the proceedings consist of two stages.[50] In the first stage, the judge can impose a protective measure, during which time the judge will order an investigation of the social and educational environment by a welfare officer connected to the juvenile court. Protective measures include: community service, an educational course, house arrest, placement in an (partially or fully closed) institution. The second stage concerns the merits of the case, where the guilt and the necessity of an additional

---

[47] Art. 29 § 1 of the Royal Decree of 1 May 1965 on the general regulation of penitentiary institutions stipulates that lawyers can have a private consultation at every hour of the day with those detainees who are not finally sentenced, and by whom they are called, or to whom they were appointed, but only after their first interrogation (also see art. 20 of the Law of 20 July 1990 on pre-trial detention).

[48] The law of 12 January 2005 on the penitentiary system and the rights of detained persons stipulates in art. 67 (which has not yet entered into force) that the lawyers can visit the detainees 'during the hours of the day which, for each prison, are determined by the King').

[49] A juvenile is defined by law as a minor (below 18) who has committed a 'fact described as an offence' (a fact explicitly defined in the Penal Code). This group should be distinguished from those minors in a problematic educational situation (according to art. 2, a and 4 of the decree on the Special Youth Assistance this is 'a situation where the physical integrity, the affective, moral, intellectual or social chances for development of minors are threatened, due to special circumstances, relational conflicts or the circumstances in which they live'). The protective measures determined by law are largely the same for both categories. The distinction between both categories is often vague and, in practice, a considerable number of the latter category (who are often placed in foster families or educational institutions) reappear before the juvenile judge for having committed a fact described as an offence.

[50] See the law of 8 April 1965 on youth protection, adjusted by the law of 15 May 2006 and 13 June 2006.

measure will be determined, and where civil parties can make their claim. In both stages, the assistance of a lawyer is mandatory.

Unless the parents have appointed a lawyer themselves (which is rather exceptional), a lawyer will be appointed and paid for by the state in the (second-line) legal aid system.[51] With regard to the legal assistance of minors, it is legally stipulated[52] that, 'in each judicial or administrative procedure where a minor is a party or wherein he is involved of during his/her interrogation, the minor is assisted by a specialized lawyer except when he chooses another lawyer'. However, this bill has not yet been approved. Recently, the local legal aid bureaus of the Flemish local bars have begun to draw up a list of lawyers specialising in providing assistance to juveniles.[53]

A special protection in the form of legal assistance is accorded to mentally vulnerable persons.[54] When an offender is found to be mentally impaired his/her internment can be ordered following a special procedure. In the course of this procedure, there is a mandatory legal assistance for the mentally vulnerable person. Many of the questioned professionals (mainly judges) were critical about the performance of lawyers appointed under second-line legal aid in internment procedures. The defence of mentally vulnerable offenders by lawyer-trainees is too often seen as inadequate. A number of young lawyers handle these cases 'too lightly'. They hardly ever visit their client before the hearing (this could be partially explained by the late notification) and sometimes do not even appear at the hearing.

Legal assistance of indigent suspects/defendants

If a person required to appear before a court has been found in need of legal aid, and asks for the assistance of a lawyer at least three days before the court hearing, the President of the court will send the request to the legal aid bureau, which will then appoint a lawyer. A similar request can be made by a suspect (whether or not arrested) in the course of a judicial investigation.[55]

While suspects or defendants in principal have the right to choose their own lawyer, this is not (always) the case for indigent persons. If they are accorded a lawyer under the legal aid system, they cannot choose which lawyer is appointed. The lawyer is appointed from a list of lawyer-trainees or other lawyers who are registered unless they choose a lawyer they know (under the condition that this lawyer is registered, in the legal aid system). Suspects/defendants always have a right to ask for a replacement (for example, if they do not trust the appointed

[51]   Art. 52*ter* and 54*bis* of the law of 1965.
[52]   Law of 22 December 1999.
[53]   In practice this will be those lawyers who have attended the recently introduced special course on juvenile law which is held annually and is organized by the Flemish lawyer association in cooperation with all Flemish universities.
[54]   According to art. 1 of the Law of 1930, a mentally vulnerable person is someone who, due to a mental illness, is not capable to control his deeds and is a danger for society (this last criterion was developed by the jurisprudence). According to art. 8 of the Law of 2007, this is a person who suffers from a mental illness which seriously affects his judgment capability or the control of his deeds.
[55]   Art. 184*bis* CPC.

lawyer), although this can be a time consuming process (the appointed lawyer first has to be relieved from the case before a new lawyer can be appointed).

Representation

The legal provisions on representation have fundamentally changed, following the case law of the ECtHR. In the old system, the defendant who did not appear could not be represented by a lawyer, except in a few limited circumstances, such as *force majeure*.[56] In the *Van Geyseghem* case,[57] the ECtHR ruled that the right to legal advice contained in article 6(3)d ECHR also included the right to representation. This right is not lost solely by the fact that the defendant was absent from the hearing.[58] Following this judgment, representation by a lawyer is now principally allowed, unless the court orders the personal appearance of the defendant.[59] Only at the Assize court is the personal presence of the accused still obligatory.

The right to representation is not absolute. In cases of pre-trial detention, the presence of the suspect at the hearing before the investigating courts is required. If, however, the suspect is unable to appear (for example, because of a strike that makes it impossible to transport the suspect between prison and court), the investigating court will allow the lawyer to represent his/her client. If the lawyer (who was duly notified) does not appear, or does not request permission to represent his/her client, the investigating court can decide in absence of the suspect and his/her lawyer.[60] The same is possible when the suspect refuses to appear.

2.3. Procedural rights

2.3.1. The right to release from custody pending trial

Prior to 1990, there were no alternatives to pre-trial custody. The investigating judge only had two options: either to release the suspect, or to order the arrest. At present, suspects can be released from pre-trial custody under certain conditions, in all cases where the pre-trial custody can be ordered or continued. The release from custody pending trial (with or without conditions) can now be ordered by the investigating judge,[61] the investigating courts (at one of the regular appearances for continuation

---

[56] If the defendant did not appear in person, he/she was convicted *in absentia*, even if the lawyer was present at the hearing. If the defendant did not appear on the hearing in opposition to the default judgment, the opposition was declared inadmissible.

[57] ECtHR 21 January 1999, *Van Geyseghem* v. *Belgium*, No. 26103/95.

[58] Other cases on this point include ECtHR 20 March 2001, *Goedhardt* v. *Belgium* and *Stroek* v. *Belgium*, Nos. 36449/97 and 36467/97; ECtHR 8 July 2004, *Pronk* v. *Belgium*, No. 51338/99 and ECtHR 24 February 2005, *Stift* v. *Belgium*, No. 46848/99.

[59] Art. 152 § 1 and 185 §§ 1 and 2 CPC.

[60] If the investigating court wants to decide on the pre-trial detention, in the absence of a suspect who is unable to appear and who is not represented by a lawyer, the decision to continue the detention must determine that the court is unable to vary the current position move (Cass. 7 May 2003, P.03.0607.F).

[61] Since the Law of 31 May 2005 (S.B. 16 June 2005), there is no possibility for an appeal against this decision of the investigating judge.

of the arrest, or at the hearing when the 'arrangement of proceedings' decision is taken) and the trial judge.[62] When the release from custody pending trial is ordered, there are three possibilities: (1) the arrest warrant is lifted; (2) the arrest warrant is continued but the suspect is released under conditions; or (3) the arrest warrant is continued, but the suspect is released after payment of bail (a combination of (2) and (3) is possible).

In case of a conditional release, the conditions under which the release can be ordered are not expressly defined in the law, but are determined by the judge. The judge is, however, not totally free in this respect: the conditions must relate to one of the circumstances named in the legislation: risk of absconding, risk of recidivism, risk of misappropriation, or risk of collusion.[63] The conditions therefore vary according to the specific circumstances of the case and the personal situation of the suspect.[64] The conditions are valid for three months, after which they can be renewed or changed.[65]

Release after payment of bail can be ordered at all stages of the criminal proceedings. The Supreme Court has ruled that the right contained in article 5.3 ECHR is not an absolute right, but that the judge should consider whether the aim of the pre-trial custody can be achieved in this way.[66] The judge freely determines the amount of bail and can base the decision on serious suspicions that money or valuables originating from the offence have been placed abroad or are kept in hiding. The money must be deposited in cash in a closed account of a specific institution (the *Deposito- en Consignatiekas*). From the moment that the original proof of payment is submitted at the prosecutor's office, the release is ordered. The right can be exercised regardless of the financial situation of the suspect/defendant. In theory, every person can apply for bail. In determining the amount, the judge/court can take account of the financial situation of the applicant (there are no minima or maxima).

The fact that legislation expressly foresees alternatives for the pre-trial detention, implies an obligation for the competent judicial authorities to consider these alternatives whenever possible. Extremely long periods of pre-trial detention

---

[62] See arts. 25, 27 and 35 of the Law of 20 July 1990.
[63] See arts. 16 § 1 and 35 § 3 of the Law of 20 July 1990. Unless the maximum sentence of the offence for which the suspect is arrested exceeds 15 years of imprisonment, the arrest warrant can only be issued if there are serious indications to suggest that the suspect who is released would commit new crimes, would abscond, would try to make evidence disappear, or would collude with third parties.
[64] They can include *inter alia* a prohibition to frequent a certain area or establishment, or to contact a certain person (or group of persons), a prohibition to use or abuse alcohol or drugs, an obligation to reside at a specific address, an obligation to find work (and not to lose this due to his/her own fault), an obligation to attend a specific course (for drug addicts or sexual offenders). If the conditions oblige the suspect to follow guidance or treatment, the suspect is expected to choose a competent person or institution. This person or institution is then obliged to report regularly to the judicial body that imposed the condition.
[65] The suspect can ask for a change in the conditions, or can oppose the renewal or change (with the exception of conditional release ordered by the investigating judge: if the judge decides to renew the conditions, there is no possibility to appeal).
[66] Cass. 7 May 2003, P.03.0620.F.

can only be justified in exceptional circumstances. Belgium has already been found in violation of the law on this point by the ECtHR.[67]

Although there is a wide range of alternatives for pre-trial detention, the practical implementation poses many problems. All professionals involved (judges, investigating judges, prosecutors and lawyers) regret the lack of institutions that can be used as a basis for guidance or treatment of suspects who are eligible for conditional release. In particularly access to services for mental health care (for treatment of sexual offenders or drug offenders) have a shortage of available places and can therefore not be used immediately if a judicial body considers a conditional release.

All professionals indicate this as an area where intervention by policymakers is urgently needed. The difficulties in implementing alternatives to pre-trial detention are not only caused by organisational (capacity) problems. All too often, lawyers do not seem to be aware of the various institutions that can be contacted, in order to prepare for conditional release. Instead of being offered a viable alternative, judges often have to make suggestions to lawyers as to how to prepare these alternatives.

The illegal status of many (foreign) suspects makes a conditional release impossible. This is due to the conflict between the law on pre-trial detention and the Aliens Act. The latter makes it impossible for an illegal person to be required by judicial bodies to reside at a particular address within the country (which is one of the conditions automatically included when a conditional release is ordered). The only alternative is to release the foreigner under bail, although for a large group of suspects, this is not possible because they lack the financial resources to pay (even a very limited) bail.

Moreover, many judges are not easily convinced to release illegal suspects under bail. As a result, Belgian prisons are, to a large extent, filled with foreign suspects in pre-trial detention. A possible option to counter this would be to make use of international criminal law, namely by transferring the criminal proceedings to the countries of origin. Another option would be to make an amendment to the Aliens Act so as to permit a judge to require an alien to reside at a particular address for the purpose of conditional release in criminal proceedings.

---

[67]   In the case of Michel Lelièvre, an accomplice in the notorious *Dutroux* case, the pre-trial detention of seven years, ten months and eight days was deemed excessive. The ECtHR considered that the Belgian courts had never seriously considered the question of alternatives to his detention, although the defence appeared to have put forward proposals in that respect. The ECtHR also considered that the proceedings had not been conducted with 'special diligence', noting in particular that almost two years had passed between the transmission of the file and the opening of the trial (ECtHR 8 November 2007, *Lelièvre* v. *Belgium*, No. 11287/03). In the *Grisez* case, the ECtHR held that there had been no violation of art. 5 §3 ECHR: the Court found that, although the medical examinations had caused delays in the proceedings, other steps had been taken in the investigation during that period. Furthermore, the total length of the detention pending trial (two years, three months and nineteen days) did not appear unreasonable in view of the seriousness of the charges and the number of matters requiring investigation (ECtHR 26 September 2002, *Grisez* v. *Belgium*, No. 35776/97).

2.3.2. The right of a defendant to be tried in his/her presence

Although defendants have the right to be tried in their presence, they are not obliged to be present. If a defendant, or a lawyer representing the defendant, does not appear at the court hearing as determined in the summons, the defendant can be tried in absentia. The defendant who was tried in absentia can oppose his conviction.[68] The right to opposition against judgments in absentia is not an internationally guaranteed procedural right. The ECtHR has, on the contrary, repeatedly underlined the importance of the presence of a defendant at trial.

2.3.3. The right to be presumed innocent

The presumption of innocence applies from the moment a person is suspected, and continues to apply until the criminal procedure has been concluded by a final conviction.[69] A violation of this principle will not, however, always lead to the nullity of a procedure. In some cases, a violation will be easily remedied.[70] In other cases, the remedy will leave damage. In some cases, the inadmissibility of the prosecution is the only suitable remedy.[71] This will only be the case when the breach of the presumption of innocence has irrevocably violated the right of defence, in other words when the later or higher jurisdiction can no longer repair the situation.

The presumption of innocence implies that judges (Bench or investigating judges) must refrain from making statements (in court or in the press) that could amount to a declaration of the suspect's or defendant's guilt.[72]

Particularly at a time when criminal law is a popular media topic, it is evident that declarations of guilt in the press are very common.[73] The question arises whether such press campaigns could have procedural consequences. Although such a thesis could be argued on the basis of jurisprudence of the ECtHR, the Supreme Court has ruled that respecting the presumption of innocence is an obligation for the judges who must make a judgment on the merits of the accusation, and that this is judged by taking account of the proceedings as a whole. The circumstance that

---

[68]   See arts. 149, 151, 186 and 187 CPC. If the opposition was done in a timely manner, the opposed judgment no longer exists and the case will be tried again before the same court. The new judgment 'on opposition' will be a judgment in first instance and is subject to appeal. If the opposing defendant does not appear at the court hearing on which his opposition will be considered, the opposition is considered 'not done'. The right to opposition is not absolute. If the defendant or his/her lawyer do not appear at a later hearing, after he/she or his/her lawyer have appeared at the initial hearing, the judgment will not be regarded as a judgment *in absentia* and opposition will not be possible (art. 185 §2 CPC).

[69]   Cass. 19 May 1981, *Pas.* 1981, I, 1089.

[70]   In some cases, the reasons used to arrive at a certain decision can disregard the presumption of innocence, for example in the issuing of an arrest warrant by the investigating judge, or in the extension of the pre-trial custody by the investigating court: such breaches can be solved by the investigating courts (in first instance or in appeal respectively).

[71]   Verstraeten & Traest 2008, p. 90.

[72]   ECtHR 21 September 2006, *Pandy* v. *Belgium*, No. 13583/02.

[73]   See Taevernier 2005, p. 33.

the presumption of innocence has not been respected in the public opinion does not necessarily imply that the trial judge has violated this same principle.[74]

Belgium has been found by the ECtHR to have violated article 6 §2 ECHR with regard to the statutory requirement for persons who have claimed compensation for unfounded pre-trial detention.[75]

2.3.4. The right to silence (including the prohibition of self-incrimination)

The right to silence is recognised in Belgium as an aspect of the right of defence.[76] It is said to follow from article 6.1 ECHR.[77] This means *inter alia* that a suspect cannot be interrogated under oath. The suspect determines the extent to which he/she makes use of this right (he/she can choose to answer some questions and not to answer others). Although the right is recognised by the Supreme Court, there is no legal obligation requiring the police (or the investigating judge) to inform the person of his/her right to silence.

Although there is no legal provision stipulating that the exercise of the right to silence can have adverse consequences for the suspect, such effects are possible in practice. When a person refuses to cooperate with the authorities, it will often be more difficult for that person to be released from pre-trial custody, and it could also influence the sentencing afterwards.

The right to silence has not been found irreconcilable with the use of a polygraph, if the concerned person has agreed to this voluntarily, if no pressure or force was used and if the person can decide to stop at any moment.[78] The person has to consent after being sufficiently informed. The same rules apply for those DNA analyses where consent of the person is required (which means *inter alia* that the person is informed of the reasons for taking the sample).[79]

An important question is whether the right to silence can be used by a person who is interrogated within the framework of other procedures that could lead to criminal prosecution. Belgian jurisprudence has repeatedly stated that, when cooperation with the government can imply that a person would be forced to confess to certain criminally relevant facts, that person can use his right to silence in the non-penal procedure (for example, civil, fiscal and social cases). If the investigating (non-judicial) authority is aware of a possible interference with a

---

[74]   Cass. 15 December 2004, A.R. No. 9.04.1198.F.
[75]   The applicant had been placed in pre-trial custody from 29 March 1994 until 21 April 1994, but at the end of the judicial investigation, the case was dismissed. His claim was rejected on the ground that he had not provided evidence of his innocence in his application in the Belgian courts, as required by art. 28 § 1 b of the Law of 13 March 1973. Such a requirement, which suggested that the applicant was guilty, seemed unreasonable, and was found to infringe the presumption of innocence (ECtHR 13 January 2005, *Capeau* v. *Belgium*, No. 42914/98).
[76]   Cass. 13 January 1999, *Arr. Cass.* 1999; Kuty 2000, p. 309.
[77]   Cass. 11 March 1992, *Arr. Cass.* 1991-92, 657.
[78]   Cass. 15 February 2006, *R.W.* 2006-07, 1039.
[79]   Cass. 31 January 2001, *Arr. Cass.* 2001, No. 61.

pending or planned prosecution, expressly informing the person regarding the right to silence seems an essential prerequisite.[80]

2.3.5. The right to reasoned decisions

Various legal provisions specify the obligation to make a reasoned judgment concerning guilt and the sentence.[81] The Supreme Court has repeatedly ruled that the obligation of a reasoned judgment also implies that the judge should answer the defence that was argued by way of written conclusions. The essential criterion applied by the Supreme Court is that the judgment should meet the specific requirements of the applicable legal provisions. The judge should investigate and answer the plea in law of the parties, rather than the arguments that support this plea.[82] Whether a certain defence is a plea in law or (merely) an argument depends on the circumstances of the particular case.

2.3.6. The right to appeal

The right to appeal is legally guaranteed. Each party in principle has the right to appeal, but only concerning their own interests. This means *inter alia* that the public prosecutor can only appeal in regard to a criminal prosecution, and not a civil claim;[83] that the defendant who was acquitted cannot appeal; and that a civil party can only appeal in regard of its claim. In principle, all judicial decisions are subject to appeal (provisional judgements as well as final judgements; judgements after trial as well as judgements in absentia). There are some exceptions, however, such as judgments of the Assize court and decisions of the penitentiary courts.

The right of appeal of suspects in the pre-trial stage is restricted in two ways. First, the right of suspects to appeal against the decision of the investigating court that refers them to the trial court is subject to certain conditions: appeal is only possible if there are grounds of non-admissibility or prescription of the prosecution, or in case of irregularities, negligence or nullities with regard to an investigative deed, the gathering of evidence or the referral decision itself. In the latter case, an appeal is only admissible if these arguments have been submitted in writing before the investigating court at first instance.[84]

Secondly, if referral of the suspect to the trial court is combined with the continuation of his/her pre-trial detention, the suspect cannot appeal against the part of referral decision where his/her arrest was continued. On the contrary, if the suspect is referred and his/her release is ordered, this part of the decision is subject to appeal by the prosecutor.[85]

The appeal cannot harm the party appellant. This principle, however, only applies when that party was the only appellant. If the public prosecutor appeals,

---

[80]   Cass. 16 February 1996, *Arr. Cass.* 1996, No. 82.
[81]   See art. 149 of the Constitution.
[82]   Cass. 18 December 2007.
[83]   Cass. 23 May 2001, *J.T.* 2001, 716.
[84]   Art. 135 § 2 CPC.
[85]   Art. 26 §§ 3 and 4 of the Law of 20 July 1990 on the pre-trial detention.

then the sentence can become more severe. In that case, there is an important exception to the principle that judgments should be made with an absolute majority: the appeal judges can only decide upon a harsher sentence by unanimity.[86] The unanimity requirement generally applies to all cases where the defendant's position on appeal is changed in an adverse way (for example, a conviction after acquittal; an additional sentence is given (such as confiscation); imprisonment instead of internment; an effective sentence instead of a suspended sentence).

2.4. Rights relating to effective defence

2.4.1. The right to investigate the case

Suspects

The pre-trial investigation is principally non-adversarial: the investigation is secret and the suspect is not allowed to be present during inquiries such as line-ups, searches and interrogation of witnesses. This principle is said to be compensated by the fact that the prosecutor or investigating judge are obliged to investigate the case by gathering all useful elements *à charge* and *à décharge*. The only way in which suspects can participate in the investigation is indirectly, by requesting that additional inquiries are made. Even then, this right is not absolute. It depends on the type of the investigation.

If the investigation is prosecutor led, there is no possibility to submit formal requests for additional inquiries. Only informal requests are possible. In the case of a judicial investigation, there is a formal possibility for all suspects targeted by the investigation – whether or not they are officially accused – to demand that certain additional inquiries be made. This right is subject to certain (formal) conditions, and the investigating judge can refuse the request if he/she does not deem the inquiry necessary to reveal the truth, or if he/she deems the inquiry prejudicial to the investigation at that particular moment.[87]

The right to request additional inquiries exists until the time when the investigating court makes the 'arrangement of proceedings' decision. If the court decides that the investigation is not complete, the file is sent back to the investigating judge, who is then ordered to carry out certain additional inquiries. The proposal for a new CPC intends to narrow the differences between both types of investigation on the point of requesting additional inquiries.[88]

---

[86] Art. 211*bis* CPC.
[87] The judge's decision is subject to appeal by the prosecutor and the applicant within 15 days following the decision. A new request is only possible after a period of three months since the last decision on the same subject.
[88] Art. 125 introduces the formal possibility for a suspect ('anyone who is suspected of having committed an offence which is punishable with a sentence of one year imprisonment or higher') to request the prosecutor to make an additional inquiry. The injured person would have the same right. The Prosecutor would have the possibility to refuse the request, if he/she would not deem the inquiry necessary to reveal the truth, or if he/she would deem the inquiry prejudicial to the investigation at that particular moment. No appeal is possible against the Prosecutor's decision. A new request would only be possible after a period of
→

An important question related to the non-adversarial character of the pre-trial stage is whether this is compatible with the aims of the specialised judicial expertise (i.e. a court appointed expert) required during this stage. According to the recent jurisprudence of the Supreme Court, the judicial expertise ordered in the pre-trial investigation remains in principle non-adversarial. This does not, however, prevent the investigating judge from ordering the expert to hear the parties, or to give the parties the opportunity to contest the preliminary expert report.[89] The jurisprudence of the Supreme Court does not seem compatible with the present view of the ECtHR, which appears to require an accusatorial expert, particularly when the expertise is related to the appraisal of the prosecution. It should be noted that the proposal for a new CPC sets forth the principle of an accusatorial judicial expert during the trial, as well as the pre-trial phase, meaning that it would be possible for a suspect to be heard by the expert, or to make remarks regarding the preliminary findings.

Defendants

In the trial stage, the entire criminal file (containing the results of the investigation) is presented to the court. Defendants (as well as civil parties) have the right to ask additional inquiries of the prosecutor (after the pre-trial stage has been closed, but before the court hearing), or to the court itself. The prosecutor decides whether to comply with the request without possibility for appeal. The same goes for the trial court: it decides freely whether to order the prosecutor to make the additional inquiry.[90] The Supreme Court has ruled that neither article 6.3.d ECHR, nor the general principle of respect for the rights of the defence, deprives the judge of the freedom to decide on the relevance of a request for additional inquiries.[91]

---

three months since the last decision on the same subject. Art. 130 of the Proposal extends the right of suspects to ask for additional enquiries to be made up to the time of the 'arrangements of proceedings' decision to all prosecutor led investigations: each suspect would have the possibility to ask for additional inquiries at this stage. This may slow down the treatment of such cases significantly (every suspect – even in relation to a mere shoplifting – confronted with an imminent direct summons, would be able to ask for additional inquiries).

89   Cass. 7 May 2002, *Pas.* 2002, 1106.

90   An interesting example of the freedom of courts on this point is the *Van Ingen* case. Following the opening of an investigation in the United States in relation to international drug trafficking, the applicant was charged in Belgium and was sentenced in June 2002 by the Antwerp Court of Appeal to seven years imprisonment. The applicant complained of the refusal of the Court of Appeal to reopen the proceedings to give the prosecution the opportunity to adduce new evidence transmitted by the American authorities in May 2002. He alleged that this had prevented him from presenting his case effectively. The ECtHR considered that the applicant had not indicated how the new evidence could have assisted in changing the verdict against him by the Belgian courts, if it had been adduced in the proceedings before them. It further noted that the prosecution did not appear to have relied on the evidence contained in the documents. In conclusion, it considered that the proceedings had observed the adversarial principle and equality of arms (ECtHR 13 May 2008, *Van Ingen v. Belgium*, No. 9987/03).

91   Cass. 16 June 2004, *Arr. Cass.* 2004, 1094.

The defence always has the possibility to gather evidence (*à décharge*) on its own initiative, which can be submitted at trial (and is then added to the file). A lawyer is not allowed, however, to interview prospective witnesses. The defence has the right to consult and use the reports of (unilaterally appointed) experts (for example, psychiatrists). The evidentiary value of defence instructed experts is deemed lower by most judges than those of judicial experts, since it is assumed that the latter will be more objective. In practice, the report of a defence instructed expert can be useful to result in a request for a (court instructed) counter expert.

In answer to the criticism of some lawyers regarding the absolute freedom of judges to decide on requests for additional inquiries, it was pointed out by some judges that the Belgian criminal justice system foresees many possibilities for the defence to make such a request, and to appeal against the rejection by the judge,[92] although most of these only apply to judicial investigations, which constitute about 10% of all cases.

2.4.2. The right to adequate time and facilities for the preparation of the defence

Suspects

In the pre-trial stage, the defence is offered time to prepare the case in two ways. First, if the person is in pre-trial custody, the defence is notified at least two days before the appearance before the investigating court (one day in case of the first appearance), that the criminal file can be consulted. Secondly, when the judicial investigation is closed, the defence is notified at least fifteen days before the appearance before the investigating court, which will decide on the 'arrangement of proceedings'. This period is reduced to three days if one of the persons involved is in pre-trial custody. During this period, the defence has the right to view and to take a copy of the file.

Defendants

In the trial stage, a period of ten days has to be left between the notification (by a summons) and the first appearance before the police court or trial court. Non-compliance with this period is sanctioned by the nullity of the conviction in absentia of the defendant. In urgent matters, this period can be reduced by court order. The period can be reduced if the defendant or one of the defendants is in custody,

---

[92]   First, a request for additional inquiries can be made every three months, with the possibility to appeal. Secondly, when the investigation is closed and the parties are notified of the date on which the procedure will be arranged, each party again has the right to make a request, with the possibility to appeal. Finally, when there is an admissible appeal against a referral decision, a request can be made to the investigating court on appeal. Requests can later be repeated to the trial judge. If the trial judge (at first instance) rejects the request, this will either be done by means of a provisional judgment, or in the final judgment. In both cases, an appeal is possible.

without being any shorter than three days.[93] The period of notification before the Assize court is two months, unless the parties expressly waive this right.

Two important remarks should be made in this respect. First, when the case is brought before the trial court after referral by an investigating court, there is no indication in the legislation as to whether the ten day period should be counted from the referral order, or from the day on which the summons is served (which, in such cases, only counts as a fixation of date). Secondly, when a suspect who is referred by an investigating court is kept in custody pending trial, the legislation does not foresee a maximum period within which the case must be brought before the trial court by summoning the defendant. This means that such a person can be kept waiting in prison for weeks (even months) without knowing when the case will be tried or without the possibility to view the file (this right only exists from the moment that the date of the initial court hearing is fixed). In such cases, the defence can submit a petition for conditional release to the trial court.

With regard to the delay/adjournment of a hearing on request of the defence, there is no specific legal provision regulating this. The judge decides if the suspect/defendant and his/her lawyer have had enough time and facilities to prepare the case.[94] This depends on the circumstances of the case, including such considerations as the size of the file, the nature and complexity of the case and the legal questions at hand. The argument of the defence that it wants to have the same amount of time to prepare as the prosecutor has had is not a relevant criterion.[95] A change of lawyer can be a reason to adjourn the hearing, if this has truly left insufficient time to prepare the defence.[96]

The majority of the questioned professionals agree that the lack of facilities offered to the defence to prepare the case in the pre-trial stage is an obstacle for the effective defence of suspects. On each occasion where the defence has access to the case file in the course of an investigation, there is no possibility to take a copy of the file. This possibility is only offered for the first time at the end of the investigation. This means that, in all other cases where the defence has access to the file in the pre-trial stage, the content of the file has to be copied in writing by the lawyers at the court registry (some registries allow the use of dictaphones).

Taking account of the fact that there is only a limited amount of time available and that cases are increasingly extensive, this system is completely inefficient. The fact that lawyers are obliged to gather at the registry in order to take notes in stressing circumstances has been rightly described by some as 'prehistoric'. Taking into account the current technical possibilities, it would not require a great investment or significant manpower to deliver digital copies of files to lawyers. At the least, the right to a copy of the file should be ensured from the first moment the lawyer has access to the file in the pre-trial stage.

The comment of some professionals that the complaints of lawyers regarding lack of time are largely inspired by their own agenda cannot be seen as a convincing argument. The interests involved in cases of pre-trial detention should make

---

[93]   Art. 184 CPC.
[94]   Cass. 14 September 2004, *Pas.* 2004, 1332.
[95]   Cass. 15 December 2004, *J.T.* 2004, 4.
[96]   Cass. 9 February 2005, *Pas.* 2005, 329.

lawyers give these cases priority and should require their full attention. This does not, however, mean that these lawyers would be prevented from demanding the best possible facilities for preparing the case.

2.4.3. The right to equality of arms in examining witnesses

Although the trial stage in the Belgian criminal procedure is (theoretically) said to be adversarial, trial proceedings have some clearly non-adversarial characteristics. One of these is the active role of the trial judge, whose mission consists of discovering the truth (rather than passively judging the presented evidence). To accomplish this, the court should use whatever means it has to investigate the case, while respecting the defendant's fair trial rights.[97]

This active role, and consequently the non-adversarial character of the proceedings, is strongly present in the hearing of witnesses at trial. The judge decides on the necessity and opportunity of hearing witnesses (*à charge* and *à décharge*) at trial. This very broad competence is not deemed to be incompatible with the ECHR.[98] The Assize court is an exception to this general rule: the defence and the prosecutor have an equal right to call witnesses. Although the court is free to make its decision, it is obliged to indicate the reasons why a request for hearing witnesses is denied. Not justifying this decision can lead to a violation of article 6 ECHR.[99]

The active role of the Belgian trial judge is also illustrated in the examination of witnesses. The defence has the right to (cross-)examine witnesses at trial. This is, however, firmly controlled by the presiding judge. This means that the judge usually asks the questions suggested by the parties, although in practice the judge sometimes allows direct examination of witnesses by the parties.

A specific regulation exists regarding anonymous witnesses. Under clearly defined conditions, the investigating judge can decide to hide (certain elements of) the identity of particular witnesses. During the pre-trial stage, certain possibilities exist for the parties to interrogate the witness in the presence and under control of the investigating judge.[100] A similar right exists during the trial stage: at the request of the defence, the court can decide to interrogate the witness (while preserving his/her partial or full anonymity) and allow the defence to ask certain questions of this witness.

---

[97] Belgium has already been found in violation by the ECtHR in a case where a court of appeal, which convicted a defendant (after an acquittal in first instance) for deprivation of the fortune of a civil party, failed to arrange a 'confrontation' between the civil party and the defendant on three of the five charges (ECtHR 7 July 1989, *Bricmont* v. *Belgium*, No. 10857/84).

[98] ECtHR 27 July 2000, *Pisano* v. *Italy*, No. 36732/97.

[99] ECtHR 22 April 1992, *Vidal* v. *Belgium*, No. 12351/86.

[100] See arts. 86*ter* and 235*ter* § 2 CPC.

2.4.4. The right to free interpretation of documents and translation

The right to interpretation

Each suspect who does not understand the language in which the investigation is carried out has the right to ask that the criminal proceedings are continued in another of the three official languages (Dutch, French or German).[101]

When the suspect does not speak any of the three Belgian languages, or does not request that the proceedings are continued in another of the three official languages, the law guarantees the right to an interpreter. With regard to interrogations, a sworn interpreter is commonly used to assist a suspect who wishes to use a language different from the procedural language.[102]

An interesting question, particularly in respect of the increased internationalisation of crime, concerns the situation where it is impossible to find an interpreter for the language chosen by the suspect who has been deprived of his liberty within the period of 24 hours from the moment of deprivation of liberty. Should this suspect then be released from custody? It has been suggested instead to interrogate the person in another language that he understands and for which an interpreter is available. This does not, however, work in all circumstances (for example, when the suspect only speaks one language, or when the suspect is not able to communicate and does not have any papers so as to help the police to know which language he speaks).

It has been accepted by the jurisprudence that, in those situations where, despite all possible efforts, it is impossible to find an interpreter within the 24 hour period, it is possible to issue an arrest warrant, because it concerns a matter of *force majeure*. It should then be clear from the file that all possible efforts were made to find an interpreter. This solution could be seen as contrary to the law on the pre-trial custody. In any case, the investigating judge would be obliged to continue his/her search for an interpreter, in order to allow the interrogation of the suspect as soon as possible.

If the suspect has already been interrogated with the assistance of an interpreter regarding the facts that have led to his arrest, the Supreme Court has ruled that is it not required that a translation of the arrest warrant is attached to the warrant that is served to the suspect.[103]

At the Assize court, the President is obliged to appoint an interpreter *ex officio* when the accused, the civil party, the witnesses, or one of them, do not speak the same language, or the same 'idiom' (dialect).[104] For the normal trial courts, there is no similar legal provision. The judge decides whether the defendant has sufficient knowledge of the procedural language and whether he/she wants to proceed with

---

[101]   The Law of 15 June 1935 on the use of the language in judicial affairs.

[102]   Another option is to note the suspect's declarations in his/her own language. This last option is only possible when the police/investigating judge adequately speaks the language chosen by the suspect. A final option is to request the suspect to write his/her declaration himself/herself.

[103]   Cass. 2 December 1987, *Arr. Cass.* 1987-88, No. 205.

[104]   Art. 332 CPC.

the case without the use of an interpreter.[105] In practice, most judges will want an interpreter to be present, because this enables them to interrogate the defendant more efficiently. In any case, parties have to ensure their own defence rights: they cannot invoke for the first time before the Supreme Court that an interpreter should have been appointed.[106] The law does not prescribe any sanction if the right to an interpreter is not respected. This could, however, lead to a nullity of the prosecution or conviction if it constitutes a violation of the defence rights.

Many questioned professionals pointed to the fact that, in cases of legal aid, suspects in pre-trial detention have the right to free assistance of an interpreter for a period of only three hours. This does not seem sufficient in complex cases, or when interpretation is required in certain 'exotic' languages (of which the lawyer does not even have a basic knowledge).

In the current legislation, there is no specific regulation for persons acting as interpreter or translator in judicial proceedings. There is no official statute for sworn interpreters or translators.[107] If an interpreter is not competent, the suspect/defendant can complain about this, but only in extreme circumstances will a replacement immediately be appointed. The total lack of any selection and quality criteria, education, code, control and complaints procedure, clearly indicates the need for legislative intervention.[108]

The right to translation of documents

The Supreme Court has ruled that article 6.3.a ECHR does not require a translation to be attached to the summons. The fact that defendants have been informed in such a way that they are able to ensure their defence is sufficient.[109] Information regarding the accusation can, if necessary, be provided with the assistance of an interpreter at the court hearing.

The translation of documents is a sensitive issue. Depending on the court's location, the trial will be held in Dutch, French or German. According to the law,[110] every suspect who only understands Dutch and German, or one of these languages, can demand that a Dutch or German translation of the interrogation reports, witnesses or injured parties statements, and expert reports that are drawn up in French, are included in the criminal file. The same evidently goes, mutatis

---

[105]   Cass. 2 January 1996, *Arr. Cass.* 1996, 6.
[106]   Cass. 28 January 2004, *Arr. Cass.* 2004, 141.
[107]   In practice, interpreters and translators who are used in criminal proceedings are appointed by the prosecutor's office from a list. To be included on this list, the interpreter has to prove his/her clear criminal record and has to submit degrees/diplomas. If the interpreter is accepted by the prosecutor, he/she will take an oath before the Justice of the Peace.
[108]   In the Antwerp Court of First Instance, a specific service 'Sworn Interpreters and Translators' has been in place since 1 January 2008. This service covers four aspects: managing the list of sworn interpreters and translators; organizing their selection, education and appointment; guaranteeing the quality and integrity; and acting as ombudsman. Moreover, cooperation between magistrates, prosecutors, lawyers, police and the Lessius College in Antwerp has elaborated a test project for better training of judicial interpreters and translators.
[109]   Cass. 17 October 1972, *Arr. Cass.* 1973, 173.
[110]   Art. 22 of the Law of 15 June 1935 on the use of the language in judicial affairs.

mutandis, for those who only speak French and/or German, or those who only speak French and/or Dutch.[111]

In a recent judgment, the Supreme Court gave a very narrow interpretation of this legal provision: a Lebanese citizen who also spoke French had asked for a French translation of the file. The courts of first and second instance rejected this, and the Supreme Court did not quash these judgments. The Supreme Court used the remarkable argument that article 22, according to its express wording, was applicable to all suspects who only (read 'exclusively') understand Dutch, French or German, and not those who speak another than one of these three languages and also only understand Dutch, French or German. According to this interpretation, this legal provision would only be useful for unilingual Belgians.[112]

In the same ruling the Supreme Court remarked that the fact that a suspect who speaks a foreign language cannot demand a translation on the basis of the provision, does not diminish the need to respect his right of defence. This implies that non-Belgian defendants who speak one of the three official Belgian languages could still, depending on the circumstances, request the judge to order the translation of documents from the procedural language into another Belgian national language. This also seems to imply that a defendant who does not speak one of the Belgian languages cannot request the translation of documents in the case file into his/her native language. The assistance of a lawyer seems crucial in those cases.

The law on the use of the language in judicial proceedings is very strict. Its rules are prescribed with the sanction of nullity. However, each non-purely preparatory judgment after trial applies to the nullity of the writ of summons and the other procedural acts that have preceded that judgment. Often, defendants try to call upon too strict an interpretation of the law. The Supreme Court has clearly ruled that the circumstance that the summons mentions the place of birth and the residence of the defendant in the language of this place, rather than in the procedural language, does not lead to the nullity of the summons.[113]

In another judgment, the Supreme Court decided that the sole circumstance that documents that were drawn up in the framework of a foreign prosecution have afterwards been included in the criminal file (of a Belgian prosecution) does not imply that the defendant has not been informed without delay of the nature and cause of the accusation against him.[114]

3. Professional culture of defence lawyers

3.1. Introductory remarks

There has been little study undertaken in Belgium on the role played by the various actors within the criminal justice system and the perception of and among these

---

[111]   Cass. 1 December 1982, *Arr. Cass.* 1982-83, No. 233.
[112]   Cass. 18 December 2007.
[113]   Cass. 12 April 2005, *Pas.* 2005, 850.
[114]   Cass. 24 September 2002, *Arr. Cass.* 2002, 1934.

actors. This is to be regretted, since this forms an important part of the general situation in a country regarding compliance with fair trial rights. Defence rights may well be recognized by law, but their application in practice is determined to a large extent by the actions of the specific actors dealing with them every day, and the underlying relationships between these actors. This interaction, together with the opinions of the various actors within the criminal justice system, can be referred to as the 'professional culture' within a particular system.

The professional culture in the Belgian criminal justice system will briefly be touched upon below. This part of the report does not provide a definitive account, nor does it present the total picture. Moreover, none of the viewpoints expressed can be regarded as representative for a particular professional group. Nevertheless, the text (which is largely the result of interviews with, and the practical experience of criminal justice actors, such as prosecutors, judges, criminal defence lawyers, interpreters) offers some remarkable insights into some of the main areas of concern. No specific actor is targeted or blamed for any of the defaults within the system which are described. The insights provided can merely serve as a basis for instigating future work in this field.

3.2. *Obstacles for criminal defence lawyers*

Although all actors involved in criminal proceedings should respect defence rights 'spontaneously', practice shows that fair trial rights are at constant risk of being neglected and violated, possibly due to the complexity of (some) criminal proceedings, the pressure to bring suspects to justice as soon as possible, and the increasing workload. Within this difficult context, criminal defence lawyers have to serve as the first guardian of fair trial rights in practice, which puts them in a very specific position.

The task of criminal defence lawyers is far from easy. Their autonomous position is a crucial element in accomplishing the task of acting in the best interests of their clients. This autonomy also brings with it some difficulties. In defending their clients, lawyers often have to challenge the normal course of criminal proceedings: this may involve the submission of extensive written conclusions on procedural discussions that can lead to enormous delays, adopting a critical attitude towards the prosecution and sometimes even towards the judge, questioning the quality of the work done by police and investigating judges.

Moreover, there are often situations where fair trial rights are not directly violated, but where measures of a practical and organisational nature hinder criminal defence lawyers in doing their job. First, requests for adjournments of cases seem to be increasingly denied, although they may have very well founded reasons (lack of time for preparation of a complex case, clients who first contact their lawyer a few days before the hearing). The flexibility of judges on this point is clearly decreasing.

Although a minority of these requests may be unfounded, the majority of lawyers handle such requests with the necessary care. Judges sometimes appear to forget that lawyers are often obliged to prepare (increasingly complex) cases at very short notice, while the prosecution has had months or years to prepare the case for trial. It is remarkable in this respect to note that demands for adjournments made by the prosecution (to further investigate a certain fact, or to answer the arguments of the defence) are almost always accepted by the judge, while defence lawyers often have to fight a constant battle to justify similar requests. Secondly, criminal defence lawyers who enter the court are sometimes confronted with the fact that their case has already been treated in their absence. An increasing number of cases arise where the judge, despite notification by the lawyer, has already started dealing with the case.

These examples illustrate the need for all actors to step up their efforts in trying to establish a work environment of mutual respect, with at least a minimum of flexibility and courtesy on all sides. While lawyers are obliged to act firmly in order to protect the interest of their clients, this should be done with courage, prudence and skill. The main challenge for judges is to differentiate these reasonable efforts from those that are intended to misuse procedural guarantees in an unfounded way.

A final obstacle for effective criminal defence work relates to police performance in relation to fair trial rights. Taking account of the significance of the case file within Belgian criminal proceedings, the way in which the content of the file (i.e. the results of investigative actions by the police) is presented is of utmost importance. In drawing up their reports, investigators sometimes cross the border of what is expected from them. They often take on the role of the judge themselves, by drawing suggestive conclusions and by expressing statements on the guilt of the suspect, instead of merely giving an objective presentation of the information that was collected. This trend indicates the need for increased education and training of police investigators with regard to basic skills, such as conducting interrogations and with regard to the fundamental principles of criminal procedure. Insufficient performances at these levels have a negative impact on the entire criminal proceedings and can be damaging for the fair trial rights of suspects/defendants.

3.3.   *Perception of criminal defence lawyers*

Although the majority of lawyers appear to adequately assist their clients in criminal cases, there seems to be a considerable group of lawyers who are not specialized in criminal cases and therefore often lack the knowledge of elementary principles of both criminal law and criminal procedure. This ignorance and incompetence is, according to several judges, particularly present among somewhat older lawyers who are no longer (actively) aware of, or skilled in, new evolutions or matters of a high technical nature (for example, special investigative techniques, clearing of irregular evidence from the file, the European dimension of criminal procedure, such as the European arrest warrant, complex new legislation on substantive criminal law, such as human trafficking or criminal organisations). A number of judges reported that they frequently have to make 'corrections' *ex officio* in criminal cases, in order to respect the fair trial rights of suspects (when their lawyer was not even aware of the need to make this correction).

There seems to be an increasing repressiveness among a proportion of (mostly young) lawyers towards their clients ('they deserve to be in prison', 'they have themselves to blame'), which could lead to a decreased engagement with them. Moreover, some young lawyers (in particular trainees) also seem to be increasingly unaware of various fundamental requirements to assist their client (the word 'naive' was used by one particular judge), such as their client's background (particularly when it concerns minority groups such as Roma gypsies), and are perceived as lacking a critical and interested attitude. This is illustrated by the fact that too few (young) lawyers communicate adequately with their clients, particularly if they are detained in prison.

Many young lawyers do not seem capable of making an essential contribution to the debate before (particularly investigating) courts, because they have no knowledge outside the file (leaving aside the question of whether, in most cases, the file has been sufficiently studied). These elements seem to necessitate a more thorough education and training of young lawyers, starting already at university and continuing in the professional education of lawyers during their traineeship. These findings also support the call for the restriction of criminal defence work only to specialized lawyers.

3.4. Limitation of criminal defence work to specialized criminal defence lawyers

In Belgium, the provision of legal services is not limited to qualified (specialised) criminal defence lawyers. There are no minimum quality requirements for lawyers doing criminal defence work. Particularly in the framework of (second-line) legal aid, this can be problematic. Every lawyer-trainee, as well as those totally inexperienced in, or even reluctant to do criminal defence work, must in principle accept every case appointed to them during their traineeship, and will thus inevitably be appointed to indigent suspects/defendants in criminal cases. This system is often criticized, due to the fact that some of these lawyers appear incapable of protecting the interests of their clients in (often) complicated criminal cases.

Due to the increasingly technical nature and complexity of criminal cases, and with the aim of providing clients with a lawyer who is sincerely engaged (which implies *inter alia* that the lawyer actively gathers information on the client's background and personal situation), a strong argument can be made for limiting criminal defence work to specialized lawyers, at least in the legal aid system (where at present all trainees can/must do criminal defence work). All questioned professionals agreed with such a proposal. Moreover, most trial judges expressly welcome such an idea, because for them 'it is more agreeable to lead a trial where prosecution and defence can perform with equal arms'.

3.5. Comments on the legal aid system in relation to criminal defence work

The idea of limiting the appointment of lawyers under legal aid for criminal defence work to those trainees (or other lawyers who have registered in the legal aid system) with a specialisation in criminal defence was welcomed by the overall majority of questioned professionals.

As has already been indicated throughout this report this could significantly improve the quality of legal aid in criminal affairs. Such a specialisation would not require radical change.

Most questioned professionals agree that the legal aid system should be made more attractive. First, the remuneration of lawyers doing criminal defence work under legal aid should be increased. Since the average remuneration per case for the year 2006-07 was around 400 Euro, it is evident that specialised criminal defence lawyers are not always enthusiastic about assisting indigent defendants. Secondly, the payment should also be made sooner (for example, on a monthly basis) than at present (where lawyers are usually paid 1 to 1,5 years after they have worked in the case).

Thirdly, the 'point system' used as the basis for determining the remuneration should be made more flexible, in the sense that a differentiation should be introduced according to the nature, complexity and size of the case. The current system (where a huge drug trafficking case with several defendants is valued no higher than a mere shoplifting case) is neither realistic nor adequate.

4.   Political commitment to effective criminal defence

4.1.   Public attitude

The political culture regarding fair trial rights can obviously not be seen separately from the attitude of the public to criminal justice. Since the 1970s, the theme of insecurity due to crime has gradually taken a more prominent place in the broad social debate, the political discussion and media coverage. In the Belgian, context the rise of crime and feelings of insecurity have from the start been associated with the (increased) presence of (particularly) Turkish and Moroccan migrants and, from the 1990s, also illegal persons and asylum seekers.

On 19 October 2007, the results of the second justice barograph were presented.[115] An important aspect of the research is the view regarding the severity of sentencing. For five of the six groups of offences measured (organized crime, sexual offences, murders, drug-related crime and financial crime), a large majority (up to 87%) thought that judges are too lenient. Only for the sixth category, traffic offences, was a majority opposed to more severe sentencing. Furthermore, according to 68% of respondents, disrespect for criminal procedure rules cannot legitimate an acquittal (elders and young people, persons professionally tied to justice and those who had already experienced a criminal trial favoured a more severe sanctioning of violation of criminal procedure).

A clear conclusion can be made concerning the execution of sentences: 60% of respondents thought that convicted persons should be obliged to serve their full sentence (in 2002 this was only 53%). Only 35% favour conditional release (in

---

[115]   In 2004, the Universities of Leuven and Liège developed a 'justice barograph' to map the average citizen's attitude towards the judicial system. The barograph research involves a telephonic inquiry of a representative sample of the Belgian population.

particular, people aged 26 to 45 and people with a lower or secondary education call for a more strict prison policy).

Regarding youth delinquency, 80% of respondents want to preserve the model that places young offenders in an institution where education and guidance are central (this is an increase compared to 2002 (76%), despite greater media attention on youth delinquency cases).

4.2. The current political climate: shifting towards or moving away from fair trial rights?

A quick scan of the viewpoints of some of the major political parties immediately shows that there is no attention to fair trial rights, apart from in a negative way. Beside the main themes that can be found in almost every party's programme (reform of the prosecution and police, elaboration of alternative sentencing and mediation, better regulation of the serving of sentences), the fair trial rights of suspects/defendants are remarkably absent.

The apparent current (political) shift towards victims' rights, a more effectively working judicial apparatus, and away from the procedural guarantees, could be explained by the increasingly critical attitude among the general public. It is alarming, however, that this discourse often undermines some of the fundamental principles of a modern criminal justice system. Proposals by political parties stating that acquittals should be made impossible in the case of procedural errors are not only (politically) cheap, but also dangerous.

Procedural rules form the fundamental guarantee against unlawful actions of the police and prosecution. A strict application of the sanctions in the case of procedural errors is therefore a condition sine qua non in order to ensure a fair trial for every suspect/defendant, regardless of their origin, income, status or background. Acquittals of defendants (sometimes even in serious cases such as drug trafficking or organized crime), due to procedural errors, can seem unreasonable and even unacceptable to the general public.

It should be stressed however that such acquittals are rare and that the current system of excluding irregular evidence functions adequately and is capable of restricting such cases to an absolute minimum.[116] If, nevertheless, the trial judge is confronted with a flagrant procedural error, which leads to the inadmissibility of the prosecution, this is the price that should be paid in order to effectively preserve the right to a fair trial. One can only hope that those with political power and

---

[116] At present, the issue of irregular obtained evidence in criminal affairs is dominated by the jurisprudence of the Supreme Court, which is based on the following rules: in principle, the use of evidence (by the judicial authorities) that was produced through committing a crime, or by violating a criminal procedural rule, through violating the right to privacy, or the right to human dignity, is not allowed. The judge can, however, *only* exclude irregularly achieved evidence if (1) the disrespect for certain formalities is sanctioned (by the law) by nullity; or (2) if the irregularity affects the credibility of the evidence; or (3) if the use of the evidence violates the right to a fair trial. According to this doctrine, the judge decides on the admissibility of irregularly obtained evidence in light of the art. 6 ECHR, taking into account the elements of the case as a whole, including the way in which the evidence was obtained and the circumstances in which the irregularity was committed.

responsibility do not ignore these unpopular, but fundamental, arguments in their quest for the electorate's vote.

5.   Conclusions

In assessing the quality of a criminal justice system, it is tempting to look at other systems and to select those aspects that seem better and more effective. No system is perfect, however, and each system must be analysed from its own historic, cultural and social background. Merely criticising a system by comparing it to the best practice of other systems is therefore both insensitive and difficult.

Although, in the last 10 years, some adversarial elements have been introduced into the investigation stage, the bulk of the criminal investigations in Belgium are still characterised by the inquisitorial nature of the pre-trial stage. As such, this gives rise to certain obstacles to an effective defence. Suspects in principle do not have access to the case file during the investigation, and requests for additional inquiries are still largely dependent on the goodwill of the magistrate leading the investigation. In a system where the investigative proceedings often (solely) determine the outcome of the trial, the recognition and implementation of effective defence rights in the investigative stage are vital. On this point in particular, the Belgian system has many shortcomings.

Apart from a notification of certain rights at the start of an interrogation, suspects who are taken into pre-trial custody are not expressly informed of their procedural rights. Belgium does not have a letter of rights. There is no legal obligation to inform suspects of their right to remain silent. Limited access to the file during the investigation is only legally guaranteed for suspects in pre-trial custody. Moreover, there are no adequate facilities for the defence for the preparation of the case in the pre-trial stage. Belgian practice in this respect is totally outdated and involves a pointless waste of time and resources. There is no right to a (digital) copy of the file until the end of the investigation. There is no right for a lawyer to be present during interrogations by the police, or the investigating magistrate, although this will have to change as result of recent ECtHR case law.

Although the right to an interpreter is legally recognized at every stage of the proceedings, the quality and practical organisation of the profession of interpreters and translators is problematic. There is a clear need for legislative action in this field. At present, many suspects who are eligible for conditional release remain in pre-trial detention, due to the shortage in capacity of those institutions offering guidance or treatment. Increased funding of, and support in this field is essential for effectively implementing the legally available alternatives for pre-trial detention. Finally, a limitation of criminal defence work in the legal aid system only to those lawyers who have a special qualification and specialization in this field would generally be seen as an improvement. This should be accompanied by measures to make the remuneration for lawyers in second-line legal aid more attractive.

There is an urgent need for systematic consultation between the various criminal justice actors (in particular judges, prosecutors and lawyers), in order to guarantee a reasonable and professional interaction between them. Continuous training and education are key elements, in order to guarantee an acceptable qualitative performance of the various criminal justice actors and, as such, are inextricably bound to the fair trial rights of suspects and defendants. Improvement in this area is particularly necessary for trainee-lawyers and police investigators.

The political discourse on criminal justice legislation should give greater attention to fair trial rights. The current approach is often (mainly) victim oriented. Moreover, in preparing new legislation in the field of criminal (procedural) law, more attention should be paid to the input of the various relevant actors.

In general, it can be concluded that the Belgian criminal justice system is, in several ways, inadequate in guaranteeing effective defence rights. Although a number of rights are both sufficiently recognized in law and implemented in practice, improvements on various levels are necessary if Belgium wants to meet ECHR standards. Apart from the necessary changes in order to strive for full compliance with the ECHR, a supporting professional culture and sufficient political commitment are crucial, in order to achieve an effective defence for all suspects and defendants in criminal proceedings.

6.   Bibliography

Books

Beyens, Snacken & Eliaerts 1993
Beyens, K., Snacken, S. & Eliaerts, C., *Barstende muren. Overbevolkte gevangenissen: omvang, oorzaken en mogelijke oplossingen*, Antwerp: Kluwer, Gouda: Quint, 1993.

Articles in Journals

Daems 2007
Daems, T., 'Strafuitvoeringsrechtbanken, overbevolkte gevangenissen & compatibele slachtoffers', *Panopticon*, 3, 2007, p. 41-57.

De Smet 1996
De Smet, B., 'Het onmiddellijkheidsbeginsel in het strafproces: een anachronisme of een waarborg voor een kwalitatief goede rechtspleging?', *Rechtskundig Weekblad*, 1996-97, p. 65-76.

Kuty 2000
Kuty, F., 'L'étendue du droit au silence en procédure pénale', *Revue de Droit Pénal et de Criminologie*, 2000, p. 309-334.

Schuermans 2005
Schuermans, F., 'Donkere onweerswolken boven het Belgisch strafvorderlijk landschap', *Panopticon*, 5, 2005, p. 39-54.

Taevernier 2005

Taevernier, B., 'La présomption d'innocence et la médiatisation de la justice: une cohabitation précaire', *Revue de Droit Pénal et de Criminologie*, 2005, p. 33-85.

Traest & De Tandt 2004

Traest, P. & De Tandt, I., 'Het voorontwerp van wetboek van strafprocesrecht: een kennismaking', *Panopticon*, 4, 2004, p. 6-24.

Van Puyenbroeck & Vermeulen 2009

Van Puyenbroeck, L. & Vermeulen, G., 'Het recht op bijstand van een advocaat bij het politieverhoor na de arresten Salduz en Panovits van het EHRM', *Nullum Crimen*, 2, 2009 , p. 87-97.

Verstraeten & Traest 2008

Verstraeten, R. & Traest, P., 'Het recht van verdediging in de onderzoeksfase', *Nullum Crimen*, 2, 2008, p. 85-105.

7.   Annex

Extract from the Ministerial Decree of 21 August 2006 on the determination of the list of points regarding the performance by lawyers responsible for fully or partially free second-line legal aid

The list below only covers performance in the field of criminal law, youth protection and the assistance of mentally impaired persons. The average value per point is between 24 and 25 Euro.

1. Mentally impaired persons

First appearance   12p
Subsequent appearance   + 6p

2. Criminal cases

   1)   Criminal defence

Police court: 8 points

With civil party (irrespective of the number of civil parties): + 7 points

Additional hearing (other than an adjournment or a mere pronouncement of the judgment): + 3 points

Dealing with the civil case following involvement of a judicial expert: + 10 points

Correctional court: 20 points

With civil party (irrespective of the number of civil parties): + 7 points

Additional hearing (other than an adjournment or a mere pronouncement of the judgment): + 3 points

Dealing with the civil case following involvement of a judicial expert: + 10 points

Investigating court: 6 points (per appearance)

Assise court: per day (defence and civil party): 25 points

   2)   Civil action

Civil action in the hands of an investigating judge: 6 points

Civil action (apart from the Assise court): 10 points

   3)   Petition for clemency: 5 points

   4)   Rehabilitation: 10 points

   5)   Commission of social defence: 6 points

   6)   Conditional release (per appearance): 6 points

   7)   Commission of financial help for victims of deliberate violence: 10 points

   8)   Mediation in criminal affairs: 6 points

   9)   Restorative mediation: 8 points

   10) Appearance for bodies competent for provisional or conditional release: 6 points
   11) Petition according to the Franchimont Law: 5 points

Petition restricted to viewing the file: 5 points (maximum 10 points per appointment)

   12) Extradition: 10 points

   13) Swift justice (appearance during the weekend) + 4 points

   14) Probation commission (per hearing): 6 points

3. Youth cases (other than civil)

   1)   Juvenile court: 10 points

With a civil party (irrespective of the number of civil parties): + 7 points

Additional hearing (other than an adjournment or a mere pronouncement of the judgment): + 3 points

2) Juvenile judge (appearance in cabinet)

First appearance: 6 points

Additional appearance: + 3 points

Appearance during the weekend: + 4 points

3) Defence in the Special Committee for youth care / mediation commission of special youth care (per appearance): 6 points

4) Restorative mediation / Restorative group consultation: 8 points (+ 6 points if the mediation or consultation is followed by a public hearing)

5) Civil action: 8 points (10 points for dealing with the civil case after involvement of a judicial expert)

4. Opposition as defendant: half of the points that would be accorded for a new procedure

5. Appeal: the same points as for the procedure in first instance

6. Supreme Court

1) Request for legal aid (to be freed from paying the procedure costs): 10 points

2) Supreme Court procedure: 25 points

7. International courts: 40 points

8. Reimbursement of transport costs: a half point per 20km starting from the lawyer's office

8. Abbreviations

Journals

Arr. Cass.: Arresten van het Hof van Cassatie

J.T.: Journal des Tribunaux

N.C.: Nullum Crimen

N.J.W.: Nieuw Juridisch Weekblad

Pas.: Pasicrisie Belge

R.D.P.: Revue de droit pénal et de criminologie

R.W.: Rechtskundig Weekblad

Other

CPC: Criminal Procedure Code

ECHR: European Convention on Human Rights and Fundamental freedoms

ECtHR: European Court of Human Rights

LAB: Legal Aid Bureau

S.B.: Statute Book

Ed Cape

CHAPTER 4 ENGLAND AND WALES*

1.   Introduction

1.1.   Basic demographic information

England and Wales constitutes one of the three major legal jurisdictions in the United Kingdom, the other two being Scotland and Northern Ireland, each having its own separate and distinctive criminal justice system.[1] The population of England and Wales is just over 52 million, with slightly more females than males. Approximately one fifth of the population is aged 15 years or under. In the 2001 census 91.3 per cent identified themselves as white, 2.2 per cent as black, 4.4 per cent as Asian, and 2.4 per cent as mixed or other. However, the distribution is uneven, and about 40 per cent of the population of London identified itself as other than White British.

1.2.   The nature of the criminal justice system

The English and Welsh system of criminal procedure is rooted in the adversarial tradition, but over the past couple of decades or so it has been undergoing significant change, largely informed by managerialist values. There are many strands to this. The resources and the powers of the police have been continually enhanced, giving them the ability to arrest, detain, control and keep under surveillance suspects and others to a greater extent than ever before. The Crown Prosecution Service (responsible for most, but not all, state prosecutions) has been given a greater role in criminal investigation and charging, raising important questions (that have largely gone unanswered) about independence and accountability. Suspects and defendants have increasingly been required to provide

---

[*]   This country report has been reviewed by Michael Zander, Emeritus Professor, London School of Economics.

[1]   The Welsh Assembly now has legislative responsibility for a number of areas of policy but not for criminal justice, although a number of its powers have implications for criminal justice.

information to the police and prosecution in advance of trial. Mechanisms designed to encourage early guilty pleas have been developed without adequate safeguards designed to ensure that the innocent do not plead guilty. Legislation and policies have been introduced that are directed either at dealing with 'offenders' outside of the criminal justice system or at encouraging non-court disposals for criminal offences.[2]

Over the same period, however, there have been three key developments which have, to a greater or lesser extent, enhanced the position of those suspected or accused of crime. First, in the mid-1980s comprehensive statutory regulation of the investigative stage of the criminal process was introduced.[3] Whilst this legislation increased certain police powers, such as those concerning stop and search, arrest, searches, and the taking of samples, using a combination of statutory regulation and codes of practice it created a regulatory regime dealing with, *inter alia*, review of and maximum length of pre-charge detention; responsibility for the detention and care of suspects, and the recording of detention and detention decisions; the conduct and recording of police interviews of suspects; rights for, and protection of, suspects, including the right to information about rights, the right to legal advice before and during police interviews, the right to have family and friends notified of a suspect's detention, and the right of vulnerable suspects to the presence of an appropriate adult. In addition, evidential rules were introduced which can, although not necessarily, result in exclusion of evidence obtained in breach of the regulations. In the period since the introduction of this regime, many police powers have been enhanced, and there have been significant developments such as enabling courts to draw adverse inferences from 'silence' of a defendant in police interviews. However, the basic structure of the regulatory regime remains in place, and the rights of suspects at the investigative stage have become entrenched.[4]

Second, the European Convention on Human Rights (ECHR) was, in effect, incorporated into domestic law in 2000.[5] It is unlawful for public authorities, including the police, prosecution, and the courts, to act in a way that is incompatible with a Convention right.[6] Legislation must, as far as is possible, be read in a way that is compatible with Convention rights, and courts must have regard to European Court of Human Rights (ECtHR) jurisprudence.[7] Although the courts do not have the power to strike down legislation on the grounds that it is incompatible with the ECHR, the higher courts do have the power to make a declaration of incompatibility[8] which, whilst not affecting the instant decision and although little used, would have the effect of bringing the issue to the attention of Parliament. Whilst opinion is divided on the effects of incorporation of the ECHR on criminal

---

[2]   See, for example, Duff et al. 2004, 2006 and 2007; Young 2008; Cape 2008; Jackson 2008; Solomon et al. 2007; and Morgan 2008.

[3]   By the Police and Criminal Evidence Act (PACE) 1984. See generally Zander 2005.

[4]   For a recent analysis of PACE 1984 and developments since it was introduced, see Cape & Young 2008.

[5]   By the Human Rights Act 1998.

[6]   Human Rights Act 1998 s. 6.

[7]   Human Rights Act 1998 ss. 3 and 2 respectively.

[8]   Human Rights Act 1998 s. 4.

procedure, there have been a number of clashes between the government and the judiciary particularly in relation to responses to terrorism.

Third, spending on criminal legal aid significantly increased over the period up to about 2003, and currently amounts to almost 1,4 billion Euro per annum.[9] One of the consequences of this level of spending is that the Legal Services Commission, which has responsibility for administering legal aid, has taken a close interest in value for money and quality of service provided by lawyers paid from the legal aid fund. Although highly controversial for a number of reasons, firms of solicitors carrying out legally-aided work are required to comply with a variety of quality assurance standards, and individual criminal defence lawyers (especially solicitors) are required to satisfy certain minimum standards through a number of post-qualification accreditation schemes.[10]

1.3.   The structure and processes of the criminal justice system

The police have extensive powers of summary arrest, and whilst they may apply to a court for an arrest warrant, most arrests are carried out under legislation that permits arrest without a warrant.[11] In 2006/7 there were 1,48 million arrests for notifiable offences, a four per cent increase on the previous year, continuing a trend of increasing numbers of arrests over the past few years, despite a declining crime rate.[12] Most arrests are of males (83 per cent in 2007/8), and just over one fifth arrests are of persons under the age of 18 years (and about 36 per cent are of persons under the age of 21 years).[13] Once a person has been arrested, they must normally be taken to a police station as soon as practicable, where a custody officer may authorise their detention for the purpose of investigation and/or questioning.[14] Such detention may be for up to an initial period of 24 hours from the time of arrival at the police station, although this may be extended to a total of 36 hours by a senior

---

[9]   £ 1.2 billion. See further section 1.5.

[10]   See further Section 3.

[11]   The main power of arrest is governed by the Police and Criminal Evidence Act 1984, s. 24 which, broadly, empowers police officers to arrest without a warrant provided that the officer has reasonable grounds for suspecting that an offence has been, is being or is about to be committed, and has reasonable grounds for believing that arrest is necessary for one or more of a number of reasons set out in s. 24(5).

[12]   In 2007/8 the number of arrests fell marginally compared to the previous year, whilst recorded crime decreased by 9% over the same period. Most arrests are for 'notifiable offences' (broadly those offences for which a person can receive a sentence of imprisonment), but there is an unknown number of arrests for non-notifiable offences. Although the crime rate has been declining for more than a decade, government policies encourage the police to 'bring more people to justice', with incentives on the police to meet targets on the number of offences brought to justice. In fact, in the most recent year for which statistics are available, the target has been more than met. See Home Office 2008a, p. 78.

[13]   Ministry of Justice 2008a.

[14]   This process is governed by PACE 1984, Part IV. For a description and analysis see Cape & Hodgson 2007.

police officer, and thereafter for a further 72 hours on the authority of a magistrates' court.[15]

Evidence obtained from the suspect whilst in police detention, including the product of police interviews, is generally admissible at trial, although confession evidence may be excluded on grounds of oppression or unreliability.[16] If the defendant represents to the court that a confession was or may have been obtained in such circumstances, it is not admissible unless the court is satisfied beyond reasonable doubt that it was not so obtained.[17] This potentially provides a powerful safeguard against police misconduct in securing confessions, although courts sometimes appear to be reluctant to exclude evidence of confessions under these provisions. Confession evidence has, for example, been excluded where the police interviewed a man with borderline learning difficulties for 13 hours spread over five days in a manner that was bullying and verbally threatening,[18] but not in a case where the police were 'rude and discourteous.'[19] The mere fact that a suspect was withdrawing from the effects of drugs at the time of the police interview may not be treated by the courts as rendering a confession unreliable, but such a confession may be excluded if the police deliberately denied such a suspect access to a doctor.[20]

In addition, courts have a discretion to exclude any prosecution evidence (including evidence of a confession) if, having regard to all the circumstances including the circumstances in which it was obtained, they are satisfied that the admission of the evidence would have such an adverse effect on the fairness of the proceedings that it ought not to be admitted.[21] Judicial approaches to this rule vary considerably, but generally prosecution evidence should be excluded if it was obtained as a result of a significant and substantial breach of procedural rules and admission of the evidence would have a serious adverse effect on the fairness of the trial.[22] For example, the Court of Appeal has decided that evidence should have been excluded where a suspect was wrongly denied access to legal advice before being interviewed by police,[23] but in a similar case the court decided that the trial judge was right not to exclude evidence where the accused knew what his rights were.[24] In addition, courts have the power to 'stay' (i.e., stop) a prosecution on the

---

[15]   Police and Criminal Evidence Act 1984, ss. 41-44. Where a person is arrested on suspicion of terrorism, they can be detained without charge for up to 28 days. Government proposals to extend this even further were defeated in Parliament in 2009. Statistics on length of detention without charge are not routinely collected (although there are statistics on the number of people detained beyond 24 hours and who are not charged), but the vast majority of suspects are charged or released within 24 hours of arrival at the police station. See Ministry of Justice 2009a.

[16]   Police and Criminal Evidence Act 1984, s. 76(2).

[17]   *Ibidem.*

[18]   *R* v. *Paris, Abdullahi and Miller* (1993) 97 Cr App R 99.

[19]   *R* v. *Emmerson* (1991) 92 Cr App R 284.

[20]   *R* v. *Crampton* (1990) 92 Cr App R 369.

[21]   Police and Criminal Evidence Act 1984, s. 78.

[22]   *R* v. *Walsh* (1989) 91 Cr App R 161, and *R* v. *Keenan* (1989) 90 Cr App R 1. For an analysis of these provisions see Mirfield 1997 and Sharpe 1998.

[23]   *R* v. *Samuel* (1988) 87 Cr App R 232.

[24]   *R* v. *Alladice* (1988) 87 Cr App R 380, and see also *R* v. *Dunford* (1990) 91 Cr App R 150. For a discussion of this case see Hodgson 1992.

grounds of abuse of process. For example, in one case a prosecution was stayed where the police had covertly kept a lawyer and their client under surveillance during consultations at a police station.[25] However, this power is used relatively rarely, being available only where the accused has been prejudiced by delay by the prosecution, or where the prosecution has manipulated or misused the court process so as to deprive the defendant of a protection provided by law or to take unfair advantage of a technicality.[26]

These evidential provisions only apply where there is a trial (i.e. a suspect is charged with a criminal offence and pleads not guilty), and are therefore not directly relevant in terms of regulating the conduct of investigations. There is no equivalent of the evidentiary motion at the investigation stage, as found in some other jurisdictions. Habeas corpus is available in respect of unlawful detention, and actions of the police and prosecution may be subject to judicial review. However, whilst the police are under a duty to pursue all reasonable lines of enquiry, including those suggested by the accused,[27] the accused cannot apply to a court to require them to conduct a particular investigation or interview a particular witness.

Criminal investigation is the responsibility of the police,[28] although they may seek advice from a prosecutor. There is no investigating judge in the English and Welsh system and prosecutors (known as Crown Prosecutors, who work for the Crown Prosecution Service or CPS) have no formal supervisory powers over the police. Generally, the police can exercise most investigative powers without authorisation from a prosecutor or a judge although they do have to apply to a judge in order to exercise a limited number of powers.[29] Police investigation is regulated by a number of key pieces of legislation, the most important being the Police and Criminal Evidence Act (PACE) 1984. The custody officer (a police officer of at least the rank of sergeant) plays an important role in regulating the detention of suspects and ensuring their overall welfare. Historically, the custody officer made the decision whether to charge[30] a suspect with a criminal offence but recent legislation has modified this procedure so that prosecutors now take the decision whether or not to charge in all but the most minor offences, and they are also becoming increasingly involved in advising the police on their investigations. About 60 per cent of those arrested for notifiable offences are charged with one or

---

[25]   R v. *Grant* [2006] QB 60. The House of Lords has since decided that such surveillance may be lawful. See section 2.2.2.

[26]   R v. *Derby Crown Court*, ex parte Brooks (1985) 80 Cr App R 164.

[27]   Code of Practice § 3.5, issued under the Criminal Procedure and Investigations Act 1996 Part II.

[28]   Although certain offences are investigated by other agencies such as HM Revenue and Customs, the Serious Fraud Office and the Serious Organised Crime Agency.

[29]   In particular, to enter and search property where the owner or occupier has not been arrested. Further, interception of telecommunications or post can normally only be carried out on the authority of a warrant issued by the Home Secretary.

[30]   The 'charge' is one of two ways by which criminal proceedings may be commenced, the other being by summons (which is being replaced by a similar procedure known as 'written charge'). The majority of people appearing in magistrates' courts do so as a result of a summons (57%) rather than charge (43%), although the summons procedure tends to be used for traffic and minor offences.

more offences, but extensive use is made of 'diversionary' disposals such as cautions and fixed penalties, and about half of all criminal cases where formal action is taken against the accused are dealt with without them going to court.[31]

There are two levels of first instance criminal courts. The lower level, dealing with less serious cases, is comprised of magistrates' courts. These are presided over by lay magistrates, who deal with most cases, or by 'District Judges', who sit in only a few courts and who deal with a small minority of cases. The office of lay magistrate, or Justice of the Peace, has existed for centuries and represents a key, and largely respected, element of lay involvement in the criminal justice process in England and Wales. Lay magistrates are drawn from the local community and sit as magistrates on a part-time, unpaid, basis. They are not legally qualified but are advised by a legally qualified clerk. The Crown Court[32] is presided over by professional judges, who sit with a jury for the purpose of conducting trials. Both District Judges and Crown Court judges are appointed on a full time basis from the ranks of practising lawyers, and their numbers are bolstered by practising lawyers who sit part-time as Deputy District Judges or Crown Court Recorders.

Where a person has been charged with a criminal offence, they will initially appear in a magistrates' court.[33] However, the court in which the accused is tried and/or sentenced depends upon the offence charged. Offences are classified as either 'summary' or 'indictable' offences, but indictable offences are sub-divided into 'indictable-only' and 'either-way' offences. A summary offence normally may be dealt with (i.e., the trial and/or sentence) only in a magistrates' court. Most motoring offences are summary offences, as are relatively minor offences such as taking a motor vehicle without consent, minor public order, public drunkenness, and also a large number of regulatory offences. An either-way offence is one that may be tried either in a magistrates' court or the Crown Court. There is a fairly complex mechanism by which this is determined. Essentially, if a defendant intends to plead guilty the case is dealt with in a magistrates' court but they may be 'committed' to the Crown Court for sentence if the court believes that its power of punishment is inadequate having regard to the nature and seriousness of the crime and the previous criminal record of the defendant.[34] If the defendant does not intend to plead guilty, or will not indicate a plea, their case must be sent to the Crown Court[35] unless both the court and the defendant agree that it should be dealt with in the magistrates' court. An indictable-only offence can only be dealt with by

[31]   The proportion of cases dealt with without court proceedings is even greater if traffic offences are included. For critical analyses of this phenomenon, see Young 2008 and Morgan 2008.

[32]   Technically there is one Crown Court which sits in a number of towns and cities round the country.

[33]   This is also the case if criminal proceedings are commenced by way of summons or written charge.

[34]   Generally magistrates' court sentencing powers are limited to six months imprisonment, or 12 if the accused pleads guilty to, or is found guilty of, more than one indictable offence.

[35]   The case will, in fact, only go to the Crown Court if the magistrates' court, sitting as examining magistrates, are satisfied that there is sufficient evidence to establish a prima facie case. This was of historical significance, but most defendants now agree to an abbreviated form of committal proceedings in which there is no examination of the evidence, so that committal to the Crown Court is routine.

the Crown Court, irrespective of plea, although the first court appearance is always in a magistrates' court which, in particular, may deal with the issue of bail. In practice, the vast majority of cases are dealt with in magistrates' courts.[36]

There is a guilty plea system, and if the accused pleads guilty the court will not be informed of the evidence but will accept the plea as sufficient evidence of guilt. In practice, most criminal cases are dealt with in this way,[37] and in such cases the court deals only with procedural issues such as bail, and with sentence. There is no formal system of plea bargaining, but evidence demonstrates that informal plea bargaining (and other forms of bargaining, such as charge bargaining) is a central feature of the criminal justice process. This was demonstrated by research in the late 1970s, and later research conducted in the early 1990s showed that defence lawyers often ignored clients' protestations of innocence, and failed to emphasise to their clients that they should only plead guilty if they were guilty.[38] A major incentive to plead guilty is the prospect of sentence discount. In determining sentence in respect of a defendant who has pleaded guilty the court is statutorily required to take into account the stage in the proceedings that they indicated their intention to plead guilty.[39] Guidance from the Sentencing Guidelines Council indicates that the discount can be up to one third of the sentence that otherwise would have been imposed.[40]

If the accused pleads not guilty, a trial is conducted, before (normally) three lay magistrates or a District Judge in magistrates' courts, or a judge and jury in the Crown Court. Broadly, the judge makes decisions of law and the jury decisions of fact. It is for the prosecution and defence to determine what evidence to adduce at trial, and they lead the examination of their witnesses, with judges having only a limited power to call witnesses on their own account (a power which they rarely exercise). The orality principle is reflected in a general rule that the trial court can only rely on evidence given by, or produced by, witnesses giving oral evidence during the course of the trial. However, there are important exceptions to this, including where both prosecution and defence agree to witness statements being read to the court, in certain cases where a witness is unable or unwilling to give evidence, and in some cases involving child or vulnerable witnesses (see further section 2.4.3).

There is a common perception, although not universally held, that magistrates' court proceedings are highly routinised, are dominated by a concern to process defendants and cases quickly, and are less concerned than the Crown Court with procedural and evidential requirements. The Crown Court deals more satisfactorily with evidential and legal issues, but cases take longer and trials cost considerably more than those in magistrates' court although, of course, the court deals with more serious cases. A greater proportion of defendants appearing in magistrates' courts

---

[36]   About 2 million cases are dealt with my magistrates' courts each year, compared to about 80,000 by the Crown Court.

[37]   Well over 90% in magistrates' courts, and about 64% in the Crown Court. See Ministry of Justice 2007a, and Ministry of Justice 2007b.

[38]   See Sanders & Young 2007, p. 430 for a summary of the research, and Bridges 2006.

[39]   Criminal Justice Act 2003 s. 144(1).

[40]   Sentencing Guidelines Council 2007.

plead guilty than those appearing in the Crown Court (about 90 per cent in magistrates' courts compared to about 60 per cent in the Crown Court), and the acquittal rate (where the defendant pleads not guilty) is significantly lower in the former compared to the latter.[41]

1.4. Levels of crime and the prison population

There are two major measures of crime levels in England and Wales: recorded crime (i.e. crime recorded by the police), and a major self-report series known as the British Crime Survey (BCS). Recorded crime relies on a crime (a) being reported, and (b) being recorded as such by the police, and there is evidence of both significant under-reporting and under-recording. The BCS only surveys people aged 16 years and above,[42] does not capture crime for which there is not a human 'victim', and does not capture 'victimless' crime. However, the BSC is regarded as the most reliable measure of the extent of victimisation and of national trends over time.[43] According to the BSC there were 10.1 million crimes in 2007/8, and in that year just under five million crimes were recorded by the police. The BSC showed that crime increased between 1981 and 1995, and then fell sharply up to about 2004/5, since when it has stabilised. There was an overall fall in crime of 48 per cent from 1995 to 2007/8. Although violent crime receives a lot of media coverage, the BSC has shown a significant fall since the mid 1990s, and the most serious violence against the person accounted for only two per cent of total violence against the person offences in 2007/8. There is a great deal of regional variation, and in 2007/8 nearly two thirds of all recorded robberies in England and Wales were recorded by just three police forces: the Metropolitan Police, Greater Manchester and the West Midlands.

Ethnic minorities are over-represented at all stages of the criminal process. In 2007/8 black people were eight times more likely to be stopped and searched by the police than white people, and Asians twice as likely as white people. In the same year black people were nearly four times more likely than white people to be arrested, and less likely to be diverted from court proceedings by way of a police caution. Twenty five per cent of the male prison population were black or minority ethnic, as were 29 per cent of the female prison population. For British nationals, the population of black prisoners relative to the population was 6.8 per 1,000, compared to 1.3 per 1,000 for white people. By way of contrast, five per cent of those working for the prison service were black or minority ethnic, four per cent of police officers and four per cent of the judiciary came from these groups.[44]

The prison population has been rising for more than a decade, and now stands at about 83,000, compared to 61,470 in June 1997. Out of that total just over 13,000 were on remand either awaiting trial (8,549) or awaiting sentence (4,527).[45] The

---

[41]   See generally Sanders & Young 2007, chs. 9 and 10.
[42]   Although there are plans to extend it to victims of crime under 16 years.
[43]   See Home Office 2008b.
[44]   All these statistics taken from Ministry of Justice 2009b.
[45]   Ministry of Justice 2009c.

prison population is projected to rise to up to 88,000 by June 2010.[46] The increase in the population is largely a result of increasing numbers of people being given custodial sentences and an increase in average sentence length. Other factors result directly from government policy and legislation: for example, the introduction of indeterminate sentences for public protection in 2005, and an increase in the number of people recalled to prison for breach of their licence following early release.

1.5. Legal aid for persons suspected or accused of crime

As noted earlier, expenditure on criminal legal aid is high by international standards, as is eligibility. Legal aid is available for suspects and defendants at all stages of the criminal process, from the time that a person is arrested and detained at a police station through to appeal. At the investigative stage and in the Crown Court it is available without a means test, whereas legal aid for magistrates' court proceedings is means-tested.[47] The means test was abolished in 2001, but re-introduced for magistrates' court cases in 2006[48] as part of a programme designed to reduce legal aid expenditure. Defendants with a gross annual income of less than 14,160[49] Euro automatically satisfy the means test, and those with an annual gross income of 25,340[50] Euro or more are ineligible. For those with gross incomes between these limits a calculation of net income is made in order to determine eligibility.[51] There is no contribution system so if the defendant is not eligible on financial grounds they have to pay privately if they want to be legally represented. Certain defendants, such as those under 18 years who are in full time education, and those in receipt of certain state benefits, automatically satisfy the means test.

The system is administered by the Legal Services Commission (LSC) which is established under statutory authority.[52] The LSC has a close relationship with its sponsoring department, the Ministry of Justice, and receives all of its monies from the state. In 2007/8 annual expenditure on all forms of criminal legal aid was about 1,390 million Euro,[53] which amounted to expenditure of 26.7[54] Euro per head of population. After a decade of rising expenditure on criminal legal aid up to 2006, expenditure now appears to be falling, probably as a result of a number of initiatives designed to contain or reduce cost.

---

[46]   Ministry of Justice 2008b.

[47]   The government is currently planning to re-introduce means-testing for Crown Court legal aid.

[48]   By the Criminal Defence Service Act 2006.

[49]   £ 12,007.

[50]   £ 21,487.

[51]   The government estimates that just over half of defendants appearing in magistrates' courts are eligible on financial grounds. See *Criminal Defence Service Act 2006 Final Regulatory Impact Assessment*, available at <http://www.dca.gov.uk/risk/crime-defence-act-ria.pdf>.
        However, a leading advice organisation, the Citizens Advice has recently estimated it to be under half. See <www.citizensadvice.org.uk/index/campaign/s/evidence-journal.htm>.

[52]   Access to Justice Act 1999.

[53]   £ 1,179 million. See generally Legal Services Commission 2008a, p. 10.

[54]   £ 22.67.

Traditionally, legally-aided criminal defence work has exclusively been provided by lawyers (i.e., solicitors or barristers)[55] in private practice. The government experimented with a Public Defender Service in the early years of the twenty-first century, but there are currently only four public defender offices and the service is unlikely to be expanded. Thus most legally-aided criminal defence services continue to be provided by private lawyers. There are about 2,510 solicitors' offices providing legally-aided criminal defence services, probably involving about 6,000 to 7,000 solicitors, which is about six per cent of all solicitors in practice.[56] A greater proportion of barristers, nearly 40 percent, do some criminal work,[57] but this includes both prosecution and private defence work. Nevertheless, the vast majority (about 93 per cent) of those barristers doing criminal work do some of it for legally aided clients.[58]

Since changes to the system of procuring criminal legal aid services were introduced in 2001, solicitors can only be paid under the criminal legal aid schemes if their office has a contract with the LSC. The contract is highly detailed and contains provisions regulating the work that can be done under the contract and, to an extent, how it can be done. It also regulates remuneration for solicitors, and most work is now covered by standard fees rather than on a 'time spent' basis. Barristers are not directly covered by this contracting system, but in order to do legal aid work they must be instructed by a solicitor whose office has a contract with the LSC. Much of their work is also covered by a standard fee system. There is a separate system, involving individual contracts with the LSC, for very high cost criminal cases (VHCCC).[59]

As in many jurisdictions, remuneration for legal aid work is highly controversial, with lawyers' complaining that they are not paid adequately, and whilst some leading criminal barristers are well remunerated, undoubtedly legal aid rates are significantly less than the fees charged for private work. The average value of lawyers' claims for advice and assistance at police stations in 2006/7 was 263 Euro[60] (including profit costs, travel, waiting and disbursements). In January 2008 a fixed fee scheme was introduced for police station advice and assistance. The fee covers profit costs, travel and waiting time (but not disbursements). The fee differs in different parts of the country: in central London it is currently 345[61] Euro, and in

---

[55] See section 3 for a brief description of the legal profession.

[56] Legal Services Commission 2007, p. 22. The LSC is currently consulting on a new system of contracting for criminal legal aid called Best Value Tendering. If introduced it is likely to significantly reduce the number of solicitors' firms able to conduct legally-aided criminal defence work.

[57] Legal Services Commission 2007.

[58] Tam 2008, p. 14 and 20. One leading academic expert suggests that all leading barristers who undertake criminal defence work spend most of their working lives working on legally-aided cases.

[59] Defined as cases where the trial is likely to last for more than 40 days, or in some circumstances, where the trial is likely to last for more than 25 days. See note 56 regarding the planned introduction of a tendering system for legal aid.

[60] £ 223.

[61] £ 293.

Bristol (a provincial city) 206 Euro.[62] The average claim for magistrates' court work in 2006/7 was 643 Euro,[63] and the average claim for Crown Court work was 5,307 Euro.[64] However, for a variety of reasons, these figures must be treated with some caution.[65]

2. Legal rights and their implementation

2.1. The right to information

In the English and Welsh context, it is important to distinguish between four stages: arrest, police interview, charge (or summons), and trial preparation (i.e., between charge (or summons) and trial).

2.1.1. Arrest

When a person is arrested they must be told that they are under arrest as soon as is practicable after the arrest (even if the fact of arrest is obvious), and the arrest is not lawful unless this is done.[66] In addition, they must be informed of the ground for the arrest at the time of, or as soon as is practicable after, the arrest and, again, the arrest is not lawful if this is not done.[67] PACE Code of Practice C states that the level of information that must be given is 'sufficient information to enable [the suspect] to understand that they have been deprived of their liberty and the reason they have been arrested, [for example] . . . the suspected offence's nature, when and where it was committed. The suspect must also be informed of the reason or reasons why the arrest is considered necessary. Vague or technical language should be avoided'.[68] However, there appears to be no obligation at this stage to provide the information in a language that the suspect understands. The requirement at this stage is to give the information orally, but it must also be recorded in the custody record which is opened if and when the person is detained at a police station.[69] The custody record is available for inspection by the suspect's lawyer whilst they are in police

---

[62]   £ 175. There is an escape clause, which enables a higher amount to be paid if the work necessarily done on a case is worth more than three times the fixed fee.

[63]   £ 545.

[64]   £ 4,500. Average figures were produced by dividing total expenditure by number of claims. See Legal Services Commission 2008a, p. 23. As an example of fee levels, for cases outside the standard fee scheme in magistrates' courts, preparation is paid at 58.61 Euro (£ 49.70) per hour (or 61.97 Euro (£ 52.55) in London), and advocacy is paid at 73.53 Euro (£ 62.35) per hour (national rate)).

[65]   In particular, the number of claims is not the same as the number of cases since, on the one hand, a claim may be only for part of a case and, on the other, one claim may cover a number of clients where they are jointly accused.

[66]   Police and Criminal Evidence Act 1984, s. 28(1) and (2).

[67]   Police and Criminal Evidence Act 1984 s. 28(3).

[68]   PACE Code C, Note for Guidance 10B. For police powers of arrest, see section 1.3 above.

[69]   PACE Code C, § 3.4 and 10.3, and PACE Code G, § 2.2 and 4.3.

detention, and the suspect is entitled to a copy of it (and to inspect the original) once they leave detention.[70]

There does not appear to be research evidence on these information requirements. The requirement to make a written record of the information given provides for some accountability, although the fact that a record is made does not guarantee that the information was given at the requisite time. However, since the requirements are mandatory, if the suspect can establish that they were not complied with, it may provide them with a defence if they are prosecuted for an offence such as assault on a police officer in the execution of their duty, and the person may sue the police for trespass to the person and/or false imprisonment (although the level of damages tends to be relatively low).[71] If the arrest is unlawful for this reason, a subsequent detention will be unlawful, although it may be made lawful if and when the information is given.[72]

In addition to information regarding the arrest, where a person is taken to a police station under arrest, or is arrested at a police station, they must be told clearly about the following rights, and that they may exercise them at any time whilst they are in police custody:

- the right to have someone informed of their arrest;[73]
- the right to consult privately with a solicitor, and that this is free of charge; and
- the right to consult the PACE Codes of Practice.

The suspect must also be given a written notice which sets out these rights, and which informs them of the arrangements for accessing legal advice, the right to a copy of the custody record, and the caution, and they must be asked to sign the custody record to acknowledge receipt.[74] There is no explicit enforcement mechanism in relation to this obligation although breach, especially in respect of the right to advice and the caution may, but would not necessarily, result in evidence obtained from a subsequent interview being excluded at trial.

2.1.2. Police interview

There is no further obligation on the police to provide information to the suspect about the allegation or evidence relating to it prior to any police interview.[75] This is in stark contrast to the position of the suspect, who may suffer adverse

---

[70]   PACE Code C § 2.4 and 2.4A.
[71]   See, for example, *Wood* v. *DPP* [2008] EWHC 1056 (Admin).
[72]   *Lewis* v. *Chief Constable of South Wales Constabulary* [1991] 1 All ER 206.
[73]   This right is governed by PACE 1984, s. 56. There are limited exceptions to this right but only on the authorisation of a police inspector who has reasonable grounds for believing that it would lead, for example, to interference with evidence or alerting a person not yet arrested.
[74]   PACE Code C § 3.1 and 3.2. The caution is prescribed by PACE Code C § 10.5 as follows: 'You do not have to say anything. But it may harm your defence if you do not mention when questioned something which you later rely on in Court. Anything you do say may be given in evidence'.
[75]   Confirmed in *R* v. *Imran and Hussain* [1997] Crim LR 754.

consequences if they do not disclose to the police in interview the facts upon which they subsequently rely at their trial (see section 2.3.4). However, the general rule is subject to two specific exceptions. First, as noted above, a suspect and their lawyer are entitled to inspect the custody record, although this rarely reveals anything concerning the evidence. Second, prior to an identification procedure, the suspect must be shown a copy of the description given by an identifying witness, provided this is practicable.[76] There is no specific enforcement mechanism in respect of either of these exceptions, although failure by the police to permit inspection or to provide the witness description may, but will not necessarily, lead to exclusion of evidence subsequently obtained.[77]

In practice, the police often do provide some information to the suspect about the evidence prior to a police interview. Police interview training encourages officers to consider what information to divulge, having regard to the fact that this may lead to admissions being made and, if not, may make adverse inferences from 'silence' more likely.[78] However, from the defence perspective, the problem is that it cannot be known whether disclosure given by the police is accurate or complete since there is no right to inspect the investigator's file or to read witness statements.

2.1.3. Charge

Where a person is charged with a criminal offence (which is a procedure conducted by a police custody officer, although the decision whether to charge is normally made by a Crown Prosecutor) they must be told that they are being charged, and told the offence with which they are being charged. In addition, they must be given a written notice setting out the precise offence with which they are being charged together with brief details of the offence.[79] They must also be cautioned.[80] Where the summons (or written charge) procedure is used to commence criminal proceedings, similar information must be given which, given the nature of the process, will be given in writing.[81] If the charge or summons does not contain the requisite information it may be treated as a nullity although, depending on the nature of the missing information, this could be 'cured' if the information is supplied in sufficient time.

2.1.4. Pre-trial

Material collected in a criminal investigation can be broadly divided into two categories – 'used' and 'unused' material. 'Used' material is that which the

---

[76]   PACE Code D § 3.1.

[77]   Exclusion of evidence is unlikely in respect of the right to inspect the custody record, and will normally not result from failure to show a suspect an identifying witness's description. See, for example, *Marsh* v. *DPP* [2006] EWHC 1525.

[78]   See further section 2.3.4.

[79]   PACE Code C § 16.2 and 16.3.

[80]   For the wording of the caution see note 74.

[81]   For the form and content of a written charge see Criminal Justice Act 2003 ss. 29 and 30. See also Criminal Procedure Rules 2005 rule 7.2(1)(a).

prosecution intends to use as evidence at a trial, for example, statements taken by the police from witnesses who the prosecution would call to give evidence if there is a trial. 'Unused' material is that which 'may be relevant to the investigation [and] has been retained but does not form part of the case for the prosecution against the accused'.[82] Unused material would include statements taken from people who the prosecution would not call as a witness because, for example, they do not contain relevant information or they do not support the prosecution case.

The obligation to disclose used material depends upon the category of offence with which the defendant is charged. If they are accused of a summary-only offence,[83] guidance from the Attorney-General provides that the prosecution must supply to the defence all evidence on which they intend to rely at trial, in sufficient time for the defence to give it proper consideration.[84] In principle, this only applies where an accused has already pleaded not guilty, although in practice prosecutors are often willing to allow a defence lawyer to look at their file. In the case of an either-way offence,[85] the accused is entitled to a copy of the statements of witnesses that the prosecution intends to call, or a summary of such evidence, prior to the mode of trial decision.[86] In the case of an indictable-only offence, or in the case of an either-way case which is to be committed or transferred to the Crown Court, the prosecution must disclose sufficient evidence to establish a *prima facie* case in order for the case to be committed or transferred, and are under a continuing duty to disclose used material as it becomes available.

Disclosure of unused material is governed by the Criminal Procedure and Investigations Act (CPIA) 1996, section one of which provides that the primary prosecution disclosure obligation arises where a defendant pleads not guilty to an offence which is to be tried in a magistrates' court, or is committed or transferred for trial to the Crown Court. As a result, other than in the case of an indictable-only offence, a defendant is asked to plead, or at least to indicate a plea, before they have a right to look at unused material. There is no time limit for prosecution disclosure. The law merely provides that it must be disclosed as soon as is reasonably practicable.[87] Where, under these provisions, the prosecution are obliged to provide disclosure of unused material to the accused they 'must disclose to the accused any prosecution material which has not previously been disclosed to the accused and which might reasonably be considered capable of undermining the case for the prosecution against the accused or of assisting the case for the accused . . .'.[88] This is a continuing obligation[89] and applies until the case is concluded. If a defendant

---

[82] The Crown Prosecution Service *Disclosure Manual*, § 5, available via <http://cps.gov.uk>.

[83] I.e., an offence that can only be tried in a magistrates' court. See section 1.3.

[84] See Attorney General's *Guidelines on Disclosure*, § 58, available via <http://www.cps.gov.uk/legal/d_to_g/>.

[85] I.e. an offence that may be tried either in a magistrates' court or the Crown Court. See section 1.3.

[86] Criminal Procedure Rules 2005, rule 21(3). The mode of trial hearing determines whether the case is to be tried in a magistrates' court or in the Crown Court. See section 1.3.

[87] Criminal Procedure and Investigations Act 1996 s. 13(1). This is contrast to the obligation on the accused to disclose their defence, in respect of which there is an explicit time limit.

[88] Criminal Procedure and Investigations Act 1996 s. 3(1)(a).

[89] Under Criminal Procedure and Investigations Act 1996 s. 7A.

serves a defence statement,[90] the CPIA 1996 Code of Practice requires the police officer in charge of the investigation to review the material and inform the prosecutor if there is any further material that satisfies the test for disclosure. If there is any such material, the prosecutor is then obliged to disclose it to the defence.

In order to achieve a degree of transparency, when the prosecutor serves primary prosecution disclosure on the accused, they must also serve a schedule (a 'non-sensitive schedule') which lists all material collected by the police during the investigation. However, 'sensitive' material, that is, material in respect of which the police believe there is a real risk of serious prejudice to an important public interest if disclosed, is listed in a separate 'sensitive schedule' that is not disclosed to the accused. This might include material relating to national security, but also material given in confidence, or which relates to informants, undercover police officers, premises used for police surveillance or techniques used in the detection of crime.[91] The prosecutor must then determine whether such material satisfies the test for disclosure (see above). If not, it is not disclosed. If the prosecutor believes that it does satisfy the test, but should not be disclosed, he or she must make an application to the court for a decision on whether it is covered by public interest immunity.[92] The court will make its decision by reference to whether there is a real risk of serious prejudice to an important, and identified, public interest.[93]

There are no explicit sanctions if the prosecution fails to comply with the disclosure obligations. The court does have power to order disclosure on an application by the accused,[94] although there are practical difficulties if, as a result of lack of disclosure, the accused is unable to specifically identify the material which they believe may exist and which ought to be disclosed. A court may also adjourn a trial in order to give time for disclosure to be made and for this to be considered by the defence. The court also has power to stay a prosecution on the grounds of abuse of process, for example, where relevant evidence has not been disclosed, and this would also provide good grounds for appeal.[95]

Research conducted in the late 1990s showed that the police and prosecution were poor at identifying unused material that should be disclosed and that there was little faith in the system, even amongst prosecutors.[96] The law was subsequently amended by the Criminal Justice Act 2003 to widen the prosecution disclosure obligation (and also the disclosure obligation on the defence). However, the latest review by the CPS Inspectorate has found little improvement, finding

---

[90]   Which is compulsory where a person is being tried in the Crown Court, but voluntary in magistrates' court trials (Criminal Procedure and Investigations Act 1996 ss. 5 and 6).

[91]   Criminal Procedure and Investigations Act Code of Practice § 6.12.

[92]   Criminal Procedure and Investigations Act 1996 s. 8.

[93]   *R* v. *H and C* [2004] AC 134.

[94]   Criminal Procedure and Investigations Act 1996 s. 8.

[95]   See, for example, *R* v. *Hadley* [2006] EWCA Crime 2544 in which the court held that it would be difficult to accept that a conviction was safe where the prosecution had failed to disclose a significant volume of material that should have been disclosed.

[96]   Crown Prosecution Service Inspectorate 2000, and Plotnikoff & Woolfson 2001. The research also found significant non-compliance or poor compliance by the defence in fulfilling defence disclosure obligations under the legislation.

significant non-compliance with the disclosure regime by both the police and the CPS.[97] It has been persuasively argued that the prosecution disclosure obligation cannot work effectively because responsibility is placed on the police and prosecution to disclose material that may benefit their adversarial opponent.[98]

There is no specific evidence that any of the information or disclosure requirements operate unfairly in respect of poor suspects or defendants. There is evidence from the 1990s that a significant minority of suspects did not understand the police caution,[99] and this is likely also to be the case in respect of the other disclosure requirements described. However, as noted elsewhere, defendants facing more serious offences, in the Crown Court, are normally entitled to legal aid so that most such defendants will have the assistance of a lawyer in understanding and enforcing prosecution disclosure obligations. Similarly, there is no specific evidence that the provisions operate unfairly in respect of ethnic minorities although since, as noted earlier, ethnic minorities are over-represented at all stages of the criminal process, they disproportionately face the issues identified as a matter for concern.

2.2. The right to defend oneself

2.2.1. The right of a person to defend him/herself

It is a long established common law rule that a person accused of a crime has a right to defend him/herself, and this is given statutory force by the fact that the Human Rights Act 1998 'incorporates' the ECHR in domestic law.[100] However, the right has traditionally been conceived of as a trial right, or probably more accurately, a right that exists once court proceedings have commenced. Thus, whilst during the investigative stage there are certain specific provisions that entitle a suspect to make representations to the police,[101] generally there is no such right.[102]

2.2.2. The right to legal advice at the investigative stage

The right of a defendant to legal advice and representation has long been regarded as a fundamental right, but again this was traditionally conceived of as a right that applied where a person was taken before a court. In theory there was no need for the right to apply at an earlier stage because historically the police were permitted to arrest and detain a person only for the purpose of producing them before a court (and not for the purpose of investigation). Whilst the role of the police in crime investigation developed during the twentieth century it was not until the 1980s that it was given statutory recognition. Since legislation was introduced in 1984, a

---

[97]   HM Crown Prosecution Service Inspectorate 2008.

[98]   Quirke 2006. See also Taylor 2006.

[99]   See Gudjonsson 2003, p. 73.

[100]   See further § 1.2 above.

[101]   For example, the right to make representations on review of pre-charge detention, under PACE 1984 s. 40(12).

[102]   Thus there is no explicit right for a suspect to make representations regarding a charge decision, nor in respect of decisions regarding police bail.

person who has been arrested and who is detained at a police station (or other premises) is entitled, at their request, 'to consult a solicitor privately at any time'.[103] Similarly, although not provided for by statute, a person who is interviewed by the police without being arrested (a 'volunteer') is also entitled to legal advice.[104] The major difference between them is that in the case of a detained person, they must be informed of their right to legal advice when their detention at a police station is authorised,[105] whereas a volunteer does not have to be told of the right unless they ask or are cautioned (which the police are not required to do unless they want to question them about an offence in circumstances where they have grounds to suspect that they committed it).[106] There are no special provisions regarding legal advice for vulnerable suspects except that in the case of juveniles and suspects who are mentally vulnerable the police must ask an 'appropriate adult' to attend, and they have a separate right to request legal advice.[107]

Where a suspect has asked to consult a solicitor the police are required to allow a consultation as soon as practicable unless delay in access to a lawyer is permitted.[108] Delay, up to a maximum of 36 hours, is only permitted if authorised by a senior police officer who has grounds for believing that access will lead to one of a number of specified consequences, such as interference with or harm to evidence or the alerting of persons wanted by the police but not yet arrested.[109] Following a request for legal advice, the suspect normally cannot be interviewed, or continue to be interviewed, until they have received advice although there are exceptions where: (i) delay in access to legal advice has been authorised in accordance with the above provisions; (ii) it is authorised by a senior officer on the grounds that delay might lead to one or more of the consequences that would permit access to a lawyer to be delayed or that waiting for the lawyer to arrive would cause unreasonable delay to the investigation; (iii) where the nominated solicitor cannot be contacted or will not attend and the suspect refuses advice from a duty solicitor; or (iv) where the suspect changes their mind and confirms this to a senior officer and in writing.[110] These exceptions have been interpreted strictly by the courts,[111] and evidence suggests that formally delaying access to legal advice is

---

103   Police and Criminal Evidence Act 1984 s. 58(1).
104   PACE Code C Note for Guidance 1A.
105   PACE Code C § 3.1. As noted at section 2.1.1, notice of the right must also be given in writing. They must also be reminded of their right to legal advice at the beginning of a police interview, when detention is reviewed, and when certain police investigative powers are exercised, for example, before a person is asked to provide an intimate sample. For a summary of the circumstances where a suspect must be told of their right to legal advice see Cape 2006a p. 82. The suspect must be asked to sign the custody record showing whether they have requested legal advice (Code C § 6.17).
106   PACE Code C § 3.21 and 3.22.
107   For an explanation, see Cape 2006a, ch. 11.
108   Police and Criminal Evidence Act 1984 s. 58(4).
109   See Police and Criminal Evidence Act 1984 s. 58(8)-(11). There are similar provisions applying to persons arrested on suspicion of terrorism under the Terrorism Act 2000.
110   PACE Code C § 6.6.
111   See, for example, R v. Samuel [1988] QB 615.

rare.[112] However, although inferences from 'silence'[113] are not permitted where a suspect is interviewed under (i) and (ii) above, the product of any such interview may be used as evidence at trial.[114]

Failure by the police to inform a suspect of their right to consult a solicitor, or failure to facilitate or permit access to a solicitor who has been requested by a suspect may, but will not necessarily, lead to the exclusion of evidence obtained following the breach. Breach of PACE or the Codes of Practice does not automatically lead to exclusion of evidence, nor does it necessarily give rise to civil liability. Exclusion of evidence is principally governed by the two statutory provisions explained in section 1.3. Breach of the right to legal advice has led to the exclusion of evidence,[115] but not always.[116]

A person who has been arrested and detained by the police, or a volunteer, is entitled to legal aid without reference to their financial means and without a financial contribution.[117] Although statistics are not routinely kept, it would seem that about 50 per cent of persons arrested and detained by the police ask for legal advice, and that the majority (although not all) of them actually receive it.[118] Again, although statistics are not kept, it is likely that in the vast majority of cases the lawyer acts under legal aid rather than privately. Whilst in the past lawyers acting under legal aid were paid on the basis of time spent, they are now normally paid a fixed fee,[119] and there are concerns that this will lead to a decline in quality.

Until the beginning of 2008, when a suspect requested legal advice the custody officer was required to contact the solicitor nominated by the suspect, or contact the duty solicitor scheme if the suspect did not know of, or did not wish to instruct, a particular solicitor. The duty solicitor scheme was, and continues to be, operated by solicitors in private practice who have been accredited following examination under a scheme run jointly by the Law Society and the Legal Services Commission.[120] However, as a result of the introduction of two schemes by the Legal Services Commission, the Defence Solicitor Call Centre (DSCC) and CDS Direct, the police now contact the DSCC which either directs the request to the nominated or duty solicitor, or if the case is covered by the CDS Direct scheme, refers it to the CDS

---

[112] Although there is evidence, from the 1990s, that the police use informal 'ploys' to deter some suspects from seeking legal advice. For a critical account see Sanders & Young 2007 ch. 4.

[113] See § 2.3.4.

[114] *R v. Ibrahim, Omar, Osman and Mohamed* [2008] EWCA Crim 880.

[115] For example, *R v. Samuel* [1988] QB 615; *R v. Williams* [1989] Crim LR 66.

[116] For example, *R v. Alladice* (1988) 87 Cr App R 380; *R v. Walsh* [1989] Crim LR 822.

[117] See generally the Access to Justice Act 1999 and the regulations made there under. As noted in § 1.5, legal aid services can only be provided either by a lawyer from a firm that has a contract with the Legal Services Commission or who works for the Public Defender Service.

[118] In 2006/7 there were 788,430 claims by solicitors' firms for police station legal aid compared to 1,43 million arrests for notifiable offences. The total cost of police station legal aid in 2007/8 was just over £ 170 million (Legal Services Commission 2008b).

[119] See § 1.5. They may also claim for disbursements, for example, in respect of medical examination or an interpreter, although in practice such claims are minimal. As indicated in note 56, the government is planning to replace this system of payment with a system of best value tendering

[120] Rota or panel arrangements ensure that a duty solicitor is always available to provide advice at all police stations.

Direct telephone advice service.[121] It is too early for evidence to be available as to the impact of these schemes, but they restrict choice for those suspects covered by the CDS Direct scheme and there is concern that they will lead to delay and to a decline in quality. There is also suspicion that the government intends to use them to reduce demand for police station legal advice.

The CDS Direct scheme also raises concerns about confidentiality. As noted above, the suspect has a statutory right to advice in private. This is reinforced by PACE Code C which describes it as a fundamental right, although it appears to permit a consultation to be observed provided that it cannot be overheard.[122] The Code also provides that where the consultation is conducted by telephone, which is the case where advice is given under the CDS Direct scheme, this should be in private unless impracticable (although this qualification of the right is arguably unlawful). In practice, private telephone facilities are often not available in police stations,[123] and it has been held that the absence of private facilities does not contravene ECHR article 6.[124] Although concern periodically surfaces, it is impossible to know the extent of any interference with the right to a private consultation. Covert surveillance of solicitor/client consultations was condemned by the Court of Appeal in a 2005 judgement as 'categorically unlawful'.[125] However, the House of Lords has more recently held that covert surveillance is permissible provided that it is properly authorised under the relevant legislation.[126]

2.2.3. The right to legal representation at the trial stage

The right to legal representation at the trial stage, and on appeal, is still largely governed by the common law, and there is no explicit statutory right to legal advice and representation. There is no formal obligation requiring defendants to be informed of their right, but in practice a court is likely to inform an unrepresented defendant of their right to consult a lawyer, especially where they are at risk of losing their liberty by a remand in custody during an adjournment, or by being given a custodial sentence. In magistrates' courts this is facilitated by the fact that duty solicitor schemes ensure that a defence solicitor is normally available. In practice a court is likely to adjourn a case to give an unrepresented defendant the

---

[121] The CDS Direct scheme applies where a person is arrested for a non-imprisonable offence where the police do not intend to interview them, and to drink-driving cases. In such cases publicly funded advice is restricted to advice by telephone from a CDS Direct adviser. For an explanation and critique of the new schemes see Bridges & Cape 2008.

[122] PACE Code C Note for Guidance 6J. Note that there is an exception to the right to a private consultation in the case of people detained on suspicion of terrorism, where it is possible for authorisation to be given for a consultation to be held within the sight and hearing of a police officer (Terrorism Act 2000 Sch. 8 § 9(1) and (2), and PACE Code H § 6.5).

[123] See Bridges & Cape 2008, p. 29.

[124] *R (on the application of M)* v. *Commissioner of Police for the Metropolis* [2002] Crim LR 215.

[125] See *R* v. *Grant* [2005] EWCA Crim 1089. As a result, the prosecution was stayed on the basis that it amounted to an abuse of process even though the prosecution did not seek to use any evidence obtained from the surveillance.

[126] *In re McE; In re M; In re C (AP) and another (AP)* [2009] UKHL 15. Covert surveillance is governed by the Regulation of Investigatory Powers Act 2000.

opportunity to obtain legal advice unless, perhaps, they are using the lack of legal advice or representation to abuse the legal process, for example, by deliberate delay. Although there is no explicit statutory basis for the right to legal representation, nor any specific limitation on the powers of the court if a defendant is not represented,[127] the right appears to be so firmly entrenched that there is little, if any, evidence of breach of the right. Of more practical significance is the issue of whether legal aid is available and, if not, whether a defendant could afford to instruct a lawyer.

In accordance with the principle that a person should be free to choose whether they wish to be legally represented, and free to instruct a lawyer of their choice, there is generally no system of mandatory legal representation and the courts do not have powers to appoint lawyers to act for defendants. Vulnerable defendants are in no different a position in this respect, although they may be informally assisted by the court. There are certain statutory exceptions to the right of a defendant to cross-examine a witness in person (mostly sexual offences and offences against children).[128] As a result, if the defendant is unwilling to instruct a lawyer, the court may appoint a lawyer to cross-examine on their behalf, although strictly the appointed lawyer does not act for the defendant. It is also possible, but rare, for a court to appoint a lawyer as 'special advocate' in cases involving national security, and such advocates are subject to restrictions in speaking to and obtaining instructions from the defendant.[129] In principle, defendants have complete freedom of choice in instructing a lawyer to act for them,[130] and even if they are legally-aided, the appointment of the lawyer is made by them rather than the court or legal aid authorities.[131] However, this is subject to a number of restrictions where the defendant is legally-aided. First, as a result of the system of legal aid contracting described in section 1.5, a legally-aided defendant can only instruct a solicitor from a firm that has a legal aid contract. Second, legal aid regulations provide that co-accused should have the same lawyer unless there is a conflict of interest.[132] Therefore, a defendant who applies for legal aid after another co-accused has already been granted it may be directed to be represented by the lawyer already assigned.

---

[127] Other than some relatively minor procedural consequences. For example, if a defendant is not legally represented they cannot be committed for trial to the Crown Court without the magistrates hearing sufficient evidence to satisfy them that there is a prima facie case. See Magistrates' Courts Act 1980 s. 6(2).

[128] Youth Justice and Criminal Evidence Act 1999 ss. 34-39.

[129] This is not governed by statute, nor is it subject to formal rules of procedure. See further Boon & Nash 2006. The legality of this system has recently been questioned by the House of Lords in *Secretary of State for the Home Department* v. *(1) AF (2) AM (3) AN; AE* v. *Secretary of State for the Home Department and Justice* [2009] UKHL 28.

[130] Other than in respect of special advocates.

[131] Although a solicitor can refuse to act for a particular person. Barristers are, in theory, governed by a professional conduct rule known as the 'cab rank' rule which requires them to act, within their specialism, for any client. However, in practice there are informal mechanisms that undermine this rule including the fact that appointment of a barrister is mediated by solicitor since in criminal cases defendants cannot instruct a barrister directly.

[132] Criminal Defence Service (General) (No. 2) Regulations 2001, reg. 16A.

In principle there is no restriction on the right of a defendant to communicate with their lawyer and to do so privately. Legal professional privilege, which covers communications between a defendant and their lawyer made for the purpose of obtaining or giving legal advice, and communications between a defendant or their lawyer and third parties for the sole or dominant purpose of advising or acting in an actual or pending case, is well-established and jealously guarded.[133] As a result, neither a defendant nor their lawyer can be required to divulge the content of a privileged communication. Until recently it was thought that lawyer/client communications could not be subjected to covert surveillance by the police, but as noted earlier, it has recently been held that this can be lawfully carried out.[134] There are practical and procedural limitations on lawyer/client privilege. Courts often have inadequate facilities for consultation, and where a defendant is remanded in custody, defence lawyers complain that it is often difficult to hold a timely and adequate consultation with their clients in prison. Although privilege may only be waived by a defendant, or by their lawyer on their behalf, they may do so inadvertently or, in particular, in an attempt to avoid adverse inferences being drawn from 'silence' in a police interview.[135]

Statistics are not routinely kept on the number or proportion of defendants who are legally represented. In 2006 1,78 million people were proceeded against in magistrates' courts, and in 2006/7 there were 503,578 legal aid claims by solicitors' firms for representation in magistrates' courts. Whilst this indicates that approximately one third of defendants in magistrates' courts were represented under legal aid, in addition 79,536 duty solicitor sessions were paid for by legal aid in that year,[136] and it is not known how many more defendants are privately represented (although this is likely to be relatively few).[137] A means test for legal aid in magistrates' courts was re-introduced in 2006 with the explicit aim of reducing the number of legal aid orders granted, so it is likely that the proportion of

[133] See R v. *Derby Magistrates' Court, ex parte B* [1996] AC 487, in which the House of Lords held that there should be no exception to the absolute and permanent nature of legal professional privilege. There is an important exception where the communication is made to further a criminal purpose, as where a lawyer is suspected of committing a criminal offence. The law in this area is complex. See further Hooper & Ormerod 2008, p. 2495.

[134] See the text to note 126.

[135] A defendant may wish to give evidence of the reasons given for advice to remain 'silent' in a police interview in an attempt to avoid adverse inferences being drawn, but this has the effect of waiving privilege. See, for example, R v. *Condron* [1997] 1 WLR 827; R v. *Bowden* [1999] 1 WLR 823; and R v. *Louizou* [2006] EWCA Crim 1719.

[136] Legal Services Commission 2007, p. 23. The court duty solicitor scheme provides legal representation for defendants appearing in a magistrates' court who have not arranged for a lawyer to represent them, normally where they are appearing for the first time in relation to a case, and either they have been produced in court from police custody and did not have a lawyer advising them at the police station, or because they are accused of a relatively minor offence. Statistics are not routinely collected on the average number of clients advised and/or represented in each court duty solicitor session.

[137] A survey conducted in 2008 found that 85% of defendants in a magistrates' court were legally represented, but this was based on only one London court. See Fewkes, Lomri & White 2008.

defendants who are legally represented has declined.[138] The number of defendants proceeded against in the Crown Court in 2006 was 75,700.[139] No statistics are available on the proportion of those who were legally represented, but it is likely that, since there is currently no means test for legal aid for Crown Court proceedings,[140] the vast majority are legally represented. In the same year, 95 per cent of defendants facing trial in the Crown Court were represented under legal aid, as were 77 per cent of those committed to the Crown Court (from a magistrates' court) for sentencing, and 57 per cent of those appealing to the Crown Court from a decision of a magistrates' court.[141]

As noted earlier, legal aid is available in respect of proceedings in all criminal courts, including appeal courts. There is no formal mechanism for a defendant to be informed of the availability of legal aid but in practice, other than in minor cases, the court will normally advise an unrepresented defendant of the availability of the duty solicitor and/or the legal aid scheme, and will normally adjourn a case to enable the defendant to consult with a solicitor and make an application for legal aid. Although formally the application is made by the defendant, the application forms are normally completed by the lawyer who will act in the case, and the application is determined by the court on behalf of the LSC.[142]

It was explained in section 1.5 that legal aid for proceedings in magistrates' courts, is means-tested, but not in respect of other forms of criminal legal aid. There is also a merits test. This has the effect of preventing many defendants from receiving legal aid for magistrates' court proceedings, but most applicants for legal aid in the Crown Court will satisfy the merits test on the grounds of the risk of loss of liberty. The merits test does not necessarily depend upon whether the defendant intends to plead not guilty, but is based upon the interests of justice. The relevant criteria are set out in statute, and are as follows:

- whether the person would, if the case were to be decided against them, be likely to lose their liberty or livelihood of suffer serious damage to their reputation.
- whether the determination of any matter arising in the proceedings may involve consideration of a substantial question of law;
- whether the person may be unable to understand the proceedings or to state their own case (for example, because of mental vulnerability or language difficulties);
- whether the proceedings may involve the tracing, interviewing or expert cross-examination of witnesses on behalf of the person;

---

[138]   In September 2008 the Legal Services Commission, which has responsibility for magistrates' court legal aid, proclaimed 'The new scheme has been a success in operational and financial terms. It has led to a 15 per cent reduction in the number of grants.' See <www.legalservices.gov.uk/criminal/cds_news_8750.asp?page=1>.

[139]   Ministry of Justice 2007a.

[140]   But see note 47 regarding plans to introduce a means test for Crown Court proceedings.

[141]   Ministry of Justice 2007b, p. 172.

[142]   A court, other than a magistrates' court, also has power to grant legal aid even though no application has been made: Criminal Defence Services (General)(No. 2) Regulations 2001, reg. 7.

- whether it is in the interests of another person (for example, a complainant in a sexual assault case) that the person be represented (Access to Justice Act 1999 Sch 3).

Research has shown that the first criterion is regarded by decision-makers as the most important.[143] Whilst Labour government rhetoric has tended to describe magistrates' courts as being too generous in granting legal aid on the basis of the merits test, research conducted for the Legal Services Commission in 2005 concluded the opposite, although it found wide variation in the application of the criteria.[144]

2.2.4. Independence and competence of defence lawyers

Since most criminal defence work is funded by legal aid, the independence and competence of criminal defence lawyers needs to be analysed and understood by reference to the structure of the legal aid schemes and legal aid remuneration. As noted in section 1.5, solicitors' firms that undertake legally aided criminal defence work must have a contract with the Legal Services Commission (LSC). Many such firms are specialist criminal defence firms (or specialist legal aid firms) and are therefore dependant on the LSC for most if not all of their income. Barristers often carry out work both for the defence and the prosecution, and are therefore arguably less dependant on the LSC. On the other hand about 93 per cent of barristers that do criminal work earn at least some of their fees from legal aid, and the profession as a whole is probably more dependant on legal aid than the solicitors' profession.[145]

Thus the LSC has the capacity to influence the work of criminal defence lawyers through contract mechanisms and price mechanisms. During the 1990s[146] the LSC and its predecessor, the Legal Aid Board, sought to influence the legal professions in order to improve the quality of their work. A police station accreditation scheme was introduced which initially applied to non-qualified advisers who gave advice at police stations employed by solicitors' firms, but was subsequently extended to all criminal defence lawyers providing police station advice under legal aid. The accreditation scheme requires candidates to submit a reflective portfolio of cases they have worked on, pass a legal knowledge test,[147] and also pass a 'critical incidents test' which uses role play to test representation skills. A similar accreditation scheme also applies to magistrates' court duty solicitors. The LSC is currently piloting a quality assurance scheme for court advocacy which, if adopted, will apply to criminal defence advocates (solicitors and barristers) at all levels of experience.[148] In addition the LSC uses a system of peer review, based on

---

[143]   Wilcox & Young 2006.
[144]   Young & Wilcox 2007.
[145]   Tam 2008.
[146]   For an explanation of the system of contracting legal aid services see § 1.5. Prior to 2001, legally- aided criminal defence work could be conducted by any solicitor or barrister.
[147]   Solicitors and trainee solicitors are exempted from this test.
[148]   For further information see
       <https://consult.legalservices.gov.uk/inovem/consult.ti/quality.assurance/listdocuments>.

solicitors' case files, as a quality assurance mechanism.[149] The only scheme to have been evaluated in terms of its impact on quality is the police station accreditation scheme[150] and, in particular, important questions about the efficacy of peer review remain largely unexplored.[151]

Since the turn of the century, the LSC has sought to contain the growth of legal aid expenditure, and has used both contractual (for example, the DSCC and CDS Direct schemes) and price mechanisms (for example, the introduction of fixed fees) to control the amount of work that defence lawyers carry out.[152] No research has been conducted to assess what impact these have had on the quality and independence of defence lawyers' work but there is clearly a tension between these policies and the quality assurance mechanisms described. What they both demonstrate is the potential for the LSC, and the government, to have a significant impact on the work of criminal defence lawyers via legal aid.

In recent years the government, together with elements of the judiciary, has also sought to limit, or redefine, the role of criminal defence lawyers in ways which arguably compromises their independence. In particular, the government has sought to co-opt lawyers into its policy of changing the criminal justice system traditionally based upon adversarial principles into one that is informed principally by managerialist imperatives. There are a number of dimensions to this.[153] For example, the Criminal Defence Service (the division of the LSC that is responsible for criminal legal aid) regards itself as bound by the government's targets of, *inter alia*, increasing the number of crimes for which an offender is brought to justice.[154] In 2005 Criminal Procedural Rules were introduced, requiring all parties to the proceedings, including criminal defence lawyers, to assist the criminal courts in achieving the overall objectives, defined as acquitting the innocent and convicting the guilty, dealing with the prosecution and defence fairly, and dealing with the case efficiently and expeditiously.[155] Whilst the rules cannot require defence lawyers to breach professional privilege, they do appear to require them to breach the professional duty of confidentiality by, for example, disclosing information about the defence in advance of trial. This has been enthusiastically taken up by some members of the judiciary. For example, in a case presided over by a senior judge, the lawyer was criticised for not informing the prosecution that they had indicted the defendant for the 'wrong' offence in the following terms: 'for defence advocates

[149] Further information about the LSC's approach to quality assurance is available at <http://www.legalservices.gov.uk/criminal/quality_performance.asp>.
[150] See Bridges & Choongh 1998.
[151] For example, the criteria adopted by peer reviewers, how the standards applied by peers relate to other standards, and the impact on peer review of a declining resource base.
[152] In principle, the LSC cannot control the amount of work that a lawyer does on a particular case, but in practice it can do so by restricting the work for which the lawyer will be paid. For more detailed analyses see Cape 2004, and Bridges & Cape 2008.
[153] Examined in more detail in Cape 2006b.
[154] The then head of the Public Defender Service was so concerned by the implications of this that he issued guidance to PDS lawyers that this objective was to be regarded as subordinate to the objective of providing advice and assistance to clients. See Public Defender Service Guidance 1/2005, § 14.
[155] Criminal Procedure Rules 2005, rule 1.1(1) and (2).

to seek to take advantage of such errors by deliberately delaying identification of an issue of fact or law in the case until the last possible moment is… not longer acceptable, given the legislative and procedural changes to out criminal justice process in recent years'.[156] So far, the response of the legal professions has been muted, vulnerable to the charge that that they do not have democratic legitimacy and are motivated by the desire to protect vested interests.

2.3. Procedural Rights

2.3.1. The right to release from custody pending trial

Where a person has been charged with a criminal offence the police must decide whether to detain them in custody or release them on bail pending their first court appearance. Where a defendant appears in court, either having been kept in custody or released on police bail, if the case is adjourned the court must make a similar decision for the period of the adjournment. It should be noted that in the English and Welsh context the term 'bail' refers to a release from custody subject to a legal obligation to surrender either to a police station or to a court on a future date. Although bail may be granted on condition that the defendant pays a financial security, or that a third party offers a financial surety, bail is normally granted without such conditions. As a result, there is no equivalent of the American 'bondsman'.[157]

The police have extensive powers to impose[158] bail on a suspect, with conditions, during the investigative stage. Where a person has been arrested at a place other than a police station they must normally be taken to a police station as soon as practicable after the arrest.[159] However, the police officer who carries out the arrest can, alternatively, bail the arrested person to appear at a police station on a future occasion (known as 'street bail'),[160] and can impose conditions for the purposes of securing surrender, preventing further offences, preventing interference with witnesses or obstruction of the administration of justice, or for the person's own protection.[161] Almost any condition can be imposed provided that it is for one of these purposes, but the officer cannot require the payment of money in the form of a security or surety. The arrested person can make an application to a police custody officer or a court to vary or remove the conditions, but generally a

---

[156]   R v. Gleeson [2004] 1 Cr App R 29, § 34, per LJ Auld.

[157]   A security is a sum of money, or other valuable thing, which the defendant must deposit prior to their release. A surety is the promise by a third party to forfeit a specified sum of money if the defendant absconds.

[158]   The term 'impose' is used rather than 'grant' because bail prior to charge is normally used as an alternative to unconditional release rather than to custody. Therefore, it is a mechanism for imposing restrictions on a person who has not been convicted of an offence, rather than as an alternative to keeping the person in pre-trial detention. The power to impose conditional 'street bail' has been brought to the public attention as a result of the police using it to prevent climate change protesters from going within the vicinity of power stations.

[159]   PACE 1984 s. 30(1).

[160]   PACE 1984 s. 30A(1)-(3).

[161]   PACE 1984 s. 30A(3B).

court has no power to order unconditional release. There is no time limit on the period for which bail can be imposed. The person can be arrested for failure to comply with the conditions or failure to attend the police station on the due date, but neither amounts to an offence in its own right.[162] There is no statistical evidence of the use of 'street bail' but it appears that it has not frequently been used, and the government has sought ways of increasing its use since they believe that it would lead to the more efficient use of resources.[163]

Where an arrested person is in police detention (i.e., detained at a police station for the purposes of an investigation), the police have a variety of powers to grant them bail, with an obligation to return to the police station on a future occasion.[164] This form of bail is normally imposed to enable the police to continue with their investigations without detaining the suspect at a police station whilst the investigations are being carried out. There is no limit on the period for which bail can be imposed. The decision is made by a police custody officer. In most (but not all) circumstances where bail can be imposed prior to charge, conditions can also be imposed for similar purposes as for street bail.[165] Any condition can be imposed for these purposes other than a condition that the person reside at a bail hostel, make him/herself available for the purposes of a court report, or attend an interview with a lawyer.[166] Although a financial surety or security can be required, this is relatively unusual. The person can make an application to a police custody officer or a court to vary or remove the conditions, but cannot apply for bail to be removed altogether. A person released on bail in these circumstances may be rearrested if new evidence justifying a further arrest comes to light after their release.[167] Further, they may be arrested if a police officer has reasonable grounds for suspecting that they have broken any of the conditions,[168] or if they fail to attend the police station at the appointed time.[169] Whilst breach of conditions is not an offence, failure to surrender to bail is. There is no statistical evidence available as to the use of these powers, although they are used quite frequently. A major concern of defence lawyers is that suspects can be, and are, repeatedly bailed for lengthy periods of time, running into months and, in a few cases, years. The courts have made it clear that they will not interfere with decisions to grant bail under these powers other than in exceptional circumstances, and it appears that a court has never determined that the circumstances are so exceptional that they should interfere.[170]

Where a person has been charged with a criminal offence they must be released pending their first appearance in court unless the custody officer

---

162 Although the government is proposing to give the police power to arrest for anticipated breach of conditions or failure to surrender, and to make breach of conditions or failure to surrender criminal offences.
163 See Home Office 2007a, § 3.19.
164 PACE 1984 s. 34(2) and (4), s. 37(1), and s. 37(7)(a) and (b).
165 PACE 1984 s. 47(1A) and Bail Act 1976 ss. 3(6) and 3A(5).
166 Bail Act 1976 s. 3A(2).
167 PACE 1984 s. 47(2).
168 PACE 1984 s. 46A(1A).
169 PACE 1984 s. 46A(1).
170 See R (C) v. Chief Constable of A [2006] EWHC 2352 (Admin). For a critical analysis of these powers see Cape 2007.

determines that one or more of a number of conditions is satisfied. These include: that the person's identity or address has not been ascertained or there are reasonable grounds for doubting the name or address given; the officer has reasonable grounds for believing that the person will not turn up in court; (where the person is arrested for an imprisonable offence) that the officer has reasonable grounds for believing that detention is necessary to prevent the person from committing an offence; (where the person is arrested for a non-imprisonable offence) the officer has reasonable grounds for believing that detention is necessary to prevent the person from causing physical injury to any person or from causing loss of or damage to property; the officer has reasonable grounds for believing that detention is necessary to prevent the person from interfering with the administration of justice or with the investigation of offences; or the custody officer has reasonable grounds for believing that detention is necessary for the persons own protection (or if a juvenile, for their own welfare or protection).[171] In circumstances where a person is charged with certain serious offences (such as murder or manslaughter), and they have a previous conviction for another such serious offence, they may only be granted bail in exceptional circumstances.[172]

Conditions can be attached to bail if it appears necessary for the purpose of securing that the person surrenders to custody, does not commit an offence on bail, does not interfere with witnesses or otherwise obstruct the course of justice, and/or for their own protection (or, in the case of a person under 17 years, for their own welfare or in their own interests).[173] Although a financial surety or security can be required, this is relatively unusual. A person on whom conditions have been imposed can make an application to another custody officer or to a court to remove or vary the conditions of bail. Failure to attend court at the appointed time is an offence. A person can be arrested for failure to attend or an anticipated failure to attend court, and they can also be arrested for failure or anticipated failure to comply with conditions. Most people[174] charged with a criminal offence are bailed pending their first court appearance rather than being kept in custody, although it is not known how often this is subject to conditions.

Once a person appears in court, bail is principally governed by the Bail Act 1976. The accused normally has a prima facie right to bail. The prima facie right can be displaced, and bail need not be granted, if the court is satisfied that there are substantial grounds for believing that the defendant, if granted bail, would: fail to surrender to custody; commit an offence whilst on bail; or interfere with witnesses or otherwise obstruct the course of justice. In making a decision the court must take into account the nature and seriousness of the offence and the probable method of dealing with it; the character, antecedents, associations and community ties of the accused; their record for having answered bail in the past; and the strength of the evidence against them. Bail may also be refused if it is necessary for the accused's own protection, or if they are already serving a custodial sentence. There are similar

---

[171] PACE 1984 s. 38(1).
[172] Criminal Justice and Public Order Act 1994 s. 25.
[173] PACE 1984 s. 47(1A) and Bail Act 1976, ss. 3(6) and 3A(5).
[174] In 2006 about 85% of persons charged with an offence were bailed pending their first court appearance. See Ministry of Justice 2007a.

restrictions on bail for those accused of certain serious offences that apply to bail after charge (see above). There are also restrictions if the person is accused of an offence that carries a life sentence (for example, murder, manslaughter, rape, robbery), if they have already failed to surrender to bail granted previously in the same proceedings, and in certain cases where the person has tested positive for the presence in their body of a Class A drug (for example, heroin, cocaine) and they do not agree to undergo a drugs assessment. The grounds for withholding bail where a person is facing a non-imprisonable offence are more limited.

When granting bail, the court may impose a security or surety,[175] or conditions where the court believes that they are necessary to ensure the person surrenders to custody, to prevent further offences, or interference with witnesses, or for their own protection. Commonly imposed conditions include a condition of residence at a specified place (including a bail hostel), a condition of reporting to the police, a curfew, a condition that the accused does not go to a specified locality or address, a condition that they do not have contact with specified persons, or a condition that they surrender their passport. Failure to appear at court on the due date is an offence. Breach of conditions is not an offence, but a person may be arrested for a failure or anticipated failure to comply with conditions, and may also be arrested for failure or anticipated failure to surrender to custody. The court may then remand them in custody.

There is statutory restriction on the period for which a defendant can be kept in custody pending various stages of the criminal process. Broadly, the maximum period between first appearance in court and committal to the Crown Court is 70 days; between first appearance and summary trial is 70 days; and between committal and trial on indictment is 112 days. If the custody time limit expires, the defendant must be released on bail. However, courts have the power to extend the custody time limit if satisfied that the prosecution has acted with due diligence and expedition, and there is good and sufficient cause for extending the time limit,[176] and it appears that they are often willing to do so.

It is estimated that 28 per cent of all persons proceeded against in magistrates' courts are remanded in custody at some stage during proceedings. Of those who are committed for trial from magistrates' courts to the Crown Court (i.e. for more serious alleged offences) about a third are committed in custody.[177] The average time from charge to completion of the case (other than motoring offences) in magistrates' courts was about 62 days in 2006.[178] Equivalent data are not available in respect of cases in the Crown Court. In 2002 the average period of remand in custody for those committed to the Crown Court was over 12 weeks.[179] Whilst the average time spent in custody pending final disposal of the case has reduced over recent years, it is still a matter of great concern given that the majority of adult defendants, and three-quarters of defendants under 18 years, who are kept in

---

175   For an explanation, see note 157.
176   Prosecution of Offences Act 1985.
177   Ministry of Justice 2007a, ch. 4.
178   Ministry of Justice 2007a, p. 29.
179   Ashworth & Redmayne 2005, p. 220.

custody pending trial or sentence do not receive a custodial sentence (because they are either acquitted or receive a non-custodial sentence).[180]

There is relatively little research evidence available regarding bail/remand decision-making. Such evidence as there is suggests that magistrates take very little time in making bail decisions in the majority of cases.[181] This is due, in part, to the fact that most remand hearings are uncontested. One study found that the prosecutor did not seek a remand in custody in 85 per cent of cases, and only just over half of cases where they did were opposed by the defence. Furthermore, magistrates normally agreed with the decision recommended by the prosecution.[182] In fact the key decision-makers appear to be the police: their initial decision whether to grant bail to a person who has been charged is the most important determinant of whether a court will grant bail.[183] It also appears that bail decisions are not routinely monitored by reference to race or ethnic origin, and the Ministry of Justice admits that recording of ethnicity in magistrates' courts is poor.[184] However, official statistics show that black people are 3,6 times more likely to be arrested than white people, and are less likely to be diverted from prosecution.[185] Therefore, it is almost certain that they are less likely to be granted bail (both by the police and by the courts) and, if granted bail, probably more likely to be made subject to conditions, than white defendants.

2.3.2. The right of a defendant to be tried in their presence

The right of a defendant to be tried in their presence differs as between trials on indictment (i.e., trials in the Crown Court), and summary trials (i.e. trials in magistrates' courts). In trials on indictment, the defendant must be present at the commencement of the trial in order to enter a plea (of guilty or not guilty). If the defendant has absconded, a warrant may be issued for their arrest and the trial delayed until they are detained. However, following the taking of a plea a trial can proceed in the absence of the accused in a number of circumstances, including: where the accused acts in an unruly fashion or if he/she is apparently trying to intimidate jurors or witnesses by their conduct; or where the accused, having been present at the commencement of the trial, later voluntarily absents him/herself by escaping from custody or (if they are on bail) by failing to surrender to custody. If convicted, the accused can then be sentenced in their absence.[186] However, if the accused is absent for reasons beyond their control (for example, they are too ill to attend court), the trial may not continue in their absence unless they consent. There are no special protections concerning trial in absentia, but in most circumstances the accused will be represented by a lawyer.

---

[180] Sanders & Young 2007, p. 476, and Gibbs & Hickman 2009.
[181] For a summary of the research evidence see Sanders & Young 2007, p. 473.
[182] Hucklesby 1997.
[183] Burrows, Henderson & Morgan 1994.
[184] Ministry of Justice 2007c, p. ix.
[185] Ibidem.
[186] The principles to be applied in deciding whether to proceed in the absence of the accused are set out in R v. Hayward [2001] QB 862.

By contrast, in summary trials, the trial may proceed in the absence of the accused, although if the proceedings have been commenced by summons (or written charge and requisition, which replaces the summons procedure) the court must be satisfied that the summons (or written charge and requisition) was served on the accused a reasonable time before the hearing.[187] If the trial does proceed in the absence of a defendant a not guilty plea is entered on their behalf, and the burden is then on the prosecution to adduce sufficient evidence to prove guilt beyond reasonable doubt (the normal standard of proof). If the case is proved, the court may then proceed to sentence the accused, although a custodial sentence cannot be imposed in their absence.[188] As an alternative to proceeding in the absence of the defendant, the court can issue a warrant for their arrest. Case law shows that the power to proceed in the absence of the accused must be exercised with caution, and should not be done where there are genuine reasons for absence, such as illness.[189] There is a statutory procedure enabling a conviction to be set aside where the accused makes a statutory declaration that they did not know of the summons (or requisition) until after the date of the trial.[190] Quite separately from the procedures just described, there is a well-established statutory procedure that applies to certain (generally relatively minor) offences, such as many traffic offences, allowing the defendant to notify the court by post that they plead guilty, and in such cases the court can then proceed to sentence in the absence of the defendant.

2.3.3. The right to be presumed innocent

The presumption of innocence, at least in the context of literature on the subject in England and Wales, is a difficult concept both theoretically (for example, its relationship with the privilege against self-incrimination, and with the 'right to silence') and in practice.[191] In a formal sense, under the common law, a person is presumed to be innocent unless and until they are proved to be guilty of one or more offences. Therefore, again in a formal sense, they cannot be punished by the state unless and until they are proved to be guilty. However, this requires qualification for a number of reasons.

First, if the presumption of innocence means that a person should not be treated as a suspect unless there are good grounds for doing so, this is not always the case under English and Welsh law. Whilst most powers of arrest require reasonable suspicion that an offence has been, is being or is about to be, committed, the police do not have to establish reasonable suspicion if it is subsequently established that the suspect was in fact about to commit, or had committed, an

---

187   Magistrates' Courts Act 1980 s. 11.
188   The court in these circumstances could adjourn sentence, and issue a warrant for the arrest of the accused.
189   See *R* v. *Dewsbury Magistrates' Court, ex parte K* (1994) The Times 16 March 1994, and *R* v. *Bolton Magistrates' Court, ex parte Merna* (1991) 155 JP 612.
190   Magistrates' Court 1980 s. 14.
191   For a brief but useful discussion see Ashworth & Redmayne 2005, p. 129-137.

offence[192] (in other words, an *ex post facto* justification for the arrest can be sufficient to make the arrest lawful). Furthermore, there is extensive evidence to suggest that even where reasonable grounds for suspicion is required, it is not very effective in preventing arrest on the basis of mere suspicion.[193]

Second, as described in section 2.3.1, the police and the courts have extensive powers to detain people, or to release them subject to (possibly) stringent conditions, both prior to charge and following charge, but before a determination of guilt by a court. Formally, the justification for this is protection of the community (or of the person themselves), rather than punishment. However, to the suspect or defendant it is likely to feel like punishment and, indeed, is *de facto* punishment in that time spent in police custody or custody pending trial counts as sentence served if the person is subsequently made the subject of a custodial sentence.[194]

Third, there is a variety of mechanisms for imposing restrictions on liberty and freedom of movement on people who are suspected of 'quasi-criminal' conduct without the need to establish guilt or culpability, either at all or to the criminal standard: for example, anti-social behaviour orders,[195] and control orders in respect of persons suspected of terrorist activities.[196] Again, these are justified by reference to protecting the community and controlling risk, but from the individual's perspective it would be difficult to discern the difference between that and punishment.

Fourth, whilst the primary principle is that the legal burden of proving every element of an offence lies on the prosecution,[197] there is a relatively large number of circumstances where the defence has the legal burden of establishing a defence.[198] Where the legal burden of proof is on the prosecution, the relevant standard is 'beyond reasonable doubt'.[199] In those exceptional cases where the legal burden rests on the accused, the standard is a 'balance of probabilities'.[200] In such cases, if the prosecution can prove the essential elements of the offence, the defendant will be found guilty unless they can adduce sufficient evidence to establish their defence to the required standard.

Broadly, the circumstances where the accused has a legal burden of proof are as follows –

---

[192] Police and Criminal Evidence Act 1984 s. 24(1)(a) and (b) and (3)(a).
[193] See Sanders & Young 2007, ch. 3. The case law also indicates that the reasonable suspicion requirement is not very stringent. See, for example, *O'Hara* v. *Chief Constable of the Royal Ulster Constabulary* [1997] AC 286, and *Alford* v. *Chief Constable of Cambridgeshire* [2009] EWCA Civ 100.
[194] See also Choongh 1997, who argues that the police use arrest and detention as a way of disciplining 'undesirables'.
[195] Crime and Disorder Act 1998, s. 1.
[196] Prevention of Terrorism Act 2005.
[197] *Woolmington* v. *DPP* [1935] AC 462.
[198] The leading case is *R* v. *Lambert* [2002] 2 AC 545.
[199] See *Miller* v. *Minister of Pensions* [1947] 2 All ER 372.
[200] See *R* v. *Carr-Briant* [1943] KB 607.

- If a defendant raises the defence of insanity.
- If a statute expressly provides that the burden of proof in relation to a defence lies on the defendant. For example, the burden of proving a defence of diminished responsibility is expressly placed on the defendant.[201] Similarly, where a person is accused of being in possession of an offensive weapon, the burden of proving that they had lawful authority or reasonable excuse to possess the weapon rests on them.[202]
- In relation to trials in magistrates' courts the Magistrates' Courts Act 1980 s. 101 provides that where a defendant relies on any exception, exemption, proviso, excuse or qualification, the burden of proving that exception etc. rests on them. For example, if a person is prosecuted for driving without a licence, the burden of proving that they had a licence at the relevant time will rest on the accused.

These 'reverse-onus' provisions have generated a large number of appeals by reference to the Human Rights Act 1998, the argument being put by the appellants that the provisions are contrary to ECHR article 6. In most cases, the appeal courts have found that such provisions do not contravene article 6.[203]

In some circumstances, whilst not bearing a legal burden of proof, the defendant has an evidential burden. For example, if a defendant accused of assault wishes to raise a defence of self-defence, they must produce some credible evidence of the defence in order to make it a live issue. If they fail to do so, the prosecution can succeed without adducing evidence to disprove self-defence.

2.3.4. The right to silence

English and Welsh law, prompted by a decision of the ECtHR, distinguishes between whether a person can be convicted on evidence obtained from them by compulsion,[204] and whether a court can treat 'silence' as evidence of guilt.

In relation to the former, it was held in *Saunders* v. *UK*[205] that using evidence that was obtained from a person under compulsion[206] in a subsequent criminal trial of them was contrary to ECHR article 6. As a consequence, a number of statutes that permitted compulsion were amended so that answers given by a person under compulsion could not be used in evidence against them. However, the courts have treated traffic offences differently, so that a person may be convicted, for example, of exceeding the speed limit on the basis of information obtained from them as to the identity of the driver of the vehicle at the relevant time, where failure to provide

---

[201] Homicide Act 1957 s. 2(2).
[202] Criminal Justice Act 1988 s. 139.
[203] See, for example, Attorney-General's Reference (No 4 of 2002); *Sheldrake* v. *DPP* [2004] UKHL 43 and *Lynch* v. *DPP* [2002] 2 All ER 854.
[204] I.e., evidence obtained by questioning. There has been no real dispute that evidence obtained under compulsion that has an existence separate from the person's will, for example, blood, DNA samples, etc., can be used as evidence against them.
[205] (1997) 23 EHRR 313.
[206] In this case a refusal to answer questions put to him in an enquiry under the Companies Act 1985 could be punished as a contempt of court.

Ed Cape

the information is a criminal offence.[207] It is not clear whether the courts will be willing to extend this exception beyond traffic offences.

Treating 'silence' as evidence of guilt has been a very controversial issue. Legislation was introduced in the mid 1990s which enables a court to draw 'proper' inferences in a number of circumstances.[208] Under the Criminal Justice and Public Order Act (CJPOA) 1994 inferences may be drawn in four circumstances.

- (a) If a defendant relies on facts in their defence at trial which they did not tell the police about on being questioned under caution or on being charged, provided that it is reasonable to expect that they would have mentioned those facts.
- (b) If a defendant, having been arrested and given a special warning informing them of the consequences of non-response, fails to account for an object, substance or mark on their clothing or in their possession.
- (c) If a defendant, having been arrested and given a special warning informing them of the consequences of non-response, fails to account for their presence at a place at or about the time that an offence was committed.
- (d) If a defendant fails or refuses to give evidence at their trial.[209]

Under the Criminal Procedure and Investigations Act (CPIA) 1996 'proper' inferences can be drawn if a defendant fails in the pre-trial phase to provide to the prosecution a defence statement setting out the general nature of their defence, the matters on which they take issue with the prosecution, and the reasons why, and details of alibi (if relevant), if such a statement is filed outside the time limit, or it is inconsistent with the defence put forward at trial.[210]

A person cannot be convicted on the basis of an inference alone; there must be some other credible evidence sufficient to establish a prima facie case. However, it is obvious that provided the prosecution can establish a prima facie case on the basis of other evidence, an inference can provide enough to convict the person. Case law has established, in relation to the CJPOA 1994, that in order to draw an inference a jury or court must be satisfied that the reason for the 'silence' was that the defendant had no innocent explanation or none that would stand up to scrutiny.[211]

---

[207]   *Brown* v. *Stott* [2003] 1 AC 681. It was held in ECtHR 29 June 2007, *O'Halloran and Francis* v. *UK*, No. 15809/02 and 25654/02, that this did not contravene ECHR art. 6.

[208]   In addition, 'proper' inferences can be drawn if a suspect fails to permit an intimate sample to be taken at the police station (PACE 1984 s. 62(1)). Note that a person cannot normally be interviewed after charge. If, in exceptional circumstances, they are questioned after charge, inferences cannot be drawn from 'silence' under such questioning.

[209]   CJPOA 1994 ss. 34, 36, 37 and 35 respectively.

[210]   CJPOA 1996 ss. 5, 6 and 11. The requirement to give such information is compulsory in the Crown Court, but not in magistrates' courts.

[211]   ECtHR 2 May 2000, *Condron* v. *UK*, No. 35718/97, followed in *R* v. *Betts and Hall* (2001) 2 Cr App R 257.

It has also established that the fact that a person remained 'silent' on legal advice does not necessarily prevent inferences from being drawn.[212]

The inference provisions, especially those under the CJPOA 1994, have generated a large number of appeals, much academic interest, but relatively little research. Research in England and Wales, and in Northern Ireland where there are almost identical provisions, has shown that after introduction of the legislation more suspects do speak during police interviews, but that there is no measurable effect in terms of the confession rate or conviction rate. To an extent this is not surprising since the number of people who remained completely silent before the legislation was introduced was relatively low anyway.[213] It has been convincingly argued, however, that the provisions have changed the relationship between the police and suspects (and their lawyers), increasing the effective power of the former, and have created a normative expectation that suspects will answer police questions (which accords with the managerialist developments discussed earlier, and which itself makes adverse inferences more likely). Given, as noted earlier, that the police are under no obligation to disclose evidence to suspects at the investigative stage, this places suspects in a disadvantageous position, and 'sidelines' the impact of legal advice. Furthermore, it effectively brings the trial forward to the investigative stage, but without most of the safeguards that apply at trial, such as disclosure of prosecution evidence.[214]

2.3.5. The right to reasoned judgements

ECtHR jurisprudence requires courts to give reasons for their judgements and, as noted in section 1.2, the courts in England and Wales must not act in a manner that is incompatible with a convention right.[215] This right to a reasoned judgement created a challenge to a system where most decisions as to fact are made by lay people, either lay magistrates or juries. Even now there is no general statutory duty on magistrates or judges to give reasons for their decisions, and no obligation on juries to give reasons for their decisions as to guilt. It follows that a defendant convicted or acquitted following a trial in the Crown Court will not know with certainty why that decision was made. However, it has come to be accepted that judges must give reasons for their decisions and this is supported, for example, by guidance issued by the Judicial Studies Board.[216] Therefore, following a trial in a magistrates' court reasons for a decision, or at least for a conviction, should be given. In fact one of the mechanisms for appeal from a magistrates' court, an appeal by case stated to the High Court, requires the magistrates to 'state a case', that is, give reasons for the decision appealed against.

---

[212]   *R* v. *Howell* (2005) 1 Cr App R 1 and *R* v. *Hoare and Pierce*, [2005] 1 WLR 1804.
[213]   Research evidence shows that prior to the CJPOA 1994 10% of suspects refused to answer all questions, and 13% refused to answer some. After the CJPOA 1994 the figures were 6% and 10% respectively. See Bucke, Street & Brown 2000.
[214]   See, in particular, Jackson 2001, Leng 2001 and Cape 1997.
[215]   Human Rights Act 1998 s. 6.
[216]   See, for example the Judicial Studies Board guidance, *Sitting as a District Judge in a magistrates' court*, p. 21, available via <www.jsboard.co.uk>.

There are statutory requirements to give reasons in respect of certain decisions. For example, a judge must normally give reasons for and explain the effect of the sentence that they impose,[217] although failure to do so does not render the sentence invalid.[218] Similarly, where a court withholds bail from a person who has a prima facie right to it, or imposes conditions on bail to such a person (or varies conditions already imposed), it must give reasons, and these must be recorded in writing.[219]

In fact, there appears to be little concern about the issue of reasons for decisions. In part this may result from the fact (explained in the next section) that a defendant has an absolute right to appeal against a finding of guilt following a trial in a magistrates' court, and an acceptance in respect of trials on indictment that it is unrealistic to expect that juries, consisting of lay people, should have to give reasons for their verdicts.

2.3.6. The right to appeal

A person tried or sentenced in a magistrates' court has a right to appeal to the Crown Court, although appeal against conviction is normally only possible if they pleaded not guilty. If they were legally-aided in the magistrates' court, the legal aid order covers advice on appeal, but a separate application for legal aid must be made in respect of the appeal itself, which is decided on the normal criteria as to merits (see section 2.2.3). In 2007 there were just over 5,800 appeals against conviction, of which 37 per cent were successful, and nearly 6,600 appeals against sentence, of which 44 per cent were successful.[220] Appeal may be on a matter of law or fact, and no leave is required. In the case of the latter, the matter is tried de novo by a judge, normally sitting with two lay magistrates (who must not have been involved in the decision which is the subject of the appeal). If conviction is then upheld, and also in the case of appeals against sentence, the court may impose any sentence that a magistrates' court could have imposed.[221] Therefore, an appellant faces the risk that their sentence may be increased, although this is probably relatively unusual.

Appeal to the Crown Court from a magistrates' court is only open to the defence, but either prosecution or the defence can appeal 'by case stated' to the High Court on the grounds that a magistrates' court acted in excess of its jurisdiction or its decision was legally incorrect. Appeal thereafter lies to the Supreme Court.[222] There are relatively few appeals by case stated. In 2007, for example, just 87 such appeals were dealt with, of which 35 were allowed.[223] It is also

---

[217]   Criminal Justice Act 2003 s. 174.
[218]   *R* v. *McQueen* (1989) 11 Cr App R (S) 305.
[219]   Bail Act 1976 s. 5.
[220]   Ministry of Justice 2008c.
[221]   Powers on appeal are governed generally by the Supreme Court Act 1981.
[222]   Under the Constitutional Reform Act 2005, the Supreme Court replaced the judicial committee of the House of Lords as the final court of appeal in October 2009.
[223]   Ministry of Justice 2008c. The statistics do not show how many were appeals by the defence and how many by the prosecution.

possible for either the prosecution or defence to seek judicial review of a magistrates' court decision, but the numbers of such applications are very small.

Appeals from the Crown Court lie to the Court of Appeal, Criminal Division. A convicted person may appeal against conviction (normally, only if they had pleaded not guilty) or against sentence, or both. In order to appeal, the trial judge must issue a certificate stating that the case is suitable for appeal or leave of the Court of Appeal must be obtained.[224] If they were legally aided in the Crown Court, that legal aid order will cover the drafting of grounds for appeal, but not the appeal itself, and the likelihood of legal aid being granted depends upon whether the court registrar refers the case to a single judge or the full court. If the trial lawyer advises against appeal, there is no prospect that the defendant will be granted legal aid for the appeal. Although there is no recent evidence, research in the early 1990s found significant problems with the quality of legal advice regarding appeal.[225] The only ground for appeal against conviction is that the conviction is unsafe.[226] Generally, the Court of Appeal does not hear evidence, although it has the power to do so in limited circumstances, and the appeal consists essentially of a review of the original trial.

If the appeal is upheld the conviction is quashed, but the court has the power to order a re-trial. If an appeal is unsuccessful, the court can order than any time served in custody between commencing the appeal and consideration of leave for appeal is deemed not to have been served (known as the 'loss of time' rule), thus effectively lengthening the sentence. The court rarely uses this power, although recent case law has encouraged its greater use.[227] However, the court has limited itself to a maximum of 28 days, and loss of time is rarely ordered unless the court concludes that the appeal was wholly without merit. In an appeal against sentence the court may quash the original decision and may substitute any sentence that could have been imposed in the Crown Court. Normally a person is only able to appeal once (but see below).

There are relatively few appeals to the Court of Appeal, Criminal Division. For example, in 2007 a total of 2,774 appeals were heard, 523 against conviction and 2,252 against sentence. Of the former, 196 were successful (with retrials ordered in 83 of them), and of the latter 1,632 were successful.[228] Appeal lies from the Court of Appeal to the Supreme Court, but only if the case involves a point of law of public importance.[229] A leading academic researcher in this field commented in the early 1990s that 'The appeal process can be likened to an obstacle race: only the determined, strong and well prepared will reach the end – and they are likely to be

---

224 Appeal is governed by the Criminal Appeal Act 1968. Research evidence from the early 1990s showed that applications for leave were given very brief consideration by judges.
225 Plotnikoff & Woolfson 1993.
226 A recent attempt by the government to change the ground for appeal which would have prevented the Court of Appeal from allowing an appeal on 'procedural grounds' was abandoned after overwhelming opposition from, amongst others, the judiciary and the legal profession.
227 See, for example, R v. Kuimba [2005] EWCA Crim 955.
228 Ministry of Justice 2008c.
229 In contrast to the Supreme Court in the USA, criminal cases make up a very small proportion of cases heard by the UK Supreme Court (formerly judicial committee of the House of Lords).

found in the higher reaches of the offence and sentence scale'.[230] More recently, Sanders and Young in their book *Criminal Justice*, conclude that the appeals process largely reflects 'what can be seen as [England's] crime control heritage'.[231]

Generally, the prosecution cannot appeal, but they have been given increasing power to do so over the past decade or so. Thus the prosecution can appeal against 'terminating rulings' (for example, a decision to stop a case from proceeding because of an abuse of process, or a decision to exclude evidence which leads the prosecution not to continue with the case);[232] and can effectively appeal against 'unduly lenient' sentences.[233] Furthermore, the Criminal Justice Act 2003 s. 75 introduced a procedure whereby the prosecution can apply to the Court of Appeal to order a re-trial of a person who has been acquitted of certain serious offences on the grounds that there is new and compelling evidence justifying a re-trial. This legislation overturned the fundamental principle that an acquittal is final, and was highly controversial. It is likely that it will be used relatively rarely, in respect of as small number of exceptional cases.[234]

A major innovation introduced in 1997 was the creation of the Criminal Cases Review Commission (CCRC). This was established following concern about a number of high profile miscarriages of justice in which people who had served a considerable number of years in prison following conviction for serious offences were eventually exonerated. A person who has exhausted their rights of appeal can make an application to the CCRC, which has powers and resources to investigate the circumstances of the conviction (or sentence). The CCRC can refer a case back to the Court of Appeal if it considers that there is a 'real possibility' that the appellate court will not uphold the conviction. Whilst the Commission has been the subject of criticism, particularly that it is under-resourced and too cautious, a significant number of people have had their convictions overturned as a result.[235]

2.4. Rights relating to effective defence

2.4.1. The right to investigate the case

In English and Welsh law, although not expressly stated in any statute, there is formal recognition of equality of arms between defence and prosecution. However, its meaning is not precise, and the extent to which it is recognised in practice depends upon a variety of factors including the stage of the criminal process.

---

[230] Malleson 1991, p. 328.
[231] Sanders & Young 2007, p. 595.
[232] Criminal Justice Act 2003, s. 58.
[233] Criminal Justice Act 1988, ss. 35 and 36. There is also a power to refer a case to the court for an opinion on a point of law following an acquittal, although this has no effect on the particular person who has been acquitted: Criminal Justice Act 1982, s. 36. Applications under these provisions can only be made by the Attorney General.
[234] A prediction reinforced by recent case law. See *R v. G (G) and B (S)* [2009] EWCA Crim 1077, and *R v. JB* [2009] EWCA Crim 1036.
[235] For a review of the issues, see Sanders & Young 2007, ch. 11.

At the investigative stage, the suspect and/or their lawyer has the right to be present whilst some, but by no means all, investigative acts are conducted. For example, a suspect has the right to have their lawyer present during any interview of them by the police (subject to exceptions noted in section 2.2.2), and when fingerprints or samples are taken, although in the case of the latter two procedures, it is probable that the police do not have to delay the procedure pending the arrival of a lawyer unless they are readily available. The suspect or their lawyer has the right to be present at certain identification procedures, such as a video identification, although the government is proposing to remove this right provided that the identification procedure itself is video-recorded.[236] Whether there is a right to be present at the search of premises depends upon the power under which it is conducted but generally there is no right for either the suspect or their lawyer to be present. Similarly, there is no right for them to be present when prospective witnesses are interviewed by the police. For the right to be present when witnesses give evidence at court, see below.

Whilst there are no specific rights of the defendant or their lawyer to seek evidence, investigate facts, interview witnesses, or instruct experts, it is accepted that there is a common law right to do so and, in the case of defence lawyers, that they have a professional obligation to do so in that they are required to act in their clients' best interests. It is said that there is 'no property in a witness' and, for example, the Solicitors' Code of Conduct states: 'You are permitted, even when acting as an advocate, to interview and take statements from any witness or prospective witness at any stage in the proceedings…'.[237] Furthermore, there is case law that suggests that the police must not interfere with defence attempts to interview witnesses by, for example, warning witnesses not to speak to a defence lawyer. The defence can ask the police to investigate particular aspects of the case, and there is a statutory duty on the police to pursue all reasonable lines of enquiry.[238] However, there is little confidence amongst defence lawyers that the police would pursue such enquiries with vigour.

In practice there a number of limitations on the defence right to investigate. At the investigative stage, there is no obligation on the police to permit the defence access to the crime scene, nor to inform them of details concerning witnesses they have interviewed or identified, and during pre-trial disclosure the addresses of witnesses are normally withheld by the prosecution. Witnesses are under no obligation to speak to a defendant or their lawyer, and in view of the risk of allegations of interfering with witnesses or perverting the course of justice the Law Society advises defence lawyers to be cautious about interviewing witnesses who may be called to give evidence by the prosecution.[239] If the defendant is legally-aided, the fixed fee schemes that cover most criminal defence work mean that lawyers may be reluctant to be pro-active because the fee may not cover the additional work carried out. Although the cost of an expert witness may be claimed

---

[236] PACE Code D, Annex A. For government proposals Home Office 2008c, p. 49.
[237] Rule 11, Guidance Note 18. For guidance for lawyers on their role in this respect see Ede & Shepherd 2000, especially ch. 14.
[238] Criminal Procedure and Investigations Act 1996 s. 23.
[239] See Ede & Edwards 2008, p. 22.

in addition to a fixed fee, in order to guarantee that the LSC will pay the cost (on the basis it was reasonably incurred), lawyers frequently request prior authority from the LSC and if that is not forthcoming, it is likely that a lawyer would not take the risk of incurring the cost. There is no up-to-date evidence on these issues, but research conducted in the early 1990s found that lawyers were insufficiently adversarial, and insufficiently active in investigating cases on behalf of clients.[240] The criteria used for the purposes of peer review[241] of criminal defence solicitors do include consideration of whether the lawyer has done all the work that should reasonably have been done, but there is no evidence as to how peer reviewers relate this to the pro-active investigation of the defence case.

2.4.2. The right to adequate time and facilities for preparation of defence

At the investigative stage the major issue, as explained in section 2.1.2, is lack of disclosure by the police. Since a suspect has a right to consult a solicitor 'at any time',[242] in principle there are no limits on the time that the lawyer can spend on taking instructions and giving advice, although in practice the police may place pressure on the lawyer to speed up the process if the consultation interferes with their investigative timetable or a detention time limit is close to expiry.[243] Most police stations have consultation rooms where a private consultation can take place, although facilities are often limited.

There is no set period of notice that must be given to a defendant before a court appearance. Where a person is charged with an offence[244] and held in custody pending their first court appearance, they must normally be produced in court no later than the following day, unless the following day is a Sunday or Bank Holiday.[245] If they are released on bail following charge the first hearing must normally be within the same period, although it may be marginally longer.[246] In practice, these provisions are complied with and there appears to be no concern either as to delays in the first court appearance, or lack of time for preparation by the defence. If a person is summonsed to appear in court, the period before their first court appearance will be longer, but they will neither be in custody nor on bail during this period. Courts have wide powers to adjourn cases and regularly do so in order to give defendants time to instruct a solicitor, or to enable the solicitor to prepare the case. Both the accused and the prosecution can apply for an adjournment, and an application must not be unreasonably refused. The higher courts are reluctant to interfere with a court's refusal to adjourn a case unless the decision was clearly unreasonable.[247] Although there is no research evidence on the

---

240 McConville et al. 1994. For earlier findings see Baldwin & McConville 1977, and for a more recent consideration of the professional and ethical issues involved, see Bridges 2006.
241 See section 2.2.4 for an explanation of peer review.
242 PACE 1984 s. 58(1), and see section 2.2.4.
243 See section 1.3 for detention time limits.
244 For an explanation of 'charge' and 'summons' see note 30.
245 PACE 1984 s. 46.
246 PACE 1984 s. 47(3A).
247 *R (CPS)* v. *Uxbridge Magistrates* (2007) 171 JP 279. See also *R* v. *Kingston-upon-Thames Justices (ex p Martin)* [1994] Imm AR 172 and *CPS* v. *Picton* (2006) 170 JP 567.

point, defence lawyers complain that periods of adjournment are too short for adequate preparation – in less serious cases an adjournment may only be granted for a matter of hours – and that this is getting worse since courts have to meet efficiency targets. There is also anecdotal evidence that where a defendant is remanded in custody it is often difficult for lawyers to make appointments to see their clients, a problem that is exacerbated by serious prison overcrowding.

2.4.3. The right to equality of arms in examining witnesses

The basic rule is that it is for the prosecution and defence to decide what evidence to adduce at trial and, broadly, they are permitted to do so provided that it is relevant and does not offend an evidential rule (for example, the rule against hearsay). If a witness is reluctant to attend court to give evidence, the prosecution or defence can apply to the court to issue a summons requiring the witness to attend. Criminal defence lawyers are often loathe to use this procedure because they believe that a reluctant witness may not serve the interests of the accused. Judges do have a discretion to call witnesses, although in practice they do so very infrequently. It would seem, however, that judges are increasingly asking questions of witnesses called by the prosecution or defence. It may be that one reason for this is the government's desire to encourage judges to be more 'activist' trial managers as part of its policy of increasing speed and efficiency of the trial process.

If a defendant is not legally represented the judge should assist them.[248] Whilst generally unrepresented defendants can call and examine witnesses, and cross-examine witnesses called by the prosecution and any co-defendant, they are prohibited from cross-examining complainants and child witnesses in trials for certain offences, and there is provision for the appointment of counsel to conduct the cross-examination in such circumstances.[249]

Apart from these limitations in respect of unrepresented defendants, defendants (personally, or by their lawyer if represented) have a right to cross-examine any witness called by the prosecution or a co-defendant. However, there are a number of statutory measures designed to protect 'vulnerable' witnesses, including those who are vulnerable on the grounds of youth, incapacity or because of the fear or distress they are likely to suffer when giving evidence.[250] If the conditions are satisfied, a variety of 'special measures' are available including screening the witness from the defendant, giving evidence by live video link, and pre-recorded video-recording of evidence-in-chief. In addition courts have an inherent power to modify the normal procedure of giving evidence even if the witness does not fall within one of the statutory categories.[251] When first introduced

[248]   See Hooper & Ormerod 2008, p. 1744.
[249]   Youth Justice and Criminal Evidence Act 1999 ss. 34-39, and Criminal Procedure Rules 2005 rule 31.4.
[250]   Youth Justice and Criminal Evidence Act 1999 ss. 16 and 17.
[251]   Youth Justice and Criminal Evidence Act 1999 s. 19(6)(a). A recent House of Lords decision, *R v. Davis* [2008] UKHL 36, which decided that measures to protect the identity of certain prosecution witnesses in a murder trial resulted in an unfair trial, led the government to introduce temporary emergency legislation, the Criminal Evidence (Witness Anonymity) Act

→

the special measures did not apply to vulnerable defendants when giving evidence, although subsequent amendment of the legislation allows a court to permit certain categories of defendant to give evidence by live video link.[252] However, in practice they are mostly used in respect of prosecution witnesses.

A further impediment to the ability of the accused to cross-examine witnesses is the widening of the circumstances in which hearsay evidence is admissible, as a result of changes introduced by the Criminal Justice Act 2003. For example, this permits a statement made by a witness who has since died, or who is too frightened to give evidence, to be used as evidence. The Court of Appeal has decided that despite the fact that in *Al-Khawaja* v. *UK*[253] the European Court of Human Rights found that a conviction based solely or to a decisive degree on such statements contravenes the article 6 right to fair trial, domestic courts could admit such evidence provided that there are sufficient counter-balancing measures.[254]

2.4.4. The right to free interpretation of documents and translation

Generally, other than in relation to the Welsh language, in respect of which there is specific legislation, the right to interpretation and translation is not governed by statute but appears to be largely a matter of common law. There is specific provision for interpretation at the investigative stage in that PACE Code of Practice C provides that 'a person must not be interviewed in the absence of a person capable of interpreting if . . . they have difficulty understanding English . . . the interviewer cannot speak the person's own language . [and]. . the person wants an interpreter present'.[255] In addition, the notice of suspects' rights[256] should be available in Welsh and the main ethnic minority and principal European languages.[257] There appears to be no specific requirement that reasons for arrest or grounds for detention be translated, but the caution given at the beginning of a police interview should be translated.[258] Anecdotal evidence suggests that whilst defence lawyers advising at police stations can instruct their own interpreter (and claim for the cost under legal aid), they frequently rely on the interpreter obtained

---

	2008 designed to reverse the effects of the decision. The government has indicated that it will introduce permanent legislation to permit anonymous evidence, but in a recent decision on the 2008 legislation the Court of Appeal held that the legislation did not extend to permitting anonymous hearsay evidence to be adduced. See *R* v. *Mayers* [2008] EWCA Crim 2989.
252	Those who are under 18 years and whose ability to participate is limited by their intellectual ability or lack of social function, and those over 18 years who suffer from a mental disorder that prevents their effective participation (Youth Justice and Criminal Evidence Act 1999 ss. 33A and 33B).
253	ECtHR 20 January 2009, *Al-Khawaja* v. *UK*, Nos. 26766/05 and 22228/06.
254	*R* v. *Horncastle* [2009] EWCA Crim 964.
255	PACE Code of Practice C, § 13.2.
256	See § 2.1.1.
257	PACE Code of Practice C Note for Guidance 3B.
258	There is no specific requirement in this regard, but PACE Code C Note for Guidance 10D provides that if a person does not understand the caution the person giving it should explain it in their own words, and if a court accepted that a suspect did not understand the caution it is likely that evidence of the interview would be excluded as evidence.

by the police. This is partly because of the difficulty of securing the services of an interpreter at short notice, especially for less common languages.

In court proceedings it is up to the court to decide whether a witness requires an interpreter and can make its own assessment.[259] An agreement between criminal justice agencies sets out responsibility for arranging an interpreter as follows:

- the police or other prosecuting agency in respect of a defendant who is charged with an offence and is to appear in court within two working days of charge;
- the court for a defendant in all other circumstances;
- the prosecution, for a prosecution witness; and
- the defence lawyer, for a defence witness.[260]

The agency that has responsibility for organising an interpreter, according to the above agreement, has responsibility for the cost. In the case of a legally-aided suspect or defendant the cost of an interpreter can be claimed for as a disbursement provided that the amount is reasonable, and the cost is reasonably incurred.

In relation to translation of documents there appears to be no set procedure for determining whether translation is necessary, for arranging translation or for determining who bears the cost, and there is no specific requirement that a charge or indictment be translated. In the case of a legally-aided defendant the cost of translation of documents (for example, witness statements, or documents disclosed by the prosecution) can be claimed for under the legal aid contract provided that the amount is reasonable, and the cost is reasonably incurred.

A number of bodies have some responsibility for regulation or registration of interpreters and translators.[261] Such organisations have requirements as to minimum quality. However, there is no requirement that the police, courts or defence lawyers to use interpreters or translators registered with such organisations, although they are encouraged to do so.

There is no explicit sanction where an interpreter, or translation, is not provided. Where a police interview is conducted without an interpreter in circumstances where the suspect needed a translator, evidence of what was said in the interview may be excluded on the grounds of unreliability or unfairness.[262] If a defendant was convicted in circumstances where an interpreter should have been appointed, the defendant could appeal (from the magistrates' court as of right, and from the Crown Court on the basis that lack of an interpreter rendered the conviction unsafe).

---

[259]   *R* v. *Sharma* [2006] EWCA Crim 16.
[260]   *National Agreement on Arrangements for the Use of Interpreters, Translators and Language Service Professionals*, available via <http://frontline.cjsonline.gov.uk/guidance/race-confidence-and-justice/>.
[261]   Such as the National Register of Public Service Interpreters (NRPSI), the Council for the Advancement of Communication with Deaf People (CADCP), and the Directory of British Sign Language/English Interpreters. See the *National Agreement on Arrangements for the Use of Interpreters, Translators and Language Service Professionals*, Annex G.
[262]   Under PACE 1984 ss. 76(2) or 78(1). See § 1.3 above.

3.   The professional culture of defence lawyers

In order to understand the professional culture of criminal defence lawyers in England and Wales, it is important to understand that the legal profession is a 'divided' profession: lawyers may be either barristers or solicitors.[263] Barristers have rights of audience in all courts and in relation to criminal defence work, tend to carry out most of the advocacy in cases that go to the Crown Court. Normally, they can only act for a defendant if instructed by a solicitor. Barristers are generally self-employed, but organised into chambers, sharing administrative and other resources. Strictly, they are bound by a professional rule known as the 'cab rank' rule, meaning that they have to take any case that is referred to them, but in practice there is a fair degree of specialisation. Nearly 40 per cent of barristers report undertaking some criminal work, although it is not possible to distinguish between work for the prosecution and criminal defence work.[264]

Solicitors do not automatically have rights of audience in the Crown Court and appeal courts, but can obtain a qualification to carry out advocacy in the higher courts.[265] They may operate as 'sole practitioners' but most are either partners in law firms, or employed by such firms.[266] Defence solicitors advise in police stations (although many employ non-solicitor representatives for this purpose), do most of the representation in magistrates' court cases, and act for clients in cases that go to the Crown Court, although they normally instruct barristers both to advise and to conduct the court advocacy. Only about eight per cent of solicitors in practice claim that they do some criminal work, and criminal defence work tends to be carried out by solicitors in firms that specialise in such work, or in legal aid work generally. See further section 1.5.

Both professions have professional rules that set out in some detail the professional obligations of lawyers, including criminal defence lawyers.[267] They also have complaints and disciplinary procedures, but whilst the number of complaints against solicitors is relatively large, there are no figures for either profession on the proportion of complaints that relate to criminal defence work. There are no specific associations of criminal defence lawyers. Both the major professional bodies have criminal law committees or sections which give guidance to their members regarding criminal defence work,[268] but these are open to lawyers who work for both prosecution and defence. There is also a Criminal Law Solicitors Association

---

[263]   The legal profession is relatively large, with over 108,000 practising solicitors, and 15,000 practising barrister, so that there is approximately one lawyer for every 420 of the population.

[264]   See further § 1.5.

[265]   Known as obtaining 'higher rights'.

[266]   There is also a small Public Defender Service. See § 1.5.

[267]   See the Bar Standards Board Code of Conduct, available via <http://www.barstandardsboard.org.uk/standardsandguidance/>, and the Solicitors Regulation Authority Code of Conduct, available via <http://www.sra.org.uk/solicitors/code-of-conduct.page>.

[268]   The Law Society also publishes a number of good practice guides including Ede & Edwards 2008; Ede & Shepherd 2000; Keogh 2002; and Shepherd 2004. There are also a number of 'unofficial' good practice guides such as Cape 2006.

(and a London equivalent) which, although open to all criminal lawyers, tends to be dominated by criminal defence lawyers.

The professional codes of conduct governing both legal professions require lawyers to act in their clients' best interests. However, until the 1990s, the meaning of this in the context of criminal defence work was not articulated in detail and defence lawyers were criticised for being insufficiently adversarial and too willing to pressure clients to plead guilty.[269] Criticism of solicitors (and their representatives) in respect of advising clients at police stations in the early 1990s led to the creation of an accreditation scheme for representatives, which was later extended to all solicitors doing police station work, and to duty solicitors in magistrates' court. This required the Law Society to set out in detail the role of the solicitor at the police station, and as court duty solicitor, and this incorporated the concept of the lawyer as 'defender' rather than merely 'adviser'.[270] There is no similar accreditation scheme for barristers, although the LSC and the Ministry of Justice are currently piloting a quality assurance scheme for both barristers and solicitors who perform advocacy in legally aided cases.

The predecessor of the LSC (the Legal Aid Board) played a significant role in the development of the accreditation schemes during the 1990s, and with the introduction of contracting in 2001, the LSC used the contract to impose a number of minimum performance standards, particularly in relation to police station work.[271] The LSC also introduced a quality assurance mechanism known as 'peer review' under which solicitors' files are assessed by experienced criminal lawyers.[272] These measures, together with a high degree of specialisation and recognition by the legal professions of the need for defence lawyers to act in a pro-active manner, has almost certainly resulted in a good general standard of criminal defence work. However, more recently the LSC has changed its focus from improving quality to reducing legal aid expenditure, using mechanisms such as fixed fees (and, in the future, a system of competitive price tendering), and call centres for providing advice, and there is concern that this is leading to a reduction in quality.[273] There is also concern that the development of managerialism at the expense of adversarialism in the criminal justice system, exemplified by the Criminal Procedure Rules 2005, is having an adverse effect on the ability of defence lawyers

[269]   See, in particular, Baldwin & McConville 1977, and McConville et al. 1994. For a more recent consideration of the professional and ethical issues involved, see Bridges 2006.

[270]   For a slightly more detailed explanation, see Cape & Hodgson 2007. Research indicated that the introduction of the police station accreditation scheme did lead to an improvement in standards. See Bridges & Choongh 1998.

[271]   These included response times and use of non-lawyers for police station work, and management mechanisms such as supervision of casework.

[272]   For further information see <http://www.legalservices.gov.uk/civil/how/mq_peer review.asp>. Statistics supplied by the LSC show that of the 876 firms peer reviewed between 1 April 2005 and 17 June 2008, 2% were classed as 'excellent', 49% as attaining 'competence plus', 42% as being of 'threshold competence', and 7% as 'below competence'.

[273]   See, for example, Bridges & Cape 2008.

to act in their clients best interests.[274] However, there is a paucity of recent empirical evidence on the quality of the work of criminal defence lawyers.[275]

4.   Political commitment to effective criminal defence

It is, perhaps, ironic that whilst crime rates have fallen, fear of crime has increased, although this phenomenon has also been encountered in other jurisdictions.[276] There is almost certainly a dynamic relationship between such fears and the criminal justice policies of the government. The Labour government, and all of the major political parties, want to be seen to be in tune with the concerns of citizens, but adopting policies, and a rhetoric, that is perceived as 'hard on crime' almost certainly increases fear of crime. When the Labour government came to power in 1997 the then Prime Minister, Tony Blair, was well known for his slogan 'tough on crime, tough on the causes of crime'. It has been said by many informed commentators that the emphasis of government policy since then has been on the former rather than the latter. The Labour government increased spending on the criminal justice system significantly. According to a recent report, the United Kingdom 'now spends proportionately more on law and order than any other country in the OECD, including the United States and major European Union members such as France, Germany and Spain'.[277] Spending on the criminal justice system in 2007/8 was estimated to be £ 22.7 billion, of which two thirds was spent on the police, 'which benefited from a 21 per cent real terms increase in funding between 1997 and 2005'.[278] It has been estimated that the Labour government has introduced over 3,000 new criminal offences since it came to power in 1997, and also that between 1997 and 2004 there were nearly 50 Acts of Parliament concerned with crime, disorder, policing, criminal justice and punishment.[279]

In addition to policies and legislation on terrorism, the three major planks of the Labour government's criminal justice strategy have been policing, youth crime and drugs. Such policies have been target driven, and targets have been imposed on

[274]   See Cape 2006. The Law Society has recently published two practice notes dealing with the conflicts between the duty to the client and the duty to the courts and to the administration of justice. See *Anti-terrorism practice note: The conflicting duties of maintaining client confidentiality and reporting terrorism*, 19 July 2007, and *Criminal Procedure Rules: impact on solicitors' duties to the client*, 31 March 2008.

[275]   The Legal Services Research Centre, the research department of the Legal Services Commission, is currently conducting research on users' perspectives of criminal defence services but whilst this is likely to provide insights into what suspects and defendants want of their lawyers its findings have not yet been published. See also Skinns 2009, whose research examines the impact of privatisation of police custody suites on suspects' request for legal advice, and also shows that suspects' perceptions of delay resulting from a request for legal advice is probably more important than perceptions of quality of that advice.

[276]   Two thirds of people asked say that crime nationally has risen in the previous two years, with one third believing that it has risen a lot, although when asked about crime locally far fewer believe that it has risen. Generally, people overestimate the likelihood of being a crime victim. See Home Office 2008b.

[277]   Solomon et al. 2007, p. 10.

[278]   Ibidem.

[279]   Loader 2006.

many criminal justice agencies, in particular the police. One such target, the 'offences brought to justice' target, committed criminal justice agencies, and in particular the police, to increasing the number of offenders brought to justice annually from one million in 2002 to 1.25 million by 2007/8. This target was exceeded in the 12 months to June 2007 during which period the number of offences brought to justice was 1.434 million.[280] A large number of legislative developments, including increased police powers, new forms of diversion (for example, conditional cautions and fixed penalty fines that avoid court proceedings), and evidential changes such as permitting trial courts to know about a defendant's previous history of misconduct, may be understood in the context of the current government's imperative to meet this and other targets.[281]

During the 1990s, although the major political parties competed to be seen as adopting tough policies on crime,[282] a number of policies were adopted that were designed to improve access to effective criminal defence, particularly by the legal aid authorities. Spending on criminal legal aid increased significantly and, as was indicated in the previous section, criminal defence lawyers were subjected to a number of quality enhancement and assurance policies. However, the advent of a new government in 1997 signalled a significant shift. A central theme, adopted by both the Labour government and others, was that the criminal justice system had tipped too far in favour of suspects and defendants and that the system needs to be 're-balanced'. Most starkly, this came from the then Prime Minister himself who said, in a major newspaper interview in 2002 that 'Justice [is] weighted towards the criminal and [is] in need of rebalancing towards the victim'.[283] In his major review of the criminal courts Lord Justice Auld, a senior judge, said that it had to be remembered that criminal processes 'are not just there to protect defendants'. Until recently, he said, the focus had been on the criminal or alleged criminal, 'leaving the victim, or alleged victim, with only a walk-on part'.[284] At around the same time the then president of the Association of Chief Police Officers stated that 'it is already acknowledged in this country that victims' rights appear to come second to the defendant's in court'.[285] There was also, for a time, an argument at the political level about whether incorporation of the ECHR had led to a 'criminals' charter' and at one stage the government indicated that it might modify the Human Rights Act 1998, although no changes were made.[286]

To an extent, these attitudes and policies reflect (or are reflected by) public attitudes to the criminal justice system. Around eight in ten people are confident

---

[280] Home Office 2008d. An offence is brought to justice where a person is arrested and convicted of a recordable offence or is dealt with by a formal method of diversion (for example, a caution). The government has recently signalled a move away from targets, both in relation to criminal justice and other areas of government policy.

[281] For an analysis of some of these issues see Cape & Young 2008. The government has recently signalled a move away from targets, both in relation to criminal justice and other areas of government policy.

[282] See Downes & Morgan 1997.

[283] *The Observer*, 10 November 2002, p. 26.

[284] Auld 2001, p. 11, 13 and 496.

[285] Quoted in an Association of Chief Police Officers press release dated 10 January 2002.

[286] For analyses of this, see Tonry 2004, and Morgan 2006.

that the criminal justice system respects the rights of those accused of committing crime and treats them fairly. On the other hand, only a quarter have confidence in the way the system deals with young people accused of crime; a third have confidence that the system meets the needs of crime victims; just over a third believe that it is effective in reducing crime; and 40 per cent confident that the system is effective in bringing people who commit crime to justice. Those who have been the victim of crime in the previous 12 months have lower confidence on all of those measures. Interestingly, particularly given the over-representation of people from ethnic minorities as suspects, defendants and prisoners, people from non-white groups have higher levels of confidence than those from white groups other than in relation to whether the system respects the rights of people accused of committing crime.[287]

5. Conclusions

The shift in focus of the criminal justice process from the trial to the investigative stage has been marked by, and has resulted in, the police being given greater investigative powers, the independence of prosecutors being compromised by being required to work more closely with the police and being made subject to targets designed to increase the rate of convictions, and in suspects and defendants being increasingly required to divulge information at the pre-trial stage and to assist the prosecution by pointing out weaknesses in their case. Yet there have been few, if any, safeguards introduced in response. The police have limited obligations of disclosure to suspects at the investigative stage, many dispositive[288] decisions are made by the police and prosecutors without the involvement of judges, and the courts are reluctant to supervise police or prosecution decision-making through mechanisms such as the exclusion of evidence or by judicial review. Whilst the criminal justice process is formally based on adversarial principles, in practice managerialist objectives of economy and system efficiency are increasingly displacing mechanisms that take account of the disparity of power and resources between prosecution and defence.

This report has identified a number of positive features concerning access to effective defence rights in England and Wales, the importance of which should not be underestimated. Police powers, especially at the investigative stage, are regulated in a way which, overall, has been regarded as successful. In particular, suspects normally have a right to legal advice both before and during police interviews, and such interviews must normally be audio-recorded. Legal aid is, at present, still available to a large proportion of suspects and defendants, and in more serious cases both suspects and defendants are almost always legally represented. There is a cadre of specialised criminal defence lawyers who (currently) make a reasonable living from legal aid income and who are subject to a variety of quality assurance mechanisms. Defendants who believe that they have been wrongly convicted, and who have exhausted their appeal rights, can refer their case to the

---

287 See Home Office 2007b, ch. 5.
288 That is, decisions that 'dispose' of cases by, for example, formal cautions and fixed penalties.

Criminal Cases Review Commission. The Commission has powers of investigation, and can send the case back to the Court of Appeal if it concludes that there is a real possibility that the Court will not uphold the conviction. The ECHR has effectively been incorporated into domestic law, and all public authorities are required to respect Convention rights.

However, the report has also identified a number of major concerns about ways in which access to effective criminal defence is limited, or is in danger from recent or proposed developments.

- Whilst failure by a suspect to tell the police what their defence is going to be may be used as evidence against them, there are limited disclosure obligations on the police and prosecution, particularly at the investigative stage, and relatively weak sanctions. Although recent legislation has increased the pre-trial disclosure obligations on the prosecution, the evidence demonstrates that the police and prosecution routinely do not comply with their obligations.
- A suspect or defendant has no right to require the police to pursue a particular line of enquiry or interview a particular witness, and cannot make an application to a court to require them to do so. Whilst in theory the accused has the power to conduct their own enquiries, they have limited powers (and if legally-aided, resources) to do so.
- Whilst an accused has a theoretical right to defend him/herself, this is not clearly expressed in law, and tends to be focused on the trial stage. In particular, a person has no right to make representations in relation to the extensive powers the police have to impose conditional bail on them prior to charge, nor as to the charge itself. People who voluntarily subject themselves to police questioning do not have to be told that they have a right to legal advice even though they may, in fact, be a suspect.
- About half of persons arrested and detained by the police do not have legal advice at the investigative stage, and probably less than half of those appearing in magistrates' courts are legally represented and, as a result of the re-introduction of the means test, this proportion is almost certainly increasing. The planned re-introduction of means-testing for Crown Court cases is likely to have a similar effect.
- The police and prosecution are increasingly being given powers to impose punishment outside of the court system and this, together with incentives to indicate a guilty plea at an early stage, jeopardise the right to fair trial.
- Defence lawyers are increasingly limited in terms of their ability to act in the best interests of their clients, especially as a result of the introduction of the Criminal Procedure Rules, the use of fixed fees for legal aid lawyers (and, in future, competitive tendering), and the changing attitudes of the judiciary.
- Whilst expenditure on 'law and order' has increased substantially and is very high compared to that in other countries, the government regards

increases in expenditure on criminal legal aid as unsustainable.[289] The focus in recent years has been on capping or reducing legal aid expenditure by reducing eligibility, introducing schemes that limit choice of lawyer, and controlling the work of defence lawyers through contractual mechanisms.

- Police investigative powers have been subject to continual expansion, at the expense of the rights and liberties of suspects. The extensive powers the police now have to impose conditional bail on suspects who have not been charged with a criminal offence are neither subject to time limits nor effective control by the courts. In addition, statistics on the use of police bail are not routinely collected so that effective monitoring, for example, in relation to their use in respect of ethnic minorities, is impossible. There are similar concerns in relation to court bail, in respect of which police decision-making is very influential.

- A high proportion of defendants who are kept in custody pending final disposal of their case (i.e., trial and/or sentence), are either acquitted or do not receive a custodial sentence. This is particularly true for young defendants.

- Changes to evidential rules have compromised the privilege against self-incrimination, and have arguably undermined the presumption of innocence. Failure of the accused to disclose their defence at the investigative and pre-trial stages can, in effect, be used as evidence of guilt. The principle of orality has been compromised by a series of legislative provisions enabling evidence to be given other than in the presence of the accused, and by weakening of the rule against hearsay evidence.[290] Evidence of previous misconduct of defendants, which in the past was generally prohibited at trial, is now admissible in a broad range of circumstances.[291]

- Whilst rights of appeal for defendants have not been reduced, a person wishing to appeal against conviction or sentence imposed by a magistrates' court in respect of a relatively minor offence may well not be granted legal aid and whilst there is no firm empirical evidence it is likely, as a result, that their chances of successful appeal are diminished. However, of greater concern is the fact, identified in section 2.3.6, that legal aid for appeals from the Crown Court which, of course, concern more serious offences, is seriously deficient. Prosecution appeal rights have been increased and in limited circumstances it is now possible for the prosecution to appeal against an acquittal.

- As demonstrated in section 2.4.4, whilst it can be argued that a right to interpretation and translation derives from the common law (and ECHR)

[289] As the Justice Secretary said in March 2008, 'The complexity of the criminal justice system means that it is difficult for researchers and others in the field to isolate the cost drivers behind increases in legal aid expenditure. It is likely that there are a range of interconnected factors, but the fact remains that costs have been rising greatly in recent years and this level of increase cannot be maintained going forward'.
[290] Criminal Justice Act 2003 Part 11 ch. 2.
[291] Criminal Justice Act 2003 Part 11 ch. 1.

right to fair trial, there is no clear, comprehensive, or detailed statutory right applying to all stages of the criminal process. Nor are there adequate mechanisms for ensuring that competent interpretation and translations services are available. Whilst there is a lack of firm empirical evidence, the evidence that does exist suggests that those suspects and defendants who do not have an adequate understanding of spoken or written English suffer a particular disadvantage. This is probably particularly true for asylum seekers and those of uncertain or unlawful immigration status.

Given the widespread availability of legal aid, and because there is a well established section of the legal profession that engages in legally-aided criminal defence work, it is difficult to compare the position of poor defendants with those who are better off in terms of access to effective criminal defence. Whilst it is almost certainly the case that most people arrested and prosecuted (leaving aside traffic offences) are relatively poor, those who are better off nevertheless qualify for legal aid at the investigative stage and in respect of the more serious offences that are dealt with in the Crown Court.[292] Whilst there is some (probably justified) suspicion that rich defendants who pay privately secure a higher level of service from lawyers than those who are reliant on legal aid, there is little evidence that those better off suspects and defendants who could afford to pay privately opt to do so in large numbers. There is a fear amongst many lawyers, and informed commentators, that legal aid contracting and fixed fees are leading to a decline in the quality of work carried out by criminal defence lawyers but as yet there is little, if any, empirical evidence of this.

Criminal law and law enforcement are not equal opportunity phenomena and they apply, and are applied, disproportionately to those who are poor and marginalised.[293] Therefore, in addition to the particular concerns about legal aid identified in this report, to the extent that the conditions for effective criminal defence in England and Wales are deficient, those deficiencies apply disproportionately to poor people. This is particularly the case for poor people from most (but not all) ethnic minority populations since they are much more likely to be treated as suspects and defendants than white people.

6.   Bibliography

Books

Ashworth & Redmayne 2005
Ashworth, A. and Redmayne, M., *The Criminal Process*, Oxford: Oxford University Press, 2005.

---

[292]   Although, as noted earlier, this will change when means-testing in the Crown Court is re-introduced.

[293]   See, for example, Tombs & Whyte 2008, and Karstedt & Farrall 2007.

Auld 2001

Auld, L.J., *Review of the Criminal Courts*, London: TSO, 2001.

Baldwin & McConville 1977

Baldwin, J. & McConville, M., *Negotiated Justice*, London: Martin Robertson, 1977.

Bridges & Cape 2008

Bridges, L. & Cape, E., *CDS Direct: Flying in the face of the evidence*, London: Centre for Crime and Justice Studies, King's College, 2008, available via <http://www.crimeandjustice.org.uk/pubs.html>.

Bridges & Choongh 1998

Bridges, L. & Choongh, S., *Improving Police Station Legal Advice*, London: Law Society, 1998.

Bucke, Street & Brown 2000

Bucke, T., Street, R. & Brown, D., *The right of silence: the impact of the Criminal Justice and Public Order Act 1994*, London: Home Office, 2000.

Burrows, Henderson & Morgan 1994

Burrows, J., Henderson, P. & Morgan, P., *Improving Bail Decisions: the bail process project, phase 1*, London: Home Office, 1994.

Cape 2006a

Cape, E., *Defending Suspects at Police Stations*, London: Legal Action Group, 2006.

Cape & Young 2008

Cape, E. & Young, R., *Regulating Policing: the Police and Criminal Evidence Act 1984 Past, Present and Future*, Oxford: Hart Publishing, 2008.

Choong 1997

Choongh, S., *Policing as Social Discipline*, Oxford: Clarendon, 1997.

Crown Prosecution Service Inspectorate 2000

Crown Prosecution Service Inspectorate, *Thematic Review of the Disclosure of Unused Material*, London: CPSI, 2000.

Duff et al. 2004

Duff, A., Farmer, L., Marshall, S. & Tadros, V., *The Trial on Trial Volume One*, Oxford: Hart Publishing, 2004.

Duff et al. 2006

Duff, A., Farmer, L., Marshall, S. & Tadros, V., *The Trial on Trial Volume Two*, Oxford: Hart Publishing, 2006.

Duff et al. 2007
Duff, A., Farmer, L., Marshall, S. & Tadros, V., *The Trial on Trial Volume Three*, Oxford: Hart Publishing, 2007.

Ede & Edwards 2008
Ede, R. & Edwards, A., *Criminal Defence*, London: Law Society, 2008.

Ede & Shepherd 2000
Ede, R. & Shepherd, E., *Active Defence*, London: Law Society, 2000.

Gibbs & Hickman 2009
Gibbs, P. & Hickman, S., *Children: Innocent Until Proven Guilty?*, London: Prison Reform Trust, 2009, available at <www.prisonreformtrust.org.uk>.

Gudjonsson 2003
Gudjonsson, G., *The Psychology of Interrogations and Confessions: A Handbook*, Chichester: Wiley, 2003.

HM Crown Prosecution Service Inspectorate 2008
Disclosure: A thematic review of the duties of disclosure of unused material undertaken by the CPS, London: HMCPSI, 2008, available via <http://www.hmcpsi.gov.uk/>.

Hooper & Ormerod 2008
Hooper, L. & Ormerod, D., *Blackstone's Criminal Practice 2009*, Oxford: Oxford University Press, 2008.

Karstedt & Farrall 2007
Karstedt, S. & Farrall, S., *Law-abiding majority? The everyday crimes of the middle classes*, London: Centre for Crime and Justice Studies, King's College, 2007.

Keogh 2002
Keogh, A., *CLSA Duty Solicitors' Handbook*, London: Law Society, 2002.

McConville et al. 1994
McConville, M., Hodgson, J., Bridges, L. & Pavlovic, A., *Standing Accused*, Oxford: Clarendon, 1994.

Mirfield 1997
Mirfield, P., *Silence, confessions and improperly obtained evidence*, Oxford: Clarendon, 1997.

Morgan 2008
Morgan, R., *Summary justice: Fast – but Fair?*, London: Centre for Crime and Justice Studies, King's College, 2008.

Plotnikoff & Woolfson 1993

Plotnikoff, J. & Woolfson, R., *Information and Advice for Prisoners about Grounds for Appeal and the Appeal Process, RCCJ Research Study No. 18*, London: HMSO, 1993.

Plotnikoff & Woolfson 2001

Plotnikoff, J. & Woolfson, R., *'A Fair Balance'? Evaluation of the Operation of Disclosure Law*, London: Home Office, 2001.

Sanders & Young 2007

Sanders, A. & Young, R., *Criminal Justice*, Oxford: Oxford University Press, 2007.

Sharpe 1998

Sharpe, S., *Judicial Discretion and Criminal Investigation*, London: Sweet and Maxwell, 1998.

Shepherd 2004

Shepherd, E., *Police Station Skills for Legal Advisers*, London: Law Society, 2004.

Solomon et al. 2007

Solomon, E., Garside, R., Eaves, C. & Rutherford, M., *Criminal Justice Under Labour: an independent audit*, London: Centre for Crime and Justice Studies, King's College, 2007.

Tam 2008

Tam, T., *Barrister Workforce Profile*, London: The Bar Council, 2008.

Taylor 2006

Taylor, C., *Criminal Investigation and Pre-Trial Disclosure in the United Kingdom: How Detectives Put Together a Case*, Lampeter: Edwin Mellen, 2006.

Tombs & Whyte 2008

Tombs, S. & Whyte, D., *A crisis of enforcement: The decriminalisation of death and injury at work*, London: Centre for Crime and Justice Studies, King's College, 2008.

Tonry 2004

Tonry, M., *Punishment and Politics: Evidence and emulation in the making of English crime control policy*, Cullompton: Willan, 2004.

Wilcox & Young 2006

Wilcox, A. & Young, R., *Understanding the interests of justice*, London: Legal Services Commission, 2006.

Zander 2005

Zander, M., *The Police and Criminal Evidence Act 1984*, London: Sweet and Maxwell, 2005.

Chapters in Compilations

Cape 2008
Cape, E., 'PACE then and now: 21 years of 're-balancing', in: E. Cape and R. Young, *Regulating Policing: the Police and Criminal Evidence Act 1984 Past, Present and Future*, Oxford: Hart Publishing, 2008, p. 191-220.

Cape & Hodgson 2007
Cape, E. & Hodgson, J., 'The investigative stage of the criminal process in England and Wales', in: E. Cape et al. (eds.), *Suspects in Europe: Procedural Rights at the Investigative Stage of the Criminal Process in the European Union*, Antwerp: Intersentia, 2007, p. 59-78 .

Downes & Morgan 1997
Downes, D. & Morgan, R., 'Dumping the "Hostages to Fortune"? The Politics of Law and Order in Post-War Britain', in: M. Maguire et al., *The Oxford Handbook of Criminology*, Oxford: Oxford University Press, 1997, p. 87-134.

Jackson 2008
Jackson, J., 'Police and Prosecutors after PACE: The Road from Case Construction to Case Disposal', in: E. Cape and R. Young, *Regulating Policing: the Police and Criminal Evidence Act 1984 Past, Present and Future*, Oxford: Hart Publishing, 2008.

Morgan 2006
Morgan, R., 'With Respect to Order, the Rules of the Game have Changed: New Labour's Dominance of the 'Law and Order' Agenda', in: T. Newburn and P. Rock, *The Politics of Crime Control: Essays in Honour of David Downes*, Oxford: Oxford University Press, 2006, p. 91-116.

Young 2008
Young, R., 'Street Policing After PACE', in: E. Cape and R. Young, *Regulating Policing: the Police and Criminal Evidence Act 1984 Past, Present and Future*, Oxford: Hart Publishing, 2008, p. 149-189.

Articles in Journals

Boon & Nash 2006
Boon, A. & Nash, S., 'Special Advocacy: Political Expediency and Legal Roles in Modern Judicial Systems', *Legal Ethics*, 9(1), 2006, p. 101-104.

Bridges 2006
Bridges, L., 'The Ethics of Representation on Guilty Pleas', *Legal Ethics*, 9(1), 2006, p. 80-100.

Cape 1997
Cape, E., 'Sidelining Defence Lawyers: Police Station Advice After Condron', *International Journal of Evidence and Proof*, 1(5), 1997, p. 386-402.

Cape 2004
Cape, E., 'The Rise (and Fall) of a Criminal Defence Profession', *Criminal Law Review*, 2004, p. 401-416.

Cape 2006b
Cape, E., 'Rebalancing the Criminal Justice Process: Ethical Challenges for Criminal Defence Lawyers', *Legal Ethics*, 9(1), 2006, p. 56-79.

Cape 2007
Cape, E., 'Police Bail and the Decision to Charge: Recent Developments and the Human Rights Deficit', *Archbold News*, 2007, p. 6-9.

Fewkes, Lomri & White 2008
Fewkes, V., Lomri, S. & White J., 'YLAL surveys unmet legal need at court', *Legal Action*, 2008, p. 9-11.

Hodgson 1992
Hodgson, J., 'Tipping the Scales of Justice: The Suspect's Right to Legal Advice,' *Criminal Law Review*, 1992, p. 854-862.

Hucklesby 1997
Hucklesby, A., 'Remand Decision Makers', *Criminal Law Review*, 1997, p. 269-281.

Jackson 2001
Jackson, J., 'Silence and proof: extending the boundaries of criminal proceedings in the United Kingdom', *International Journal of Evidence and Proof*, 5(3), 2001, p. 145-173.

Leng 2001
Leng, R., 'Silence pre-trial, reasonable expectations and the normative distortion of fact-finding', *International Journal of Evidence and Proof*, 5(4), 2001, p. 240-256.

Loader 2006
Loader, I., 'Fall of the platonic guardians: liberalism, criminology and political responses to crime in England and Wales', *British Journal of Criminology*, 46(4), 2006, p. 561–586.

Malleson 1991
Malleson, K., 'Miscarriages of Justice and the Accessibility of the Court of Appeal' *Criminal Law Review*, 1991, p. 323-332.

Quirke 2006

Quirke, H., 'The significance of culture in the criminal procedure reform: why the revised disclosure scheme cannot work', *International Journal of Evidence and Proof*, 10(1), 2006, p. 42-59.

Skinns 2009

Skinns, L., 'I'm a Detainee; Get me out of here', *British Journal of Criminology*, 49(2), 2009, p. 399-417.

Young & Wilcox 2007

Young, R. & Wilcox, A., 'The Merits of Legal Aid in the Magistrates' Courts', *Criminal Law Review*, 2007, p. 107-128.

Official Sources

Home Office 2007a

Modernising Police Powers: Review of the Police and Criminal Evidence Act (PACE) 1984 Consultation Paper, London: Home Office, 2007.

Home Office 2007b

Crime in England and Wales 2006/7, London: Home Office, 2007.

Home Office 2008a

Home Office Departmental Report 2008, London: Home Office, 2008.

Home Office 2008b

Crime in England and Wales 2007/08: Findings from the British Crime Survey and police recorded crime, London: Home Office, 2008.

Home Office 2008c

PACE Review: Government proposals in response to the Review of the Police and Criminal Evidence Act 1984, London: Home Office, 2008.

Home Office 2008d

Home Office Targets Report 2007, London: Home Office, 2008.

Legal Services Commission 2007

Legal Services Commission Annual Report and Accounts 2006/07, London: Legal Services Commission, 2007.

Legal Services Commission 2008a

Annual Report and Accounts 2007/08, London: Legal Services Commission, 2008.

Legal Services Commission 2008b

Statistical Information 2007/08, London: Legal Services Commission, 2008.

Ministry of Justice 2007a
Criminal Statistics 2006, London: Ministry of Justice, 2007.

Ministry of Justice 2007b
Judicial and Court Statistics 2006, London: Ministry of Justice, 2007.

Ministry of Justice 2007c
Statistics on Race and the Criminal Justice System 2006/7, London: Ministry of Justice, 2007.

Ministry of Justice 2008a
Arrests for Recorded Crime (Notifiable Offences) and the Operation of Certain Police Powers under PACE 2006/07, London: Ministry of Justice, July 2008.

Ministry of Justice 2008b
Prison Population Projections England and Wales 2008-2015, London: Ministry of Justice, 2008.

Ministry of Justice 2008c
Judicial and Court Statistics 2007, London: Ministry of Justice, 2008.

Ministry of Justice 2009a
Police Powers and Procedures: England and Wales 2007/08, London: Ministry of Justice, April 2009.

Ministry of Justice 2009b
Statistics on Race and the Criminal Justice System 2007/8, London: Ministry of Justice, 2009.

Ministry of Justice 2009c
Population in custody monthly table April 2009 England and Wales, London: Ministry of Justice, May 2009.

Sentencing Guidelines Council 2007
Reduction in Sentence for a Guilty Plea, London: Sentencing Guidelines Council, 2007, available via <http://www.sentencing-guidelines.gov.uk/>.

Matti Tolvanen

CHAPTER 5 FINLAND[*]

1. Introduction

1.1. Basic demographic information

The population of Finland is about 5.3 million inhabitants. At the end of 2008, about 2.7% of the total population were foreigners. Most of the foreign inhabitants came from Russia, Estonia, Sweden and Somalia. Finnish is the mother tongue for 90.9%, Swedish for 5.4% and Lappish for 0.03% of the population. Apart from the official languages of Finland (Finnish and Swedish), 3.6% of the inhabitants have some other native language. Around 16% of the population are under 15 years of age and the proportion of elderly persons within the population is growing.[1]

The biggest cities, including the capital Helsinki, are located in the south of Finland, as well as most of the population in general. In contrast, the north and the east of Finland are very sparsely populated areas, where the number of inhabitants has been decreasing over the past decades. It seems that this process will continue in the future and it has left its mark on the Criminal Justice System as well; judiciary functions are being reduced in the more rural areas and have been shifted to more densely populated regions.[2]

---

[*]   This country report has been reviewed by Jussi Tapani, professor of criminal law at the university of Turku.
     Maija Helminen, M.Sc., B.A., researcher, has given her considerable contribution to the author of this report.

[1]   Statistics Finland, 2009.

[2]   For example, recently the number of police departments was reduced from 90 departments into 24 departments in the whole Finland. The strongest influence of this reform will be felt in sparsely inhabited regions, in which the area of operation of a single police department continues to grow significantly larger.

1.2. The nature of the criminal justice system

The current Finnish Criminal Code[3] was adopted over 100 years ago in 1889. The Code has gone through several amendments during the past decades and has now been reformed almost completely.[4] Originally, the Code leaned heavily on the ideas of the classical school of penal law; the purpose of the punishment was to be retribution for the offence, and punishment should have a deterrent effect (general prevention). However, soon after the Criminal Code was adopted, the principle of individual prevention began to affect criminal law thinking and practice. As a result, various measures, for example, probation order and special sanctions for young offenders, were introduced. Due to the increase of the criminality in the 1940s, the criminal policy in Finland became more severe, but moderated again in the 1960s and 1970s. For example, the death penalty was abolished by law in 1972. In the 1970s, the criminal policy once again began to emphasize the idea of retribution, and that punishment should be measured in relation to the crime and, thus, not based on personal characteristics of the offender.[5]

A typical feature of Finnish criminal policy and practices has been that different trends and changes in general criminal policy have not been fully realized. In a way, the Finnish legislator has sought to choose the best traits from each trend. Although the leading principle in the Finnish criminal policy is still the idea of prevention and justified retribution, this has not prevented the introduction of rehabilitating punishment, as well as punishment based on characteristics of the individual.[6] The most recent of this type of punishment is juvenile punishment, which was introduced in 2005.

Previously, it has been said that the purpose of criminal proceedings is to find the material truth. In practice, this has in many ways proven to be an unrealistic and even misleading definition of the purpose of pre-trial investigation and criminal proceedings, although it is quite often claimed to be the case, particularly in criminal procedure.[7] Of course, the police and the prosecutor are striving to find the relevant facts of a given case as effectively as is both possible and reasonable. The suspect or the accused, however, never has an obligation to contribute to this purpose. He or she has no obligation to give a statement in his/her matter, and even has no obligation to give true statements (if they give statements at all).

In the pre-trial investigation, the police have an obligation to take into account facts and evidence both against and in favour of the accused. The prosecutor is bound by the principle of objectivity and must act in an impartial and unprejudiced manner. The value of rights affected naturally raises the level of legal requirements. The more valuable the rights affected are, the more detailed shall be the pre-investigation and proceedings in court.

The presumption of innocence has an essential importance in criminal proceedings. An important component of this principle is the *in dubio pro reo* rule. In

---

3   Criminal Code (39/1889).
4   Frände 2005, p. 15.
5   Heinonen et al. 1999, p. 93-98.
6   Heinonen et al. 1999, p. 99.
7   See, for example, Jokela 2008, p. 12-13.

case of any reasonable doubt concerning the evidence presented, the accused must be acquitted. The European Convention on Human Rights (ECHR) is directly applicable in Finnish law and is applied by the court in practice. This has been affirmed and stressed in several interviews we have conducted.

Criminal proceedings are oral. According to the primary rules, the parties may not read out or present to the court a pre-written trial document, nor otherwise present their case in writing. There are only certain written documents allowed at the trial, including expert statements. In addition, other kinds of written documents are allowed as evidence, provided that they are not given in order to be used as evidence in criminal proceedings. All criminal proceedings are usually open to the public, including the pre-trial proceedings *in court*. The pre-trial investigation conducted by the police cannot, of course, be open to the public, and this is highly also recognised by judges and advocates.[8]

The principles of orality,[9] immediacy[10] and concentration[11] aim to ensure the best possible examination of the evidence. In most criminal cases, the main hearing lasts only a few hours, or at most one day. The main hearing of an extensive or complex case may take several days or even weeks. The membership of the court may not change during the proceedings.

Prior to the extensive reform of the Finnish criminal procedure in 1997, the roles of the prosecutor and defence attorney were passive compared to the role of the judge. The main task for the prosecutor was to read the written indictment and to help the judge to find the truth. The judge could procure evidence *ex officio*, although it may have been detrimental to the suspect.

The roles of the judge, the attorneys and the prosecutor changed dramatically when reform concerning criminal matters was enacted. The prosecutor is now an active party to the case, ensuring the implementation of criminal liability and actively promoting the progress of the proceedings. It is the duty of the prosecutor to prove the charge, by procuring sufficient evidence in support of the charge and by presenting it to the court. The court itself is neutral; it does not support or assist the prosecutor. The judge cannot hear a witness *ex officio* if the hearing is to be detrimental to the suspect.

One may say that the main tasks of the judge in a criminal case are to safeguard (formally) a fair trial, and to decide the case by reflecting the evidence that the prosecutor and the attorneys have procured and presented to the court. Communication, co-operation, interaction and a fair trial as a whole are the main features of Finnish criminal procedure.

The victim is a party in criminal proceedings. The right of the victim to prosecute not only covers only the alleged offences, but extends to all categories of offences. Under the new criminal procedure, the complainant's independent right of prosecution has been restricted so that he/she no longer has an independent right to prosecute. This right of the complainant is therefore now *secondary* and can be

---

8   The interviews are referred to at the end of this report.
9   Finish Criminal Procedure Act, ch. 6, sec. 6.
10 *Ibidem.*
11 Finish Criminal Procedure Act, ch. 5, sec. 9.

used only *if the District Prosecutor decides not to bring charges* or decides to withdraw charges during the trial.

The amount of damage caused by the crime is investigated by the police as a part of the pre-trial investigation. The police have the obligation to determine what the victim's civil claims are in a case. The victim may claim damages in criminal proceedings. According to the principle of adhesion, civil demands based on a crime may be – and in practice almost always are – investigated in the course of criminal proceedings.

Civil claims are normally proved and decided as a part of criminal proceedings. At the victim's request, *the public prosecutor has an obligation to pursue the civil claims* cost-free, if this is possible without major inconvenience and if the claim is not obviously ill-founded. This right can be seen in the light of fundamental human rights – a fair trial necessitates an easy and cheap procedure for the victim.

1.3. The structure and processes of the criminal justice system

Finnish procedure law is arranged according to the accusatorial system; the tasks of finding the evidence, prosecuting and deciding a case are each separated. When deciding the case, the court is bound by the arguments of the parties.[12] The criminal process can be divided into four parts: 1) pre-trial investigation; 2) consideration of charges; 3) trial; and 4) enforcement.

The police has the main responsibility over pre-trial investigation. The purpose of the investigation is to determine whether or not a crime has been committed, the circumstances in which it has happened, what is the advantage of the crime, who are the parties in the case, and other important matters necessary to decide the appropriate charge.[13] The person of the enquiry is known as the suspect. The head of the inquiry, who is usually a police officer in command, leads the pre-trial investigation.[14] The police have the obligation to inform the prosecutor as soon as they receive details of a possible crime to investigate, unless the alleged crime is a simple one.[15] The police must also inform the prosecutor how the investigations are progressing and obey instructions given by the prosecutor,[16] if the prosecutor so requires. The prosecutor also has a right to be present at the interrogations,[17] but this right is only rarely used.

The authority conducting pre-trial investigations has a right to use coercive measures in order to gather the necessary information to solve the crime and carry out the investigations. Coercive measures may, for example, be divided between those that limit one's personal freedom and those that are directed towards items. The most important coercive measures that set limitations on personal freedom are apprehension, arrest and remand in custody. Only the court may remand a person

---

[12]   Jokela 2008, p. 22.
[13]   Criminal Investigations Act (449/1987), sec. 5.1.1.
[14]   Criminal Investigations Act, sec. 14.1.
[15]   Criminal Investigations Act, sec. 15.1.
[16]   Criminal Investigations Act, sec. 15.1.
[17]   Criminal Investigations Act, sec. 32.2.

in custody. The use of other coercive measures – wire-tapping and other 'metering' of telecommunications requires authorization by the court.[18]

The suspect has a right to counsel already during the pre-trial investigations, and the police officer has a duty to inform the suspect of this right when he/she has been apprehended, arrested or remanded in custody.[19] Furthermore, the suspect, or counsel, has the right to demand that the police conduct extra interviews and other pre-trial investigative measures that may influence the outcome of the case, provided that these do not incur unreasonable costs.[20] Nonetheless, advocates have been rather reluctant to take an active role during the pre-trial investigation and co-operation with prosecutors has been quite rare.

There are several possible reasons for this, including the fact that the work outside court is not well paid, the work load of lawyers is too heavy, and that the defence counsel are reluctant to show their hand too early (they want to wait and see how the prosecutor evaluates the evidence).[21] This certainly is a frailty in the Finnish defence system, because the absence of the counsel at the pre-trial investigation stage weakens the defence.[22]

The prosecutor decides, based on the evidence provided in the pre-trial investigation, whether or not charges should be pressed against the suspect. The trial in a court can be divided into the hearing of the case and the enforcement stage. Enforcement means that either a judgment will be passed on the accused, or that the accused is cleared of charges.[23] In the trial, the accused person is known as the accused, and if he/she is convicted, is then referred to as a convict.

In Finland, courts dealing with criminal cases are the general courts of law – district courts, courts of appeal and the Supreme Court. A district court is headed by the Chief Judge, and the other judges have the title of District Judge. In certain cases, the district court may also have Lay Judges.[24] The number of district courts was reduced from 51 to 27 at the beginning of 2010.[25]

Criminal cases in district courts are usually dealt with, and resolved by a chairman and three Lay Judges. However, recently the law was amended so that simple criminal cases can be dealt by one legally trained judge sitting alone, if the maximum punishment for the offence referred in the charge is a fine or imprisonment for 24 months.[26] A combination of three trained judges can, however, be used, if it is considered necessary.

Furthermore, since October 2006, it has been possible to decide some minor criminal cases solely on the basis of a written procedure, without a main hearing. Crimes handled via written procedure include drunken driving, theft, embezzlement and assault for which a maximum penalty would be imprisonment

---

[18] Coercive Means Act (450/1987), ch. 1, sec. 9.
[19] Criminal Investigations Act, sec. 10.1.
[20] Criminal Investigations Act, sec. 12.
[21] According to an interview of two prosecutors.
[22] Tolvanen, Kosonen & Helminen, p. 73.
[23] Jokela 2008, p. 5−6.
[24] Code of Judicial Procedure (4/1734), ch. 1, sec. 2.
[25] Judicial System, 2009.
[26] Code of Judicial Procedure, ch. 2, sec. 1 and 6. Previously, the maximum penalty for one trained judge was a fine or imprisonment for 18 months.

of two years. As a result, a relatively large part (30% in 2007)[27] is handled in this manner. The written procedure always requires the consent of the accused, and it is not possible if the crime has been committed by a person less than 18 years of age.[28] According to the judges, prosecutors and defence counsel that we interviewed, the written procedure has not caused problems in terms of the protection of defence rights.

There are six courts of appeal, which primarily deal with appeals against decisions of district courts. In addition, courts of appeal decide at first instance matters of treason and high treason, as well as certain offences in public office. Another task of the courts of appeal is to supervise the operations of the district courts in their jurisdiction on a general level.[29] The members of a Court of Appeal are the President of the Court of Appeal, the Senior Justices of the Court of Appeal and the Justices of the Court of Appeal. A Court of Appeal has a quorum with three members present, although there are exceptions to this rule.[30] A large part of the cases in appeal courts are decided by way of a written procedure.

The final instance in criminal proceedings is the Supreme Court.[31] As well as being the last instance of appeal, the Supreme Court establishes judicial precedents in leading cases, thus ensuring uniformity in the administration of justice by the lower courts. Decisions of the courts of appeal may be appealed to the Supreme Court, subject to the Supreme Court granting leave to appeal. The Supreme Court grants leave to appeal to cases that have a special value as a precedent. This means that it is quite difficult to get the case into the Supreme Court, and the decision of the appeal court is therefore usually the final decision.[32]

According to the principle of immediacy, the court must base its decision solely on what has been presented in the trial. Hearsay testimony is excluded in the Finnish legal system. This refers to the statements by the parties, as well as presentation of the evidence; the court may take into its consideration only the evidence presented in the court session. In addition, the presented evidence must be original and first hand information, and the decision must be made immediately after the presentation of the evidence. In some situations defined by law, it is possible to deviate from the principle of immediacy (for example, if a witness cannot, for some acceptable reason, be present in the trial).[33]

It is the duty of the court to decide what material is to go before the trial court, although providing evidence is task of the parties. Prior to the trial, the court must ensure that the case has been prepared (either by way of written or oral material) in such a way that it can be handled without interruptions, and that all of the evidence will be available at the main hearing. This presumes that the parties are aware of all the evidence that will be presented in the trial. The court also must determine if some of the evidence turns out unnecessary, or if the evidence requires to be

---

[27]   Jokela 2008, p. 451.
[28]   Criminal Procedure Act (689/1997), ch. 5a, sec. 1.1.3.
[29]   Court of Appeal Act (56/1994), sec. 2.
[30]   See Code of Judicial Procedure, ch. 2, sec. 8.
[31]   Finnish Constitution (731/1999), Sec. 99; Supreme Court Act (665/2005) sec. 1.
[32]   Lappalainen et al. 2003, p. 208.
[33]   Jokela 2008, p. 19-20.

supplemented to some extent. For example, a party may attempt to present evidence that has not been part of the pre-trial investigations.[34]

In principle, all witnesses are heard orally in the main hearing, although there are some exceptions to this rule.[35] If the witness cannot appear in the main hearing owing to illness or another reason, or if the appearance of the witness in the main hearing would result in unreasonable expense or undue inconvenience out of proportion to the significance of the evidence, the court may order that the witness be heard outside of the main hearing.[36] In addition, it is possible for expert witnesses to give testimony outside the actual trial.[37] The suspect and defence counsel have the right to be present at such events. It is, however, quite exceptional not to arrange hearings outside the criminal trial.

A criminal matter becomes pending when the prosecutor or complainant has delivered a written application for a summons to the registry of the district court.[38] The court must inform the defendant about the charge brought to the court and ask the defendant to give his/her statement of defence. In the statement, the defendant must indicate whether or not he/she admits the charge, give reasons if he/she denies the charge, and present the evidence which he/she is going to use to indicate his or her innocence.[39]

The court – or a judge, since the preparation is conducted by a judge – must check the application for summons and ensure that the main hearing can be carried out without interruption.[40] If the court notices that weaknesses are present in the summons that may cause a postponement of the trial, the court must inform the prosecutor and suggest that he/she complete the investigations.[41] An example of this is when the defendant or prosecutor pleads to such matter that has not been clarified in the pre-trial investigation. The court cannot advise the prosecutor to obtain additional evidence, if it believes that there is not enough documentation to prove the defendant guilty, as this would be against the principle of objectivity. It can only request those measures from the prosecutor that are indispensable for a successful main hearing.[42]

However, the court can decide that further evidence must be obtained if the evidence may lead to a dismissal of the charge. This idea is based on the principle of *favor defensionis*. The preparation is usually handled without an oral hearing, unless the complexity of matter requires one to be held.[43] The parties are, of course, involved in preparation, which can be done either on paper or orally.

In the summons, the defendant is asked to:

---

[34]   Criminal Procedure Act, ch. 5, sec. 11.
[35]   Code of Judicial Procedure, ch. 17, sec. 32.
[36]   Code of Judicial Procedure, ch. 17, sec. 41.1.
[37]   Code of Judicial Procedure, ch. 17, sec. 51.2.
[38]   Criminal Procedure Act, ch. 5, sec. 1.1 and ch. 7, sec. 1.1.
[39]   Criminal Procedure Act, ch. 5, sec. 9.
[40]   Criminal Procedure Act, ch. 6, sec. 1.
[41]   Criminal Procedure Act, ch. 5, sec. 7.
[42]   Jokela 2008, p. 296.
[43]   Criminal Procedure Act, ch. 5, sec. 10.1.

- state his/her position as regards the claims filed against him/her;
- state the reasons for the position, if he/she objects to the charge or to the other claims;
- specify the evidence that he/she intends to present and state what he/she intends to prove with each piece of evidence, unless it is clear, owing to a confession by the defendant or to other circumstances, that there will be no need for evidence; and
- deliver to the court any written evidence to be relied on.

A preparatory (oral) hearing is to be arranged in the case, whenever necessary, in order to secure the immediacy of the main hearing.

The court must order a main hearing immediately after the preparation is completed.[44] The law obligates the court to handle urgently any case where the defendant is under 18 years of age and is charged with an offence that, under the circumstances referred to in the charge, is subject to a penalty more severe than imprisonment for six months, or if the defendant is in detention, under a travel ban or suspended from public office.[45]

The preparation is led by a judge, in accordance with claims made by the prosecutor and defence counsel. Nowadays, in many minor cases, it is also possible to handle the case in a written procedure, which is conducted more swiftly than normally. The conditions that must be fulfilled in order to use a written procedure are defined in the law but its use is regulated very strictly.[46]

The presentation of evidence commences by hearing the parties, if their stories are used as evidence,[47] and the complainant, tells his/her story before the accused, though the order of events is not set in store.[48] Parties must give their testimony orally, like witnesses.[49] The accused, however, is not under an obligation to tell the truth, or even say anything while being examined.

In some criminal cases, mediation is also an option. If the parties of the case agree to mediation, and they reach an agreement, it may curtail the criminal proceedings in cases of lesser crimes.[50] At a later stage, mediation can lead to non-prosecution, waiving of sentence, or to a more lenient punishment. Mediation is possible at any stage of the criminal proceedings prior to the judgment.[51] The types of crime that are particularly well suited to mediation are assault, theft and criminal damage. Other types of offences can also be dealt with via mediation, if the crime is assessed as eligible.

---

[44] Criminal Procedure Act, ch. 5, sec. 12.1.
[45] Criminal Procedure Act, ch. 5, sec. 13.
[46] Criminal Procedure Act, ch. 5a, sec. 1.1. Conditions for written procedure are explained above.
[47] Criminal Procedure Act, ch. 6, sec. 7.2.
[48] Government Bill 82/1995, p. 82, 85.
[49] Code of Judicial Procedure, ch. 17, sec. 32.
[50] There are, unfortunately, no reliable statistics available. According to the Mediation Offices, mediation is often applied in minor cases.
[51] Act on Mediation in Penal and Certain Civil Matters (1015/2005), sec. 3.3.

However, in serious crimes, the possibility of mediation is usually excluded.[52] Mediation services are provided free of charge by municipal social authorities, under the control of the Ministry of Social Affairs and Health.[53]

Traditionally, the public prosecutor was bound *by the principle of legality*. He/she was obliged to bring charges whenever the evidence was sufficient and the act in question fulfilled the conditions of criminal liability. However, in the 1990s, the public prosecutor's right to waive charges was significantly extended (the *principle of opportunity*) and it can now be said that, in practice, the prosecutor has a great deal of discretion to drop a charge.

More specifically, the prosecutor may waive charges on the following grounds:

- *Pettiness* – The anticipated penalty *in concreto* would be a fine, and the offence is deemed of little significance in view of its detrimental effects and the degree of culpability of the offender (for example, petty theft committed for the first time, or use of drugs); or
- *Youth* – The offender was under 18 years at the time of the offence, and the offence is deemed to be the result of a lack of judgment or negligence, rather than conscious disregard for the prohibitions and commands of the law (for example, joy riding in a group of youngsters).

The prosecutor may also waive prosecution, unless important public or private interests otherwise require, on the basis of the following grounds:

- *Equity* – The trial and punishment are deemed unreasonable or pointless, in view of the settlement reached by the offender and the complainant (particularly victim-offender reconciliation), the actions of the offender to prevent or remedy the effects of the offence (voluntary compensation for the damages), the personal circumstances of the offender (for example, advanced age or weak health), other consequences of the offence to the offender (for example, injuries to the offender him/herself arising when assaulting another), the welfare and health care measures undertaken (particularly voluntary drug and alcohol rehabilitation measures), and the other circumstances; or
- *Procedural economy* – Due to the provisions on joint punishment, as well as the consideration of previous punishments in sentencing, the offence would not have an essential effect on the total punishment (for example, in complex economic or narcotics offences).

1.4.   Levels of crime and the prison population

In 2008, police registered 876,000 crimes, which was 61,000 more than the year before.[54] The rise seems to be due to the increase in traffic violations, which is a

---

[52]   Judicial System, 2009.
[53]   Act on Mediation in Penal and Certain Civil Matters, sec. 5 and 8.

result of more intensive traffic controls. In the last ten years, minor changes have occurred in crime levels; the number of assaults, malicious damage and traffic offences has increased and the number of larcenies and robberies has decreased.[55] Foreigners are 1.3–1.5 times as likely to be suspects as Finnish citizens, based on their proportion to the total population.[56]

The Finnish prison population is one of the smallest in Europe, along with the other Nordic countries.[57] In May 2009, the total prison population was 3,583, the equivalent of 67 prisoners per 100,000 inhabitants.[58] The prison population began to decrease in the 1970s and, since the 1990s, it has been around 3,500 prisoners, sometimes reaching even less then 3,000 prisoners.[59]

The proportion of foreign prisoners has increased. In 2000, the percentage of foreign prisoners was 6.1 and, in 2009, it was 10.3.[60] The percentage of women prisoners is currently 6.8 and, like the proportion of foreign prisoners, has also slightly increased.[61]

As well as prison, around 3,300 people were sentenced to community service in 2007, a similar number to previous years.[62] Community service is an alternative to a prison sentence when the prison penalty would be eight months or less.[63]

1.5. The organization of legal aid

A right to a legal help regardless of one's economic situation is guaranteed by the Finnish Constitution, as well as by international human rights conventions.[64] The system is, in a way, bipolar. In most cases, the right to legal aid depends on the monthly salary of the suspect. However, in many cases (see footnote 73 below), the suspect is entitled to legal help regardless of his/her economic situation. The Legal Aid Act regulates the conditions upon which legal aid can be allotted, as well as also the organization of the legal aid.[65]

Legal aid covers legal advice, necessary measures and representation in court, or other authorities, and release from certain expenses relating to the case.[66] Thus, legal aid is available in all stages of legal proceedings in one way or another, depending on the help required.[67]

[54] Statistics Finland, 2009.
[55] Sirén 2008, p. 9-11.
[56] Niemi, Honkatukia & Lehti 2008, p. 251. Statistics about crimes committed other than by Finnish citizens have been systematically compiled only since the mid 1990s.
[57] Wamsley 2009, p. 5.
[58] The number does not include 86 remand prisoners in police establishments. King's College London 2010.
[59] Statistics Finland, 2009.
[60] King's College London, 2010.
[61] King's College London, 2010; Statistics Finland, 2009.
[62] Statistics Finland, 2009.
[63] Criminal Code, ch. 6, sec. 11.
[64] Finnish Constitution, ch. 2, sec. 21; art. 6 ECHR; art. 14 ICCPR.
[65] Legal Aid Act (257/2002).
[66] Legal Aid Act, sec. 1.
[67] For example in first stage the client may ask help to his or her problem in legal guidance phone service. Until present the phone service has been in test use in part of the public legal
→

Responsibility for legal aid in Finland lies with the Public Legal Aid Office, which is under the authority of Ministry of Justice. The head of the Public Legal Aid Office is the country's leading public legal aid attorney. There are 60 legal aid offices around the country, organised into six legal aid districts. A legal aid director is in charge of each legal aid district.[68]

The Finnish Legal Aid system has a so-called dual nature. This means that legal aid is provided by public legal aid offices, as well as by private attorneys. However, private attorneys give legal aid only in court cases, whereas public legal aid attorneys provide legal aid in all kinds of cases.[69] The dual system originates from the fact that public legal aid offices could not cover the whole country – which still is the case.[70] Private attorneys are advocates or other lawyers providing legal services, while public legal aid attorneys are lawyers employed by the public legal aid offices. A public legal aid attorney must hold a Master of Law degree and have adequate experience in advocacy or adjudication.[71] Public legal aid attorneys are appointed by the Minister of Justice and are subject to supervision by the Finnish Bar Association and the Chancellor of Justice. In addition, many public legal aid attorneys are members of the Bar Association.

To be entitled to legal aid, the suspect/defendant's monthly available means must be less than 1500 Euro or, if the suspect/defendant lives with a spouse, domestic partner or registered partner, their monthly available means must be less than 2600 Euro. Nevertheless, the income of the spouse is not taken into account if the spouses are opposing parties in the case. The means are tested by making a calculation of the funds available to the suspect/defendant per month. The calculation is based on the monthly income, necessary expenses, wealth and maintenance liability of the applicant, his or her spouse, or his or her domestic partner.[72] Legal aid is applied from one of the legal aid offices, whether or not the

aid offices, but from the end of the year 2009 it will be expanded to cover the whole country. In the phone service a person receives directions how and where to find legal advice and assistance. However, direct legal advices are not given via telephone. Legal guidance phone service is free of charge (Legal Aid Act, sec. 3a).

[68] Act on State Legal Aid Offices (258/2002); Ministry of Justice Decree on legal aid districts and places of legal aid offices (13/2009).

[69] Legal Aid Act, sec. 8.

[70] Rosti, Niemi & Lasola 2008, p. 64.

[71] Act on State Legal Aid Offices, sec. 3.

[72] Government Decree on Legal Aid, sec. 6. The basic deductible is calculated as a percentage of the costs of the legal aid, determined on the basis of the applicant's available means. The deductible charts are as follows:

Single person:	For a couple, per person:
available means less than 700 €: 0%	available means less than 600 €: 0%
available means less than 900 €: 20%	available means less than 700 €: 20%
available means less than 1100 €: 30%	available means less than 850 €: 30%
available means less than 1300 €: 40%	available means less than 1100 €: 40%
available means less than 1400 €: 55%	available means less than 1200 €: 55%
available means less than 1500 €: 75%	available means less than 1300 €: 75%

applicant is using public legal aid attorney or a private attorney. In 2008, queuing time for legal aid decisions was, on average, 11.5 days.[73]

The legal aid system was reformed in 2002. Prior to this, it was estimated that legal aid would cover a little less than 80% of the population.[74] By looking at the current average income in Finland, it seems that the estimation was correct. In 2007, the average income was 23,992 Euro per year,[75] which implies that an average person has monthly income of about 2000 Euro. Thus, after deducting necessary expenses from this amount, a person with average income receives legal aid in Finland. The annual overall cost of legal aid is approximately 60 million Euro.[76] This amount includes also civil and administrative cases, and it is not possible to give the amount used only in criminal cases.

1.6.   Legal aid for persons suspected or accused of crime

Legal aid is available for the suspect/defendant at all stages of the criminal process. Nevertheless, legal aid does not cover an attorney's services in simple criminal cases. The case must also be such that prevailing penal practice indicates that the foreseeable penalty to be no more severe than a fine or where, in view of the foreseeable penalty and the results of the investigation of the matter, access by the defendant to justice does not require an attorney. Although the case would be simple, the suspect is still entitled to other legal aid, which involves advice from the public legal aid attorney.[77] Offences regarded as simple are, for example, drunk driving and larceny.[78] In practice, assault has also been held to be a simple crime that may not require legal aid.[79]

The 'simplicity' of the case is always estimated separately in each case,[80] either by Legal Aid Office or by court.

Apart from legal aid, an important part of defence rights is access to a free public defender, who can be appointed in certain cases[81] that are not dependent on

---

[73]   Ministry of Justice, 2009, p. 26.
[74]   Government Bill 82/2001, p. 62.
[75]   Statistics Finland, 2009. In 2007, the average income was 19,648 Euro for a woman and 28,619 Euro for a man.
[76]   Budget Proposal, 2010.
[77]   Legal Aid Act, ch. 1, sec. 6.2.2. Also, legal aid is not allotted if 1) the matter is of little importance to the applicant; 2) it would be clearly pointless in proportion to the benefit that would ensue to the applicant; 3) the pursuit of the matter would constitute an abuse of process; or 4) the matter is based on an assigned right and there is reason to believe that the purpose of the assignment was the obtainment of legal aid (Legal Aid Act, ch. 1, sec. 7).
[78]   Government Bill 82/2001, p. 84.
[79]   Supreme Court Precedent 25:1999. However, in this case, legal aid was granted to the defendant, because there were evidentiary issues that required assistance of an attorney.
[80]   See, for example, Supreme Court Precedent 1996:8, in which a young person with a criminal record was charged with drunk driving and larceny (among other things). Because of the amount involved, nature and motives and the defendant's personal circumstances and criminal record, the sanction was not easy to predict and thus, the court assessed the defendant's legal protection to require counsel.
[81]   At the request of the suspect, a defence counsel is to be appointed for him/her, if: (1) he/she is suspected of, or charged with an offence punishable by no less than imprisonment for four

→

the financial situation of the suspect/defendant. In these cases, a court may even appoint a public defender for a suspect/defendant who would not wish this. The Public defender system is explained below in paragraph 2.2.

In 2008, criminal matters covered about 18% of all cases handled by the legal aid offices, which is quite similar compared to prior years.[82] In court cases, however, criminal matters are the biggest group by number and costs.[83] Criminal cases, of course, quite often require a main hearing in court and thus, more working hours.

In addition, in criminal cases, the clients are many times entitled to legal aid free of charge. One should also remember that the legal aid statistics about costs and numbers of criminal matters include legal aid that has been allotted to the victim of the crime.[84]

2. Legal rights and their implementation

2.1. The right to defend oneself and the right to legal advice and/or representation

According to the ECHR and the Finnish Criminal Procedure Act, the suspect/defendant has a right to defend him/herself at all stages of the criminal proceedings. Thus, legal representation in court is not mandatory in Finland. However, the suspect/defendant has a right to legal advice/representation, and the suspect must be immediately informed of his/her right to use counsel when he/she has been apprehended, arrested or remanded in custody.[85] The pre-trial authority must inform the suspect verbally and record his/her request on the examination record. The pre-trial authority also notifies the suspect of the possibility to apply legal aid, and helps the suspect to contact a lawyer by showing him/her a list of advocates who work in the area.[86] This service is, in principle, available a round-the-clock. And, according to the interviews we have taken, the system is working sufficiently well.

---

months, or with an attempt of, or participation in such an offence; or (2) he/she is under arrest or in detention. (3) A defence counsel is to be appointed to a suspect *ex officio*, when: (1) the suspect is incapable of defending himself/herself; (2) the suspect, who has not retained a defence counsel, is under 18 years of age, unless it is obvious that he/she has no need of a defence counsel; (3) the defence counsel retained by the suspect does not meet the qualifications required of a defence counsel, or is incapable of defending the suspect; or (4) there is another special reason for the same. Criminal Procedure Act, ch. 2, sec. 1.

[82]   18% equates to about 9,300 cases. Ministry of Justice, 2009, p. 24.

[83]   In 2008, 5% of the criminal cases handled by legal aid offices resulted in settlement where there was no hearing in court (Ministry of Justice, 2009, p. 25).

[84]   Rosti, Niemi & Lasola 2008, p. 94, 96. About right to a counsel for a victim see Criminal Procedure Act, ch. 2, sec. 1a.

[85]   Criminal Investigations Act, sec. 10.1.

[86]   Although the suspect/defendant has a right to legal advice and representation, using legal representation in a court is not currently mandatory in Finland and also a close relative may act as a representative if the defendant wants this (Code of Judicial Procedure, ch. 15, sec. 2.3). However, if the court appoints a public defender for the suspect/defendant this person must be a person holding a law degree.

If the suspect/defendant is indigent and cannot afford to pay for legal representation, and the matter is such that it requires legal representation, the suspect/defendant may obtain the services of legal counsel either by virtue of Legal Aid Act or Criminal Procedure Act. The difference between these two laws is that, when a person obtains the services of legal counsel under the Criminal Procedure Act, he/she receives it *free* and the suspect/defendant's financial situation is irrelevant. If the suspect/defendant is not entitled to a free legal representation under the Criminal Procedure Act, he/she may be still eligible for legal aid according to Legal Aid Act, either partially or wholly, depending on his/her income.[87]

A defence counsel appointed under the Criminal Procedure Act is called *a public defender*. He/she is either a public legal aid attorney,[88] an advocate, or if suitable, public legal aid attorney. If an advocate is not available, another person with the degree of Master of Laws who by law is competent to act as an attorney may be appointed as a public defender. The suspect/defendant must be given an opportunity to be heard regarding the appointment.[89] As the right to a public defender may already arise at the pre-trial stage, the pre-trial authority must inform the suspect of the possible public defender, even if the suspect would not want this.[90]

A public defender is appointed for the suspect/defendant either where the court appoints the defender on request, or where it appoints the defender for the suspect/defendant *ex officio*. The court appoints a public defender for the suspect/defendant *on request* if; 1) he/she is suspected of, or charged with an offence punishable by no less than imprisonment for four months, or an attempt of or participation in such an offence; or 2) he/she is under arrest or in detention.

The court *orders* a public defender for the defendant if; 1) the suspect is incapable of defending him/herself; 2) the suspect, who has not retained defence counsel, is under 18 years of age, unless it is obvious that he/she has no need of a public defender; 3) the defence counsel retained by the suspect does not meet the qualifications required for such representation, or is incapable of defending the suspect; or 4) there is another special reason for the this.[91]

Thus, the right to a public defender is bound in with circumstances other than the financial position of the defendant, in order to secure a fair trial. The public defender may be appointed already at the very beginning of the criminal investigations.

If the suspect/defendant is not provided with a public defender under the Criminal Procedure Act but obtains the services of legal counsel according to Legal Aid Act, he/she may choose either *a private legal aid attorney* or *a public legal aid attorney*. Private attorneys are advocates, or other lawyers providing legal services and public legal aid attorneys are lawyers employed by the public legal aid offices.

---

87   Regarding eligibility, see footnote 69.
88   See the following paragraph.
89   Criminal Procedure Act, ch. 2, sec. 2.1.
90   However, in practice, such procedure has apparently been rare (Halijoki 2001, p. 1038-1066).
91   Criminal Procedure Act, ch. 2, sec. 1.

When a person receives legal aid, both the private attorney and public legal aid attorney receive remuneration from their work from the state.

However, in matters other than court cases, legal aid is provided solely by public legal aid attorneys.[92] It seems that, when it is possible, clients tend to use a private attorney in criminal cases; over two-thirds of the legal aid orders made in relation to the private attorneys in the period 2003 – 2005 have related to a criminal matter.[93]

Currently, legal aid covers a maximum of 100 hours of work done by the attorney, but this will be reduced to 80 hours at the end of 2009. The court may, however, still decide that legal aid is to be continued after 80 hours, if there are special reasons in view of the person's need for access to justice and the nature and extent of the case. In this event, the court can set a maximum for the billable hours of the attorney at 30 hours per order, although if necessary, more hours can be allotted.[94]

The basic remuneration for defence counsel is 100 Euro per hour. However, remuneration is dependent on the type of the work that the lawyer does, as well as the stage of the proceedings. For example, the remuneration in an oral hearing in a district court is at least 400 Euro, and at least 600 Euro if the court session lasts longer than three hours.[95] If the case is very difficult, requiring special skills or some extra effort, the fee of the attorney is assessed up to a maximum of 20% higher than the normal fee.[96]

In addition, the Finnish Bar Association monitors the compensation of advocates and public legal aid attorneys to ensure it is reasonable and in accordance with the guidelines of the Bar Association, in circumstances where the remuneration of the lawyer is not based on the Legal Aid Act (for example, where the person is not entitled to legal aid or to a public defender).[97]

At the moment, the qualification requirements for representatives in court are not consistent. This means, for example, that not all lawyers are subject to the same supervision as advocates and public legal aid attorneys, since membership of the Finnish Bar Association is not a precondition to working in a court. In addition, the level of knowledge and skills may vary, although this is probably more in the case

[92] Legal Aid Act, sec. 8.
[93] Litmala, Alasaari & Salovaara-Karstu 2007, p. 37.
[94] Amendment on Legal Aid Act (927/2009).
[95] Government Decree on Legal Aid Fee Criteria (290/2008), sec. 7.
[96] Decree on Legal Aid Fee Criteria, 8.1. The fee of the attorney is assessed at a maximum of 20% higher than the normal fee, if; 1) the task, for reasons not attributable to the attorney, must be performed in a foreign language, under exceptional circumstances, or particularly urgently; 2) the task is exceptionally difficult and its performance requires special expertise, experience and skill; or 3) the responsibility of the attorney is considerably heavier than normal, either because of the scope of the financial interest at stake, or because the matter is otherwise of special importance to the client.
[97] If the client and his/her advocate/public legal aid attorney do not reach an agreement about compensation, the client has a right to take the case to the Disciplinary Board of the Finnish Bar Association, the court, or the consumer complaint board. If the lawyer is not a member of the Finnish Bar Association, or a public legal aid attorney, they can only try to resolve the dispute in court or in the consumer complaint board (Finnish Bar Association 2009a).

of a civil procedure;[98] in criminal proceedings, the competence of the defence counsel is more strictly supervised (since, for example, the court must appoint a public defender for the suspect/defendant).

Recently, the Ministry of Justice appointed a working group to consider the qualification requirements for legal representation in court and how they should be adjusted. In future, the proposed tightening of qualification requirements (a common licence given by a public authority) may mean that only advocates and public legal aid attorneys have a right to represent a client, or that a separate licence is required in order to be an advocate.[99]

The suspect has a right to consult with his/her representative during the investigation stage, as well as during the trial stage. The suspect and his/her representative also have a right to a private consultation if he/she has been be apprehended or is under custody. The meetings or other communication (phone calls, exchange of letters) between the suspect and his/her representative are not allowed to be restricted or supervised.[100]

2.2.   Procedural rights

2.2.1. The right to respond to charges without restrictions on personal freedom

In Finland, the suspect or defendant has a right to answer the charges against him/her without any restrictions being imposed on his/her personal freedom. A system of bail does not exist.[101] However, if securing the pre-trial investigations or the main hearing so requires, the pre-trial authority can argue that the suspect should be remanded in custody or order a travel ban. The preconditions for custody and a travel ban are the same;[102] nevertheless, if the pre-trial investigations or main hearing can be secured in a more lenient way, a travel ban should be used instead of custody. If the suspect violates the conditions of the ban, he/she can be arrested and remanded in custody.[103]

A person can be remanded in custody if he/she is suspected on balance of probabilities of an offence with a minimum sentence of at least two years imprisonment. In addition, a person can be remanded in custody if he/she is suspected on balance of probabilities of an offence with a maximum sentence of

---

[98]   See, for example, Committee Report 2003:3, p. 264.

[99]   Ministry of Justice 2009.

[100] Detention Act (768/2005) ch. 8, sec. 4 and ch. 9, sec. 1. The meetings can be supervised, if there is a justified reason to believe that the law would be breached in an unsupervised meeting. In addition, a letter or other mail delivery from a suspect's attorney may be checked for forbidden items or substances. Nevertheless, the contents of the letter may not be read (Detention Act, ch. 9, sec. 1.3 and ch. 8, sec. 4.2).

[101] However, under the Customs Act (1466/1994) sec. 44, bail can be imposed on a person who has been arrested or remanded in custody, in order to secure his/her appearance in the court. The scope of application of this section is very narrow and it has not been applied in practice (see, for example, Committee Report 2009:2, p. 128-129).

[102] Coercive Means Act, ch. 1, sec. 3.1 and sec. 8.

[103] Coercive Means Act, ch. 2, sec. 8.

imprisonment for at least one year, and it is probable that the suspect; 1) will seek to escape or evade justice; 2) will seek to tamper with the evidence, or influence witnesses or other parties; or 3) will continue criminal activity.

In addition, if someone is suspected of an offence (it does not have to be on balance of probabilities), he/she may be remanded in custody if it is important for impending investigation in the case. In this situation, the above mentioned requirements must also be fulfilled.

The police may apprehend a person for whom an arrest or remand warrant has been issued, or if the conditions for an arrest are present and the situation cannot wait. Such an action must be reported to a commanding officer, or another authority with powers to arrest, who shall decide within 24 hours whether the suspect shall be released or arrested. A decision to arrest must be made by a commanding officer. The decision to detain a suspect is always made by a *court* on the *request of the police or the prosecutor*. The request for detention must be presented to the court without delay, and in any case by noon of the third day from the date of apprehension. The court must decide on the matter within four days of the apprehension of the suspect.

During the investigations, any decision about a travel ban belongs with to the pre-trial authority. During the consideration of the charges, the prosecutor makes the decision about a travel ban and, after bringing the charges, a travel ban is ordered by the court.[104] The court always makes the final decision regarding custody.[105] A travel ban is valid up to the main hearing, unless it has been ordered to expire earlier, or has been rescinded.[106]

The pre-trial authorities (police, Boarder Guards and customs) have tended to use detention rather then a travel ban. In 2008, remand in custody was utilised 2,263 times, and a travel ban 667 times. This is similar to previous years. A travel ban was violated in about 140 cases.[107] It should be noted in this context that total number of criminal cases handled each year by Finnish courts is approximately 70,000.

2.2.2. The right of a defendant to be tried in his/her presence

The presence of the defendant is generally considered to be important when determining a case in court. In the past, the absence of the defendant has often resulted in the adjournment of main hearings.[108] It is now possible to hold and decide some cases, despite the defendant not being present. A precondition of this is that the case must be such that the presence of the defendant is not necessary for its resolution, and the defendant must be informed in the summons about the possibility that the case may be resolved and judged without his/her presence. In

---

[104]   Coercive Means Act, ch. 2, sec. 3.
[105]   Coercive Means Act, ch. 1, sec. 9.1.
[106]   Coercive Means Act, ch. 2, sec. 7. The maximum length of travel ban is 60 days. However, the court can prolong the ban on request of a pre-trial authority (Coercive Means Act, ch. 2, sec. 6.2).
[107]   Statistics Finland 2009.
[108]   Government Bill 82/1995.

this situation, the defendant may be sentenced to a fine or to imprisonment for a maximum of three months and a 10,000 Euro forfeiture.

If the defendant has also given his/her *consent* to the court, he/she may be sentenced to imprisonment for a maximum of six months.[109] Counsel for the defendant has a right to represent the defendant if they themselves are absent, but in practice the presence of the counsel has been rather rare. However, according to the interviews we have conducted where there are more complicated cases, defence counsel usually is present.

Some situations in which the defendant may be tried without his/her presence are, for example, those where the defendant has confessed to the act described in the summons in the pre-trial investigations. In addition, there is a well established practice as to how acts of this kind are to be judged, and the presence and comments of the defendant are considered not to have much influence on the decision. However, the court must consider each case separately to determine if it can solve the case without the presence of defendant. The court must pay particular attention to the nature of the crime and of the defendant. For example, if the defendant is young, the court should think very carefully, as to whether he/she should be tried without being present.[110]

Initially, this procedure was intended only as an exception, but in practice it has been used quite often. About 20% of cases in Finnish courts were heard without the presence of the defendant, following the introduction of the new procedures. However, the practice varied greatly between different courts at that time, particularly in smaller courts.[111] Most of the crimes judged in this way were drug offences, traffic offences and drunk driving.[112]

In 2006, in order to make the main hearings in court more 'expeditious, functional and cost-effective' the written procedure was introduced.[113] This is a criminal procedure in which no oral main hearing is held, but the case is handled and decided via the use of documents. The handling of these cases is faster, compared to normal criminal procedure.[114] Crimes processed via a written procedure are similar to those that can be handled when the defendant is absent from the main hearing.

The preconditions for a written procedure are that; 1) the maximum penalty for the crime described in the summons is two years of imprisonment; 2) the accused confesses to the crime specified in the charges and gives his/her consent to deciding the matter without a main hearing before the court; 3) the accused was 18 years of age or older when the criminal act was committed; 4) the victim, or the injured party, has given his/her consent to the written procedure; and 5) taking

[109] Criminal Procedure Act, ch. 8, sec. 11 and sec. 12.
[110] Government Bill 82/1995.
[111] Alternation was between 40% and 10% (de Godzinsky 2000), p. 33.
[112] De Godzinsky 2000, p. 32-33.
[113] Government Bill 271/2004, p. 22.
[114] In the year 2008, the average time for handling a criminal case in district court was 2,8 months and if the case was handled via written procedure the average time was 1,6 months (Statistic Finland 2009).

account of the matters that have been already clarified in the case, an oral hearing is not considered necessary.

The maximum penalty that can be imposed on the basis of a written procedure is a fine or nine months (conditional or unconditional) imprisonment. Community service is also possible.[115]

The purpose of the written procedure was not to compromise as regards principles of orality, immediacy and centralisation. However, it is obvious that some of the leading principles of criminal process have been waived when forgoing a main hearing in criminal cases. It is also unclear whether an accused use the assistance of attorneys in written procedures, but it is quite likely that this does not happen very often. Nevertheless, in 2008, written procedures were used in 19,958 cases, out of the total number of criminal cases decided in district courts of 66,961.[116] Thus, if about one-third of all criminal cases are solved via a written procedure, in practice it can hardly be regarded as an exception to the main rule of orality.

2.2.3. The right to be presumed innocent and the right to silence

The foundation of all criminal proceedings is the presumption of innocence: a suspect/defendant must be treated as innocent until his/her culpability has been legally proven.[117] An important component of this principle is the *in dubio pro reo* rule. In case of any reasonable doubt concerning the evidence presented, the accused must be acquitted.

The presumption of innocence also includes the rule that the suspect cannot be forced to incriminate him/herself. This rule was fully applied in a recent decision of the Supreme Court.[118] The former practice regarding this rule was vague, but since this decision the interpretation of the rule should be quite clear.

The right to be presumed innocent is closely related to the right to silence, under which the suspect/accused is not obligated to say or do anything that would contribute to determining the case, either in the pre-trial investigation stage, or in the trial. The right to silence binds Finnish authorities via international human right conventions, but, for example, the Criminal Investigations Act does not obligate a criminal investigator *expressis verbis* to inform the suspect of this right.

The right is absolute. However, it is possible that silence may have certain consequences. If the prosecutor has presented aggravating evidence against the defendant, he/she is supposed to give an explanation of what has actually happened.

---

[115]   Criminal Procedure Act ch. 5a, sec. 1.
[116]   Statistic Finland, 2009.
[117]   ECHR, art. 6.2; ICCPR, art. 14.2; Finnish Constitution, sec. 21 and 22; Criminal Investigations Act sec. 7.2.
[118]   KKO 2009:90, decision of 20 October 2009. The case concerned Kari Uoti who was a suspect in criminal proceedings regarding his acts in some companies. At the same time he was obliged to reveal his economic relations to these companies when he was being heard in an insolvency procedure which concerned his private economy. The Supreme Court decided that this obligation was in breach of the principle not to incriminate oneself.

2.2.4. The right to reasoned decisions

The right to reasoned judgements is one cornerstone of a fair trial. This right is guaranteed in the Finnish constitution in the section 21. A judgement must disclose the grounds upon which the act described in the charge is a crime; how the evidence has been gathered and on which grounds the punishment has been imposed.

From the point of view of legal policy, an obligation to give a reasoned decision is intended to promote the following purposes:

- Provide information to the parties of a criminal case;
- Develop legal reasoning, particularly in cases of prejudicial interest;
- Evaluate the effects of legislation and case law;
- Inform the media and the public as a whole;
- Instil trust (confidence) in the courts;
- Control the function of judges and parties;
- Emphasis legitimacy and possibility of democratically controlled courts;
- Encourage predictability and rationality of the criminal justice system

According to the Criminal Procedure Act, the reasons for the judgment are to be stated. The statement of reasons is to indicate the circumstances and the legal reasoning upon which the decision is based. The statement is also to indicate the basis on which a contentious issue has been proven or not proven. The judgment in a criminal case is either a conviction or acquittal.[119]

The legal culture of court reasoning in Finland has experienced radical changes over the past 20 years. Previously, it was quite usual that the court did not reveal its reasoning as to how it had concluded a crime was proven. Nowadays, the situation has totally changed. The basis is an adversarial criminal procedure. After the trial, it is for the court to decide whether to dismiss or uphold the charge, to determine the type and measure of the penalty, and to assess the damages and the other possible sanctions. The court can uphold the charge only on the basis of 'complete proof', and decides the case by reflecting upon the evidence that the prosecutor and the attorneys have procured and presented.

2.2.5. The right to appeal

In Finland, the system of appeal is arranged at three levels. A person tried in a district court has a right to appeal to one of the six courts of appeal. The appeal can be categorized into 'ordinary' and 'extraordinary' means of appeal. In criminal proceedings, the ordinary means of appealing is to *appeal*.[120] An extraordinary means of appeal is a complaint on the basis of a grave procedural error, reversal of a final judgement and granting a new deadline.[121]

---

[119]   Criminal Procedure Act ch. 11, sec. 4.
[120]   Code of Judicial Procedure ch. 25, sec. 1.
[121]   Code of Judicial Procedure ch. 31, sec. 1, 7 and 17.

From a court of appeal, a person can appeal to the Supreme Court, but must first obtain *leave to appeal*. Apart from being the final court of appeal, the Supreme Court establishes judicial precedents in leading cases, in order to ensure uniformity in the administration of justice by the lower courts.

In 2008, the courts of appeal passed judgement in 7,919 criminal cases, of which 53 cases were declared inadmissible.[122] The average length of the proceedings in the courts of appeal was seven months.[123] Annually, the Supreme Court receives about 2,500 requests for leave to appeal, with less than 10% of all requests (including civil matters) being granted.[124] The reason for such a low acceptance rate is that the Supreme Court only grants leave in cases that have a special value as a precedent. This has, however, increased the importance of courts of appeal in legal practice.[125]

2.3. *Rights relating to effective defence*

2.3.1. The right to information

The right to information is crucial for the suspect/defendant, in order to be able to prepare his/her defence. The right arises immediately when a person becomes subject to criminal investigative measures. The manner of imparting the information depends on the stage of the proceedings and must be done in a language that the suspect understands. The information is given orally.

If the suspect has been apprehended or arrested, he/she must be informed of the grounds,[126] in a language that he/she understands. If the police request someone to attend an interrogation, he/she must be told what his/her is position in the investigation. Before commencing the interrogation, the pre-trial authority also has to describe to the suspect the type of act in relation to which he/she is being interrogated.[127]

During the pre-trial investigation, it is not necessary to define the exact accusation that the person is being suspected of, because this may not yet be possible if the investigations are still ongoing and further evidence about the crime may be found. The investigators have a duty to inform the parties about progress in the investigation, as long as this does not impede solving the crime.[128] According to the interviews we have undertaken, there are sometimes problems regarding the giving of information during the pre trial phase.

There is no obligation to provide information about a suspect's/defendant's rights in written form. However, this is currently under consideration. In the future, the suspect or other person in the investigation might have to be provided with a written notice, in which he/she has been informed about the right to use counsel.

[122]   These numbers include those matters that the court of appeal has handled as a first instance.
[123]   Statistic Finland 2010.
[124]   The Supreme Court 2009.
[125]   See, for example, Jokela 2008, p. 670.
[126]   Coercive Means Act, ch.1, sec. 2.2 and 7.1.
[127]   Criminal Investigations Act, sec. 29.1.
[128]   Criminal Investigations Act, sec. 11.

However, if the case is dealt with as a summary penal proceeding, there would be no obligation to provide such a notice.[129] The planned amendment has been proposed following criticism of Finland by the European Committee for the Prevention of Torture, but also because suspects tend not to use the help of attorneys in the pre-trial investigation stage.[130]

In the summons, the defendant must be given detailed information about the charge that has been brought against him/her. The summons must include, among other things, the accusation against the accused, the act for which the charge is being brought, the time and place of commission and other information necessary to specify the act, as well as the evidence that the prosecutor intends to present and what he/she intends to prove with each piece of evidence. If the suspect has been under arrest over 24 hours, the summons must also include the time of arrest.[131] In principle, there is no obligation to inform the accused about the possible sentence that he/she might face.

2.3.2. The right to investigate the case

The suspect and his/her representative have the same right to seek evidence as the pre-trial authorities. It is primarily the task of the police to seek evidence if the defendant asks for it. In that case, it is also financed from public funds. All the evidence that has come up in the investigation must be brought to the attention of the suspect and his/her representative as soon as it does not jeopardise solving the crime.[132] According to the interviews we have undertaken, this exception is used fairly often, particularly at the beginning of the investigation. However, the pre-trial authorities are also obliged to notify the suspect of those matters that are in favour of the suspect, and they must carry out the measures that the suspect or his/her lawyer requests where they have an influence on the matter and do not give rise to unreasonable expenses.[133] The leader of investigation decides on these requests. There is no possibility to appeal in case of denial, but the defendant may ask the prosecutor to order the measures to be done. A similar obligation applies for expert evidence.

The suspect/the defendant and his/her lawyer have a right to attend the interviews of witnesses or other parties involved in the case and, with certain restrictions, to put questions to them. The police can restrict the right to put questions, if they are inappropriate (for example, suggestive or penetrating). Attendance at the interviews may be restricted, if it is considered to harm either the

---

[129] Committee Report 2009:2, p. 75, 247, 316, 623.
[130] European Committee for the Prevention of Torture 2009, p. 5. In the report it was stated that 'access to a lawyer continues in most cases to be granted only at the beginning of the first formal interview by the investigator (which could happen as late as three days after the actual apprehension). The delegation also heard several allegations from persons who were or had recently been in police custody that they had only been able to meet a lawyer after they had signed a statement, or at the beginning of the first court hearing'.
[131] Criminal Procedure Act, ch. 5, sec. 3.
[132] Criminal Investigations Act, sec. 11.
[133] Criminal Investigations Act, sec. 7.1 and sec. 12.

investigations or the solving of the crime.[134] In this case, however, the defendant must be informed upon request about the issues dealt with in the interview, and must be given an opportunity to present questions to the witness via an examiner. This also applies to a suspect/accused.[135]

In Finland, attorneys are little used in the pre-trial stage.[136] This can be seen, for example, from the statistics of legal aid offices that deal with those clients entitled to free legal aid,[137] Which indicate that a lawyer has been used during the pre-trial investigation only nine times during 2007, although, where coercive means have been used, the number is 2,205.

Hence, suspects tend to resort to legal help only if they are subject to restrictions of personal freedom. In these situations, suspects more often seek the help of a private attorney, namely an advocate, rather than of a public legal aid attorney.[138]

Before closing a pre-trial investigation, each of the parties will be given an opportunity to produce a final statement on the material gathered thus far, if this would expedite or assist in handling the case in court. The prosecutor can arrange a negotiation meeting with defence counsel, for example, in order to find out how much oral testimony will be necessary in court. defence counsel has the right to suggest that such meetings be arranged. Thus, defence counsel has an opportunity to influence the course of the pre-trial investigation and the decision-making of the prosecutor.

These negotiation meetings are not to be used for plea bargaining. It is, however, possible to reduce the punishment on account of reconciliation between the offender and the injured person, or due to the offender's attempts to mitigate the effect of his/her actions on the victim and/or society. Reduction of the sentence mostly applies when the suspect helps the police clear up the crime/the effects of the crime during the pre-trial investigation.

It should, however, always be kept in mind that it is the court that decides the sanction to be imposed. The prosecutor can, of course, suggest to the court that punishment be reduced on one of the grounds detailed above.

Overall, it is reasonable to conclude that the guarantees (in law) for effective defence are quite comprehensive during the pre-investigation.

According to the interviews of judges and prosecutors we have undertaken, defence lawyers are, in general, clearly prepared to represent their client in the oral hearing, with some exceptions. Defence counsel also follow high ethical standards and have an honest way of proceeding, which does not, however, imply that they neglect to defend of their clients rights as efficiently as possible.

---

[134]   Criminal Investigations Act, sec. 32.1.
[135]   Criminal Investigations Act, sec. 34.
[136]   For example, the Finnish Bar Association has pointed out this problem and has advised attorneys to attend pre-trial investigations more often (Finnish Bar Association, 2000, p. 67).
[137]   These statistics do not show whether the figures also include those suspects entitled to legal aid under the Criminal Procedure Act, ch. 2.
[138]   Ministry of Justice, 2007.

2.3.3. The right to adequate time and facilities for the preparation of the defence

After receiving the summons, the defendant must be given enough time to prepare his/her defence.[139] The summons, the application for a summons (including the indictment), and the claim are to be served on the defendant. The defendant is also entitled to receive the entire pre trial material at no cost. There are no precise timelines for this, but the court must consider, based on the circumstances in each case, what period of time is sufficient. This has not been regulated in the law, but if the defence needs more time to prepare, the court may set a new time for a hearing.[140]

The defence can, of course, also conduct its own enquiries, interview witnesses, or instruct experts. According to one prosecutor, it sometimes happens that the judge orders the day of the oral hearing (in cases in which the accused person is in custody) without consulting defence counsel. This may cause difficulties for counsel (he/she may already been involved in another case on the same day).

2.3.4. The right to equality of arms in examining witnesses

The accused or his/her lawyer has a right to examine witnesses that they have called, as well as witnesses of the opposing party. Witnesses are, of course, also questioned in the pre-trial investigation, mainly by the police. Defence counsel is always allowed to be present and can also ask questions. The party that has named the witness begins the examination, and after this, the opposing party has an opportunity to examine the witness. If the opposing party is not present in the main hearing, the court examines the witness. After examination by both parties, the parties and the court have a right to ask further questions from the witness.[141]

The presence of the witness in the main hearing may be secured by bringing him/her to the court, imposing upon him/her a conditional fine, or taking him/her into custody. If the witness has failed to appear in the court, or leaves the court without permission, he/she will be imposed with a fine and will be ordered to be brought to the court immediately, or else the hearing will be postponed. The witness can be taken in to custody for a maximum of five days, if it is likely that he/she will not comply with the invitation to testify in the court.[142]

2.3.5. The right to free interpretation of documents and to translation

The suspect/accused has a right to use his/her own language in the interrogation and in court. Depending on his/her native language, Finnish officials are obliged by the Language Act to use either Finnish or Swedish (the official languages in

---

139   Criminal Procedure Code, ch. 5, sec. 8.
140   Jokela 2008, p. 298.
141   Code of Judicial Procedure, ch. 17, sec. 33.1-33.3.
142   Code of Judicial Procedure, ch. 17, sec. 36.1-36.2.

Finland).[143] In addition, Sámi people have a right to use the Sámi language or Finnish.[144] In bilingual municipalities, the language of the interrogation or main hearing is chosen according to the native language of the defendant.[145]

If the pre-trial authority or court cannot arrange interpretation themselves, or if the suspect's native language is not any of the above mentioned, the pre-trial authority or court must provide a free interpreter for the suspect, or attend to the interpretation themselves.[146] The interpreter does not have to speak the native language of the suspect/defendant, but it is enough that the interpretation is done in a language in which the suspect is capable of expressing him/herself. The pre-trial authority or court must ensure that an interpreter is suitable for the task. However, there are no official proficiency requirements for interpreters.[147]

Before commencing the interrogation, the person being interrogated must be asked what his/her native language is, and what language he/she would like to use during the interrogation and in any possible main hearing. Apparently, in the education of the police it has been recommended that, in those situations in which the person being interrogated does not use Finnish or Swedish the interrogation should either be recorded or the main points should be written down.

The actual examination record is written in one or the other of the official languages, but a record made in a foreign language is attached to the Finnish or Swedish version and the interrogated person signs only the version made in the language that he/she has used in the interrogation.[148]

A party to the case has a right to a free official translation of the documents in the criminal process (examination record, application for summons, court record) into Finnish or Swedish.[149] If the suspect speaks some other language, the interpreter or his/her attorney, if they are able to, usually translates the documents for the suspect/defendant. A party to the case can also request the decision of the court to be translated to some other language.[150]

3.   Professional culture of defence lawyers

In Finland, the pre-trial investigation and court work is not a question of directing, but rather are of co-operation. In recent years, the role of the prosecutor in police investigations and criminal proceedings in general has been strengthened, on the basis of mutual confidence and co-operation. It is the task of a police officer to decide the investigation tactics, but at the same time, it is a task of a public prosecutor to ensure that the requirements of a fair trial are already fulfilled in the pre-trial investigation phase.

---

[143]   Language Act (423/2003), ch. 2, sec. 10.
[144]   Sámi Language Act (1086/2003), ch. 2, sec. 4. The Sami language is spoken mainly in Lapland.
[145]   Language Act, ch. 3, sec. 14.
[146]   Criminal Investigations Act, 37.3; Criminal Procedure Act, ch. 6a, sec. 2.
[147]   Helminen, Lehtola & Virolainen 2005, p. 310.
[148]   Helminen, Lehtola & Virolainen 2005, p. 309, 342.
[149]   Language Act, ch. 4, sec. 20.
[150]   Criminal Procedure Act, ch. 6a, sec. 2.3.

One could have some doubts as to how division of power works in real life. Much depends the on personal capacity and readiness to co-operate of the police officers and prosecutors. There have been attempts to develop positive attitudes concerning co-operation during pre-investigation by arranging common training for police officers and prosecutors. The results have been promising: it seems that prosecutors and police officers can work together for a common goal, despite being separate organisations.

This kind of arrangement underlines the need for effective defence for the suspect. The high procedural position of the prosecution office must be balanced with the absolute right to use a lawyer on the side of the suspect. In a state governed by law, defence attorneys also have a central role in implementing and developing the rules of law and the administration of justice, as well as in avoiding and resolving disputes. These principles are expressed in Finnish legal writing and included in the professional culture of defence counsel.

The main rule is that the suspect or the defendant has a right to choose the person to assist him/her. This person does not even have to be a lawyer. According to the rules governing good professional conduct of the members of the Finnish Bar Association (and thus also public legal aid attorneys), the advocate has a freedom to decide whether or not he/she takes the case, unless they have a legal obligation to represent the suspect (as, for example, a public defender).[151] If the advocate considers that he/she is biased in the particular case, he/she must deny the request.

An advocate may not, in proceedings before a court, make statements that he/she knows to be untrue, nor contest information that he/she knows to be true. An advocate does not have an obligation to verify the accuracy of information provided by the client, unless he/she has specific reasons to do so. An advocate may not contribute to the destruction or distortion of evidence. He/she is not obligated, nor entitled, to present evidence or information detrimental to the client against the client's wishes, unless so obligated by law.

Finnish criminal proceedings are accusatorial, which means that the prosecutor has the responsibility to prove the defendant's guilt beyond reasonable doubt, and the court remains quite passive throughout the whole proceedings. The main task of defence counsel is to defend his/her client, not to seek the truth.

It is the duty of the prosecutor to prove the charge, by procuring sufficient evidence to support it, and by presenting it to the court. At the trial stage, defence counsel has the right – and even the obligation – to suggest alternatives to conviction. The duty of the defence counsel is thus to promote the best interests of the client. Nevertheless, this does not mean that advocates can present evidence that they know to be illegal or untruthful; advocates are bound by the ethics of their profession. This means, for example, adhering all of the obligations of an advocate referred to above.

An advocate must be independent and autonomous in relation to the government and elsewhere with the exception of his client. Thus, in order to secure the task of a defence lawyer – defending the client – advocates are also independent from other criminal justice actors. However, the court decides about the fees of

---

[151]   Finnish Bar Association, 2009b.

counsel,[152] and the members of the Finnish Bar Association are subject to the supervision of the Bar Association and the Chancellor of Justice. This does not cause any problems regarding the independence of lawyers.[153]

The Bar Association has approximately 1800 members. In Finland, there are no specified associations for defence lawyers. The main reason for this is that most advocates represent both complainants and suspects (though, of course, not in a same case). Those lawyers who do not belong to the Bar Association are not subject to supervision as advocates. This has caused some problems, for example, as far as the fees, or the quality of work are concerned.[154]

The Disciplinary Board of the Bar Association, which deals with the more important matters concerning the supervision of advocates, consists of a chairman and eight members. Two of these members are elected from outside the profession; before their election, the Ministry of Justice will issue an opinion on their suitability. The Board appoints a number of committees to assist it. The Disciplinary Board decided 312 supervision cases in 2008. It ordered warnings in 55 cases, a caution in 31 cases and a monetary penalty in two cases.

The Finnish professional legal ethics standards consist of several ordinances, specific combinations of instructions and practice.[155] An advocate shall honestly and conscientiously fulfil the tasks entrusted to him/her and shall at all times observe the rules of proper professional conduct for advocates.[156] The main elements of proper professional conduct for advocates have been summarized in these Rules of Conduct, although they do not, however, constitute an exhaustive description of proper professional conduct. Therefore, what has not been specifically prohibited in the Rules of Conduct cannot necessarily be considered as being permissible.

The decisions and other opinions of the executive bodies of the Bar Association include interpretations of proper professional conduct. In addition to legal provisions on the performance of assignments (the latest published version accepted by the Bar Association is from this year), an advocate shall observe proper professional conduct.

Disciplinary proceedings relating to the professional supervision of advocates are also of importance in this respect. The basic requirements established for an advocate by the rules of professional ethics are honesty, professional secrecy regarding confidential information of the client, and the preservation of his/her confidence more generally. An advocate must try to achieve a solution that is most favourable for his/her client.

An advocate's fee for each mandate is determined by the amount and quality of the work required. The degree of difficulty of the mandate and the interest involved are also relevant. As noted above, citizens who are unable to pay legal expenses may be granted legal aid. In addition, legal expenses insurance may cover

---

152   Criminal Procedure Act, ch. 9, sec. 5.
153   Virolainen & Pölönen 2004, p. 395-404.
154   Interview with advocates 1 and 2.
155   See web page of the Finnish Bar Association:
        <www.asianajajaliitto.fi/ asianajajaliitto/in_english/ethics>.
156   Advocates Act (1958/496), sec. 5.1; Rules of the Finnish Bar Association, sec. 35.1.

the expenses of a legal dispute (also in some criminal matters) exceeding the excess payable by the insured.

A binding decision in a dispute regarding an advocate's fee can only be issued by a court. The client may ask the Disciplinary Board of the Finnish Bar Association for a recommendation regarding the fee. According to information provided by the Disciplinary Board, advocates normally comply with these recommendations. Disputes can also be taken up by a consumer complaint board, which likewise only issues recommendations.

Advocates, prosecutors and judges are considered to be similarly valued legal professions. This means that being an advocate is not understood as 'a stepping stone' towards a career as a prosecutor or judge. There is a transition among the professions, but this does not occur only in one direction; advocates may become judges or prosecutors, and prosecutors and judges may become advocates.[157]

4. Political commitment to effective criminal defence

Criminal policy in Finland covers social decision making concerning crime and the discussion attached thereto. Criminal policy is a form of guidance by which we attempt to promote the attainment of the goals of other policies accepted in a given society. Criminal political considerations, and the general principles of criminal law, may restrict the use of criminal justice as an instrument of economic policy, for example, even though all the tools would be effective as far as economic policy is concerned. The way in which criminal policy is defined has also consequences regarding defence in criminal matters. The Government is not attempting to reduce the crime rate as such, but rather the total cost associated with criminality. According to a generally accepted dogma, it is necessary to guarantee the legal rights of a person suspected or accused of crime.

The goals of criminal policy can be defined as follows: 1) to minimise the harm and other costs of both crime and the controlling of crime; and 2) to share the costs of protecting basic rights and justice in general. The basis of this policy is the fact that behaviour deviating from the norm cannot be completely abolished at a reasonable cost. When reducing the costs, we have to consider the goal and the objectives of, for example, economic policy, and the costs of making the economy more effective on the one hand and the costs incurred when regulations are broken on the other. Both preventive measures and the breaking of the regulations impose significant costs on society. These are the leading principles for criminal policy in Finland, not only in theory, but also in legislative and court practice.

Derived from basic human rights, the state has the obligation to protect its citizens from violations of their rights. In the process of criminalisation, the state has to respect basic rights by refraining from imposing too extensive restrictions on the freedom to act. In a wider perspective, the state must guarantee the exercise of basic rights. The principles of criminalisation must be defined on the basis of fundamental human rights.

---

[157]   See, for example, Ohisalo 2008, p. 38-49.

The starting point in Finnish criminal policy is the pragmatic and rational justification of criminal law. Criminal law is necessary to safeguard organised society, safety and our life together in general. Criminal law can be used a) only to protect rightful advantages; b) on the assumption that no other mechanism is available that is more morally acceptable, as effective as criminal law and as viable at a more moderate cost; and c) the advantages obtainable by punishment are greater than the disadvantages brought by them.

These criminalisation principles are political gauges by which an attempt is made to define the factual criteria of behaviour threatened by punishment. The issue regarding the criminalisation principles is both when to prescribe something as punishable, and how the conditions of penal responsibility are generally defined. The starting point of criminalisation should thus be the protection of rightful advantages. If it can be proved that there is no need for rightful protection, criminalisation should be abandoned.

The central point is perhaps not deterrence, but trust. By imposing punishment, the state tries to tell citizens that no-one can act against legal rules without consequences. Social life is crucially based on mutual trust. If someone betrays that trust, a sanctioning system is required. Punishment demonstrates that anyone acting against the common rules has to pay for his/her actions. A summary of the main features of the Finnish criminal justice system produces the following list of 'slogans':[158] humanity; basic rights; rationality; pragmatism; prevention; integration; trust; adversarial procedure; and cost/benefit calculation.

There are also some threats, as far as legal policy is concerned. The main concern: management-thinking; zero tolerance; increasing prison population; efficiency considerations; budget cuts; over sanctioning; international crime; and the fight against terrorism.

In Finland, the constitutional protection of fundamental rights is based on a wide understanding of those rights that deserve protection including, in addition to traditional civil and political rights, economic, social, cultural and environmental rights as well. Section 8 of the Constitution (731/1999), and chapter 3, section 1 of the Criminal Code (39/1889), define the principle of legality in criminal matters, including the prohibition against retroactive criminal laws. According to Section 22 of the Constitution, it is a constitutional obligation of all public authorities – including the judiciary – to guarantee the observance of constitutional rights and internationally recognized human rights. The Finnish criminal justice system relies heavily on principles of equality, humanity and legality, which are based on human and constitutional rights provided in the Finnish Constitution.

The principle of equality demands that everyone should be treated in the same way, without unjustified discrimination in the face of the law – all cases falling within a specific category are dealt similarly.[159] The respect for humanity requires that no one shall be sentenced to death, tortured or otherwise treated in a manner violating human dignity.[160] Legality in criminal cases means that no one shall be

---

[158]   See, for example, Tapani & Tolvanen 2008, p. 21-109.
[159]   Finnish Constitution, sec. 6.
[160]   Finnish Constitution, sec. 7.

found guilty of a criminal offence, or be sentenced to a punishment, on the basis of an act that, which has not been determined punishable by Law at the time of its commission.[161]

Under the influence of the section 21 of the Constitution, and article 6 of the ECHR, the principle of the right to a fair trial is fully accepted in Finland. Both provisions have direct effect in Finnish court proceedings, and the jurisprudence of the Finnish Supreme Court and the ECtHR is an important source of the fair trial rights in criminal proceedings, in cases where the domestic legislation gives room for several interpretations. The Constitution guarantees a fair trial for everybody as laid down by law.

In addition, the victim or the injured party has the right to a fair trial, which means that the Finnish Constitution goes in some respects even further than the ECHR (which only regulates the rights of the defendant). In Finland, fair trial rights extend beyond court proceedings and cover the proceedings as a whole, from the pre-trial investigation to the enforcement of punishment.

A large part of Finnish population is entitled to legal aid in criminal matters. In addition, if a person is held in custody, he/she always has a right to counsel in the pre-trial stage and in court. This right does not depend on how much the suspect is earning or how rich he/she is, and the state always pays the fees of counsel. In Finland, all lawyers can act as public defenders, not only those who work in public legal aid offices. There are currently over 2000 lawyers providing public defender services, a significant number given that the total population in Finland is approximately five million inhabitants. The territorial distribution of defence lawyer services is also guaranteed. It is therefore reasonable to conclude that the political commitment to effective criminal defence is quite strong.

5.   Conclusions

Let us first list the main positive features in the Finnish legal system regarding effective defence rights.

The basic rights of individuals suspected of a crime are guaranteed and defined in an appropriate way in the legislation of Finland. The suspect has the right to legal counsel during the pre-trial investigation, right from the very beginning. The police must inform the suspect of his/her right to defence counsel. The accused always has the right to legal counsel during the trial. An advocate must be independent and autonomous in relation to the government and elsewhere, with the exception of his/her client.

Defence counsel has the right to attend the investigation and to be present during police questioning of any other parties, unless there are special investigative reasons for excluding him/her. The suspect's counsel also has the right to demand that the police conduct additional interviews, as well as other pre-trial investigative measures that may influence the outcome of the case, provided that these do not incur unreasonable costs.

---

[161]   Finnish Constitution, sec. 8; Criminal Code ch. 3, sec. 1.

A suspect and defence counsel have the right to be informed of the outcome of the pre-trial investigation as soon as possible, without hindering the criminal investigation. Before closing a pre-trial investigation, each of the parties will be given the opportunity to produce a final statement on the material gathered thus far, if this would expedite or assist in the handling of the case in court. In general, final statements are written by defence counsel.

The new Finnish criminal procedure system places an emphasis on the prosecutor and defence counsel. The main tasks of the judge in a criminal case are to safeguard (formally) the right to a fair trial, and to decide the case by reflecting on the evidence that the prosecutor and the attorneys have procured and presented to the court. Witnesses are examined by the parties. Defence counsel has the right to present his/her own witnesses, and also to cross-examine witnesses called by the prosecution. The main task of defence counsel is to defend his client, not to seek the truth. It is the duty of the prosecutor to prove the charge by procuring sufficient evidence to support it, and by presenting it to the court. At the trial stage, defence counsel has the right – and even the obligation – to suggest alternatives to conviction.

Concerning some very serious crimes, the court can also make decide to allow the police to undertake technical surveillance – even at the home of the suspect. When this happens, the court will nominate a defence lawyer to supervise the work of the police during surveillance. The lawyer is not allowed to be in contact with the suspect in these cases. The lawyer cannot function as defence counsel in a case where he has been working as a supervisor of the technical surveillance.

The suspect receives details of the information procured by such technical surveillance at the very latest when the police send the documents to the prosecutor in order to consider the charges. It should be considered that such an arrangement is also applicable to other secret coercive methods.

In both criminal proceedings and the pre-trial investigation, the defendant is, under certain circumstances, entitled to a public defender regardless of his financial situation. A public defender will be appointed on request for a suspect of an aggravated offence and for a person who has been arrested or detained. The court may, on its own initiative, appoint a public defender for a person under 18 years of age or a person incapable of seeing to his/her own defence.

There are, however, some unsatisfactory practices in the Finnish legal system that need further consideration. In general, it is problematic that police investigative powers have been expanding, which has usually meant a reduction of the rights and liberties of suspects. It seems highly probable that this kind of development is still continuing. Particularly vulnerable areas are surveillance, and the use of covert human intelligence sources (private informants, policemen as covert informants).

The use of covert methods also raises the question of the use of illegal obtained evidence. As a rule, relevant evidence is admissible even though it has been obtained illegally. This rule is, however, applicable only in cases involving serious crime (for example, murder, drug trafficking, money laundering). In minor cases, it is probable that the court will exclude illegally obtained evidence. Of course, the court must reflect on the importance of criminal liability in a given case and how seriously the police have breached the rules when obtaining evidence. It should be stressed that the court always has discretion, having regard to all circumstances of a case, to exclude evidence, if it would operate unfairly against an accused.

Defence counsel cannot, according to Finnish law, make any application for a court order in order to force certain action (during the pre-trial investigation). He/she can, however, ask the prosecutor or higher police official to give such an order, if the leader of the investigation does not accept a request made by defence counsel for a certain investigative measure to be undertaken. It is worth considering whether the court should have powers to order the police to perform necessary investigative measures when required by defence counsel.

Another issue that needs further consideration in the future is the so called privilege against self-incrimination. As noted above (1.2), the suspect/accused never has an obligation to contribute to finding relevant facts in a case. He/she has no obligation to give a statement in the matter – he/she even has no obligation to give true statements if he/she decides not to be silent. There are, however, some obligations to give true statements, for example, to taxation officials during an insolvency procedure and as a debtor in bankruptcy proceedings. This obligation may cause problems if the police want to use the same facts provided under this obligation as evidence in criminal investigation. The recent practice of the Supreme Court of Finland tends to prefer excluding this kind of evidence in criminal matters.[162] The practice is, however, still rather vague and remains to be seen how far the privilege against self-incrimination will develop.

The Government is already planning to further reform law, which would make it possible for the accused person to appeal to a higher court in order to get his/her case proceeded with without unreasonable delay. The state would have a responsibility to pay compensation if the process were then to take an unreasonably long time. The ECtHR has repeatedly criticized Finland for not guaranteeing legal remedies against unreasonable delay of criminal proceedings.[163]

As noted above (2.1), the qualification requirements for representatives in court are not consistent and not all lawyers are subject to the same supervision as advocates and public legal aid attorneys, since membership of the Finnish Bar Association is not a precondition to work in a court. This may cause problems since, according to our research (interviews), the knowledge and skills may vary as far as so called 'wild' attorneys are concerned. The client does not always understand the difference between members of the Bar and other lawyers. If the wild attorney does not handle the case professionally and in an appropriate manner, this may negatively tarnish the reputation of the legal profession in general, and thus weaken trust of legal system as a whole.

According to procedural law, a person involved in a criminal case has a right to a free interpreter if he/she does not speak Finnish or Swedish. There have, however, been problems in cases in which the accused person speaks a very uncommon language (for example, a rare Indian dialect), and does not speak or even understand other languages. The court has little possibility to control the real

---

[162] See, for example, precedents of the Supreme Court 2009:27 and 2002:116.

[163] See, for example, ECtHR 9 December 2008, *Danker* v. *Finland*, No. 39543/04, ECtHR 13 January 2009, *Sorvisto* v. *Finland*, No. 19348/04, ECtHR 9 December 2008, *Jussi Uoti* v. *Finland*, No. 43180/04, and ECtHR 9 January 2007, *Uoti* v. *Finland*, No. 61222/00.

skills of a person who is suggested as an interpreter and there are no written qualifications for interpreters.

A foreigner as an accused person, of course, usually has a right to legal aid and a defence attorney paid by the state. It is, however, important in criminal cases that the court has a possibility to hear the statement of the accused person personally, and this is not possible if the defendant does not have proper translation services available.

As noted above (2.1), according to Finnish law, all criminal proceedings are as a rule public. The court has, however, the power to exclude the public partly or totally from the hearing in cases defined by law. The courts have had some tendency to apply the law in a way that in fact restricts the public nature of court hearings. This is rather apparent as far as pre-trial proceedings involving coercive measures, the use of which require court approval, are concerned, but the courts have occasionally also restricted public access in main hearings, even if it was not necessary for reasons of privacy and despite the important public interest in a particular case.

Despite the existence of free legal aid and public defence, defence is perhaps the weakest part of Finnish criminal procedure. Advocates have been rather reluctant to conceive an active role during the pre-trial investigation, and co-operation with prosecutors has taken place on an occasional basis. According to Haavisto,[164] it has also been difficult for some judges to understand the new role (since the beginning of 1990s) of defence counsel in the adversarial criminal procedure. Judges should always keep in mind that defence counsel must act only in the interests of the accused.

At the same time, advocates are bound by the ethics of their profession. Defence counsel is bound by the Criminal Procedure Act and it is not his/her task to cause undue delay in the process. The situation is, however, slowly changing. Advocates are beginning to understand just how crucial it is for the defence to outline alternative hypotheses from the outset (during the preliminary investigation), and judges have now realized that the main task of defence counsel is to defend her/his client. It is the task of the prosecutor to ensure that criminal liability is correctly attributed and to support the state authority in criminal cases (Act on Public Prosecutors, Section 1).

Finland thus represents a system of criminal procedure based on co-operation and on mutual trust. This kind of system is, on the one hand, flexible but, on the other, also rather vulnerable. Very much depends on the personal capacities and ability of actors in a given case. With united efforts, shared values and a common professional education, it is possible to have an efficient and, at the same time fair, criminal procedure. The results of this report give quite strong support to this assumption.

It is, however, reasonable to ask if the situation really is so unproblematic (as stated in legal writing), or are we simply lacking sufficient facts and research data to properly evaluate the situation of defence rights as a whole. Comprehensive data collection and reliable information systems should be essential prerequisites for

---

[164]   Haavisto 2002.

developing the necessary self-awareness and understanding of legal policy, criminal justice systems and procedure and their outcomes. All in all, there is an urgent need for a reliable empirical study regarding the realization of defence rights in the Finnish legal system.

6.   Bibliography

Books

de Godzinsky 2000
de Godzinsky, V., *Tietoa uudesta rikosasioiden oikeudenkäynnistä, Oikeuspoliittisen tutkimuslaitoksen tutkimustiedonantoja*, Helsinki: Oikeuspoliittinen tutkimuslaitos, 47, 2000.

Finnish Bar Association 2000
Finnish Bar Association 2000, *Suomen asianajajaliiton oikeusturvaohjelma 2000*, Helsinki: Suomen asianajajaliitto, 2000.

Frände 2005
Frände, D., *Yleinen rikosoikeus*, Helsinki: Edita Publishing Oy, 2005.

Haavisto 2002
Haavisto, V., *Court Work in Transition*, Helsinki: University of Helsinki. Department of Education.. 2002.

Heinonen et al. 1999
Heinonen, O., Koskinen, P., Lappi-Seppälä, T., Majanen, M., Nuotio, K., Nuutila, A.M., Rautio, I., *Rikosoikeus*, Juva: WSOY Lakitieto, 1999.

Helminen, Lehtola, & Virolainen 2005
Helminen, K., Lehtola, K. & Virolainen, P., *Esitutkinta ja pakkokeinot*, Helsinki: Talentum Media Oy, 2005.

Jokela 2008
Jokela, A., *Rikosprosessi*, Jyväskylä: Talentum Media Oy, 2008.

Lappalainen et al. 2003
Lappalainen, J., Frände, D., Koulu, R., Niemi-Kiesiläinen, J., Rautio, J., Sihto, J., Virolainen, J., *Prosessioikeus*, Juva: WSOY Lakitieto, 2003.

Litmala, Alasaari & Salovaara-Karstu 2007
Litmala, M., Alasaari, K. & Salovaara-Karstu, C., *Oikeusapu-uudistuksen seurantatutkimuksen osaraportti II. Oikeuspoliittisen tutkimuslaitoksen tutkimustiedonantoja 77*, Helsinki: Oikeuspoliittinen tutkimuslaitos, 2007.

Ohisalo 2008

Ohisalo, J., J´accuse! Kahden syyttäjän näkemyksiä syyttäjätoiminnasta. Teoksessa: Jussi Ohisalo ja Matti Tolvanen (toim.) Consilio manuque, Joensuu: Department of Law. 2008, p. 38-44.

Rosti, Niemi & Lasola 2008

Rosti, H., Niemi, J. & Lasola, M., *Legal Aid and Legal Services in Finland*, Research report No. 237, Helsinki: National Institute of Legal Policy, 2008.

Tapani &Tolvanen 2008

Tapani, J. & Tolvanen, M., *Rikosoikeuden yleinen osa*, Helsinki: Vastuuoppi, 2008.

Virolainen & Pölönen 2004

Virolainen, J. & Pölönen, P., *Rikosprosessin osalliset, Rikosprosessioikeus II*, Porvoo: WSOY, 2004.

Wamsley 2009

Wamsley, R., *World Prison Population List*, London: King's College London – International Centre for Prison Studies, 2009.

Chapters in Compilations

Niemi, Honkatukia & Lehti 2008

Niemi, H., Honkatukia, P. & Lehti, M., 'Ulkomaalaiset, maahanmuuttajat ja rikollisuus', in: H. Niemi, P. Honkatukia and M. Lehti, *Rikollisuustilanne 2007*, Helsinki: Oikeuspoliittinen tutkimuslaitos.. 2008, p. 249-277.

Sirén 2008

Sirén, R., 'Rikollisuuden rakenne ja kehitys', in: *Rikollisuustilanne 2007*, Helsinki: Oikeuspoliittinen tutkimuslaitos. 2008, p. 9-14.

Articles in Journals

Halijoki 2001

Halijoki, J., 'Epäillyn asema rikosprosessuaalisen vapaudenriiston yhteydessä', *Defensor Legis*, 2001, p. 203-227.

Official Sources

Ministry of Justice 2009

Oikeusaputoimistojen toimintakertomus vuodelta 2008. Toiminta ja hallinto 2009:7. Helsinki: Oikeusministeriö, 2009.

Internet Sources

Judicial System: <http://www.oikeus.fi> (12.1.2009).

King's College London, World Prison in Brief, Europe, Finland, 2010, <http://www.kcl.ac.uk/depsta/law/research/icps/worldbrief/wpb_country.php ?country=137>.

Ministry of Justice: <http://www.om.fi> (13.11.2009).

Police: <http://www.poliisi.fi> (13.1.2009).

Statistics Finland: <http://www.stat.fi> (21.1.2010).

The Supreme Court: <http://www.kko.fi/27080.htm> (16.1.2009).

The Finnish Bar Association: <http://www.asianajajat.fi> (15.1.2009).

The Office of the Prosecutor General: <http://www.vksv.oikeus.fi> (14.1.2009).

Unpublished sources

Tolvanen, M., Kosonen, H. & Helminen, M., *Rethinking European Criminal Justice, Country Report on Finland*, Unpublished report, 2009.

Interviews (11 persons)

State Prosecutor.

District Prosecutors 1 and 2.

Advocates 1 and 2.

District Court Judges 1 and 2.

Judge, Court of Appeal.

Police Officers 1, 2 and 3.

Cases

Supreme Court Precedent KKO 25:1999.

Supreme Court Precedent KKO 1996:8.

Supreme Court Precedent KKO 2009:27.

Supreme Court Precedent KKO 2002:116.

ECtHR 9 January 2007, *Uoti* v. *Finland*, No. 61222/00.

ECtHR 9 December 2008, *Danker* v. *Finland*, No. 39543/04.

ECtHR 9 December 2008, *Jussi Uoti* v. *Finland*, No. 43180/04.

ECtHR 13 January 2009, *Sorvisto* v. *Finland*, No. 19348/04.

Legislation

Act on Mediation in Penal and Certain Civil Matters 1015/2005.

Act on State Legal Aid Offices 258/2002.

Advocates Act 1958/496.

Amendment on Legal Aid Act 927/2009.

Code of Judicial Procedure 4/1734.

Coercive Means Act 450/1987.

Court of Appeal Act 56/1994.

Criminal Investigations Act 449/1987.

Criminal Code 39/1889.

Criminal Procedure Act 689/1997.

Customs Act 1466/1994.

Detention Act 768/2005.

Finnish Constitution 731/1999.

Government Decree on Legal Aid Fee Criteria 290/2008.

Language Act 423/2003.

Legal Aid Act 257/2002.

Ministry of Justice Decree on legal aid districts and places of legal aid offices 13/2009.

Sámi Language Act 1086/2003.

Supreme Court Act 665/2005.

Other official sources

Government Bill 271/2004.

Government Bill 82/1995.

Committee Report KM 2003:3, *Tuomioistuinlaitoksen kehittämiskomitean mietintö*, Helsinki: Oikeusministeriö, 2003.

Committee Report KM 2009:2, *Esitutkinta- ja pakkokeinotoimikunnan mietintö*, Helsinki: Oikeusministeriö, 2009.

Other sources

Ministry of Justice 2007, Maksuton oikeudenkäynti avustajaryhmittäin 2007, käräjäoikeudet.

European Committee for the Prevention of Torture report on its fourth visit to Finland, Council of Europe, 2009.

Pascal Décarpes

CHAPTER 6 FRANCE[*+]

1.   Introduction

1.1.   *Basic demographic information*

As at 1 January 2008, there were approximately 63,750,000 persons living in France, making it the second largest country in Europe. In 2007, the population increased by 0.55% (340,000 additional) inhabitants. This was made up by net immigration of 70,000, plus a natural increase by the birth of 270,000 – the natural growth is also the second fastest in Europe behind Ireland.

At the same time, an important factor of the social development over the last century has been the migration from countryside to cities. This phenomenon can be observed all around the world. This growing urbanity is thought to be a factor for the rising crime rate against persons[1] and robberies, particularly in areas with a high population density.[2]

In that context, the number of young people has remained stable over the last ten years. In 2008, 15.3 million people under 20 lived in France.[3] However, there is a long term trend showing a slight decrease of the proportion of youth in the French population, from 32.2% in 1962 to 24% in 2008 (European average 21.9%). On the other hand, 16.4% of the population are older than 65 (European average 16.9%).

The proportion of immigrants in/to France has not changed much since the 1980s, due to stricter immigration laws. There were 4 million immigrants (persons

---

[*]   This country report has been reviewed by Jackie Hodgson, professor of law Universtity of Warwick.

[+]   The report was written with substantial contributions from Morgane Landel, Associate Legal Officer at the Open Society Justice Initiative and Anna Ogorodova, PhD researcher at the Maastricht University.

[1]   The French term *aggressions* covers robbery, assault, insults, etc.

[2]   The risk for a Parisian to be attacked is four times higher than for someone living in the countryside; INSEE (*Institut National de la Statistique et des Études Économiques*, National Institute for statistics and economic studies), INSEE Première, No. 1124, May 2007.

[3]   This data is issued by the INED (*Institut national d'études démographiques*, National Institute for demographic studies), <http://www.ined.fr/fr/pop_chiffres/france/>.

born abroad) in 1982, 4.3 million in 1999 and 4.9 million in 2006 (an increase of 22%, whereas the whole population increased by 15%). Specifically, 1.8 million are from Europe, 1.4 million from North Africa, 500,000 from elsewhere in Africa and 600,000 from Asia. On the other hand, in 2005 the number of foreigners (persons with another citizenship) remained stable at 2.9 million. It should be noted in this regard that 41% of immigrants obtained French citizenship.

These figures represent a continuous and integrated population that is not considered as a potentially criminal one, but more as a 'second-class-population' that is overrepresented in low socio-economic groups. One viewpoint is to blame foreigners for crime, based on a supposed *communautarisme*, where foreign persons refuse to integrate into society and hence do not respect the French Republic.

An opposite issue is mixed marriage. In 1973, the proportion of mixed marriage was only 5%, but it has increased to 16% in 2002 and 14.3% in 2006, which speaks of a relative but increasing integration.

1.2.   The nature of the criminal justice system[4]

The French criminal justice system is a mixture of inquisitorially rooted procedures with increasingly accusatorial aspects. This is defined in the preliminary article of the French Criminal Procedure code as a procedure which must be *contradictoire*.[5] Historically, the preliminary police investigation and the investigating judge (*Juge d'instruction*) were striking examples of a system where one figure conducted an investigation on his/her own and in relative secrecy. However, as a response to this concentration of power, in 1897, the defence lawyer was given a role during the investigation, by allowing him/her to consult the case file before his/her client's interrogation and to be present during the interrogation.[6] In addition, in later stages of the criminal process, many adversarial techniques have been integrated, and the trial before a jury (*cour d'assises*) applies the principle of *contradictoire*.

In addition, French criminal legislation is codified. Thus, judges were traditionally required to apply the law literally. Among politicians however, there has always been a spectre of a *gouvernement des juges*,[7] which partially explains the current debate about the investigating judge and the (in)dependence of public prosecutors.[8] The investigating judge has an ambiguous role that requires him/her both to investigate and take judicial decisions that may raise questions about his/her ability to act with complete neutrality. In addition, there is no clear definition of tasks as between the investigating judge, the prosecutor and the judiciary police.[9]

---

[4]   Interviews for this research were conducted in August and September 2009. The interviewees were two magistrates (one *procureur* and one trial judge) and three lawyers who undertake criminal defence work.

[5]   Preliminary article of the Criminal Procedure Code (*Code de Procedure Penale*), (CPP).

[6]   Hodgson 2005, p. 27.

[7]   Hodgson 2005, p. 17.

[8]   See under 5 'Conclusions'.

[9]   *Léger* Report, named after Phillipe Léger, drafted by a commission called by the French President to propose a comprehensive reform of criminal proceedings, published in September 2009, available at <http://www.justice.gouv.fr/art_pix/1_sg_rapport_leger2_ →

However, jurisprudence, and thus the power of judges, has become more important over recent decades, and under the influence of the institutional European framework represented by the European Convention on Human Rights (ECHR). In 2000, the legislator introduced into the code of criminal procedure a preliminary article setting out a list of fundamental defence rights that were directly inspired from the ECHR.[10] The authority of European Court on Human Rights (ECtHR) is also a recent development in criminal law and defence rights, since the *Cour de cassation* applies the ECHR rules and ECtHR decisions,[11] examining all relevant ECtHR decisions in criminal matters within its commission *juridictionnelle*.[12]

Legal culture also strongly varies from one court district to another and depends on the attitude and the practice of local prosecutors and presidents of the local bar (*bâtonniers*). The practice regarding defence rights depends on the acceptance and mobilisation of lawyers within the local judicial system. Although training and career development are based on a national centralized framework, all judicial actors operate differently according to the size, location and criminal background of their jurisdiction.[13] For instance, small structures can either facilitate contacts and cooperation between lawyers and magistrates, or give a strong power to a single prosecutor, when he is the only one working at a local court.

1.3.   The structure and processes of the criminal justice system

A criminal case begins when a complaint is made to the police. However, before setting out the procedure, it is helpful to describe the various state actors involved in the criminal justice system.

State actors

In most cases, in large urban areas complaints have to be made and recorded by the *Police Nationale* (National Police), whereas the *Gendarmerie* covers small cities and the countryside. The *Gendarmes* are members of the army, supervised by the

---

20090901. pdf>, p. 6-7. See generally the full report, which makes a number of recommendations in relation to these issues, including replacing the *juge d'instruction* with a judge who deals only with jurisdictional and procedural issues during the investigation, such as granting search or arrest warrants, bail, etc; creating one authority allowed to investigate, namely the prosecutor acting under the Ministry of Justice; creating safeguards for the rights of the accused and the victim; reinforcing the right of the accused during *Garde à Vue* (GAV), including the increased role of the defence lawyer; simplifying the rules in relation to bail and length of pre-trial detention and generally simplifying pre-trial procedures.

10   Law of 15 June 2000. The principle of *contradictoire* is also inspired by the ECHR.
11   See, for example, Crim., 15 May 2002, Bull. crim., No. 114 (reasonable time); Crim., 29 February 2000, Bull. crim., No. 86 (right to appeal); Crim., 27 June 2001, Bull. crim., No. 164.
12   Article 626-1 CPP: 'The reconsideration of a final criminal decision may be requested for the benefit of any person judged guilty of an offence, where this conviction is held [...] to have been declared in violation of the provisions of the ECHR or its additional Protocols, and where the declared violation, by its nature or seriousness, has led to harmful repercussions for the convicted person.'
13   Interviewed magistrates, August and September 2009.

Ministry of Defence.[14] A third force is the municipal police, which operates under the authority of the Mayor and only has administrative functions.

As at 1 September 2008, there were 143,965 persons working for the National Police: 128,006 of them working 'in the field' and the remainder (11%) working on administrative, technical and scientific projects.[15]

Both the National Police and the *Gendarmes* have two distinct functions: administrative and judicial. The administrative role is preventative and the judicial role relates to criminal investigations. There are obvious overlaps between the two roles; for instance, where a police officer is on street patrol (administrative part of his/her duties) and witnesses a crime (judicial part of his/her duties).[16]

A difficulty with this distinction is that supervision of the National Police is done through a different hierarchy, depending on the function.[17] In its administrative capacity, the National Police is supervised by the Ministry of the Interior, which has led to claims of undue interference from politicians on this aspect of the police work.[18] In their judicial capacity, the National Police answer to the Ministry of Justice.[19] In this capacity, 'the judicial police (many are officers from the National Police) are charged with the task of discovering violations of the criminal law, of gathering evidence of such violations and of identifying their perpetrators'.[20] Officers of the judicial police detect and track crime, gather evidence, fulfil investigations and proceed to coercive measures, such as search, arrest, hearings, etc.

Procureurs (Prosecutors) oversee the work of the judicial police.[21] Each local court (*tribunal de grande instance*) has one public prosecutor. Prosecutors are *magistrats* (magistrates) and, as a result, are trained in the same school as judges (*Ecole Nationale de la Magistrature*). Although they specialise in different areas, they follow common courses. Prosecutors are judicial officers and are required to protect the public interest and apply the law.[22]

Prosecutors are accountable to the Ministry of Justice, which has led some commentators to question some of their decisions as being political, or at least

---

14 The National Police is a larger force, and is sometimes considered more professional, whereas the *Gendarmes* operate more locally and are considered to be non-political. There are tensions and mutual distrust between members of the National Police and *Gendarmes*, as they often compete for cases (Hodgson 2005, p. 86-89).

15 For a detailed analysis of policemen's profile, see Pruvost 2009.

16 See Hodgon 2005, p. 93. The role of police officers is defined by the law of 21 January 1995, art. 4. These are the 'fight against urban violence, petty delinquency and traffic-road insecurity; control of illegal immigration and the fight against employment of illegal aliens; the fight against drug, organised and white-collar crime; protection of the country against terrorism and maintaining public order'.

17 Hodgson 2005, p. 93.

18 Hodgson 2005, p. 95.

19 Hodgson 2005, p. 93.

20 Art. 14, which also states: 'Where a judicial investigation is initiated, they carry out the duties delegated to them by the judicial investigation authorities and defer to their orders'.

21 See, for example, Bénec'h-Le-Roux 2007. There were 1,834 prosecutors in 2006; CEPEJ 2008.

22 Hodgson 2005, p. 69.

subject to political pressure and control from the executive branch.[23] Indeed, lawyers and magistrates have regularly condemned the interference of the Ministry of Justice, or the President of France, in their work.[24]

Until the 1980s, the role of the public prosecutor was mainly to prosecute or to close a criminal case and then to request a trial. During recent decades, they also have had to deal with public policy, judicial urban policies and judicial investigation. Their work has been particularly extended to include alternative procedures to prosecution such as mediation, restoration, guilty pleas and conditional suspension of the prosecution.[25]

Prosecutors have also been given a stronger role in police investigations, both in the preliminary phase and the police report summons. The prosecutor decides which procedure is best adapted to cases received from police officers, according to the nature of the offence. Some cases will be charged as middle ranking criminal cases, instead of serious ones, since the costs of a procedure before a *cour d'assises* (delays, money and public attention) would be too high in comparison with expected results.[26]

The prosecutor delegates many powers to the judiciary police officer,[27] principally because prosecutors are overworked.[28] Therefore, officers of judicial police (OPJ) and prosecutor assistants (*susbstitut du procureur*) are required to work together.

The third actors are the judges, who are constitutionally independent.[29] The *Conseil supérieur de la magistrature* is in charge of the independence by assisting the French President.[30] On the one hand, there are the judges sitting in the court (*Juge du siège*) who conduct trials and read judgments. On the other hand, the investigating judge (*Juge d'instruction*) conducts the proceedings when the prosecution phase has begun.[31] The French President announced in January 2009 his intention to abolish the investigating judge, leading to almost immediate opposition from all justice professionals.

---

[23] Hodgson 2005, p. 75-81, describes various instances where the French president and the government have inappropriately interfered in decisions made by the Judiciary. See also, the so-called 'Clearstream Affair', in which there were accusations of undue pressure and involvement from the government and French President Nicolas Sarkozy, <http://www.guardian.co.uk/world/2010/jan/28/france> and <http://www.guardian.co.uk/world/2009/oct/23/france-clearstream-sarkozy-de-villepin>.

[24] See, on this question, the protest from the main magistrates' union (USM), 4 October 2007, or recently from the left-wing-oriented union *Syndicat de la magistrature*, 23 April 2009.

[25] Law No. 2004-204 of 9 March 2004 on adaptation of Justice to criminality evolutions (so-called Loi Perben II) and Law No. 2005-847 of 26 July 2005 on plea bargaining.

[26] S. Portelli, heard on the website 'Bibliothèque Zoummeroff', interviewed by S. Enderlin in December 2008.

[27] Officier de police judiciaire (OPJ).

[28] See Mouhanna 2004; Hodgson 2005.

[29] *Ordonnance* No. 58-1270 of 22 December 1958.

[30] Art. 64 of the 1958 Constitution.

[31] Under arts. 49 to 52-1 and arts. 79 to 84 CPP.

Investigation

In practice, either the police conduct the investigation under the supervision of the prosecutor or of the investigating judge.[32] At the outset, the offence must be classified into one of three categories, as this will impact on how the investigation is conducted and the venue for any court appearances: *crime* (serious such as homicide), *délit* (petty or middle ranking such as theft, with a maximum sentence of up to 10 years imprisonment), or *contravention* (misdemeanour or minor offence, such as threats of violence, with a maximum sentence of a fine up to 1,500 Euro.).

There are two procedures for investigations, the *Garde à Vue* (GAV) and the *instruction*, which determine who is responsible for the investigation. The two procedures are not mutually exclusive and a suspect may be first dealt with under the GAV procedure and then through the *instruction*.[33] As will be discussed later, the accused has different rights under both procedures. The GAV is more oppressive than the *instruction*, thereby leading some prosecutors to delay as much as possible resorting to the *instruction*.[34]

The GAV is used in 95% of cases,[35] when the police investigate a case under the supervision of the prosecutor. The prosecutor is responsible both for the conduct of the investigation and the way in which the GAV is conducted. A police official will make the initial decision to detain someone and subject them to the GAV procedures, but he/she must inform the prosecutor of this decision from the beginning of the GAV.[36] By law, the suspect must be brought before the prosecutor within 20 hours after the start of GAV (or shall be released);[37] if not, the complete proceedings are a nullity, which means that he/she must be released from detention and that information gathered during the GAV cannot be used against him/her.[38]

The prosecutor must give his/her express authority for detention beyond 24 hours. The maximum amount of time someone can spend in GAV is 96 hours for serious offences. Although the prosecutor has an obligation to ensure that the GAV is conducted properly, he/she is not obliged to attend the police station in person or check how the evidence is being gathered.[39] Evidence shows that prosecutors rarely visit police stations and, in a majority of cases, announce their visit beforehand, thereby preventing any meaningful supervision on their part.[40] As a result, the GAV procedure continues to allow the police to exercise power with minimal supervision.[41]

---

[32] Hodgson 2005, p. 93-94.
[33] Hodgson 2005, p. 212-213.
[34] Hodgson 2005, p. 213-214.
[35] Data from *Annuaire Statistique de la Justice* 2008.
[36] Hodgson 2005, p. 145-146.
[37] Art. 803-3 al. 1 CPP; except for terrorism cases, art. 803-3 al. 4 CPP.
[38] Crim., 6 December 2005, Bull crim., No. 321. In practice, the suspect is almost never brought before the *procureur* and exceptional circumstances are invoked systematically; see Hodgson 2005, p. 161-177.
[39] Hodgson 2005, p. 143-146.
[40] Hodgson 2005, p. 157. Data collected by researchers and the author through a questionnaire.
[41] Hodgson 2005, p. 159.

In practice, supervision by the prosecutor deals with legal issues and requests for evidence. The prosecutor rarely supervises the police on the way in which they obtain this information.[42] There is no input from the defence lawyer during the GAV about the direction of the investigation, which contradicts the judicial role that the prosecutor should have during the GAV.[43]

France has regularly been criticised for the condition of police detention and police treatment during the GAV.[44] As will be discussed in paragraph 2.2.2, the French courts have taken different approaches to the GAV and whether the system complies with the ECHR.

There were 564,934 GAV[45] from April 2007 to March 2008, which represents a rise of 5% within one year and 60% since 2001 – in fact there were 800,000 GAV if road traffic related GAV is also included.

At the end of the GAV, the prosecutor has five options: to close the case (*classement*), to propose a *médiation pénale* (guilty plea), to give the suspect a return date for court (*citation directe*), to impose an expedited hearing for trial on that day (*comparution immédiate*), or to pass the case to the investigating judge.[46] Once one of these procedures has started, the case can always be closed (a *non-lieu*).

If the case is referred to the investigating judge, the investigation continues through a process known as the *instruction*, which, as seen above, takes place in about 5% of cases. A suspect dealt with in this way is *Mis en Examen* (*MEE*). In 2008, there were 609 investigating judges and each had 50 cases. From this number, 11,000 were closed without charge, after an average of 20 months spent on the investigation.[47] The difference with the GAV procedure is that, once a suspect is an MEE, he/she can only be interrogated by the investigating judge.

Under this procedure, the investigation is led by the investigating judge, although he/she does not have the power to open an investigation. Instead, the prosecutor must open an *information*, which officially refers the case to the investigating judge. In cases of *crimes*, the prosecutor must refer the case to the investigating judge whilst in cases of *délits* and *contraventions*, this is discretionary. Resources sometimes determine whether or not a prosecutor will refer a case to the investigating judge, who is often overworked and may not be able to deal with a case in a timely fashion.[48] The prosecutor or the investigating judge have the power to re-classify an offence from a *délit* to a *crime* and *vice-versa*. In certain areas,

---

[42]   Hodgson 2005, p. 164.

[43]   Hodgson 2005, p. 171.

[44]   See European Committee for the Prevention of Torture and Inhuman or Degrading Treatment or Punishment, 2001 (§ 22). See also ECtHR 28 July 1999, *Selmouni* v. *France*, No. 25803/94, where the ECtHR stated that France had violated art. 3 of the Convention, because of the treatment received by the applicant whilst he was in police detention. See also Jean-Marie Delarue, general controller of imprisonment places, Le journal du dimanche, 19 December 2009.

[45]   This covers police detention and interview. Since 2002, there have been instructions to increase police and *gendarmerie* activities, so that some local police offices have to fulfil a quota of, for example, five *gardes à vue* per day; see Portelli 2007, chapter XI.

[46]   Hodgson 2005, p. 236.

[47]   Data from *Annuaire Statistique de la Justice* 2008.

[48]   Hodgson 2005, p. 209-212.

prosecutors will systematically downgrade offences to avoid having to open an *information*, as there are not enough resources to deal with serious cases as *crimes*.[49]

Although this investigation is led by the investigating judge, he/she can use a *commission rogatoire* to delegate powers to the police. In practice, the police carry out much of the investigation, except for questioning the suspect, as this cannot be delegated to the police. One of the problems in practice is that the police will still lead these investigations by requesting the investigating judge to delegate his/her powers to them. This has the impact of negating the effective supervisory role that the investigating judge should have in making decisions about the direction of the investigation.[50]

Victims can also be part of the *instruction* as third parties. They can be represented by lawyers and have the right to ask the investigating judge to order certain actions as part of the investigation.

Pre-trial detention

The procedure for placing a suspect in pre-trial detention is detailed below, but it is worth setting out some statistics about pre-trial detention. In 2005, 60,948 persons were placed in pre-trial custody.[51] In 2006, of the 24,363 investigations completed by the judge or prosecutor, 34.5% of the concerned persons remained in pre-trial custody after the investigation was completed.

In 2005, the national average length of pre-trial detention was 8.7 months. For those awaiting trial in *Cour d'assises* (for serious crimes), it went up to 16.8 months, whereas the average length before a *tribunal correctionnel* was 7.9 months.[52] Almost all persons remanded in custody pending trial in 2006 (94%) were convicted, while only 574 were released without being convicted.[53] In *correctionnel* proceedings, the detention delay may not exceed four months; it can be prolonged every four months up to one year in case of recidivism, and up to two years in case of drug trafficking or organized crime.

In *crime* cases, the delay varies from one to three years.[54] Once the investigation is closed, two years is the maximum time until the trial before a *cour d'assises* takes place; otherwise the detained person must be released.[55] Before a *tribunal correctionnel*, the delay is two months (plus a maximum of another two months) once the prosecutor has decided to send a person to court (*ordonnance de renvoi*).

---

[49]   Hodgson 2005, p. 212.
[50]   Hodgson 2005, p. 212-213.
[51]   Commission de suivi de la détention provisoire (CNSDP), 2007. There is no available data on the proportion of those arrested who are then proceeded against.
[52]   *Répertoire de l'instruction* and CNSDP 2007.
[53]   CNSDP 2007.
[54]   Art. 145-1 CPP.
[55]   Art. 181 CPP.

210

Court Procedure

When the prosecutor or investigating judge decides that there is sufficient evidence to justify bringing the case before the court, there are three possible venues, corresponding to the three types of offences defined above. The *tribunal de police* is for misdemeanours and is presided by one professional judge; the *tribunal correctionnel* is for petty crime and consists of three magistrates; the *cour d'assises* is for serious crime and consists of three magistrates and nine jurors (12 on appeal).[56]

There are a number of procedures available at court. In 2007 there were 49,712 guilty plea procedures (*comparution sur reconnaissance préalable de culpabilité*),[57] many more when compared to 2001 (31,600).[58] The advantage to the defendant is a discounted sentence– the public prosecutor can propose a lower prison sentence that 'may not exceed either a year or half the prison sentence incurred'.[59] The defendant admits the facts and accepts the proposal as to sentence made by the public prosecutor. He/she is then brought before the correctional court, where the judge must check 'the truth of the facts and their legal qualification, [and] may decide to approve the penalties proposed by the district prosecutor'.[60] The judge issues his/her ruling the same day.

Another procedure is the expedited hearing procedure (*comparution immédiate*), which is used for almost all middle ranking offences, since it concerns sentences of at least six months.[61] In many cases, a social enquiry about the defendant will be made.[62] Usually, the lawyer takes notice of the file just a few hours before the court hearing. It has to be judged and decided on the same day, but only if the defendant agrees to it. When the case has to be postponed, this must be for a period of between two to six weeks.[63] 'Where the penalty incurred is greater than seven years' imprisonment', the case must be held within two to four months'.[64] When the case is postponed and the defendant is in pre-trial detention, the judgement must occur 'within two months from the day of his first appearance before the court'.[65] Prosecutors present before the court an average of 15-25 cases a day/hearing,[66] so that judges never know how many they will have to deal with. Some cases are even introduced pending a court session.

---

[56] When the suspect is acquitted, it will be a *relaxe* before the *tribunal de police* and the *tribunal correctionnel*, and an *acquittement* before the *cour d'assises*.

[57] Art. 495-7 CPP.

[58] There is no data available as to whether these procedures were linked to pre-trial detention, and the measure is too recent to draw conclusions as to its practice; see J. Danet, daily newspaper Le Monde, 18 August 2009.

[59] Art. 495-8, al. 2 CPP.

[60] Art. 495-9 al. 2 CPP.

[61] Arts. 388 and 395 CPP.

[62] *Enquête sociale rapide*, compulsory for recidivism offence. In Paris, an association is paid by the Ministry of Justice to establish the file, which takes generally thirty minutes per defendant.

[63] Pre-trial detention shall not last more than two months in an expedited hearing proceeding.

[64] Art. 397-1 al. 2 CPP.

[65] Art. 397-3 al. 3 CPP.

[66] Figures for the Paris court district.

One of the problems with this system is that the prosecutor cannot carry out a comprehensive review of the file, and therefore depends completely on the information received from the OPJ. As discussed above, prosecutors are overworked and generally do not carry out a meaningful review of the police files during the GAV. As a result, when the case gets to court, they are not familiar with the intricacies of the case and are likely to rely on the police file as the basis for the court hearing.

For the expedited hearing, the only incentive for the defendant is the short period in police or prison custody before being judged, since all persons in expedited hearing procedures have been arrested by the police and are detained.

The French system gives less importance to the judgment, since judicial theory is not based on case law. Thus, there is not the same dynamic between judges and lawyers as in an Anglo-Saxon trial, the French judge being more isolated in the individual decision process. As a consequence, lawyers seek and gain more prestige and acknowledgment in direct opposition to the court in the name of defence rights by acting adversarially.[67] Furthermore, criminal procedure has become very important and can result in an automatic nullity of the case. In other cases, breach of procedure may lead to nullity, but only if certain consequences flow from such breach.[68]

1.4. Levels of crime and the prison population

At least with regard to murder and homicide, the numbers of committed crimes have decreased over the past 30 years and are now under 1,000 cases per year (826 in 2007).[69] However, the number of convictions has grown: in 2006 there were 3,300 convictions for *crime* (serious offence) and 582,761 for *délit* (misdemeanour).[70] Statistics from the police, the attorneys or the National Observatory for Criminality (OND) cannot be used as such without any scientific and critical analysis, because of bias linked to the data collection.[71]

The increase in the prison population in France corresponds to a common trend in many European countries. As at 1 November 2008, there were 67,545

---

[67] Darrois 2009, p. 6. The Bar has been involved in the work of the Commission Darrois through proposals and hearings; see, for example, *Bulletin du Barreau de Paris*, No. 31, 16 September 2008.

[68] Article 174 al. 2 and 3 of the CPP stipulates that 'the investigating chamber decides whether the annulment should be limited to all or part of the vitiated procedural instruments or documents, or should extend to all or part of the later proceedings, and proceeds as stated in the third paragraph of article 206. The annulled instruments or documents are withdrawn from the case file of the investigation and filed in the court office of the court of appeal. The procedural instruments or documents annulled in part are cancelled after the taking of a copy certified true to the original, which is filed with the court office of the court of appeal. It is prohibited to draw any information against the parties from the annulled procedural instruments or documents or from the annulled parts of such instruments or documents, under penalty of disciplinary proceedings for the advocates and the judges or prosecutors.'

[69] Mucchielli 2008.

[70] *Crime* is, for instance, murder or rape; *délit* is, for instance, assault or drug consumption.

[71] Mouhanna & Matelly 2007; Aubusson de Cavarlay 1997. For instance, reported crimes are not recorded by the police (*principe d'opportunité*), or prosecutors can close cases (art. 40-1 CPP).

inmates in French prisons, of which 3,333 were under electronic supervision and 386 were serving custodial sentences outside of prison (so called *placement à l'extérieur sans hébergement pénitentiaire*).[72] The prison capacity was 51,000, making the occupancy rate approximately 120%.[73] In November 2008, the occupancy rate was 200% or more in 16 prisons, between 150% and 200% in 45 prisons and between 100% and 150% in 82 prisons. Since 2004, the rate of remand prisoners decreased from 37% to 26% (November 2008). Since 1980, the rate of prisoners per 100,000 inhabitants rose from 66 to 100 and all in all, the prison population rose by 88%.

Despite a lower number of convictions and prison sentences,[74] the prison population rose between 1986 and 2000 by about 20,000 inmates, mainly because serious crimes leading to convictions (such as sexual offences) are more regularly reported by victims[75] and also because such crimes are being treated as more serious by the courts. Four phases should be mentioned: a decrease of about 13% between 1996 and 2000, an increase about 24% between 2001 and 2003, a phase of stability in 2004 and 2005,[76] and a subsequent increase since then.

In that context, within ten years, the number of convicted inmates for rape and other sexual offences has doubled in percentage terms and tripled in absolute numbers.[77] As at 1 January 2000, almost one fourth of inmates – precisely 22.6%, (7,499 people) – were convicted of sexual offences. As at 1 January 2007, this number had slightly decreased to 19.5%.

Another trend is the criminalisation of more behaviour. For instance, it is now an offence to insult a civil servant. The law has been misused by policemen, since any conflict or protest from citizens is interpreted as an insult against the State and then brought as such to the court.[78] This raises the question of whether the law has simply dealt with an existing problem, or whether the police have (mis)used this law by prosecuting behaviour that had not been criminalised until that time.

A clear case is the criminalisation of domestic violence. It has exposed a current issue and thus multiplied corresponding criminal procedures. A tangible effect on prison rate is illustrated by the criminalisation in 1998 of driving over 40 km/h speed limit, and the re-classifying as a *délit* of road traffic offences that were previously only considered *contraventions*.[79]

The criminalisation of sexual harassment and, in 1994, of other sexual offences such as rape, have significantly changed inmates' profiles. The prison population now comprises a larger proportion of sexual offenders with longer prison sentences. Criminalisation serves as a lawful recognition of a wrongful act by the offender and often means for the victim a *legitimation* of his/her complaint and an automatic increase of public acknowledgment of such issues.

---

[72]   Article 132-43 to 132-46 Criminal Code.

[73]   Pierre V. Tournier calculated an overcrowding of around 14,000 inmates as at 1 of November 2008; see Tournier, *Arpenter le Champ Pénal*, 1 December 2008.

[74]   Peyrat 2002.

[75]   Leturmy 2009.

[76]   Tournier P. V., *Informations Criminologiques Hebdo*, 2 February 2006.

[77]   Prison administration, *Chiffres clefs de l'administration pénitentiaire* 1990, 2000 and 2007.

[78]   Jobard 2004.

[79]   This re-classification has led to prison sentences being imposed for crimes that previously did not carry prison sentences.

As to drug policy, the drug act of 31 December 1970 (*Loi sur les stupéfiants*) is still operative. Voted to maintain the post-1968s order, this conservative and punitive oriented act does not take into consideration health policy issues.[80] It has been tightened several times over the last 40 years (1986, 1987, 1992 and 1996), which had served to increase the punitive nature of drug policy.[81]

However, over the last 30 years, some alternative measures have been implemented in parallel to laws lengthening prison sentence,[82] mostly in relation to offences leading to short prison sentences. Nevertheless, these policies were not sufficient to stop the prison rate expansion.[83]

Regarding rehabilitative sentences, the suspension of a verdict (*ajournement du prononcé de la peine*) was introduced in 1975. Community service was introduced in 1983 (*travail d'intérêt general, so-called TIG*) and the fine instead of imprisonment (*jour-amende*). Therefore, the number of short prison sentences has slowly decreased, influenced also by the decriminalisation of cheque fraud in 1991.

Alternative measures were also developed between 1990 and 2005. However, whereas the total number of alternative measures has increased, the absolute number and percentage of people released on parole has decreased.[84] In addition, support and supervision measures for sexual offenders are rarely implemented.[85]

1.5. Legal aid for persons suspected or accused of crime[86]

The total public budget for legal aid (*aide juridictionnelle*) was 306,760,000 Euro in 2008 (+ 36% compared to 1998), with one third of it (103,000,000 Euro) spent on criminal legal aid.[87]

Of the approximately 900,000 grants of legal aid in 2006, 50% were granted for civil procedure, and 7% for administrative cases. The 43% granted for criminal cases[88] represents a growth of one fourth since 2000. Legal aid is granted in one third of criminal cases that go to court.[89] Around 95% of legal aid beneficiaries in criminal cases received full legal aid. Since 1996, about 8% of legal aid applications

---

[80] See Bergeron 1999; Beauchesne 2003.

[81] See Faugeron 1999.

[82] See Tournier 2001.

[83] One reason is that work outside of prison (*placement à l'extérieur*) is too rarely used as a sentence alternative; see Dünkel & Fritsche 2005a; 2005b.

[84] For the first quarter of 2007, conditional release represented only 2.7% of all releases; Tournier 2007.

[85] See Act of 17 June 1998 introducing the *suivi socio-judiciaire*; which that is social and legal monitoring for sexual offenders needing treatment.

[86] It was not possible to find public access to the supposed yearly report of the *Conseil national de l'aide juridique* (national council for legal aid), although this institution has existed since the law No. 91-647 of 10 July 1991, and although mention is made of recent members' nominations. The *Conseil national de l'aide juridique* (CNAJ) is a consultative institution reliant on the Ministry of Justice. It is in charge of collecting data, suggesting ameliorations and guaranteeing harmonisation among legal aid offices. The CNAJ is composed of 24 members, half of them representing the legal profession.

[87] Ministry of Justice 2009.

[88] Poutet C., Blandin A., Infostat Justice No. 85, 2006.

[89] *Annuaire statistique de la justice* 2008.

have been refused.[90] In 2004, full legal aid represented 88% of all legal aid grants, an increase of 21% since 2001. From 2001 to 2004, the legal aid budget rose by 35.4%.[91]

Article 6-3c ECHR remains the fundamental provision guaranteeing legal. There is no difference between investigative and trial stage, or between the first instance and appeal or cassation stage.[92] The legal framework for legal aid has two aspects. The first is for all judicial matters, except the criminal ones for which the State pays partly or totally the costs of a chosen lawyer.[93] The second concerns criminal matters with a chosen or a court appointed lawyer (duty lawyer, called *avocat commis d'office*): the State pays a lawyer where the defendant does not know any. Both financial calculations are made on the basis of the *aide juridictionnelle*.

There is no legal obligation to inform a person of the provisions concerning legal aid. Suspects or defendants are, in practice, usually informed by the officer of judicial police, the prosecutor or, where applicable, the investigating judge. As to lawyers, there is no obligation to provide legal advice and/or representation, but they have ethical rules that oblige them to inform defendants about legal aid.[94]

The office of legal aid (*bureau d'aide juridictionelle*)[95] is in charge of decisions as to whether somebody satisfies the means test, and makes the decision regarding entitlement to free or subsidised legal representation.[96] The means test is based on income during the year preceding the application. For applications made in 2009, in order to qualify for full legal aid, the applicant must have had an average monthly income during 2008 of less than 911 Euro; for partial legal aid, it must have been between 912 and 1.367 Euro. The applicable average monthly income increases based on the number of the defendant's dependents.

---

90   *Annuaire statistique de la justice 2008.* Denials are based on the applicant having too high an income in half of the cases, the lack of relevant documents for one third, and inadmissible/ungrounded reasons for 20%.

91   Conseil National des Barreaux (National Bar Association), Observatoire, Statistiques, *L'aide juridictionnelle et les avocats en France*, Septembre 2006.

92   In two cases, the supreme administrative court stressed that any legal proceeding must be suspended until the legal aid demand has been examined; *Conseil d'Etat*, avis No. 322713 of 6 May 2009.

93   See law No. 91-647 of the 10 July 1991 (*relative à l'aide juridique*), completed and implemented by the decree No. 91-1266 of the 19 December 1991.

94   Art. 3 of decree No. 2005-790 of 12 July 2005.

95   Regulated by the decree No. 91-1266 of 19 December 1991 implementing the law No. 91-647 of 10 July 1991 on legal aid.

96   The procedure is the same at the investigative and trial stage, and there is there no difference between the first instance and appeal or cassation stage. A decree sets each year the conditions of income.

Dependants of the person in custody (child, parents, etc.)	Average monthly income Full legal aid	Average monthly income Partial legal aid
0	911 Euro	1,367 Euro
1	1,075 Euro	1,531 Euro
2	1,239 Euro	1,695 Euro
3	1,343 Euro	1,799 Euro
4	1,447 Euro	1,903 Euro
5	1,551 Euro	2,007 Euro
6	1,655 Euro	2,111 Euro

(Figures for 2009)

From 2001 to 2005, the minimum income that still allows a defendant to receive legal aid increased by 11.5%. The revaluation occurs automatically, following the law of 10 July 1991, and is based on the indexed income tax (*impôt sur le revenu*). Comparing the eligibility level with other relevant data, the minimum wage is about 1,000 Euro, the poverty level 800 Euro, the median wage 1,500 Euro and the mean wage 2,000 Euro (excluding taxes).[97] The defendant applies himself/herself the means test at the office of legal aid.[98] He/she must supply a copy of any decision made in the case indicating the stages of the proceedings, a copy of his/her last three pay slips, or proof of actual income, as well as proof of persons living in the same house and a copy of the last income declaration. The first step is to fill a form. It is available online, at the local bar association (although only at some of them), or at the legal aid office (located at the district court). This form must be handed in to the local bar association at least 15 days before the convocation by the investigating judge or the court. A copy of the convocation and the last tax declaration must be added to it.

Then, a lawyer will be automatically appointed (*commis d'office*) to assist the suspect or the defendant. The lawyer, once he/she has been appointed by the penal office of the bar association, contacts with the person. There is no means test for representation in 'emergency' situations, like a GAV.[99]

When legal aid is granted only partially, the beneficiary may be required to pay back the costs incurred by the other party, if he/she is convicted. The judge can also ask the beneficiary to pay back a part of State expenses other than legal aid.[100] When a person is granted full legal aid, they cannot be required to pay costs, even if they are convicted, except if the proceedings were considered as a waste of time. Legal aid can be withdrawn when the defendant is considered to be abusing the

---

[97] There exists no assessment of the proportion of the population who are eligible for legal aid, but the 911 Euro limit corresponds to the monthly income of 20% of the French population.

[98] In the case where the defendant has previously chosen a lawyer, the latter might help him/her to fill in the application.

[99] See generally, <http://www.vos-droits.justice.gouv.fr/index.php?rubrique=10062&ssrubrique=10207&article=11139> and <http://www.vos-droits.justice.gouv.fr/art_pix/Notice51036n02.pdf>.

[100] Art. 42 of law No. 91-647 of 10 July 1991.

process and wasting time. In that case, the defendant must reimburse immediately all legal aid costs and expenses.[101]

There is no merits test for full or partial legal representation. A defendant is always eligible for legal aid if he/she fulfils formal criteria, irrespective of how minor the alleged offence is. Because legal residence is a condition to the grant of legal aid, persons illegally residing in France will only be granted legal aid on a discretionary basis.[102]

There is a long list of the work covered by legal aid.[103] There are restrictions on the amount of work that can be done and will be paid for since expenses are based on units for each type of work, according to the proceedings, and these units are fixed. This means that only the listed tasks are remunerated,[104] no matter the amount of work done.[105]

The basic fee is 8.84 Euro per case under the title *droits de plaidoirie* (pleading's rights).[106] A complex system of remuneration then deals with each type of case, stage of proceedings, etc. Legal aid is paid on a unit base. Each unit for partial legal aid is 22.50 Euro (tax free). It may be more for full legal aid. The unit base is multiplied by a coefficient, depending on the type of case.

For example, in the first half hour of the GAV, the lawyer receives 61 Euro (travelling expenses or night shift), which means an hourly rate of 122 Euro which is more than the hourly rate of legal aid (45 Euro).

Before the correctional court, the remuneration is 8 UV[107]– a UV is about 22 Euro. Before the *cour d'assises*, it is 50 UV for the first day, and 16 UV for the following ones. An *instruction* is worth 50 UV, a correctional one 20 UV with pre-trial detention and 12 without. A simple appeal will result in a payment of about 150 Euro, a more complex one about 250 Euro.

Recently, in a trial that lasted over two months, the defence lawyer was paid about 70,000 Euro and the victim's lawyer was paid more than 100,000 Euro.[108] However, there are no relevant widespread statistics on a national and global scale. Lawyers in private practice are free to charge as much as they want. A typical hourly rate is 200-300 Euro, which represents more than 129 Euro for a complete

---

[101] Art. 52 of law No. 91-647 of 10 July 1991.
[102] There is no special restriction on the availability of legal aid, legal advice or representation or choice of lawyer, in terrorist cases, but there are special proceedings in terrorist cases under art. 706-16 ff. CPP.
[103] Art. 90 of decree No. 91-1266 of 19 December 1991.
[104] For instance, legal aid does not cover tracing and/or interviewing witnesses, carrying out other investigations, or instructing experts.
[105] This means that a lawyer has to be effective, fast or neglectful in order to reach a substantial financial payment based on an hourly rate. However, legal aid is predominantly carried out by lawyers who are successful in running private client practices.
[106] Decree of 29 May 1989 fixing it to 58 Francs (around nine Euro).
[107] For a charge case, the remuneration is about 75 Euro (excluding taxes), plus 50 Euro when there is a contradictory debate before the judge of liberties and detention. As to expedited hearings, it as about 300 Euro (excluding taxes) for a hearing session, and *gardes à vue* are paid case by case (63 Euro at day and 92 Euro at night).
[108] Darrois 2009, p. 98.

case, which is the average remuneration for a *contravention* case.[109] For serious crime, it might be around 1,000 Euro.[110] For a 129 Euro case, there are often unpaid hours, since remuneration is not directly linked to the complexity of a case – particularly cases with numerous files or requiring bail applications. In Paris, the average remuneration for a case is 190 Euro. For an instruction by an investigating judge, it is 200 Euro and 400 Euro when the defendant is in detention.[111]

Concerning the practice of legal aid, there is no existing evidence about how the decision making and appointment process works. According to the liberal and non-restrictive conditions relating to receiving legal aid, and with regard to the number of beneficiaries, many lawyers and judges appear to be satisfied with the way that legal aid works (see interviews). There are, however, some problems. Lawyers complain about the low remuneration from legal aid,[112] although they have to undertake some training (including legal dispositions concerning proceedings such as *garde à vue*, expedited hearings, etc.) of, for instance, 24 hours for lawyers working in Paris. It is often also wrongly assumed that legal aid is only performed by lawyers who are not good enough to earn a living from private work.[113] As to the subjective perception of legal aid, some lawyers lose motivation and defendants are sometimes disrespectful to them, since they pay nothing or very little.[114]

2.   Legal rights and their implementation

The rules on nullity[115] are often used by lawyers at the pre-trial, investigation and trial stages[116] although they are rarely admitted by courts.[117] The importance of the principle of nullity is that, once it has been recognised that a nullity was committed, it cannot be rectified by compliance with other obligations. Further, evidence obtained through a breach of procedure must be excluded at trial, while evidence

---

[109]   Interviewed lawyers were critical of the low remuneration rate of legal aid; 129 Euro is the average remuneration per case in misdemeanour matter; Darrois 2009, p. 115.
[110]   Interviewed lawyers 1 and 2.
[111]   Interviewed lawyer 1. The remuneration remains the same, even if the *instruction* lasts several months, or if there are several hearings with the judge.
[112]   Art. 37 of the law on legal aid enable a lawyer paid by legal aid to ask the judge to sentence the adverse party to pay compensation corresponding to the costs he/she would have charged his/her client if the client had not benefitted from legal aid; Ordonnance No. 2005-1526 of 8 December 2005 and decree No. 2007-1151 of 30 July 2007 have simplified this disposition.
[113]   Eolas, 25 March 2009, <http://www.maitre-eolas.fr/>. This experienced lawyer indicates that, in 2008, he earned 4,500 Euro with legal aid representation.
[114]   Interviewed lawyer 2. The remuneration of legal aid is not sufficient to sustain a living. It is more a complementary income needed mostly by young lawyers. Many of them quit legal aid as soon as they earn enough on their own, Eolas, 16 September 2008, <http://www.maitre-eolas.fr/>.
[115]   Art. 171 CPP represents the general ruling if an obligation is not complied with: 'There is a nullity when the breach of an essential formality provided for by a provision of the present Code or by any other rule of criminal procedure has harmed the interests of the party it concerns.'
[116]   Interviewed lawyer 2.
[117]   Interviewed lawyer 1.

illegally obtained cannot be produced before the court. According to article 206 CPP, 'subject to the provisions of articles 173-1, 174 and 175, the investigating chamber examines the lawfulness of the proceedings of which it is seized.

If it discovers a ground of nullity, it pronounces the nullity of the instrument vitiated and, where necessary, of all or part of the subsequent proceedings'.

For instance, when a suspect in a GAV is presented with unjustified delay before an investigation judge or a court, he/she must be released. The correctional court and the investigation chamber (*chambre de l'instruction*) are responsible for annulment proceedings.

2.1. *The right to information*

There is no obligation to give a suspect or defendant a 'letter of rights' informing him/her of his/her rights. Rules on written information are found in diverse proceedings and measures, such as GAV (art. 63-1 CPP), charge (art. 116 CPP), pre-trial detention (art. 145), etc.

The general term for a person suspected of an offence is a *mis en cause*, which means 'somebody who is put into question'. This applies to persons who have not been charged by the investigating judge, including suspects under preliminary enquiry (*enquête*) and in a GAV.

There is no obligation to inform a person under preliminary investigation about the nature and cause of the accusation against him/her.

The only rights of the suspect are during 'searches, house visits and seizures of exhibits [that] may not be made without the express consent of the person in whose residence the operation takes place'.[118] Consent must be handwritten. An exception is made in the case of an offence punished by a prison sentence of five years or more: the decision is taken by the liberty and custody judge. Further, according to article 78 CPP, the police officer may compel a suspect to attend an interrogation. In practice, although there is no legal provision to this effect, at the stage of search or interview with a police officer, the suspect will often be verbally informed about why an inquiry is being conducted.

The right to information during the preliminary investigation only applies to suspects in GAV. Suspects must be informed about the following rights at the outset of the GAV: the right to notify his/her relative by telephone about the arrest; to contact his/her lawyer or to have a duty lawyer appointed for a 30-minute consultation before the start of the interrogation; to request a medical examination.[119] The notification of these rights must be in the language that the suspect understands, and the fact of notification should be noted in the record of the interrogation.[120] Importantly, there is no obligation to notify suspects in GAV about the right to remain silent (see 2.3.4 below).

Suspects charged by an investigating judge acquire the procedural status of *mis en examen*. The suspect may be *mis en examen* only after an interrogation by the

---

[118]   Art. 76 CPP.
[119]   Art. 63-1 CPP.
[120]   *Ibidem.*

investigating judge.[121] From this moment, the obligation exists to inform the suspect about the nature and cause of the accusation, and to grant him/her access to the file.[122]

The evidentiary standard for being *mis en examen* is quite high: a person is *mis en examen* when there is serious or corroborated evidence indicating that he/she has probably participated in the events under investigation.[123] This means that many suspects would be charged as late as several months after the commencement of the investigation. Until recently, they would have had no access to procedural rights, and no knowledge about the investigation, until it has reached a quite advanced stage.

In an attempt to address this problem, the procedural figure of an 'assisted witness' (*témoin assiste*) was introduced in 2000.[124] An assisted witness is an intermediary in terms of procedural status between the *mis en cause* and the *mis en examen*. A suspect should be granted the status of *témoin assiste* when there is evidence indicating the probability of his/her participation in the crime(s) that he/she is suspected of.[125] The *témoin assiste* acquires some of the procedural rights of the *mis en examen*, namely the right to be informed about the nature and cause of the accusation, to have access to the case file and to legal assistance.[126]

There is a legal obligation to inform the *mis en examen* of the nature and cause of the accusation against him/her, in accordance with either article 80-2 CPP (when it deals with a written convocation), or article 116 when the *mis en examen* operates consequently to hearing, detention or arrest (*mandat d'amener or mandat d'arrêt*).

The duty to inform arises either in the written convocation that takes place between ten days and two months before the first appearance (*comparution*) before the investigating judge, or as soon as the *comparution* has begun (the relevant provision also concerns suspects who are deprived of their liberty).[127] However, it is

---

[121] Art. 80-2 CPP.
[122] Art. 114 CPP. The moment of *mettre en examen* triggers other procedural rights of a suspect, such as the right to legal assistance, or the right to request the *juge d'instruction* to undertake investigative acts; arts. 116 and 82-1 CPP.
[123] 'A peine de nullité, le juge d'instruction ne peut mettre en examen que les personnes à l'encontre desquelles il existe des indices graves ou concordants rendant vraisemblable qu'elles aient pu participer, comme auteur ou comme complice, à la commission des infractions dont il est saisi'; art. 80-1 CPP.
[124] Pradel 2002, p. 578-579.
[125] 'Toute personne mise en cause par un témoin ou contre laquelle il existe des indices rendant vraisemblable qu'elle ait pu participer, comme auteur ou comme complice, à la commission des infractions dont le juge d'instruction est saisi peut être entendue comme témoin assisté'; art. 113-2, al. 2, *in fine* CPP. Thus, the difference in the evidentiary standard required for *mis en examen* and *temoin assiste* is that, for *mis en examen*, 'serious or corroborative' evidence of his/her probable involvement in the crime is required, while for *temoin assiste*, the requirement of seriousness or corroboration of evidence is absent.
[126] Art. 113-3 CPP. However, a *temoin assiste* does not have the right to request that investigative actions to be undertaken or to apply for nullity; Pradel 2002, p. 579.
[127] Art. 116 al. 2 CPP stipulates that 'the investigating judge [...] expressly informs [the person] of each of the charges of which he is seized and for which placement under judicial examination is contemplated, specifying their legal qualification. A record of these charges and their legal qualification is made in the official record'.

not compulsory that the information is given in writing.[128] There is a continuing obligation to provide information as the investigation or case develops.

Further, there is no explicit rule concerning the obligation to inform the *mis en examen* of the accusation. However, since the lawyer has a continuing and complete right of access to the file and the defendant and the lawyer are free to communicate, the right to be informed is absolute and complete as soon as the lawyer has accepted the defence.[129] Yet, despite the fact that the ECtHR criticised the lack of opportunity for a defendant without a lawyer to have access to his/her case file in order to prepare a defence,[130] the practice has not changed, so that a defendant is still dependent on a lawyer to have access to the file.[131] The file given to the lawyer must be complete and up-to-date.[132]

Research shows, however, that in practice judges delay attaching evidence to the case file in order to keep it from lawyers.[133] The transmission of the file to the lawyer must be recorded in written form, or risk leading to a nullity.[134] The only exception to this principle is in an emergency, but the judge must prove its necessity, in order to otherwise guarantee the defence rights.[135]

As to legal aid, there are no rules setting at differences either between poor or legally-aided suspects and defendants and those who are able to pay privately, or when the legal aid is total (100% of costs). On the other hand, when legal aid is partially granted, some suspects or defendants are not able to make up the financial difference by paying for extra expenses, particularly since the corresponding fees do not allow for straight forward prediction of costs. Indeed, there is no clear access to information on lawyers' remuneration (hour based rate), or on specific legal actions to seek evidence that can be more complex than expected (for example DNA analysis).

2.2. The right to defend oneself

2.2.1. The right of a person to defend him/herself

Defendants have the general right to participate in the proceedings by making representations, providing explanations, requesting certain investigative acts to be undertaken, commenting on the evidence, and so forth.[136] The CPP gives defendants the same rights to participate in the trial proceedings as their lawyers, with one important reservation. Defendants cannot – unlike their lawyers – pose questions to

---

[128] Crim., 18 April 1972, Bull. crim., No. 130; Crim., 6 January 1989, Bull. crim., No. 3; Crim., 8 October 1998, Bull. crim., No. 250.
[129] Art. 114 al. 3 CPP stipulates that 'after the first appearance of the person under judicial examination […], the case file is also put at the permanent disposal of the advocates during working days […]'.
[130] ECtHR 18 March 1997, *Foucher* v. *France*, No. 22209/93.
[131] Pradel 2002, p. 673.
[132] Crim., 28 July 1958, Bull. crim., No. 589.
[133] Hodgson 2001, p. 354-355.
[134] Crim., 27 July 1906, Bull. DP 1907, I. 334.
[135] Conseil Constitutionnel, 11 August 1993, JO 15 August 1993, p. 11600.
[136] Vogler 2008, p. 192.

witnesses and experts directly, but only through the presiding judge (arts. 312 and 442-1 CPP).

At the pre-trial stage, the opportunities for suspects to act in their own defence are limited. During the preliminary enquiry (*enquête*), suspects are not informed about the content of the dossier and the course of the investigation. In these circumstances, even though suspects have a theoretical right to defend themselves against a suspicion – for instance, by suggesting explanations of the imputed events that would exonerate them, or naming witnesses who are likely to testify in their favour – this is difficult to do in practice.

At the stage of the *instruction*, suspects acquire greater possibility to conduct their defence. It is during the instruction that they are granted access to the case file and to legal assistance.[137] Furthermore, the 1993 and 2000 reforms introduced a special defence right to request the investigating judge to undertake a particular investigative act.[138] If the investigating judge refuses the request, he/she must give reasons for the refusal, and the refusal may be appealed to the *chambre d'instruction*.[139]

In 1996, suspects for the first time acquired the right of access to the *dossier*, which was originally granted only to a lawyer, albeit that the right can only be exercised through the lawyer.[140] Despite these important advances, the pre-trial participation rights of the defence remain auxiliary to the power of the investigating judge to conduct the inquiry. In the words of one commentator, 'the right to participate is not the right to conduct the procedure, for it is the judge who directs the investigation. This right is simply the one to propose and to suggest.'[141]

2.2.2. The right to legal advice at the investigative stage

During the preliminary investigation (enquête) and the GAV

Traditionally, suspects have not enjoyed the right to legal assistance during the preliminary investigation (*enquête*).[142] However, the reforms of 1993 and 2000 afforded a (very limited) right to legal advice to a special category of suspects who are subject to a preliminary investigation, namely for those held in GAV. The jurisprudence underlines that the police officer must inform the suspect of his right

---

[137]   Articles 80-2 and 114 CPP.

[138]   The law of 4 January 1993 permitted the defence to request the *juge d'instruction* to conduct an interrogation of a suspect, an interrogation of a witness, a confrontation and a site examination. The 2000 reform extended the scope to all other acts that the defence believes necessary for the establishment of truth; Pradel 2002, p. 595.

[139]   The *chambre d'instruction* is part of the appellate court (*cour d'appel*) and consists of three judges; art. 191 CPP.

[140]   Hodgson 2005, p. 120. The right of access to the dossier may only be exercised through a lawyer, which means that an unrepresented suspect would not have such access; Pradel 2002, p. 593.

[141]   'Le droit de participer n'est pas celui de conduire la procedure, puisque c'est le juge qui mene l'instruction. Ce droit est simplement celui de proposer, de suggérer.'; see Pradel 2002, p. 594.

[142]   See Devreux 2002, p. 238.

to consult a lawyer immediately after his placement under GAV, otherwise the procedure will face being considered a nullity.[143]

The extent of the legal assistance provided during the GAV, however, remains nominal: some call him/her a 'social worker'[144] or even a 'tourist'.[145] It is limited to a 30 minute private consultation[146] with a lawyer prior to the first suspect's interrogation by police, at the expiry of first 24 hours of the GAV, and after 12 hours if the GAV is prolonged. In special circumstances, such as organized crime, the lawyer can intervene only 48 hours after the beginning of police custody, and only after 72 hours for drug and terrorist cases.[147]

However, an interrogation can commence prior to any consultation with a lawyer.[148] Lawyers are excluded from the interrogation of suspects. They are also not given access to the case file. The lawyers' role during the GAV is not to participate in the police inquiry or to defend a suspect, but to monitor that the GAV was conducted in conformity with the formal rules and that no excesses occurred, thus contributing to the credibility of police inquiries.[149] Lawyers themselves reportedly see their primary role during the GAV as providing moral and psychological support, rather than legal advice, to the suspect.[150]

The information concerning the right to a lawyer must be written and signed by the suspect. An oral notification is exceptional and temporary.[151] The request for a lawyer must be written down in an official report (procès-verbal) of the interrogation and be signed by the suspect.[152]

In practice, legal advice during police custody is requested in a minority of those criminal cases that result in the GAV.[153] While it is plausible that the majority of suspects do not ask for an interview with a lawyer during the GAV because they believe that such interview would not be necessary in their case, empirical research found that, occasionally, police officers were actively discouraging suspects from calling a lawyer.[154] Suspects may opt for an interview with a lawyer of their own choosing. If they do not have one, a duty lawyer will be appointed to them.[155] Local bar associations are responsible for organising emergency legal assistance,[156] and

---

[143]   Crim., 6 May 2003, Bull. crim., No. 93.

[144]   Soulez La Rivière 2009.

[145]   Portelli 2009. See also Hodgson 2005, p. 131-139.

[146]   The client-suspect interviews observed by Field and West in 1996-7 were brief, with many lasting no longer than 15 minutes; Field and West 2003, p. 287.

[147]   Art. 706-88 al. 6 CPP.

[148]   Crim., 13 December 2006, Bull. crim., No. 312.

[149]   This is important since mistreatment can occur; see the condemnation for violation of art. 2 in ECtHR 1 June 2006, Taïs v. France, No. 39922/03. See also Hodgson 2005, p. 133-134.

[150]   Field and West 2003, p. 287-288.

[151]   Circular CRIM 00-13 F1 of 4 December 2000, 2.1.

[152]   Art. 63-1 CPP.

[153]   According to the Rapport Lazerges No. 1 486 sur la presomption d'innocence et la reforme de la procedure penale, Assemblee Nationale, a lawyer is requested in 40% of criminal cases which result in a GAV; see Danet 2001, p. 39.

[154]   Hodgson 2004, p. 190.

[155]   Vogler 2008, p. 198.

[156]   Field & West 2003, p. 272.

the responsibility of police ends with the notification of the local bar about a suspect in the GAV who has requested legal advice.[157]

Legal assistance during the GAV is provided predominantly by inexperienced lawyers (*avocats-stagiaires*), or by non-criminal law specialists.[158] Lawyers who specialize in criminal law would normally participate in the GAV only if requested by their (paying) clients. Naturally, this places persons who, for various reasons – lack of financial means, first contact with criminal law – do not have their own lawyer, in a disadvantaged position compared to those who may know a lawyer from a former case, or through their social network.

There is an ongoing debate in France about the role of the lawyer in the GAV. The debate was initiated by lawyers' groups,[159] following a series of ECtHR judgments emphasising the need for legal advice from the outset and throughout police detention.[160] The debate coincided with the larger movement against the excessive use[161] and harsh conditions[162] of the GAV, coupled with ongoing public discussion of the Criminal Procedure Code reform.[163] Not surprisingly, the police are reluctant to allow lawyers a greater presence during the GAV than they have at present,[164] and are opposed to the proposed changes.

The response from the government has been mixed. Some concessions have been made – such as tightening the legal grounds for the GAV, audio recording of GAV interviews in serious matters (*crimes*), the possibility for a lawyer to access his client at the 12th hour of the GAV, etc. At the same time, the government is not prepared to allow a lawyer' presence at the first interrogation and continuously throughout the GAV.[165]

---

[157]   Pradel 2002, p. 458.
[158]   Field & West 2003, p. 272.
[159]   See Le Figaro, 17 November 'L'offensive des avocats pour reformer la GAV' available at <http://www.lefigaro.fr/actualite-france/2009/11/16/01016-20091116ARTFIG00313-l-offensive-des-avocats-pour-reformer-la-garde-a-vue-.php>.
[160]   ECtHR, Grand Chamber, 27 November 2008, *Salduz* v. *Turkey*, No. 36391/02; ECtHR 18 December 2008, *Panovits* v. *Cypruz*, No. 4268/04 and others.
[161]   In 2008, for example, there were about 800,000 cases of GAV. GAV may be applied to minors as young as 10 years old.
[162]   Such as the indiscriminate use of the handcuffs and strip searches. See *Commission Nationale de Déontologie de la Sécurité, Rapport 2008 Remis au Président de la République et au Parlement* available at <http://lesrapports.ladocumentationfrancaise.fr/BRP/094000187/ 0000.pdf>.
[163]   For details, see the Conclusions to this report.
[164]   At the end of December 2009, for example, there was a conflict between a *juge d'instruction* and some police officers who refused to obey the *juges d'instruction* and to arrest suspected persons in drug trafficking and organised crime. They explained their refusal by a lack of staff, but in a letter of 11 January 2010, the *juges d'instruction* condemned this refusal, arguing that the head of judicial police has declared that he did not want to arrest anybody, since the magistrates were requesting the effective presence of a lawyer at the very beginning of and during all the hearings of the *garde à vue*. The *juges d'instruction* have officialy ordered this requirement to cope with the latest decisions of the ECtHR, whereas the police head office relies only on the provisions in the CPP.
[165]   See the statement of the Minister of Justice, Michele-Alliot Marie, of 12 February 2010 about the proposed reforms, available at <http://www.presse.justice.gouv.fr/index.php?rubrique=11603&article=18947>.

The reaction from courts has also been mixed. A recent court decision condemned a GAV that was 'incompatible with human dignity' because; the suspect had not eaten or drunk during the 48 hours detention at the station office in Nancy.[166] In the cell, there was one bed that was already occupied by another suspect. The person has since been released without charge, as the court considered the conduct of this GAV lead to the nullity of the entire procedure.

Further, the *cour d'appel* of Nancy has ruled, in a decision dated 19 January 2010, as inadmissible statements made in GAV where suspects had not had access to a lawyer for 72 hours, again following the jurisprudence of the ECtHR.[167] In addition, the Paris court (*tribunal de Grande Instance*) on 28 January 2010 nullified 5 GAV, as being incompatible with European Law. The court said that legal assistance during a GAV – only 30 minutes at the beginning of detention – did not constitute a proper consultation between a lawyer and a defendant.[168] Despite these rulings, the Paris appeal court recently confirmed the compliance of the GAV regime with the ECHR.[169]

Outside of the GAV, lawyers play a modest role in the *enquête*. In cases where no *instruction* is envisaged, lawyers would only appear at the end of the investigation, when a suspect is brought before the *procureur* with the view to refer the case to court.[170]

During the judicial investigation (instruction)

The right to legal assistance is significantly broader during the *instruction* than during the preliminary investigation. However, it should be kept in mind that the *instruction* is only undertaken in approximately 5% of all criminal cases.[171] The first interrogation (*première comparution*), with the view to charge (*mis en examen*), and

[166] *Tribunal correctionnel* of Nancy, 9 September 2009.
[167] *Cour d'Appel de Rennes, Arrêt* N 350/2009, 17 December 2009; *Cour d'Appel de Nancy, Arrêt* N 10/72, 19 January 2010 available at <http://cnb.avocat.fr/Presence-de-l-avocat-des-le-debut-de-la-Garde-a-vue-la-Cour-d-appel-de-Nancy-dit-oui,-la-Cour-de-Cassation-devra-a-se_a796.html>.
[168] <http://www.maitre-eolas.fr/post/2010/02/06/Cinq-gardes-%C3%A0-vue-annul%C3%A9es-par-le-tribunal-correctionnel-de-Paris>. Quoting extracts of the judgement: '[...] This 30 minutes interview obviously does not cope with the European requirements. The lawyer can't fulfil his tasks which are listed by the ECtHR. He has no possibility to discuss the case – he has no information about it but the day/time of the offense and its nature and what the defender knows about it. It is impossible for him to organise the defence since he doesn't know the accusation grounds brought by the police officer who decided the garde à vue. Seek for evidence favourable to the accused remains very random since he doesn't know the unfavourable evidence and the circumstances of the case. The French judge has to guarantee the principle of a fair trial, especially with regard to defence rights. The French judge has to apply the ECHR'.
[169] *Cour d'Appel de Paris*, 9 February 2010, unpublished; available at <http://www.maitre-eolas.fr/post/2010/02/11/La-chambre-de-l-instruction-de-Paris-juge-la-garde-%C3%A0-vue-sans-avocat-conforme-%C3%A0-la-CEDH>.
[170] Art. 393 CPP, art. 41-2 § 5 CPP.
[171] See *Ministere de la Justice, Annuaire statistique de la Justice, Édition 2008*, p. 109, available at <http://www.ladocumentationfrancaise.fr/rapports-publics/094000150/index.shtml>.

any subsequent interrogations of the suspect by the investigating judge, are conducted in the presence of a lawyer, unless the suspect expressly waives this right.[172] The decision to waive the assistance of a lawyer must be written in the interview file. Any violation of the right to the presence of a lawyer leads to nullity of the respective investigative act.[173]

Before proceeding to the first interrogation, the investigating judge will verify whether the suspect is assisted by a lawyer.[174] If the suspect has already engaged a lawyer, a notification about the time and place of the interview must be sent to the lawyer by registered post no later than five days in advance.[175] The lawyer is not obliged to appear, however, and if he fails to do so, or departs during the course of the interrogation, it may proceed without him.[176] The same rules apply to all subsequent suspect interrogations.

If a suspect has not engaged a lawyer by the moment of the first interrogation, the investigating judge must inform him/her about his/her right to choose a lawyer, or to request a duty lawyer to be appointed. If the person under judicial examination is held in custody, his/her choice of lawyer may also be made by means of a statement before the governor of the prison.[177]

In relation to the first hearing before the investigating judge, article 116 CPP stipulates only that the suspect has a right to have a lawyer present with whom he/she can freely communicate, but there is no mention of a private consultation. In practice, lawyers' interviews with their clients before the first interrogation tend to be very short.[178] When duty lawyers are involved, they are often subject to significant time pressures: the notice period, for example, is usually no more than one or two hours before the appearance.[179] If the suspect is in custody (remand), the consultation takes place only after the first hearing.[180]

During the *instruction*, lawyers may have access to the *dossier* at any time. They can participate in some investigative acts, such as the interviews of suspects and witnesses, make procedural objections (for example, request to annul a certain procedural step – *nullite*) and request that a certain procedural step is undertaken.

However, the conduct of the *instruction*, the collection of evidence, and the construction of the dossier are firmly controlled by the investigating judge. The role of the defence lawyer during the *instruction* is thus to influence the construction of the *dossier* by the investigating judge, and in this sense their role is supplementary to that of the judge.[181] Empirical studies report that defence lawyers do not attempt

---

172   Art. 114 al. 1 CPP.
173   Crim., 4 January 1994, Bull. crim., No. 2.
174   Stefani 2008, p. 625.
175   Art. 114, § 2 CPP. However, if it is sent less than five days in advance, the results of interrogation would not be nullified, unless the defendant's interests were prejudiced; Pradel 2002, p. 590.
176   Stefani 2008, p. 629.
177   Art. 115 al. 3 CPP.
178   Field and West report that these interviews lasted no longer than half an hour; Field & West 2003, p. 300.
179   *Ibidem.*
180   Pradel 2002, p. 590.
181   Hodgson 2005, p. 124.

to actively shape the content of the *dossier*, or to perform fact finding on their own. Rather, they strive to reconstruct the *dossier* in the way that is most favourable to the defendant. When criticising the *dossier*, they mostly focus not on its content, but on its consistency and comprehensiveness, the presence of the standard supportive documents etc.[182]

Research indicates that, at the first interrogation, lawyers tend to be passive, and limit their interventions to a few questions at the end of the interview.[183] This is partly due to the established practice that an investigating judge controls the conduct and pace of the interview, and lawyers are expected to speak only when invited by the judge, normally towards the end of the interrogation. Another reported reason is that the first interrogations are served mostly by the duty lawyers, who tend to be less specialized and/or less experienced.

On a more general note, a Field and West study found a lack of continuity in legal representation throughout the pre-trial investigation. Investigating judges are not obliged to secure the attendance of a suspect's lawyer beyond sending him/her a notification about the prospective interview. In fact, the CPP explicitly states that, if a suspect's chosen lawyer does not attend, the judge may appoint a duty lawyer to assist the suspect during the interrogation. This often results in situations where suspects are represented by different duty lawyers at the GAV, at the bail hearings and at the premiere *comparution*.[184]

For certain groups of people

There are special rules for access to a lawyer for certain classes of people, in which case a lawyer is compulsory: in juvenile cases,[185] before military courts,[186] for vulnerable adults (*majeur protégé*),[187] and for a guilty plea.[188] Further, there is an obligation to have a lawyer at the cassation stage.[189] Finally, according to article 417 CPP, a lawyer is 'compulsory where the defendant suffers of an infirmity liable to compromise his defence'.[190]

Juveniles are persons under 18 years.[191] For juvenile defendants, special provisions apply. If a juvenile suspect is held in the GAV, the public prosecutor, the parents, a doctor and a lawyer must be immediately informed. Pre-trial interrogations of juvenile suspects are videotaped. In addition, 'the minor must be assisted by his legal representative except where this is impossible'.[192] Further, the provisions of 'fast-track' proceedings are not applicable to minors.

---

[182]   Field & West 2003, p. 293-294.
[183]   Field & West 2003, p. 301.
[184]   Field & West 2003, p. 304.
[185]   Art. 13 al. 1 of *Ordonnance* of 2 February 1945.
[186]   Art. 22 of *Code de justice militaire*.
[187]   Art. 706-116 CPP.
[188]   Art. 495-9 CPP.
[189]   Art. 973 of *code of civil procedure*.
[190]   Art. 417 al. 4 CPP.
[191]   There is no age of criminal responsibility for children since only the judge estimates his/her capacity of understanding his/her acts.
[192]   Art. 78-3 CPP.

There are also special provisions for mentally vulnerable suspects and defendants.[193] They were introduced in the CCP by the law No. 2007-308 of 5 March 2007, which provided reforms for the protection of adults, following a condemnation by the ECtHR.[194] Called *majeur protégé*,[195] this concerns adults whose mental or psychological state could endanger their own person or property. The public prosecutor must inform the guardian and the judge of guardianship about the proceedings. The guardian has access to all files and permission to visit the person in custody. There must be a medical report before any judgment evaluating the criminal responsibility of the person. Failure to apply these rules results in a nullity.

2.2.3. The right to legal representation at the trial stage

Although the assistance of a lawyer is, in general, not compulsory before a *tribunal correctionnel*, there have been only isolated cases where the defendant has waived his/her right to legal representation at trial stage – either he/she benefits from legal aid or can afford to pay for a lawyer. When the defendant is not assisted at the hearing, but demands a lawyer, the judge has to appoint one; if this causes logistical problems, the hearing must be postponed.[196] Those proceedings for which a lawyer must be present concern expedited hearings (*comparution immediate*) and a guilty plea (*comparution sur reconnaissance préalable de culpabilité*).

In practice, it happens quite often that lawyers are called to different hearings before different courts concerning different clients on the same day.[197] Some jurisdictions organize meetings to set hearings dates, others send proposals in advance, but some decide unilaterally within a short time frame and without informing lawyers. When there is no possibility to postpone a hearing, the jurisprudence admits that, because of 'continuity of justice' and 'judgment in reasonable time', either an appointed lawyer will be chosen before the *cour d'assises*,[198] or a defendant will be heard without his lawyer.[199]

2.3. *Procedural rights*

2.3.1. The right to release from custody pending trial

The right to release from custody pending trial is linked to the restrictive conditions for the use of pre-trial detention.[200] A suspect must be released as soon as the

---

[193]   Art. 706-112 CPP.
[194]   ECtHR 30 January 2001, *Vaudelle* v. *France*, No. 35683/97.
[195]   Under Titre XI of Livre I of the civil code.
[196]   Crim., 22 September 1999, Bull. crim., No. 196.
[197]   See, for more details, Saint-Pierre 2007.
[198]   Crim., 31 March 2005, Bull. crim., No. 114.
[199]   Crim., 20 December 2006, Bull. crim., No. 7.
[200]   Art. 144 CPP.

grounds for his/her detention no longer apply.[201] This right is also supported by the obligation of 'reasonable time'.[202] Any prolongation of pre-trial detention must be balanced with the possibility of foreseeable delay to finish the investigation.[203] In addition, release can occur through a nullity of the detention itself, since the lawyer must be duly informed of the hearing that decides on detention, and may therefore participate in this hearing and challenge the grounds for pre-trial detention.[204]

Courts may apply a number of measures as alternatives to pre-trial detention (conditional release or bail). For example, a suspect may be ordered to 'abstain from seeing, meeting and contacting persons',[205] abstain from holding or carrying any weapons. There are 15 different conditions that can be imposed when a person is released on bail. Surety (*cautionnement*) is 'determined [...] by the liberty and custody judge, taking into account the income and outgoings of the person'. This means that payment must correspond to the financial resources of the defendant and that the judge must provide reasons for his/her decision of the relevant amount.[206] In addition, the provisional reimbursement of the financial damage suffered by the *partie civile* can also be taken into account.[207]

In 2006, 35,000 persons had been convicted after pre-trial detention – 2,500 for *crime*. The average length of pre-trial detention in the context of an *instruction* was about 7.3 months; 15 months for the *cour d'assises* and six months for the *tribunal correctionnel*. The average length of pre-trial detention for crime was 26 months.

The decision on pre-trial detention or (conditional) release is rendered by the liberty and custody judge (*juge des libertés et de la détention*) or, in certain circumstances, by the *Chambre d'Instruction* or the *tribunal correctionnel*. The liberty and custody judge was introduced in 2000, in response to a concern that the independence of the investigating judge, who had been deciding on pre-trial detention prior to 2000, was compromised by his investigative functions.[208] Empirical research undertaken in 1997-1999 – shortly before the introduction of the liberty and custody judge – found that decisions to place a suspect in pre-trial detention had been largely pre-determined in consultations between the prosecutor

---

[201] Art. 144-1 al. 2. The grounds for pre-trial detention are listed in art. 144: 'Pre-trial detention may only be ordered or extended if it is the only way: 1° to preserve material evidence or clues or to prevent either witnesses or victims or their families being pressurised or fraudulent conspiracy between persons under judicial examination and their accomplices; 2° to protect the person under judicial examination, to guarantee that he remains at the disposal of the law, to put an end to the offence or to prevent its renewal; 3° to put an end to an exceptional and persistent disruption of public order caused by the seriousness of the offence, the circumstances in which it was committed, or the gravity of the harm that it has caused.'

[202] Art. 144-1 al. 1 CPP; art. 5-3 ECHR, see ECtHR 26 September 2006, *Bernard* v. *France*, No. 27678/02. On this issue (reasonable time), reference is made by French jurisprudence to the ECHR; see Crim., 15 May 2002, Bull. Crim., No. 114.

[203] Art.145-3 CPP, see Crim., 21 June 2005, Bull crim., No. 182.

[204] Arts. 197 and 803-1 CPP, see Crim., 10 December 2008, *pourvoi* No. 08-86.668.

[205] Art. 138 al. 2, 9 CPP.

[206] Crim., 4 November 2008, *pourvoi* No. 08-85.724.

[207] Crim., 23 August 1994, Bull. crim., No. 292.

[208] Hodgson 2005, p. 215.

and the investigating judge (but without defence counsel) prior to a detention hearing. Thus, the pre-trial hearing was more of a procedural formality.[209]

The study also reported that, contrary to the presumption of innocence, the suspect's perceived guilt or innocence was central to the discussion of whether or not he should be placed in pre-trial detention.[210] Furthermore, it transpired from interviews with prosecutors and investigating judges that the threat of pre-trial detention was commonly used to extract confessions.[211]

Given that the liberty and security judges share close educational and professional ties with the prosecutors and investigating judges (they all belong to the corps of the *magistrature*, follow the same educational path, socialise together and sit in the same office), it is unlikely that the introduction of this new figure effectively addresses the problem described in the Hodgson study. Indeed, it appears that prosecutors continue to discuss pre-trial detention outside of the courtroom, only now not with the investigating judges, but with the liberty and security judges.[212]

2.3.2. The right of a defendant to be tried in his/her presence

Rules relating to the need for the presence of the defendant in court differ according to the jurisdiction before which they appear. As a general principle, his/her presence shall be the rule, but the accused can also be tried in his/her absence. Based on formal criteria, the protection or guarantees are the same with or without the accused. The court can decide to 'defer the case to a latter session'[213] if it considers that there can be no fair trial without the accused.

The trial procedure is different when a defendant is not present. First, interrogations of a defendant can not practically take place. Second, as to serious crimes, the jurors do not examine the case, but only professional judges.[214] Lawyers have the same powers in a trial *in absentia* as in a normal one, but when there is no lawyer defending the accused, the 'court rules on the accusation'.[215] Moreover, there is no possibility of appeal for persons tried *in absentia*.[216]

In trials before the *tribunal correctionnel*, the lawyer is entitled to represent his client, no matter if the latter has known about the trial or not. When the sentence rendered is more than two years imprisonment, the court can issue an arrest warrant. In serious criminal matters (*crimes*), the defendant must be present and representation by his lawyer alone is not allowed. However, when the defendant refuses to participate in the trial, the court can decide to hear the case with only his/her lawyer present.

---

[209]   *Ibidem.*
[210]   Hodgson 2005, p. 216.
[211]   Hodgson 2005, p. 218-219.
[212]   For example, Hodgson cites an example of a *Cour de Cassation* decision (9 July 2003) where the fact that the *procureur* met with the liberty and security judge before a custody hearing did not result in a nullity of the custody decision; Hodgson 2005, p. 215.
[213]   Art. 379-2 CPP.
[214]   Art. 379-3 CPP.
[215]   Art. 379-3 al. 3 CPP.
[216]   Art. 379-5 CPP. See also Crim., 30 January 2008, Bull. crim., No. 26; D. 2008. AJ. 788.

In 2007, there were 33 people convicted for *crimes* (5 years imprisonment and more) *in absentia*. The sanction if any required protections or guarantees are breached is to quash the proceedings by appealing on a point of law under a so-called *cassation*.[217]

2.3.3. The right to be presumed innocent

The presumption of innocence is regularly questioned in criminal proceedings, since the media often have access to information that puts suspects or defendants under a negative light.[218] It is considered a fundamental right that protects any suspect or defendant from guilt, as long as a criminal court has not decided whether he/she is guilty or not, and is elevated to the status of the 'general principles governing the procedure'.[219] Further, the jurisprudence regularly confirms this right.[220] In its broadest possible meaning, the presumption of innocence may be understood as protecting any person from being publicly accused of a crime, no matter whether or not there is an ongoing criminal investigation against him/her. In the context of criminal proceedings, however, the presumption of innocence means that the authorities taking procedural decisions should not pre-empt the question of guilt, until it is proven beyond a reasonable doubt.

Empirical studies into the decision making processes of police, prosecutors and judges, demonstrate that the presumption of innocence may be compromised in a number of significant ways. Firstly and perhaps most importantly, the research casts doubt on the 'neutrality' and 'objective nature' of the pre-trial investigation, which is meant to examine the circumstances inculpating and exonerating the suspect with equal care.[221]

In reality, investigations are geared towards constructing a *dossier* that would include sufficient material to convict a suspect, and preferably a confession. The tension between decisions on pre-trial detention and the presumption of innocence has been discussed above (2.3.1).

On a technical level, the burden of proof of defendant's guilt generally lies on the prosecution,[222] with the consequence that the defendant has the benefit of the

---

217   Art. 591 CPP.
218   N. Sarkozy, President of the Republic and Head of the judicial authorities, declared on television the 22 September 2009, about a running case before the *tribunal correctionnel* where former Prime Minister D. de Villepin was a defendant: 'Two independent judges have brought the guilty parties before the court'. There was a previous condemnation, because of a Minister presenting a suspect as a murderer; ECtHR 10 February 1995, *Allenet de Ribemont* v. *France*, No. 15175/89).
219   'As all persons are held innocent until they shall have been declared guilty'; art. 9 of the *Déclaration des droits de l'homme du citoyen* of 26 August 1789; 'Everyone charged with a criminal offence shall be presumed innocent until proved guilty according to law'; art. 6 § 2 ECHR; 'Every person suspected or prosecuted is presumed innocent as long as his guilt has not been established', preliminary art. III. CPP.
220   Crim., 29 May 1980, Bull. crim., No. 164; Crim., 22 February 1993, Bull. crim., No. 84.
221   See e.g. Hodgson 2005, p. 225-226.
222   Crim., 24 March 1949, Bull. crim., No. 114.

doubt, even if guilt is seen as probable.[223] There are, however, some exceptions, where the suspect or defendant is under a presumption of guilt and thus must prove his/her innocence, for instance, in cases of smuggling,[224] procuring, and drug trafficking.[225] In addition, defences such as self-defence or necessity[226] have also to be raised and proven by the defendant.[227]

2.3.4. The right to silence

The right to silence during a criminal procedure is considered as a fundamental right. It means that a suspect or a defendant cannot be obliged to confess, or to answer questions from a police officer, a prosecutor or a judge. This right has existed since 1897.[228]

Notification of the right to silence at the outset of the GAV was introduced in 2000, but then narrowed down in 2002 and repealed in 2003.[229] If a lawyer-client interview in the GAV takes place, lawyers would normally inform their client about their right to remain silent. However, even if clients decide to exercise this right, it is difficult to maintain silence under the significant psychological pressure to speak that is often exerted by the police.[230]

Before an investigating judge, the defendant must be informed of his/her right to silence.[231] During the investigation proceedings, the defendant can be heard only when his/her lawyer assists him/her in the judge's office. He/she always has the right to refuse to answer questions. Further, the right to silence also applies at the trial stage (*tribunal correctionnel* and *cour d'assises*), even if there is no statutory provision relating to this.[232]

2.3.5. The right to reasoned judgements

There is an obligation for a reasoned judgement in the *tribunal correctionnel* (*motivation du jugement*),[233] but not in a *cour d'assises*, where the jury is only required to answer (yes or no) a list of questions on the offence and the guilt.

[223]   Crim., 22 June 1960, Bull. crim., No. 339.
[224]   Crim., 5 October 2005, Bull. crim., No. 252.
[225]   The presumption of responsibility is also recognized by the ECtHR 30 March 2004, *Radio France* v. *France*, No. 53984/00.
[226]   *Etat de nécessité*, for example to steal food to avoid starvation or to feed children.
[227]   It is not known whether these apparent conflicts with the presumption of innocence have been challenged at the ECtHR.
[228]   Art. 3 of law of 8 December 1897. The right to silence is, for instance, mentioned under art. 116 al. 4 CPP.
[229]   Vogler 2008, p. 194.
[230]   For an account of an empirical study into the conduct and tactics of police interrogation in France, see Hodgson 2004.
[231]   Art. 116 al. 4: 'The investigating judge then informs the person of his choice to remain silent, to make a statement, or to be interrogated'.
[232]   Interviewed judge 1 considers this non-written right like the right to drink or to eat during the trial, both essential rights without statutory provision.
[233]   Crim., 23 January 1963, Bull. crim., No. 39.

The judgements rendered by correctional courts, 'must include reasons and enacting terms. The reasons form the basis of the decision'.[234] The court must recognize the characteristics of the offence, to reason in relation to them[235] and to detail them.[236] Further, a *motivation* is also required in the proceedings involving a guilty plea.[237]

As to serious crimes, a cause of the lack of a reasoned judgement[238] is the unprofessional and heterogeneous character of juries, and thus a greater difficulty to find a common agreement.[239] There are merely some formal criteria to fulfil. The decision consists only in either retaining (or not) any offence dealt with before the court. The juror 'writes or causes to be secretly written the word "yes" or "no" on a table' (art. 357 al. 2 CPP).

A recent report of the Committee for criminal procedure reform (*Léger* Report)[240] suggests that, relying on the recent ECtHR case law,[241] the decisions of the *cour d'assises* should be reasoned, in order to guarantee the parties' right to appeal against such decisions, which was introduced in 2000.[242]

2.3.6. The right to appeal

An appeal for misdemeanour offences can be undertaken by all parties to the trial: the defendant (on criminal and civil matters), third party (only civil interests), the prosecutor, the prosecutor-in-chief and other public bodies involved in the prosecution.[243] The right to appeal was only recently granted for convictions before the *cour d'assises*.[244] In contrast to other types of appeal before a higher court (*appel hiérarchique*), the appeal lies to another *cour d'assises* and is thus called 'turning' (*tournant*).

The appeal form made by the defendant or his/her lawyer is a declaration to file with the clerk of the court that took the contested decision. An appeal of a judgment made by a *tribunal correctionnel* does not require much formality. Even a guilty plea can be reviewed on appeal.[245] The normal maximum time limit within which a defendant may appeal is 10 days, even though the prosecutor-in-chief has

---

[234] Art. 485 CPP. Even a *motivation spéciale* is required in case of a prison sentence, art. 132-19 CCP.
[235] Crim., 22 September 1999, Bull. crim., No. 195.
[236] Crim., 6 March 1996, Bull. crim., No. 105.
[237] 'The criminal order must be reasoned', art. 495-9 al. 2 CPP.
[238] 'The law does not ask the judges to account for the means by which they convinced themselves; it does not charge them with any rule from which they shall specifically derive the fullness and adequacy of evidence', article 353 al. 2 CPP.
[239] See Pradel 2008, p. 877.
[240] *Rapport de Comite de Reflection sur la Justice Penale, remis a le President de la Republique et a le Premier Ministre le 1er septembre 2009* (hereinafter – *Léger* Report), available at <http://www.ladocumentationfrancaise.fr/rapports-publics/094000401/index.shtml>. For a more detailed discussion of the reform proposals, see below Section 4.
[241] ECtHR 13 January 2009, *Taxquet* v. *Belgium*, No. 926/05.
[242] *Léger* Report, p. 37-39.
[243] Art. 497 CPP.
[244] Law of 15 June 2000.
[245] Art. 495-11 CPP.

two months for it, which violates the equality of arms principle.[246] An appeal is not possible when a person has been sentenced *in absentia*.

During an appeal and until a new judgement, the enforcement of the contested judgement is suspended.[247] An appeal cannot raise a new issue before the appeal court. If an appeal is upheld before the *Cour de Cassation*, then the conviction is quashed.

An appeal can be made by the prosecutor against a conviction of guilt, the sentence or against an acquittal.[248] A convicted person can appeal against the conviction and sentence but not against an acquittal. In addition, when the convicted person is the only party to the appeal, then he/she cannot receive a harsher sentence than rendered at first instance. In general, the prosecutor always appeals when the defendant does, and vice versa, so that the court of appeal has the possibility to review all decisions.

Recently, the Ministry of Justice directly and publicly decided to appeal in an *assises* case where all accused were convicted to prison sentences.[249] The Ministry took this decision under the pressure of the victims' representatives, who were not entitled to appeal, although the prosecutor had declared after the court's decision that he was satisfied with it.

In 2006, there were 600 appeals in criminal matters, which represent 23.8% of all decisions before a *cour d'assises*. In the same year, 48,873 decisions were made by *chambre des appels correctionnels*. Further, 9,767 decisions were made on appeal against measures of the investigating judge. Finally, 9,205 new cases have been received and 9,047 closed by the *cour de cassation*.

2.4. Rights relating to effective defence

2.4.1. The right to investigate the case

Defence lawyers have limited opportunities to influence the collection of evidence in the *dossier*. Since 1993, for example, there exists the possibility to ask for *actes d'instruction* (investigation measures) and, since 2000, for *expertises* (expert reports), meaning that the defence is able to request that experts be appointed and suggest what issues they should deal with (art. 161-1 CPP). Specifically, according to article 156 al. 1 CPP, 'any investigating or trial court may order an expert opinion where a

---

[246] Crim., 10 February 2009, *pourvoi* No. 08-83.837; see also ECtHR 22 May 2008, *Gacon v. France*, No. 1092/04.
[247] Art. 30-4 CPP: 'During the time limit for an appeal and during the appeal itself, execution of the decision reached in the criminal proceedings is suspended. However, the committal order remains in force against a convicted person sentenced to imprisonment'. This means that the defendant can be kept in custody pending the appeal hearing. Art. 506: 'During the time limits for appealing and during the appeal itself, the enforcement of the judgment is suspended'.
[248] Art. 380-2 CPP.
[249] 13 July 2009. 14 sentences were lower than the demand of the prosecutor, for example 15 and 18 years prison instead of 20. As a consequence, only 15 accused (14 accomplices and the main defendant) out of 28 will stand before the next *cour d'assises*.

technical question arises, either upon the application of the public prosecutor, of its own motion, or on the application of the parties.'

However, the decision as to whether to undertake a certain act suggested by the defence, and to attach its results to the dossier, belongs to the authority that conducts the inquiry. For example, only the investigating judge, or the court judge, is entitled to decide whether or not such expert reports will be conducted. When the defence demands an *expertise* and there is a delay of one month, this constitutes as implicit denial of the demand by the investigating judge.[250] There is the possibility for a defendant to appeal against a decision of the judge refusing his/her application. If a DNA examination is requested by the defence, the defence party must pay for it, unless the defendant is benefiting from legal aid.

For a variety of reasons, defence lawyers usually do not conduct their own (private) investigations.[251] Duty lawyers, who handle the majority of criminal cases, are not motivated professionally (these are usually lawyers who are not specialized or interested in criminal matters), or financially,[252] to pursue a costly and time consuming independent investigation. On the other hand, specialist criminal lawyers acting for private clients may be deterred from pursuing their own investigation by cultural or deontological reasons. The use of private investigators in high profile cases, for example, is seen with suspicion in French legal culture.[253] Similarly, prior contact by defence lawyers with witnesses is regarded by courts as tainting the quality of the testimony given by such witnesses.[254]

Thus, it is usually the officers of the judicial police (art. 62 CPP) who interview witnesses, even if the defence can ask the investigating judge to conduct an interview on behalf of the defence.

2.4.2. The right to adequate time and facilities for the preparation of the defence

During the *instruction* phase, the investigating judge must notify the suspect 'by a registered letter that he will be called, within a period of not less than ten days or longer than two months, for a first appearance'.[255] If a suspect has a lawyer, the latter must be notified no later than five days prior to the interrogation;[256] if by the time of the first interrogation a suspect has not hired a lawyer, but wishes to do so, or requests a duty lawyer to be appointed, a chosen lawyer or local *batonnier* must be notified 'without delay'.[257] In practice, duty lawyers are often notified about the first interrogation too late to adequately prepare (see Section 2.2.2.).

Further, if it is impossible for the investigating judge to undertake in person all the investigative steps, 'he may give a rogatory letter (*commission rogatoire*) to

---

[250] Crim., 25 April 2006, Bull. crim., No. 109, D.2006. IR.1636.
[251] *Ibidem.*
[252] Legal aid fees are on a flat basis - fixed per case rather than per hour worked.
[253] Field & West 2003, p. 296.
[254] Field & West 2003, p. 296-297.
[255] Art. 80-2 CPP.
[256] Art. 114-2 CPP.
[257] Art. 116-4 CPP.

judicial police officers in order to have them perform the necessary investigative steps' (hearing, interview, search, where the lawyer can be present).[258] As discussed above, the investigating judge uses the *commission rogatoire* systematically for all acts of investigation other than those that he/she is not permitted to delegate in this way. The period of notification is the same as for articles 80-2 and 114. The obligation to notify a suspect and his/her lawyer is, however, not on the investigating judge, but on the person who conducts the *acte rogatoire*.[259]

The investigating judge has other means to secure a person's attendance. The subpoena (*mandat de comparution*) is 'designed to give to the person against whom it is made a notice to appear before the judge at the date and time specified by this warrant'.[260] Failure to comply with the subpoena is illegal, although there is no penalty for such a failure. A summons can also be used.[261] In both cases, there is no specific time period for notification.

During the trial phase, there are several statutory notice periods to ensure that defendants have time to prepare their defence. Under the *citation directe* procedure before the correctional court, 'the time between the date when the summons is served and the date fixed for the appearance before the correctional court or police court is at least ten days', or one month if the defendant resides outside of metropolitan France.[262] The same notice periods apply to summonses before the *tribunals de police* and *tribunals correctionnel*.[263]

Before the *assises*, 'the public prosecution informs the accused of the date at which he must appear'. In addition, the president of the *cour d'assises* discusses with both parties the date at which the trial will be held – which can be up to three months later. Article 277 stipulates that the defendant must be informed at least five days before the first hearing.

There is no provision for the defence to delay an *assises* session. Only 'the president may order any cases […] to be adjourned to a later session'.[264] The defendant is not qualified to make such a demand.[265] Throughout the proceedings, the right of a private consultation is absolute, since 'the accused is allowed to communicate freely with his lawyer at any time'.[266]

There is, however, no adequate time and facilities for the preparation of the defence for expedited hearings (*comparutions immediates*),[267] since the prosecutor has 24 or 48 hours to build a case, but the defence lawyer only a few hours to read the file and prepare. Under the CPP, defendants have an option to request an adjournment of a hearing for two to six weeks,[268] but this is rarely used. There is a

---

258   Art. 81 al. 4 CPP.
259   Stefani 2008, p. 714.
260   Art. 121-2 al. 4 CPP.
261   *Mandat d'amener*, art. 122 al. 5 CPP.
262   Art. 522 al. 1 CPP.
263   Art. 180 CPP.
264   Art. 287 CPP.
265   Crim., 5 December 1990, Bull. crim. No. 419.
266   Art. 278 CPP.
267   In 2006, *comparution immediate* was used in 8.2% of cases before the *tribunals correctionnels*; Ministere de la Justice. Annuaire Statistiques de la Justice. Edition 2008, 109.
268   Art. 397-1 CPP.

great deal of pressure on the defence lawyers (who are usually duty lawyers) and judges to dispose with the cases dealt by the *comparution immediate* procedure in the most expedient manner.[269] In some busier courts, multiple cases are heard simultaneously.[270] Thus, parties have no time to study the *dossier* and to adequately prepare for the hearing.

As to the *comparution sur reconnaissance préalable de culpabilité* (guilty plea), it is possible for a lawyer to negotiate the sentence with the prosecutor, which must be endorsed by a judge.[271] This is a relatively new procedure, introduced only in 2004, which is being used increasingly more often.[272] By definition, plea bargaining, in order to serve the interests of the defendant effectively, must be conducted by an adversarial and proactive defence lawyer. This image conflicts with traditional French defence culture. Unfortunately, there has been no research into whether defence lawyers are taking a more adversarial stance in guilty plea proceedings, and whether the interests of the defendants are protected effectively in such proceedings.

Magistrates interviewed for this report claimed that, in several cases, the defendant accepted a higher sentence than he would have received if he had followed the regular proceedings in a trial before the court. For instance, where the maximum sentence is ten years imprisonment, the prosecutor might propose seven years, whereas the established case law indicates five years. Lawyers and prosecutors are both aware of this, but the defendant is willing to finish with the proceedings as quickly as possible – and consequently to avoid further pre-trial detention.

2.4.3. The right to equality of arms in examining witnesses

With regard to evidence put before a trial court, and witnesses giving oral evidence at court, the court president decides upon the evidence permitted before the *tribunal correctionnel* and the *cour d'assises*. However, the court president must respect article 6 § 3d ECHR,[273] as well as corresponding French legal sources and jurisprudence that are in line with the ECHR.[274]

In expedited hearings, the defendant or his lawyer can 'ask the court to order any investigative action', including examining witnesses, and any refusal must be

---

[269] In some courts, expedited hearings sometimes take place after the end of the working day and continue into the night until around 3 or 4 a.m. The 'record' in Paris is 6 a.m.; Portelli 2009. See also Viennot 2007.

[270] Vogler 2008, p. 216.

[271] Art. 459-9 CPP.

[272] According to the statistics, in *tribunals correctionnels*, 2,187 such proceedings took place in 2004, 27,500 in 2005 and 50,250 (about 9% of all cases) in 2006; see *Ministere de la Justice. Annuaire Statistiques de la Justice*. Edition 2008, 109.

[273] The right 'to examine or have examined witnesses against him and to obtain the attendance and examination of witnesses on his behalf under the same conditions as witnesses against him'.

[274] Under arts. 329 (*assises*), 397-5 and 435 CPP (*correctionnel*). The jurisprudence refers to the same principle stipulated in art. 6 § 3 ECHR and art. 444 CPP.

reasoned.[275] Further, the defendant or his lawyer can request witnesses to 'be summoned forthwith and by any means available', which means that he/she has the possibility to demand a postponement of the trial.[276]

In regular proceedings in *tribunals correctionnels*, examining witnesses are not often used, because judges consider that all evidence is to be found in the investigation file. Still, when witnesses are called, the presiding judge first hears the defendant, then the witnesses, who are examined by all parties.[277] The witnesses from the accusing and defendant parties are to be accepted by the judge, but not those called by the prosecutor. Until 2000, only the presiding judge could pose questions to witnesses. Since 2000, representatives of the parties, including defence lawyers, may question witnesses, but with the prior permission of the presiding judge (art. 442.1 CPP).[278] Defendants may not pose questions to witnesses directly, but only through the presiding judge.

The jurisprudence has dealt with the examination of witnesses. A court can make a decision without having heard witnesses, if this testimony was not the only evidence to prove guilt.[279] However, the court must provide reasons for its refusal to hear witnesses; the consequent need to delay a hearing is not a sufficient reason to justify such a decision.[280] Instead, only serious reasons may be accepted to refuse to hear witnesses.[281]

In addition, the testimony of a witness who has not been examined at any time during the proceedings by the defendant or his/her lawyer cannot constitute the sole basis for conviction.[282] The principle of *contradictoire* requires the parties to inform each other about the witnesses who would attend the hearing, even though there is no explicit provision in the CPP to this effect

There is no possibility of cross-examination of the witnesses in the legal tradition of the North American system. Once the judge, the accusing parties and the prosecutor have examined witnesses, the defence lawyer has only the opportunity to raise questions 'for the information of the court'. Generally, the procedure of evidence taking is less formal and more conversational than in the courts of the common law countries.[283]

Some specific rules governing witness examination before a *cour d'assises* apply. Each party can call witnesses – the prosecutor and the defence lawyer each draft a list of witnesses. However, over recent years, managerial concerns and pressure from the Ministry of Justice has lead to a reduction in the number of witnesses who are heard in person because this makes the trial last longer.[284] The

---

[275] Art. 397-1 al. 3 CPP.

[276] Crim., 18 April 1988, Bull. crim., No. 161.

[277] All parties must ask the judge 'for leave to speak', art. 442-1 CPP. In addition, witnesses 'swear an oath to speak the whole truth and nothing but the truth before starting to give their evidence', article 446 CPP.

[278] Vogler 2008, p. 217.

[279] Crim., 10 May 2006, Bull. crim., No. 123.

[280] Crim., 29 March 2006, Bull. crim., No. 93.

[281] Crim., 9 November 2005, Bull. crim., No. 287.

[282] ECtHR 13 November 2003, *Rachdad* v. *France*, No. 71846/01.

[283] Vogler 2008, p. 217.

[284] Interviewed judge, August 2009.

costs of witnesses' attendance are borne by the defence, or are paid from the legal aid budget. In addition, defendants who are not eligible for legal aid and represented by private lawyers may ask the public prosecutor to call up to five witnesses on behalf of the defence.[285] Since defence lawyers do not interview prospective witnesses, they cannot be sure what evidence they will give in court.

The presiding judge can call at any time any witness he/she wants. A lawyer can contact his/her own expert. During the trial, a lawyer can call witnesses before the court after having informed the prosecutor. Witnesses are interrogated by the judge and other parties, and the lawyer can cross examine them. He/she can also submit *expertise* he/she has ordered or written testimony.

2.4.4. The right to free interpretation of documents and translation[286]

For the suspect, the right to have access to an interpreter is based on article 102 (hearing as a witness)[287] and article 121 (interrogation and confrontation by the investigating judge) of the CCP. For the defendant, this right is stipulated under article 272 (interpreter in the court office), articles 344 (interpreter or translation of documents by the production and discussion of evidence), 407 (hearings) and 443 (administration of evidence).

The jurisprudence on the right to an interpreter[288] refers on the one hand to the right of free communication with a lawyer (art. 116) and on the other to article 6 § 3 (e) of the ECHR. A suspect or defendant has a right to free assistance of an interpreter, if he/she cannot understand or speak the language of his/her lawyer, the investigator, the person conducting an expert report or the court.[289] A person has a right to an interpreter to enable him/her to communicate with his/her lawyer. A defendant is also allowed to speak before the court in another language, which the interpreter translates into French.[290] However, the jurisprudence[291] has held that a defendant is not entitled to a translation of all the documents.[292]

The need for an interpreter is determined if it is established that the suspect or defendant is not able to understand what he/she is being told or cannot express him/herself in the local language.[293] The responsibility for determining this lies

---

[285] Art. 281-4 CPP.

[286] In 2006, around 7,000 foreign persons were under investigation by a *juge d'instruction*, and 73,489 were found guilty of *délit*.

[287] All arts. referred to here are from the CPP.

[288] Crim., 6 December 1994, D., 1995, Somm. p.146, commented by J. Pradel.

[289] For example, in a case of a sexual offence, the interview of the non French speaking defendant by experts without the assistance of an interpreter has lead to the nullity of the expert report; Crim., 21 March 2007, Bull. crim. No. 90, D.2007. AJ. 1271.

[290] Crim., 13 February 1993, B.C., No. 73.

[291] *Cour d'assises spéciale*, Paris, 2 November 1994, D., 1995, Somm. p.139, commented by J. Pradel, confirmed by Crim., 4 October 1995, B.C., No. 293.

[292] Article 279 CPP: 'copy of the official records establishing the existence of the offence, of the written statements of witnesses and of any experts' reports'. This is the practice, according to our interviews.

[293] For example, art. 272 al. 4 CPP.

with the investigating judge,[294] the public prosecutor or the court judge,[295] depending on the stage of the proceedings. During the trial proceedings, the president of the court makes this determination. Judges and lawyers are of the opinion that the right to interpretation is complied with.[296] The state must pay all expenses, but it sometimes takes several months for the remuneration of interpreters. In addition, some interpreters or translators are not aware of the criminal procedure, and have no specific training to translate legal terms, which complicates communication between the parties.[297]

To ensure quality control, some provisions[298] require that interpreters and translators are registered on a list established by the public prosecutor of each district court (*tribunal de grande instance*). This list is updated once a year. Interpreters and translators must fulfil three criteria: to live or work in the area of the district court, to prove their skills by diploma or experience in the interpretation/translation field, and to be without a criminal record. Normally, interpreters and translators are asked to take an oath, although according to the jurisprudence, this is not compulsory.[299]

Some interpreters and translators are also recognised as judicial experts working for appeal courts and the cassation court. They may also be registered on the above mentioned list if they wish to be. Registration requires that an investigation is conducted by the public prosecutor, who must consult the president of the district court. The public prosecutor can remove from the list those who no longer fulfil the criteria. He can also remove those who have not properly fulfilled their duty. The interpreter or translator must be informed of the decision of withdrawal and is able to respond to it. The decision must be reasoned.

Since they are appointed by the Ministry of Justice, it is difficult for a suspect or defendant to criticize or challenge an interpreter or a translator. It might be problematic for a suspect to point to the inaccuracies in the interpretation/translation, because his/her knowledge of the French language is, by definition, limited. Another problem lies in the complexity of languages and dialects, which makes it difficult for judges and court employees to define which language the defendant speaks and what interpreter shall be called. Some interpreters also do not speak good French.

If there is a problem with the interpretation/translation, the procedure will be annulled.[300] Finally, the delays of remuneration for interpreter or translator are sometimes very long and some persons refuse to come before court, or voluntarily take themselves off the list.

---

[294]   Art. 102 al. 2 CPP.

[295]   The judge alone decides this; Crim., 21 December 1977, Bull. crim. No. 409.

[296]   See, among others, our interviews 2009; Portelli 2009.

[297]   Difficulties also observed by interviewed magistrates.

[298]   Decree No. 2005-214 of 3 March 2005 concerning interpreters and translators.

[299]   Crim., 12 January 1966, Bull. crim., No. 8; Crim., 7 September 1974, Bull. crim., No. 268.

[300]   *Cour de cassation*, 13 February 1974, Bull. Crim.ndeg.65.

3.   Professional culture of defence lawyers

The profession of lawyer is ruled by the law of 31 December 1971.[301] In 2007, there were 47,765 lawyers in France (23,619 are women), which represents a rise of 40% within 10 years, out of a population of 63 million inhabitants (1 lawyer per 1,318 inhabitants). They are all required to be members of the single official bar association: the *Conseil national des barreaux* (CNB).[302] The CNB is independent of government and government institutions. The National Bar Council is a recognised public institution and represents all lawyers in France, even if each lawyer remains personally registered with one of the 181 local bars (*barreau*).[303] Lawyers are affiliated to a local committee in each court district (*tribunal de grande instance*). There is no specialised criminal defence bar,[304] and the bar association has exclusive responsibility for the discipline of the legal profession.[305]

[301]   This law has been significantly modified by the law of 31 December 1990, and by three decrees of 27 November 1991, 20 July 1992 and 25 March 1993, in addition to a normative decision of the national bar, No. 2005/003, adapting the internal ruling.

[302]   This was established by the law of 31 December 1990, modifying art. 21-1 of the law No. 71-1130 of 31 December 1971.

[303]   This number will change within the next years through the closure of many local courts (TGI). The number of TGI will be of 158 in 2011. *Barreaux* vary in size. Around half of them have less than 50 lawyers, whereas in ten there are more than 500.

[304]   The CNB has a section dedicated to criminal matters called the *Commission Libertés et Droits de l'Homme* (commission freedom and human rights). The function of this Commission is to assess legal acts concerning, in particular, criminal law and criminal procedure law, and to present comments and proposals to the members of Parliament.

[305]   Disciplinary provisions are under chapter III of the law No. 71-1130 of 31 December 1971. There is a disciplinary council in each appeal court district. The disciplinary council is composed of representatives of all bar councils present at the appeal court. No bar council can designate more than half of the disciplinary council's members, and each bar council must have at least one representative in the disciplinary council. The disciplinary council meets with at least five members. It is called on either by the dean of the bar or by the general prosecutor of the appeal court and must take a decision within 15 days. The *conseil de l'ordre* as a disciplinary council, and also the *bâtonnier* (president of the bar), are in charge of the disciplinary procedure. The committee and the president hold the functions of implementation, investigation and judgement. The president can initiate autonomously an inquiry, or do so when the public prosecutor requires it. The disciplinary procedures have been modified in accordance with the jurisprudence of the ECtHR with regard to art. 6-1 of the ECHR (see, for example, ECtHR 16 July 1971, *Ringeisen* v. *Austria*, 13; ECtHR, 23 June 1981, *Le Compte* v. *Belgium*, 43) in 2004 (Lecerf, 2003. See the corresponding law No. 2004-130 of 11 February 2004, reforming the status of some judicial professions.). In addition, disciplinary proceedings are now public (see Decision Cour de Cassation, civ. Rennemann, 10 January 1984; Decision *Conseil d'Etat*, Maubleu, 14 February 1996). The disciplinary council must render its decision after an adversarial (*contradictoire*) investigation conducted by a member of the disciplinary council. The misconduct can result from negligence, fault, breach of the oath obligations, but also of all rulings and laws, and from any infraction to honour, or probity, and even for behaviour outside of work. Four sanctions can be imposed by the disciplinary committee against the accused lawyer: complete exclusion from the bar, a temporary bar to practice (maximum 3 years), criticism and warning, without direct effects – although they are recorded into the lawyer's file. In parallel, a lawyer can be provisionally suspended throughout the investigation by the disciplinary committee (see art. 184 of decree of 27 November 1991). The lawyer's misconduct is sanctioned by the *conseil de l'ordre*

→

Criminal defence work is carried out by lawyers in private practice. There are no special qualification requirements, or certification system, for lawyers doing criminal defence work,[306] only that they hold a Bar licence.[307] Criminal defence work has low prestige among lawyers.[308] It is mostly undertaken by young lawyers, who either serve as duty lawyers as an obligatory part of their *pupilage* (*stage*), or seek to establish their own practice; or by generalists with insufficient or unstable clientele.[309] There is only a small minority of lawyers for whom crime is a main interest, and even they retain 20-40% of their practice in other areas, according to a study by Field and West.[310]

The professional culture of criminal defence lawyers in France is rooted in the inquisitorial model of justice, which is centred on the judge who directs the inquiry, looks after the defendants' interests, and guarantees that the procedures are adhered to. The presence of such an omnipotent figure leaves little room for a defence lawyer to act.[311] This results in a passive defence culture based on dialogue and compromise – rather than opposition and argument – with the prosecution and the judiciary.

Furthermore, the written and formalized nature of inquisitorial procedures has an inevitable effect on the culture of criminal defence. For instance, research indicates that French lawyers exercise the same formalistic approach to reading the *dossier* – focusing on the deficiencies in its form but not in its content – as practiced by prosecutors and judges.[312]

Further, the occupational culture of other criminal justice actors – judges and prosecutors – has a strong impact on criminal lawyers' behaviour. There is a longstanding history of professional separation[313] of *avocats* from the rest of the legal

---

[ ] (disciplinary committee of the bar) in the first instance, then before the appeal court and further to the cassation. As to sanctions, the number of examined 'deontological files' rose from 3,972 in 2001 to 5,110 in 2006. Compared to 2001 (42), almost 50% more sanctions have been applied in 2006 (60). Of these, 16 were criticisms, 12 warnings, 2 permanent exclusions and 28 temporary bars (three years maximum). Two sanctions are missing. Our interviewees criticise the sanction system, because of its partiality within colleagues. Moreover, disciplinary decisions are not published.

[306] There exists, however, a voluntary scheme, under which lawyers may apply for a specialization certificate (the so-called *mention*). About 26% of all lawyers participate in this scheme. Out of them, only 4.9% obtained a *mention* in criminal law.

[307] Such licence may be obtained after four years of legal experience and some examinations, without any further training or competence requirements. Edict (*arrêté*) of 8 June 1993 sets out the list of specialisation used in the profession of a lawyer. In 2007, 22,976 lawyers worked for legal aid, which constitutes about 45% of all licensed lawyers; Conseil National des Barreaux, Observatoire, Statistiques, *L'aide juridictionnelle et les avocats en France*, Octobre 2008.

[308] See Hodgson, citing Kaprik 1999, p. 198, that of the 14 fields of law, crime ranked 12th in terms of prestige; Hodgson 2005, p. 115.

[309] *Ibidem.*

[310] Field & West 2003, p. 283.

[311] For a discussion of the role of defence in inquisitorial criminal justice systems, see Hodgson, 'The Role of the Criminal Defence Lawyer in Adversarial and Inquisitorial Procedure', unpublished, electronic copy available at <http://ssrn.com/abstract=1504000>.

[312] Field & West 2003, p. 293-294.

[313] This dates back as for as the 16th century; see Kaprik 1999, p. 27.

profession, namely the *magistrature*[314] and, correspondingly, of the professional unity between prosecutors and judges. Moreover, the profession of *avocats* is less prestigious compared to the *magistrature*.[315] This is due to the professional dominance of judges and prosecutors, who treat lawyers as inferior and as 'professional outsiders'.[316] The relationships between judges and prosecutors are based on a great degree of mutual confidence and trust. They regard as complementary their professional goals of protecting the public interest. At the same time, lawyers are seen as 'partisan' and serving their own financial interest, and therefore not to be trusted.[317]

Some recent criminal justice reforms – notably, those of 1993 and 2000, or the introduction of the guilty plea proceedings in 2004 – cast the role of a defence lawyer in more proactive and adversarial terms. However, for the lawyers to adopt this behavioural style, a change in the professional cultures of all criminal justice actors is required.[318] The recent *Outreau* case is an illustration of the inter-professional relationships described above, and of the lawyers' inability to effectively challenge the actions of the investigating judge, due to the established criminal justice culture, where prosecutors and judges heavily rely on each other's conclusions, overlooking arguments made by defence lawyers.[319]

4. Political commitment to effective criminal defence

Over recent decades, the French criminal justice system has developed along contrasting lines. On the one hand, the need to ensure compliance with the ECHR, in particular given a large number of judgments condemning France for its systemic failure to guarantee individual rights in criminal proceedings,[320] has led to a number of successful reforms that strengthen individual liberties and the rights of the defence.[321] For example, the reforms of 1993 and 2000 described in this report, which extended the rights of defendants and their lawyers in the GAV and

---

[314] For more detailed accounts of the professional culture and role of criminal defence lawyers, see Hodgson 2005, p. 101-143; Field & West 2003; Kaprik 1999; Danet 2004.

[315] Hodgson 2005, p. 115.

[316] *Id.*, p. 112.

[317] Regarding the attitudes of other criminal justice actors towards criminal defence lawyers, see *id.*, p. 139-141.

[318] For a similar argument, see, for example, Hodgson 2007.

[319] In the *Outreau* case, 17 people were accused of participation in a child rape gang, seven of whom were eventually acquitted. The investigation was heavily criticized by the accused and their lawyers as being one sided and partial. However, neither the *juge d'instruction* nor the numerous *magistrats* who handled the case at various times adhered to the requests of the accused to conduct a more comprehensive inquiry.

[320] Among the most notable cases are ECtHR 27 August 1992, *Tomasi* v. *France*, No. 12850/87 ECtHR 28 July 1999, *Selmouni* v. *France,* No. 25803/94, which condemned France for the use of brutal interrogation techniques by police; ECtHR 25 September 1992, *Pham Hoang* v. *France*, No. 13191/87) a case concerning deficiencies in the legal aid system; ECtHR 26 June 1991, *Letellier* v. *France*, No. 12369/86), on the length of pre-trial detention.

[321] See Hodgson 2005, p. 32-38.

instruction proceedings, were the result of discussions framed around compliance with the requirements of the ECHR.[322]

On the other hand, and particularly since the centre right government has come to power, the debate about crime and justice has been increasingly dominated by the security and crime control agenda.[323] A number of measures have been introduced since 2002 that aim at more rapid detection and suppression of crime, and quicker disposal of criminal cases.[324] These measures have resulted *inter alia* in the significant widening of police powers; further limitations on the degree and amount of judicial control in criminal proceedings, and the marginalization of the defence role.

In addition, during the same period, a plethora of new criminal offences were introduced,[325] and new rules allowing for harsher treatment of juvenile defendants were adopted.[326] In that context, effective defence rights are not the priority. Indeed, criminal lawyers are still perceived in some political circles as blocking the path to the 'real' truth.[327]

A new challenge for criminal law is posed by the French safety retention law called the *rétention de sûreté*, passed in February 2008.[328] This may be imposed on an offender serving a custodial sentence, if it was provided for in the sentencing judgment, and if the convicted person is particularly dangerous and highly likely to reoffend, because he suffers from a serious personality disorder. At least one year prior to the offender's scheduled release date, he is placed under observation. A commission assesses the extent of the danger posed by the offender and may recommend precautionary detention in a secure socio-medico-judicial facility, where he/she will be offered medical, social and psychological care. The regional *rétention de sûreté* tribunal, comprising three judges, may order a *rétention de sûreté* for an initial period of one year. This may be renewed indefinitely.

In its opinion of 8 February 2008, the CNCDH[329] held that the bill called into question the principles of certainty of the law and the presumption of innocence. It also held that it broke the causal link between an offence and the deprivation of liberty, since *rétention de sûreté* was based on a possible future offence, rather than one already committed. This was also criticised by the report of the Commissioner for Human Rights.[330]

[322]   Hodgson 2005, p. 32.
[323]   Hodgson 2005, p. 45.
[324]   For a more detailed overview, see Hodgson 2005, p. 45-65.
[325]   A controversial 2003 law for interior security (*Loi pour la securite interieure* No. 2003-239 of 18 March 2003) criminalised such behaviour as prostitution, begging, wandering or threatening and hostile gatherings.
[326]   For example, allowing children as young as 10 years to be kept under a *GAV*; see Hodgson 2005, p. 43.
[327]   See Thomas More in *Utopia* ('They have no lawyers among them, for they consider them as a sort of people whose profession it is to disguise matters, and to wrest the laws'); quoted by Saint-Pierre 2007, p. 66. Also see Hodgson 2001.
[328]   Law No. 2008-174 of 25 February 2008. It took its inspiration from the German *Sicherungsverwahrung:* Leblois-Happe 2008, p. 210. It also has similarities to the Imprisonment for Public Protection (IPP) in England and Wales.
[329]   National Consultative Commission on Human Rights.
[330]   CommDH(2008)34, Hammasberg, § 53 ff.

The political attitude towards effective criminal defence within recent years can perhaps best be illustrated by the example of the recent *Léger* report, which was immediately and harshly criticized by the judiciary and lawyers' professional associations.[331]

The main source of controversy regarding the *Léger* report is the proposed abolition of the investigating judge, and the delegation of the power to direct and oversee investigations to prosecutors. Both judges and lawyers argued that this would create a risk of political (executive) interference with investigations, because prosecutors are hierarchically dependent on the Ministry of Justice, and the guarantees for their independence are lacking.[332] In addition, the *Léger* report does not specify whether and how the defence would participate in prosecutor supervised investigations.[333]

Another important criticism of the *Léger* report, voiced primarily by the National Bar Council, is that it does not go far enough in strengthening the position and role of the defence lawyer during the GAV.[334] In addition to the existing defence rights during the GAV, the report proposes introducing the possibility for a

---

[331]   See Le Monde, 3 September 2009, 'Avocats et Magistrat Critiquent Vivement le Rapport Léger', available at <http://www.lemonde.fr/societe/article/2009/03/09/avocats-et-magistrats-critiquent-vivement-le-rapport-leger_1165610_3224.html>.

[332]   *Ibidem*. It should be noted that, in 1987 for example, the commission Delmas-Marty already suggested the abolition of the investigating judge and its replacement by the prosecutor to lead investigations. However, the necessary pre-condition was to guarantee the independence of the public prosecutor, which is not the case in the latter report. The ECtHR has pointed out that the 'public prosecutor is not a 'competent legal authority' [and] he lacks the independence in respect of the executive to qualify as such'; see ECtHR 10 July 2008, *Medvedyev* v. *France*, No. 3394/03. After an appeal by France, and examination in Grand Chamber on 6 May 2009, the final decision is pending as at the date of this report.

[333]   A recent example of the confusion due to this reform period is the *Dray* case. Julien Dray, a politician and member of the Socialist Party, had been suspected of abuse of funds. Information about the preliminary investigation against Dray became known to the media and was published, along with some sensitive personal information. Dray and his lawyers criticised the closed nature of the preliminary inquiry, because it did not allow him to defend against the investigation and the media attacks. As a result, the public prosecutor decided to disclose, for the first time in an *enquête préliminaire*, a part of the case file to Dray, his lawyers and other persons implicated in the *dossier*. The magistrates' associations criticised this decision, because of the risk of legal uncertainty they argued might result from it. Eventually, the prosecutor decided not to refer Dray's case to the correctional courts and the investigation was closed in December 2009; see Le Monde, 20 July 2009, 'L'Affaire Dray: Le Procureur Accorde L'Acces au Dossier a Toutes les Parties', available at <http://www.lemonde.fr/societe/article/2009/07/20/affaire-dray-le-procureur-accorde-l-acces-au-dossier-a-toutes-les-parties_1220717_3224.html>. The prosecutor declared that the reasons for this were to give more rights to the defence in the preliminary investigation, and saw this decision as a kind of 'experimentation and innovation', but denied acting under political or public pressure. Because this isolated decision was not foreseen in any law, many questions remained unclear: how one-sided are preliminary investigations? Can a defence lawyer ask for any investigative act to be undertaken? Who can guarantee the quality of evidence? Another problem was the prohibition to communicate parts of the investigation files to third parties: in legal terms, since Dray had not been a suspect, he and his lawyers were to be considered as third parties and therefore were not legally entitled to have access to the case file.

[334]   *Conseil National des Barreaux*, Communiqué de presse, 1 September 2009.

lawyer to intervene during the 12th hour of the GAV,[335] and to be present at suspect interviews if the GAV is prolonged beyond 24 hours.[336] Lawyers argue, however, that the standards of the ECHR require that defence counsel can participate during the entire GAV proceedings, including in any interrogation of the suspect.

On 1 March 2010, the Ministry of Justice published for public consultation the preliminary draft of the Criminal Procedure Code on its website.[337] The proposed text mostly endorses the proposals made in the *Léger* report. The draft has been criticised – largely for the same reasons as the *Léger* report itself – by the *Syndicat de la Magistrature*,[338] *Conseil National de Barreaux*[339] and human rights organisations.[340]

5. Conclusions

The report has identified the following problems related to the effective exercise of criminal defence in France:

The obligation to inform suspects about their rights at certain stages of the proceedings, such as the GAV, are limited. In particular, suspects do not have to be informed about the right to remain silent during the GAV. There is no obligation to give a person a 'letter of rights'.

Access to a lawyer is virtually non-existent during the GAV. Limited access to the client during the GAV, and the exclusion of lawyers from suspect interviews during the GAV, are clearly in violation of the ECHR.[341] Moreover, the police use ploys to discourage suspects from requesting legal assistance during the GAV.

On a more positive note, in March 2010, the *Conseil Constituonnel* was seized to examine whether the GAV procedure complies with the Constitution.[342] If the

---

[335]   Currently, a lawyer may only intervene at the beginning of the GAV, after the first 24 hours, and at every prolongation of the GAV.

[336]   See Léger Rapport, p. 9.

[337]   Available at <http://www.justice.gouv.fr/art_pix/avant_projet_cpp_20100304.pdf>.

[338]   See the statement of the *Syndicat de La Magistrature*, 'Avant-project de la procedure penale: chronique d'un disastre annonce', 2 March 2010, available at <http://www.syndicat-magistrature.org/Avant-project-de-reform-de -la.htm>.

[339]   See the Resolution *sur l'avant-project de reforme du Code de procedure penale*, Assemblee Generale des 12 and 13 March 2010, *Conseil National des Barreaux*, available at <http://cnb.avocat.fr/L-avant-projet-de-reforme-du-code-de-procedure-penale-soumis-a-l-examen-de-l-Assemblee-generale-du-Conseil-National-des_a830.html>.

[340]   See, for example, Human Rights Watch, *France: L'avant-project de Reforme de la Justice Ne Vas Paz Assez Loin*, 4 March 2010, available at <http://www.hrw.org/fr/news/2010/03/02/france-l-avant-projet-de-r-forme-de-la-justice-ne-va-pas-assez-loin>.

[341]   ECtHR 27 November 2008, *Salduz* v. *Turkey*, No. 36391/02, confirmed by ECtHR 24 September 2009, *Pishchlanikov* v. *Russia*, No. 7025/04 and ECtHR 13 October 2009, *Danayan* v. *Turkey*, No. 7377/03. Despite the strong efforts by criminal lawyers to reform the *garde à vue* (see <http://www.jeneparleraiquenpresencedemonavocat.fr/index.php> [18 January 2010]) the Ministry of Justice issued a circular on 17 November 2009 reaffirming that French criminal proceedings of *garde à vue* fully comply with the decisions of the ECtHR and with the ECHR.

[342]   This was possible due to the entry into force of the new procedure, which allows the Constitutional Council to review compliance of enacted legislation with the Constitution; art. 61-1 Constitution. See also, <http://www.lepoint.fr/actualites-societe/2010-03-01/reforme-constitutionnalite-de-la-garde-a-vue-le-tgi-de-paris-saisit-la/920/0/429064>.

Constitutional Court decides that a legal disposition violates fundamental rights, it can abolish it. The government must then pass a new law within a reasonable timeframe. The Constitutional court will render its judgement in summer 2010.

Lawyers and defendants often lack adequate time and facilities to prepare their cases. There is no right of access to the file during the GAV and preliminary investigations, and for those defendants who are not represented by a lawyer, also during the *instruction* stage. Duty lawyers are often notified very late about the upcoming interrogation or hearing, and thus often have no time to adequately prepare. This problem is particularly acute in relation to expedited hearings (*comparutions immediates*) before the correctional courts, where duty lawyers are often appointed to cases 'on the spot'. In addition, the fast track proceedings, which are used increasingly, do not provide for sufficient time for the defence to prepare, and do not ensure a real equality of arms between the defence and prosecution, as they are based mostly on material gathered during the preliminary police enquiry.

There are serious concerns about the quality of the services provided by duty lawyers, who are mostly young lawyers-*stagiaires*, or generalists who have no special interest or expertise in criminal cases. The problem is exacerbated by the low level of legal aid fees, which do not attract qualified and experienced lawyers and do not stimulate quality services. The judges' failure to discuss the dates of hearing with defendants' lawyers often results in the latter's inability to attend. In such cases, a duty lawyer is usually appointed, which is arguably in breach of the defendant's right to choose his/her lawyer and may prevent that lawyer from providing quality representation, as he/she may not be able to prepare adequately.

Defence lawyers have limited possibilities to investigate the case and to examine witnesses. Prior contact with witnesses by the defence is regarded with strong suspicion. During the trial, defence lawyers or defendants do not have the possibility to cross examine prosecution witness. These procedural barriers, combined with a legal culture that does not value an active defence, mean that the equality of arms principle is lacking from the trial process and the investigation phase.

6.   Bibliography

Books

Beauchesnes 2003
Beauchesne, L., *Les drogues. Les coûts cachés de la prohibition*, Québec: Lanctôt Éditeur, 2003.

Bergeron 1999
Bergeron, H., *L'État et la toxicomanie, histoire d'une singularité française*, Paris: PUF, 1999.

Cusson 1990
Cusson, M., *Croissance et décroissance du crime*, Paris: PUF, 1990.

Danet 2004
Danet, J., *Défendre – Pour une défense pénale critique*, Paris: Dalloz-Sirey, 2004.

Faugeron 1999
Faugeron, C. (ed.), *Les drogues en France. Politiques, marchés, usages*, Genève: Georg Éditeur, 1999.

Garçon 1957
Garçon, M., *Défense de la liberté individuelle*, Paris: Fayard, 1957.

Godefroy & Laffargue 1991
Godefroy, T. & Laffargue, B., *Changements économiques et répression pénale. Plus de chômage, plus d'emprisonnement?*, Paris: CESDIP, 1991.

Hodgson 2005
Hodgson, J., *French criminal justice. A comparative account of the investigation and prosecution of crime in France*, Oxford: Hart Publishing, 2005.

Kaprik 1999
Kaprik, L., *French Lawyers: a Study in Collective Action, 1274-1994*, Oxford: Oxford University Press, 1999.

Mouhanna & Matelly 2007
Mouhanna, C. & Matelly, J.-H., *Police. Des chiffres et des doutes*, Paris: Michalon, 2007.

Portelli 2007
Portelli, S., *Ruptures*, <http://www.betapolitique.fr>, 2007.

Pradel 2002
Pradel, J., *Manuel de procédure pénale*, Paris: Editions Cujas, 2002.

Pradel 2008
Pradel, J., *Procédure pénale*, Paris: Editions Cujas, 2008.

Saint-Pierre 2007
Saint-Pierre, F., *Le guide de la défense pénale*, Paris: Dalloz, 2007.

Stefani 2008
Stefani, G., Levasseur, G. & Bouloc, B., *Procedure Penale*, Paris: Dalloz, 2008.

Tournier 2007
Tournier, P., *Loi pénitentiaire. Contextes et enjeux*, Paris: L'harmattan, 2007.

Chapters in Compilations

Devrieux 2002
Devrieux, V., 'The French system', in: M. Delmas-Marty and J.-R. Spenser, *European Criminal Procedures*, Cambridge: Cambridge University Press, 2002, p. 218-292.

Leturmy 2009
Leturmy, L., 'La répression de la délinquance sexuelle', in: M. Massé, J.-P. Jean and A. Giudicelli (eds.), *Un droit pénal postmoderne? Mise en perspective des évolutions et ruptures contemporaines*, Paris: Presses Universitaires de France, p. 125-147.

Salas 2009
Salas, D., 'Le droit pénal à l'ère du libéralisme autoritaire', in: M. Massé, J.-P. Jean and A. Giudicelli (eds.), *Un droit pénal postmoderne? Mise en perspective des évolutions et ruptures contemporaines*, Paris: Presses Universitaires de France, p. 111-124.

Vogler 2008
Vogler, R., 'Criminal Procedure in France', in: R. Vogler and B. Huber (eds.), *Criminal Procedure in Europe*, Berlin: Duncker & Humblot, 2008, p. 171-269.

Articles in Journals

Aubusson de Cavarlay 1997
Aubusson de Cavarlay, B., 'Les statistiques policières: que compte-t-on et comment?', *Questions pénales*, 1997.

Bénec'h-Le-Roux 2007
Bénec'h-Le-Roux, P., 'Procureur de la République: une identité professionnelle renforcée', *Questions Pénales*, 2007.

Dünkel & Fritsche 2005a
Dünkel, F. & Fritsche, M., 'L'aménagement de la peine et la libération conditionnelle dans les systèmes pénitentiaires allemand et français', *Déviance et Société*, 2005, p.335-348.

Dünkel & Fritsche 2005b
Dünkel, F. & Fritsche, M., 'Vollzugslockerungen and bedingte Entlassung in Frankreich im Vergleich zu Deutschland', *Zeitschrift für Strafvollzug und Straffälligenhilfe*, 2005, p. 208-215.

Field & West 2003
Field, S. & West, A., 'Dialogue and the inquisitorial tradition: French defence lawyers in the pre-trial criminal process', *Criminal Law Forum*, 14 2003, p. 261-316.

Hodgson 2001
Hodgson, J., 'The police, the prosecutor and the juge d'instruction: judicial supervision in France, theory and practice', *The British Journal of Criminology*, 41 2001, p. 342-261.

Hodgson 2002
Hodgson, J., 'Constructing the pre-trial role of the defence in French criminal procedure: an adversarial outsider in an inquisitorial process?', *International Journal of Evidence and Proof*, 1 2002, p. 1-16.

Hodgson 2004
Hodgson, J., 'The detention and interrogation of suspects in police custody in France: a comparative account', *European Journal of Criminology*, 2004, p. 163-199.

Kensey 2004
Kensey, A., 'Longues peines: 15 ans après', *Cahiers de démographie pénitentiaire, direction de l´administration pénitentiaire*, 2004.

Jobard 2004
Jobard, F., 'Der Ort der Politik. Politische Mobilisierung zwischen Aufstandsversuchung and Staatsgewalt in einer Pariser Vorstadt', *Berliner Journal für Soziologie*, 2004, p.319-338.

Leblois-Happe 2008
Leblois-Happe, J., 'Rétention de sûreté vs Unterbringung in die Sicherungsverwahrung: les enseignements d'une comparaison franco-allemande', *Actualité Juridique Pénal*, 2008, p. 209-220.

Maillard & Roché 2004
Maillard de, J. & Roché, S., 'Crime and justice in France: time trends, policies and political debate', *European Journal of Criminology*, 2004, p. 111-151.

Mouhanna 2004
Mouhanna, C., 'Les relations police-parquet en France: un partenariat mis en cause?', *Droit et Société*, 2004, p. 505-520.

Mucchielli 2008
Mucchielli, L. 'L'évolution des homicides depuis les années 1970. Analyse statistique et tendance générale', *Questions Pénales*, 2008.

Peyrat 2002
Peyrat, D., 'La société face à la délinquance', *Cahiers français*, 2002, p. 12-18.

Porteron 2009a
Porteron, C., 'La violation du secret professionnel doit être rendue nécessaire par l'exercice des droits de la défense', *Actualité Juridique Pénal*, 2009, p. 26-28.

Porteron 2009b
Porteron, C., 'Le secret professionnel de l'avocat', *Actualité Juridique Pénal*, 2009, p. 159-163.

Pruvost 2009
Pruvost, G., 'Les conditions de vie et d'emploi des policiers en 2003. Enquête sociodémographique', *Questions Pénales*, 2009.

Tournier 2001
Tournier, P., 'Détenus hors les murs. Des substituts du troisième type', *Revue nationale des barreaux*, 2001, p.153-159.

Viennot 2007
Viennot, C., 'Célérité et justice pénale: l'exemple de la comparution immédiate', *Archives de politique criminelle*, 2007, p. 117-143.

Official Sources

Annuaire Statistique de la Justice 2008
Annuaire Statistique de la Justice, Paris: La Documentation Française, Ministère de la Justice, 2009.

CEPEJ 2008
European Commission for the Efficiency of Justice, European Judicial Systems, Council of Europe, 2008.

CSM 2008
Conseil supérieur de la magistrature, *Les Français et leur Justice: restaurer la confiance*, Paris: La documentation française, 2008.

Darrois 2009
Darrois, J.-M., *Rapport sur les professions de droit, remis au Président de la République*, 2009.

Lecerf 2003
Lecerf, J.-R., *Rapport sur le projet de loi réformant le statut de certaines professions judiciaires ou juridiques, des experts judiciaires et des conseils en propriété industrielle*, Sénat, 2003.

Other Sources

Hodgson 2007
Hodgson, J., *Recent Reforms in Pre-Trial Procedure in England and Wales*, Paper presented to the international seminar 'Best Practices in Latin America's New Criminal Procedure Systems', 22-25 May 2007, Santiago, Chile, unpublished, available at <http://ssrn.com/abstract=1494391 at 10>.

Portelli 2009
Website Bibliothèque Zoummeroff, interviewed by S. Enderlin in December 2008, <http://www.collection-privee.org/>.

Soulez La Rivière 2009
Website Bibliothèque Zoummeroff, interviewed by S. Enderlin in July 2009, <http://www.collection-privee.org/>.

Dominik Brodowski
Christoph Burchard
Nathalie Kotzurek
Jochen Rauber
Joachim Vogel

CHAPTER 7 GERMANY[*]

1.   Introduction

1.1.   Basic demographic information

Germany has a total population of approx. 82,217,800 (40,274,300 men and 41,943,300 women).[1] The average age is 42.9.[2] 19.4% of the population is under the age of 20.[3] The number of foreigners represents about 8.83% of the general population at large.[4] The foreign population is mainly to be found in urban areas in the former western states of Germany,[5] and consists approximately of 1,688,370 persons of Turkish origin (23.3% of the foreign population and 2.1% of the general population), 815,050 from the former Yugoslavia (11.2%; 1%), 523,162 Italians (7.3%), 393,848 Polish (5.4%), 287,187 Greeks (3.7%).[6] Further, 8,131,000 German citizens are from a migrant background (9.9% of the total population).[7]

1.2.   Basic statistical information on crime and punishment

Generally, the number of investigated possible criminal offences is decreasing (2007: 6,284,661 total, representing 7,634.9 offences per 100,000 inhabitants).[8] From the total

---

[*]   This country report has been reviewed by Thomas Weigend, professor of criminal law and criminal procedure at the University of Köln. We would like to thank our student research assistants Roschan Babat, Hannah Epple, Kathrin Groß, Karen Häußer, Friedrich Kern, Sebastian Ritter, Amina Slawitsch and Ina Vedie for their diligent support.

[1]   Statistisches Bundesamt 2007a, p. 9, 6.

[2]   Statistisches Bundesamt 2007a, p. 10.

[3]   Statistisches Bundesamt 2007a, p. 8.

[4]   Statistisches Bundesamt 2008, p. 23.

[5]   See the illustration by the Federal Office for Statistics at Statistisches Bundesamt 2008, p. 12.

[6]   Statistisches Bundesamt 2008, p. 30 *et seq.*

[7]   All dates refer to 31 December 2007 and can be found at Statistisches Bundesamt 2007b, p. 32.

[8]   Cf. the statistics of the Federal Office for Statistics at <http://www.destatis.de/jetspeed/portal/cms/Sites/destatis/Internet/DE/Content/Statis tiken/Rechtspflege/Content75/AktuZusatz.psml> (last visited 29 April 2010) – see also Chart 1 and 2 in the Appendix.

number of 2,294,883 suspects in 2007, 1,804,605 were of German (78.6%) and 420,278 of foreign[9] nationality (21.4%).[10] In 2006, the total number of convicted persons was 751,387, comprising 580,202 of German (77.2%) and 171,387 of foreign (22.8%) nationality.[11] Incarceration rates are also decreasing (2008: 61,900 total, representing 75.29 per 100,000 inhabitants).[12]

1.3. Basic constitutional information

1.3.1. Federalism and its discontents

The (western) Federal Republic of Germany was reunited with the (eastern) Democratic Republic of Germany in 1990. Germany has a federal constitutional structure, with 16 states and a federal level, all constituting – unlike, for example, in the United States – one overarching jurisdiction in the sense of one criminal justice system.[13] Nevertheless, many – albeit not all – administrative, investigative, prosecutorial, adjudicative and legislative authorities are dispersed over the various state/federal levels, and allocated to various actors. This dispersion of authority not only complicates – and, for the purpose of this report, indeed renders impossible – precise account of the governance framework of the German criminal justice system. The federal structure moreover also impedes a uniform – let alone centralized – gathering of data and information, which in turn is a precondition for evidence based criminal policy making, as well for translational monitoring and evaluation regimes.

1.3.2. Codifications and the role of the courts of law

Within the traditional categories of comparative (criminal) law, Germany belongs to the circle of Civil Law countries. This is to say, in principle, the rights and obligations of law enforcement agencies on the one hand, and those of the defence on the other, are codified. From a more normative constitutional vantage point, interventions in a citizen's freedom require a prior mandate by a democratically legitimized regulatory act.

In the hierarchy of norms, and as concerns the law as codified, the German Federal Constitution is the supreme law of the land and prescribes general – yet often very broad – fundamental rights and principles, as well as institutional guarantees and processes, which all pertain to the administration of criminal justice. Investigative, prosecutorial, judicial and defence rights/obligations, as well as institutional settings, are codified in more depth and detail in various statutes. For the purpose of this report, the most important German Federal Statutes are the Code of Criminal Procedure (CCP – *Strafprozessordung*) and the Act on the

---

9   108,055 were of Turkish (23.8%) and 33,291 of Polish (7.8%) nationality.
10   Bundeskriminalamt 2007, p. 26.
11   Statistisches Bundesamt 2006, p. 16 *et seq.*
12   See Chart 3 in the Appendix.
13   FHCJ, 3 BGHSt, p. 137.

Organization of the Judiciary (AOJ – *Gerichtsverfassungsgesetz*). Federal Statutes rank below the German Federal Constitution but are above State legislation.

The European Convention for the Protection of Human Rights and Fundamental Freedoms (ECHR) has been transformed into a German Federal Statute. The ECHR formally has the rank of a Federal statute and would thus normally be superseded by the Constitution and any subsequently enacted Federal statute. However, the German Constitutional Court has ruled that German courts and agencies are constitutionally normally required to interpret domestic law in a way that it complies with Germany's obligations under international law, including the ECHR, if this does not run contrary to constitutional principles.

It can be argued that most, if not all, of the specific statutory rights/obligations are but an extension of the general principles as contained in the German Constitution and the ECHR. Both serve, at a minimum, as supplementary sources for (public and individual) rights/obligations and institutional guarantees.

Despite far-reaching codification, courts of law play an increasingly important role in the German domestic legal order. Statutory interpretations by upper courts are not *de iure* binding on lower courts (in the sense of *stare decisis*) or the prosecution, yet they are *de facto* commonly followed by all legal practitioners. What is more, many rights/obligations, as well as their technical specificities, have been judicially developed, particularly in the jurisprudence of the Federal High Court of Justice (FHCJ – *Bundesgerichtshof*) and the Federal Constitutional Court (FCC – *Bundesverfassungsgericht*). This jurisprudence is thus also an important source of the operation of the law.

The role of the European Court of Human Rights (ECtHR) merits special attention, as German courts are constitutionally obliged to take into account the ECtHR's jurisprudence – even with respect to cases to which Germany was not a party – although they are not formally bound by the rulings of the ECtHR.[14]

1.4. Basic information about the administration of criminal justice

1.4.1. Phases of the criminal proceeding; the use of the 'deal'

German criminal procedure can best be described as a 'hybrid' system,[15] which for the sake of classification leans towards the inquisitorial paradigm. The prototypical criminal proceeding has the following stages, involving their principal actors:

The investigation of low and mid-level criminality rests *de facto* with the respective State police force. In theory, but still valid for complicated and grave criminality, investigations are under the supervision and control of the respective State offices of the public prosecutor. Investigations of national security cases rest with the Federal Office of the Public Prosecutor General (*Generalbundesanwalt*). For certain investigative measures that prove particularly intrusive into human and fundamental rights – such as search and seizure, wire tapping, etc. – the police or prosecution must obtain a judicial warrant from an investigative judge.

14   See generally FCC, *Juristenzeitung* 2004, p. 1171.
15   Huber 2008, p. 283.

The investigative phase ends with the prosecutorial decision to either (1) file a writ of indictment (*Anklageschrift*);[16] (2) drop the case due to an insufficient conviction probability;[17] or (3) move for alternative sanctioning modes,[18] or for an alternative discontinuance of the proceedings.[19] As a theoretical starting point, this decision is informed by the principle of mandatory prosecution and trial,[20] while in practice the prosecutor enjoys a certain degree of discretion in cases of low and mid-level criminality.[21]

If the prosecutor files a writ of indictment, there is a procedure for the confirmation of charges (*Zwischenverfahren*)[22] conducted by the later trial court, which reviews the validity and legality of the indictment. The court can either dismiss, confirm or amend/change[23] the indictment; the latter two decisions constitute orders to commence a public trial.

The public and oral main trial (*Hauptverfahren*) is not premised upon a guilty plea system, and combines the finding of guilt and sentencing – it is not bifurcated as in some jurisdictions in the United States. The trial starts with the indictment being read out by the prosecution. Thereafter, the defendant is interrogated by the bench and the parties (prosecutor/defence counsel); since the defendant enjoys the right to remain silent, the interrogation only takes place if he/she declares that he/she is willing to make a statement. This is followed by the evidentiary phase. Witness examination is but one of the formal modes of evidence accepted in a trial, together with expert testimony, documentary evidence and sensory inspection of individual pieces of evidence (*Augenschein*). The hearing comes to a conclusion with the closing statements of the parties and the final words of the defendant.

The trial ends with the determination of the verdict and, where necessary, the sentence; the judgment is also to be argued and explained in writing.[24] The determination of guilt and of the appropriate sentence is premised upon the principle of a free and encompassing evaluation of the evidence brought before the court (*Grundsatz der umfassenden und freien Beweiswürdigung*); this effectively means that there are no preset rules by which a fact is proven or disproven (for example, if it is one person's word against another), and the bench is free to determine – on objective grounds – that one piece of evidence is better than a contradicting one. This freedom is compensated by the *in dubio pro reo* principle, by which overall reasonable doubt as to the accused's guilt must lead to an acquittal.

---

16   See § 170 (1) CCP.
17   See § 170 (2) CCP.
18   Such as the written summary sanctioning order (*Strafbefehl*), see §§ 407 *et seq.* CCP, or a summary fine, see § 153a CCP.
19   See, for example, § 153 CCP (dismissal due to the insignificance of the case).
20   See §§ 152 (2), 170 (1) CCP (*Legalitätsprinzip*).
21   See §§ 153 *et seq.* CCP (*Opportunitätsprinzip*).
22   See §§ 199 *et seq.* CCP.
23   The trial court cannot 'change' an indictment in the sense of redefining its factual scope. The trial court can, however, give a different legal interpretation to the facts brought forward by the prosecution, and the prosecution is legally obliged to amend the indictment in accordance with the trial court's interpretation. The trial court can also refuse to admit for trial one or more of several charges.
24   See § 267 CCP.

The composition of the bench, and the inclusion of lay jurors (*Schöffen*), depends *inter alia* on the court; in cases of low-level criminality, the trial will regularly be before a single professional career judge, who has qualified by passing the so called First and Second State Examination in Law. A multi-person bench is presided over by the presiding judge. Following the inquisitorial paradigm, judges – and not the parties – are responsible for court and trial management. Judges will also do most of the examination of witnesses, although the parties can intervene with questions, statements and motions.

After the main trial, the prosecutor and the defence can both move for post-trial review by filing – depending on the particular court of first instance – an appeal of fact (*Berufung*) and/or an appeal of law (*Revision*).[25]

Many criminal proceedings are now brought to a more or less (semi-)consensual ending by way of a 'deal' (*Verfahrensabsprache; Verständigung*). The 'deal' and its requirements are now regulated in § 257c CCP, but have been accepted by the FHCJ for years.[26] In so doing, the FHCJ had also set certain limits in respect of 'deals' reached in and during trial, which still represent good law:

- The 'deal' is to be finalised, disclosed to and documented in a public trial, whereas preliminary discussions can take place out of trial. All parties (judges, lay judges, prosecutor, accused, counsel, co-accused) must be given the opportunity to make declarations in response.
- The verdict cannot be consensually agreed upon, but rests with the court to determine. This means that, even where the accused confesses in accordance with a 'deal', the trial court is still obliged to examine the facts and legal qualifications of the case before it, so as to verify that the confession is actually factually and legally correct.
- With regard to the sentence, the court must not agree to a fixed sentence, but may only announce a certain margin, particularly a maximum sentence, which in turn is to be equitable and proportionate (particularly in light of the harm of the offence and the level of responsibility of the accused); it goes without saying that this represents a major incentive for the defendant to enter into a 'deal'. On the other hand, there must be no threat that, to not enter into a 'deal' would lead to a disproportionately high sentence for the accused (thus guaranteeing his/her freedom of will).
- The court is allowed to break from the 'deal', if new factual or juridical circumstances emerge; if the court wishes to do so, it must inform the accused accordingly, and any confession the accused has made in reliance on the agreement will be inadmissible as evidence.

25   An appeal of law can either be reasoned with a relative or an absolute ground of appeal, the latter always leading to a reversal of the challenged verdict, whereas the former justifies a reversal only if the verdict is normatively based (*beruhen*) on the challenged violation.

26   See the landmark decisions of the FHCJ, 43 BGHSt, p. 195-211; FHCJ (Grand Chamber), 50 BGHSt, p. 40-64; see also Beulke 2008, marginal No. 396 for further references.

- If the verdict is based upon a 'deal' pursuant to § 257c CCP, the law rules out any (agreed upon) waiver of the right to appeal this verdict.[27]

1.4.2. Provisional detention and provisional arrest

During all phases of the proceedings, the accused may be taken into provisional detention (*Untersuchungshaft*)[28] on the basis of an arrest warrant by a judge. An arrest warrant can only be issued (by the competent judge), and an accused can only be taken into provisional detention, if (1) it is highly likely that he/she committed the crime (*dringender Tatverdacht*); (2) certain conditions justifying detention are satisfied;[29] and (3) provisional detention does not represent a disproportionate measure, particularly in light of the presumption of innocence and the gravity of the crime.[30]

During provisional detention, the investigative authorities are allowed to continue their investigations, and the charge does not have to be finalized before the issuance of the arrest warrant.

Prosecutors and police officers are allowed to provisionally arrest (*vorläufige Festnahme*) an accused under these very same substantive preconditions (i.e. if an arrest warrant could be issued), if the arrest must not be delayed.[31]

1.4.3. The court system

The AOJ confers jurisdiction to courts on four different levels: District Courts (DC – *Amtsgerichte*), Regional Courts (RC – *Landgerichte*), Higher Regional Courts (HRC – *Oberlandesgerichte*) and the FHCJ:[32]

- The DC is the regular court of first instance for low and mid-level criminality. Misdemeanours will regularly be heard in front of a single

---

[27]   § 303 (1) CCP.

[28]   German criminal procedure – with the exception of provisional arrest (*vorläufige Festnahme*) – does not conceptually distinguish between different modes of custody in the investigation, the confirmation of charges, the trial, and the post-trial review phase; rather, only one custody regime attaches, which we (crudely) translate as 'provisional detention' (*Untersuchungshaft*); translations such as 'pre-trial custody' or 'remand' fail to recognise that under provisional detention, the arrestee can be confined until a final determination of the case.

[29]   These conditions are enumerated, *inter alia*, in §§ 112, 112a CCP and comprise scenarios where the accused is a fugitive or is likely to flee; is likely to interfere with the administration of justice (for example, by intimidating witnesses, or by interfering with evidence); is alleged to have committed one the offences enumerated in § 112 (3) CCP (for example, murder, manslaughter, or participation in a terrorist organization); is likely to re-commit one of the offences enumerated in § 112a CCP (for example, repeated aggravated assault).

[30]   §§ 112 *et seq.* CCP.

[31]   § 127 CCP.

[32]   Only the FHCJ is a federal court, while the others are, formally speaking, state courts; the states are also responsible for financing and staffing these courts. However, all German courts are governed and organized by the Federal AOJ. The German court system will be only rudimentary laid out in this report.

judge. In all other cases, one judge sits with two lay jurors. In rare circumstances, two judges decide together with two lay jurors. DC judgments can be appealed to the RC (appeal of fact) or the HRC (appeal of law). There are 663 DCs in Germany.

- The RC is – apart from when it is hearing appeals of fact from the DC – the regular court of first instance *inter alia* for grave crimes (for example, murder or rape). As a court of first instance, the RC decides with either two or three judges and two lay jurors, depending on the particularities of the case. RC Judgments can be appealed to the FHCJ (appeal of law only). There are 116 RCs in Germany.
- The HRC is – apart from when it is hearing appeals of law from the DC – the regular court of first instance for national security cases, such as terrorism. As a court of first instance, the RHC decides with three or five judges, depending on the particularities of the case. Judgments can be appealed to the FHCJ (appeal of law only). There are 24 HRCs in Germany.
- The FHCJ hears appeals of law. Decisions are normally rendered by a panel of five federal judges. For cases of special significance, an *en banc* procedure exists, which is only used infrequently. Decisions are final and are not open to ordinary judicial review; extraordinary remedies can be sought before the FCC or the ECtHR.

1.5. The status of the accused

Several defence rights in the investigation phase – *inter alia* the right to information – are only enjoyed by an accused (*Beschuldigter*),[33] but not by a mere suspect (*Tatverdächtiger*), who is – as it holds true for many, if not most foreign jurisdictions – considered an ordinary witness.[34] Since investigations and proceedings against accused involve certain complications for law enforcement agencies, they might seek to avoid the accused status and to proceed against mere suspects; to forestall that law enforcement agencies arbitrarily deny a person status of an accused, several protections are in place, and it is wrong that the investigation authority enjoys the unfettered power to classify someone as either a suspect or an accused.

Leaving theory and its doctrinal starting points aside, a person becomes an accused if any one of the three following conditions is satisfied:

- A person acquires the status of an accused if a law enforcement agency initiates a formal investigation or prosecution against him/her, thus linking this person to a criminal offence. The determination to initiate formal proceedings requires a positive act of the law enforcement agency (for example, qualifying the person concerned as an accused

---

[33] This status is a technical legal concept, which for the sake of this report we equate – disregarding all possible semantic and comparative legal objections – with the English term *accused*.

[34] At later stages of the proceedings, this distinction becomes moot; a trial cannot by definition be conducted against a mere suspect.

during an interrogation). Note that law enforcement agencies are obliged to initiate formal proceedings, once there are sufficient factual indications about the person being criminally linked to an offence.[35]

- A person can also acquire the status of an accused, despite the law enforcement agency failing – for whatever reason – to formally qualify the person concerned as an accused. The accused status is acquired if the law enforcement agency applies for, or implements, an investigative measure that by law must only be administered against an accused. For example, an arrest warrant must only be issued, or provisional detention must only be executed against an accused; if the police therefore apply for an arrest warrant, this effectively – and objectively – makes the person an accused.

- A person can finally also acquire the status of an accused if a law enforcement agency has – objectively – collected sufficient factual indications that the person concerned has committed a crime, but – illegally (see *supra*) – does not initiate a formal proceeding. In a recent case,[36] the police suspected a father of having murdered his wife and daughter; instead of interrogating the father as an accused, and informing him of his defence rights, he was ordered to appear at an ordinary witness examination that lasted for some 10 hours, where he was pressed to disclose the location of the bodies. The FHCJ held that a person must not be arbitrarily denied the accused status, particularly with the aim of denying his/her rights to information. Therefore, a certain (objective and judicially reviewable) level of suspicion by the investigating authorities effectively brings with it the accused status, irrespective of the determination to formally initiate proceedings against the person concerned.[37] In the case at hand, the police did not properly inform the father of his defence rights. Thus, since German law does not provide for any formal act of accusation, case law often turns on the question of whether a person should have been 'treated as' an accused, and particularly whether he/she should have been warned of his/her right to remain silent and to consult with a lawyer. The 'objective' strength of suspicion at any given point in time is the main criterion for making that determination.

The latter – objective – condition for acquiring the status of an accused is a particularly viable deterrent against the arbitrary – subjective – denial of this status in practice by law enforcement agencies. However, the requirement that the law enforcement agency has 'sufficient factual indications that the person concerned has committed a crime' of course represents a concept that can only be resolved from case to case and by taking into account ordinary investigative experience; to this extent only criminal justice actors still enjoy certain margins of appreciation as to

---

[35]   See § 152 (2) CCP.
[36]   FHCJ, 51 BGHSt, p. 367.
[37]   But also see FHCJ, 38 BGHSt, p. 228 (noting that investigative authorities retain a margin of appreciation).

whom to classify as an accused and against whom to proceed against as a mere suspect.

1.6. *Legal aid*

It is understood in the English legal system, 'If you have to go to court, you can get legal aid to pay for a solicitor and a barrister if you can't afford it.'[38] This system resembles the German civil legal aid system, but German criminal justice does *not* have a legal aid scheme. However, the German criminal justice system knows a complex *functional equivalent*;[39] the findings of our field research in this regard will be outlined in *infra* 1.6.4.

1.6.1. State spending on the German criminal legal aid equivalent

Since the financial administration of the German criminal legal aid equivalent falls to the individual German states, no comprehensive and uniform statistics on spending are available.[40]

1.6.2. The German criminal legal aid equivalent

The German legal aid equivalent only applies to cases of so called mandatory legal representation (*notwendige Verteidigung*), such as felony,[41] or otherwise complex proceedings.[42] Such cases may arise in all phases of the proceedings (including the

---

[38] See the official Legal Aid homepage: <http://www.legalaid60.org.uk/whatis/> (last visited 29 April 2010).

[39] Also see § 2 (2) ALAR which pertains directly, i.e. is only open to both indigent accused and indigent suspects; is only available during the investigation and the confirmation of charges phase, and only if the accused is not represented by a court appointed counsel; covers (almost) free of charge legal advice, including related preparatory work (for example, access to the case file, or representation during an interrogation to enable counsel to properly advise his/her client); representation during trial is expressly excluded in matters of criminal law (while it is allowed for in matters of administrative law or social welfare). Note that this Act does not apply to Hamburg and Bremen, which have special systems for legal advice (§ 12 [1] ALAR); special regulations also apply for Berlin (§ 12 [2] ALAR).

[40] As to the data available, see chart 4 of the appendix.

[41] German substantive criminal law distinguishes between felonies (*Verbrechen*) and misdemeanours (*Vergehen*). A felony is an offence punishable with a minimum of one year imprisonment (or more).

[42] A court appointed counsel must only be appointed in cases of mandatory legal assistance. Scenarios of mandatory legal assistance during the (normal) trial phase are enumerated in § 140 (1) CCP; the most pertinent are: the trial of first instance takes place before the Higher Regional Court or before the Regional Court, in cases of grave crimes; the accused is charged with a felony; the accused is in provisional detention. In addition, pursuant to § 140 (2) CCP, cases of mandatory legal assistance during the trial phase also arise: if the assistance of defence counsel appears necessary, because of the seriousness of the offence; if the assistance of defence counsel appears necessary, because of factual or legal difficulties (for example, in the appeal of law or cassation stage); or if it is evident that the accused cannot defend him/herself, for example, because of mental vulnerability. During the investigation phase, under § 141 (3) CCP the prosecution may – and in certain cases must – bring a motion to

→

261

investigation phase). Irrespective of indigence, every accused in a case of mandatory legal representation, has the right to a court appointed counsel; as a corollary to this, due to its mandatory nature, in such cases an accused is precluded from conducting his/her own defence without a defence counsel, even if he/she does not want one.

Every lawyer may be appointed as court appointed counsel; there is no public defender scheme in Germany. In cases on non-mandatory legal representation (which represent most cases of low and mid-level criminality), the German legal aid equivalent does not apply.

What is more, it only applies when a court appointed counsel (*Pflichtverteidiger*) has been assigned to the accused; hence, when the accused chooses his/her own counsel (*Wahlverteidiger*) in cases of mandatory legal representation, he/she has to pay for the assistance him/herself. It should be noted, however, that the accused may indicate to the competent court who is to become his/her court appointed counsel; this request is normally granted, except where serious grounds (for example, incompetence or lack of expertise) lead the court to appoint a different counsel. This effectively means that the accused may seek to have his/her hired attorney become his/her court appointed counsel in cases of mandatory legal representation.

The primary objective of the German legal aid equivalent is *not* to ultimately determine who will bear of costs at the beginning of the proceedings, or at the time of the assignment of the court appointed counsel. Rather, it is solely to remove the risks associated with the client's insolvency, in order to ensure unimpeded legal representation during the proceedings; questions about the indigence of the accused are adjourned until after the proceedings have ended. This objective is accomplished in that the state guarantees to court appointed counsel the remuneration of the codified fees for statutorily enumerated defence services;[43] although it should be critically observed that the remuneration regime focuses too much on the trial stage, and does not provide adequate remuneration for defence services in the investigation phase.

All of this effectively means – *ex positivo* – that the court appointed counsel can always rely on having a solvent debtor (the state), even where his/her client is or appears indigent, yet – *ex negativo* – only to the extent of the codified ordinary fee remuneration scheme. The court appointed counsel may also apply for an 'adequate

---

    appoint counsel, if the trial is expected to meet the requirements of mandatory legal assistance (§ 140 [1], [2] CCP).

[43] Regulations are to be found in § 45 LRA and provisions # 4100 *et seq.* of the additional LRI (online available at <http://bundesrecht.juris.de/rvg/anlage_1_80.html> last visited 29 April 2010). The number of working hours is *not* a decisive indication for the remuneration. Rather, the above mentioned regulations differentiate between more than 60 different fees for the same number of different services. Some examples with regard to court appointed counsel are: The ordinary fee for familiarizing oneself with the case is 132 Euro (# 4100 LRI). The ordinary fee for legal representation during the examination by public prosecution is 112 Euro (# 4102 LRI). The ordinary fee for legal representation in a trial before the district court is 184 Euro a day. If the trial session lasts for more than 5 hours, there will be additional payment of 92 Euro, and if last for more than 8 hours, the additional payment is 184 Euro (# 4108 LRI).

advance payment' from the treasury for the services he/she provides to the accused.[44] What is more, counsel can also move for lump-sum remuneration in particularly complicated or extensive cases, where the workload is considerably higher than under the ordinary fee remuneration scheme.[45] The codified ordinary fees of a court appointed counsel are normally considerably lower than the codified ordinary fees of a hired counsel, let alone the negotiated fees charged by high-quality criminal defence lawyers and firms.[46]

Under this regime, it is thus irrelevant whether the person accused of murder (which qualifies as a case of mandatory legal representation, since it is a felony) is a beggar or a millionaire – both have the right to a court appointed counsel, who in turn can safely provide defence services, knowing that he/she will be remunerated by the state under the codified ordinary fees scheme. On the other hand, the hired counsel of a person accused of ordinary petty theft (which normally does not qualify as a case of mandatory legal representation) is not absolved from the risk of her client's indigence and thus insolvency.

Just like in ordinary private law, the ultimate bearing of costs and the existence of a claim is to be distinguished from any defence of indigence against the levy of execution (*Zwangsvollstreckung*) of this claim.

The court is legally bound to impose the costs of court proceedings and of defence on the defendant if he/she has been convicted.[47] Conversely, if the defendant has been acquitted or proceedings have been dismissed, the CCP requires the court to impose costs (including ordinary costs of defence services, which are calculated by reference to the codified ordinary fees for statutorily enumerated defence services) on the state.[48] If the case has been dismissed under a provision that leaves it to the court's discretion whether to dismiss, however, the court can refrain from imposing lawyer's fees on the state.[49]

Convicted persons – irrespective of whether they are indigent or not – are thus faced with claims of remuneration (be it by counsel directly, or by the state, to the extent it had advanced the ordinary fees to a court appointed counsel).

What is more, even acquitted persons may be faced with claims of remuneration from counsel, but only to the extent that this claim goes beyond the codified ordinary fees for defence services (for example, because counsel and the client negotiated higher fees than statutorily guaranteed). Whether counsel's financial demands fall under the ordinary fees regime is often only determined *ex post facto*, that is after the proceedings, which leaves a financial risk with those counsel who provide extraordinary defence services. Finally, court appointed counsel can claim his/her fees from the client after conviction, only if the trial court

---

[44]   § 47 LRA.

[45]   § 51 LRA.

[46]   Suffice to raise one example: The ordinary fee for attending a trial hearing is 184 Euro for a court appointed counsel, while a hired counsel can charge an average fee of 230 Euro; negotiated fees can be much higher.

[47]   § 465 (1) CCP. As to the exceptions, see § 465 (2) CCP.

[48]   § 467 (1) CCP.

[49]   § 467 (4) CCP.

has made a finding that the client can pay the fee, in one payment or in instalments, without jeopardising him/her or his/her family's subsistence.[50]

In terms of the indigence of the accused, any remuneration claim – be it brought against the accused directly by his/her counsel or, more importantly, by the state to the extent it advanced fees to a court appointed counsel – falls under the protective standards of the Code of Civil Procedure (CCivP). This means that indigent persons are protected against the levy of execution under the ordinary civil procedure regime; indeed, the test for indigence at this stage is one of civil and not criminal procedure. Under this test, for example, the prescribed social minimum (currently 985.15 Euro for a single person; 1,769.03 Euro for a person who has to support a spouse and two children) of a person's monthly salary is safe from levy of execution.[51]

In summary, if an indigent person thus faces criminal proceedings, he/she is only entitled to a (temporary) state sponsored defence counsel, if it is a case of mandatory legal representation. Then, the indigent accused may request that his/her hired counsel will be appointed as his/her court appointed counsel. This will shift the risk of the accused's insolvency away from counsel and onto the treasury.

After a conviction, a court appointed counsel can choose whether to execute his/her claim against the treasury or against the convicted client; if the client is indigent, counsel will – for obvious reasons – normally seek to execute his/her claim against a solvent debtor – the state treasury – which will then try to execute the reclaim the amount from the accused.

If the case is not one of mandatory legal representation, the risk of the client's insolvency lies with the accused's hired counsel, who nevertheless can perhaps rely upon an acquittal (in which case, the treasury again remunerates the codified ordinary fees for statutorily enumerated defence services).

1.6.3. Organizational responsibility for administering the German criminal legal aid equivalent

The organizational responsibility for administering the German criminal legal aid equivalent must be distinguished between the three tenets outlined above:

- In all phases of the proceedings, including the investigation phase, the determination of whether a case is one of mandatory legal

---

[50]   § 52 (2) LRA.

[51]   §§ 850, 850c [1] CCivP. This is not to say that the state proceeds before civil courts to execute its claims. Rather, the state directly executes its claim according to § 1 (1) # 4 Court Execution Act (*Justizbeitreibungsordnung*). An appointed lawyer's statutory fee, if paid by the state, is regarded as part of the 'costs and fees' of the proceedings in accordance with § 464a CCP. These costs and fees are levied against the defendant, if he has been convicted (see *supra*). However, the regulations of the Code of Civil Procedure concerning income protected from execution of claims are also applicable with respect to the execution of court costs (§ 6 Justizbeitreibungsordnung). Execution thus will be effected only if the convicted defendant is no longer indigent. Therefore, the German scheme is deemed to be in agreement with art. 6 (3) (c) ECHR.

representation and whether the accused is not represented by his/her hired counsel, as well as the appointment of a court appointed counsel, rests with the presiding judge of the chamber that has jurisdiction over the case. The accused may seek to have his/her hired appointed as court appointed counsel.[52] In the determination and assignment of court appointed counsel, questions about who ultimately bears the costs, as well as the possible indigence of the accused are irrelevant, particularly where the presiding judge does not enjoy discretion in the determination.[53] Moreover, in the appointment process, the presiding judge has no fixed (for example, yearly) budget, and must make his/her considerations solely in the interests of the fair administration of justice.

- The decision of who has to eventually bear the costs for ordinary defence services (the state in case of an acquittal, and the accused in case of her conviction) is made in the judgment and thus rests with the deciding court; the indigence of the accused is normally of no relevance for this decision.

- The decision as to whether indigence is a valid defence against the levy of execution of a remuneration claim against the accused follows the sophisticated rules of German civil procedure. For example, if the state has advanced or remunerated a court appointed counsel, it may move to seize a convict's wage. The local and material competence to decide then falls to the civil section of the district court in the jurisdiction of which the applicant resides. The personal competence falls to a judicial officer (*Rechtspfleger*).

1.6.4. Results of field research

In the course of writing this report, basic field research was conducted, based upon interviews with legal practitioners, which were meant to provide a qualitative sample of the professional experiences, status and roles of the German legal staff (*Rechtsstab*).[54] These interviews shed some light on how the criminal legal aid equivalent is handled in practice, as well as the quality and role of defence counsel in general and of court appointed counsel in particular (on the latter see *infra* 3.4).

Our field research is ambivalent about how criminal defence lawyers explain its complexity to clients. It was often indicated that only minimal information will be passed along, and that clients – including indigent ones – are often not particularly interested in the details of the remuneration process, due to the stress of the ongoing criminal proceedings against them.[55]

Although remuneration according to the codified ordinary fees scheme is seen as very bureaucratic, defence lawyers indicated that it can be, and often is dealt with handled by secretaries and law clerks who have the necessary experience and

---

[52]   See *supra* 1.6.2.
[53]   See the scenarios set forth in § 140 (1) CCP.
[54]   See chart 5 of the appendix.
[55]   Interview # 5.

technical support. Rather than the actual calculation, defence lawyers mainly criticised the long time span between filing a remuneration claim to the competent court, the court's determination about the validity of the claim, and the actual payment. The opinions of our interviewees regarding the actual amount of remuneration in legal aid cases differ starkly.[56]

1.7. Additional challenges to the German criminal justice system

The ongoing European and international integration, and, as a consequence, the increasing Europeanization and internationalisation of the administration of criminal justice, brings with it new challenges to criminal defence services and rights. It is yet to be determined if ever closer cooperation and coordination between formerly impenetrable sovereign states, and the risks for a defendant stemming there from, can indeed be compensated by merely national procedural safeguards and their (European) harmonization or convergence. Rather, it is submitted that, for translational cases, a novel set of truly translational procedural fundamental rights should at least be discussed.

Not only in terms of legal doctrine, but also with regard to the practice of criminal justice, European and international concepts erode one of the fundamental pillars of traditional German penal culture: the distinction between the proactive pre-emption and prevention of impending threats to society on the one hand (a task that was hitherto assigned to intelligence agencies and the police), and the repression of *and the reaction to past crimes* (a task assigned to the criminal justice apparatus) on the other. The rise of incapacitation as a legitimate purpose of criminal justice (preventive detention, *Sicherungsverwahrung*) and of outwardly preventive coercive measures (for example, DNA-databases) (*Strafverfolgungsvorsorge*), symbolises a new understanding of criminal acts, which are not (only) to be readdressed retrospectively, but represent occasions to identify dangerous persons. Thus, criminal law and procedure transforms into a tool for social control.

On a purely national level, the codification of the 'deal' (see *supra* 1.4.1) in § 257c CCP has been critically appraised as a symbol of the erosion of another pillar of traditional German penal legal culture: the quest for material truth by independent organs of the criminal justice system, by 'neutral' prosecutors and defence counsel. Yet, since 'deals' are now common practice, their positive regulation is not so much a proactive legislative revolution, but rather 'only' retraces this common practice and tries to set certain limits.

It seems curious that the right to a speedy trial is, in practice, developing into a handicap for the defence, since courts and prosecutors are under severe pressure to present results, particularly in ordinary cases; investigations, 'deals', and trials are administered principally with time efficiency, rather than objectives such as rehabilitation of the accused or a general coming to terms with the past, in mind. On the other hand, and by contrast, particularly in difficult and complex cases like

---

[56] Interviews # 1, 2, 3 and 5 on the one hand (the compensation is inadequate); interview # 7 on the other hand (adequate).

white collar crime, practitioners compromise the right to a speedy trial, and in prominent cases many years may pass until an indictment is filed or a trial hearing scheduled. In summary, German criminal justice should develop a more balanced understanding of the right to a speedy trial, which must neither be turned upside down to the disadvantage of the accused in ordinary cases, nor be violated in difficult cases.

Eventually, effective defence not only requires a set of defence rights in the statute books, but also their implementation in practice, which in turn requires truly independent, professional and high-quality defence counsel. There is credible anecdotal evidence reporting of an almost symbiotic relationship between the courts and their 'chosen' counsel, who are regularly appointed in cases of mandatory legal representations and so earn their living, but who dare not stand up against the court or make use of their rights, such as to bring evidentiary motions.

Similarly, there are no hard qualitative standards, and great differences between the skills of lawyers prevail. On the other hand, the professionalisation of defence counsel is clearly increasing. In order to secure the services of an independent and high-quality counsel, the financial resources of the accused are determinative, and well paid counsel can and do make a difference in effective defence. That is why Germany needs to consider addressing the factual discrimination against indigent persons, for example, by raising the ordinary fees of court assigned counsel. This might be a politically unpopular demand, but the recent rise of the fees seems to have only been a drop in the ocean, at least with regard to fees as they are guaranteed for defence services in the investigative phase.

With regard to institutional safeguards, the system of judicial warrants (see *supra* 1.4.1.) needs to be rethought. While theoretically sound, in practice judges do not or cannot review all of the material submitted before issuing a judicial warrant – particularly when time is pressing, where the case and evidence is complex (for example, in cases of organized crime), or where judges, who do not necessarily serve in the criminal department, are called in on emergency service (for example, over the weekend). From a very critical point of view, the judicial warrant may only be – metaphorically speaking – a 'fig leaf'; it may thus radiate a certain normative legitimacy that is factually groundless.

On the other hand, with regard to certain coercive measures, there seems to be systemic non-compliance with the judicial warrant, particularly by the police in cases of physical examination of the accused (more concretely; the taking of blood samples for alcohol or drug testing). German criminal procedure needs to develop better sanctioning instruments, for example, the exclusion of the evidence as some German courts currently accept.

As concerns technological developments, these need to be considered in securing and monitoring the proper administration of justice (for example, by producing video or audio transcripts of trials at the regional court level), but they also lead to new challenges and problems for criminal investigations, particularly when it comes to 'criminal' data (for example, deploying 'Trojan horses' in computers to intercept communications). These challenges are further amplified, since criminal justice actors often depend on the cooperation of private actors (for example, when accessing data of mobile phones), which in turn gives rise to the risk of private abuse (for example, private telecommunication corporations accessing databases that were originally foreseen for the use of investigative authorities only). German criminal procedure again needs to balance the fundamental German right to informational self-determination, with investigative interests into 'criminal' data and with the proper control of cooperating private actors.

The proper regulation and governance of private actors who enter the criminal justice arena becomes more pressing bearing in mind the fact that private law firms or internal compliance offices are increasingly involved in private investigations into white collar crime (for example, grand corruption). It is an imperative to positively determine the scope of their powers (for example, compliance officers examining and interrogating corporate personnel and staff), the corresponding 'defence' rights, and the transferability of privately obtained 'evidence' to the criminal justice apparatus.

2. Legal rights and their implementation

2.1. The right to information

It is important to distinguish between the *positive duties* of the investigating authorities to inform the accused (be it in the context of the interrogation, upon provisional arrest, or provisional detention, in the writ of the indictment, or in the trial) and the active right of the defence to access the case file (during all stages of the proceedings).

2.1.1. Interrogation by the investigating authorities (police, prosecution, investigating judge)

In (most) cases, where the accused is not caught red-handed but only in the course of ongoing investigations, he/she will be ordered in writing to appear at an interrogation (*Ladung*)[57] in the offices of either the police, the prosecution, or the investigating judge; the first interrogation may often be the first contact between the accused and the investigating authorities in the investigation phase.[58] The police have less rigorous duties to inform than the prosecution and investigating judge; this is partially compensated by the fact that the accused only has to follow the order to appear before the prosecution and the investigating judge, but not an interrogation before the police.

In (most) cases, where the accused is caught red-handed, that is particularly where investigating authorities identify an accused in the course, or in the immediate aftermath of a criminal offence, the first interrogation can be conducted in the field without a prior written order to appear at an interrogation; the accused

---

[57]   Many commentators agree that this order to appear at an interrogation must already outline its subject matter; see Gleß 2007a, marginal No. 3; Meyer-Goßner 2008, § 133 marginal No. 4. Contra Meyer-Goßner 2007, § 133 marginal No. 4.

[58]   The accused is to be interrogated before the end of the investigation phase, if the proceedings are to be continued (for example, by filing a writ of indictment); see § 163a (1) CCP.

need not be provisionally arrested prior to the commencement of the interrogation, and the accused is under no legal duty to talk to the police.

Where the investigating authorities have not identified an accused, or have not gathered sufficient evidence to link a person to an offence, mere informational questioning (*informatorische Befragung*) of witnesses or suspects is still permissible. Such questioning does not qualify as an interrogation[59] *strictu sensu*, so that no information duties whatsoever emerge;[60] however, once sufficient factual indications that the questioned person has committed a crime become apparent during the informational questioning, duties to inform then arise.

Likewise, there are no duties to inform in case of so called spontaneous testimony (*Spontanäußerungen*)[61] – where the person concerned testifies before the investigating authorities were able to inform and caution that person. Spontaneous testimony normally occurs only vis-à-vis police officers, for example, when a man walks into a police station and tells the desk officer 'I just killed my wife'. Such declarations can be used as evidence. But the police officer would then immediately have to tell the citizen that he is an accused and inform him about his rights.

In the first police interrogation, the accused is to be informed about the (1) *criminal conduct* that he/she is suspected of;[62] as well as the (2) *right to consult with a defence counsel*; (3) the *right to remain silent*; and (4) the *right to bring motions* to gather specific evidence.[63] What is more, during every police interrogation, the accused shall normally be informed about the (4) *causes of the suspicion* (*Verdachtsgründe*);[64] however, according to the jurisprudence of the FHCJ and FCC, evidence shall not be disclosed to the accused if this would jeopardize the investigations.[65] These duties to

---

[59]   Meyer-Goßner 2008, Einl. marginal No. 79.

[60]   For a critique, see Beulke 2008, marginal No. 118 (duties to inform and to instruct may be circumvented in practice by not initiating a formal interrogation and, instead, conducting general informational questioning).

[61]   See Krehl 2001, marginal No. 2; Griesbaum 2008, marginal No. 32; Wohlers 2008a, marginal No. 46.

[62]   § 163a (4) CCP. The information is to be so precise and determinate as to dispel all doubts about the subject matter of the interrogation, and hence enable the accused to effectively defend him/herself; the naming of, particularly legal, keywords (like murder, robbery, petty theft) is not enough; rather, the factual circumstances of the criminal conduct, as they are understood thus far by the investigating authorities, are to be disclosed. On the other hand, this disclosure must not jeopardize further investigations.

[63]   §§ 163a (4), 136 (1) CCP.

[64]   §§ 163a (4), 136 (2) CCP; the latter reads: 'The interrogation shall enable the accused to rebut all causes of the accusation and to assert facts which are in his/her favour.'

[65]   The fact that any interrogation shall present the suspect with an opportunity to put forth circumstances in his/her favour does not mean that the police must actively offer him/her material for exoneration. Only in extreme cases can withholding exonerating evidence known to the police amount to 'deception', which would lead to the inadmissibility of any ensuing statement under § 136a (1) CCP. Indeed, criminal justice actors enjoy investigative and tactical discretion, and may keep an accused in the dark on particular facts. This discretion, in turn, is limited to the extent that non-disclosure of evidence must not amount to (willful) deception, or to an infringement of the accused's freedom to testify; see § 136a (1) CCP. See also FHCJ, 37 BGHSt, p. 53; FCC, *NStZ*, 1984, p. 228, but cf. Meyer-Goßner 2008, § 136 marginal No. 13. Further cf. (on academic critique of this jurisprudence) Gleß 2007b, marginal No. 22, 56.

inform also arise in interrogations by the prosecution or the investigating judge, who additionally have to inform the accused in their interrogations about (5) the general legal qualification of the accusation, and about potentially aggravating penal provisions, so as to enable an effective defence.[66]

The information can be provided orally[67] and must be presented in a clear and understandable manner. Except where the accused is arrested, there is no duty to hand the accused a letter of rights, but in practice the standard forms used to record the interrogations may[68] spell out certain defence rights in writing. On these standard forms, the observance of duties to inform, as well as all significant parts of an interrogation, will in practice be recorded.[69]

There is no codified enforcement mechanism in relation to these duties to inform during interrogations by investigative authorities, and it is yet to be decided by the FHCJ exactly which violations may principally lead to the exclusion of evidence gathered during the interrogation. It has been established that the failure to inform the accused about his/her right to counsel (with few exceptions) triggers the exclusionary rule. It is further safe to assume that this exclusionary rule would apply if the authorities consciously mislead the accused, by obfuscating the nature and cause of the accusation, thus interfering with his/her freedom to testify.

Apart from such extreme cases, it is also safe to assume that courts would not apply an absolute exclusionary rule, but rather would apply a balancing test and only exclude evidence if the accused's interest in effective defence outweighs the social interests of a fair and effective prosecution. The FHCJ has repeatedly decided that an omission to inform the accused of his/her right to remain silent makes any ensuing statement inadmissible, unless it can positively be shown that the accused was aware of this right.[70]

2.1.2. Provisional arrest and provisional detention

After taking the accused into provisional detention, or after he/she has been provisionally arrested, he/she must be brought before the competent detention judge. Provisional detention is ordered by an arrest warrant (*Haftbefehl*), which must spell out the facts that substantiate both the evidence suggesting that the accused is

---

[66] §§ 136a (1) CCP and §§ 163a (3), 136a (1) CCP. Disregarding the wording of these provisions, there is growing agreement that the fair trial principle requires that *new qualifications of the nature of the offences*, as they develop during or after the first interrogation, are to be disclosed to the accused, at least if the nature of penal provisions that may have been violated changes fundamentally, be it that the accusation becomes graver or pettier; see for example, Wagner 1997, p. 569 *et seq.*

[67] In exceptional cases – particularly where the accused suffers from speech or hearing impairments – the information is to be provided in writing, § 186 AOJ. Also see *infra* 2.1.2 on the new § 114b CCP and the letter of rights in case the accused is arrested.

[68] Note that, due to German federalism, there is no uniform standard police interrogation form throughout the country.

[69] See Rule 45 of the Rules for Proceedings in Criminal and Administrative Sanctioning Matters (RPCASM), stipulating certain documentation duties for interrogations by the prosecution and the investigating judge.

[70] See Meyer-Goßner 2008, § 136 marginal No. 20.

highly likely to have committed a crime, as well as the conditions justifying provisional detention (see *supra* 1.4.2).[71]

According to § 114b CCP, which entered into force on 1 January 2010, the arrested accused is to be informed in writing and in a language he/she understands about (1) the right to appear before a judge without undue delay and, at the latest, one day following the day the arrest took place; (2) the right to remain silent; (3) the right to bring motions to gather evidence; (4) the right to consult counsel; (5) the right to be examined by a medic; (6) the right to inform a relative, as long as this does not jeopardize the investigations; (7) the right to free interpretation (if the accused does not have a command of the German language); and (8) the right to inform the relevant consulate (if the accused is a foreign citizen).

Pursuant to the newly introduced § 140 # 4 CCP, the execution of the provisional detention of the accused now also triggers mandatory legal representation.

The first appearance before the detention judge is to take place without undue delay and at the latest before the end of the day following arrest.[72] If the first appearance coincides with the first interrogation before a judge, the general duties to inform emerge (see *supra* 2.1.1). Additionally, at the first appearance, the judge has to substantiate the accusation thoroughly: all incriminating, as well as exonerating evidence – relevant to both the subject matter of the case and the substantive conditions justifying detention – are to be presented; the accused is hence to be given the opportunity to rebut all grounds of suspicion and all grounds for provisional detention. This information must be supplied orally (in addition to the information already contained in the written arrest warrant).

The right of the accused to detailed information is even more extensive if the decision regarding provisional detention is reviewed (*Haftprüfung*) by a court. During the review hearing,[73] the accused is to be informed comprehensively about the facts of the case,[74] as well as the pertinent results of the ongoing investigation,[75] even if – in principle –the investigations are thus jeopardised.[76]

Our field review revealed that the practical problem in common cases is not a lack of information. However, criminal defence lawyers[77] were in broad agreement that, particularly in complex cases, provisional detention is often used as an investigative measure to 'motivate' as accused to give a (partial) confession and that the grounds for provisional detention are interpreted broadly and liberally. One criminal defence lawyer[78] criticised the fact that the police often point to provisional detention in order to motivate an accused to a confession, although the police are not competent to move for, let alone order, provisional detention.

---

[71]   § 114 (2) CCP.
[72]   §§ 115, 115a CCP.
[73]   §§ 118a (3), 122 (2) CCP.
[74]   Hilger 2007a, marginal No. 24.
[75]   Paeffgen 2007a, marginal No. 6.
[76]   Paeffgen 2007a, marginal No. 6; Hilger 2007a, marginal No. 24.
[77]   Interviews # 1, 2, 3, 5, 7, 8, 9.
[78]   Interview # 8.

Nevertheless, other criminal defence lawyers[79] commended the good cooperation with prison staff, while others were critical of the fact that these facilities are often too far away. One federal prosecutor,[80] on the other hand, pointed to the benefits of provisional detention for the accused, while state prosecutors[81] emphasized that provisional detention is only ordered, if its substantive legal preconditions are met; nevertheless, they also admitted that the police occasionally use the wrong tone when introducing provisional detention to interrogations. One federal judge[82] did not agree that provisional detention is reinterpreted as an investigative measure, because it is only rarely challenged on the ground that the preconditions are/were lacking.

A frequent problem is the lack of the detainee's information about the progress of the investigation, when the detention order is reviewed. The FCC, in accordance with a judgment of the ECtHR, has decided that the judge cannot base an order to uphold detention on material that has not been made known to the detainee. It is possible to withhold sensitive information from him/her, but in that case, the judge cannot rely on such information to the detainee's detriment.[83]

2.1.3. The writ of indictment

There is an unconditional obligation[84] on the prosecution to spell out, in the writ of indictment, all pertinent incriminating and exonerating evidence (the latter also encompassing evidence that may challenge the reliability of incriminating evidence),[85] as well as the essential results of the investigation in more complex or grave cases. This is to satisfy the so called informational function of the writ of indictment. This information is to enable the accused to prepare his/her defence and to bring motions to gather additional evidence. The prosecution enjoys a certain degree of discretion as to which evidence it deems pertinent for an efficient, speedy and fair trial. The prosecution must specify all of the contact details of witnesses (except if there are reasons for witness protection) and the identity of experts; it must also specify the documents in the case file (which, however, are not to be reprinted).

The correct remedy for a deficient writ of indictment, which does not satisfy its informational function, is controversial. The FHCJ has held that such deficiencies do not render the writ of indictment invalid, because it can supposedly be rectified by a clarification during the trial.[86] Only if this clarification is missing, can a verdict be

---

79   Interviews # 1, 2, 7, 9.
80   Interview # 6.
81   Interviews # 10, 11.
82   Interview # 4.
83   See *infra* 2.1.5.
84   §§ 170 (1), (2), 200 (1) CCP.
85   A written summary sanctioning order (*Strafbefehl*) is to contain comparable information (§ 409 [1] [#5] CCP) about the evidence.
86   FHCJ, 40 BGHSt, p. 45. This line of reasoning faces serious challenges by courts and academics.

challenged on appeal of law.[87] Nevertheless, the court is free to return the writ of indictment to the prosecution and ask for amendments.[88]

2.1.4. Confirmation of the charges and the trial phase

If the court orders further evidence to be obtained in the confirmation of charges phase,[89] the accused is to be informed about the results of the investigation.

The prosecution is obliged to read out the writ of indictment (and thus the information contained therein) to the accused in the beginning of the trial (just after the identification of the accused).

To a certain extent, § 246 CCP prohibits 'surprise evidence' that is produced by either the prosecution or the defence *during trial*.[90] On the one hand, the court must not decline evidence simply because it is produced too late. On the other hand, if new evidence is produced by one side, the court must also[91] ensure that the other side has sufficient time for effective preparation of its case; this may require the court to suspend the trial. To forestall this, the order to appear at trial, or the hearing notification (*Terminsmitteilung*), must inform the parties about the evidence that will be dealt with during trial.[92]

Violations of the duties to inform during the confirmation of charges and the trial phase may be challenged by an appeal of law, particularly if the defence was impermissibly constrained.[93]

2.1.5. Access to the Case File

The rights of accused and counsel to access to the case file – which are complemented by right to be positively informed about the evidentiary basis of the accusation during an interrogation (see *supra* 2.1.1), in the arrest warrant (see *supra* 2.1.2), or in the writ of indictment (see *supra* 2.1.3) – differ significantly, depending on whether it pertains to the accused or counsel, on which phase of the criminal proceedings it is, and the status of the accused.

After the investigation has been officially closed (that is, particularly during the trial), the right *of counsel* to access the case file is no longer subject to any restrictions.

---

[87]   Stuckenberg 2008, marginal No. 93.
[88]   Meyer-Goßner 2008, § 200 marginal No. 27.
[89]   § 201 CCP.
[90]   It is the responsibility of the presiding judge to make sure that all necessary evidence is presented in court (§ 244 [2] CCP). There does exist a right for the defence and the prosecution to ask the court to introduce *additional* items of evidence. Only if the court grants such a motion, or belatedly introduces new evidence *sua sponte*, can the judge grant the affected party additional time to prepare or re-adjust its argument.
[91]   Note that, according to the jurisprudence of the FHCJ, a court is to ensure a speedy trial. This consideration might clash with the guarantee of effective defence preparation. See *NJW*, 1990, p. 1124.
[92]   Rule 118 RPCASM.
[93]   § 338 (#8) CCP.

During the investigation phase, the extent of the *right of counsel* to access the case file primarily depends on whether the accused is kept in provisional detention:[94] As a general rule, if the accused is not kept in provisional detention, access to the case file can be restricted, in order not the jeopardize the investigation; this is in accordance with the German Constitution and has so far not been challenged successfully before the ECtHR. A determination that the investigation would be jeopardised must not be based on vague and remote reasons; however, counsel's access to the file can be restricted if the authorities plan investigative measures that, to be successful, depend on the accused not being aware.[95]

If the accused is kept in provisional detention, the ECtHR ruled in 2001 that restrictions of the right to access the case file violate article 5 ECHR, to the extent that access is necessary to ensure effective defence[96] – that is: the ECtHR effectively demanded that the defence be granted access to those parts of the case file upon which an arrest warrant is based. In heeding this jurisprudence, which was accepted by the FCC in 2006 and applied to the provisional freezing of assets,[97] it is now[98] well accepted that access to the case file will be granted to counsel if the accused is kept in provisional detention, and (only) to the extent that the arrest warrant is based (or upheld) on the case file's evidence regarding both the accusation and the reasons justifying provisional detention. This means that sensitive evidence can still be withheld from counsel, in order not to jeopardize the investigation, but in that case, the judge cannot rely on such evidence to the accused's detriment, for example, in issuing or upholding an arrest warrant against him/her.

The CCP[99] regulates the *right of the accused* to access the file in a more restrictive manner.[100] An *accused without legal representation* shall only be provided with information or excerpts/copies from the file, and only if this does not jeopardise the investigation, or does not go against the interests of third persons (for example, witnesses). If this restriction infringes upon the accused's right to effective defence, this may constitute a case of mandatory legal representation, so that court appointed counsel will be granted access to the file. If this procedure is

---

94   At no stage of the proceedings may defence counsel be refused access to records concerning the examination of the accused, acts in the judicial investigation at which defence counsel was or should have been allowed to be present, or expert reports.

95   Meyer-Goßner 2008, § 147 marginal No. 25.

96   ECtHR 13 February 2001, *Lietzow* v. *Germany, Schöps* v. *Germany, Garcia Alva* v. *Germany*, Nos. 24479/94, 25116/94, 23541/94. A German translation of the judgments is reported in *StV*, 2001, p. 201 *et seq.*; see also ECtHR 30 March 1989, *Lamy* v. *Belgium*, No. 10444/83, also reported in German in *StV*, 1993, p. 283.

97   FCC, *NStZ*, 2006, 459.

98   The latest decision of the ECtHR against Germany – ECtHR 9 July 2009, *Mooren* v. *Germany*, No. 11364/03 – pertains to a 2002 case, and is thus not indicative of the present practice.

99   § 147 (7) CCP.

100   In this context, the ECtHR has only ruled on counsel's right to access the file in Germany; therefore, this jurisprudence must not be too quickly applied to the accused's access rights. In *Mooren* (see *supra* note 98), the ECtHR heard complaints that, in the review proceedings of provisional detention, counsel was refused access to the case file, which made it impossible for the applicant to defend himself effectively (§ 108 of the decision).

inappropriate, for example, due to the criminal accusation being only of a petty nature, the accused is to be granted full access to the file.[101]

An *accused with legal representation* has no own right to access to the case file; however, if necessary for the effective exercise of counsel's right to access to the file, counsel has the right to demand that the accused also be present;[102] counsel may also provide his/her client with copies from the file.[103] The restrictions on the accused's right to access the file are compensated to a certain extent by the more far-reaching access rights of counsel – who are considered more trustworthy due to their role as independent organs of the criminal justice system (see *infra* 3.3) – and by the fact that counsel are generally obliged to inform the client about the content of the file.

The restrictions on the accused's right to access the case file face possible challenges alleging a violation of article 6 (3) (c) ECHR and corresponding ECtHR jurisprudence. To be in compliance, commentators suggest treating counsel and accused alike; namely that access shall only be denied in the investigation phase, only if the investigation would be jeopardized,[104] and only if the accused is not (to be kept) in provisional detention.[105]

The *case file covers* all pieces of incriminating or exonerating evidence that are relevant to the case.[106] Counsel may also access the criminal record of the accused, reports of the juvenile court assistance agency (*Jugendgerichtshilfe*) and case files concerning co-accused, if they are tried in common proceedings.[107] However, files relating to other suspects, whom public prosecution has decided not to prosecute (*Spurenakten*), are only covered if they have been presented to the court.[108] Further, certain pieces of information must not be included in the case file, in order to ensure confidentiality; this applies *inter alia* in cases of witness protection, in relation to very limited information about personal data obtained during telephone surveillance measures,[109] to information about the identity of undercover agents,[110] and to matters of national or public security.[111] Information gained from telephone surveillance and undercover informers is, of course, not *per se* excluded from the file and hence from inspection by defence counsel.

---

[101] See also ECtHR 17 February 1997, *Foucher* v. *France*, No. 10/1996/629/812.
[102] HRC Köln, *StV*, 1999, p. 12.
[103] Donath & Mehle, p. 1399.
[104] Wohlers 2008b, marginal No. 14.
[105] Meyer-Goßner 2008, § 147 marginal No. 25a.
[106] FHCJ, 42 BGHSt, p. 72.
[107] If the co-accused are tried in different proceedings the files may – if relevant to the case – be called in. If this is done, the access rights of the defence counsel also extends to the case file of the co-accused. This also applies if the two or more co-accused are originally tried in the same proceedings, but in the course of proceedings, the court decides to try them separately. Then, the file up to the date of separation is covered by the defence counsel's access right. Elements of the file of the co-accused added after the date of separation may be called in; see Wohlers 2008b, marginal No. 52.
[108] Krekeler & Werner 2007, marginal No. 10 with references in footnote 14.
[109] § 101 (4), (8) CCP: Namely personal data (*personenbezogene Daten*) that is no longer of significance for the criminal investigation.
[110] § 110b (3) CCP.
[111] § 96 CCP.

Access to the case file must be granted under *reasonable conditions*. If the file does not exist in hardcopy form, the authorities have to provide the necessary technical facilities to make the file accessible. The courts agree that neither the accused, nor counsel, have a right to free copies of the file;[112] however, under normal circumstances, counsel has the right to keep the file (not the evidence) for a reasonable time in his/her office, and to make copies of the file, a task for which he/she can claim remuneration.[113]

2.2.   The right to defend oneself

In the German context, the accused's right to defend him/herself in person must be distinguished from, and is less far-reaching than, the accused's right to legal representation at all stages of the proceedings.

2.2.1. The right to defend oneself in person at all stages of the proceedings

There is at least no *codified overarching right* of the accused (see *supra* 1.5) to defend him/herself in person during all stages of the proceedings, although one might deduce such an overarching right *inter alia* from the ECHR and the rule of law principle as enshrined in the German Constitution; there exists, however, a conglomerate of codified particular rights, such as:

Facilitative rights, including (1) the accused's right to be informed about the accusation (see *supra*); (2) the accused's right to be personally present during examination of the evidence, or during interrogations of witnesses and experts (but not of co-accused) by an investigative judge;[114] and (3) the accused's right, but normally also the duty, to be present during the trial.[115]

Positive rights, including (1) the accused's right to bring general motions (for example, to disqualify biased judges) during trial; (2) the accused's right to bring motions to gather, produce and introduce evidence (*Beweisantragsrecht*) during the investigation,[116] the confirmation of charges,[117] or the trial phase;[118] (3) the accused's right to personally question witnesses and experts during the trial;[119] (4) the

---

[112]   FHCJ, *MDR*, 1973, p. 371.

[113]   § 147 (4) CCP; # 7000 LRI.

[114]   § 168c (2) CCP. § 168c (3) CCP sets forth conditions under which the accused shall not be present, for example, if his/her presence would intimidate the witness; § 168c (5) CCP states that the accused is to be informed in a timely manner – and in whatever form suitable – about the upcoming interrogation. There is no corresponding right with regard to interrogation of witnesses and experts by the police or the prosecution.

[115]   A trial *in absentia* is allowed only under very limited circumstances, see §§ 231, 231a, 231b, 232 CCP. Also see § 247 CCP, which allows the temporal exclusion of the accused for limited reasons.

[116]   §§ 163a (2), 166 CCP. Pursuant to § 136 (1) CCP, the accused is to be informed about this right at the first interrogation.

[117]   § 201 (1) CCP.

[118]   § 244 (2) CCP. § 244 (3)-(5) set forth conditions under which the court is, by way of exception, *not* obliged to gather this evidence, for example, if the evidence cannot be obtained, or if the motion is only to willfully delay trial.

[119]   § 240 (2) CCP; this right does not pertain to co-accused.

accused's right to make additional remarks after the examination of individual pieces of evidence during the trial;[120] and (5) the accused's right to a closing statement (*letztes Wort*) at the very end of the trial.[121]

In cases of mandatory legal representation, for example, in felony or complex cases or if the accused has been taken into provisional detention, legal representation is mandatory, particularly during the trial; the accused must not defend him/herself in person alone and without counsel.

The fact that the accused has a lawyer does not curtail his/her personal rights as described *infra*. The defendant can, for example, personally question a witness, even when his/her lawyer has already interrogated that witness.

2.2.2. The right to legal representation at all stages of the proceedings

Pursuant to § 137 CCP, there is a general overarching right of an accused – but not of a mere suspect (see *supra* 1.5) – 'to avail him/herself of legal representation at every stage of the proceedings.'[122] Any suspect – in fact, any person – has, of course, the right to avail him/herself of the services of a lawyer. However, it is the special right to a defence lawyer that applies only when the client has acquired the status of an accused.

This gives the accused the right to seek the advice of, and to consult with, counsel during all phases of the proceedings, and to appear before the authorities only in the presence of counsel. The latter has an important exception[123] with regard to police interrogations during the investigation phase, where counsel does not enjoy a right to be present.[124] This is partially compensated both by the fact that the accused is not obliged to appear at a police interrogation, and that a (police) interrogation shall normally (see *infra* at 2.2.3) not be continued if the accused asks for a lawyer; since the accused is to be informed accordingly, he/she can effectively 'compel' the presence of counsel during a police interrogation. However, it is common knowledge that police officers sometimes try to persuade the person being interrogated that they might as well do without a lawyer 'for now'.

The accused is free to contact and appoint up to three hired counsel at all times.[125] He/she also has some, although limited, influence on the assignment of court appointed counsel. Court appointed counsel must only be assigned in cases of mandatory legal representation, for example, in felony or complex cases or if the

---

120   § 257 (1) CCP.
121   § 258 (1) CCP.
122   The right to the assistance of a lawyer is also constitutionally warranted. Both the *fair trial* and *rule of law principles* embodied in arts. 2 (1), 20 (3) German Constitution (GC), and the right to a fair hearing, art. 103 (1) GC, guarantee the right to legal assistance.
123   Also see § 228 (2) CCP: in cases of *optional legal representation,* it is the responsibility of the accused to secure a hired counsel; if he/she fails to do so, despite the order to appear at trial giving adequate time for preparation of defence, he/she loses the right to move for an obligatory adjournment. Also see § 168c (5) CCP for cases where counsel are not informed of the upcoming examination of evidence by the investigative judge, where counsel may factually be excluded from such examinations.
124   §§ 168c (1), 163a (3) CCP *e contrario.*
125   § 137 CCP.

accused has been taken into provisional detention. If the accused already has hired a counsel, an additional court appointed counsel will only be assigned in exceptional cases, and only if this is necessary to ensure the fair and effective administration of justice (for example, because hired counsel ideologically sides with his/her clients or delays the proceedings);[126] the practice of appointing counsel even when the defendant appears with hired counsel is not limited to terrorism cases. Judges also may do so if they suspect that hired counsel, at some point, may 'drop out', thus jeopardizing the continuity of the trial, because a lawyer appointed mid-trial can demand an adjournment, in order to have sufficient time for preparation.

The accused can also request that hired counsel will become his/her court appointed counsel; this request will normally be granted in practice, and triggers the German legal aid equivalent (see *supra* 1.6). Decisions and determinations about mandatory legal representation, and the assignment of court appointed counsel, rest with the presiding judge of the chamber having jurisdiction of the case.[127]

If indigent accused cannot afford legal representation, the German legal aid equivalent takes effect (see *supra* 1.6).

If the accused is not represented during an ordinary trial of a case of mandatory legal representation, such as in a felony or complex case, the court can either assign a court appointed counsel on the spot, or adjourn or impose a stay of the proceedings.[128] Otherwise, in cases of optional legal representation, it is the responsibility of the accused to secure a hired counsel; the fact that hired counsel does not appear in court does not give the defendant the right to have the trial adjourned or postponed, although the court may grant this so as to ensure a fair trial.[129]

2.2.3. Access to legal representation in the investigation phase (particularly during interrogation)

As a rule, it is up to the accused to secure defence services in all phases of the proceedings, including the investigation phase. However, German criminal procedure conspicuously lacks positive legal regulations – be they contained in law, procedural rules, or protocols[130] – about the *factual facilitation* of the right to freely choose counsel, particularly where the accused asks for, but does not know and/or cannot easily contact, counsel (for example, because he/she has been arrested in the middle of the night).

Facilitation of access to legal representation is not on the political agenda, but the case law of the FHCJ offers some general duties on the part of the authorities,

---

126   Meyer-Goßner 2008, § 141 marginal No. 1a.
127   § 142 CCP.
128   § 145 CCP.
129   § 228 (2) CCP.
130   As to a minor exception, see Rule 106 RPCASM: The accused's request for the details of a competent lawyer is to be rejected. However, an alphabetical register of all lawyers in the Regional Court's jurisdiction can be presented to the accused, so that she can choose counsel.

although the details are yet to be developed and decided.[131] Flagrant violations of these duties may lead to the exclusion of the evidence obtained, which raises the incentive to comply in practice; our field research indicates, however, that the police in particular may sometimes lack serious motivation to facilitate effective contact with counsel during interrogation; there is, however, no empirical data that suggests that accused are routinely interrogated and held in custody for long periods without seeing a lawyer.

According to the FHCJ, state authorities are obliged, at least under certain circumstances, to 'seriously' and 'effectively' support the accused in contacting counsel.[132] In a prominent case, it was held that effective support was withheld, where the accused was simply given the yellow pages of Hamburg, because the huge amount of entries, combined with the insufficient language skills of the accused, actually deterred – rather than facilitated – contacting counsel.[133]

At any rate, the accused should be in a position where he/she is able to contact counsel by phone.[134]

Continuing with the interrogation despite the accused's express request for a lawyer is only permissible if the accused clearly agrees to it, and only after the state authorities have made serious efforts to facilitate access to counsel;[135] violations of this rule lead to the exclusion of the evidence obtained in any irregular interrogation.[136] However, in one – albeit heavily criticized[137] – decision, the FHCJ deemed the continuation of the interrogation permissible, where the efforts to procure legal representation did not seem promising due to the lateness of the hour.[138]

In order to afford serious and effective support to indigent accused who want to consult with a lawyer but are afraid to do so due to financial constraints, state authorities 'may' be required (*kann es angezeigt sein*) to give information about the possibility to appoint a – at least temporarily state subsidized – court appointed counsel[139] (see *supra* 1.6), as well as the possibility to consult with a defence emergency service.[140]

Such private defence emergency services are available in many – but not all – regions in Germany.[141] These are privately organized networks of regional lawyers – occasionally with the support of the regional bar association – that are intended to ensure easy access to defence services. Their effectiveness has not recently been empirically researched, and our field research indicates that there appear to be

---

[131]   See Gleß 2007b, marginal No. 43.
[132]   See FHCJ, 42 BGHSt, p. 15.
[133]   FHCJ, 42 BGHSt, p. 20.
[134]   Meyer-Goßner 2008, § 136 marginal No. 10.
[135]   Meyer-Goßner 2008, § 136 marginal No. 10.
[136]   There are no positive legal regulations for such a scenario, which is 'only' governed by the case law of the FHCJ.
[137]   See Meyer-Goßner 2008, § 136 marginal No. 10.
[138]   FHCJ, 42 BGHSt, p. 172.
[139]   FHCJ, *StV*, 2006, p. 566.
[140]   FHCJ, *StV*, 2006, p. 567. See also Mehle 2007, p. 973.
[141]   A complete list can be found online at <http://www.ag-strafrecht.de/Notdienst.aspx> (last visited 29 April 2010).

considerable regional discrepancies (particularly between areas with high population densities and rural areas).

2.2.4. Right to consult and communicate in private with a lawyer

§ 148 (1) CCP ensures the 'fundamental'[142] right of the accused to communicate freely with counsel during all phases of the proceedings. This includes a prohibition against infringing upon any oral or written communication between counsel and the accused,[143] particularly where the accused is in provisional detention.[144]

Where the right to communicate freely with counsel is violated in order to obtain evidence (for example, by opening a letter), that evidence is excluded from the trial.[145] Where the accused is in provisional detention, factual infringements of this right are open to judicial review; where the infringement is due to a directive of the relevant custodial facility, the directive is also open to judicial review.[146]

The right to free and unimpeded consultation is only limited in highly exceptional *terrorism scenarios* enumerated and regulated by positive law; such limitations are scarce in reality, and no empirical data is available:

- According to § 148 (2) GCCP, the right to free *written* communication can be limited where the accused is in provisional detention, if he/she is highly likely to have participated in a terrorist organization: Documents and other objects must not be passed along, if the addressor has not accepted prior screening by a judge. This does not limit the right to free oral consultation, which must not be supervised.
- According to §§ 31 *et seq.* Introductory Act to the AOJ, where there is an imminent and substantiated danger of bodily harm in terrorist cases, the provisionally detained accused can be completely cut off from any communication with other inmates and the outside world, which includes any oral or written communication with counsel (*Kontaktsperre*).

2.2.5. The independence and competence of defence lawyers: Theory and practice

While the independence and competence of defence lawyers might be an important subject matter in German legal theory and is reflective of German legal self-image, their respective empirical foundation has hardly been the subject of research and they may not live up to the high self-expectations.

In theory, defence lawyers are *independent* actors in the German criminal justice system. As such, they are, on the one hand, independent from any interventions by state authorities, yet, on the other hand, they are also independent

---

142   Beulke 2008, marginal No. 153.
143   Wire tapping is thus disallowed, as is the opening of letters.
144   § 37 (1) RPD.
145   RC Munich #1, *StV*, 2005, p. 38.
146   See Meyer-Goßner 2008, § 148 marginal No. 24 *et seq.*

from their clients. Under German criminal procedure, lawyers must not consider themselves the adversarial representative of the interests of their clients, but are to act as 'organs of the criminal justice system' (*Organe der Rechtspflege*) and thus in the furtherance of the collective interest in the proper administration of justice.

Hence, lawyers must not wilfully counteract this collective good; otherwise, they may incur criminal responsibility, particularly as accessories after the fact, which can lead to their exclusion in the trial at hand and, ultimately, from the Bar. Some examples may illustrate the thin red line between permissible and impermissible (and even criminal) conduct. According to the rich catalogue developed by German courts, it is permissible to (1) explain the legal situation, particularly the legal consequences of different versions of the facts; (2) suggest using the right to remain silent; (3) suggest an exculpatory testimony, even where the lawyer thinks it might be a lie; or (4) plead for an acquittal, even where the lawyer deems his/her client to be guilty, but considers this unsubstantiated by evidence presented at the proceedings.

However, it is impermissible for the lawyer to (1) construe lies favourable to the accused, or to suggest lying; or (2) work in concert with other co-accused and their counsel to distort the facts of the case, the latter pertaining to the still undetermined boundaries of impermissible joint defence work (*Sockelverteidigung*).

The *quality* of lawyers is ensured predominantly by their compulsory membership of the Bar, which in turn requires the lawyer to have passed both German State Examinations in Law. Although lawyers are legally obliged[147] to continue their studies as long as they practice, this obligation is often disregarded and can – due to the lack of binding criteria on how it must be undertaken – only be insufficiently made subject to judicial review. Thus, once a member of the Bar, the quality of the lawyer can hardly be monitored at all. This has been criticised by representatives of the Bar,[148] but so far no viable and serious quality assurance schemes have found their way onto the legislative/political agenda.

Even though in practice there is no effective – let alone compulsory, uniform, and overarching – independence monitoring and no quality assurance mechanism, in a tentative normative assessment, confirmed by our field research,[149] defence work became far more professionalised over the last decade.

This development, as well as the independence and competence of defence lawyers, should be seen within the perspective of the German legal aid equivalent (see *supra* 1.6); three of its core characteristics raise impediments to factual independence and (high) quality defence work:

- The German legal aid equivalent only benefits court appointed counsel. Although an accused may request a hired counsel to be assigned as court appointed counsel, there are still many cases[150] where accused do not have a lawyer, and thus rely solely on the court appointment process. The most far-reaching anecdotal evidence, which has been

---

[147] § 43a (6) FLA.
[148] See, on this point, Johnigk 2006, p. 349.
[149] Interview # 5.
[150] Empirical data is not available.

confirmed in some of our interviews,[151] but so far has not seen hard empirical verification, suggest almost symbiotic relationships between individual courts and their 'chosen' counsel, who are regularly appointed in cases of mandatory legal representation and so earn their living, but who dare not stand up against the court or make use of their rights e.g. to bring evidentiary motions etc. This seriously curtails the factual independence of a certain class of defence lawyers. This problem is, however, not on the political or jurisprudential agenda, and academics often turn a blind eye to it.

- The German legal aid equivalent only guarantees codified ordinary fees for enumerated defence services; even if these fees are 'adequate' for a normal life style, they are considerably lower than the codified ordinary fees of a hired counsel, let alone the negotiated fees charged by high quality criminal defence lawyers and firms;[152] even the Federal Bar Association, however, could not provide empirical data on the average remuneration of court appointed counsel. From a policy point of view, this is why Germany may need to consider addressing discrimination against indigent persons, for example, by raising the ordinary fees of court assigned counsel, particularly where defence services in the investigative phase are concerned. Many defence lawyers consider – in our point of view; at least partially correctly – the remuneration regime to be financially inadequate. While it can be argued that the remuneration of defence services at the trial stage is adequate, the same does not, in our opinion, hold true for defence services in the investigation phase, which we deem of supreme importance for an effective defence.

- Finally, the ordinary fees for court appointed counsel will be much higher if the case goes to trial, while the crucial defence work in the investigation phase is remunerated comparably poorly. There is thus a strategic disfunctionality inherent in the German legal aid equivalent.

2.2.6. Vulnerable persons

Vulnerable groups subject to special provisions under German law are juveniles[153] and mentally vulnerable accused.

---

[151]   Interview # 2, 13.
[152]   Suffice to give one example: The ordinary fee for attending a trial hearing is 184 Euro, for a court appointed counsel, while a hired counsel can charge an average fee of 230 Euro; negotiated fees can be much higher.
[153]   Pursuant to § 1 (2) JCA a juvenile (*Jugendlicher*) in the strict legal sense of the term is a person who is 14 but not yet 18 years of age at the time of the commission of the crime. Additionally young adults (*Heranwachsende*) are also partly subject to the special protections enjoyed by juveniles. A young adult is a person who is 18 but not yet 21 years of age at the time of the commission of the crime (§ 1 (2) JCA). To them the JCA's special provisions on substantive and procedural criminal law apply only if either the accused is not mature enough to be prosecuted under the adult regime or if the crime's nature is typical for juveniles (§§ 105 (1), 109 JCA respectively).

Like every accused, a juvenile has the right to a defence lawyer of his/her choice at any time of the proceedings. Additionally, the legal representative (*gesetzlicher Vertreter*),[154] as well as the legal guardian (*Erziehungsberechtiger*),[155] can appoint a hired counsel for a juvenile. In juvenile cases, § 68 JCA enumerates additional scenarios[156] of mandatory legal representation, including *inter alia* if (1) the case is one of mandatory legal representation for adult accused, for example, in felony or complex cases; or if (2) every legal representative and legal guardian is excluded from the proceedings (for example, because they are likely to have participated in the crimes concerned); or if (3) the juvenile is taken into provisional detention.

Mental vulnerability of the accused makes the case one of mandatory legal representation – in all phases of the proceedings – if the accused cannot defend him/herself.[157] This is already the case if there are considerable doubts about the accused's ability for self-representation,[158] for example, because the accused's procedural demeanour is unintelligible and disadvantageous for the defence.[159]

2.3. Procedural rights

2.3.1. The right to release from custody pending trial

During all phases of the proceedings, the detained accused has the right to have the arrest warrant revoked – and thus to be released from provisional detention – if one of the following conditions is met:

- one (or more) of the prerequisites for provisional detention is no longer satisfied (for example, because the accused has been acquitted, because all pertinent evidence as been accumulated and the accused had originally been taken in provisional detention in order to avoid any tampering with the evidence, or because the time spent in provisional detention is disproportionate to the expected sanction);[160]
- the prosecution moves to have the accused released;[161]
- provisional detention has already lasted for more than six months, and no special ground (such as the complexity of the case, or the extensiveness of the investigations) justifies a prolonged

---

[154] § 137 (2) CCP.
[155] § 67 (3) JCA.
[156] These are often criticized as insufficient, but a broad, juvenile-specific interpretation of the general clause in § 140 (2) CCP helps to guarantee appropriate defence for juvenile accused; see Ostendorf 2007, marginal No. 75; Streng 2008, marginal No. 134.
[157] § 140 (2) CCP.
[158] Meyer-Goßner 2008, § 140 marginal No. 30.
[159] HRC Zweibrücken, *NStZ*, 1986, p. 135.
[160] § 120 (1) CCP.
[161] § 120 (3) CCP.

confinement;[162] if such special grounds are met, however, provisional detention may well last longer.

What is more, the detainee has the right to have the execution of the arrest warrant temporarily discontinued (*Aufhebung des Vollzugs des Haftbefehls*) – and thus be released from provisional detention – in several circumstances, which include:

- if the reason for detention was the *likelihood of escape or flight*, the execution of the arrest is to be discontinued if a less strict method to ensure the presence of the accused is available.[163] These methods include *inter alia*[164] the directive (1) to report to certain government agencies at certain times; (2) to not leave a certain place without prior approval; (3) to not leave home without supervision; and (4) to furnish an adequate financial deposit.[165] With regard to the latter, release from provisional detention may – but does not have to – be dependent on the payment of money.
- if the reason for detention was the *likelihood of interference with the administration of justice*, the execution of the arrest is to be discontinued if a less strict method than provisional detention is available to ensure the correct proceedings, for example, the directive not to communicate with co-accused, witnesses, or experts.[166] A financial deposit is not considered a suitable method to frustrate any attempts by the accused to interfere with the proper course of events.[167]

The judge or court decides either *ex officio* (1) after three months of provisional detention if the accused does not have legal representation and if no motion to review the grounds of detention has been filed;[168] or (2) after the sixth month of provisional detention,[169] or upon an *motion* by the (3) prosecution; or the (4) accused/defence, to revoke the arrest warrant.[170]

In 2006,[171] out of 947,837 persons who were processed by investigative authorities, 24,352 were kept in provisional detention (approximately 2%). Out of these 24,352 persons, 12,141 (49.86%) were detained for less than three months, 4,485 (18.42%) between six and twelve months, and 1,499 (6.15%) more than one

---

[162] § 121 (1) CCP.
[163] § 116 (1) CCP.
[164] The judge can combine two or more of these methods.
[165] Also see § 127a CCP with regard to persons who do not have a permanent German domicile. Other possible conditions are the deposit of an ID card or passport, the instruction to report to a private body (for example, the employer), the freezing of a bank account, the implementation of a withdrawal treatment such as electronic shackles. Cf. Paeffgen 2007b, marginal No. 15 *et seq.*
[166] § 116 (2) CCP.
[167] Meyer-Goßner 2008, § 116 marginal No. 16.
[168] § 117 (5) CCP.
[169] § 121 CCP. There are no other scenarios where the judge or court can act *ex officio*.
[170] §§ 117, 304 CCP.
[171] Statistisches Bundesamt 2006, p. 340 *et seq.*

year. In 1,360 cases, the time served in provisional detention[172] was longer than the eventual sentence, in 22,820 cases it was shorter, and in 172 cases both were of equal length. There is no empirical data available as to persons who are subject to conditional release from provisional detention.

Indigent defendants enjoy the right to initiate a review of the detention or to file a custodial complaint. In practice, there are no indications of factual discrimination against them. Suspension of provisional detention upon payment of a financial deposit naturally favours the financially well-off.[173] However, according to jurisprudence and most commentators, this is not a constitutionally (art. 3 German Constitution) relevant discrimination against indigent persons, because the amount of the financial deposit is to be determined based upon the financial resources of the provisionally detained person.[174] Although the financial deposit is intended to exert a strong compulsion on the accused to stand trial after his/her release from provisional detention,[175] no inadequate and/or excessive demands may be directed against the accused.[176]

What is more, the deposit may also be sponsored by a third person, as long as the relationship between this person and the accused is close enough to guarantee that the latter will not harm the former and thus that the accused can be expected to stand trial.[177]

With regard to *foreign nationals* who do not have family ties to Germany, the practice more easily justifies the use of provisional detention to prevent the likelihood of flight.[178] Courts tend to impose provisional detention against foreign nationals more often than against German nations.[179] Nevertheless, the simple fact that a foreign national returns to his/her home country does not of itself constitute a likelihood of flight, as long as it can be expected that the foreign national will return to Germany to stand trial.[180]

Similarly, it does not constitute likelihood of flight if the accused's place of residence is known to the investigative authorities and if there are no indications that he/she will abandon his/her home.[181] With regard to all accused, any foreign relationship, foreign language skills, or financial resources abroad may constitute a likelihood of flight, if it can be reasonably expected that the accused will be able to settle in a foreign country[182] – this may more often be the case for foreign ethnic minorities.

---

[172] As to the concept of provisional detention, see *supra* at 1.4.2.

[173] Meyer-Goßner 2008, § 116 marginal No. 10 with further references.

[174] Hilger 2007b, marginal No. 2; Paeffgen 2007b, marginal No. 14.

[175] Meyer-Goßner 2008, § 116a marginal No. 10.

[176] HRC Berlin, 8 February 2000, 1 AR 160/00 – 5 Ws 139/00 (not reported).

[177] Graf 2008a, marginal No. 3.

[178] Graf 2008b, marginal No. 22.

[179] Bleckmann 1995, p. 552; Gercke 2004, p. 676.

[180] HRC Stuttgart, *StV*, 1999, p. 34; HRC Naumburg, *StV*, 1997, p. 138; HRC Bremen, *StV*, 1997, p. 533. Critically reviewing this HRC Köln, *NStZ*, 2003, p. 219 with further references. See also Hilger 2005, p. 36 *et seq.*

[181] FHCJ, *StV*, 1990, p. 309; HRC Offenburg, *StV*, 2004, p. 326 *et seq.*

[182] Graf 2008b, marginal No. 22 with further references.

2.3.2. The right of a defendant to be tried in his/her presence

In principle, a trial must be held while the accused is present. However, there are some exceptions that allow – under certain *very limited* and codified circumstances – for trials *in absentia*.[183] The general principle, which guarantees the defendant a right to be present, is found in § 230 (1) GCCP and reads: 'There is to be no trial hearing against an accused who is not present.'

The resulting rule that criminal proceedings shall not be held *in absentia* and the corresponding right of the accused to be present while his/her case is tried, is, however, subject to a few exceptions. As the FHCJ has repeatedly stressed, these exceptions are to be interpreted narrowly;[184] in practice, trials *in absentia* are very rare, illustrating the strength of the rule that the accused is to be present during the trial.

Three groups of exceptions to this rule can be distinguished: The court can (1) *temporarily exclude the accused* from the hearing, or certain periods thereof, *even though the accused is willing to be present*;[185] (2) continue with the hearing *in absentia*, if the *accused fails to be present* due to his/her own fault;[186] or (3) *grant the accused a leave of absence*.[187]

Infringements of defence rights, such as trials *in absentia* necessarily imply, are (somewhat) *compensated* in that the verdict must stay within the limits set by the writ of indictment; since an absent accused cannot be given prior fair warning,

---

[183]   For a brief overview, see Kühne 1993, p. 159 *et seq.*

[184]   See, on the exception enshrined in § 247 CCP, *inter alia*, FHCJ, 15 BGHSt, p. 195; FHCJ, 21 BGHSt, p. 333; FHCJ, 26 BGHSt, p. 220; FHCJ, *StV*, 1987, p. 377.

[185]   § 247 CCP allows for the temporary exclusion of the accused from the examination of witnesses, or of co-accused, under any of the following circumstances: (1) There is concrete evidence that a witness or co-accuse will not testify truthfully in the presence of the accused; (2) the exclusion is necessary to protect the, particularly mental, health of a witnesses, particularly those of a young age; (3) the exclusion is necessary to protect the health of the accused him/herself. The temporary exclusion is compensated by various procedural protections, such that the court is to inform the accused about the substance of any testimony he/she was excluded from.

[186]   § 231 (2) CCP. The accused leaves the hearing without permission, or had already been heard on the indictment, and the court deems her presence unnecessary. § 232 (1) CCP. The accused, without due excuse, fails to follow a order to appear at trial that had instructed him/her about the possibility of a trial *in absentia*, and which gave him/her fair warning about the expected (and relatively) light sentence that must not exceed, *inter alia*, a fine of 180 days' income (*Tagessätze*); the verdict must stay within the limits indicated in the order to appear to trial. § 231a CCP. The accused intentionally and culpably made him/herself unfit to undergo trial (and thus knowingly prevented the proper administration of justice), the court deems his/her presence unnecessary, and the accused had the opportunity to express him/herself on the indictment before the court or a court commissioned judge. § 231b CCP. The accused demonstrates improper behaviour, fails to comply with court orders issued to preserve court order and, as a consequence, is removed from the court room; the court deems his/her presence unnecessary, and he/she is given the opportunity to express him/herself on the indictment.

[187]   §§ 231c, 233 CCP.

he/she must not be convicted under an altered set of facts, or an altered legal evaluation of the original facts.[188]

The permissibility of a trial *in absentia*, as well as compliance with the compensatory scheme, are open to judicial review in an appeal of law; if there was a violation that determined the verdict, it will be nullified and the accused remanded for a new trial.

2.3.3. The right to be presumed innocent; *in dubio pro reo*; burden of proof

The presumption of innocence is amongst the most basic principles of German criminal procedure; it is not contingent on a criminal indictment and thus applies during all stages of the proceedings, but ends once a conviction becomes final and is no longer open to ordinary appeal.[189] The presumption of innocence is enshrined in both a rule of law principle and the constitutionally guaranteed right to human dignity. The right to be presumed innocent translates into the right not to be treated as an offender until criminal guilt has officially been proven. The presumption of innocence hence sets normative limits to those investigative and procedural measures that criminal justice authorities may take with regard to the accused. This excludes measures that would not be justifiable, in case the accused turns out to be innocent;[190] for instance, the accused in provisional detention must be granted as much freedom as possible.[191] The practical implications of the right to be presumed innocent are rather limited, and the fact that courts frequently cite the presumption to add weight to their argument, does not mean that it has great practical relevance.

According to the *in dubio pro reo* principle, which is often grounded in the presumption of innocence,[192] the accused must be acquitted if there are any *reasonable doubts* concerning his/her guilt. The eventual decision on whether a doubt is, in fact, reasonable, remains with the trial court.[193] However, the *in dubio pro reo* principle is not applicable to all kinds of doubt. It applies to the question of guilt, to sentencing, and to certain questions of jurisdiction and admissibility (*Prozessvoraussetzungen*) (such as whether a statute of limitation applies).

Doubts concerning questions outside of these categories may be decided against the accused, without constituting a violation of the *in dubio pro reo* principle. Judicial compliance with the in dubio pro reo principle is subject to full judicial review and constitutes – given that the court convicted the accused notwithstanding some doubt – a reason for appeal on law.[194]

Furthermore, in theory, the parties do not carry a *burden of proof* under German criminal procedure law. It is the court that must find the facts on its own initiative; it must do so even if neither the prosecution nor the defence has presented any

---

[188]   As an exception, if the absent accused has legal representation, it suffices that counsel is given fair warning. § 234a CCP.

[189]   Jarass 2009, marginal No. 108; Schädler 2008, marginal No. 43.

[190]   Volk 2008, p. 31 *et seq.*

[191]   Jarass 2009, marginal No. 108.

[192]   See Beulke 2008, marginal No. 25 with further references.

[193]   Kühne 1993, p. 148.

[194]   Schoreit 2008, marginal No. 59.

evidence. This means in particular that the accused does not have to prove grounds for excluding criminal responsibility. In practice, however, the accused may have a factual burden to come forward (but not prove) with grounds for excluding criminal responsibility, or with their evidentiary foundation, where the court would otherwise not be able to find these facts on its own initiative.

The presumption of innocence also relates to a general *reluctance to inform the general public about ongoing investigations* and proceedings. The exact remedies for violations of this reluctance, for instance where the authorities inform the general public too hastily with information about proceedings against persons of public prominence, are yet to be determined.

2.3.4. The right to silence

The accused enjoys the right to remain silent during all stages of the proceedings.[195] This comprises the right to either remain fully silent during all interrogations/ examinations by the authorities. This right extends to mimic, gesture, and other related behaviour (for example, the accused's right not to release privileged persons such as medical personnel from their privilege).[196] It equates to remaining silent if the accused generally denies his/her criminal participation in an offence or generally asserts that he/she not guilty.

The right to remain silent is absolute and no inferences – neither incriminating nor exonerating[197] – must be drawn from the accused's use of it. Therefore, (1) state authorities must not ask for the accused's reasons for remaining silent;[198] (2) the accused's full silence must not to be treated as evidence (the latter overriding the principle of a free and encompassing evaluation of the evidence brought before the court);[199] and (3) the time of an exculpatory statement must not be treated as an incriminating indication (such as if the accused only offers exculpatory explications late in the proceedings, for example, if he/she remained silent during the investigation phase only to defend him/herself actively during trial). The latter suggests that, unlike the situation in England and Wales, no inferences whatsoever may be drawn if an accused fails to provide the investigative authorities with any grounds excluding criminal responsibility.

If the accused chooses to remain fully silent, a statement by defence counsel in his/her name must not be used as evidence, unless the accused expressly confirms it.[200]

The position is different, however, if the accused is not fully, but only partially silent (*teilweises Schweigen*) with regard to one and the same factual accusation;[201] if

---

[195] This right is implied by § 136 CCP. The exact legal basis of this right remains subject to considerable academic controversy. The FHCJ relies on the rule of law principle, while others appeal to the Latin principle *nemo tenetur se ipsum accusare*, which states that the accused shall not be forced to actively support the proof of his/her guilt.
[196] Beulke 2008, marginal No. 495.
[197] Meyer-Goßner 2008, § 261 marginal No. 16.
[198] Meyer-Goßner 2008, § 261 marginal No. 16.
[199] Beulke 2008, marginal No. 511.
[200] Meyer-Goßner 2008, § 261 marginal No. 16a.
[201] Beulke 2008, marginal No. 495.

there are more independent accusations (for example, several independent theft allegations), and the accused only chooses to answer some of them (for example, to the other points one and four of the accusation), while otherwise remaining silent (to points two and three), inferences must only be drawn with regard to the allegations in relation to which he/she has made him/herself available as evidence (i.e. points one and four).

Partial silence means that the accused actively supports the investigation of an accusation in certain respects, while not answering other questions or not mentioning certain factual circumstances (for example, the accused proffering an alibi, yet not mentioning a name). If partial silence leaves open several inferences, all of these must be discussed in the free evaluation of the evidence (for example, not mentioning the name of an alibi witness because there is none or in an attempt to protect an *affaire de coeur*).

The accused is to be orally informed about his/her right to remain silent at the very beginning of the first interrogation by the judge, the prosecution, and the police in the investigation phase, as well as at the very beginning of the trial. Any interrogation without informing the accused about his/her right to silence will normally cause an exclusion of any evidence obtained under the violation of this duty, unless it can positively be shown that the accused was aware of this right.[202]

The same applies – *a maiore ad minus* – if state actors force the accused to testify by violence or threat. In such cases, too, all evidence illegally obtained will be excluded. It is permissible to explain to the accused that remaining fully silent is not always the best and most helpful defence. However his/her free decision as to whether to exercise the right must not be violated.[203]

In our field research, criminal defence lawyers[204] agreed that accused persons are often only crudely aware of the rights to remain silent and to consult a lawyer and that they tend to 'forget' these rights in the heat of action. Some believe that accused persons even think that exercising these rights can and will be used against them; this renders compliance with information duties particularly important. Moreover, some criminal defence[205] lawyers believed that the police instruct accused persons properly, but doubt that the accused understand these instructions, particularly accused with limited intellectual abilities. One criminal defence lawyer[206] disagreed, and told an anecdote that police officers taking the stand could not repeat proper instructions and information.

One federal judge[207] also considered inadequate instructions about defence rights a problem, since the police often aim to obtain confessions and, in the course of doing so, limit access to defence services; thus, the judge opted for better documentation of police work and for signboards with defence emergency services at police stations.

---

[202]   Beulke 2008, marginal No. 468.
[203]   Meyer-Goßner 2008, § 136 marginal No. 8.
[204]   Interviews # 5, 7, 8 and 9.
[205]   Interviews # 7, 8 and 9.
[206]   Interview # 3.
[207]   Interview # 4.

Recent case law deals with police violations of duties to inform, particularly the duty to inform the accused that his/her prior testimony is excluded, because of a prior violation of the duties to inform (*qualifizierte Belehrung*); in order to enforce compliance with such duties, the FHCJ has called on the public prosecution to increase supervision over the police, while at the same time denying an absolute exclusion of the evidence obtained.[208] This balanced approach implies that the FHCJ deems violations of duties to inform by the police a problem, but not a grave and systemic one.

2.3.5. The right to a reasoned decision

According to the jurisprudence of the FCC, the rule of law includes the obligation of every state authority to give reasons for the decision it takes.[209] The corresponding right of the accused to a reasoned decision is an element of the right to be heard.[210] The obligation of state authorities, particularly of courts, to thoroughly reason their decisions and judgments is an integral check and balance in the German criminal justice system, which obliges state authorities to, at least in their external presentation of their actions, follow the substantive requirements of criminal law and procedure. It is also a precondition for an effective system of judicial review, which can only be successful if the parties and the reviewing body are in a position to attack a decision based upon its reasons.

For criminal proceedings, this precept is given special expression in § 267 CCP, pursuant to which the trial court is under the obligation to give a reasoned judgment.[211] The reasons given in the judgment have to be clearly worded and are to be independently understandable, without having to take any other documents into consideration.[212] In its reasoning, the judgment has to specify, *inter alia*, (1) all the facts establishing the statutory elements of the criminal offence, (2) the penal provisions that have been applied to the case, and (3) the circumstances that were decisive in assessing the penalty.

Moreover, there is also an obligation to explain the evaluation of the evidence. The listing of the facts alone is not sufficient. Rather, the court has to consistently communicate all aspects relevant to the evaluation of the evidence.[213] The evaluation of the evidence must be logical and coherent,[214] otherwise it can be overturned in an appeal of law. A judgement is insufficiently reasoned if it leaves undiscussed a fact that was used in the judgment,[215] or does not discuss all obvious or reasonable possible inferences that may be drawn from the evidence presented.[216]

---

[208]   FHCJ, *NJW*, 2009, p. 2612.
[209]   FCC, 40 BVerfGE, p. 286; FCC, 71 BVerfGE, p. 135 *et seq*. See also Sachs 2009a, marginal No. 164.
[210]   Art. 103 GC.
[211]   It is still unclear whether § 267 CCP in fact constitutes *an individual right* in itself or simply a *legal obligation* on the court.
[212]   Ranft 2005, marginal No. 1852.
[213]   FHCJ, 14 BGHSt, p. 165; Gollwitzer 2001, marginal No. 51.
[214]   FHCJ, 3 BGHSt, p. 213; Gollwitzer 2001, marginal No. 55.
[215]   FHCJ, *NJW*, 1967, p. 1140.
[216]   FHCJ, 25 BGHSt, p. 367.

In particular, the confession of the accused must be discussed and evaluated as to its credibility.[217] Witness statements must be discussed and evaluated in detail, if the statement has a high relevance, or if other (for example, contradicting) evidence suggests so;[218] otherwise, witness statements do not have to be reconsidered in every point.

The court also has to communicate the decisive considerations for choosing a certain sanction and for determining the sanction's severity/leniency. However, it is not necessary to provide a detailed enumeration of all causes leading to the decision.[219] If the imposed punishment deviates from the usual punishment in similar cases, the court has to reason its judgment thoroughly.[220]

The obligation to a reasoned judgment finds a notable exception, in that a court does not have to give the full line of reasoning if a judgment cannot be appealed, particularly if all parties waive their right to appeal. In this case, it is sufficient for the court to give a shortened reasoning.[221]

In practice, the right to a reasoned judgment is generally complied with, for the simple reason that it is enforced by upper courts, which are (self-)interested in supervising lower courts.

2.3.6. The right to appeal

Article 19 (4) of the German Constitution contains the individual right to effective[222] judicial review of all acts by state organs, to the extent that they infringe the applicant's individual rights.[223] The CCP also provides for an encompassing[224] right to challenge court decisions (for example, decisions in the investigation phase, such as judicial warrants on search and seizure measures), or to have verdicts judicially reviewed (by an appeal of fact and/or an appeal of law; see *supra* 1.4.3).

This right is generally enjoyed by both the prosecution and the defence. Pursuant to the German understanding, the prosecution may challenge acquittals without violating the *ne bis in idem* principle, since the accused would only face double jeopardy if a second set of proceedings on the same facts would be initiated against her. The prosecution, as an independent and neutral actor of the German

---

[217] FHCJ, *NStZ-RR*, 1997, p. 172.

[218] FHCJ, 12 BGHSt, p. 315.

[219] FHCJ, 3 BGHSt, p. 179; Gollwitzer 2001, marginal No. 83.

[220] Gollwitzer 2001, marginal No. 84; Meyer-Goßner 2008, § 267 marginal No. 18.

[221] § 267 (4) CCP. A further and minor exception to the general rule that a decision has to be reasoned is enshrined in § 322a CCP: If *certiorari* to hear an appeal of law is granted, this decision does not need any reasons. However, this *certiorari* regime only applies to cases where the sanction imposed by the court of first instance is (extremely) low (see § 313 CCP).

[222] Sachs 2009b, marginal No. 143.

[223] Note that the FCC has repeatedly held that this right does not apply to court decisions. FCC, 15 BVerfGE, p. 280 *et seq.*; FCC, 25 BVerfGE, p. 365; FCC, 49 BVerfGE, p. 340; FCC, 76 BVerfGE, p. 98.

[224] It is only in cases regulated by § 313 CCP that the right to appeal is restricted and that the court of appeal of law has to grant *certiorari*. This *certiorari* regime is only applicable in cases of minor sanctions, for example, where the accused has been sentenced by the court of first instance to a fine not exceeding fifteen daily units (*Tagessätze*), or where only a regulatory fine has been imposed.

criminal justice system, may, in theory, also file for judicial review in favour of a convicted accused.[225] Defence counsel must not lodge appeal proceedings contrary to the express will of the accused.

Pursuant to § 35a CCP and Rule 142 of the Rules for Proceedings in Criminal and Administrative Sanctioning Matters (RPCASM), an accused present at the rendition of judgment will be informed about his/her right to appeal; he/she will also be given a leaflet listing the procedural details as they are to be observed. What is more, the accused's right to appeal is procedurally protected, in that (1) the possibility to withdraw appeals and (2) the possibility to waive the right to appeal is restricted. It merits special observance that a court shall not prompt the accused to waive her right to appeal,[226] and that a waiver is invalid if it is part of a 'deal' between the court and the parties pursuant to § 257c CCP.[227] While the latter may be an important theoretical protection of the accused, our field research – as well as common sense – suggests that, in practice, a 'deal' will often include an accord that the right to appeal shall not be used, in order to consolidate the 'deal'.

Leaving appeals to Regional and Higher Regional Courts aside, the FHCJ alone hears some 3,100 appeals of law every year,[228] thus consolidating the law into action; the right to appeal is thus an integral module in the overall German administration of criminal justice. Credible anecdotal evidence suggests, however, that appeals of law filed by the defence to the FHCJ will often be rejected and verdicts upheld, and that there is an increasing overall punitive trend in the jurisprudence. The FHCJ makes frequent use of the statutory option to unanimously dismiss an appeal without giving reasons, when it deems the appeal to be evidently unfounded.[229]

2.4. Rights relating to effective defence

2.4.1. The right to investigate the case; equality of arms; line-ups

Equality of arms between the prosecution and defence is generally recognized as one of the major objectives of criminal procedure.[230] It finds expression in, and is safeguarded by, independent rights of the accused and counsel to be present during all stages of the proceedings (particularly at certain investigative acts in the investigation phase), as well as procedural rights to seek evidence (including interviewing prospective witnesses) and investigate facts.

In the *investigation phase*, both the accused and counsel enjoy independent rights to be present during *examinations of evidence, or during interrogations of*

---

[225]   If the prosecution has filed an appeal in favour of the accused, the prosecution must not withdraw it without the consent of the accused. § 302 (1) CCP.

[226]   Rule 141 (2) RPCASM.

[227]   § 302 (1) CCP.

[228]   2008: 3,167. 2007: 3,104. See <http://www.bundesgerichtshof.de/cln_136/DE/BGH/Statistik/Taetigkeitsberichte/FruehereJahre/Taetigkeit2008/taetigkeit2008_node.html#Strafsenate> (last visited 29 April 2010).

[229]   § 349 (2) CCP.

[230]   Beulke 2008, marginal No. 148.

witnesses and experts (but not of co-accused), if these are conducted by an investigative judge (but not by the police or prosecution).[231] However, a provisionally detained accused, who is represented by counsel, only enjoys the right to attend such acts, if they are conducted at the court with jurisdiction of his place of custody.[232]

The judge can only refrain from notifying the accused or his lawyer of an impending judicial act of investigation if such notification would impede the investigation, that is, when the judicial act needs to be undertaken immediately.

The accused, but not defence counsel, can be excluded from an investigative measure, in order not to jeopardize the investigation.[233]

If the right to be present during such investigative measures is violated, the evidence obtained so must not be submitted at the trial as having the significant probative value normally attached to investigative acts conducted by an investigative judge. According to the FHCJ, however, such evidence (for example, the minutes of a witness statement) may be presented at the trial as 'ordinary' evidence, if the prerequisites of § 251 (1) CCP are met.[234]

Further, counsel enjoys an independent right to be present at interrogations of the accused by the prosecution or an investigative judge (but not by the police, see *supra* 2.2.2).

Participation in *line-ups* can be ordered either against witnesses[235] or the accused. There is no positive legal basis upon which to order the accused's participation in a line-up, and thus the authorisation to do so is disputed.[236] Many commentators, however, regard § 81a CCP (physical examination of the accused) to constitute the pertinent authorisation. Thus, a line-up with the accused could normally only be ordered by a judge, while the prosecution or the police would only be entitled to issue a comparable order if undue delay (due to involving a judge) would jeopardize the investigation;[237] whether counsel has the right to be present during physical examinations of the accused is not seen as a positive regulation, and is thus disputed.[238] A 1993 ruling by the FHCJ, however, found a proper basis to order the accused's participation in a line-up comparable to ordering him/her to participate in a regular interrogation.[239] Thus, the accused would need to follow the order of a judge or the prosecution,[240] but would not be obliged to

---

[231]   §§ 168c (2), 168d CCP.

[232]   § 168c (3) CCP.

[233]   § 168c (3) CCP.

[234]   This holds especially true where a witness or expert has died, or cannot be examined before the court in due time, see § 251 (1) #2 CCP.

[235]   During the investigation phase pursuant to § 58 (2) CCP, and the during trial pursuant to § 244 (2) CCP.

[236]   See Eisenberg 2008, marginal No. 1193.

[237]   § 81a (2) CCP.

[238]   See Bosch 2007, § 81a marginal No. 38, arguing that such a positive right of counsel should be affirmed.

[239]   FHCJ, 39 BGHSt., p. 96: '… die Neuregelung des § 163a Abs. 3 StPO [hatte] auch den Zweck […], einen Beschuldigten, der Angaben zur Sache verweigert, zur Teilnahme an einer Wahlgegenüberstellung mit Zeugen zwingen zu können.'

[240]   §§ 133, 163a (3) CCP.

follow an order by the police. If this view were to prevail, counsel would enjoy a right to attend the line-up as ordered by a judge or the prosecution,[241] but not by the police.

During house searches (*Durchsuchungen*), only the proprietor (*Inhaber*) enjoys the right to be present.[242] If the accused is not the proprietor – as is also the position, for example, with regard to search measures in the cells of provisionally detained persons – neither the accused nor counsel have a right to be present, except where the proprietor allows their presence.

Our field research indicates that, in practice, the defence right to be present is generally observed by law enforcement agencies.

Although it is sometimes disputed[243] and often not positively regulated,[244] counsel[245] has the 'self-evident'[246] and 'unchallenged'[247] right to (1) *investigate* facts,[248] in particular to *seek evidence*; (2) *interview* prospective witnesses, although not in an official interrogative capacity;[249] (3) *obtain expert evidence*;[250] and (4) mandate any capable *third person to investigate*.[251]

However, the state is not obliged to positively support any private investigations or interviews (for example, by providing rooms), nor is the communication *per se* protected against any intrusion (such as wire tapping of witnesses). Defence counsel cannot compel the cooperation of any witness, and has no right to require a judge interrogate a witness before trial. This is different for the public prosecutor, who can demand that an investigative judge interrogate specific witnesses and experts.[252]

The right of defence counsel to investigate finds is limited only by (1) the general provisions of the German Criminal Code;[253] (2) the general personal rights of those being investigated;[254] and (3) professional rules and regulations.[255]

---

[241] §§ 168c (1), 163a (3) CCP.

[242] § 106 CCP. Note that a violation of this right will not lead to the exclusion of the evidence obtained so.

[243] HRC Schleswig, *NStZ*, 1996, p. 443.

[244] The right to investigate, particularly to interview prospective witnesses and obtain expert evidence, seems to arise from the right to a fair trial, the equality of arms principle, and defence counsel's position as an 'organ of the criminal justice system'.

[245] Since counsel exercises most of the following rights on behalf of the client, it is evident that the latter enjoys similar rights.

[246] Wächtler 2007, p. 141.

[247] Dahs 1999, marginal No. 285.

[248] HRC Frankfurt, *StV*, 1981, p. 28.

[249] FHCJ, 46 BGHSt, p. 4.

[250] FHCJ, 46 BGHSt, p. 4; Dahs 1999, marginal No. 285-294; Neuhaus 2006, marginal No. 11; Beulke 2008, marginal No. 159; all with further references.

[251] Dahs 1999, marginal No. 287.

[252] § 162 CCP.

[253] For example, §§ 239 (deprivation of liberty), 240 *et seq.* (coercion), 257 (accessory after the fact), 258 (obstruction), 267 *et seq.* (falsification of documents).

[254] For example, the right to privacy, the right to informational self-determination (*Recht auf informationelle Selbstbestimmung*), the right to visual and verbal self-determination (*Recht am eigenen Bild und Wort*).

[255] Meyer-Goßner 2008, Vor § 137 marginal No. 2 with further references; Neuhaus 2006, marginal No. 22.

Our field research indicates that, irrespective of the possible indigence or vulnerability of a particular accused, counsel's right to investigate is rarely exercised in practice,[256] perhaps with the exception of high profile cases and accused. This can be explained by the fact that many prosecutors and judges are critical, sceptical, and even distrustful vis-à-vis the results of private investigations,[257] particularly vis-à-vis the results of private interviews with prospective witnesses (because of possible defects in the way the interviews are conducted),[258] and privately commissioned expert evidence (because of possible bias).[259] By contrast, documents produced by the defence are considered of (greater) evidentiary value.[260]

2.4.2. The right to adequate time and facilities for preparation of the defence

The right to *adequate time* for preparation of the defence is protected by legal regulations providing for *notifications* before any appearance before a prosecutor, judge or court; these regulations differ, dependent on the particular stage of the proceedings. Moreover, there are *provisions for hearings to be suspended or adjourned*, in order to give the accused and/or counsel sufficient time to prepare.

In the investigation phase, no 'rigid' periods of notification exist; this is compensated by the fact that, for example, (1) an order to appear at a police interrogation generally need not be followed, although the police are under no duty to instruct the requested person accordingly; (2) a compulsory order to appear before a judge or prosecutorial interrogation incorporates a 'soft' period of notification (the appearance must not be scheduled too soon, otherwise, non-appearance is justified and must not be sanctioned by arresting the accused to secure his/her appearance);[261] and (3) a notification of an examination of evidence by an investigative judge similarly has a 'soft' period (the examination must normally[262] not be scheduled too soon; if the accused or his/her counsel files a reasoned request, the examination is to be rescheduled, otherwise evidence obtained may not be submitted as having the high(er) evidentiary value accorded to judge obtained evidence).[263]

With regards to notifications in the trial phase, the presiding judge has discretion in scheduling the (normal) trial.[264] However, the initial summons to appear at trial has a minimum notification period of one week;[265] this is to ensure an

---

[256]   Neuhaus 2006, marginal No. 16 with further references.
[257]   Dahs 1999, marginal No. 285.
[258]   Dahs 1999, marginal No. 288.
[259]   Dahs 1999, marginal No. 289.
[260]   Dahs 1999, marginal No. 290.
[261]   Gleß 2007a, marginal No. 5.
[262]   An exception is warranted by investigative necessity (for example, a foreign witness travelling home).
[263]   Meyer-Goßner 2008, § 168c marginal No. 6.
[264]   § 213 CCP.
[265]   § 217, 218 CCP. If the actual period of notification falls short of the minimum period of one week, the presiding judge is to inform (§ 228 (3) CCP) the accused that he/she is entitled to

→

effective preparation of the defence and, thus, must be further prolonged due to the (factual or legal) complexity of the case, or the personal circumstances of the accused (for example, illness).[266] One defence lawyer pointed out that this period specified by law would often be too short for an adequate preparation of the defence, but that the periods applied in practice by the judges are often longer and sufficient.[267]

The initial summons must also include a trial plan (delineating what evidence, and particularly which witnesses are to be examined during any specific trial session), if the trial is expected to last for several trial sessions.[268] Finally, the scheduling of the trial is to take account of other commitments of counsel.[269]

In simple cases, that are unlikely to result in sentences exceeding one year imprisonment, the prosecution may seek an accelerated trial (*beschleunigtes Verfahren*). The minimal notification deadline is 24 hours;[270] however, in order to comply with article 6 (3) (b) ECHR, commentators agree that this deadline must be prolonged, or the application for a accelerated trial dismissed, if the defence requires more time for preparation.[271]

A verdict cannot be challenged on appeal of law solely on the ground that the minimum, or reasonable, periods of notification were denied. The appeal of law is likely to succeed, however, where there was an infringement of the accused's right to reasonable time of preparation or of general defence rights.[272]

During the trial, § 246 CCP prohibits, at least to a certain extent, 'surprise evidence' produced either by the prosecution or the defence.[273] On the one hand, the court must not decline evidence simply because it is produced (too) late. On the other hand, if new evidence is produced by one side, the court also must ensure that the other side has sufficient time for effective preparation; this may require the court to suspend the trial (*Aussetzung*), if a party brings a motion:[274] Suspension of trial means that it is to start all over again.[275]

The court enjoys certain discretion to reconcile the right to effective preparation with the expeditious trial principle.[276] If the court unreasonably exercises this discretion, and rejects a motion to suspend the trial, the defence can challenge an eventual conviction, if its rights were seriously infringed.

Further, the court is to suspend the trial, if the defence did not have sufficient and reasonable time to prepare against (1) an altered legal evaluation of the facts

     move for an adjournment (§ 217 (2) CCP); the accused may, however, waive this right (§ 217 (3) CCP).
[266] Gmel 2008a, marginal No. 1.
[267] Interview # 8.
[268] § 214 (2) CCP.
[269] Gmel 2008b, marginal No. 4b.
[270] § 418 (3) CCP.
[271] Meyer-Goßner 2008, § 418 marginal No. 8.
[272] Gmel 2008b, marginal No. 9.
[273] See *supra* at 2.1.4. and *supra* note 90.
[274] The court is generally under no obligation to instruct the accused about this, except where the accused does not have legal representation; Meyer-Goßner 2008, § 246 marginal No. 3.
[275] § 228 CCP.
[276] See FHCJ, *NJW*, 1990, p. 1124.

originally contained in the indictment;[277] (2) any significant factual alteration of, and in, the indictment;[278] or (3) any significant procedural developments during the trial.[279] If the rejection of a motion to suspend infringes defence rights, an eventual (partial) conviction can be challenged on appeal of law.

§ 266 (3) CCP obliges the court to adjourn the proceedings, if a new indictment seeking to extend the trial to a different transaction (which concerns events other than those initially charged) is to be merged into, and processed by, the original trial (*Nachtragsanklage*). A *Nachtragsanklage* can only occur with the consent of the defendant, and the adjournment is to ensure adequate time for preparing against the newly filed charges. If the rejection of a motion to adjourn infringes defence rights, an eventual (partial) conviction can be challenged on appeal of law.

German criminal procedure does not know a general right of the accused or counsel *to adequate facilities for the preparation of the defence*. This finds a notable exception only if the accused is kept in provisional detention: in that case, the accused and counsel normally have a right to a room, in order to talk and prepare the defence in private, and without state supervision.[280]

2.4.3. The right to equality of arms in examining witnesses

The inquisitorial paradigm, which guides the German criminal justice system, inspires the so called principle of official investigation (*Amtsermittlungsgrundsatz*), as well as the principle of material truth (*Prinzip der materiellen Wahrheit*). Therefore, the police, the prosecution and, in particular, the courts are obliged to gather, produce and introduce all evidence potentially relevant to 'discover' the facts of the case, and the guilt or innocence of the accused.

Nevertheless, the accused and counsel both enjoy the right to bring motions requiring that (specific) evidence be gathered, produced and introduced (which includes witness testimony) in each of the investigation,[281] confirmation of charges[282] and trial[283] phases.

In the investigation phase, the prosecutor shall consider exculpatory evidence suggested by the suspect 'if it is relevant'.[284] The courts leave the determination of relevance to the prosecutor's discretion.

During the trial, in order to satisfy formal requirements, this motion is to contain a specific factual contention (for example, that the accused was sleeping at home while the robbery was committed), substantiated by legitimate evidence (for

---

[277]   For example, an initial charge of 'reckless manslaughter' becoming 'murder' during the trial. § 265 (1) CCP obliges the court to give the accused *fair warning*, if it becomes apparent during the trial that the accused may be convicted for the *violation of penal provisions that were not named or described in the indictment*.

[278]   For example, the initial indictment identifying alleged co-perpetrators and, during the trial, the prosecution describing them as unknown.

[279]   For example, the prosecution only disclosing exculpatory evidence during the trial.

[280]   § 148 (1) CCP.

[281]   § 136, 163a CCP.

[282]   § 219 CCP.

[283]   § 244 (2) CCP.

[284]   § 163a (2) CCP.

example, a specific person testifying to this end). Defence motions for the introduction of additional evidence at the trial can be rejected by the trial court for a variety of reasons (which have been detailed by meticulous case law).[285] These reasons are limited, however, with respect to suggested witness testimony; in particular, the court cannot refuse to hear a witness merely because it deems that witness to be unreliable.

If the motion is illegally rejected, and thus not all relevant evidence is used to find material truth, the court violates the principle of official investigation; this may be challenged upon an appeal of law.

In practice, the exercise of the right to demand that evidence be produced and introduced is somewhat related to the financial resources of the accused, since the drafting of an non-rejectable motion to gather, produce and introduce evidence is an art of its own, which not all defence lawyers have developed to perfection. What is more, a court is normally required to introduce all available evidence to the trial, so that the accused is free to deploy his/her own financial resources to make certain evidence available (for example, to fly-in foreign witnesses[286]).

Our field research indicates a change of perception about defence motions to gather, produce, and introduce evidence. Trial courts increasingly tend to perceive such motions as uncooperative and unfriendly acts, particularly because they fear reversal upon an appeal of law, or delays in the proceedings, or are getting used to managing the trial in advance. As a reaction, upper courts give trial courts greater leeway for rejecting such motions. This change of perception has also influenced the behaviour of defence lawyers, who are – particularly in low-profile cases – more careful and hesitant to stand up to the court and file such motions.

The inquisitorial paradigm further dictates that there does not exist a prosecution or defence 'case', and accordingly no prosecution and defence evidence (which includes witness testimony). The examination of witnesses, both favourable and detrimental to the accused, first of all falls to the presiding judge, with the accused and counsel having the right to ask questions. As a consequence, a formal adversarial system of cross-examination does not exist.

2.4.4. The right to free interpretation of documents and translation

Criminal proceedings are to be conducted in German.[287] If an accused does not have a command of the German language, he/she has far-reaching rights to free interpretation and translation. These rights are interlinked, however, with the

---

[285]   § 244 (3)-(5) CCP. For example, motions to gather, produce, and introduce evidence may be rejected, if (1) the formal requirements of the motion are not met; (2) the factual contention is irrelevant, or already established; (3) the factual contention will be the accepted by the court; (4) the evidence submitted is impermissible (for example, involving the torture of a specific witness); 5) the evidence demanded is evidently superfluous; (6) the evidence demanded does not have any evidentiary value (such as polygraph evidence); (7) the evidence demanded is inaccessible (which is difficult to ascertain with regard to witnesses living abroad); or (8) the motion is only intended to wilfully delay the proceedings.

[286]   The court may refuse to hear such witnesses for the same reasons that enable the court to reject a defence motion to call additional witnesses, § 245 (2) CCP.

[287]   § 184 AOJ.

former sometimes overriding the latter. It is expressly regulated[288] that the costs for interpretation and translation services will normally be paid by the state,[289] irrespective of whether the accused is found guilty or innocent,[290] and irrespective of the financial resources[291] of the accused.[292]

If an accused does not have a command of the German language, he/she has the *right to free translation* in all phases of the proceedings (including the investigation phase, be it outside or inside a trial hearing), in order to communicate with either a law enforcement agency (police, prosecution, court), or with counsel (irrespective of whether the case is of one of mandatory legal representation or not).

The substantive test is that the accused does not have a command of the German language. This comprises (1) the ability to passively understand – from a merely linguistic rather than a cultural point of view[293] – the proceedings; and (2) the ability to proactively convey his/her own points of view (the accused must not be 'degraded to an non-understandable object of the proceedings', and accordingly it is not sufficient that the accused can shake or nod his/her head in reply).[294]

The determination rests with the court that either tries the case or, in the investigation phase, has jurisdiction to try the case subsequently. In exercising due judgment, the court is to decide upon, and appoint an interpreter, either *ex officio*, or upon an informal request by the parties. This effectively means that an accused or counsel cannot appoint an interpreter themselves, but instead must request a court appointed interpreter.

Where an accused has a partial command of the German language, the court is to decide – again in exercising due judgment – the extent to which an interpreter is necessary;[295] in such circumstances, an interpreter may only be appointed for particular sessions.

There seems to be no duty on state actors to inform the accused of his/her right to translation during interrogation, hearings and communications with counsel. However, if the court is convinced that the language skills of the accused are not sufficient, it is obliged to appoint an interpreter *ex officio*.[296] This duty is unconditional and cannot be waived by an accused who has insufficient command of the German language.[297]

---

[288]   § 464c CCP and # 9005 (4) of the Cost Index of the Court Cost Act (CICCA).
[289]   FCC, *NJW*, 2004, p. 50; FHCJ, *NJW*, 2001, p. 309; Diemer 2008, marginal No. 2; Frister 2006, marginal No. 10.
[290]   ECtHR 28 November 1978, *Luedicke, Belkacem and Koç v. Germany*, Nos. 6210/73, 6877/75 and 7132/75; for a German report of the judgment see *NJW*, 1979, p. 1091; Diemer 2008, marginal No. 2.
[291]   Kissel & Mayer 2008, § 184 marginal No. 19.
[292]   This is in full compliance with the rules of the ECHR, cf. ECtHR 28 November 1978, *Luedicke, Belkacem and Koç v. Germany*, Nos. 6210/73, 6877/75 and 7132/75; ECtHR 18 May 1977, *Luedicke, Belkacem and Koç v. Germany*, Nos. 6210/73, 6877/75 and 7132/75 and the German decisions implementing this rule: FCC, *NJW*, 2004, p. 50; FHCJ, *NJW*, 2001, p. 309.
[293]   Cultural miscommunication is compensated by mandatory legal representation; see Kissel & Mayer 2008, § 185 marginal No. 5.
[294]   Kissel & Mayer 2008, § 185 marginal No. 5 *et seq.*
[295]   FHCJ, *NStZ*, 2002, p. 275; FHCJ, *NStZ*, 1984, p. 328; Diemer 2008, marginal No. 4.
[296]   Diemer 2008, marginal No. 1, 4.
[297]   Diemer 2008, marginal No. 4.

With regard to the investigation phase, it is yet to be decided whether evidence obtained during an oral interrogation (conducted either by the police, the prosecution, or a judge) is to be excluded, if the accused did not have sufficient command of the language used. Yet, it has been held that an exclusionary rule generally applies, where the accused, due to a mental disorder, does not understand instructions about his/her freedom to testify.[298] Some commentators deem this situation analogous to a lack of understanding due to insufficient language skills.[299]

With regard to the trial phase, there is an absolute ground for an appeal of law if the trial takes place without an interpreter, despite the accused not having command of the German language. However, appellate review is limited to the question of whether the trial court violated due judgment in its determination of the language skills of the accused. If the trial takes place without an interpreter, despite the accused having only a partial command of the German language, a verdict can be challenged by an appeal of law, if the trial court did not exercise due judgment when not appointing an interpreter.[300]

The *right to free interpretation of documents* is also well accepted, but its exact scope is still to be determined. Until 2004, the right had not been codified and had only been generally deduced from the fair trial principle; it was understood rather restrictively, an approach that still prevails today although the right to translation was enshrined in § 187 AOJ in 2004.

If the accused does not have a command of the German language, the court orders the translation of documents, to the extent necessary for the effective exercise of defence rights. The determination again rests with the court that either tries the case or, in the investigation phase, has jurisdiction to try the case subsequently.

With regard to official documents to be served on the accused, the court must ensure that their substance is summarily communicated (either by interpretation or translation); to the extent to which the original wording is decisive, a literal translation becomes necessary. Therefore, in practice, the following documents are usually to be translated literally: summons, arrest warrants, written summary sanctioning orders (*Strafbefehl*), writs of indictment, and all decisions on the merits of the case.[301]

As to the written reasons of the judgment, older but still unchallenged jurisprudence – by various Higher Regional Courts and the FCC – denies a right to their translation, if the accused has (German) legal representation.[302] The reason for this is that the verdict is orally explained by the court. This restrictive approach is

---

[298] FHCJ, 39 BGHSt, p. 349. For this principle to apply, certain procedural originalities must be observed (for example, counsel must object to the use of the evidence, the so-called 'Widerspruchslösung').

[299] Kiehl 1994, p. 1267. See also Frister 2008, marginal No. 62.

[300] Kissel & Mayer 2008, § 185 marginal No. 25.

[301] See Rule 181 [2] RPCASM, which, however, only directly pertains to 'foreigners'; the debate has not yet sufficiently addressed accused who hold the German citizenship, and who do not have a command of the German language.

[302] HRC Hamburg, *NJW*, 1978, p. 2462; HRC Stuttgart, *NStZ*, 1981, p. 225 *et seq.*; HRC Düsseldorf, *StV*, 1985, p. 361 and FCC, *NJW*, 1983, p. 2764. See further Frister 2006, marginal No. 5 with further references.

rightly criticised, because an effective preparation of an appeal of law can only be based on the written reasons.[303]

With respect to instructions about available legal remedies, particularly involving impending deadlines, older but still unchallenged jurisprudence denies that an accused, who does not have command of the German language, be served with a translated letter of instructions;[304] the reason for this is that the accused can reasonably be expected to organize translations of written instructions him/herself.[305] This is rightly criticised as being contrary to the spirit of § 187 AOJ.[306]

With regard to documentary evidence, the court is again to ensure that their substance be summarily communicated to the accused (either by interpretation or translation); but only to the extent to which the original wording is decisive for the case and thus for effective defence, a literal translation becomes necessary. The accused thus generally cannot demand a translation of the entire case file, or every piece of evidence. What is more, according to the leading case on the point, the defence lawyer is to summarise orally the substance of the case file; the free interpretation of this oral out-of-court summary is deemed sufficient to ensure the effective exercise of defence rights.[307]

With regard to his/her written communications with the court (for example, motions, declarations, pleadings), older but still unchallenged jurisprudence does not afford to the accused any right to translation, particularly on the ground that German is the official court language; this jurisprudence counts such communications as void. This is rightly criticised as being contrary to the spirit of § 187 AOJ.[308]

There also seems to be no duty on state actors to inform the accused of the right to free translation of documents. If the court decides to deny translation (in general, or in relation to specific documents), this may be challenged on appeal of law, if the decision represented an unacceptable infringement of defence rights.

---

[303] Frister 2006, marginal No. 5.
[304] HRC Köln, *VRS*, 1972, p. 251; see also Meyer-Goßner 2008, § 35a marginal No. 9 with further references.
[305] Meyer-Goßner 2008, § 35a marginal No. 9.
[306] Frister 2006, marginal No. 6.
[307] HRC Hamburg, *NJW*, 2005, p. 1138: 'Die erforderliche Dolmetscherleistung i.S. des § 187 GVG umfasst eine Übersetzungshilfe bei die Hauptverhandlung sowie eigene Verfahrenshandlungen vorbereitenden Gesprächen mit einem Verteidiger oder Vertreter. Durch die Übersetzung der ihm dabei von seinem Verteidiger oder Vertreter zu erstattenden zusammenfassenden Berichte über den Akteninhalt wird der Berechtigte in der Regel ausreichend in die Lage versetzt, seine strafprozessualen Rechte wahrzunehmen. Die – wörtliche – Übersetzung der gesamten Akte oder einzelner Aktenbestandteile gehört regelmäßig nicht zu den nach § 187 GVG erforderlichen Dolmetscherleistungen.'
[308] Frister 2006, marginal No. 3.

3. Professional culture of defence lawyers

3.1. Bar associations

In Germany, every lawyer is required by law[309] to become member of one of the 28 regional bar associations (*Rechtsanwaltskammern*), which are in turn united under the Federal Bar Association (*Bundesrechtsanwaltskammer* – BRAK). The BRAK is a public legal entity (*Körperschaft des öffentlichen Rechts*).[310]

The major role of the Federal Bar Association is to politically represent the professional interests of German lawyers on a federal level.

Moreover, the regional bar associations and the Federal Bar Association have the right – but not the absolute duty – to investigate complaints of alleged professional misconduct.[311]

While ordinary courts decide on civil cases, (for example, torts, claims or violations of penal law), the boards of the bar associations have exclusive competence to discipline lawyers for minor violations of professional rules and duties.[312] In order to supervise lawyers and to review complaints, the board can oblige the lawyer to provide more information and to produce his/her case file, except where this would violate counsel-client confidentiality.[313]

The Bar also staffs, to a significant extent,[314] the so called Lawyers' Disciplinary Courts (*Anwaltsgericht*), which discipline lawyers for major violations of professional rules and duties. Proceedings before a Lawyers Disciplinary Court very much resemble – in terms of rights and procedures – a criminal trial (including a prosecution and quasi-indictment). These courts may impose cumulative sanctions (for example, in addition to those imposed by a criminal court), if this is

---

[309] This is due to § 6 (2), § 12 (3), § 60 (1) 2 FLA. The regional bar associations are competent in relation to the admission of lawyers in their district. With admission, lawyers become members of the relevant bar association.

[310] § 176 (1) FLA.

[311] § 56 (1) FLA.

[312] § 74 FLA.

[313] § 56 FLA. – Decisions about questions of law or fact are rendered as follows (cf. Kleine-Cosack 2006, marginal No. 63 *et seq.*): A simple instruction (*Belehrung*) – for example, on whether a certain conduct would entail a violation of professional obligations – is not *per se* binding, does not entail any negative consequences for the lawyer, and hence cannot be reviewed by an appellative body. A ruling (*Bescheid*) on a disputed question of professional duties – for example, on whether a certain conduct would entail a violation of professional obligations – has a binding effect and can thus be challenged by the lawyer and brought to the review of the competent appellative body (§ 223 FLA). A reproof (*Rüge*) formally establishes a minor violation of professional obligations of which the lawyer is guilty. The reproof must not be rendered without a prior hearing of the lawyer. It can be challenged and brought before a lawyers tribunal for judicial review (§ 74a FLA).

[314] Lawyers Disciplinary Courts are first instance courts and are exclusively staffed by members of the Bar (§ 94 FLA). The Lawyers Disciplinary Supreme Court (*Anwaltsgerichtshof*) acts as the court of appeal; pursuant to §§ 101 *et seq.* FLA, the president, the presiding judges, and in total 50% of all judges shall be recruited from the Bar, while the other 50% are professional/ordinary judges. A special chamber in the Federal High Court of Justice acts as the (final) court of cassation; pursuant to § 106 FLA, seven judges sit on the bench, of which three are to be members of the Bar.

necessary to ensure that a lawyer complies with her professional duties and to protect the reputation of the Bar.[315] A Lawyers Disciplinary Court has the right, *inter alia*, to prohibit the lawyer from providing legal assistance in a specific field of law, or to exclude him/her from the Bar altogether.[316] A verdict is open to judicial review by the Lawyers' Disciplinary Supreme Court (*Anwaltsgerichtshof*) and, as the final arbiter, the Federal High Court of Justice in Lawyers' Matters (*Bundesgerichtshof in Anwaltssachen*).

Trials before the Lawyers' Disciplinary Court are held in camera. They can be made public on a motion by the prosecution, and must be made public on a motion by the lawyer.[317] Therefore, disciplinary proceedings are only published infrequently.

The primary statutory condition for becoming a member of the Bar is the passing of both German State Examinations in law.[318] Currently, 150,377 lawyers are registered at the German Bar.[319]

According to our field research, there seems to be very little interest among lawyers in the bar associations themselves and the opportunities of advanced training that they offer.[320] It was suggested that compulsory membership of the bar association was simply an inconvenient duty.[321]

3.2. Specialisation in criminal law, legal aid equivalent, and quality assurance

The German tradition is that every lawyer is regarded as qualified to provide every type of legal service. Hence, aside from the general legal qualifications necessary to become a lawyer, special qualifications are not required to provide defence services. Where a lawyer has acquired special skills and expertise, he/she can apply for a special title – that of counsel specialised in criminal defence (*Fachanwalt für Strafrecht*). The required theoretical, as well as practical, skills and expertise are determined by a specific set of rules.[322] Currently, 2,276 lawyers have qualified for this title.[323]

---

[315]   § 115b FLA.

[316]   § 114 (1) FLA.

[317]   § 135 FLA.

[318]   § 4 FLA. Admission is to be rejected, *inter alia*, if (1) the applicant does not have the right to take public office on grounds of a criminal conviction (§ 7 #2 FLA); (2) the applicant has been excluded from the Bar within the past eight years (§ 7 #3 FLA); (3) the applicant is or appears unworthy to practice as a lawyer (§ 7 #5 Federal Lawyers' Act); (4) the applicant opposes the system of free and democratic fundamental order in a way punishable by law (§ 7 #6 FLA); (5) the applicant is bankrupt (§ 7 #9 FLA).

[319]   See <http://www.brak.de/seiten/pdf/Statistiken/2009/MGg2009.pdf> (last visited 29 April 2010).

[320]   Interviews # 1, 2 and 7.

[321]   Interview # 8.

[322]   § 2 SLA. Cf. on this topic and suggesting that the special title has insufficient minimum quality standards; Johnigk 2006, p. 349 *et seq.*

[323]   <http://www.brak.de/seiten/pdf/Statistiken/2009/10_FA_2009.pdf> (last visited 29 April 2010).

German lawyers are statutorily obliged to render pre-trial legal advice under the Act on Legal Advice and Representation for Indigent Citizens. What is more, lawyers are under a similar obligation to accept the assignment as 'court assigned counsel', and may only move to revoke the assignment for serious reasons.[324] In practice, however, lawyers will not be so assigned if they do not wish to be.

Although lawyers are legally obliged[325] to continue their studies as long as they practice, this obligation is often disregarded and can – due to the lack of binding criteria on how this must be undertaken – only insufficiently be made subject to judicial review. Thus, once a member of the Bar, the quality of the lawyer can hardly be monitored at all. This is criticised by representatives of the Bar,[326] but no viable and serious quality assurance schemes have so far found their way onto the legislative/political agenda.

3.3.   Role of defence lawyers

German law[327] describes the role of lawyers in general, and criminal defence lawyers in particular, as an independent 'organ of the (criminal) justice system' (*unabhängiges Organ der Rechtspflege*). This is a highly ambivalent und controversial concept, which is fleshed out by jurisprudence about the specific duties and obligations towards both the client and the administration of criminal justice.

There is broad agreement that this concept must not unreasonably prejudice defence rights and prerogatives in the interests of efficient and effective criminal justice; on the other hand, defence lawyers must not be seen simply as mere representatives of their clients' interests. There is also an imperative to remain objective (*Sachlichkeitsgebot*).[328] This ambivalence creates thin red lines between what the lawyer must and must not do, and what his/her concrete, and possibly contradicting, obligations towards his/her clients and the administration of criminal justice are.

Suffice to provide some examples:[329] while lawyers are allowed to give broad advice (including about the right to remain silent), and to explain the legal situation of a hypothetical factual scenario, they must not induce the accused or witnesses to lie; neither must lawyers lie themselves in favour of their clients. While they are allowed to move for an acquittal even though they are certain of their client's guilt, they must not bring motions to hear witnesses who they know are likely to commit perjury.

What is more, courts have (although one could argue, rarely) obliged lawyers to mediate the courts' relationship towards the accused by requiring that an accused who excessively uses, and thus abuses, his/her right to bring motions to gather, produce, and introduce evidence, is no longer able to bring these motions in person,

[324]   §§ 49 (2), 48 (2) FLA.
[325]   § 43a (6) FLA.
[326]   See, on this point, the criticism by Johnigk 2006, p. 349.
[327]   § 1 FLA.
[328]   § 43a (3) FLA.
[329]   See *supra* 2.2.5.

but only via counsel.[330] More importantly, the FHCJ requires that the defence objects to the introduction of (certain) inadmissible evidence (*Widerspruchspflicht*), and that failure to do so carries a waiver to object or appeal against this inadmissible evidence.[331] This creates serious legal problems, which not only impact upon the lawyer/client relationship, but also – and arguably more importantly – the inquisitorial character of German criminal proceedings. Courts also impose certain duties to inform on the lawyer, for example, by requiring that former counsel informs a newly assigned court appointed counsel about the previous proceedings.[332]

Defence lawyers provide their clients with legal assistance. They advise the accused on issues concerning substantial and procedural law, make statements in favour of the accused (for example, pointing out his/her positive characteristics), represent the accused to the extent legally possible or obligatory, and exercise those procedural rights that they share with the accused, as well as procedural rights only they have by virtue of being defence counsel.[333] Among those rights that the defence lawyer may exercise are, *inter alia*, the right to bring motions with regard to evidence, the right to access the case file and the right to appeal a decision.[334]

Defence lawyers have a right to be present during interrogation of the accused by a judge or public prosecution, but not the police. Defence lawyers have right to be present during court proceedings; there are also cases of mandatory legal representation (such as felony or complex proceedings), where the trial hearing must only be conducted in the presence of counsel.

3.4. Perception of defence lawyers (particularly in cases of mandatory legal representation)

In our field research, although everyone interviewed took a different position about the quality of defence lawyers, they were in agreement that the last 15 years have seen a greater professionalisation of defence work.

Some criminal defence lawyers,[335] particularly those who are not representatives of the bar, considered the quality of those colleagues who practice in all branches of law, including criminal defence, to be just mediocre to bad quality. Some[336] regarded court appointed counsel in particular to often be only of mediocre quality, due to economic pressure in legal aid cases.

Some criminal defence lawyers[337] regarded the ordinary fees of court assigned counsel as being too low; what is more, they pointed out that the governance

---

[330]   See FHCJ, 38 BGHSt, p. 114.
[331]   Without raising an objection, the defence may – depending on the evidence in question – lose the right to challenge the introduction of illegally obtained evidence in an appeal of law.
[332]   See HRC Berlin, *JR*, 1981, p. 86.
[333]   Beulke 2008, marginal No. 149.
[334]   Only the right to inspect the file relates exclusively to counsel; all other rights can also be exercised by the accused personally.
[335]   Interviews # 3, 8 and 9.
[336]   Interviews # 5 and 7.
[337]   Interviews # 1, 2, 3 and 5.

strategy for these fees is incorrect, because it, for example, does not reward intensive defence services in the investigation and confirmation of charges phases.

One person interviewed[338] convincingly portrayed (some) court appointed counsel as not being factually independent from 'their courts', which appoint them on a regular basis and for many cases; that person reported of almost 'symbiotic relationships' between courts and court appointed counsel (see *supra* 2.2.5). This leads to court assigned counsel entering into less favourable 'deals' for their clients and not availing themselves of all the rights and possibilities under the CCP.

By contrast, other interviewees[339] regarded the institution of court appointed counsel as important in ensuring good legal representation and enforcing quality control. The ordinary fees for court assigned counsel were described by one person interviewed[340] as 'adequate' (*auskömmlich*), particularly since they were only recently raised under new reforms.

One criminal defence lawyer[341] said that one-third of all prison sentences results from poor defence work. He/she explained that this was a consequence of the varying degrees of experience between defence lawyers, rather than any different qualities between hired counsel and court assigned counsel.

According to a federal judge,[342] varying quality is not linked to differences between hired counsel and court appointed counsel, but rather to age and experience. Young defence lawyers 'fight' more determinedly, due to increased competition, and will use all possibilities provided for by the CCP, in order to obtain a positive result for their clients. Normal and non-specialized defence lawyers can very well be successful at trial courts, but appeals of law should be handled by specialists, due to the intricacies of appeal of law procedures.

4.   Political commitment to effective criminal defence and public perception about crime

Our field research indicates that practitioners, including defence lawyers, are in broad agreement that the legislature has closed most gaps in the codification of essential defence rights. As a most recent development, the Federal legislature has continued on this path, by regulating the 'deal' under § 257c CCP, and by making mandatory legal representation compulsory in cases of provisional detention.[343]

Nevertheless, defence rights, and in particular their European harmonization or supervision, represent a highly sensitive political issue. It thus proves difficult to acquire explicit and concrete statements by political actors, such as the Federal Ministry of Justice. To a considerable degree, this is due to German federalism, because the implementation and financing of cost-intensive, but federally legislated defence rights (for example, the right to free translation and interpretation), or of federally legislated extensions of the legal aid equivalent, are under the authority of

[338] Interview # 3.
[339] Interviews # 9, 10 and 11.
[340] Interview # 7.
[341] Interview # 7.
[342] Interview # 4.
[343] Beginning as at 1 January 2009.

German states. Explanations of the political difficulties, with more far-reaching and liberal legislation and implementation of defence rights, thus must take account of the multitude of political state and federal actors involved.

What is more, on a rather tentative assessment, recent political campaigns, as well as much of the legislation in the context of criminal justice, rather tend towards the security and 'tough on crime' paradigm. These paradigms erode the liberal protection of the accused, who in turn does not have a strong political lobby. It is yet to be determined whether this increasingly punitive tenor has actually been well received by the population at large. Based on attitudes during the election campaign in Hesse in 2008, when the conservative Roland Koch promoted a tough crime policy, it is more likely that the people are indeed sceptical and dismissive of an increasingly punitive tenor.

During the campaign, 'infratest dimap'[344] carried out a public opinion poll in Hesse. According to this analysis, people named faster and more effective court proceedings (92%) and support for children and adolescents (82%) as the most important methods to combat juvenile crime. So called 'Youth Camps' and tougher laws had the lowest results within the poll; however about 50% of the interviewees still considered these methods effective. The broad opinion (61%) seems to be that preventive sanctions are more likely to be successful than strong repressive penalties (25%).[345]

By contrast, an analysis of the criminology institute of Niedersachsen pointed out that the sanctions imposed are regarded as being too low. On a scale from 1 (far too low a penalty) to 7 (too high a penalty), people evaluated the sanctions at an average of 2.03. Sanctions for rape and sexual abuse were rated at 1.46, while theft related offences were rated at 2.95.[346]

The phenomenon that the population misjudges the increase/decrease of crime also holds true for Germany. According to one study, 90% of the population estimates that the crime rate in Germany rose at least marginally between 1993 and 2003, while 27% think there was a considerable rise. In reality, crime rates dropped by 2.6%.[347] Another study found that the population significantly overestimates the number of criminal offences committed by foreigners. The estimated rate was 37.3%,[348] while in reality it was only 22.5%.[349]

However, the general fear of crime seems to be decreasing. According to one study, while in 1994, 60% of the population was concerned about crime, in 2004 this number decreased to 42%.[350] Further, a public opinion poll that was conducted by the European Commission in 2008 points out that only 16% of Germans consider crime as one of the most important problems for the EU; this is lower than the

---

[344] 'Infratest dimap' is a highly-renowned German institute specialised in electoral and political research.
[345] All statistics taken from Schöneborn 2008.
[346] Windzio et al. 2007, p. 39.
[347] All statistics taken from Bundesinnenministerium & Bundesjustizministerium 2006, p. 493.
[348] Windzio et al. 2007, p. 37.
[349] Bundeskriminalamt 2005, p. 109.
[350] Bundesinnenministerium & Bundesjustizministerium 2006, p. 498.

European average (20%).[351] A different study reveals that the fear of becoming the victim of a crime is similarly decreasing.[352]

5.   Conclusions

It can be concluded that the German legal order has established defence rights to a point where Germany is in compliance with the ECHR in most cases. Occasional exceptions (leading to verdicts of the ECtHR against Germany) rather prove this rule, and are no indications of the overall deficiency of the German criminal justice system.

The German legal aid equivalent not only proves complex in theory, but also raises many administrative barriers in practice. Indigent defendants are effectively deterred from obtaining legal representation during the trial in cases of non-mandatory legal representation, because the German legal aid regime does not apply in those situations. For defence lawyers, obtaining remuneration under the German remuneration scheme is often lengthy and time consuming. Many defence lawyers consider – in our point of view at least partially correctly – the statutory remuneration to be inadequate, and while it can be argued that the remuneration of defence services at the trial stage is adequate, the same does not, in our opinion, hold true for defence services in the investigation phase, which we consider to be of supreme importance for an effective defence.

With regard to foreign nationals, courts tend to impose provisional detention more often than against German citizens, due to the alleged higher likelihood of flight.

The ethos of all criminal justice actors, and the changes that have taken place over recent years, creates challenges to the attitudes and practice of defence rights. Courts and/or judges have increasingly become used to (semi-)consensual 'deals', and consider previously 'normal' and active defence behaviour, for example, the bringing of motions to gather, produce, and introduce new evidence, as overly time consuming. One of the pressing challenges for the structure of the German criminal justice system therefore seems to be finding a new balance between the economic effectiveness of 'deals', and the right to a fair and unbiased trial.

Further, there is no comprehensive quality assurance (regular monitoring and assessment) of German defence lawyers, so that the quality of defence services (particularly where lawyers act as court appointed counsel on a regular basis, which in turn creates unhelpful dependencies), may vary.

The federal Constitutional setup of Germany impedes a uniform – let alone centralized – gathering of data and information, which in turn is a precondition for evidence based criminal policy making, as well for translational monitoring and evaluation regimes.

---

[351]   European Commission 2008.
[352]   Bundesinnenministerium & Bundesjustizministerium 2006, p. 519.

6.   Bibliography

Books

Beulke 2008
Beulke, W., *Strafprozessrecht*, Heidelberg: C.F. Müller, 2008.

Dahs 1999
Dahs, H., *Handbuch des Strafverteidigers*, Cologne: Verlag Dr. Otto Schmidt, 1999.

Kissel & Mayer 2008
Kissel, O. & Mayer, H., *Gerichtsverfassungsgesetz*, Munich: C.H. Beck, 2008.

Meyer-Goßner 2007
Meyer-Goßner, L., *Strafprozessordnung*, Munich: C.H. Beck, 2007.

Meyer-Goßner 2008
Meyer-Goßner, L., *Strafprozessordnung*, Munich: C.H. Beck, 2008.

Ostendorf 2007
Ostendorf, H., *Jugendstrafrecht*, Baden-Baden: Nomos, 2007.

Ranft 2005
Ranft, O., *Strafprozessrecht*, Stuttgart: Boorberg Verlag, 2005.

Streng 2008
Streng, F., *Jugendstrafrecht*, Heidelberg: C.F. Müller, 2008.

Volk 2008
Volk, K., *Grundkurs StPO*, Munich: C.H. Beck, 2008.

Chapters in Compilations

Diemer 2008
Diemer, H., '§ 185 GVG', in: R. Hannich (ed.), *Karlsruher Kommentar zur Strafprozessordnung*, Munich: C.H. Beck, 2008.

Frister 2006
Frister, H., '§ 187 GVG', in: W. Frisch, K. Rogall, H.-J. Rudolphi, E. Schlüchter, H. U. Paeffgen and J. Wolter (eds.), *Systematischer Kommentar zur Strafprozessordnung und zum Gerichtsverfassungsgesetz*, Munich: Luchterhand, October 2006.

Frister 2008

Frister, H., '§ 163a StPO', in: W. Frisch, K. Rogall, H.-J. Rudolphi, E. Schlüchter, H. U. Paeffgen and J. Wolter (eds.), *Systematischer Kommentar zur Strafprozessordnung und zum Gerichtsverfassungsgesetz*, Munich: Luchterhand, June 2008.

Gleß 2007a

Gleß, S., '§ 133 StPO', in: V. Erb , R. Esser, U. Franke, K. Graalmann-Scheerer, H. Hilger and A. Ignor (eds.), *Löwe-Rosenberg StPO. Die Strafprozessordnung und das Gerichtsverfassungsgesetz. Großkommentar*, Vol. 4, Berlin: De Gruyter, 2007.

Gleß 2007b

Gleß, S., '§ 136 StPO', in: V. Erb, R. Esser, U. Franke, K. Graalmann-Scheerer, H. Hilger and A. Ignor (eds.), *Löwe-Rosenberg StPO. Die Strafprozessordnung und das Gerichtsverfassungsgesetz. Großkommentar*, Vol. 4, Berlin: De Gruyter, 2007.

Gmel 2008a

Gmel, D., '§217 StPO', in: R. Hannich (ed.), *Karlsruher Kommentar zur Strafprozessordnung*, Munich: C.H. Beck, 2008.

Gmel 2008b

Gmel, D., '§ 213 StPO', in: R. Hannich (ed.), *Karlsruher Kommentar zur Strafprozessordnung*, Munich: C.H. Beck, 2008.

Gollwitzer 2001

Gollwitzer, W., '§ 267 StPO', in: V. Erb, R. Esser, U. Franke, K. Graalmann-Scheerer, H. Hilger and A. Ignor (eds.), *Löwe-Rosenberg StPO. Die Strafprozessordnung und das Gerichtsverfassungsgesetz. Großkommentar*, Vol. 4, Berlin: De Gruyter, 2001.

Graf 2008a

Graf, J.-P., '§ 116a StPO', in: R. Hannich (ed.), *Karlsruher Kommentar zur Strafprozessordnung*, Munich: C.H. Beck, 2008.

Graf 2008b

Graf, J.-P., '§ 112 StPO', in: R. Hannich (ed.), *Karlsruher Kommentar zur Strafprozessordnung*, Munich: C.H. Beck, 2008.

Griesbaum 2008

Griesbaum, R., '§ 163a StPO', in: R. Hannich (ed.), *Karlsruher Kommentar zur StPO*, Munich: C.H. Beck, 2008.

Hilger 2007a

Hilger, H., '§ 118a StPO', in: V. Erb, R. Esser, U. Franke, K. Graalmann-Scheerer, H. Hilger and A. Ignor (eds.), *Löwe-Rosenberg StPO. Die Strafprozessordnung und das Gerichtsverfassungsgesetz. Großkommentar*, Vol. 4, Berlin: De Gruyter, 2007.

Hilger 2007b

Hilger, H., '§ 116a StPO', in: V. Erb, R. Esser, U. Franke, K. Graalmann-Scheerer, H. Hilger and A. Ignor (eds.), *Löwe-Rosenberg StPO. Die Strafprozessordnung und das Gerichtsverfassungsgesetz. Großkommentar*, Vol. 4, Berlin: De Gruyter, 2007.

Huber 2008

Huber, B., 'Criminal Procedure in Germany', in: R. Vogler and B. Huber (eds.), *Criminal Procedure in Europe*, Berlin: Duncker & Humblot, 2008, p. 269-371.

Jarass 2009

Jarass, H., 'Art. 20 GG', in: H. Jarass and B. Pieroth, *Grundgesetz*, Munich: C.H. Beck, 2009.

Kleine-Cosack 2006

Kleine-Cosack, M., 'Berufsrechtliche Risiken', in: G. Widmaier (ed.), *Münchener Anwaltshandbuch Strafverteidigung*, Munich: C.H. Beck, 2006, p. 2078-2097.

Krehl 2001

Krehl, C., '§ 163a StPO', in: K.-P. Julius, B. Gercke, H.-J. Kurth, M. Lemke, H. Pollähne and E.C. Rautenberg (eds.), *Heidelberger Kommentar zur Strafprozessordnung*, Heidelberg: C. F. Müller, 2001.

Krekeler & Werner 2007

Krekeler, W. & Werner, E., '§ 147 StPO', in: W. Krekeler and M. Löffelmann (eds.), *Anwaltskommentar StPO*, Bonn: Deutscher Anwaltsverlag, 2007.

Neuhaus 2006

Neuhaus, R., 'Eigene Ermittlungen des Verteidigers', in: G. Widmaier (ed.), *Münchener Anwaltshandbuch Strafverteidigung*, Munich: C.H. Beck, 2006, p. 689-729.

Paeffgen 2007a

Paeffgen, H.-U., '§ 118a StPO', in: W. Frisch, K. Rogall, H.-J. Rudolphi, E. Schlüchter, H.U. Paeffgen and J. Wolter (eds.), *Systematischer Kommentar zur Strafprozessordnung und zum Gerichtsverfassungsgesetz*, Munich: Luchterhand, September 2007.

Paeffgen 2007b

Paeffgen, H.-U., '§ 116 StPO', in: W. Frisch, K. Rogall, H.-J. Rudolphi, E. Schlüchter, H.U. Paeffgen and J. Wolter (eds.), *Systematischer Kommentar zur Strafprozessordnung und zum Gerichtsverfassungsgesetz*, Munich: Luchterhand, September 2007.

Sachs 2009a

Sachs, M., 'Art. 20 GG', in: M. Sachs (ed.), *Grundgesetz Kommentar*, Munich: C.H. Beck, 2009.

Sachs 2009b

Sachs, M., 'Art. 19 GG', in: M. Sachs (ed.), *Grundgesetz Kommentar*, Munich: C.H. Beck, 2009.

Schädler 2008

Schädler, W., 'Art. 6 EMRK', in: R. Hannich (ed.), *Karlsruher Kommentar zur Strafprozessordnung*, Munich: C.H. Beck, 2008.

Schoreit 2008

Schoreit, A., '§ 261 StPO', in: R. Hannich (ed.), *Karlsruher Kommentar zur Strafprozessordnung*, Munich: C.H. Beck, 2008.

Stuckenberg 2008

Stuckenberg, C.-F., '§ 200 StPO', in: V. Erb , R. Esser, U. Franke, K. Graalmann-Scheerer, H. Hilger and A. Ignor (eds.), *Löwe-Rosenberg StPO. Die Strafprozessordnung und das Gerichtsverfassungsgesetz. Großkommentar*, Vol. 5, Berlin: De Gruyter, 2008.

Wohlers 2008a

Wohlers, W., '§ 163a StPO', in: W. Frisch, K. Rogall, H.-J. Rudolphi, E. Schlüchter, H.U. Paeffgen and J. Wolter (eds.), *Systematischer Kommentar zur Strafprozessordnung und zum Gerichtsverfassungsgesetz*, Munich: Luchterhand, June 2008.

Wohlers 2008b

Wohlers, W., '§ 147 StPO', in: W. Frisch, K. Rogall, H.-J. Rudolphi, E. Schlüchter, H.U. Paeffgen and J. Wolter (eds.), *Systematischer Kommentar zur Strafprozessordnung und zum Gerichtsverfassungsgesetz*, Munich: Luchterhand, June 2008.

Articles in Journals

Bleckmann 1995

Bleckmann, A., 'Verbotene Diskriminierung von EG-Ausländern bei der Untersuchungshaft', *Strafverteidiger*, 1995, p. 552-555.

Donath & Mehle 2009

Donath, A. & Mehle. B., 'Akteneinsichtsrecht und Unterrichtung des Mandanten durch den Verteidiger', *Neue Juristische Wochenschrift*, 2009, p. 1399-1400.

Gercke 2004

Gercke, B., 'Der Haftgrund der Fluchtgefahr bei EU-Bürgern', *Strafverteidiger*, 2004, p. 675-679.

Hilger 2005

Hilger, H., 'Anmerkung zu OLG Hamm', *Strafverteidiger*, 2005, p. 36-38.

Johnigk 2006
Johnigk, F., 'Verteidiger – nicht nur erster und zweiter, sondern auch dritter und vierter Klasse?', *Strafverteidiger*, 2006, p. 347-353.

Kiehl 1994
Kiehl, W., 'Neues Verwertungsverbot bei unverstandener Beschuldigtenbelehrung – und neue Tücken für die Verteidigung', *Neue Juristische Wochenschrift*, 1994, p. 1267-1268.

Mehle 2007
Mehle, B., 'Zeitpunkt und Umfang der Pflichtverteidigerbestellung', *Neue Juristische Wochenschrift*, 2007, p. 969-974.

Wächtler 2007
Wächtler, H., 'Informationsgewinnung durch die Verteidigung', *Strafverteidiger-Forum*, 2007, p. 141-148.

Wagner 1997
Wagner, H., 'Rechtliches Gehör im Ermittlungsverfahren', *Zeitschrift für die gesamte Strafrechtswissenschaft*, 1997, p. 545-592.

Official Sources

Bundesinnenministerium & Bundesjustizministerium 2006
Bundesinnenministerium and Bundesjustizministerium, Zweiter Periodischer Sicherheitsbericht, 2006, available online at <http://www.bmj.bund.de/enid/Kriminologie/Zweiter_Periodischer_Sicherheitsbericht_der_Bundesregierung_131.html> (last visited 09 October 2009).

Bundeskriminalamt 2005
Bundeskriminalamt, Polizeiliche Kriminalstatistik 2005, 2005, available online at <http://www.bka.de/pks/pks2005/index.html> (last visited 9 October 2009).

Bundeskriminalamt 2007
Bundeskriminalamt, Polizeiliche Kriminalstatistik 2007, 2007, available online at <http://www.bka.de/pks/pks2007/index.html> (last visited 09 October 2009).

European Commission 2008
European Commission, Eurobarometer 69 – Factsheet Germany, 2008, available online at <http://ec.europa.eu/public_opinion/archives/eb/eb69/eb69_sheet_de.pdf> (last visited 09 October 2009).

Statistisches Bundesamt 2006
Statistisches Bundesamt, Strafverfolgung – Fachserie 10 Reihe 3 – 2006, 2006, available online at <https://www-ec.destatis.de/csp/shop/sfg/bpm.html.cms.

cBroker.cls?cmspath=struktur,vollanzeige.csp&ID=1021380> (last visited 09 October 2009).

Statistisches Bundesamt 2007a
Statistisches Bundesamt, Bevölkerungsfortschreibung – Fachserie 1 Reihe 1.3 – 2007, 2007, available online at <https://www-ec.destatis.de/csp/shop/sfg/bpm.html.cms.cBroker.cls?cmspath=struktur,vollanzeige.csp&ID=1023172> (last visited 09 October 2009).

Statistisches Bundesamt 2007b
Statistisches Bundesamt, Bevölkerung mit Migrationshintergrund – Ergebnisse des Mikrozensus 2007 – Fachserie 1 Reihe 2.2 – 2007, 2007, available online at <https://www-ec.destatis.de/csp/shop/sfg/bpm.html.cms.cBroker.cls?cmspath=struktur,vollanzeige.csp&ID=1023127> (last visited 09 October 2009).

Statistisches Bundesamt 2008
Federal Office for Statistics (*Statistisches Bundesamt*), Ausländische Bevölkerung – Fachserie 1 Reihe 2 – 2008, 2008, available online at <https://www-ec.destatis.de/csp/shop/sfg/bpm.html.cms.cBroker.cls?cmspath=struktur,vollanzeige.csp&ID=1023732> (last visited 09 October 2009).

Other Sources

Schönenborn 2008
Schönenborn, J., *Lieber Vorbeugen als härter strafen*, 11.01.2008, available online at <http://www.tagesschau.de/inland/deutschlandtrend/deutschlandtrend90.html> (last visited 09 October 2009).

Windzio et al. 2007
Windzio, M., Simonson, J., Pfeiffer, C. & Kleimann, M., *Kriminalitätswahrnehmung und Punitivität in der Bevölkerung – Welche Rolle spielen die Massenmedien?*, Forschungsbericht No. 103 des Kriminologischen Forschungsinstituts Niedersachsen, 2007, available online at <http://www.kfn.de/versions/kfn/assets/fb103.pdf> (last visited 09 October 2009).

7.   Annex

Chart 1: Absolute number of recorded criminal offences	
Year	Number of criminal offences recorded
2004	6,663,156
2005	6,391,715
2006	6,304,223
2007	6,284,661

Chart 2: Recorded criminal offences per capita	
Year	Criminal offences per capita
2004	8,037.1 offences per 100,000 inhabitants
2005	7,747.4 offences per 100,000 inhabitants
2006	7,647.2 offences per 100,000 inhabitants
2007	7,634.9 offences per 100,000 inhabitants

Chart 3:
Incarceration rates

Year (as at 31 March of each year)	People in prison	People in preventive detention (Sicherungsverwahrung)
2004	63,372	305
2005	63,183	350
2006	64,137	375
2007	64,273	427
2008	61,900	448

Chart 4:
State spending on legal aid

Baden-Württemberg, Budget 2007/2008, sect. 0503, p. 39: 18,100,000 € (based on court appointed counsel as at 2007); spending per inhabitant: 1.68 €

Bavaria, Budget 2007/2008, sect. 0404, p. 40: 18,000,000 € (2007); spending per inhabitant: 1.44 €

Berlin: no particularized data available

Brandenburg, Budget 2007, sect. 04 040, p. 63: 6,600,000 € (2007); spending per inhabitant: 2.60 €

Bremen: no particularized data available

Hamburg: no particularized data available

Hesse: no particularized data available

Lower Saxony, Budget 2008, sect. 1116-1118, p. 86, 96, 104: 59,500,000 € (2007); spending per inhabitant: 7.47 €

Mecklenburg-Western Pomerania, Budget 2006/2007, sect. 0902, p. 40: 4,500,000 € (2007); spending per inhabitant: 2.68 €

North Rhine-Westphalia, Budget 2007, sect. 04.210, p. 73: 44,787,000 € (2007); spending per inhabitant: 2.49 €

Rhineland-Palatinate, Budget 2007/2008, sect. 05 03, p. 50: 8,970,000 € (court appointed counsel and legal advisers 2007); spending per inhabitant: 2.22 €
Saarland, Budget 2007, sect. 05 60, p. 117: 2,300,000 € (2007); spending per inhabitant: 2.22 €
Saxony, Budget 2007/2008, sect. 06 04, p. 65: 8,279,500 € (2007); spending per inhabitant: 1.96 €
Saxony-Anhalt, Budget 2007, sect. 11 04, p. 42: 18,276,500 € (2007); spending per inhabitant: 7.58 €
Schleswig-Holstein, Budget 2007/2008, sect. 09 02, p. 28: 4,450,000 € (2007); spending per inhabitant: 1.57 €
Thuringia, Budget 2006/2007, sect. 05 04, p. 50: 3,500,000 € (2007); spending per inhabitant: 1.53 €

Chart 5:
Field research

# of interview	date of interview	professional experience, status and role of interviewee	interviewer(s)
1	03/04/2009	defence lawyer, member of the committee for penal law of the Federal Bar Association and member of the European Criminal Bar Association	Christoph Burchard, Nathalie Kotzurek
2	03/04/2009	defence lawyer	Christoph Burchard, Nathalie Kotzurek
3	03/04/2009	defence lawyer	Christoph Burchard, Nathalie Kotzurek
4	07/04/2009	federal judge	Christoph Burchard, Friedrich Kern
5	15/04/2009	defence lawyer	Dominik Brodowski, Nathalie Kotzurek
6	15/04/2009	federal prosecutor	Dominik Brodowski, Nathalie Kotzurek
7	14/05/2009	defence lawyer, member of the board of a regional bar association	Karen Häußer, Nathalie Kotzurek
8	14/05/2009	defence lawyer	Nathalie Kotzurek,

			Jochen Rauber
09	05/06/2009	defence lawyer	Nathalie Kotzurek, Sebastian Ritter
10	15/06/2009	state prosecutor	Friedrich Kern, Nathalie Kotzurek
11	15/06/2009	state prosecutor	Friedrich Kern, Nathalie Kotzurek
12	19/06/2009	state judge	Friedrich Kern, Nathalie Kotzurek
13	03/11/2009	defence lawyer	Christoph Burchard

8. Abbreviations and Translations

Courts	
FCC	Federal Constitutional Court (Bundesverfassungsgericht)
FHCJ	Federal High Court of Justice (Bundesgerichtshof)
HRC	Higher Regional Court (Oberlandesgericht)
RC	Regional Court (Landgericht)
DC	District Court (Amtsgericht)
Reports	
BGHSt	Entscheidungen des Bundesgerichtshofs in Strafsachen (Official Reports of the Federal High Court of Justice)
BVerfGE	Entscheidungen des Bundesverfassungsgerichts (Official Reports of the Federal Constitutional Court)
VRS	Verkehrsrechtssammlung
Journals	
MDR	Monatsschrift für deutsches Recht
NJW	Neue Juristische Wochenschrift
NStZ	Neue Zeitschrift für Strafrecht
NStZ-RR	Neue Zeitschrift für Strafrecht – Rechtsprechungs-

	Report
StraFo	Strafverteidiger-Forum
StV	Strafverteidiger
ZStW	Zeitschrift für die gesamte Strafrechtswissenschaft
Acts and Statutes	
ALAR	Act on Legal Advice and Representation for Indigent Citizens (Gesetz über Rechtsberatung und Vertretung für Bürger mit geringem Einkommen)
AOJ	Act on the Organization of the Judiciary (Gerichtsverfassungsgesetz – GVG)
CCP	Code on Criminal Procedure (Strafprozessordnung – StPO)
CCivP	Code on Civil Procedure (Zivilprozessordnung – ZPO)
CICCA	Cost Index of the Court Cost Act (Kostenverzeichnis-Gerichtskostengesetz – KvGKG)
FLA	Federal Lawyers' Act (Bundesrechtsanwaltsordnung – BRAO)
GC	German Constitution (Grundgesetz – GG)
GCC	German Criminal Code (Strafgesetzbuch – StGB)
JCA	Juvenile Court Act (Jugendgerichtsgesetz – JGG)
LRA	Lawyers' Remuneration Act (Rechtsanwaltsvergütungsgesetz – RVG)
LRI	Lawyers' Remuneration Index (Vergütungsverzeichnis)

RPCASM	Rules for Proceedings in Criminal and Administrative Sanctioning Matters (Richtlinien für das Straf- und Bußgeldverfahren – RiStBV)
RPD	Regulations of Provisional Detention (Untersuchungshaftvollzugsordnung – UVollzO)
SLA	Specialised Lawyers' Act (Fachanwaltsordnung)
Authorities	
Bundesinnenministerium	Federal Department of the Interior
Bundesjustizministerium	Federal Department of Justice
Bundeskriminalamt	Federal Criminal Police Office
Statistisches Bundesamt	Federal Office for Statistics

András Kádár

CHAPTER 8 HUNGARY[*]

1. Introduction

1.1. General data

The Republic of Hungary is a Central European Parliamentary democracy with a territory of 93,000 km[2] and a population of 10,045,400.[1]

The country is characterised by an uneven distribution of population and resources and is divided into 19 administrative units (counties) plus the capital, Budapest, which has over 1.7 million inhabitants[2] and is the country's hub for commerce, culture and transportation.[3]

The country's overall average per capita GDP is approximately 10,000 Euro. In Budapest however, it exceeds 21,000 Euro, whereas in the poorest county, it is less than 5,000 Euro.[4] Economic differences are significant between the two halves of Hungary, with higher wages and less unemployment in the country's central and western parts.[5]

Most residents (over 90%) regard themselves as Hungarian,[6] but national and ethnic minorities also live in Hungary. Their collective rights are regulated in a separate Act of Parliament[7] enumerating 13 officially acknowledged minorities, most of which are minority groups from neighbouring countries: Slovaks, Romanians, Serbs, etc.

---

[*] This country report has been reviewed by Károly Bárd, professor at the Central European University in Budapest.

[1] <http://portal.ksh.hu/pls/ksh/docs/hun/xstadat/xstadat_eves/tabl1_01ib.html>.

[2] <http://portal.ksh.hu/pls/ksh/docs/hun/xstadat/xstadat_eves/tabl1_02i.html>.

[3] By comparison; the country's second largest city, Debrecen, has a population of approximately 200,000. <http://portal.debrecen.hu/gazdasag/koncepciok/varosfejlesztesi/varosfejlesztes2007_ koncepciok.html?page=6>.

[4] <http://portal.ksh.hu/pls/ksh/docs/hun/xstadat/xstadat_eves/tabl6_03_01_02i.html>.

[5] <http://www.nepszamlalas.hu/hun/kotetek/09/09_1_osszef.pdf>.

[6] <http://www.nepszamlalas.hu/hun/kotetek/04/tabhun/tabl01/load01.html>.

[7] Act LXXVII of 1993 on the Rights of National and Ethnic Minorities.

According to the 2001 census, the Roma constitute the largest ethnic minority in Hungary, with a population of over 190,000.[8] However, according to reliable research results, the actual number of Roma people is higher; at around 620,000.[9]

The Roma constitute Hungary's most vulnerable and marginalised social group. High unemployment rates and widespread discrimination of the Roma in all areas of social life are confirmed by a number of sociological studies, the reports of domestic and international human rights NGO's,[10] the Parliamentary Commissioner for the Rights of National and Ethnic Minorities[11] and international organizations.[12] The Roma are also significantly over-represented in Hungarian penitentiary institutions.

1.2. Outline of the legal system

The Hungarian legal system is a continental legal system, following primarily German legal traditions and governed by a strict statutory hierarchy.

The most important principles are laid down by the Constitution and the constitutional rules are expanded by laws. Detailed regulation is provided by governmental and ministerial decrees. The coherence of the system is guarded by the Constitutional Court, which may annul any statute that is in conflict with the Constitution.

The legal system is structured into various legal fields (criminal law, civil law, labour law, administrative law, etc), with most fields having their own procedural codes.

The judicial system has four levels: local courts, county courts, five regional appellate courts and the Supreme Court. Labour related issues are adjudicated by labour courts which are organised separately in each county and in Budapest. There are no separate military or juvenile courts, but military offences and offences committed by juveniles are adjudicated by specially designated panels (within the general structure).

In most cases, the appeals system consists of two levels (first instance and appeal level); however in criminal law, under certain conditions an ordinary appeal against the second instance decision is also possible. Extraordinary remedies (such as re-trial and review by the Supreme Court) are also available.

---

[8]   <http://www.nepszamlalas.hu/hun/kotetek/04/tabhun/tabl05/load05.html>. In this census, the question regarding minority affiliation was answered on a voluntary basis.

[9]   László Hablicsek: Kísérleti számítások a roma lakosság területi jellemzőinek alakulására és 2021-ig történő előrebecslésére. Demográfia. - 50. évf. (2007) 1. sz., p. 7-54. See <http://www.demografia.hu/Demografia/2007_1/Hablicsek4.pdf>.

[10] See, for example; <www.neki.hu>.

[11] See the Minorities Ombudsman's annual reports: <http://www.kisebbsegiombudsman.hu/kateg-292-1-beszamolok.html>.

[12] See, for example, the Third Report on Hungary by the European Commission against Racism and Intolerance: <http://www.coe.int/t/dghl/monitoring/ecri/Country-by-country/Hungary/ HUN-CbC-III-2004-25-ENG.pdf>.

1.3.   Outline of the criminal justice system

Criminal law is governed by two important laws: Act IV of 1978 on the Penal Code (Criminal Code) and Act XIX of 1998 on Criminal Procedure (CCP),which has been in force since 1 July 2003.

A criminal offence is an intentional or, if the law expressly renders it punishable, unintentional act that poses a threat to society and is rendered punishable by the Criminal Code.[13] A criminal offence is either a felony or a misdemeanour. A felony is a criminal offence perpetrated intentionally and punishable by imprisonment of two or more years. Every other criminal offence is a misdemeanour.[14]

The possible sanctions are divided into principal and supplementary punishments and measures. The principal punishments are (i) imprisonment; (ii) public labour; and (iii) a fine. Supplementary punishments include (i) a ban from participating in public affairs; (ii) a ban from carrying on a profession; (iii) a ban from driving a motor vehicle (iv) local banishment;[15] (v) expulsion;[16] (vi) a supplementary fine (accompanying imprisonment). Imprisonment may be imposed for a definite period of time (not exceeding 20 years), or for life. In the latter case, it may be a life sentence with or without the possibility of parole.

Measures include (i) a warning; (ii) probation; (iii) compulsory psychiatric treatment; (iv) compulsory treatment for alcohol addicts; (v) confiscation of objects; (vi) confiscation of assets; (vi) supervision by probation officer or (vii) measures applicable *vis a vis* a legal person.

The investigative phase of Hungarian criminal procedure is predominantly inquisitorial with elements of the adversarial system,[17] while the court phase is mainly adversarial with certain inquisitorial elements.[18]

The criminal procedure has four phases: the investigation, the prosecutorial phase, the court phase and where the defendant is convicted the implementation phase.

The investigation[19] is aimed at establishing the facts of the case to the extent that the prosecutor can decide whether the conditions for the indictment exist.

The investigation is carried out by the prosecutor, or the investigating authority which will, in the majority of cases, be the police, upon the order of the prosecutor or independently. The investigating authority conducts the investigation independently, if (i) it detected the offence itself; (ii) the report on the offence was

---

[13]   Criminal Code 10.
[14]   Criminal Code 11. This distinction formerly had implications regarding the procedural rules (the procedure for deciding on misdemeanours was simplified in a number of ways). Today, the procedure is unified regardless of the type of offence, but the difference between misdemeanours and felonies still has some implications, for example, in relation to the strictness of the regime in which the imprisonment imposed for the offence is to be served.
[15]   A Hungarian citizen may be banned from entering a certain administrative area.
[16]   Only in the case of a foreign citizen.
[17]   For example, defence counsel's right to be present during certain investigative acts.
[18]   Such as the Judge's discretion as to what evidentiary motions of the parties the court shall accept.
[19]   CCP 164-199.

submitted to it; or (iii) the prosecutor gave it the responsibility for the investigation. In practice, investigation by the prosecutor is rare, although certain types of offences (for example, offences committed against/by police officers) may only be investigated by the prosecutor. The investigation of cases of grave importance is sometimes taken over by the prosecution. However, the majority of the cases are investigated by the police upon prosecutorial order or independently. Even in the case of independent investigations, the prosecutor supervises the legality of the investigation and is authorised to instruct the investigating authorities.[20]

The investigation must be concluded within two months following its order or launch. The deadline of the investigation may be extended, but if the investigation is conducted against a specific person, any extension may not be longer than two years following the first interrogation of the suspect.

Prosecutorial phase: the prosecutor shall examine the files of the case and may perform, or order the performance of further investigative measures, or may suspend or terminate the investigation. If there is no ground for these measures, the prosecutor may file an indictment and press charges against the defendant, or make a decision on the partial omission or, under certain circumstances, the postponement of an indictment.

Judicial phase:[21] in first instance proceedings, the court obtains evidence. The basis of this activity is the bill of indictment (which lists all the evidence upon which the accusation is built). However, the prosecutor, the defendant, defence counsel, the victim, and certain other actors (for example persons having a civil claim in relation to the offence) may, throughout the whole phase, make motions for obtaining further evidence (for example hearing witnesses who were not heard during the investigation) and observations. The necessary evidentiary actions and the order thereof will be decided by the presiding judge. If the presiding judge deems the hearing of a witness motioned by the defence to be unnecessary, he/she can dismiss the motion, although this decision may be challenged in any appeal against the decision on the merits of the case.

As a result of the immediacy principle, all evidentiary acts performed during the investigations shall be repeated in the judicial phase (for example a witness who is heard during the investigation and whose testimony serves as the basis of the accusation must also be heard by the judge in person) subject to certain exceptions (for example if the witness cannot be heard for some reason in the court phase, his/her earlier testimony may be read out).

---

[20] The prosecution has various powers in relation to the supervision of the legality of independent investigations. Under art. 28 of the CCP, he/she, among others, (i) may instruct the investigating authority to perform certain investigatory acts, to carry on with an investigation or to accomplish the investigation within a certain time period; (ii) may be present at investigatory acts, may inspect the case files or may order the investigating authority to send in certain documents; (iii) may amend the decisions of the investigating authority and decide on any complaints submitted against the decisions and actions of the investigating authority; (iv) may reject a report filed with the investigating authority; may terminate the investigation, or order the investigating authority to terminate the investigation; or (v) may take over any investigation at any phase.

[21] CCP 281-344.

Up until the close of the trial, the prosecutor may drop the charges. After the evidentiary procedure is concluded, the prosecutor and defence counsel shall deliver their closing speeches. The defendant has the right to the last word. After the closings, the judges hold a panel meeting in order to reach a decision, which is, as a general rule, announced in public without delay. After the announcement, those who are entitled to appeal may exercise their right. After the communication of the appeals,[22] the trial is closed.

The court delivers a decision on the charges, either convicting or acquitting the accused. The court shall convict the accused, if it ascertains beyond reasonable doubt that the accused committed a criminal offence and may be punished.[23] The court shall acquit the accused, if the guilt of the accused cannot be ascertained beyond reasonable doubt and the procedure has not already been terminated.[24]

Second instance proceedings:[25] an appeal may be lodged against the first instance court decision by both the prosecutor and the defence on legal or factual ground. The appellate court is bound to decide on the basis of the facts of the case as established by the first instance court, unless the first instance judgement is not properly substantiated, or the appeal states new facts or refers to new evidence. In the course of the procedure of the appellate court, the taking of evidence is restricted. The appellate court may convict a defendant who has been acquitted by the first instance court only where the prosecutor requests this in his/her appeal.

Furthermore, in the absence of the prosecutor's appeal requesting a heavier punishment, the appellate court may not increase the first instance sentence. The appellate court can uphold, alter or quash the judgement of the court of first instance (and in the latter case, shall order the first instance court to conduct a new proceeding).

Third instance proceedings:[26] appeals may be submitted to the third instance court, if the court of second instance violated the provisions of criminal law and resulting in a defendant, who was acquitted in the first instance, being convicted in the second instance, or the other way round. There is no opportunity for taking evidence in the third instance proceedings. Instead, the third instance court decides on the basis of the facts as established by the court of second instance. The court of third instance can uphold, alter or quash the judgement of the court of second instance.

---

[22] As provided by art. 325 (1) of CCP, once the decision is announced, appeals shall either be lodged immediately, or a three-day deadline may be requested. If the decision is delivered by post, appeals may be lodged within eight days of receipt.

[23] Assuming that he/she does not fall under one of the provisions excluding liability, for example, because of his/her mental condition.

[24] The court shall terminate the procedure in certain cases, for example, due to the defendant's death; in case of statutory limitation; lack of legally required private motion, complaint or request; or if the prosecutor has dropped the charge and a substitute private accusation cannot be applied.

[25] CCP 345-384.

[26] CCP 385-399.

Extraordinary remedies against final and binding judgements include the reopening of a case, re-trial[27] and review by the Supreme Court.[28] A re-trial to the onus of the defendant (i.e. requesting the punishment of a previously acquitted defendant, or requesting conviction for a more severe offence than originally established, or requesting a heavier sentence than originally imposed) is only possible within the statute of limitations, whereas a motion for review by the Supreme Court to the onus of the defendant may only be submitted within six months of the final and binding decision. There is no deadline for a re-trial or Supreme Court review to the benefit of the defendant.

There are certain *special proceedings* in the Hungarian system. In case of an *expedited hearing*,[29] the prosecutor may, without a formal indictment, decide to take the defendant to court in an expedited hearing within 15 days of the commission of the criminal offence, if the criminal offence in question is punishable with a maximum of eight years' imprisonment, the case is simple, the evidence is at hand and the defendant was caught in the act or has admitted to the commission of the criminal offence. In such cases, the prosecutor shall arrange for the suspect to retain counsel. If the suspect has no defence counsel, the prosecutor shall appoint one. The prosecutor and counsel's presence at the trial is mandatory. The rationale behind this proceeding is that the particular circumstances of a case may make it possible to reach a decision without going through the normal process. There are no particular incentives for the defendant to opt for this possibility. In fact, the decision is made by the prosecutor alone and is not dependent upon the defendant's approval or consent.

In cases of the waiver of trial,[30] the maximum sanction that can be imposed on the perpetrator is significantly lower than that applicable in a normal procedure. The defendant has to make a well informed decision on whether he/she requests a waiver. If this is done and the prosecutor accepts the request, a public session is held by the court. Defence counsel is mandatory in such proceedings, so unless the defendant has already a counsel, the prosecutor shall appoint one for the defendant. At the session, the defendant shall reiterate the wish to waive the right to trial and plead guilty. If this is not done, or if there is any obstacle to adjudicating the case in this manner, the court shall refer the case to a normal trial.

While, in the case of a waiver of trial, the defendant is actually heard by the court at the public session, in a fast track procedure,[31] upon the motion of the prosecutor the court may sentence the defendant, without hearing him/her, to a suspended imprisonment, fine, or certain supplementary sanctions, or may apply the measures listed in the Criminal Code (see above). The possibility of a fast track

[27] For example, based on evidence revealed after the decision became final and binding (CCP 408-415).
[28] If, for example, the criminal liability of the defendant was established in violation of substantive law; an unlawful punishment was imposed due to the unlawful classification of the offence, or the violation of other rules of criminal law; or the court infringed one of the fundamental provisions of the CCP (CCP 416-429).
[29] CCP 516-525.
[30] CCP 533-542.
[31] CCP 543-550.

procedure is available if the criminal offence is punishable by a maximum of three years' imprisonment, and (i) the law allows for these sanctions in relation to the given offence; (ii) the facts of the case are simple; (iii) the accused has confessed to the offence; and (iv) the objective of the punishment can be achieved without a trial. Imprisonment exceeding one year may not be imposed in a fast track procedure (in fact, only suspended imprisonment may be imposed). The ruling is not subject to an appeal; instead, upon the request of the participants in the proceeding, the court shall hold a trial.

1.4. Basic statistics of the criminal justice system

Number of reported crimes and identified offenders 2004 – 2007[32]

Year	Number of reported offences	Percentage of solved cases	Number of identified perpetrators
2004	418,883	57	130,182
2005	436,522	61	133,790
2006	425,941	61	124,171
2007	426,914	59	116,161
2008	408 407	59	116 584[33]

Number of indicted and convicted defendants who are given a custodial sentence[34]

Year	All indictments	Total number of defendants convicted[35]	Number of defendants sentenced to life-long imprisonment	Defendants sentenced to imprisonment for a definite period of time	
				Suspended	Executed
2006	102,946	97,302	17	19,399	8,740
2007	94,125	87,744	16	17,560	8,853

---

[32] <http://portal.ksh.hu/pls/ksh/docs/hun/xstadat/xstadat_eves/tabl2_08_02i.html>.

[33] No explanation has been provided by the Central Office for Statistics for the difference between the number of identified perpetrators compared to the number of solved cases (59 percent of 408,407, i.e. approximately 241,000). A possible explanation is that most identified perpetrators are responsible for more than one offence.

[34] Source: Unified Police and Prosecutors' Criminal Statistics (ERÜBS) and Prosecutors' Statistical Information, Database No. 1522.

[35] For a possible explanation of the high conviction rate, see Section 2.3.3.

Trends in the number of detainees[36]

	31 December 2005	31 December 2006	31 December 2007
Pre-trial detainees	3,981	3,786	3,822
Convicted persons	11,469	10,782	10,259
Other*	270	253	272
Total	15,720	14,821	14,353

* Compulsory psychiatric treatment, petty offence custody, etc.

Statistical data on special proceedings[37]

Year	Number of defendants whose case was adjudicated by a binding decision	Out of which					
		Expedited hearing		Fast track procedure		Waiver of trial in cases where first instance decision has been delivered	
		Number of defendants	Proportion (%)	Number of defendants	Proportion (%)	Number of defendants	Proportion (%)
2006	102,946	8,226	7.99	30,500	29.63	477	0.46
2007	94,125	7,011	7.45	27,344	29.05	439	0.47

1.5. Outline of the legal aid system

Hungary does not have a unified legal aid system. In the field of civil law, legal aid is provided through the Legal Aid Service[38] and is available for extra- and pre-judicial matters, as well as court proceedings. The same mechanism provides legal aid for indigent participants in criminal proceedings, with the exception of defendants (the victim, the private prosecutor and the supplementary private prosecutor, etc).

Legal aid is available for indigent defendants at all stages of the criminal process, through the *ex officio* appointment of private lawyers as defence counsel. This is not done by the Legal Aid Service, but by the investigating authority, prosecutor or court conducting the actual phase of the proceeding. Lawyers are selected from a list compiled by regional bar associations, but the appointing authorities are completely free in making their choice. This is characterised by a complete lack of unified management: since the payments are also made by the appointing authorities, it is not possible to acquire exact data about the average total annual amounts spent on criminal legal aid. The numbers should be collected from

[36] Source: Yearbook of the Hungarian Penitentiary Headquarters: 2005, 2006, 2007 (<www.bvop.hu>).
[37] Source: Unified Police and Prosecutors' Criminal Statistics (ERÜBS) and Prosecutors' Statistical Information.
[38] The service is set up under the Central Justice Office of the Ministry of Justice and Law Enforcement (see <http://www.kih.gov.hu/alaptev/nepugyvedje>).

three different sources (police, prosecution and courts) and attempts to do so have shown that most of these institutions do not keep separate records of the amounts they pay to the lawyers as legal aid fees and costs.[39]

In relation to eligibility, there is an overlap between legal aid for the indigent and appointment based on the principle of 'the interests of justice'. In general, it is irrelevant whether the defendant has no defence counsel either because he/she is indigent, or because he/she does not wish to retain defence counsel for any other reason. The basic principle is that, in the interests of justice, defence counsel should participate in the procedure in all cases where the defendant is for some reason 'vulnerable' (juveniles, detainees, foreigners, etc). In most cases, however, the reason why a defendant does not retain a lawyer is because he/she cannot afford it. However, if he/she belongs to one of the categories requiring mandatory defence, he/she does not have to go through an eligibility procedure, since a lawyer will be appointed anyway.

The only instance when the indigence of the defendant is taken into consideration is if he/she is eligible for personal cost exemption and requests that defence counsel be appointed. In this case, the state will cover the appointed defence counsel's fees and verified costs. In all other mandatory defence cases, these costs are only advanced by the state and must be repaid as part of the criminal costs if the defendant is found guilty.

Personal cost exemption may be granted to the defendant if (i) he/she lives together with other persons, and the per capita monthly income of the household does not exceed the legally required minimum old age pension (105 Euro); or (ii) he/she lives alone and his/her monthly income does not exceed an amount that is twice the minimum old age pension (210 Euro).[40]

2.   Legal rights and their implementation

2.1.   *The right to information*

2.1.1. Information on the nature and cause of the accusation

During the criminal proceedings, the defendant should receive information on the nature and cause of the accusation at various stages. If, based on the available data, a well grounded suspicion of a criminal offence arises with regard to a particular person, the prosecutor or investigating authority shall interrogate him/her. At the beginning of interrogation, the suspect shall be informed of the nature of the suspicion, as well as the essence of the legal regulations applicable to the offence ('communication of suspicion').[41]

This information is not prescribed as being very detailed. It is limited to a brief description of the facts underlying the allegation, and information on the relevant

---

[39]   Kádár, Tóth & Vavró 2007.
[40]   For details, see Section 2.2.
[41]   CCP 179 (1) and (2).

sections of the Criminal Code. Evidence supporting the allegation need not be presented.[42]

Any changes relating to the suspicion of a criminal offence shall also be communicated to the suspect as the investigation develops. If the reasonable suspicion alters, based on evidence obtained at later stages of the proceedings, this must be communicated at the first interrogation following the change in suspicion.[43]

The next phase when substantial information is provided is in the indictment. The bill of indictment (the document in which the prosecutor states the charges and lists the evidence) shall contain, *inter alia*, the following:

- a description of the act(s) constituting the offence for which charges are pressed;
- the article of the Criminal Code allegedly violated by the act;
- a list of persons to be summoned and notified;
- a list of the evidence to be considered by the court and an indication of which facts each piece of evidence substantiates (as will be outlined in Section 2.1.2, the defendant gets to see, for the first time, copies of the actual statements made by witnesses and other evidence after the conclusion of the investigation, when the investigating authority presents the complete case file to the defence. This takes place before the submission of the bill of indictment which therefore simply refers to what the prosecution regards as evidence supporting the charges and to the page numbers within the case file where this evidence can be found);
- a motion regarding the sequence of the evidentiary procedure.[44]

Finally, at the beginning of the trial, the presiding judge shall ask the defendant prior to his/her hearing whether he/she understands the charges and, if not, the judge shall explain the accusation.[45]

Whereas the communication of suspicion is almost always carried out properly, two practical problems should be highlighted. Under Act XXXIV of 1994 on the Police (Police Act), a person may be taken into 'short-term arrest' if he/she is caught in the act of committing a crime, or if he/she is 'suspected of having committed a crime'.[46] It is current police practice to question persons in short-term arrest without the formal commencement of the criminal proceedings. This practice[47] has no legal basis, but interviewed officers and attorneys have confirmed its existence.[48] As this informal questioning takes place before the beginning of a

---

[42]   Jakucs 2003, p. 363.
[43]   Order of the Chief Public Prosecutor No. 11/2003.
[44]   CCP 217.
[45]   CCP 288 (3).
[46]   Police Act 33 (1) (a) and (2) (b). The threshold of suspicion is lower than what is required in the CCP. A short-term arrest may not last longer than is 'necessary', but in any event shall not exceed eight or (in exceptional cases) 12 hours.
[47]   Termed 'elszámoltatás' calling somebody to account in police jargon.
[48]   For the purposes of this study, a set of interviews were conducted on the practical aspects and implementation of individual defence rights. Interviews were mostly conducted in Budapest. Altogether eight attorneys, five judges, two police officers and two prosecutors

→

criminal procedure, the police are not formally obliged to inform the arrested person about his/her rights as a suspect, or of the suspicion in the above form. Officers write a report on what the future suspect said, and the report is attached to the case file.[49]

However, information provided this way makes its way into the record of the formal interrogation, since if someone makes a confession while being 'called to account', he/she will usually be pressed quite easily to repeat it at the formal interrogation, particularly if defence counsel is not present at the first interrogation (see below).[50] If, on the other hand, there is a contradiction between the police report and the subsequent testimony of the defendant, the court is obliged to explore any reasons for this.[51]

Another problematic practice arises when prospective suspects are heard as witnesses. The CCP does not prescribe an obligation of the investigating authority to warn the witness that he/she may become a suspect (although the law poses the obligation on the investigating authority to warn a witness that he/she is not obliged to answer questions in relation to which he/she may accuse him/herself or his/her close relative with a criminal offence).[52] According to experienced defence counsel, investigating authorities do not provide information on what kind of offence they are investigating, but rather pose a series of questions, so that potential suspects are not informed about the nature and cause of the accusation.[53]

2.1.2. Detailed information concerning the relevant evidence/material available to the police/prosecutor

Joint Decree 23/2003 (VI. 24) of the Minister of Interior and the Minister of Justice on the Detailed Rules of Investigation Conducted by Organisations under the Minister of Interior (Investigation Decree) prescribes that the communication of suspicion at the first interrogation, shall be carried out such that the evidence on which the suspicion is based shall not be presented to the suspect.[54]

Until the closing of the investigation (when the investigating authority is satisfied that no further investigatory acts are needed and the case can be forwarded to the prosecution to make a decision on whether to drop the case or press charges), the defence is severely restricted in knowing the basis for the accusation since in the investigation phase access to documents is limited. The suspect and defence counsel have guaranteed access only to the expert opinions and minutes of those investigative acts where they can be present. In relation to other documents, they

---

were interviewed. The interviews were carried out in two stages, in May and September 2008.

[49] Interview with police officers.

[50] Interview with defence counsel.

[51] According to our judicial sources, it frequently happens that when heard as witnesses, the officers preparing the report do not remember the circumstances and simply say that they maintain what is included in the report, thus making it difficult for the Judge to solve the contradiction.

[52] CCP 88 (1) (b).

[53] Interview with defence counsel.

[54] Investigation Decree, 119 (1).

may be granted access only if this does not infringe upon the interests of the investigation.[55]

Since the CCP in practical terms restricts defence counsel's presence only to the interrogation of the suspect and the hearing of those witnesses whose interrogation was initiated either by him/her or the suspect,[56] this severely limits the defence's right to inspect documents, since practice shows that investigating authorities tend to reject all requests for inspection without considering the individual circumstances.[57] This is particularly problematic in relation to pre-trial detention, since evidence upon which the ordering and maintaining of detention is based, is also withheld from the defence.[58]

After the conclusion of the investigation, the investigating authority must present the complete case file to the defence. The suspect and counsel are allowed to inspect all documents[59] that may serve as the basis for indictment.[60] From this moment on, the defence has full access to the files.

2.1.3. Letter of rights (information on rights)

Defendants are entitled to be informed of their rights in the criminal procedure by the court, the prosecutor and the investigative authority.[61] The suspects/defendants must be informed of their rights, both in the investigation and the trial phases. This information is not expressly prescribed to be provided in writing, but written information can be acquired in at least two senses.

First, the required warnings are recorded in the minutes of different procedural acts and defendants are entitled to have copies of those minutes free of charge. Secondly, when the bill of indictment is delivered to them, defendants receive a written form from the court (form No. 220), which contains the most important rights and obligations, including the right to retain or ask for the appointment of a lawyer, the right to copies of the file and the right to ask for a personal cost exemption.[62]

At the commencement of the interrogation, the defendant/suspect must be advised that he/she is not under an obligation to testify, and that he/she may refuse to testify or respond to any question during the interrogation, but may freely decide to testify at any time, even if he/she has previously refused to do so. The defendant shall also be warned that anything he/she says or provides may be used as evidence. The warnings and the defendant's response shall be included in the records 'word-by-word'.[63] In the absence of such warnings, the testimony of the defendant may not be admitted as evidence.

---

[55]   CCP 186 (1).
[56]   CCP, 184 (2).
[57]   Interviews with counsels.
[58]   For more on the issue of pre-trial detention and the problems posed by the lack of access to evidence, see Section 2.3.1.
[59]   With certain very restricted exceptions, for example, data of protected witnesses.
[60]   CCP 193 (1).
[61]   CCP 43.
[62]   Interviews with Judges.
[63]   CCP 117 (2).

In the trial phase, the presiding judge shall advise the accused that he/she may pose questions to those questioned during the evidentiary procedures, and may also make motions and observations or raise objections. The accused must be warned that if he/she refuses to testify, the court shall be entitled to read aloud his/her previous testimony.[64] The defendant shall also be informed that he/she may communicate with defence counsel throughout the whole procedure, except that during his/her interrogation, this right can only be exercised with the presiding judge's prior approval.[65]

However, as experts[66] and practitioners suggest the communication of rights is in practice one of the main problematic areas of the Hungarian criminal procedure system. Reading out the text of the relevant law does not necessarily enhance the suspect's awareness of his/her rights: when being read aloud the long and complex text of the law, even educated persons may have difficulties to fully understand what they are entitled/obliged to do. In the case of uneducated defendants, without some additional explanation, the mandatory warnings almost certainly fail to achieve their intended purpose.

Counsel say that, while in the investigation phase additional explanation is rarely provided, in the court phase it depends on the individual judge: some judges go to great lengths to help the defendant understand the warnings, while others simply read out the law. One judge confirmed that, even when the records of the interrogation conducted during the investigation show that the warnings were read out, it is sometimes necessary to obtain further evidence (for example summoning the police officer who conducted the interrogation of the suspect) in order to ensure that the defendant was properly informed.[67]

A number of practitioners pointed out that, if defendants are properly prepared and aided by their lawyers, they obviously have less difficulty in understanding their rights and obligations. Since there are severe problems with the quality of performance of many legal aid lawyers, this is an issue where indigent defendants are in a disadvantaged situation, compared to those who can afford to retain a lawyer.

2.2.   The right to defence

Suspects/defendants are entitled to defend themselves and may also be defended by defence counsel at any phase of the proceedings, including the investigation.[68] The court, the prosecutor and the investigating authority shall ensure that the person against whom criminal proceedings are conducted is able defend him/herself. Due to the numerous cases of mandatory defence (described in detail below), the right to defend oneself often does not include the defendant's right to choose to go through the process without a counsel; however, the rights of the

---

[64]   CCP 289 (2).
[65]   CCP 289 (3).
[66]   See, for example, Fázsi 2008.
[67]   Interview with Judges.
[68]   CCP 5.

defendant and of counsel (for example, the right to appeal or motion witnesses, etc) are independent of each other.

2.2.1. Choice of lawyer and provision of a lawyer for the indigent defendant

Immediately after the suspicion is communicated, the defendant must be informed of his/her right to choose a defence counsel or to request the appointment of one. If the person to whom the suspicion is to be communicated is detained (for example, under a short-term arrest), this information shall be provided before the first interrogation, i.e. before the person formally becomes a suspect.[69] If the participation of defence counsel is mandatory in the procedure, the defendant has to be informed that, unless he/she retains a defence counsel within three days, the prosecutor or the investigating authority will appoint one for him/her. If the defendant declares that he/she does not wish to retain a defence counsel, the prosecutor or the investigating authority will appoint one immediately.[70] Under the Investigation Decree, the defendant's statement concerning his/her wish to retain counsel (or request for the appointment of counsel) shall be recorded in the minutes.[71]

The CCP differentiates between the investigation and the judicial stages as regards the cases and content of mandatory defence. The participation of defence counsel is mandatory in the investigation stage (i) if the criminal offence the defendant is suspected or accused of is punishable by imprisonment of five years or more; or if the defendant is (ii) detained; (iii) deaf, blind or suffering from a mental disorder; (iv) unfamiliar with the Hungarian language; (v) unable to defend him/herself in person for any other reason;[72] (vi) a juvenile;[73] or (vii) benefiting from personal cost exemption and requests defence counsel to be appointed.[74]

The scenarios of mandatory defence are wider in the judicial phase. In addition to the grounds listed above, defence is mandatory if (i) the case is before the county court acting as a court of first instance; (ii) if a supplementary private prosecutor presses charges;[75] or (iii) if the prosecutor attends the hearing and the defendant, who had not previously retained a defence counsel, requests the appointment of a defence counsel.[76] If the prosecutor attends the hearing, the presiding judge may appoint a defence counsel at his/her discretion, if he/she deems the participation of counsel as necessary for any reason.[77] Defence is also

---

[69]   Investigation Decree 6.
[70]   CCP 179 (3).
[71]   Investigation Decree 5.
[72]   CCP 46.
[73]   CCP 450.
[74]   CCP 48 (2) 74 (3) (a).
[75]   CCP 242 (1). The supplementary prosecutor must always be represented by a qualified lawyer. It is therefore the equality of arms principle that makes defence mandatory in this case.
[76]   CCP 242 (2).
[77]   CCP 242 (2).

mandatory in certain special procedures, such as expedited hearing,[78] as well as procedures carried out *in absentia*.[79]

Furthermore, the appointing authority may consider whether the principle of a fair trial requires the appointment of defence counsel: the court, the prosecutor or the investigating authority may appoint defence counsel at the defendant's request or *ex officio*, if this is necessary in the interests of the defendant.[80]

Due to the wide range of situations requiring mandatory defences, relatively few defendants are without counsel (this is true for both the investigation and the court phases). Over 70% of defendants were represented by counsel in both 2006 and 2007.[81]

2.2.2. Arrangements for access to lawyers

First of all, it should be noted that the mandatory nature of defence does not require the presence of defence counsel at individual procedural actions in the investigation stage. Thus, if the notified counsel fails to show up for any reason, it will not prevent the investigative authority from interrogating the defendant. The situation is different in the judicial phase: if defence is mandatory, no hearings may be held without the presence of defence counsel.

In relation to the issue of access to a lawyer, there is a difference between retained and appointed lawyers.

In response to numerous complaints concerning this issue, the Investigation Decree was amended as of 1 June 2007, to prescribe that, if the suspect's detention is ordered, it is guaranteed that he/she can retain a lawyer prior to the first interrogation.[82] Furthermore, if the suspect claims before the interrogation that he/she has retained counsel, and requests that he/she be notified, the investigating authority shall notify the counsel about the interrogation by fax, e-mail, or if this is not possible, by telephone.[83] This, however, still may not mean that counsel actually has the chance to be present, because there is no obligation of the investigating authority to actually wait for him/her, although under the Investigation Decree, with the exception of urgent investigative acts, counsel must be notified in due course, at least 24 hours before all investigative acts that he/she may attend.[84]

If, however, the notified counsel fails to show up, this has to be communicated to the suspect, as well as the fact that the absence of counsel does not prevent the interrogation from taking place. The facts concerning the notification, presence or absence of counsel shall be recorded in the minutes of the interrogation.[85]

When asked about the actual practice, defence counsel have said that those suspects who (usually from an earlier case) already have contacts with a lawyer, are

---

[78] CCP 518.
[79] CCP 527.
[80] CCP 48 (3).
[81] Source: National Justice Council.
[82] Investigation Decree 6.
[83] Investigation Decree 9 (1).
[84] Investigation Decree 9 (2).
[85] Investigation Decree 9 (3)–(4).

in a relatively good position. If this is the case, the investigating authority usually attempts to contact the lawyer, although the notice given is often very short, not to mention instances when a fax or e-mail is sent to the lawyer's office late at night, when the chances of the lawyer receiving notification is practically non-existent. If the suspect cannot immediately name a lawyer, he/she will not be allowed to call relatives or acquaintances to inquire about one. In such cases, the interrogation is conducted and only afterwards does the suspect have the chance to try to arrange the retainer.[86]

The situation regarding appointed counsel is even more problematic. The decision on whom to appoint is made by the appointing authority (the investigating authority at the beginning of the procedure).[87] This cannot in any way be influenced by the defendant. Under the Attorneys Act,[88] the competent bar association keeps a register of those attorneys who can be appointed as defence counsel. The authority conducting the procedure is completely free to choose from this list.

If defence is mandatory because the defendant is detained, defence counsel has to be appointed at the latest before the first interrogation.[89] Following the appointment, the defendant has to be informed of counsel's name.[90]

Practice shows that the majority of appointed counsel do not attend the first interrogation (and seldom appear at subsequent procedural acts as well). A survey carried out by the Crime Investigation Department of the National Police Headquarters, involving the 23 regional investigation units[91] of the National Police and based on targeted data collected during June and July 2006 (NPH survey),[92] showed that in 14 out of the 23 regional units, less than 50% of first interrogations were attended by the appointed counsel.

In one county, for example, only 4.54% of the first interrogations took place in the presence of the appointed counsel. There were also some counties with results either below or just over 10%. The average percentage for all 23 units was 34.9, meaning that overall almost two-thirds of indigent defendants faced their first interrogation without professional legal assistance.[93]

Similarly to the case of retained lawyers, this is partly due to late notification. The NPH survey provides convincing evidence on the issue. In one county, for example the average time between notification and the commencement of the interrogation was 30 minutes, which in most cases is obviously not sufficient for the lawyer to attend. In 16 counties, the notification was sent out on average only an hour before the scheduled time, although in 11 of these, if the lawyer indicates the intention to attend, the police are willing to reschedule the interrogation.[94] Obviously, if the notification is sent by fax and no attempt is made to reach counsel

86 Interviews with counsels.
87 CCP 48 (1).
88 Art. 35.
89 CCP 48 (1).
90 CCP 48 (1) and (8).
91 The county headquarters, the Budapest headquarters, the National Investigation Office, the Highway Police and the Airport Security Service.
92 The results of the survey are presented by Szabó & Szomor 2007, p. 19-41.
93 Szabó & Szomor 2007, p. 36.
94 Szabó & Szomor 2007, p. 35.

by phone (which is often the case), there is a good chance that counsel will not be informed about the interrogation in sufficient time to allow him/her to try to have it rescheduled.

2.2.3. The right to an independent and competent lawyer who is professionally required to act in the best interests of the client

The other reason for non-appearance relates to systemic problems in the Hungarian appointment system, which poses a threat to – at the very least – the perception of effective independence. In the investigation phase, defence counsel is selected by the investigating authority, which is not interested in efficient defence work. For the investigator, it is undoubtedly easier to deal with a defence counsel who is not too agile, who does not bombard him/her with questions, remarks and motions, or who may not even show up. In addition, it is difficult to trust counsel who was selected by the person who is in charge of the investigation against the defendant. It seems self-evident that the function of appointment should be placed with another organisation, or that the selection must be randomised, so that the investigating authority is not able to influence the result of the appointment.

In addition, there are some attorneys who base their law practice principally on appointments. Such lawyers may become financially dependent on the member of the police corps who takes decisions on appointments. According to the NPH survey, 'in Budapest 12 district police stations regularly appoint the same counsels, most of whom are retired lawyers not running separate offices any more.' There are certain counties where 'some lawyers [...] "reside" at police station and their practices are based on appointment'.[95] Dependence on appointments may obviously create a conflict of interest and is certainly capable of jeopardising the trust of the client.

Not only the rates of attendance, but also the quality of the work performed by appointed lawyers, is often criticised by practitioners. According to the NPH survey:

> the general experience [of the police] is [...] that the level of efficiency of appointed counsels is generally below that of retained counsels, and the work they perform is of poorer quality. Retained lawyers appear at procedural acts and put forth motions more frequently than their appointed colleagues.[96]

These findings substantiate the conclusions of a questionnaire based study involving 500 pre-trial detainees, carried out by the Hungarian Helsinki Committee in 2003, which revealed that defendants consider retained lawyers more active and effective than appointed counsels and have a strong mistrust *vis a vis* appointed lawyers.[97] Differences in the quality of the work of the two groups were confirmed by most, though not all, practitioners interviewed for the purposes of this study.[98]

---

[95] Szabó & Szomor 2007, p. 39.
[96] Szabó & Szomor 2007, p. 38.
[97] Kádár 2004, p. 138–142.
[98] Interview with practitioners.

Another specific problem related to the competence of acting lawyers concerns the trial phase. When participation of defence counsel is mandatory, the court hearing may not be held in the absence of such counsel. If the summoned counsel fails to appear, the judge may appoint another counsel. If this is not immediately possible, or the new counsel needs time to prepare for the defence, the hearing shall be postponed at the expense of the originally summoned counsel.[99]

If the case is simple, or if there are more defendants in the case and the specified session is not important from the point of view of the defendant whose counsel is not present, it often happens that the judge appoints a new counsel on the spot.[100] However, in cases of greater gravity and complexity, judges do not resort to this possibility, but rather postpone the hearing.

In the Budapest Bar Association, for example, trainee lawyers (lawyers with law degrees but who are undertaking their three year practice before taking a bar exam) take turns of duty, so that such immediate appointments are made possible. Thus, if a counsel fails to appear at a trial, the judge can call the bar association, and the trainee lawyers will immediately go to the court and provide defence services. Some judges have expressed their dissatisfaction with this form of substitution.[101] In their opinion, the trainee lawyers do not have the knowledge and experience that would enable them to provide effective defence under such circumstances.

It should be noted that, in the case of such appointments, even experienced counsel may have difficulties providing effective defence, as (due to the need to respect the trial schedule) the maximum time that substitute counsel have to study the case file is just 30 minutes.

Another problematic point is that, under the CCP, trainee lawyers[102] are entitled to provide defence in the local courts without limitations, although, theoretically, with the professional supervision of their principal, who is ultimately responsible for the trainee lawyer's performance. According to one police officer, the majority of cases in the investigation phase are handled by trainee lawyers, whereas a judge said that in approximately 50% of the cases, trainee lawyers substitute for their principals before the local courts. Some practitioners (particularly judges) regard this as very detrimental to the defendants, because defence may be provided by a completely inexperienced person. Interviewed counsel emphasised that, whether this is problematic depends on the trainee lawyer's individual qualities and commitment, as some trainees are in fact, more enthusiastic and knowledgeable than their principals.[103]

---

[99]   CCP 281 (3).

[100]   This is often a lawyer found in the canteen of the court. There is even a special jargon for this practice: 'grabbing someone in' (berántás).

[101]   Interview with Judges.

[102]   CCP 44 (5) Trainee lawyers are excluded from providing defence in proceedings conducted by the county courts, the appellate courts and the Supreme Court.

[103]   Interviews with practitioners.

2.2.4. The right to consult and communicate in private with the lawyer

In relation to the investigative phase, there is no express provision for the possibility of private consultation.[104] However, the experience of practicing lawyers shows that investigating police officers and prosecutors usually permit a maximum 30 minute consultation before the interrogation.[105]

Between the time of the formal procedural acts, contact with defence counsel for those in detention can be subject to a special restriction, namely that the number and duration of phone calls by the defendant can be significantly restricted by the internal regulations of the penitentiary institution. The Decree of the Minister of Justice 6/1996 (VII.12) on the Rules of the Implementation of Imprisonment and Pre-trial Detention provides that detainees may use the phone in accordance with the internal rules of the prison in which they are detained.[106] As a consequence, particular institutions severely limit the time that may be used for telephone consultation with the lawyer.

Pre-trial detainees are usually placed in prisons located in the relevant county capital, so the distance between a lawyer's law firm (if it is located in another part of the county) and the prison can be substantial, meaning that it may take an unreasonable amount of time for counsel to visit the client.[107] This often prevents contact between the appointed lawyers and their clients, as the time spent by lawyers travelling to the place of detention will not be paid for and the fee for consultation is extremely low (around 6 Euro per hour). Therefore, indigent detainees are often left without any substantial legal help while in pre-trial detention. Furthermore, in some penitentiaries, there is only one room for consultation, so it may happen that counsel travelling substantial distances and then waiting for hours may still have to leave without actually talking to his/her client.[108]

During court hearings, defendants have the right to consult with their defence counsel in private, without disturbing the orderliness of the hearing. While being questioned, the defendant can only exercise this right with the judge's prior permission.[109]

In practice, it is a problem that, due to the traditional arrangement of Hungarian court rooms, the defendant and counsel are separated (with the defence counsel located on the left side of the court room and the defendant sitting in the middle, facing the judge). In practice, therefore, they do not have the chance to talk to each other while the session is in progress.

---

[104] However, such a possibility may be inferred from the provision that suspects/defendants, at any stage of the procedure, are entitled to be granted sufficient time and opportunity to prepare for their defence (CCP 43 (2) (c)), and detained suspects/defendants shall be entitled to consult with their counsel orally and in writing without supervision (CCP 43 (3) (a)).

[105] Interviews with counsels.

[106] Art. 92.

[107] Defence counsel is not allowed to telephone their clients in the penitentiary institution.

[108] Bánáti 2005, p. 50-51.

[109] CCP 289 (3).

2.2.5. Special provisions for vulnerable suspects/defendants

There are special provisions for certain vulnerable groups, including juveniles, mentally vulnerable persons and people with disabilities and foreigners. For each of these groups, defence counsel is mandatory,[110] and additional safeguards are also in place, particularly with regard to juveniles. For example, the session on imposing a preventive measure (which includes pre-trial detention) on juvenile defendants must not be held in the absence of defence counsel (which is not the case for adults),[111] and no polygraph test may be applied to juvenile defendants.[112]

As to the practice, the same problems arise as one referred to above: due to the fact that mandatory defence during the investigation phase does not necessarily require mandatory presence, appointed counsel rarely attend procedural acts and tend to be passive. An empirical survey carried out in 1999 showed that appointed lawyers do not contact juvenile defendants and rarely lodge a complaint, or submit a motion for re-trial or judicial review of the judgement.[113] Other studies also confirmed that appointed lawyers did not contact juvenile defendants in pre-trial detention.[114]

2.2.6. Existence of legal aid schemes

As was outlined in the introduction, legal aid for the indigent defendant is applied through the appointment system, although it is primarily based on the principle of 'the interests of justice'. This means that, in general, it is irrelevant whether the defendant has no defence counsel, either because he/she is indigent or because he/she does not wish to retain defence counsel for any other reason. The basic principle is that, in the interests of justice, defence counsel should participate in the proceedings in all cases where the defendant is 'vulnerable' for some reason, either due to his situation (for example, detention), or a personal characteristic (for example, being a minor) and is therefore restricted in the ability to defend himself/herself. There is, however, a certain overlap, since in most cases the reason why a defendant does not retain a lawyer is because he/she cannot afford it. However, if he/she falls within one of the categories of mandatory defence, he/she does not have to go through an eligibility procedure – a lawyer will be appointed anyway.

The only instance when the indigence of the defendant is taken into consideration is if he/she is eligible for personal cost exemption and requests defence counsel to be appointed. In this case, the state will cover the appointed defence counsel's fees and verified costs. In all other cases, these costs are only advanced by the state and have to be repaid as part of the criminal costs, if the

---

[110] CCP 46 and 450.
[111] CCP 456 (1).
[112] CCP 453 (3).
[113] Fenyvesi 2002, p. 338.
[114] Two juvenile defendants out of nine were contacted by appointed defence counsel, and then only once or twice in the course of pre-trial detention lasting several months. See Orell 1998, p. 97.

defendant is found guilty[115] (although, in most cases, the State's claim for criminal costs remains unenforceable).

If, based on his/her financial situation, it can be expected that the defendant will not be able to pay the criminal costs, and he/she verifies this in a way prescribed by a separate statute,[116] upon the request of the defendant or counsel, the prosecutor (before the indictment), or the judge (in the court phase), may grant personal costs exemption to the defendant. If the exemption is granted, upon the defendant's request, the court or the prosecutor shall appoint defence counsel, whose fees and costs are borne by the state.[117]

Personal cost exemption may be granted to the defendant if (i) he/she lives together with other persons, and the per capita monthly income of the household does not exceed the legally required minimum old age pension (105 Euro); or (ii) he/she lives alone and his/her monthly income does not exceed an amount twice that of the legally required minimum old age pension (210 Euro). A further requirement is that the defendant may not possess properties, other than assets necessary for everyday life or used for work, or the real estate in which he/she lives.[118]

Two problems need to be highlighted regarding the actual practice. First, defendants apply for cost exemption in very few cases. In 2006, for example, only 77 requests were submitted to the prosecution.[119] When asked about the possible reasons, practitioners could not explain the low numbers. As was outlined above, along with the bill of indictment, defendants are delivered form no. 220, which contains information about applying for cost exemption. A very experienced judge has, since 2003, had only two cases when an application was submitted. One of the interviewed judges said that the relevant provisions of the Costs Exemption Decree should be included in form no. 220, because defendants are not aware of the specific conditions, which itself may be part of the problem.[120]

Another explanation may be that a great proportion of eligible defendants get legal assistance anyway, on the basis of mandatory defence, and they are probably not aware that, with cost exemption, they are exempted from costs, whereas in all other cases the State only advances the costs and if they are convicted they will have to repay these amounts.

The other issue is that the quality problem outlined above in relation to appointed counsel also pertains to counsel appointed on the basis of cost exemption.

---

[115]   CCP 338 (1).
[116]   Decree 9/2003 (V. 6) of the Minister of Justice on the Application of Personal Exemption of Costs in the Criminal Procedure (Costs Exemption Decree).
[117]   CCP 74 (3) (a) and (c).
[118]   Costs Exemption Decree 2.
[119]   Source: Chief Public Prosecutor's Office.
[120]   Interviews with Judges.

2.2.7. Remuneration of lawyers

Under the Attorneys Act, there are no fixed fees and the attorney and the client are therefore free to negotiate and decide the fee.[121] Hence, the level of legal fees varies. The fees are influenced by such things as the attorney's professional experience, the characteristics and complexity of the case and the volume of work required.

For some services, such as general legal consultation, attorneys charge fees ranging from 20 Euro to 150 Euro per hour.

In criminal cases, defence counsel will frequently charge a lump sum for each stage of the proceedings (investigation, judicial phase up until first instance decision, court of second instance). The fees will also depend on the complexity of the criminal case. Sums between 5,000 and 40,000 Euro are not uncommon.

Legal aid fees are significantly below market prices. Decree no. 7/2002 (III. 30) of the Minister of Justice on the Fees and Expenses of Ex Officio Appointed Patron Lawyers and Defence Counsels (Decree on Fees) contains detailed rules on the fees, while the law on the annual State budget sets fee levels. Presently, the hourly fee is 12 Euro (plus VAT),[122] with the exception of consultation with a detained defendant, for which counsel receives just half this amount.[123]

Upon request, defence counsel shall also be paid the hourly appointment fee for every 100 pages of case documentation studied; however, the total amount paid for this activity may not exceed the fees payable for 30 hours and documents submitted by defence counsel may not be taken into account when calculating the number of pages.[124]

Appointed defence counsel are entitled to be reimbursed for expenses arising in connection with the case, based on a detailed statement. The costs that may be reimbursed include postal, telephone, travel, parking, copying and accommodation expenses.[125] Travel and accommodation can only be reimbursed if the attorney attends a proceeding that takes place outside the place where he/she lives, or where his/her office is located.[126] If the attorney fails to submit a detailed account together with documentation verifying the costs, the court establishes the amount to be reimbursed on the basis of the available data.[127]

For certain activities, such as the drafting of petitions, or consulting with a client who is not detained, no payment is allowed.

In a 2005 article, the President of the Hungarian Bar Association stated that a fee of at least 20 Euro per hour would be necessary to ensure that appointment cases would be worthwhile for a lawyer.[128] Lawyers are thus not satisfied with the extremely low remuneration for appointed defence counsel and are of the view that

---

[121] Attorneys Act 9.
[122] See: Act CLXIX of 2007 on the 2008 Budget of the Republic of Hungary, art. 58, § (3): 'The hourly fee set forth in art. 131 Par (2) of Act XI of 1998 on Attorneys, shall be HUF 3,000 (EUR 12) in the year 2008.'
[123] Decree on Fees 6 (2)–(6).
[124] Decree on Fees 6 (7).
[125] Decree on Fees 1 (2).
[126] Decree on Fees 2 (2).
[127] Decree on Fees 4.
[128] Bánáti 2005, p. 51.

it does not properly take into account the work done and responsibilities taken on by the lawyer.[129]

According to practitioners, the low remuneration is the main reason for the differences between the quality of the performance of retained and appointed lawyers. Others think that systemic problems, such as appointment by the investigating authority and the lack of any quality assurance also contribute to the problem.[130]

2.3. *Procedural rights*

2.3.1. Right to release from custody pending trial

In this section, the term 'pre-trial detention' refers to detention before a final and binding custodial sentence of the court.[131]

In the case of an offence punishable with imprisonment, the defendant may be subjected to pre-trial detention if:

- he/she has escaped or hidden from the court, the prosecutor or the investigative authority; he/she has attempted to escape, or during the procedure, another criminal procedure is launched against him/her for an offence punishable with imprisonment;
- taking into account the risk of his/her escaping or hiding, or for any other reason, there are well founded grounds to presume that his/her presence at the proceedings may not otherwise be secured;
- there are well founded grounds to presume that, if not taken into pre-trial detention, he/she would – through influencing or intimidating the witnesses, eliminating, forging or hiding material evidence or documents – frustrate, hinder, or threaten the proceedings;
- there are well founded grounds to presume that, if not taken into pre-trial detention, he/she would accomplish the attempted or proposed offence, or would commit another offence punishable with imprisonment.[132]

Pre-trial detention is ordered by a so-called 'investigation judge' upon the prosecutor's motion in the investigation phase. After the indictment, it can be ordered or prolonged by the judge trying the case without a motion. It should be noted that investigation judges do not participate in the investigation, but perform those functions in the pre-trial phase that require judicial actions in order to meet certain fundamental standards, such as those set forth in article 5 ECHR.

Judicial decisions on pre-trial detention are subject to appeal. The longest possible term for pre-trial detention is three years, unless a first instance sentence is

[129]   The Bar Association has issued a position paper on this, published in Pesti Ügyvéd (Journal of the Budapest Bar Association), 2002/6, p. 1-2.
[130]   Kádár 2004, p. 138–142.
[131]   Thus, it includes detention during the trial and also detention after the first instance court decision, pending appeal.
[132]   CCP 129.

reached within this time period. In such cases, if the first instance court maintains or orders the defendant's pre-trial detention when announcing the sentence, the detention may last until the end of the second instance proceedings (which may be more than three years from the commencement of the detention), but in any event, may not last longer than the prison sentence imposed by the first instance court.[133] It must be noted that the term spent in pre-trial detention will be deducted from the final sentence.

Pre-trial detention needs to be prolonged and/or reviewed at intervals defined by the law.[134] A motion by the defendant or counsel for the termination of pre-trial detention shall be examined and adjudicated in a reasoned decision by the court.[135]

Alternative measures for pre-trial detention exist in the Hungarian criminal procedure system. A person under a geographical ban may not leave the designated area (usually the location where one has a registered residence) without permission, and also may not change his/her place of residence without permission. A geographical ban may be ordered if, taking into consideration the nature of the offence, the defendant's personal and family circumstances, and his/her behaviour during the procedure, the goals of pre-trial detention can be realised through this measure. The geographical ban is ordered by the court. In doing so, the court may prescribe that the defendant shall contact the police regularly, and as well as other restrictive measures intended to realise the objectives of the ban.[136]

If under house arrest, the defendant may only leave the dwelling designated by the court for a purpose specified in the ordering decision (for example, medical treatment), and for the time and distance defined in the decision. If house arrest is ordered, the ordering, prolongation and termination of the measure are governed by the rules of pre-trial detention.[137]

If the defendant violates either the geographical ban or the rules of house arrest, or fails to appear when summoned, he/she may be arrested. In this case, if he/she is already under house arrest, pre-trial detention may be ordered; if he/she is already under a geographical ban, house arrest or pre-trial detention may be ordered.[138] If the defendant's house arrest or geographical ban was ordered after pre-trial detention had to be terminated due to the passing of three years, and

---

[133] CCP 131 and 132.
[134] CCP 131 and 132: During the investigation, pre-trial detention may at first be ordered for one month, and then prolonged by a special Judge every three months for a total of one year. After one year, a judicial decision on prolongation is required every two months until – after the submission of the bill of indictment – the first instance court delivers a decision on maintaining (or, if the defendant was not in pre-trial detention, ordering) the detention. Any detention ordered or maintained by the first instance court lasts until the first instance decision (when the court can also maintain or order the detention), without further prolonging decisions, but it shall be reviewed every six months by the first instance court, and after one year by a higher court.
[135] CCP 133.
[136] CCP 137.
[137] CCP 138.
[138] CCP 139.

he/she violates the geographical ban or the rules of house arrest, pre-trial detention can be ordered again, in which case the three year time limit starts again.[139]

If the only ground for ordering pre-trial detention is the danger of absconding, the court may decide to terminate or, not to order or the defendant's pre-trial detention if, taking into consideration the offence and the defendant's personal circumstances, the payment of bail makes it likely that the defendant will appear at the procedural acts. Bail may be offered and paid by the defendant, or by any other person.

The defence may file a motion for bail with the appropriate court authorised to decide on pre-trial detention. The court holds a session at which the prosecutor, the defendant, defence counsel and the person offering the bail are heard. In its decision accepting bail, the court determines the sum of the bail in accordance with the defendant's financial situation.[140] Simultaneously with accepting bail, the court may order a geographical ban, house arrest and/or the seizure of the defendant's travel documents.[141] The court may order the released defendant's pre-trial detention if he/she fails to appear on summons, or if another ground for pre-trial detention arises. The person paying the bail loses it if the defendant's pre-trial detention is ordered due to a failure to appear.[142]

The practice of pre-trial detention leaves much to be desired. Statistics show that alternative measures are not frequently used by Hungarian judges.

Number of measures ordered by first instance courts[143]

Year	Pre-trial detention	Geographical ban	House arrest	Total
2007	4,882	125	70	5,077
2006	4,896	127	45	5,068
2005	5,166	129	38	5,333

While there were 26,475 orders of pre-trial detention between 2003 and 2007, only 464 offers for bail were accepted,[144] out of 1,139 applications. Release on bail therefore constitutes less than 2% of all preventive measures.[145]

The automatic reference to the gravity of the criminal offence and the prospective punishment, as the ground(s) for establishing the danger of absconding, coupled with the failure to consider either the defendant's individual circumstances or the possibility of alternative measures are frequently criticised characteristics of

139 CCP 132 (4).
140 CCP 147.
141 CCP 147 (4).
142 CCP 148.
143 Source: Hungarian Chief Prosecutor's Office's website, <www.mklu.hu>.
144 The number of releases on bail is not broken down by the respective year on the website of the HCPO.
145 Although it should be pointed out that, compared to the annual number of convicted defendants, the annual number of pre-trial detentions ordered is not very high. In 2007, for example, 3,505 pre-trial detentions were ordered, compared to 87,744 convictions, representing approximately 4%.

Hungarian judicial practice. Hungary in two cases,[146] has so far been found to be in breach of article 5 of the ECHR on such grounds, and further cases are still pending before the ECtHR.

One systemic problem is that, as a result of the provisions outlined in Section 2.1.2, in the investigation phase the defence does not have access to the evidence upon which the judge decides on pre-trial detention. According to the well-established case law of the Strasbourg Court, the proceedings in which a decision on detention is taken:

> must be adversarial and must always ensure 'equality of arms' between the parties, the prosecutor and the detained person. [...] Equality of arms is not ensured if counsel is denied access to those documents in the investigation file which are essential in order effectively to challenge the lawfulness of his client's detention.[147]

Obviously, Hungarian practice constitutes a breach of the equality of arms, and prevents the defence from effectively arguing against the detention.

Although most of the interviewed police officers, judges and prosecutors firmly rejected the idea that pre-trial detention may, in Hungarian practice, serve any purpose other than outlined as in the CCP, all interviewed defence counsel said that the threat of pre-trial detention is often used to put pressure on the unwilling defendant to make a confession. This is substantiated by the Hungarian Helsinki Committee's 2003 survey. 28% of interviewed detainees claimed to have been threatened by the investigator that their detention would be ordered/prolonged if they refused to confess to the offence.[148]

2.3.2. The right of a defendant to be tried in his/her presence

Whereas in the investigation phase the defence's right to presence is restricted, in the court phase, it is fully guaranteed. The CCP expressly claims that the court hearing may not be held in the absence of the defendant and, in cases of mandatory defence, counsel.[149]

There are certain exceptions to this rule. If the properly summoned defendant is not present at the beginning of the court session and it is not possible to have him/her appear before the court, the session may be held, but the evidentiary procedure may not be terminated (except when the court acquits the absent defendant). This means that the attending persons shall be heard, a new date is to be set, and the court shall order that the absent defendant be escorted by the police to the court on the new date. If, at the next session, the defendant again fails to appear and the offence is punishable with imprisonment, another date has to be set, an arrest warrant is to be issued against the defendant and defence counsel is appointed for the defendant, unless he/she already has retained counsel.

---

[146] See ECtHR 9 November 2004, *Maglódi v. Hungary*, No. 30103/02, and ECtHR 2 December 2003, *Imre v. Hungary*, No. 53129/99.
[147] ECtHR 25 March 1999, *Nikolova v. Bulgaria*, No. 31195/96, § 58.
[148] Kádár 2004, p. 70–71.
[149] CCP 240 (3).

If the defendant cannot be found in spite of the warrant, the court starts proceedings in absentia.[150] In proceedings against an absent defendant, the general provisions of the CCP shall be applied with certain derogations; for example, that at the trial held in the absence of the accused, the presence of the prosecutor and defence counsel shall be mandatory.[151] It is also required that, if the defendant is located after the delivery of the final decision, a re-trial is ordered upon his/her request.[152]

In practice, judges tend to be rather 'patient' and use in absentia procedures as a last resort.

2.3.3. The right to be presumed innocent

Under the CCP; 'Everyone shall be presumed innocent until convicted in a final and binding court verdict.'[153]

Apart from the right to silence and the prohibition against self-incrimination, the main procedural manifestation of the presumption of innocence is that the prosecution shall bear burden of the proof of the defendant's guilt and that only facts that are proven beyond reasonable doubt may be used to the defendant's detriment.[154]

According to attorneys, this principle is not always complied with, one example being the very restrictive practice followed by Hungarian courts in relation to pre-trial detention, whereby court decisions ordering pre-trial detention often imply the court's firm conviction about the guilt of the suspect or accused.[155]

Another criticism voiced by attorneys is that Hungarian courts (particularly courts of second instance) are conspicuously reluctant to deliver acquittals. This practice seems to be characterised by a presumption of guilt.[156] This is confirmed by a former judge, who says that:

> acquitting decisions have to be substantiated in much more detail than convictions. [...] The existence of this approach is highlighted by a 2006 research which proves that most county courts seem to have an 'aversion' to acquittals and a significantly larger proportion of acquitting first instance decisions are quashed than convictions.[157] This fact is important, as it does not seem likely that judges are more negligent when they acquit the defendant than when they condemn him/her. Thus, it seems that courts of second instance look at acquittal as some kind of a 'mistake'.[158]

According to attorneys, this is the main reason why the success rate of the prosecution is around 95% every year.[159] Interviewed judges and prosecutors on the

---

[150]   CCP 281.
[151]   CCP 530.
[152]   Court decision BH2005.388.
[153]   CCP 7.
[154]   CCP 4 (2).
[155]   Interviews with counsels.
[156]   Interviews with counsels.
[157]   Bencze 2005.
[158]   Ibidem.
[159]   See the table in the introduction.

other hand questioned this view and tended to attribute the high conviction rates to the fact that the prosecution does not risk to taking 'weaker' cases before the court (although one of the judges admitted that, particularly younger judges tend to rely to a greater extent on the indictment than do more experienced colleagues).[160]

2.3.4. The right to silence and the prohibition against self-incrimination

The right to silence is expressly prescribed in the CCP: 'No one shall be compelled to make a self-incriminating testimony or to produce self-incriminating evidence.'[161] This is further elaborated by the rules of interrogating the defendant; as was outlined above, at the beginning of the interrogation, the defendant must be warned that he/she may remain silent, either fully, or in relation to certain questions. He/she shall also be warned that he/she may testify, even if he/she chose earlier to remain silent, but that anything he/she says may be used as evidence against him/her. The warning and any answer shall be recorded word by word. If this does not happen, the testimony of the defendant shall not be admitted as evidence.[162]

If the defendant chooses to remain silent, he/she must be warned that this will not prevent the proceedings from continuing. No further questions may be posed to the defendant and he/she may not be confronted with other defendants and witnesses in relation to the offence concerning which he/she has decided to remain silent. The decision to remain silent does not prevent the defendant from posing questions and submitting motions in the subsequent phases of the proceedings.[163] (Further exclusionary rules are described in Section 2.4.5).

According to practitioners, the warning about the right to silence is provided in most cases. One interviewed counsel emphasised that, when counsel is present, the warning is always given. However, some of his clients complained that, during the first interrogation, which had been held without the lawyer, they had not been properly warned.[164] This coincides with the experience of some judges, who say that, while the records of the warning are always in place and duly signed, the defendant often claims that the warning was not provided orally (only the sample used for the records and containing the warning was given to the defendant to sign), or otherwise properly. In some cases, it was necessary in the court phase to summon the police officer who conducted the interrogation in order to establish whether the warning was provided in full compliance with the relevant provisions.[165]

Another criticism voiced by counsel was that the essence of this right is often not properly explained, although it is difficult to understand even for educated persons.[166]

---

[160]   Interviews with practitioners.
[161]   CCP 8.
[162]   CCP 117 (2).
[163]   CCP 117 (4).
[164]   Interview with counsel.
[165]   Interview with Judges.
[166]   Interview with counsels.

To the question of whether there may be informal consequences of the right to silence, there was a difference of opinion between prosecutors, judges and police officers on the one hand, and defence counsel on the other. While the former group emphasised that attaching negative consequences to the defendant's silence would be against the fundamental principles of the CCP, lawyers claimed that the exercise of this right can have an impact on certain decisions, particularly in the case of ordering and maintaining pre-trial detention. One interviewed lawyer pointed out that, in judicial practice,[167] a confession is regarded as an important mitigating circumstance, so the choice to testify or remain silent may therefore influence the gravity of the sentence.[168]

2.3.5. The right to reasoned decisions

The CCP does not expressly contain this right, but it can be inferred from a number of provisions. With regard to the investigation phase, the CCP prescribes those types of decisions in relation to which the investigating authority or the prosecutor shall deliver a formal decision. These include, for example, the decision on personal cost exemption, the appointment of a forensic expert, restrictive measures[169] and the decision to allow or reject the involvement of the defence's expert witness. Decisions shall be reasoned by indicating briefly those facts that made the decision necessary.[170] It is not mandatory to deliver a formal decision on the evidentiary motions of the defence, so the investigating authority therefore need not provide reasons, if it does not comply with such a motion.

The provision on the mandatory elements of the judgement expressly prescribes what the 'reasons' section shall contain. These are:

- reference to the charges and, if necessary, the summary of facts as presented in the indictment;
- the facts established in relation to the personal circumstances of the accused, and the data concerning his/her earlier convictions;
- the facts of the case as established by the court;
- the enumeration and assessment of the evidence;
- the criminal offence that the facts as established by the court amount to, and, if the court applies a punishment or measure, the reasons for this along with the legal provisions applied;
- reasons for other elements of the decision (for example, the parts relating to the costs of proceeding) as well as for those evidentiary motions that the court refused, along with the legal provisions applied.[171]

---

[167]   56/2007. BK vélemény (<see: http://www.lb.hu>).
[168]   Interviews with practitioners.
[169]   For example, the 72-hour detention preceding pre-trial detention, or seizure.
[170]   CCP 169.
[171]   CCP 258 (3).

Court decisions in relation to managing the case (for example, setting a new date) do not have to be reasoned at all, whereas the rejection of evidentiary motions (both by the defence and the prosecution) shall be explained only in the final decision.[172]

If the court violates its obligation to provide sufficient reasons for the judgement, to the extent that review by the court of second instance is not possible, or the reasons are in contradiction with the merits of the judgement, the court of second instance shall quash the first instance decision and order a re-trial.[173]

Interviewed practitioners claim that judges do usually provide reasons their judgements, although in some cases, the reasoning is insufficient and/or incoherent. Some called attention to certain clichés in the reasons section, which sometimes 'hide' the fact that the reasoning itself is not sufficiently sound. An example is the often recurring reference to the fact that because the defendant is not legally obliged to tell the truth, while the witness is, the testimony of the latter is accepted in the case of a conflict.[174]

2.3.6. The right to appeal

In the investigation stage, remedies are available in the form of a complaint against both formal and informal decisions, as well as omissions by the investigating authority or the prosecutor. Complaints against acts/omissions of the investigating authority are decided upon by the prosecutor supervising the investigation; if the investigation is conducted by the prosecutor, complaints are dealt with by a superior prosecutor.[175]

In the judicial stage, the right to appeal is also guaranteed. After the announcement of the judgement, the judge calls those who are present and entitled to appeal to declare whether they exercise this right. The order of making these statements is prescribed by law, with the prosecutor being first, the defendant and counsel being last (counsel may appeal even if the defendant accepts the verdict)[176]

Those who are present can choose to take three days to decide whether to appeal. If a person is not present, the judgement is delivered to him/her in writing, in which case he/she has eight days from delivery to submit an appeal.[177] Written arguments for an appeal announced orally (either after the promulgation of the judgement or later) may be submitted no later than eight days before the second instance court's session.[178]

In an appeal, it is possible to refer to new facts and introduce new evidence that the person submitting the appeal was not aware of at the time of the announcement of the judgement. It is also possible to present an evidentiary motion in the appeal that the first instance court had considered unnecessary.[179]

---

[172]   CCP 260.
[173]   CCP 373.
[174]   Interviews with counsels. The conclusion is supported by former Judge Mátyás Bencze.
[175]   CCP 195 and 196.
[176]   CCP 323.
[177]   CCP 325.
[178]   CCP 323.
[179]   CCP 323.

An appeal is also possible against (i) decisions that are not judgements, but concern the merits of the case;[180] (ii) decisions that do not concern the merits of the case, but are not regarded as case management decisions,[181] provided that the possibility of an appeal is not expressly excluded by the CCP;[182] or (iii) those case management decisions with regard to which the CCP expressly contains the possibility of appeal.[183] In the absence of such an express provision, case management decisions may not be appealed,[184] but may be challenged in the appeal against the judgement (or the decision on the merits of the case).[185]

Since the rejection of an evidentiary motion by the defence is regarded as a case management decision under the rule noted above, both the defence and the prosecution may only challenge it in the appeal against the judgement.[186]

Appointment gives both the mandate and the obligation to counsel to provide defence until a final and binding decision is reached (and also extends to extraordinary remedies if necessary).[187] Therefore, defence provided for indigent defendants covers appeals, both to bring an appeal and to defend an appeal by the prosecution.

2.4. Rights relating to effective defence

2.4.1. Rights to investigate the case

Equality of arms (including the right to be present at investigative acts): As was outlined above, the investigation phase is predominantly inquisitorial, meaning that the equality of arms is per se limited. The two aspects where this is most apparent are in relation to presence of counsel at procedural acts and access to the files.

The CCP restricts the presence of counsel and the defendant in the investigation stage. Counsel may be present during the defendant's interrogation, the hearing of and/or confrontations[188] with witnesses proposed by counsel or defendant, and also during confrontations between the defendant and other persons.[189] The notification of counsel regarding these is mandatory.

Both counsel and the defendant may be present at the hearing of an expert, at the inspection of a scene or object, evidentiary experiments[190] and identification

---

180 CCP 346 (for example, the termination of the case due to the statute of limitations).
181 For example, the decision on restrictive measures, such as pre-trial detention.
182 CCP 347.
183 Such as the imposition of a fine on persons violating the rules of the trial.
184 CCP 260.
185 CCP 347.
186 The rationale of the rule is that the court is not bound by its ruling rejecting the motion.
187 CCP 49.
188 Confrontation is a special procedural act by which witnesses and/or defendants whose testimony is in contradiction are heard in each other's presence so that they can try to resolve the contradiction directly.
189 CCP 184.
190 An experiment reproducing the criminal offence with the aim of determining whether a certain event or incident might have taken place at a certain time, in a certain way, under certain given circumstances.

line-ups. Their notification may be disregarded, if this is necessary due to the urgency of the investigative act.[191]

A house search shall be conducted in the presence of the person concerned. If that person, his/her defence counsel, legal representative or authorised relative is not present, another person shall be appointed who may be presumed to represent the concerned person's interests.[192]

Those persons who may be present at an investigative act have the right to inspect the records thereof (even if they were absent). Furthermore, the defendant and counsel may inspect expert opinions. They can have access to other parts of the case file (during the investigation), if it does not threaten the interests of the investigation. Counsel and the defendant are entitled to free copies of those documents they are entitled to inspect.[193]

As to the practice, the problems regarding late notification of the first interrogation were outlined in Section 2.2. Later interrogations and confrontations are less problematic. Interviewed counsel unanimously said that they make it clear to their clients that nothing should be said in their absence. Investigating officers are aware of this and, since preparing an interrogation is rather time consuming,[194] and the officers prefer not to work in vain, they usually try to make sure that the lawyer is present, by contacting him/her well in advance. Obviously, indigent defendants (who often do not meet their appointed lawyer until the court phase) are in a worse position than those who have retained lawyers.

If the mandatory notification is not sent for any reason, upon a complaint by counsel the investigating authority almost always repeats the concerned act.[195] This is due to the fact that evidence obtained by the court, the prosecutor, or the investigating authority involving substantial restriction of the procedural rights of the participants may not be admitted as evidence.[196] Thus, by not repeating the interrogation, the investigating authority would risk that the information obtained at the hearing would have to be excluded from the materials of the case. If, however, the notification is sent (even if at a time when it is practically impossible for counsel to attend), the practice indicates that the exclusion rule does not apply.

With regard to those procedural acts where notification may be disregarded in cases of urgency, interviewed practitioners unanimously claimed that this happens very rarely (according to one lawyer, such procedural acts are, in fact, performed very rarely).[197]

The limited access to case files has the practical result that, in the investigation phase, even retained lawyers refrain from being too active, since they do not know what evidence the investigating authority has against their clients. Since – according to a number of interviewed defence lawyers – the investigation is of key importance

---

[191]   CCP 185.
[192]   CCP 149.
[193]   CCP 186.
[194]   A summon must be written and sent out. If the defendant is detained, his/her transportation from the place of detention shall also be arranged and administered.
[195]   Interviews with counsels.
[196]   CCP 78 (4).
[197]   Interviews with counsels.

from the point of view of the eventual establishment of criminal liability, and the omissions committed during the investigation are very difficult to remedy in the subsequent phases, this obviously has an adverse impact on effective defence.[198]

The problem of evidence serving as the basis for pre-trial detention being kept from the defence is discussed in Section 2.3.1.

Seeking evidence, investigating facts and interviewing prospective witnesses: The defendant is entitled to present any facts substantiating his/her defence, or to make an observation related to the criminal procedure.[199]

Defence counsel is also entitled to present facts substantiating the defence. Furthermore, he/she has the right to seek information and obtain and collect evidence within the framework set by law.[200] This means, for example, that counsel may contract a private detective in line with the relevant legal provisions.[201]

There is no empirical evidence as to the extent to which lawyers avail themselves of these opportunities, but it can be clearly stated said that, in this regard, indigent defendants are obviously in a significantly disadvantaged situation, as they do not have sufficient resources to pay for a private detective, whom counsel of a more well-to-do client can commission to perform data collection.

The CCP does not contain any formalised procedure for interviewing prospective witnesses, but neither does it prohibit this. The provision on counsel's right to seek information does include the right to talk to, and gather information from prospective witnesses. On the other hand, prospective witnesses are obviously under no obligation to answer counsel's queries.

Obtaining expert evidence: Both the defendant and his/her defence counsel may present a motion requesting the appointment of an expert.[202] Furthermore, the defence can obtain an expert opinion themselves and may request the prosecutor or the court to allow the expert preparing that opinion to be involved the proceedings as an expert. If the prosecutor or judge rejects this request, the opinion prepared by the expert can be used as documentary evidence.[203] The CCP[204] specifies that, where the investigative authority or the prosecutor appoints an expert during the investigation, and the defence so requests within 15 days of receipt of the bill of indictment, the court shall appoint another expert concerning the same questions, unless it has already appointed one, or the court or prosecutor have permitted the involvement of the expert commissioned by the defence.

In this regard, indigent defendants are in a significantly disadvantaged situation compared to those who can afford to commission an expert. Although appointed counsel's possibility to have the fees of a commissioned expert reimbursed by the state is not expressly excluded, due to a number of practical

---

[198]   Interviews with counsels.
[199]   CCP 43 (2).
[200]   CCP 50 (2).
[201]   For example, Act CXXXIII of 2005 on the Rules of the Protection of Persons and Assets and on the Activities of Private Investigations.
[202]   CCP 111 (2).
[203]   CCP 112.
[204]   CCP 111 (4).

reasons (including the fact that the lawyer should advance amounts that may substantially exceed his/her total fee), it is highly unlikely that appointed counsel would ever avail themselves of this option.

Some counsel expressed the opinion that regulation of the involvement of the defence's expert is not fully in line with the equality of arms principle, and if an expert is appointed by the authorities during the investigation, it should be obligatory for the court to allow the involvement of the defence's expert, as this would create the necessary balance between the prosecution and the defence (one expert chosen by each side). They emphasised that, if there is a conflict between the opinions, the court can still appoint a third expert, or order that the experts be heard together.[205]

2.4.2. The right to adequate time and facilities for preparation of defence

Summons and notifications: The CCP gives considerable discretion to the authorities as to when they send a notification. Unless the law prescribes otherwise, the investigating authority, the prosecutor and the court must summon those whose presence at the procedural act is mandatory and notify those who may be present. A summons or notification must be in writing, or orally if the person to be summoned or notified appears before the authority in person (for example, if a person attends a court session and a new session needs to be held, the court will summon him/her orally for the next session).[206]

In urgent cases, a summons or notification can be communicated by any other appropriate means, such as fax, telephone or e-mail.[207]

In the investigation phase, there are certain provisions aimed at guaranteeing that a summons or notification is sent in a timely manner. The CCP prescribes that the investigating authority shall schedule the time of the interrogation in a way that enables the defendant to exercise his/her right to defence.[208] With the exception of urgent investigative acts, counsel shall be notified in due course, at least 24 hours beforehand, regarding all the investigative acts at which he/she may be present.[209]

In the trial phase, the summons for the court hearing has to be delivered at least five days prior to the hearing.[210]

As to delays in the notification of the first interrogation, refer to Section 2.2. In the court stage, the time requirement is respected in most cases.

The practice outlined in Section 2.1.1 (namely that, prospective suspects are summonsed as defendants) is also problematic from the point of view of the preparation of defence. The CCP allows witnesses to retain lawyers who may be present at the hearing. Lawyers aiding witnesses are authorised to provide their clients with information about witness rights, but may not perform any other

---

205   Interview with counsel.
206   CCP 67.
207   CCP 67 (3).
208   CCP 179 (4).
209   Investigation Decree 9 (2).
210   CCP 279 (3).

activity and may not influence the hearing. After the hearing, the lawyer may inspect the records and present comments orally or in writing.[211]

According to practitioners, while more and more witnesses appear with lawyers, investigating authorities as a rule do not allow the interruption of the hearing for the purposes of consultation between the witness and the lawyer.[212] This does not, however, prevent lawyers from indicating to their clients in different ways that it may be advisable to refuse to testify in relation to certain questions.[213]

Access to files: In relation to the limited access to files in the investigation phase, refer to Section 2.1.2. A positive development in relation to the access to files by appointed counsel is that they may be paid for inspecting files.[214] Another amendment that significantly enhances effective defence (particularly for indigent defendants) is that since 1 August 2006, copies of the case files have been free for the defence.[215]

Consultation between counsel and the client: Refer to Section 2.2.

On the spot appointment of counsel in the trial phase: Refer to Section 2.2 on the practice of appointing counsel on the spot, if defence is mandatory and the summonsed counsel fails to attend.

2.4.3. The right to equality of arms in examining witnesses

The right to secure the attendance of witnesses: Both the defendant and counsel are entitled to motion the performance of any procedural (evidentiary) act in any phase of the proceedings.[216]

Depending on the actual phase, evidentiary motions put forth by the defence are decided upon by the police officer, prosecutor or judge in charge of the case. It is up to the authority to decide which witnesses are to be called to give oral evidence. Thus, if the relevant authorities do not accept the defence's evidentiary motions, the defence does not possess the right to demand that the proposed evidence be produced, or a particular witness be called.

During the investigation, the suspect and defence counsel may submit a complaint if the entity conducting the investigation rejects or neglects the evidentiary motion.[217]

In the court stage, if evidentiary motions are rejected, neither the prosecution nor the defence may separately appeal this decision. The refusal can only be challenged in the appeal submitted against the decision on the merits,[218] claiming that facts of the case as established in that decision are unfounded, which may therefore serve as a basis for quashing the judgement.[219]

---

[211]   CCP 85 (4).
[212]   This is also not allowed by law.
[213]   Interviews with counsels.
[214]   This has been the position since 1 August 2006.
[215]   Act XCIII of 1990 on Fees 57 (2).
[216]   CCP 43 (2).
[217]   CCP 196.
[218]   CCP 258 (3).
[219]   CCP 350.

If the court of second instance regards as necessary for the decision of the case, the evidentiary motion rejected by the first instance court, it will quash the first instance decision and order the first instance court to repeat the proceedings, on the basis that the denial of the motion qualifies as a breach of procedural rights having a significant impact on the proceedings or its outcome. The CCP expressly states that the violation of the evidentiary rules, and the restriction of the proper exercise of rights by the participants of the proceedings, shall be regarded as a breach having such impact.[220]

Practitioners gave varied descriptions as to the practice in this regard. While police officers claimed that they always accept evidentiary motions that move the investigation further, defence counsel were of the view that, in the investigation stage, most motions by the defence are rejected or neglected. Some of the judges seemed to agree with counsel and said that, during the investigation, most motions by the defence are rejected, and therefore these motions are presented again by the lawyers in the trial stage. Police officers and counsel agreed that complaints submitted to the prosecutor supervising the investigation about the rejection of an evidentiary motion are, in most cases, unsuccessful.[221]

Regarding the court phase, judges expressed the opinion that they comply with evidentiary motions, unless they are completely unfounded. Counsel said that much depended on the individual judge. One pointed out that, if the prosecution agrees with the evidentiary motion of the defence, the court almost always accepts it; if not, approximately half of the motions are accepted. With regard to the approach of the second instance court, one counsel said that, if it has doubts about the facts as established in the first instance decision, the second instance is receptive to the argument that certain evidence should have been obtained, and consequently the first instance court's failure to do so is a ground for quashing the sentence and ordering a re-trial. If, however, the first instance decision more or less coincides with the opinion of the second instance court, it will not examine the issue in detail.[222]

Right to examine the witnesses: In the investigation stage, neither the defendant nor counsel may be present at the hearing of those witnesses who are not heard upon their motion.[223] Thus, defence counsel can only examine those witnesses whose hearing is initiated by the defence. These witnesses are first heard by the investigating authority, and then the attending defence counsel is provided with the opportunity to pose questions and/or present remarks concerning the testimony.

In the court stage, the right to examination of witnesses is guaranteed. As a rule, witnesses of both the prosecution and the defence are first questioned by the judge and, after this, the other participants of the proceedings (prosecutor, defence counsel, defendant, victim) are allowed to pose questions to the witness and/or make remarks concerning his/her testimony.[224]

---

220   CCP 375 (1).
221   Interviews with practitioners.
222   Interviews with practitioners.
223   Between 1990 and 2003, counsel had the right to be present at the hearing of all witnesses.
224   CCP 286 (3).

According to practitioners, these rules are mostly complied with, although problems sometimes arise in relation to how the testimony, questions and answers are recorded. Insufficient recording of testimony can, however, be remedied by asking for the subsequent correction of the records.[225]

2.4.4. The right to the use of the suspect's own language

Interpretation: Criminal proceedings shall be conducted in Hungarian; however, no one may be placed in a disadvantageous situation due to a lack of command of Hungarian. In criminal proceedings, all the involved parties may use their mother tongue both orally and in writing or, pursuant to and within the scope of an international agreement promulgated by law, their regional or minority language[226] or, if they do not speak Hungarian, any other language they choose.[227] If the suspect does not speak Hungarian, an interpreter shall be involved.[228] The costs of interpretation are borne by the State, even if the defendant is convicted.[229]

In terms of the Investigation Decree, the witness and defendant shall be asked whether he/she understands the appointed interpreter. The answer to this question shall be recorded in the minutes of the hearing.[230] A similar practice is conducted by the courts. In fact, as one of the interviewed judges explained, not accepting the interpreter can be used as a tool to create delays and protract the proceedings.

On the other hand, while the CCP provides that only persons having the qualifications stipulated in a specific legal regulation can be employed as an interpreter,[231] it is also specified that, if appointing an interpreter or translator with the prescribed qualifications is not possible, any other person having sufficient knowledge of the particular language can be appointed.[232] In practice, under this power, authorities and courts sometimes appoint persons with insufficient language skills. No formal quality assurance mechanism is established regarding the work of interpreters and translators. There are only informal solutions for guaranteeing the quality of their work. For example, judges keep the contact details of interpreters and translators who in their view do their job with a high level of quality, and who are easy to cooperate with.[233]

Another practical problem is that no interpreter is provided by the State for the purposes of consultation between the lawyer and the client. This creates a significant inequality between indigent and paying clients. While clients who can afford to retain a lawyer can also pay an interpreter to translate during the

---

[225] CCP 166 (7) and 254 (1).
[226] This is a reference to the European Charter for Regional or Minority Languages. The use of interpreters is mandatory when regional or minority languages are used.
[227] CCP 9.
[228] CCP 114 (1).
[229] CPP 339 (2).
[230] Investigation Decree 19 (3).
[231] CCP 114 (3). This provision is Decree 24/1986 (VI. 26.) MT of the Council of Ministers on Professional Translation and Interpretation and Decree No. 7/1986 (VI. 26.) IM of the Ministry of Justice on the implementation thereof.
[232] CCP 114 (3).
[233] Interview with Judges.

consultation, indigent defendants can, unless the lawyer speaks the relevant language, only consult with their appointed lawyer immediately before the procedural act (when the interpreter is around) and are forced to rely on interpreters chosen by the authority. This is particularly problematic in the investigation phase. Not only defence counsel, but also judges find this issue significant, with one Judge emphasising that some investigating authorities tend to always appoint the same few interpreters (which also raises the issue as to the extent to which these interpreters depend on appointments by that authority), some of whom she finds incompetent and impossible to work with.[234]

Translation of documents: Translation costs are also paid by the State, with certain restrictions. The translation of decisions (including the verdict) and other official documents to be delivered to the addressee (for example, the defendant, the victim or witnesses) shall be the responsibility of and paid by the court, prosecutor or investigating authority that has adopted the decision or issued the official document.[235] Other documents (for example, minutes of procedural actions) are not translated by the authorities, and if the suspect wishes to receive them in his/her mother tongue, he/she is required to pay for the translation.

This means that, while at the beginning of the investigation, the communication of the suspicion is translated by an interpreter, the records are not available free of charge for the suspect in his/her mother tongue. The bill of indictment is translated and those costs are borne by the state, but the records of court hearings are not available for free, whereas the verdict is again translated into the required language and paid by the state.

Indigent defendants who cannot afford to pay for the interpretation of those documents that the State authorities are not obliged to have translated are in a significantly worse position than wealthy defendants who can pay for this service.

2.4.5. The consequences of the breach of defence rights

The CCP prescribes that facts derived from evidence obtained by the court, the prosecutor or the investigating authority by way of a significant restriction of the procedural rights of the participants of the proceedings shall not be admitted as evidence.[236] Some of these procedural breaches are expressly set out in the CCP.

As was noted in the Section on the right to silence, the warning and answer on the right to remain silent shall be recorded word by word. If this does not happen, the testimony of the defendant shall not be admitted as evidence.[237]

Furthermore, the CCP prescribes that the appellate court shall quash the judgement of the first instance court and order a re-trial, if the trial was held in the absence of a person whose presence was mandatory.[238] This is a so-called 'absolute ground for annulment', which means that in such cases, the appellate court is under the obligation to quash the first instance decision.

---

[234] Interviews with practitioners.
[235] CCP 9 (3).
[236] CCP 78 (4).
[237] CCP 117 (2).
[238] CCP 373 (1) II (d).

In terms of the provision on 'relative grounds for annulment',[239] the appellate court shall quash the judgement of the court of first instance and order it to conduct a new procedure, in the case of a procedural irregularity having a significant impact on (i) conducting the procedure; (ii) establishing the defendant's guilt; (iii) the classification of the criminal offence; or (iv) the application of a sanction. The law claims that 'such irregularities are, in particular, if the provisions on the lawfulness of gathering evidence were violated or the persons participating in the proceeding were prevented from or restricted in exercising their lawful rights'. These are 'relative grounds', because in such cases the appellate court has a discretionary right to assess whether the breach had a significant impact on the listed issues.

Some examples of significant breaches of procedural rights that have arisen from judicial practice are:

- The investigating authority's failure to appoint counsel in a case when defence is mandatory;[240]
- Hearing the defendant's minor and juvenile relatives as witnesses, without the agreement of the children's guardian;[241]
- Proceeding with the trial in the absence of the summonsed defendant, whose counsel has immediately provided a reasonable explanation for the absence, also supported with medical documentation;[242]
- The court does not provide sufficient time for preparation by a trainee attorney substituting for counsel, who cannot attend the trial due to an urgent problem;[243]
- A defendant's counsel in the court phase is not present at the hearing of the other defendant, and is therefore unable to exercise his/her rights to ask questions;[244]
- The failure to provide the witness with the proper warnings regarding his/her rights;[245]
- The bill of indictment is not translated into the defendant's mother tongue, provided that as a result of the lack of translation, the exercise of the defendant's lawful rights has been restricted, or has been prevented, and it has an impact on the judgement;[246]
- Employing an interpreter who does not have a certificate or who lacks the necessary competence, provided that it results in interference with the exercise of the defendant's right to an effective defence.[247]

---

[239] CCP 375 (1).
[240] Court decision BH2007.402.
[241] Court decision BH2005.385.
[242] Court decision BH2006.271.
[243] Court decision BH2006.272.
[244] Court decision BH2007.330.
[245] Court decision BH2005.386.
[246] Court decision BH1995.450.
[247] Court decision BH2005.312.

As to the practical implementation, some of the interviewed attorneys complained that some courts are reluctant to take into consideration procedural errors committed by the investigating authority, and tend to apply the provisions on 'relative grounds of annulment' rather restrictively.[248] We have no information as to how the judges and prosecutors assess the judicial practice in this respect.

3. Professional culture of defence lawyers

3.1. The bar associations and their role in the provision of criminal defence

The legal profession in Hungary is organized into separate bar associations. Membership in a bar association is compulsory for attorneys. A bar association is a public body and is completely independent of the State. Public bodies are self-governing entities established by an Act of Parliament with registered membership.[249] Public bodies perform a public function related to their membership and activities.

A bar association's primary duty is to maintain a public register of attorneys, govern them based on the principle of self-regulation and engage in professional duties and representation.[250] The bar association organises attorneys' continuous professional development, carries out disciplinary functions through its self-elected bodies, represents attorneys and their interests in public fora and plays an active role in the education of trainee attorneys. It also makes decisions concerning the initiation and termination of attorneys' membership in the bar association.

The Hungarian bar is composed of a national association (the Hungarian Bar Association)[251] and regional bar associations.[252] The Hungarian Bar Association operates as the national body of attorneys and its members are the regional bar associations. A regional bar association is also a public body, which has a representative and administrative apparatus and an independent budget; within its operational area, it fulfils the duties assigned to its jurisdiction. The membership of the regional bar associations consists of all attorneys practicing within the territorial competence of the particular association. The operational areas of regional bar associations are the same as the jurisdiction of the Budapest Metropolitan Court and the county courts respectively. Regional bar associations are located in Budapest[253] and in the 19 counties of Hungary.[254]

The statutory conditions of becoming a member of a bar association are the following:

---

[248]   Interviews with counsels. An example supporting this view is that, as noted above, in the case, where a trainee lawyer was not provided with sufficient time for preparation, the court of second instance did not quash the first instance judgement. The Supreme Court established that this amounts to a relative ground for annulment.

[249]   Act IV of 1959 on the Civil Code 65.

[250]   Attorneys Act 12.

[251]   Chapter XIII of the Attorneys Act: website: <http://www.magyarugyvedikamara.hu>.

[252]   Chapter XII of the Attorneys Act.

[253]   Budapest Bar Association: <http://www.bpugyvedikamara.hu/>.

[254]   A list of county bar associations and their contact information can be found at: <http://www.magyarugyvedikamara.hu/?content=7x>.

- Hungarian citizenship;
- No criminal record;
- A law degree;
- Successfully completed the bar exam (taken after a mandatory three year traineeship, spent in full-time employment, which requires a law degree);
- Liability insurance;
- An appropriate office for the purposes of running a law firm;
- No exclusionary reasons.[255]

There are no further restrictions on membership of the bar association. Thus, if someone fulfils these requirements he/she must be admitted to the relevant association.

Currently, approximately 10,000 attorneys are members of the 20 regional bar associations in Hungary.[256] This means that there is one attorney for approximately every 1000 persons living in Hungary. The Budapest Bar Association is by far the largest regional bar association, with about 5,500 members; hence, there is one attorney for every 310 Budapest residents.[257]

Within the bar associations, there are no specialised sections for criminal defence lawyers. There is also no institutionalised specialisation within the legal profession. The role of the bar association in relation to criminal defence will mainly be twofold. First, the competent bar association keeps a register of those attorneys who can be appointed as defence counsel (and the appointing authority chooses from this list).

> The Attorneys Act [...] does not contain guidelines as to how the register should be put together, it simply obliges the bars to create a register that ensures the undisturbed course of the criminal proceeding. The bars [...] apply different methods in compiling the register. The most frequently used method is when members of the given bar association are included in the list. Some bars mark [...] those who expressly ask to be appointed. In larger bars [...] – where the number of lawyers is relatively high – it is possible to compile the list of [...] appointed defence counsels on the basis of voluntary enrolment.[258]

---

[255] For example, a person may not be admitted for 10 years after serving imprisonment imposed for an intentional offence, for three years after the end of the parole, if the imprisonment was suspended, or for 10 years after he/she was excluded from a bar association.
[256] See <http://nol.hu/cikk/472020/>.
[257] By contrast, the Szeged Bar Association has about 520 members, which equates one attorney for every 815 residents in that county. The Debrecen Bar Association, which covers Hungary's second largest city, only has about 400 members, equating to one member for every 1,360 residents.
[258] Bánáti 2005, p. 52. For example, out of the 5,500 members of the Budapest Bar, approximately 1,150 can be appointed as defence counsel (the list of counsel who can be appointed is available at <http://www.bpugyvedikamara.hu/valasszon_ugyvedet/kirendeles/>. This does not, however, mean that this is the number of lawyers specialised in criminal law, as some criminal lawyers do not undertake appointments and prefer to pay the annual extra fee to be exempted from this obligation.

In bar associations where voluntary enrolment is possible, there is therefore the possibility for specialisation.

The other function is the adjudication of disciplinary complaints against attorneys (acting in both civil and criminal matters). This will be dealt with in more detail below.

3.2. Lawyers' role in criminal proceedings and duty to the client as reflected in ethical standards

Criminal defence lawyers may provide defence within the framework of two different legal relationships, either as retained lawyers on the basis of a contract with the client, or as counsel appointed by the competent authority.[259] In the former case, a retainer shall be concluded and the defendant shall confer a power of attorney on counsel, while in the latter case, the source of the entitlement to provide defence is based on the official decision.[260]

The basic responsibilities of defence counsel that define their role in the criminal proceedings are prescribed in the CCP.[261] Defence counsel a) shall establish contact with the defendant without delay; b) use all lawful means of defence in the interests of the defendant in proper time; c) inform the defendant of the means of defence and his/her rights in the criminal proceedings; and d) promote the finding of facts supporting the innocence of the defendant or mitigating his/her punishment. For a detailed discussion of defence rights, see Section 2.

The Attorneys Act provides further rules concerning the obligations of lawyers to their clients, including the duty to refrain from undertaking any obligation that endangers the lawyer's professional independence;[262] the duty to act in a manner that is completely lawful and worthy of the legal profession;[263] and the obligation of confidentiality with regard to every fact/data with which the lawyer becomes acquainted in the course of carrying out his/her professional duties.[264] As far as damage caused by lawyers are concerned, attorneys shall be liable for reimbursement of any damages that arise within the scope of their practice.[265] The attorney may not accept from another party a retainer for an action to be carried out against the interests of his/her client.[266]

The Code of Ethics of the Hungarian Bar Association provides detailed norms of conduct. According to the Code, attorneys should utilise all lawful possibilities in order to enforce the interests of the client. The attorney should properly prepare for the case concerning the facts and the applicable legal rules. Acting against the interests of the client is prohibited.[267]

---

[259] CCP art. 44.
[260] In Hungary there are no public defenders, as the concept of attorneys employed by the State is regarded as a violation of the independence of lawyers.
[261] CCP 50.
[262] Attorneys Act 3 (1).
[263] Attorneys Act 3 (2)-(3).
[264] Attorneys Act 8.
[265] Attorneys Act 10 (1).
[266] Attorneys Act 25.
[267] Code of Ethics Section 3/4.

Section 8 of the Code of Ethics also contains specific rules pertaining to defence counsel. If the interests of the defendants are conflicting, defence counsel is prohibited from defending both of them as a retained or appointed lawyer. If the conflict of interest only emerges during the course of the proceedings, defence counsel shall terminate all related assignments and shall request to be dismissed from all appointments.

After the assignment or the appointment, the power of attorney shall immediately be submitted to the authorities, and defence counsel shall, without delay, contact the appointing authorities in order to get information about the case. Furthermore, defence counsel shall contact the defendant if he/she is in pre-trial detention without any delay, and shall keep in touch with the defendant according to the needs of the case.[268]

Defence counsel shall inform the defendant about the legal possibilities and obligations concerning the case, the legal circumstances of the case, and the procedural acts that are likely to take place.[269] In the course of fulfilling his/her tasks, defence counsel is prohibited from contradicting the facts as submitted by the defendant and is bound by the facts as presented by the defendant.[270] If the defendant denies the charge, defence counsel shall refrain from acting in any way that would suggest that he/she doubts the innocence of the defendant.[271] Defence counsel shall ask for remedy in all cases, when it is possible according to the law, provided that it is in line with the interests of the defendant.

As outlined in Section 2, the practical implementation of these provisions leaves much to be desired, primarily in relation to the functioning of the appointed defence counsel system Appointed defence counsel[272] often fail to attend proceedings in the investigation stage, tend to be less active during the whole proceedings, frequently fail to maintain contact with detained defendants and are often not trusted by their clients – this will be further elaborated in Section 3.4.

3.3. Perception of defence lawyers and their relationship with other legal professions[273]

Although there is a general agreement among legal practitioners that there are substantial differences between individual lawyers and that it is difficult to formulate opinions concerning attorneys in general, one judge expressed the view that the types of cases in which defence counsel specialise correspond with certain typical attitudes on their part. Whereas counsel specialising in high profile white collar offences are usually cooperative and careful to move within the framework set by the law, lawyers taking cases affiliated with organised crime and violent

---

[268]   Code of Ethics Section 8/4.
[269]   Code of Ethics Section 8/6.
[270]   Code of Ethics Section 3/3.
[271]   Code of Ethics Section 8/8.
[272]   It should be noted that the same lawyer may act on the basis of a retainer in one case, and on appointment in another, although – as mentioned above – there are certain lawyers who base their practice almost exclusively on appointment.
[273]   This Section is based on interviews with practitioners.

criminals seem to be more inclined to apply unlawful means. Cases of smaller significance are often taken by young counsel, who are still enthusiastic and motivated and therefore perform quality defence services.

The majority of the interviewed practitioners (including defence lawyers) were of the view that retained lawyers as a rule provide higher quality defence services. They also sometimes expressed strong criticism of the work performed by appointed lawyers. Our sources at the police, prosecution and courts added, however, that in their view, the greater level of activity by retained lawyers is not always in the interests of the client, and is often more motivated by the intention to impress the defendant rather than professional expedience.

As opposed to the relative unanimity of views on the performance of retained and appointed counsels, there seems to be an enormous gap between the perception of counsel on the one hand, and all other legal professions on the other, with regard to the relationship between criminal defence lawyers and other criminal justice professions and institutions.

Our police sources claimed that the relationship between investigators and defence counsel is fundamentally good. Police investigators seem to have more problems with retained lawyers than appointed ones, which is not surprising in light of the fact that they have a complete discretion in choosing appointed counsel. Both our judicial and prosecutorial sources were of the opinion that their relationship with counsel is generally good, based on mutual respect, cooperation and collegiality.

The views of counsel were fundamentally different. They see their relationship with the police as generally problematic, whereas with regard to the prosecution many pointed out the almost complete lack of communication. In relation to judges, they said that while they are not hostile towards counsel, they subconsciously fail to treat counsel and prosecutors on an equal footing. One interviewed counsel expressed the view that this is rooted in organisational culture and perceptions of procedural roles. Both prosecutors and judges are state employees, vested with the task of asserting material justice, as opposed to counsel, whose fundamental task is to assist defendants, even if they are guilty.

A telling symbol of this imbalance is the practice followed at several Hungarian courts that, before the session formally commences and when members of the judicial panel are already in the court room, the prosecutor is allowed to enter without being called, and sometimes conducts long conversations inside the court room, while counsel and the defendant are waiting outside to be called to enter. The interviewed counsel did not in any way imply that on such occasions the actual case is decided in advance or even discussed; they simply quoted this example to substantiate the claim that, while judges do not look at counsel as colleagues, their relationship with prosecutors is characterised by a strong sense of collegiality. According to one interviewed counsel, this kind of organisational tradition also contributes, on a subconscious level, to the high success rate of the prosecution.

3.4. *Legal aid and quality assurance*

As explained in detail in Section 2, criminal legal aid is provided within the framework of the system of appointed counsel: if a person is granted personal cost exemption, upon his/her request the authority appoints a defence counsel for him/her. Counsel appointed in this way receive the same remuneration and operate under the same provisions as counsel appointed based on the interests of justice (for juveniles, detained defendants, etc).

As was also noted above, the system of appointed counsel suffers from severe dysfunction, often leading to a situation where the indigent defendant's right to effective defence is not properly advanced. in addition to the lack of adequate financing, legal gaps and problems in the practice of certain authorities (for example, late notifications by the police), deeply rooted structural problems contribute to this problem.

The management of the legal aid system involves four main functions: (a) providing legal aid (a legal aid lawyer) when mandatory or otherwise necessary; (b) monitoring and guaranteeing the quality of the individual lawyer's work (individual quality assurance); (c) monitoring and guaranteeing the efficient functioning of the system (general quality assurance); and (d) devising and implementing the budget of the system (budgetary functions).

In the Hungarian system, several entities are responsible for each function, which leads to an inconsistent distribution of responsibilities.

The responsibility for the provision of legal aid is shared by the bar associations, which compile the list of legal aid lawyers, and the authorities which appoint the attorneys. Here again we emphasize the dangers arising from the fact that, in the investigation phase, the police decide whom to appoint, even though they are not interested in effective defence work.

There is currently no direct individual quality assurance in the legal aid system.[274] The bar associations could, in theory, perform indirect quality assurance through their disciplinary powers, since it is a bar association's right and duty to call its members to account for not abiding by professional rules set by the law and professional Code of Ethics.[275] However, in spite of the general dissatisfaction with the activity of appointed lawyers, there are few disciplinary procedures launched against appointed counsel who may be negligent.

The reason for this may be structural. In the investigation phase, the investigating authority and defendant are mainly in the position to judge the performance of counsel. Neither can realistically be expected to file a complaint with the bar association. The former is not really interested in effective defence work, whereas the latter is in a very vulnerable situation (particularly when detained).

---

[274]   It should be noted that 'quality control' of the work of a retained lawyer may also raise questions. Theoretically, the client exercises control over the attorney's performance (if he/she is not satisfied, he/she can terminate the retainer and retain someone else); however, professionals warn that this is an oversimplification of the problem, as people are usually unable to judge the performance of their attorneys, even when the lawyer is paid according to market prices. Furthermore, effective control over the performance of retained defence counsel can only be exercised by a defendant who, in case of dissatisfaction, can afford to hire another attorney, regardless of payments already made. If legal fees are paid in advance, many families are unable to change defence counsel.

[275]   Attorneys Act 37.

Those defendants who cannot afford to retain a lawyer usually come from poor, uneducated segments of society, with a limited capacity to assert their interests. Furthermore, they do not have a guaranteed right to request the appointment of new defence counsel. Under the Attorneys Act, the competent authority may (but is not obliged to) withdraw the appointment, if the defendant makes the request on reasonable grounds.[276] The CCP prescribes that there is no remedy against the appointment of defence counsel, but the defendant may, in a reasoned motion, request the appointment of another defence counsel. The request is decided upon by the court, prosecutor, or investigating authority before which the proceedings are in progress.[277] Thus, it may happen that the defendant requests new defence counsel, the authority rejects the request, and the defendant is forced to continue the proceedings with a counsel against whom he/she has filed a complaint with the bar association. It is therefore not surprising that virtually no defendants risk this possibility.[278]

General quality assurance is completely lacking in the Hungarian system. Although the systemic collection and analysis of data regarding the operation of the legal aid system, and the regular assessment of its functioning, could make it possible to assess whether the appointment system fulfils its role of guaranteeing the right to fair trial and effective defence to those defendants who are vulnerable, there is no entity in Hungary that would perform this function. Neither the bar associations, nor the Ministry of Justice, nor any other actor have coherent data about the number, ratio and results of cases taken by appointed defence counsel. Moreover, none of these entities has commissioned surveys aimed at an examination of the system's efficiency, and they do not operate institutionalised mechanisms to monitor and assess the system's functioning.

The area of budgetary functions is also incoherent. The Minister of Justice determines the detailed rules on fees, while the law on the annual budget sets the fee levels. Those organs that decide on the system's budget lack the tools to monitor the quality of the service they pay for, while the bar association, which performs most functions related to the operation of the system, only has a limited say with regard to budgetary issues.[279] In addition, different organisations (the investigating authority, the prosecution and the court) make the actual payments in each procedural phase. Therefore, there is no aggregated annual data on the amounts paid on fees and expenses of appointed defence counsel. These individual organisations also do not keep a transparent and updated record regarding the payments they make to appointed counsel, and a determination of the break down

---

[276] Attorneys Act 34 (3).

[277] CCP 48 (5).

[278] Highlighting the problems concerning the management of the system, in response to our request, the Hungarian Bar Association was not able to answer the question of how many of the 448 disciplinary cases conducted in 2007 concerned appointed counsel, and in how many of these cases a violation of the rules of the profession was established.

[279] The President of the Hungarian Bar Association is a member of the National Justice Council, which prepares and submits the draft budget of the judicial chapter to the Government (which contains the bulk of the money to be spent on legal aid).

of costs between fees and reimbursed expenses (travel, copying, and so on) is close to impossible.

Even if these costs were known, it would be insufficient, since the State only pays the costs of indigent (and acquitted) defendants. In all other cases (with the exception of personal cost exemption), the defendant is obliged to repay the advanced fees and costs as part of the criminal costs. No separate information is available as to what percentage of the costs advanced in this way is paid back, so the actual total budget of the system is impossible to estimate and plan.

Therefore, in addition to raising legal aid fees and eliminating problems in the legal framework and the practice of authorities, in order to set up a truly efficient criminal legal aid system, one single organization should be vested with the responsibility of appointing legal aid lawyers, monitoring their performance (and signalling their omissions to the bar association for the purposes of disciplinary sanctioning), regularly assessing the efficiency of the whole system, as well as determining and implementing the legal aid budget.[280]

4.   Political commitment to effective criminal defence

The public perception of crime and defence rights: Based on available research results, we can draw the intriguing conclusion that, while crime is not among the most important considerations for the public, there is a false sense of an increase in the number of crimes, together with strong support for strict punishment. According to the fall 2007 Eurobarometer survey, the Hungarian population ranks crime as 5th in the list of concerns behind unemployment, poverty, poor health and environmental issues.[281] At the same time, whereas data from the National Institute of Criminology shows that the number of reported offences has been more or less steady since 1998, over two thirds of the 1,200 respondents of a survey on perceptions of criminal justice (carried out by the company 'Medián') sensed an increase in criminality.[282] Furthermore, the respondents estimated the percentage of violent crimes to be 55% of the total number of offences, although the actual proportion is only 7-8%.

According to the Medián survey, this distortion may be attributed to the media, which focuses primarily on violent crimes, a finding confirmed by the interviewed professionals.[283]

---

[280]   See Kádár, Tóth & Vavró 2007, p. 133-138 and also the recent research of the Hungarian Helsinki Committee, in which 150 already closed case files were analysed through a standardised questionnaire, with the purpose of testing whether such an analysis may be an efficient tool for assessing the quality of defence work. The research: a) substantiated the already known differences between the work of retained and appointed lawyers; and b) proved that even a formal analysis reveals much about the quality of the work a particular counsel performed in a case.

[281]   It was referred to by 14% of the respondents. See
         <http://ec.europa.eu/public_opinion/archives/eb/eb68/eb68_hu_nat.pdf>.

[282]   See <http://www.median.hu/object.238a5a0a-b2e7-4e2e-9ff5-5819d1493fa0.ivy> (hereafter Medián survey).

[283]   Interviews with practitioners.

According to Medián, three quarters of those who think that the number of crimes is on the increase believe this (imaginary) trend is attributable to the lenient sanctioning practices of courts. 60% of all the respondents agreed with the statement that the courts ought to impose more severe sanctions, while 63% regarded capital punishment as acceptable even in peace time (an additional 7% only in time of war).

The results confirm the view of the interviewed professionals, according to whom Hungarian society evidently supports severe punishment and is not at all receptive to liberal ideas in relation to criminal justice. They agreed that the lay public understands almost nothing of the rationale behind guaranteeing procedural rights for defendants.[284]

Foreigners are not generally perceived as a criminal threat. According to the Eurobarometer survey, 2% of respondents indicated immigration as a main concern. However, the issue of foreign criminality resurfaces in politics from time to time.[285] On the other hand, the perception that members of the Roma minority are more inclined to criminality than the majority population, and are in general a threat to society, is a view that not only the public, but even police officers, hold openly.[286]

Changes in criminal policy: The majority of the professionals interviewed were rather critical about the treatment of criminal justice by the political forces, claiming that most politicians are driven by populist intentions based on the perceived desire of Hungarian society for a stricter criminal justice system.[287]

In fact, political attitudes have gone through several changes since the political transition of 1989 – mostly (but not always) according to the pattern that, while conservative governments tend to introduce restrictions, left wing governments are more liberal in their approaches. In 1993, the Criminal Code was amended in harmony with democratic changes, and the politics of criminal justice was liberalized. In 1997, the socialist-liberal Government strengthened criminal sanctions, with the expressly stated purpose of influencing sentencing practice, which was perceived as too light. In 1998, the new conservative Government adopted the toughest amendment to the Criminal Code since the transition, with the aim of addressing delinquency and satisfying 'pressure from the public demanding harsher sentences due to an increasing fear of crime'.[288]

As a consequence, by 2001, the number of imprisoned detainees was double the EU average.[289] In 2003, the socialist-liberal Government shifted towards a more liberal direction and mitigated the stringency of the 1998 amendments, but still retained some provisions of serious concern, such as an actual life sentence

---

[284] Interviews with practitioners.
[285] For example, in the spring of 2008, the mayor of one of Hungary's largest cities began to lobby for a local refugee camp to be closed down, on the ground that asylum seekers posed a criminal threat and committed a large number of petty thefts.
[286] Pap & Simonovits 2007.
[287] Interviews with practitioners.
[288] Nagy & Szomora 2007, p. 195.
[289] The number was 170 inmates per 100,000 citizens (source: statistics of the National Prison Administration, <www.bvop.hu>).

(imprisonment without the possibility of ever being conditionally released).[290] The ongoing process of drafting a new Criminal Code seems to continue a more liberal criminal policy aimed at reducing the role of imprisonment and encouraging the application of alternative sanctions.

With regard to amendments to the rules of criminal proceedings,[291] after the 1989 transition amendments to the Criminal Procedure Code[292] guaranteed rights for the defence greater than the European average and beyond established international standards, including counsel's right to be present at all witness hearings during the investigation and to pose questions directly to the suspect and witnesses heard.

The amendments of 1994 were intended to harmonise the code with the evolving case law of the ECtHR, and introduced further guarantees of fair trial and other procedural standards. Despite this, the old Code retained several features of socialist-type procedural laws, which made the drafting of a new law inevitable. The codification committee started its work in 1994 and prepared a draft by June 1997. The law (CCP) was adopted in March 1998 and, although it was envisaged to come into force in 1999, it only did so in July 2003, and was amended on several occasions between its passing and coming into force. In line with the increasingly stringent criminal policies, these amendments have in several respects curtailed defence rights, compared to the original concept and text. Examples include the weakening of the immediacy principle (and therefore the adversarial nature of the proceeding), by allowing the broad use of statements made before the trial stage; the failure to fully separate procedural functions, by allowing prosecutors to remain absent from certain trials and preserving the primacy of judicial interrogation instead of classical cross-examination.

According to some experts:

> those ideas [of the original concept] have become reality that aimed at increasing the efficiency of the process, [...] the position of the victim was strengthened [...and] judicial competencies in the preparatory procedure were significantly broadened.[293]

However, the intention of the original concept to bring about proposed structural changes[294] that would also have had a positive impact on the fuller implementation of defence rights, has not been completely realised.[295]

---

[290] This was criticised by – among others – the European Committee for the Prevention of Torture and Inhuman or Degrading Treatment or Punishment (CPT). See <http://www.cpt.coe.int/documents/hun/2007-24-inf-eng.htm>.

[291] The development of these amendments was outlined in Bárd 2007, p. 214-33.

[292] Act I of 1973 on the Criminal Procedure.

[293] Bárd 2007, p. 232.

[294] Such as a clearer division of procedural functions and a fuller implementation of the deciding criminal liability in an adversary trial, respecting the principle of immediacy.

[295] Bárd 2007, p. 233.

5. Conclusions

In conclusion, it may be said that, whereas the legal framework of the Hungarian criminal procedure system mostly guarantees those rights that are of crucial importance for the defence to be effective, the practice of the authorities sometimes prevents the full implementation of the right to quality defence. In addition, the severe systemic deficiencies of the ex officio appointment system undermine the right to effective defence of indigent suspects and defendants.

At the level of the legal framework, the most outstanding issues that may negatively impact upon effective defence are: (i) the restricted access of the defence to evidence serving as the basis for pre-trial detention; (ii) the possibility of appointing substitute lawyers at short notice, if defence is mandatory and the summoned lawyer fails to appear at the court hearing; (iii) the wide possibility of trainee lawyers substituting for their principals in the investigation stage and before the local courts, without effective supervision from the first day of their traineeship; and (iv) the lack of mandatory translation of some documents that may be important for the defendant to understand and assess the standing of his/her case (for example, the minutes or hearings) and to exercise some of his/her rights (for example, the right to raise a motion for the correction of the minutes).

At the level of the practice of authorities, the following undermine the right to effective defence: (i) the practice of informal questioning by the investigating authority before the formal commencement of the criminal proceeding and the provision of information about the defendant's rights; (ii) the practice of hearing prospective suspects as witnesses; (iii) the late notification of counsel about the time of the first interrogation; (iv) the defendant's restricted ability to effectively choose his/her lawyer before the first interrogation, unless he/she can name a lawyer immediately; (v) the courts' failure to assess the individual circumstances of defendants when deciding on pre-trial detention, instead relying to a great extent on the severity of the offence of which the defendant is suspected and the prospective punishment; and (vi) the organisational culture that results in a stronger sense of collegiality on the part of judges towards prosecutors than towards counsel, which may play a role in a number of problems identified by attorneys and partially substantiated by sociological research: for example, the higher rates of quashing of acquitting than condemning judgements, the higher rate of complying with evidentiary motions by the defence if supported by the prosecutor, problems in applying the *in dubio pro reo* principle, etc.

Indigent defendants are particularly vulnerable in the Hungarian system. Empirical data shows that criminal legal aid lawyers often fail to attend procedural actions during the investigation (at which stage attendance is not mandatory). Even when they do appear, they tend to be inactive, are often not trusted by their clients, and frequently fail to maintain or even establish contact with detained defendants.

Apart from the very low remuneration for appointed lawyers, the main factor behind this situation seems to be that indigent defendants do not have any choice concerning their counsel. The lawyer in the investigation stage is appointed by the investigating authority, sometimes from among attorneys who fully or almost completely base their practice on appointments, which has strong implications in relation to their actual and perceived independence. Another crucial problem is that both individual and general quality assurance is missing from the system. Individual quality assurance could be performed by a bar association through its disciplinary powers. However, experience shows that, in spite of the general dissatisfaction with the performance of appointed lawyers, complaints against them are few.

General quality assurance (the regular monitoring and assessment of the system) is not performed by any entity with a role in its operation.

In addition, the legal and material framework of criminal legal aid also contributes to the deficiencies. Examples include the logistical difficulties of consulting detained clients, the lack of payment for certain activities (such as consultations with non-detained clients, preparation of written petitions) or, in the case of indigent foreigners, the failure to provide interpretation for consultations outside procedural acts (for example, interrogations).

This means that indigent defendants have a significantly reduced chance of receiving truly effective defence: the institutional safeguards are not in place, and it fully depends on the commitment and ethical conviction of the given lawyer as to whether he/she performs a counsel's tasks at a high quality standard, in spite of the low remuneration and the difficulties stemming from the legal framework, or the practice of the authorities conducting the criminal procedure.

6.   Bibliography

Books

Bencze 2005
Bencze, M., *A jogalkalmazási folyamat szociológiai vizsgálata* (manuscript).

Fenyvesi 2002
Fenyvesi, C., *A védőügyvéd: a védő büntetőeljárási szerepéről és jogállásáról* (The defence counsel: about the defence counsel's role and status in the criminal procedure), Budapest–Pécs: Dialóg Campus Kiadó, 2002.

Jakucs 2003
Jakucs, T. (ed.), *A büntetőeljárási törvény magyarázata* (Commentary of the CCP), Budapest: KJK-KERSZÖV, 2003.

Kádár 2004
Kádár, A., *Presumption of Guilt: Injurious Treatment and the Activity of Defence Counsels in Criminal Proceedings against Pre-trial Detainees*, Budapest: Hungarian Helsinki Committee, 2004.

Kádár, Tóth & Vavró 2007
Kádár, A., Tóth, B. & Vavró, I., *Without Defence, Recommendations for the Reform of the Hungarian Ex Officio Appointment System In Criminal Matters*, Budapest: Hungarian Helsinki Committee, 2007.

Chapters in Compilations

Bárd 2007
Bárd, K., 'The Development of Hungarian Criminal Procedure between 1985 and 2005', in: A. Jakab, P. Takács and F.A. Tatham (eds.), *The Transformation of the Hungarian Legal order 1985-2005*, Alphen aan de Rijn: Kluwer Law International, 2007, p. 214-233.

Nagy & Szomora 2007
Nagy, F. & Szomora, Z., 'The Development of the Hungarian Criminal Law over the Past Twenty Years', in: A. Jakab, P. Takács and F.A. Tatham (eds.), *The Transformation of the Hungarian Legal order 1985-2005*, Alphen aan de Rijn: Kluwer Law International, 2007, p. 191-206.

Articles in Journals

Bánáti 2005
Bánáti, J., 'Szabadságkorlátozások' (Forms of detention), *Fundamentum*, 2, 2005, p. 50-51.

Fázsi 2008
Fázsi, L., 'Üres garancia – a tanú figyelmeztetésének gyakorlati kérdései' (Empty safeguard – the practical aspects of warning witnesses), *Rendészeti Szemle* (Law Enforcement Review), 2, 2008, p. 47-59.

Hablicsek 2003
Hablicsek, L., 'Kísérleti számítások a roma lakosság területi jellemzőinek alakulására és 2021-ig történő előrebecslésére', in: *Demográfia*, Budapest: KSH, 2007, p. 7-54.

Orell 1998
Orell, F., 'The right to defence of the juveniles', *Belügyi Szemle*, 12, 1998, p. 97.

Pap & Simonovits 2007
Pap, A.L. & Simonovits, B., 'Igazolt diszkrimináció: Etnikai alapú kiválasztás a magyar rendőrség igazoltatási gyakorlatában' (Verified discrimination: ethnic profiling in the practice of the Hungarian Police in relation to ID checks), *Élet és Irodalom*, 20, 2007, see: <http://www.es.hu/index.php?view=doc;16599>.

Szabó & Szomor 2007
Szabó, Z. & Szomor, S., 'Fegyveregyenlőség' (Equality of Arms), *Rendészeti szemle* (Law Enforcement Review), 3, 2007, p. 19-41.

Michele Caianiello

CHAPTER 9 ITALY*

1. Introduction

1.1. Basic demographic information

Italy is a founding member of the European Union. Notwithstanding its ancient roots, the Italian State can be considered quite young, dating back to 1861. After initially being a Kingdom, these then followed the Fascist period (1922-1943) and, in 1946, the Italian Republic was born, and its Constitution entered into force in 1948.

Italian territory measures approximately 301,200 square kilometres, with a population of almost 60 million (at 31 December 2008).[1] The number of settled immigrants is increasing: citizens of other countries holding a regular residence visa now number approximately 3.9 million, around 6.5% of the population.[2] Compared to the data of previous years (2008), the foreign population has increased by about 434,000 (7.3 per 1,000 inhabitants). It is relevant to observe that, according to the Italian Institute of Statistics (*Instituto Nazionale di Statistica* – ISTAT),[3] the growth of the population is almost entirely due to immigration.

The largest foreign communities in Italy are, in decreasing order Rumanian, Albanian, Moroccan, Chinese, Ukrainian, Philippine and Tunisian.[4] The language mainly taught and spoken is High Italian (although in Alto Adige and Valle d'Aosta, German, French and Ladin are also spoken. Ladin is a Neolatin language, spoken mainly in four valleys of the Dolomites.). Citizens are obliged to attend

---

* This country report has been reviewed by Giulio Illuminati, professor of criminal procedure at the University of Bologna.

[1] See 'Istat, la popolazione in Italia oltre il traguardo dei 60 milioni. La speranza di vita diventa più alta. Aumentano i decessi ma anche le nascite: 12mila bambini in più rispetto al 2007', *La Repubblica*, 26 February 2009, online at <http://www.repubblica.it/2009/02/sezioni/cronaca/istat-popolazione/istat-popolazione/istat-popolazione.html>.

[2] See *supra* note 1. Recent studies have affirmed that the irregular immigrant population in Italy amounts to roughly 400,000 and this must be added to the 3.9 million of regular immigrants.

[3] The Italian name is 'Istituto nazionale di statistica'.

[4] For the complete list, see the Istat site, <http://demo.istat.it/str2007/index.html> (data of 31 December 2007).

373

school until the 9th grade. A large majority of inhabitants are catholic (at least formally, since practising Catholics represent no more than one-third of the population); there is also a small group of Muslims (1.2%).

The average annual income per person is $ 26,476 (approximately 18,100 Euro) (data from International Monetary Found, World Economic Outlook, October 2007). As a member of the European Union and G8, and part of the European Union-Schengen area, in which all internal border controls have been abolished, Italy is among the most industrialized countries in the world. The official currency is the Euro.

1.2. The nature of the criminal justice system

Italy has a statutory legal system in the continental European tradition. At the peak of the hierarchy of the sources of law lies the Italian Constitution, which as part of the modern age, has a rigid form: it can only be amended after a specific and complex procedure – which is different from the ordinary procedure to approve new laws – and with a vote taken by the absolute majority of each Chamber of Parliament.[5]

The legislative power belongs to the Parliament alone. The government, however, has some subsidiary powers. According to the Constitution, the Council of Ministries has the power, to adopt *Decreti Legislativi* (Legislative Decrees), observing the following procedure: the Parliament can endorse an act – the so-called *legge delega* (delegating law) – which delegates the power to the government to regulate certain aspects of the system – including those of criminal law and justice (arts. 76 and 77(1) of the Italian Constitution). The *legge delega* must contain the principles and the general criteria that the government must respect in drafting any such legislative decree.[6]

Moreover, the government as provided for by article 77(2) & (3) of the Italian Constitution, may approve a *decreto legge* (law decree) in cases of 'necessity and urgency': the act has the force of law, but must be approved by both Chambers of Parliament within 60 days. If the decree does not receive the approval of the legislative branch, it loses its effectiveness *ex tunc* (*tamquam non esset*). For the last 30

---

[5]   According to art. 138 of the Constitution, acts amending the Constitution and other constitutional laws must be approved twice by each Chamber of the Parliament, and by the absolute majority of the members of each Chamber. Within three months of their approval, acts amending the Constitution can be submitted to a popular referendum, if one-fifth of the members of one Chamber, or 500,000 electors, or five Regional Councils present a formal request. In such a case, the entering into force of the amendments is suspended until the end of the popular vote: in case of negative outcome of the referendum, the amendments to the Constitution approved by the Parliament cannot be promulgated and do not enter into force. However, a referendum is not permitted when the amendments to the Constitutions are approved by a majority of two-thirds of the components of the each Chamber, in the second voting.

[6]   If the act of the government in whole or in part exceeds or violates these principles or criteria provided by Parliament in the delegating law, then the legislative decree must be considered, in whole or in part, constitutionally illegitimate. Therefore, it may be declared null and void by the Constitutional Court.

years, the Government has often chosen to define new crimes through the means of a *decreto legge*.[7] Finally, a legislative initiative can be brought both by a Member of Parliament and a Member of Government.

Officially, political programs influence criminal justice only when they are translated into statutes by Parliament. Formally, such a system is conceived so as to not give political discretion to judges or the prosecutor. Both of these are not, in theory, permitted to set their own agenda; neither can they take autonomous moves other than those required by the law. As the system was inspired by the Enlightenment ideology, judges should limit themselves to applying mechanically the provisions of the law. In the framework drafted by the Italian Constitution, it is thus correct to observe that it is a task of the legislature to outline the criminal policy, while the judges simply must apply the law in each case that comes before them. This is, in theory, the reason why (formally, at least) the appointment of judges and prosecutors should not be affected by any political considerations or influences.

Judges do not make political choices; they simply carry out a technical activity from which political considerations are excluded. Of course, in putting into effect the meaning and scope of criminal provisions, judicial interpretation is allowed. Notwithstanding the formal role attributed to the legality principle and to the law as the governing source of the system foreseen in the Constitution, in reality the circumstances surrounding the 'moment of the application' have, in practice, assumed a more dominant role.

In other words, a provision cannot be rendered intelligible without taking into account the prior decisions of the courts. If this is common in almost every other system of law, it is, however, possible to say that in Italy, at least in some circumstances, the interpretation given to the law by the courts has completely changed the meaning attributed to it at the outset by the legislature, sometimes rendering ineffective a reform that was approved by Parliament.

The judiciary is not held politically accountable for the decisions of its members. Paradoxically, the legality principle has been shown to have the effect of shielding the prosecutors (and the judges) from any political responsibility. The consequence is that, in the Italian system, the judiciary – and particularly the prosecutor – is independent, but not accountable, for most of the choices that are made. The unaccountability of the prosecutor, in particular, is the object of debate and is vehemently contested by a portion of Italian society.

---

[7]   Among other things, it is worth mentioning the crimes introduced by the *decreto legge* No. 306 of 8 June 1992, after the murder of Judge Giovanni Falcone, his wife and escort by the criminal organisation *Cosa Nostra*; in recent times, we can cite the *decreto legge* No. 259 of 22 September 2006, governing the illegitimate wiretapping performed by private citizen or companies. Concerning the *decreto legislativo*, it could be said that a large number of the reforms having a broad character introduced into the criminal justice system were realized through this kind of primary legislative act. For example, the new Italian Code of Criminal Procedure was endorsed with a legislative decree (No. 447 of 22 September 1988), after the approval by the Italian Parliament of a law providing for the general principles and criteria that the Italian Government would have to follow (law No. 81 of 16 February 1987 – *Delega legislativo al Governo della Repubblica per l'emanazione del nuovo codice di procedura penale*).

In the last years, the most influential association of Italian criminal lawyers, the so-called Penal Chambers (*Camere Penali*) are fighting at the political and social levels for the separation of the prosecutor from the judiciary.[8] However, many scholars and politicians consider that separating the prosecutor from the judiciary could endanger the independence of the latter, giving too much power to the government. In fact, if it was separated from the judiciary, the prosecutor would be submitted in all probability to the executive. Therefore, considering that the prosecutor is deemed to be the 'gatekeeper' of the criminal justice system, the government could end by controlling the most powerful instrument in the administration of criminal justice, a perspective that it is not suitable, according to many, in the Italian context. For this reason, it is preferable that prosecutors remain part of the judiciary, as intended by the drafters of the Italian Constitution and provided for by articles 107(4), 108(2) and 112.

In recent years, to achieve a satisfactory compromise between an unaccountable prosecutorial independence and governmental control over prosecutorial policies, many scholars have supported the use of priority criteria. In the opinion of most researchers, priority criteria could be approved via specific acts of Parliament, so as to permit efficient management of prosecutions and trials.[9] In particular, it was observed that the adoption by the legislature of priority criteria for prosecutors and judges is not, as such, incompatible with the constitutional principles defending judicial and prosecutorial independence. However, only twice in past ten years has Parliament approved specific provisions to intervene in the concrete administration of criminal justice by indicating priority criteria.[10] The results of these new provisions were considered to be quite controversial.

---

[8] In the past, more than one 'abstention from the judicial hearings' (a sort of strike) has been announced by the Penal Chambers to demonstrate their support for the separation of the office of the prosecutor from the judiciary. The argument put forward by the Penal Chambers is that the lack of separation of the prosecutor from the judiciary implies that the prosecution and defence are not substantially equal in the Italian criminal justice process. It is observed, indeed, that a judge usually tends to perceive himself more proximate to the 'colleagues' of the prosecution than to the defence. This appears particularly true – it is often said – in the initial phase of the criminal proceedings – that is, in the preliminary investigations. Moreover, it has been submitted that, being the gatekeeper of the criminal justice system, since he/she alone has the power to initiate a criminal proceeding, the prosecutor should be subject to some form of political accountability. Those who supports this opinion point out that the legality principle, which should in theory regulate all procedural phases and stages, including the filing of the indictment and the selection of the charges, relieving the prosecutor from having to make any discretionary choices, has proven itself to be quite ineffective.

[9] Notwithstanding that the issues raised by priority criteria primarily involve prosecutorial discretion, they also concern judicial tasks, as, for example, the order in which cases for which a trial is fixed must be treated: see Vicoli 2003, p. 227; Vicoli 2003, p. 258-293.

[10] In particular, some priority criteria were introduced with art. 227, Legislative Decree. n. 51, 19 February 1998, and with art. 2-*bis*, Act. No. 125, 24 July 2008. See on this matter *infra*, § 4.2.

Notwithstanding its inquisitorial traditions, Italy has, since 1988, had a new Code of Criminal Procedure (CCP), modelled on the adversarial system typical of common law.[11]

In 1955, Italy ratified the European Convention on Human Rights (ECHR). For a long period of time –until about the end of the 1970s – the efficacy of the ECHR at the national level was limited. Mostly, the value of the Convention was outlined in research,[12] while, at a practical level, it received little attention in judges' decisions and legislative choices.

The adoption of the new CCP was a turning point. In fact, article 2 § 1 of the Parliament Delegation Act 16 February 1987, No. 81 gave the Government the power to elaborate and adopt the new CCP, with the express purpose of giving effect and implementing the values and principles of the ECHR.

However, looking at the first decade after the CCP came into force, it is possible to find only a few practical references to the values of the Convention, as being useful to interpret and apply the CCP in coherence with ECHR standards. In addition, Italy has remained – at the European level – one of the worst countries in relation to the length of the proceedings, both in criminal and civil law matters.

In recent years, however, it is possible to affirm that the panorama appears to have radically changed. European sources – in a broad sense – are increasingly exercising their effect on the Italian System, so that it could be said that, at present, almost every aspect of the criminal process is strongly influenced by them, principally the ECHR. This change in the application of the European sources[13] is mainly due to a judicial activist approach to cases. It is also the consequence of reforms introduced by the legislator.

In 1999, the principles of article 6 ECHR were implemented at a Constitutional level.[14] When implementing the Convention, however, the legislator chose not to adopt the official text of article 6 ECHR. Instead, an Italian unofficial translation was preferred. This is in some passages the cause of discrepancy between the two texts. Moreover, Italian judges do not seem particularly aware of the power of article 111 § 3 of the Constitution.[15]

---

[11]　See Amodio & Selvaggi 1989, p. 1211-1240; Montagna & Pizzi 2004, p. 429-466; Illuminati 2005, p. 567-581. On the distinction between the inquisitorial and accusatorial systems, specifically referred to the Italian criminal process see Illuminati 1988; Illuminati 2008, p. 135-160; Panzavolta 2005, p. 577-622; Caianiello & Illuminati 2007, p. 129-133.

[12]　Among them, see Illuminati 1979, p. 26.

[13]　Among the European sources is the Law of implementation of the European Arrest Warrant (Act No. 69, 2005). After the *Pupino* case, we may say that all Framework Decisions of the European Union play an effective role within the Italian system, due to the principle of the conforming interpretation expressed by the European Court of Justice.

[14]　By Constitutional Act No. 2, 23 November 1999, art. 111 § 3 of the Italian Constitution.

[15]　For example, they have continued to interpret the right to be informed of the nature and causes of the charge as if it refers only to the process, and not to the legal definition (*nomen iuris*). It is only in the last few months that this jurisprudence seems to have been modified, and perhaps abandoned – at least in part - as a consequence of a decision adopted by the ECtHR with regard to an Italian case (ECtHR 11 December 2007, *Drassich* v. *Italy*, No. 25575/04. See on this decision Caianiello 2008, p. 165-176.). The accused had been convicted through an unexpected change in the legal definition of the charge, adopted by the Court of Cassation at the last stage of the criminal process. The ECtHR found Italy in violation of art. 6

→

In 2005, article 175 of the CCP was reformed so to allow for the re-opening of the criminal process – if conducted *in absentia* – when the convicted affirms that he/she never received notice of the proceedings against him. In addition, more significantly, the Court of Cassation, since 2005 (the so-called *Cat Berro Decision*), has adopted a new line of interpretation, under which no conviction can be executed, nor sentence served, if the European Court of Human Rights (ECtHR) had declared that the process violated, in at least one provision, article 6 of the ECHR.[16]

Finally, in 2007, the Italian Constitutional Court declared that the ECHR must be interpreted by Italian judges as a source of the Italian system that is superior to the law, even if inferior to the fundamental principles of the Italian Constitution. Therefore, when a text of a legal provision appears to conflict with one or more provisions of the ECHR, the judges are asked to make every possible effort to interpret and apply the Italian provision in coherence with the ECHR – as interpreted by the ECtHR. If it is not possible to solve the conflict through interpretation, the judges must submit the problem to the Constitutional Court, which may declare the Italian source to be constitutionally illegal.

1.3. Structure and processes of the criminal justice system

1.3.1. Jurisdiction

In Italy, crimes are divided in two categories: *delitti* (felonies) and *contravvenzioni* (misdemeanours). Felonies are punished with imprisonment (from 15 days up to 24 years) or with life imprisonment; they can also be punished with a fine (*multa*) of between 5 Euro and 5,164 Euro. Misdemeanours are punished with arrest (from five days up to three years) and/or with a fine, different from that provided for felonies (*ammenda*) from 2 Euro up to 1,032 Euro.

Trial courts have a general jurisdiction over the felonies and misdemeanours. However, if the crime is punishable with a penalty not greater than 10 years imprisonment, the case is decided by a single professional judge (trial court in single composition); when the crime is punishable with a penalty greater than 10

---

§ 3 *a-b* of the Convention. After the ECtHR decision, in 2008, the Cassation recognised the right of the accused to be informed of the judge's intention to modify the legal definition of the charges. On the same problem, see Parlato 2008, p. 1584; De Matteis 2008, p. 215-233; Zacché 2009, p. 781-788. See on this issue *infra*, § 2.1.3.

[16] Cass., Sect. I, 22 September 2005, n. 35616, *Guida al diritto*, n. 43, p. 84, with a comment by Selvaggi E., 'I dispositivi della Corte europea possono travolgere il giudicato', p. 86. Since then, other decisions have continued to develop the legal principle: see Cass., Sect. I, 18 May 2006, Somogyi, *Dir. e giust.*, 2006, n. 48, p. 51, commented by Ubertis G., 'Contumaci, doppia restituzione in termine. Ma la legge italiana non risulta ancora adeguata alla C.e.d.u.'. See, moreover, Cass. Sect. I, 1 December 2006, Dorigo, n. 2800 *Cass. pen.*, 2007, p. 1441, commented by De Matteis L., 'Le sentenze della Corte europea dei diritti dell'uomo ed il giudicato penale: osservazioni intorno al caso 'Dorigo''. On the same decision see Lonati 2007, p. 1538-1551. Finally, see Cass., Sect. I, 12 July 2006, n. 32678, S. T., *Dir. pen. proc.*, 2007, p. 85, with a comment by Epidendio T. E.

years imprisonment, the case is adjudicated by a panel of three professional judges (trial court in panel composition).

For the most serious crimes, punishable with life imprisonment or with not less than 24 years imprisonment, the case is attributed to the Court of Assize, a mixed panel of two professional judges and six lay judges, drawn from a list prepared by any Municipal Authority of the Italian Republic and revised by the President of each Italian trial court, with the co-operation of the local Bar Association.

Less serious offences, including both misdemeanours and felonies of minor gravity – may be handled by the *Giudice di Pace* ('Justice of the Peace'). The Justice of the Peace, created in 2001, has an *ad hoc* jurisdiction. In other words, his/her jurisdiction is delimited *per nomina delicti*, because there are specific crimes – both *contravvenzioni* and *delitti* – expressly devolved to this judge. In general, crimes devolved to the jurisdiction of the Justice of Peace are prosecutable only if the victim lodges a complaint (*querela di parte*). In such cases, if the victim and the accused find an agreement, and the victim withdraws the complaint, the case must be closed. The jurisdiction of the Justice of Peace was conceived to promote reconciliation between victims and perpetrators of the crime, so to re-establish social concordance without, if possible, applying criminal penalties.

1.3.2. Structure of the Italian criminal process

The existing Italian CCP, the *Codice di Procedura Penale*, dates from 1988. The 1988 CCP entered into force on 24 October 1989, replacing the Rocco CCP of 1930. The Rocco CCP, which had been introduced under the fascist regime and was strongly inspired by the Napoleonic CCP, reflected the inquisitorial character of the Italian criminal procedure. After World War II, and particularly since the end of the 1950s, scholars increasingly began to criticise the CCP, which was considered to be a remnant of the inquisitorial model inherited from the fascist era of the 1930s.

The post war Constitution of the Italian Republic, established in 1948, was the starting point for the rights movement in the field of criminal law and criminal procedure. The protection of the rights of the accused soon became a political issue. The initial effect of this ideological paradigm shift was that some reforms improved the rights of the defence, in particular by permitting the counsel of the indicted person to participate in actions carried by the investigating judge. After more than 20 years of political pressure, academic studies and Parliamentary debate, the drafting of the 1988 CCP replaced the modified 'old system', with the new CCP derived from the adversarial model.

Compared to the 1930 CCP, the new CCP has a completely different profile, inspired by the Anglo-American criminal procedure system.[17] Investigations are

---

[17] Many scholars wrote of an 'Americanization' of criminal procedures, particularly in Europe. See, for example, Wiegand 1991, p. 229-248. A 'weaker' version of this Americanization thesis seems more appropriate, because the import of American legal aspects does not substitute for the traditional framework; rather, the new legislative products graft onto the old framework, creating a hybrid and unique mix. In fact, the consequence of this Americanization seems to be a 'fragmentation' of the traditional legal cultures: see Panzavolta, *supra* note 11, p. 578-585.

→

carried out by the prosecutor and police, while the judge intervenes only whether requested by one or both parties. The CCP gives power to the defendant and to a victim's counsel to conduct private investigations. The judge for the preliminary investigations – usually defined as a 'judge without a file' – intervenes only in exceptional cases, when the restraint of fundamental rights is involved. This judge, however, does not have control of the investigation; on the contrary, he is a mere judge *ad acta*, who is involved only in specific acts at request of the parties (usually, at the request of the prosecutor).

The prosecutor has the responsibility for the conduct of investigations. He/she may initiate the investigation on his/her own and decide the manner in which it is to be conducted. When a complaint is lodged by a private person, or information is reported by the police, the prosecutor has the duty to investigate, in order to ascertain whether there is sufficient evidence to initiate a proceeding. Moreover, the Constitution gives the prosecutor the power to give orders directly to the police.

Consequently, in any trial court there is a 'judicial police station' whose staff is put under the authority of the prosecutor and who must comply with his/her orders and follow his/her directions. However, in practice, the police have a broad discretion in cases of relatively minor importance. In the ordinary course of the investigation, the prosecutor only conducts a brief supervision of police action: in reality, it is up to the police to set the agenda during the investigations, asking the prosecutor to issue the orders they need. Only in serious cases does the prosecutor exercise any real control over the work of the police. In these situations he/she actually directs the investigations.

Despite their general subordination to the prosecutor, and in addition to the discretion they enjoy *de facto*, the police have some formal autonomous powers during the investigation. For example, they may summon and question witnesses and the suspect.[18] In this case, the suspect has a duty to make him/herself available to the police, but also a right to remain silent. The questioning of the suspect cannot be conducted by a police officer without the presence of a lawyer, regardless of the gravity of the case: if the suspect has not yet appointed one, the police must appoint a duty lawyer. The questioning of the suspect by the police is not permitted if the suspect is under arrest, or subject to detention. However, at the moment of the arrest, the police are permitted to question the arrested person, but statements obtained can be used only to carry on the investigations. In other words, they cannot be used to adopt decisions of any sort by the judge, both during the investigations phase, as well as at trial.

At trial, the parties have the right to present evidence on their own behalf, to cross-examine witnesses, while those elements gathered during preliminary investigations and police are not admissible as evidence. The defendant may be convicted only if the judges consider him guilty beyond reasonable doubt.

As a consequence of the reforms the new CCP distinguishes between the investigation and the trial phase. Most of the information collected in the first phase

---

See, for a clear distinction between the American adversarial model and any European Continental system, Kagan 2001.

[18]   Scaglione 2001, p. 91 s.

of the proceedings – the investigation – is not admitted or used as evidence at trial. The new CCP is based on the assumption that the probative value of evidence is affected by the manner in which it is collected. The drafters of the CCP believed that the best environment for proving the facts and discovering the truth is a context in which opposing viewpoints are presented: as a consequence, the only evidence on which a decision can be based is the evidence collected orally at trial, including the use of the cross-examination, which is inspired by the Anglo-American system of criminal procedure.[19]

The symbol of the separation between the trial phase and the investigative phase is the 'double-dossier system', as opposed to the single investigative dossier that characterised the old system until 1988.[20] During the preliminary stage of the criminal proceedings, all records of evidence are collected in an investigative-dossier. At the end of the investigation, or after the preliminary hearing, in case of crimes where judicial preliminary scrutiny of probable cause is required,[21] this dossier is set aside and is available only to the parties, who can use it to prepare for trial, or to challenge a witness' credibility during trial testimony.[22]

The trial judge will never see the investigative-dossier. Instead, the trial judge is given a completely new dossier, the trial-dossier, to be filled only with the evidence collected during trial, as well as the evidence that is objectively impossible to reproduce in court (*corpus delicti*, wiretappings, records of searches performed by the police, records of prior convictions of the accused).[23]

In the Italian system a form of guilty plea is provided for, namely *applicazione della pena su richiesta delle parti* (application of punishment at the request of the parties), also-called *patteggiamento* (bargaining). It is possible to find some similarities between this and the plea bargaining carried out in the United States. In this situation, the defendant and the prosecutor agree on a penalty, without a guilty plea. The penalty is reduced by up to one-third of the ordinary amount. The judge must conduct a rapid review of the investigative file so as to ensure that there is no clear indication of innocence within the records. The judge should also verify – as a consequence of the legality principle – the consistency of the penalty and the nature of the crime.

---

[19]   Giostra 2001, p. 1; Ubertis 1992, p. 2.

[20]   For a most relevant exception to the double dossier system when pre-trial detention is applied, see *infra*, under § 2.3.3.

[21]   The Italian Code of Criminal Procedure provides that, when prosecution is commenced for crimes punishable with more than four years imprisonment, a preliminary hearing is mandatory. This hearing is held by a single judge – the judge of the preliminary hearing – who, on the basis of the elements gathered by the prosecutor during the investigation, must ascertain if there is sufficient evidence to go to trial (see, on this issue, Daniele 2005). In such cases, the judge must dispose of the trial by a decree. After that, the same judge must separate the dossiers – the trial dossier and the prosecutor's one – according to the rules described above. When the judge considers that there is not sufficient evidence to dispose of the trial, he must acquit the defendant; however, the case can be re-opened, at the request of the prosecutor, if new evidence is presented that is sufficient to reverse the previous decision.

[22]   See, Illuminati 2008, p. 730-732.

[23]   See, Cesari 1999, p. 9.

To render the system sustainable, the CCP provides for an alternative means to adjudicate the case, the so-called *giudizio abbreviato* (abbreviated trial). This can take place only under the request of the defendant, and the judgment is based on the investigative files. In other words, the defendant waives the right to trial, receiving a reduction of penalty: in the case of conviction, the penalty will be reduced by one-third of the regular sentence and life imprisonment will be converted to 30 years of imprisonment.

The adoption of these two tools is aimed at making the system sustainable, but they actually prove to be ineffective in reducing the number of trials. In general, these special proceedings are chosen in a very low percentage of cases (around 10-12%). According to the data provided by the Ministry of Justice,[24] in 2003 the percentage of the proceedings adjudicated with the *patteggiamento* was 6.46%, while those decided with the abbreviated trial was 2.40%. In 2007, the results were slightly higher. 7.27% with the *patteggiamento*, and 3.98% with the abbreviated trial.

There is also a third procedural form for adjudicating criminal cases, which applies only to minor crimes. When the judge believes that the accused may receive only a fine, the CCP permits this third form special proceeding, called *procedimento per decreto* (penal decree proceeding). In this case, the judge, at the request of the prosecutor, *inaudita altera parte* (without submissions by the accused), following a quick review of the investigative file, may, by decree order the defendant to pay a fine (the amount may be reduced up to 50% of the legal requirement). If the accused does not oppose the decree, the conviction becomes final. The percentage of cases adjudicated with the penal decree proceeding is around 5% of the cases. In 2003 it represented 4% of the all cases, in 2005 4.93% and in 2007 5.93%.

According to the Constitution (art. 112), the prosecutor is obliged to take action in criminal cases: the principle of legality applies strictly.[25] No matter how minor the offence is,[26] the law gives the prosecutor no discretion as to whether to prosecute or not, nor can the prosecutor suspend or withdraw the action, which must always end in a judicial decision. Also preserved in the CCP is the judge's power to introduce evidence when he/she cannot decide the case on the evidence submitted at trial.

Another important feature of the traditional inquisitorial system retained by the 1988 reform is that, in Italy, there is no jury system: fact finding remains in the hands of professional judges. The sole exception is the 'Court of Assise', a hybrid panel composed of six lay judges and two professional judges, which only processes major crimes. Moreover, the judge's decisions must always contain a written

---

[24]   The data is not freely available at the Ministry of Justice website. It was supplied by the Ministerial Offices only following our specific request.

[25]   On the issue concerning priority criteria, see *supra* under § 1.2.

[26]   It must be remembered that, after the coming into force of the Constitution, the Prosecutor is part of the judiciary, enjoying the same guarantees and safeguards of independence as the judges: see Illuminati 2004, p. 308-310; Caianiello 2003, p. 14-20; Caianiello & Illuminati, *supra* note 11, at p. 131.

statement.[27] The decision is also subject to the right of appeal, both for the defence as well as for the prosecutor.

1.3.3. Arrest and detention of a person suspected of a crime

When a person is discovered in the midst of committing a serious crime, the police have the power to arrest him provisionally (*arresto in flagranza*) but, within 24 hours, they must communicate the arrest to the prosecutor. In contrast to arrest, *fermo* ('stop') is permissible when the suspect is not caught red-handed, and the requirements set out in article 384 are met: in particular, in case of suspect's risk of flight. There must be a specific indication that the suspect poses a flight risk, as well as strong evidence of guilt (not mere suspicions). Finally, the committed offence must be a crime involving weapons or explosives, or a crime of similar degree.[28]

As noted above, *fermo* is possible only on the basis of a prosecutor's decree. Despite the different prerequisites, both *arresto* and *fermo* serve the same goals. These measures are used either to protect the public safety or for investigative purposes.

The proceedings following *arresto* or *fermo* are similar (see arts. 390-391 of the CCP). First of all, the police must make the suspect available to the prosecutor as soon as possible and, in any case, within 24 hours of the arrest or *fermo*. A person under arrest or *fermo* has the right to inform his/her counsel and family as soon as possible. It is up to the police to give notice to counsel and the family (the duty is usually observed and notice is given within 24 hours of the arrest or detention).[29] Subsequently, the prosecutor to whom the suspect has been made available should seek validation of the arrest or *fermo* by the judge of the preliminary investigation (art. 390 CPP).

To this end, article 390 § 1 of the CCP prescribes that the prosecutor shall bring the suspect before the judge of the preliminary investigation within 48 hours of his/her arrest or *fermo*, unless he/she has ordered the immediate release of the suspect by virtue of article 389. An arrest or *fermo* becomes ineffective if the requirements set out in article 390 § 1 are not met (art. 390 § 3).

The prosecutor who has requested the validation of the arrest or *fermo* may, at the same time, also request the judge of the preliminary investigations to order the pre-trial detention of the suspect (art. 391 § 3 and 291 of the CCP). The validation hearing should be held by judge within the following 48 hours (art. 390 § 2). In addition, article 391 § 6 of the CCP prescribes that the arrest or *fermo* will lose its effect, if the validation order has not been decreed within 48 hours after the suspect has been brought before the judge. The initial detention by the police may endure for a maximum of 96 hours (four days), starting from the moment that the suspect has been arrested or *fermato* (stopped).

---

[27]   See Iacoviello 1997, p. 9 s.

[28]   For which the law sets a punishment of life imprisonment or imprisonment for no less than a minimum of two years and a maximum of six years

[29]   For more information on this point, see *supra,* under § 2.2.2.

1.4. Levels of crime and the prison population

Data relating to crime levels reveals that Italy does not demonstrate exceptional numbers, when compared with the other States of European Union.[30] Based on information from the Ministry of Home Affairs, set out below is a graphic representation of the trend of crimes in Italy in the period 2005-2006, based on the number of crimes recorded by the police.

Italy. Total amount of crimes

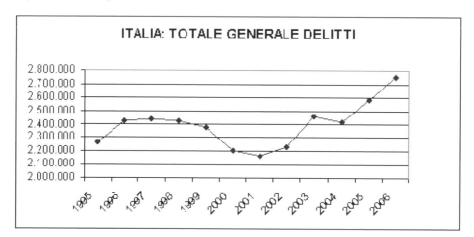

This upward trend has continued in 2007, according to the Ministry.

The total number of murders committed in 2005 was 601, and in 2006 it was 621.

Regarding violent crimes, such as serious personal injuries, kidnapping, robberies and sexual violence, it has emerged that the number of robberies has increased from 1985 to 2006. The average is 85 robberies per 100,000 inhabitants (there is a disproportion in the South, where the increase was much higher).

ISTAT conducted research concerning sexual violence against women during 2006. It emerged that 6,743,000 women suffered of acts of sexual violence, mostly committed within the family. The conclusion was that violence within the family is a national problem.

As a final consideration, the total number of crimes has not increased in the last 10 years. However, robberies and sexual violence have gone up significantly (even if, regarding the latter, some assert that the growth is due to the fact that these crimes in last years have been frequently reported by the victims to the police, while previously they largely remained unspoken).

---

[30] Data from an investigation conducted by Parliament: CAMERA DEI DEPUTATI, Indagine conoscitiva sullo stato della sicurezza in Italia, sugli indirizzi della politica della sicurezza dei cittadini e sull'organizzazione e il funzionamento delle Forze di polizia (CHAMBER OF DEPUTIES, Investigation of security in Italy, and policies concerning crime control and fight and on police functioning), 24 April 2008, <http://www.ristretti.it/commenti/2008/aprile/pdf5/indagine_sicurezza_conclusioni.pdf>.

In relation to organised crime, a recent inquiry[31] by a national statistical research centre – Eurispes – affirmed that the capability of criminal association to penetrate into civil society appears to be strengthening. In particular, the so-called *Indice di penetrazione mafiosa* (Mafia Penetration Index),[32] is 68.9 in the city of Naples and its surroundings, 60.4 in Reggio Calabria and 41.9 in Palermo. In general, the most exposed to this risk are four regions – Campania, Calabria, Sicilia and Puglia – but the entire country appears to be vulnerable to the influence of organised crime.

Finally, it should be noted that there is a dispute regarding the influence of migration on the levels of crime. One pre-eminent author[33] has asserted that migration has had a relevant impact on the rise of crime levels for certain types of crime, such as robberies, thefts and sexual violence. Others have objected to this argument, asserting that data was interpreted incorrectly. In particular, it was not taken into account that, according to other data, an immigrant has a much higher probability – around 10 times more – to be stopped, questioned and charged than an Italian.[34]

Prison overcrowding is one of the most serious problems in the Italian criminal justice system. On 31 December 2008, 58,127 persons were incarcerated in Italian prisons (as at November 2009, this rose to roughly 69,000 persons). In some cases, prison overcrowding has lead to convictions by the ECtHR, as in the recent *Sulejmanovic* case.[35] Women accounted for 2,526 prisoners, while men numbered 55,601. Ethnic minorities are over-represented. The number of foreign persons in Italian prisons is 21,562 (around 37%). Among them, the most part come from North Africa (Morocco 21%, Tunisia 11%. A rather high percentage of foreign prisoners

---

31 EURISPES, Rapporto Italia 2008. Giustizia, legalità e sicurezza, <http://www.scribd.com/doc/11570329/Sintesi-Rapporto-Italia-Eurispes-2008>.

32 This index is meant to measure the risk of penetration by organised crime into a specific territory. The parameters taken into account to elaborate the index are the unemployment rate, the number of crimes committed by criminal associations related to traditional criminal organisations, such as the *Mafia*, *'ndrangheta*, *Camorra* and *Sacra Corona*, the number of municipal administrations dismissed because of organised crime infiltration, the result of wiretapping activities and the act of terrorism.

33 Barbagli 2007, p. 53-58, 64.

34 See Melossi 2008, p. 9 and *passim*. In general, the entire issue of the review is dedicated to dispute, in many aspects, Barbagli's theses and to offer an opposite view of the immigration phenomenon.

35 ECtHR 16 July 2009, *Sulejmanovic* v. *Italy*, No. 22635/03. See Garibaldi 2009, p. 1 and 11. The prison system is under the administration of Ministry of Justice. Art. 59 Parliament Act 26 July 1975, No. 354, establishes four types of prisons: (i) *Istituti di custodia cautelare* (Preventive Detention Institutes: meant for the detention of person indicted in criminal cases, pending the investigation or trial); (ii) *Istituti per l'esecuzione delle pene* (Punishment Institutes, for the service of the sentence after the end of the criminal process); (iii) *Istituti per l'esecuzione delle misure di sicurezza* (Safety Measures Institutes, for the service of measures applied by the judge, at the end of the criminal cases, to dangerous persons either convicted or acquitted by reasons of mental insanity); (iv) *Centri di Osservazione* (Observation Centres, for the observation of the personality of detained persons. They can also be used for medical reports or psychiatric examination during the criminal process). The number of penitentiary institutions in Italy – including all of the different institutions indicated above – is 256. This data is collected from the website of the Italian Ministry of Justice site, <http://www.giustizia.it/statistiche/statistiche_dap/det/detg11_presenti.htm>.

also come from Balkans (Albania 12.1%; Former Yugoslavia 4.8%). In addition, 17.7% come from other Countries of the European Union. The Italian rate of imprisonment is almost 97 per 100,000 citizens.

More than half of prison population – 29,836 detainees – is still awaiting the final sentence, meaning that they are in custody while their criminal proceeding is still pending.

In 2006, the number of detained drastically lowered – from 59,523 in 2005 to 39,005 in 2006 – due to the Legal Pardon Act approved by the Parliament (Act No. 241, 31 July 2006). However, in the few years since then, the prison population has increased up to the same level as existed before the 2006 Legal Pardon Act. From the data emerges the fact that the overcrowding level of prisons is astonishing. In fact, it amounts to 142/100 (142 detainees actually present per 100 beds). Moreover, 20% of the prisons were built before the beginning of 20th Century.

Furthermore, 1,139 people are detained in 13 specific institutions – the so-called *Centri di Identificazione ed Espulsione* (Centres for Identification and Deportation) – used for the identification of illegal immigrants awaiting to be expelled from the Italian territory.[36]

Notwithstanding the fact that the number of crimes did not significantly increase during the same historical period, concern among the Italian population regarding crime has increased over the last decades.[37] During the 1990s, the most shared concern related to organised crime, which, as it is well known, is broadly present and developed in the Italian territory, and corruption of public officers, due to the famous inquiry called *Mani Pulite* (Hands Cleaned), which provoked a sort of earthquake in the Italian political establishment.

After 2001, the fear of crimes appears to have reduced and is often even confused with concerns regarding immigration policies. In other words, the alarm arising from the increasing immigrant population is easily expressed as apprehension for the potential risks related to the commission of crimes. This common perception has spread due to two factors. On the one hand, it is the consequence of the terrorist attacks of 11 September 2001. On the other hand, it is the result of new strategies pursued by political parties, particularly on the centre-right. In particular, one of the parties of the right hand coalition – the *Lega Nord* (Northern League) – focused its last political campaign on the fight against illegal migration, considered the main reason for social insecurity and the growth of crimes.

Moreover, recent statistical research has confirmed that, in general, crime is overrepresented in the media, and that results mostly focused on news about crime.[38] This is particularly true with regard to the period of political campaign just before the elections. The time dedicated to crime on TV in 2008 was much higher

---

[36]   See 'Immigrazione, 13 Centri di identificazione ed espulsione con 1.752 posti', *Il Messaggero*, 14 August 2009,   <http://www.ilmessaggero.it/articolo_app.php?id=20942&sez= HOME_INITALIA&npl=&desc_sez=>.

[37]   Barbagli *supra* note 33, at p. 53-58, 64.

[38]   On the over-representation of the crime in the media, see Lanzarini P., 'Come ti cucino la notizia', online at the website <www.lavoce.info>.

than the norm[39] (which is, in any event, already, excessively concentrated on this issue).

1.5. *Legal aid for persons suspected or accused of crime.*

It is important to distinguish State funded legal assistance from the function of duty counselling (or, translating literally from the Italian, counsel appointed *ex officio*). The latter is a facility provided by the State to any defendant who is not assisted by defence counsel. Since legal assistance is mandatory in criminal proceedings, defendants are provided with a duty counsel if they do not have one of their own choice already.

Duty counsels are selected from a specific list. To be included on such a list, the attorneys must have attended a specific course conducted by the Bar Association, which also keeps up to date and amends the list.

When the prosecution, police or judge need to perform an act in the presence of the defendant's counsel, and the accused has made no choice of attorney, the authority (the prosecutor, the judge or the police) must ask the Bar Association for a duty counsel. The Bar selects duty counsel according to a computer based system, which is designed to select attorneys on the basis of the competences required by the case (for example, civil cases, criminal cases, juvenile justice, immigration law).

Duty counselling is not free, nor is it paid for by the State. Although the defendant did not make a choice of his/her own, he/she has the obligation to remunerate duty counsel. The State will only cover the expenses of duty counsel if the defendant is indigent. In other words, the counsel will be paid by the State only when the defendant cannot afford one of his/her own. In all other cases, whether the defendant has chosen a counsel of his/her own or has been given a duty counsel, the defendant is required to pay for the attorney's assistance.

The counsel is paid by the State when the suspect or accused cannot afford the expenses of a criminal proceeding: specifically, when their annual income is under 9,296.22 Euro.[40] The problem is that, when the annual income of the defendant is slightly above the limit established by the law for the provision of State funded legal assistance, counsel appointed by the court must carry out every step to obtain their payment from the client – even to sue their client – and the attorneys can only ask the State to cover their fee if every legal effort has been fruitless. It is easy to understand that the obligation for counsel to collect their fee from an almost indigent client makes it difficult to build a confidential relationship between court appointed counsel and the client.

On the other hand, the lowest annual income necessary to be entitled to legal aid implies that a person slightly over the limit – for example, earning 12,000 Euro on annual basis – is obliged to borrow to pay counsel. It is relevant to note that, if

---

[39] DEMOS – OSSERVATORIO DI PAVIA – UNIPOLIS, *La sicurezza in Italia: significati, immagine e realtà -* November 2008, <www.fondazioneunipolis.org> and <www.demos.it>.

[40] For every dependent relative, the amount of income should be augmented by 1,032.91 Euro: however, if the person who asks to be admitted to free legal assistance lives with other relatives, the amount of annual revenue must be calculated by adding up the income of each cohabitant (art. 74 and 92 of President of the Republic Decree 30 May 2002, No. 115).

the defendant is entitled to legal aid, counsel cannot be paid by her/his client, not even partially. Accepting money from a client admitted to legal aid is a disciplinary offence.[41]

The distinction between mandatory counselling and free access to legal assistance should in theory imply one advantage: indigent people may elect and hire the counsel they prefer and are not obliged to accept the one appointed by the court. However, in practice, the fee paid by the State to counsel under the legal aid scheme is not very high: in a simple case (implying no more than three-five trial hearings), the average is around 1,000 – 1,500 Euro. As can be easily noted, this amount is much lower than that requested by an affirmed practitioner in the same case (which can be expected to not be less than 4,000 – 5,000 Euro). It follows that the possibility, for indigent persons, to hire the counsel they prefer is only a theoretical option.

It is possible, and it happens, that the lawyer contacted by the indigent accused refuses to take on the case, because the lawyer is aware that the fee paid by the state will be much lower than in normal cases. Formally, article 11 § II of the code of the Italian Lawyers punishes the 'unjustified' refusal of the lawyer to work for an indigent person under the provisions of legal aid. However, this provision is never applied in practice by the disciplinary authorities. In fact, in their decisions, they interpret in a broad sense the concept of 'justification', as implying that a lawyer may refuse to assist a client under the legal aid system.

If a person is facing criminal proceedings and is entitled to be under the legal aid system, he can appoint his preferred *available* counsel. In other words, there are in every Bar Associations counsel who routinely accept clients under legal aid provisions,[42] even if state remuneration for their work is lower than what they could ask (and earn) applying the ordinary fees.[43] This may happen for political reasons or for ethical ones. Lawyers often perceive it as their duty to accept cases under the legal aid system, even if the remuneration will be less than what they could have from cases in which the client has the economical resources to pay the fee.

As an example, for less serious cases, there has been a long practice to accept the defence and to apply for any remuneration at all. In general, this happens at trial, when the judge has the power to appoint on the spot a duty counsel readily available, if the accused has no counsel. At the trial, the judge asks if there is someone among the lawyers convened for a case who can accept the defence of a

---

41   This is provided for in art. 19 of the code and 85 L § 3 of the President of the Italian Republic Decree 30 May 2002, No. 115.

42   For example, the association named *'Giuristi democratici'* (Democratic Jurists – see the internet site at <http://www.giuristidemocratici.it>), open to counsel and other non practicing jurists, is engaged in improving the legal aid system. Counsel who are part of that association, which operates quite widely in the Italian territory (with 25 local cells in different trial court districts), in general routinely accept to work under legal aid provisions.

43   Lawyers' fees are determined by a decree of the Ministry of Justice, which is reviewed periodically. In general, it provides for a minimum and maximum fee for every act a counsel may perform in her/his profession. In addition, as a requirement (see art. 43 par. II of the Deontological Code of Counsels), the fee requested by counsel must not be clearly disproportionate to the work accomplished.

person who is without counsel, and usually there is always someone prepared to accept the defence (sometimes the lawyer is literally found in the corridor).

As will be discussed later, this is possible because there is a general lack of quality control on the legal profession in Italy. What matters, in other words, in such cases, is that at trial there was a lawyer of any sort; it does not matter whether the lawyer was prepared and sufficiently skilled to perform his/her duty. The accused cannot in any way appeal the issue of the incapacity or negligence of his/her counsel.

It is relevant to note that legal aid was introduced in 1990,[44] reformed in 2001, and finally settled in 2002 with Legislative Decree No. 115.

Some statistical data[45] may help to present a more detailed picture of the system. In recent years, the costs of legal aid in criminal processes have been increasing significantly, as well as the number of persons requesting legal aid and entitled to its benefits. Over the last 12 years, in 1996 there were 16,585 requests for legal aid (15,000 were accepted). In 2006, the total number of the requests was 98,329 (84,047 were accepted), and in 2007 (last available data) the number was 101,083 (accepted 94,041).

The national cost of legal aid in criminal proceedings has increased proportionally. In 1996 the Italian State spent 4,069,059 Euro; in 2006, the costs rose to 70,591,753 Euro, and in 2007 84,916,200 Euro. The *pro-capite* budget for each requesting party was 945 Euro in 1996, 754 Euro in 2006, and 879 Euro in 2007. It emerges that, with regard to 2007, the total cost was, for the North Italy 22.624,309 Euro, in the Centre 14,936,971 Euro, in the South 25,667,966 Euro and in the Islands 21,986,653 Euro (that is a sum proportionally much higher than those regarding the other areas).

Notwithstanding the increasing costs sustained by the State for legal aid and the correlative augmented number of persons admitted to it, it may be said that people do not frequently make use of legal aid, either in criminal or civil cases. Some detained persons are still perhaps not aware of their right to apply for legal aid. It may happen that counsels, too, are not prepared to properly inform their client of their right. In addition, to be paid by the State under the legal aid provisions, a counsel must be registered on a specific list kept and regularly reviewed by the local Bar Association of each trial court. Only a minimum number of the counsel practising within a trial court district is at the same time enrolled for legal aid. For example, with regard to the Milan Bar Association, of the 13,787 counsel who are part of the Bar Association – practising both in criminal and/or civil matters – only 1,258 are in the specific register.[46]

---

[44] Parliament Act No. 217, 30 July 1990.
[45] Data from the site of the Italian Minister of Justice, <http://www.giustizia.it/statistiche/statistiche_dag/2003/patrocinio.htm >.
[46] Data available at the site of Milan Bar Association, <www.ordineavvocatimilano.it>.

Regarding the nationality of persons requesting legal aid, in 2007, 80.6% were nationals, while 19.4% were foreigners. The proportion is not much different from that of 1995, when 79.9% were Italians, and 21.1% were foreigners.[47]

2. Legal rights and their implementation

2.1. *Right to information*

2.1.1. Letters of rights

The right to be informed that one is under investigation in a criminal proceeding is the first, and probably the main right recognised by the CCP, as it affects the applicability of all other rights. It implies the duty of the police, the prosecutor and/or the judge to communicate as soon as possible to the suspect that criminal investigations are underway.[48] In particular, the CCP provides that the prosecutor must give notice of the proceeding to the suspect from the time of the first act of the investigation at which his/her counsel has the right to be present.[49] In practice, this means that, at the first appearance of the suspect in front of the judicial officers or the police, the police or prosecutor must formally inform suspects of their position in the proceeding.[50]

In the course of the criminal proceeding, the suspect is entitled to receive three letters of rights, as respectively provided under articles 369, 369*bis* and 415*bis* of the CCP. The first letter – called 'information of guarantee', article 369 – must inform the suspect[51] in written form of his/her right to appoint counsel when the prosecutor intends to carry out an act for which counsel attendance is permitted. Moreover, the information must mention the legal definition of the crime alleged, the date and place of the facts that the suspect allegedly committed,[52] and the bureaucratic data of the relevant criminal proceeding (number of the case, name of the prosecutor).

---

[47]   For non EU citizens, the application must be followed by a declaration of the competent consular authority; the authority must certify that the declaration presented by requesting party – asserting that he/she did not received a salary greater than the limits provided by the law for admission to legal aid – is true. This represents a practical problem for many foreign defendants, who are irregularly present in Italy. It is often not easy, or even possible, for the applicant to obtain the necessary declaration by the consular authority.

[48]   The right to be informed that one is a suspect has a different content with regard to questioning by the police and interrogation before the prosecutor: only in the latter case must the judicial officer communicate the facts for which the person is involved in the proceeding, while, in the former, the right provided by the code includes just the juridical qualification of the charge, but not the fact: see Caianiello & Illuminati, *supra* note 11, p. 135-136, and 138-139.

[49]   The main acts at which counsel has the right to attend during the investigation are the interrogation of the suspect, the inspection of the suspect or his/her premises, the confrontation between the suspect and another person, the search and the seizure. At the first act at which the counsel of the suspect has the right to attend, the prosecutor must also give notice of the pending proceeding to the victim.

[50]   Mazza 2004, p. 36.

[51]   On that occasion, the same information must be supplied to the victim as well.

[52]   However, the suspect is not entitled to a full description of the alleged facts.

The 'letter of rights' provided for in article 369*bis* must mention the main rights of the defence in criminal proceedings: the right to appoint counsel, the right to access to legal aid, the right to an interpreter and to translation of documents, the right to silence. In particular, the letter should clearly explain the conditions for receiving State legal assistance for the costs of counsel. The letter must also inform the suspect of his/her right to hire counsel: if the defendant does not hire any, a counsel shall be appointed *ex officio*, whose name and whereabouts (firm address, telephone number) must be reported in the aforementioned document.

The right to be informed is absolute and a violation of the duty to inform the suspect of his/her position gives rise to various forms of procedural invalidity of the procedure (including nullity, inadmissibility of the statements). As can be seen, these two letters of rights are generally given to the suspect at the beginning of the investigation. The second letter contains much more information than the first, and was provided for in 1999 in order to provide the suspect more information in the initial stage of the criminal proceeding.

Finally, at the end of the investigation, according to article 415*bis*, the prosecutor must alert the accused that the prosecutor has completed all relevant investigations and intends to bring formal charges against the person (*avviso di conclusione delle indagini preliminary* – investigations closure information). The information must contain a description of the alleged facts and the legal definition of the alleged crime. It must also inform the suspect that, as from that moment, access to the Prosecutor's file is permitted, in practice without any limitations.

Failure to comply with this requirement may undermine the prosecution. In fact, the indictment filed by the prosecutor must be declared void, if it is ascertained that the suspect was not given notice of this information: in such a case, the proceedings must revert back to the investigation phase, and the prosecutor must give proper notice to the defendant of the act as provided for in article 415*bis*.

It cannot be said, at any rate, that the duty to inform the suspect during the investigation represents a continuing obligation. The duty to inform the suspect arises when it is necessary to perform an investigative act allowing for the attendance of his/her counsel. In theory, the prosecutor could conduct an investigation without carrying out a single act for which counsel attendance is requested or permitted. For example, the prosecutor could just question witnesses, or gather some documents from public offices. In such cases, the suspect would be informed only at the end of the investigation and before the presentation of the indictment, when the prosecutor must supply him/her with the investigation closure information (as provided for in art. 415*bis*).

It must be noted that each of the documents referred to in this paragraph must be translated into a language that the defendant understands. The principle also applies to the indictment formally filed by the prosecutor at the commencement of the prosecution.

2.1.2. Arrest and questioning before the police, the prosecutor and the judges

Before questioning the suspect, the police, prosecutor or judge must warn him/her of the right to remain silent and of the fact that, if a statement is made regarding other persons, the suspect may become a witness in relation to those facts (actually, a peculiar 'assisted witness', governed by rules that are, in many respects, different from that of ordinary witnesses): in these cases, the defendant loses the right to silence regarding the facts given that relate to others. However, even in the case of an 'assisted witness' the defendant has the right to remain silent in relation to the charges brought against them (art. 64 § 3).[53] The failure to give the warnings requested by the law makes any statements gathered inadmissible as evidence.

The rationale of the rights described above is that a person must be able to decide his/her own attitude towards the authority when under suspicion in a criminal proceeding and must be able to exercise his right to silence.[54]

If a person, who is questioned as a witness, gives self-incriminating statements, the prosecutor or police must immediately stop the interrogation and warn him/her that, as a consequence of the statements rendered, an investigation may begin against him/her. The person must also be notified that they have the right to appoint a counsel. Every statement given until that moment cannot be used against the defendant: instead, the declaration may only be used against other persons involved (art 63 § 1 of the CCP). If the police or prosecutor fail, either negligently or on purpose, to give the information provided for by the law, the statements gathered cannot be used at all in criminal proceedings (art. 63 § 2). This provision also applies when, from the beginning of the questioning, the police or prosecutor interrogate the suspect without informing him/her of the proceeding.

If the prosecutor intends to interrogate the suspect, he/she must summon the person, by writ, giving notice to counsel at least 24 hours in advance, except for cases of justified urgency. In general, the term provided for by the law is respected by the prosecutor, because the unjustified delay in the communication of the notice leads to the invalidity of the interrogation. If the suspect has not yet elected a lawyer, the prosecutor must appoint a duty lawyer and simultaneously inform that lawyer.

The summons must contain an exposition of the facts for which the suspect is under investigation, and may also indicate the information that has already been gathered by the prosecutor. In practice, it is unusual for the summons to contain any reference to the evidence available to the prosecutor; more usually, the prosecutor communicates the elements at his/her discretion only at the commencement of the interrogation.[55] The presence of the lawyer is not mandatory (this is the main difference between police questioning, for which the attendance of

---

[53]   The distinction between facts involving others and one's own responsibility is quite problematic in practice. Actually, a statement regarding another person may present consequences, or give rise to inferences regarding the acts performed by the person making the declaration. It is not rare, in the case law, that, when in practice a clear distinction appears impossible or at least quite difficult, the judge decides to acknowledge to the accused the right to remain silent, not only on the questions regarding the specific charges brought against the suspect, but also on those concerning other persons whose responsibility is connected with the suspect.

[54]   See § 2.3.4.

[55]   See Mazza, *supra* note 50, at p. 148.

the counsel is always mandatory, and the prosecutor's interrogation); instead, it is only mandatory for the prosecutor to give notice.[56]

After the arrest, the police must permit to the arrested person to contact a family member. In addition, the police must inform 'without delay' (in practice, within 24 hours from the arrest) the counsel of the suspect. However, in such cases, article 104 of the CCP allows the prosecutor – through a specific decree – to delay the contact between counsel and the defendant under custody for up to 48 hours, which constitutes the time that the prosecutor has at his/her disposition to interrogate the person. This provision is mostly applied for organised crime cases.

Article 104 permits the judge – except in arrest cases, in which the same power is given to the prosecutor – to prohibit any contact between counsel and his client for up to five days, when pre-trial detention is applied.[57] This constitutes the period of time within which, when pre-trial detention is applied, the defendant must be brought before the judge to be interrogated, according to article 294 CPP.

The rationale of article 104 is to avoid the suspect 'arranging' with his/her counsel a 'credible' version of the facts to be given to the prosecutor. In other words, the intent of the legislature is to stop the defendant building up his description of the facts in advance, before being interrogated, with the help of his counsel. Of course, counsel can attend the interrogation by the prosecutor, even if the prohibition provided for in article 104 is applied – he just cannot have contact with his client before the interrogations starts. In other words, what is denied to counsel is the mere possibility to contact the defendant – in custody – for a certain period of time (in practice, in the period before the interrogation by the judge or prosecutor).

By way of summary of the arguments raised in this section, the police can interrogate anyone who has not been arrested, including a person who is only suspected of an offence. In any case, the person has a right to silence of which he/she must be informed. The person has also a right to a lawyer and must be told of this right, as well as of the relevant legal aid provisions. Arrest is deemed to be 'consented' only in *flagrante delicto* (see 2.3.1), but not in any case in which there are strong elements proving the criminal responsibility of the suspect. In such cases, it is necessary to first obtain a judicial order, at the request of the prosecutor.

However, there is one case in which the police can question the suspect directly, without warning and without the presence of the lawyer. This is when the police are on the spot, performing an urgent act, such as arresting the suspect, or conducting a search or inspection. Under these circumstances, police can question the suspect without any formality (without counsel, and without previous warning), but it is prohibited to record this questioning and the results thereof can never be produced as evidence in the course of the entire criminal proceeding. The CCP states that the questioning on the spot of crime, or during a search or of an inspection can be used only 'to carry on the investigations', that is to find other sources of evidence, other persons involved, etc. However, during this questioning on the spot, the suspect can give some indirectly self-incriminating answer: for

---

[56]   Cordero 2006, p. 803-804.
[57]   See *infra*, under § 2.3.1 for the distinction between arrest and pre-trial detention.

example, he can confess to be the owner of the *corpus delicti*, or can reveal where his accomplices are hidden, and so on.

Moreover, according to article 350 § 7 CCP, the suspect may give to the police 'spontaneous statements': that is to say, he/she may present him/herself before any police station and make declarations to a police officer. According to the Court of Cassation, and despite many critics by the scholars, in case of spontaneous statements the attendance of the counsel is not necessary, neither is necessary any previous warning. In other words, if the suspect goes spontaneously to the police to make some declarations relevant for the investigations, the police are not obliged to appoint a counsel and to warn him/her of his/her rights. They can gather and record, freely and without limits, the statements the suspect spontaneously renders. The practice of spontaneous statements represents of course a critical feature for the Italian system as it can be used to disregard the suspect's safeguards and rights during investigations. It may sometimes happen that police presents a declaration as 'spontaneous' that was at least implicitly compelled, or even forced. It is not easy, in such cases to detect the violation of suspect's rights and to obtain that those statements are struck out of the prosecution file.

The fact that, 'from the first moment in which elements of a crime emerge', a person questioned by the police or prosecutor must be warned of the possibility of becoming a suspect and must have the right to counsel should lead police and the prosecutor to be cautious, and, in case of doubt, to treat the person as a suspect. In fact, if the judge subsequently finds that the person should have been interrogated as a suspect, he/she can strike out the statement from the file and declare it inadmissible as evidence. After the suspect is arrested, police cannot question him, since only the prosecutor can interrogate him.

2.1.3. Trial

After the commencement of the prosecution – which takes place with the presentation of the indictment – the proceedings take the form of the preliminary hearing[58] and the trial. During these stages, the defendant must constantly, formally and precisely be informed of any amendments to the indictment by the prosecutor. When the prosecutor amends the indictment – *rectius*, when the prosecutor modifies the material facts described in the indictment – the defendant has the right to be informed; moreover, he can ask the judge to admit new evidence, if relevant with regard to the new allegation. Under certain conditions, the defendant is allowed to make a new plea (*applicazione della pena su richiesta delle parti*) or seek an abbreviated trial,[59] in case of modification of the indictment by the prosecutor.

It should be pointed out that the Italian system does not provide for a right to be informed of the amendments of the legal definition of the crime charged in the indictment. The accused does not have any right to be informed of modifications regarding the type of crime charged. The judge may, at any time, modify the legal definition of the alleged facts, because the principle of *iura novit curia* (judges know

[58] See, on the preliminary hearing *supra* § 1.3.
[59] See *supra* § 1.3.

the law) applies without restriction. This appears in contrast with the interpretation of article 6 § 3 a-b of the ECHR. In fact, Italy has been found to be in violation of article 6 ECHR, in cases in which the judge modified the legal definition of the crimes without giving any previous advice to the accused, thus denying him/her the opportunity to discuss the legal profile of the allegations.[60]

2.2.   Right to defend oneself

2.2.1. The right of a person to defend him/herself

The right to defend oneself is not recognised in the Italian criminal process. Article 24 § 2 of the Italian Constitution declares the right to defence as inviolable in any stage and phase of the proceedings. Judges and scholars believe that this cannot be derogated from or waived. The provisions of the CCP of 1930, as well as the one now in force, specified the right to defence as a rigidly mandatory one, implying the necessary attendance of a counsel for the defendant. It is interesting to observe that the right to represent and defend oneself is also not allowed in the civil process, with the sole exception of proceedings falling within the jurisdiction of the Judge of the Peace, when the value of the case is no greater than 5000 Euro. Even in those cases, however, the decision to allow self-defence is left to the discretion of the judge, who in practice rarely grants such request.[61]

2.2.2. The right to legal advice at the investigative stage

As mentioned above, the right to the assistance of a counsel finds protection under article 24 § 2 of the Italian Constitution, as a corollary to the more general right to defence. The right to counsel formally applies from the commencement of the criminal investigations against a person, that is when the person concerned is still a mere suspect. Moreover, article 220 of the implementation rules of the CCP provides that a person must be treated as a suspect – with all the consequent guarantees, including the right to counsel – from the first moment in which elements of a crime emerge (criminis indicia). This applies in particular during a non-criminal enquiry (for example, an enquiry conducted by administrative bodies), when the first elements of a crime appear.

Both before and after the moment at which the prosecutor must inform the suspect of his/her rights, at any stage of the criminal proceedings, the suspect may appoint up to two counsel. The appointment of counsel can be effected by a written or oral declaration before the police, the prosecutor or the judge. If the declaration is made in oral form, the police or prosecutor must prepare a report, indicating the date of the appointment and other required matters (name of the counsel, name of the person under suspicion, number of the criminal proceeding, name of the

---

[60]   ECtHR 11 December 2007, *Drassich* v. *Italy*, No. 25575/04. See *supra* note 15.

[61]   Sometimes, the request is granted by the judge only when the person shows some juridical skills: for example, if the person appearing has undertaken some juridical studies during high school.

prosecutor). The report must be signed by the police officer or prosecutor, as well as by the suspect. The appointment can also be made in a form sent to the prosecutor, in which case the form must be filed in the investigation dossier under the custody of the prosecutor.

The right to appoint a lawyer does not differ depending on the financial resources of the suspect/defendant and/or whether they are entitled to legal aid.

In some parts of the investigation, attendance of counsel is mandatory. This is so when a suspect under arrest is questioned by the judge, just after the arrest, or when a suspect is called by the police – not being under arrest – to be questioned. The validation hearing after the arrest – as well as the preliminary hearing – must also be conducted with the attendance of defence counsel.[62]

Some investigations can be performed without the attendance of defence counsel. In certain cases, however, counsel must be informed before the start of the act (at least 24 hours in advance), but he/she is not obliged to attend to it. This happens with regard to the prosecutor's interrogation of the suspect and for the personal searches. In some other acts, like local searches, defence counsel is allowed to attend, but does not have a right to be previously informed. In all cases, legal assistance may be waived in theory,[63] in practice, with the exception of searches and inspections (for which the attendance of counsel is most unusual), it is quite exceptional for counsel not to attend an investigative act involving the client, albeit without any obligation to do so. This is true regardless of the gravity of the case. There is no significant distinction with regard to cases in which counsel is permitted under legal aid. In any case, most counsel attend investigative acts in which they are entitled to participate.

The defendant can, at any stage of the proceedings revoke the appointment of counsel, and nominate another. If, for any reason, the defendant remains without counsel, the prosecutor during the investigations, or the judge, must appoint a counsel on duty, who ceases when the defendant appoints one. The revoked counsel remains in charge until the new counsel has been appointed, either by the defendant or *ex officio*.

2.2.3. The right to legal representation at the trial stage

At trial, a defendant must have legal representation. If the defendant does not choose his/her own counsel, the judge is obliged to appoint one *ex officio*. The conduct of the trial – as well as any appeal stages – without the attendance of defence counsel, renders the proceedings null, requiring it to be recommenced from the moment where defence counsel must attend. In order to carry on with the trial

---

[62] As noted, under art. 104 of the CCP, the judge for the preliminary investigation, at the request of the prosecutor, may delay contact between counsel and his/her client who is under arrest for a period not longer than five days. When the suspect is arrested *in flagrante delicto*, such a decision is taken by the prosecutor and has an effect up to 48 hours.

[63] The suspect may reject the attendance of counsel, or counsel may decide not to attend. In practice, the decision is taken between the client and the lawyer.

when defence counsel is absent without any acceptable reason,[64] the judges must appoint a counsel *ex officio*.

Preparing carefully for trial is a crucial element under the present Italian criminal justice system, which attaches great importance to the principle of orality. Once the prosecutor has brought formal charges against the defendant, the attorney has a very difficult task: he/she must decide no later than the end of the preliminary hearing whether to opt for an 'alternative consensual proceeding' (the *giudizio abbreviato*, or the *applicazione della pena su richiesta delle parti*, which constitutes a form of guilty plea). This step is critical, because by choosing these consensual proceedings, the accused forgoes his/her right to go to trial and consents to being judged only on the evidence gathered during the investigation. In exchange, the accused is granted a reduction in the penalty he/she would normally receive (a reduction of one third in the *giudizio abbreviato*; a reduction up to one third in the *applicazione della pena*).

At the trial stage, counsel seeks to undermine the prosecution's case. It is quite common for Italian lawyers to attack virtually every point of the prosecutor's argumentation, even if it is supported by very strong evidence indicating the defendant's guilt or involvement. They will usually only give up the challenge when the accused has confessed. The attorney will first ask for the admission of evidence necessary to prove the issue of innocence, or to discredit the assertion of guilt.[65] When testimonial evidence is adduced at trial, the lawyer will cross-examine the prosecution witnesses, in order to challenge their veracity and credibility. He/she will then examine the witnesses he has presented for the defence. Finally, in the closing arguments, the lawyer will try to persuade the court that the prosecution's case is groundless, because it has insufficient evidence to support it, or because the arguments indicating the accused's innocence are more convincing.

There is no separation in Italy between judgment and sentencing, with the sentence determined by the judges at trial, in case of conviction, without any additional hearing. Defence counsel must therefore argue on sentencing at trial, and present relevant evidence on this issue. This aspect of the old inquisitorial system remains notwithstanding the adoption in 1989 of the CCP. The choice not to separate the trial phase from sentencing is heavily criticised by counsel, who argue that it is allowed without any restriction all evidence relevant to the previous conduct of the accused (the so-called 'bad character evidence' in common law systems) to be admitted.

---

64   When counsel is absent for a good cause, and the judges are aware of it because the defendant has duly notified them before the hearing day, the process must be adjourned. Refusal to adjourn the case can give rise to it being sanctioned as a nullity: this means that the hearing conducted notwithstanding the justified absence of defence counsel – leading to court appointed counsel *ex officio* – will be declared null and the process must recommence from that hearing.

65   Of course, this does not mean that the defendant is obliged to proof his innocence, since the presumption of innocence in Italy is duly regarded (see *infra* § 2.3.3). Actually, the defence may limit itself to undermining the prosecution case. However, when some evidence favourable to the defence arises, it will be asked to be admitted by defence counsel. The Italian trial is characterised by an adversarial structure, and it is up to the defence to build its case, while the Prosecutor must prove the defendant guilty beyond reasonable doubt.

However, rarely have these argument were taken into consideration. In general, those persons seeking to maintain the *status quo* observe that the separation between trial and sentencing is necessary when the jury adjudicates the case, while is superfluous when the decision is made by professional judges. Nevertheless, all lawyers accept that the criminal record of the accused, inserted in the judicial file since the beginning of the trial, does play a role in the adjudication of the case. The Court of Cassation itself has sometimes stated that the record of the previous convictions of the accused – as well as the one pending – can be freely evaluated by the judges, in the same manner as all the other evidence.

2.2.4. Independence and competence of defence lawyers

Criminal lawyers are not formally regulated as such. The profession, in every field of the law, has common disciplinary rules. To be admitted into practice, all counsel must belong to the Bar Association. It is necessary to have graduated in law and to have passed the bar exam, held every year in December. Italy has only one Bar Association, organised as a pyramid. At the peak, there is the National Bar Association and, at the bottom, there are local bar associations located in each trial court district. The local bar associations are submitted to the control and regulation of the National Bar Association. The National Bar Association, as well as the local bar associations at the district level, are recognized by the State. They are supervised, in some aspects, by the Government, which may have agreements with the National Bar Association in order to give directions to them in some field (for example, fiscal, contributions for retirement).

With special regard to criminal lawyers, they are for the most part – but not necessarily – associated with the Penal Chamber (*Camera Penale*), a private association organised at both the national and district level. In the last 10 years, the Penal Chamber has, in practice, exercised an important role in the reforms of criminal law and procedure: notably during the legislative drafting phase of the Constitutional reform of article 111. The Penal Chamber is not recognised as a public institution by the law: it is a mere private law association, and its lobbying influence operates only *de facto* (many of its higher representatives sit in the Italian Parliament).[66]

There is a code of professional behaviour, issued by the National Bar Association, and also a code of professional behaviour for criminal lawyers, drafted by the Penal Chamber. Both codes provide for a certain number of provisions concerning the ethical duty of counsel, in the course of his/her defence. For example, they provide for the duty to respect their counterparts and to keep secret information collected in the administration of the defence (client-counsel privilege). While the violation of the duties provided for in the Code of the Bar Association may lead to several sanctions for the counsel, the heaviest of which is a prohibition from practicing for a certain period of time or, in the most serious cases, forever, the violation of the Penal Chamber Code provisions usually only give rise to private consequences (at most, the expulsion from that association). The Penal Chamber is,

---

[66]   See Caianiello & Illuminati *supra* note 11, at p..148-149.

in fact, regulated for the most part by the provisions of the Italian civil code. However, only the violation of the Bar Association rules may give rise to a disciplinary proceeding, whose effects, and outcomes, are officially recognised by State law and are published on the local journal of the Bar Association (no statistical data is available). The disciplinary proceeding takes place before the local Bar Association of which the counsel accused of malpractice is a number. At the end of the proceeding, the sanctions adopted by the local Bar Association may be appealed before the National Bar Association and, ultimately, before the Court of Cassation.

Despite the strict rules of the CCP and the deontological code, it is rare that a lawyer is sanctioned by his/her Bar Association and, when punished, that the sentence is heavy. In particular, it is rare that the outcome of a disciplinary proceeding consists of the exclusion of counsel from the profession. The expulsion from the Bar Association, and the prohibition to act in the profession (at least for some years, for minor crimes) is generally – but not automatically – issued only in case of conviction of criminal matters.

Formally, there is no provision of legal services limited to qualified lawyers: there is a radical lack of quality control concerning legal services in Italy, and this represents one of the points of weakness in the Italian legal profession.

In general, notwithstanding their huge number (they are at the moment 213,000), counsel in Italy are, on average, competent to undertake their work, and independent from any source of conditioning or intimidation.[67] They are insured for the damages suffered by their client from their mistakes. However, in practice, the risk is higher in civil cases than in criminal ones. The criminal process is characterised by many discretional choices left in the hands of counsel that, as such, may be disputable but rarely give rise to a judicial case. It should be noted that, under the provisions of the Italian Civil Code, a lawyer can be required to pay the damages only if he acted with intent (*dolus*) of grave negligence (*gravis culpa*).

2.3. *Procedural Rights*

2.3.1. The right to release from custody pending trial

Arrest, Detention of a suspect, Pre-Trial Detention: Preliminary Distinctions

In the Italian system, a right to be released on bail or some similar condition is not provided for.[68] The current Italian CCP distinguishes between three types of preventive detention, namely: *arresto* (arrest), *fermo di indiziato di delitto* (stopping one suspected of a crime) and *custodia cautelare* (pre-trial detention). Both *arresto* and *fermo* can be categorised summarily as initial 'police detention' (actually, *fermo* can be issued only by the prosecutor, even it is executed by the police). By contrast, *custodia cautelare* may only be decreed by the court dealing with the case, or by the

---

[67]   See also, for other considerations, *infra* § 3.
[68]   See in English on this issue, 'Italy', a paper presented by the European Commission entitled *An analysis of minimum standards in pre-trial detention and the grounds for regular review in the Member States of the EU* (JLS/D3/2007/01), 2009, <http://www.ecba.org/extdocserv/projects/JusticeForum/Italy180309.pdf>.

judge and, moreover, solely upon request of the public prosecutor (art. 279 and 291 of the CCP).[69]

Pre-Trial Detention

Pre-trial detention starts with a court order of detention. At the application of the prosecutor, the judge shall issue a court order for pre-trial detention (art. 292 of the CCP), if he/she considers the conditions required by the law to be met.[70] According to article 294 of the CCP, a person held in pre-trial detention during the preliminary investigation shall immediately be interrogated by the judge and, in any case, within five days after execution of pre-trial detention. The failure to do so by the judge within the time prescribed by the law implies the end of pre-trial detention. The person must be released (but a new pre-trial detention order can be issued by the judge).

The defendant and his lawyer, separately, may submit within 10 days of the notification or execution of the decision, a request to the Court of Freedom (*Tribunale della libertà*) for review of the initial decision to pre-trial detention, on the merits of the case (art. 309). Once such a request is presented, the Court is assigned 10 days to make a decision. The defendant and his/her counsel may also appeal the pre-trial detention judicial order before the Court of Cassation, either directly or after the decision of the Court of Freedom.

There are several ways in which pre-trial detention may end. For instance, pre-trial detention ends when there is no longer a ground for (further) detention. In addition, article 299 of the CCP prescribes the immediate cancellation of pre-trial detention once the general terms stipulated in article 273 of the CCP are no longer met, or the grounds for adopting such a measure (art. 274) cease to exist. Nevertheless, if there are no longer grounds for pre-trial detention, detention will not end by operation of law. Cancellation of pre-trial detention may be decreed at the initiative of the judge, or upon request of either the public prosecutor or the accused. Subsequently, the judge should decide within five days of the request (art. 299 § 3).

Apart from the instant cancellation of pre-trial detention in default of the necessary justifiable conditions, pre-trial detention may also be replaced by another precautionary measure. Article 299 § 2 of the CCP regulates the replacement of pre-trial detention by a less severe measure, while article 299 § 4 regulates the replacement of pre-trial detention by a more severe measure. In addition, pre-trial detention should be replaced by a less severe measure (house arrest, the prohibition to leave the place in which the defendant resides, the withdrawal of the passport), or the conditions of detention should be lessened, if the grounds for detention have reduced, or if the measures are no longer appropriate or proportionate to the seriousness of the offences and the severity of sentence to be imposed.

By contrast, an aggravation of the grounds for detention may lead to the adoption of stringent precautionary measures. However, no such measure is more

---

[69] See *supra* § 1.3 c.

[70] The court order should satisfy the formal requirements listed in art. 292 of the Code.

severe than pre-trial detention. Nonetheless, if the grounds for detention have increased, the public prosecutor may still request the judge to aggravate the conditions of pre-trial detention.

The institution of pre-trial detention allows for a person to be deprived of his/her liberty, even if not yet facing formal charges. The aim of the detention is to allow the prosecuting authority to gather sufficient evidence during the preliminary investigation phase (which can last for no more than two years). However, when imposing pre-trial detention, there are some essential legal principles that should be taken into account by the judge, including the presumption of innocence, the principle of adequacy, the principle of proportionality and the principle of last resort.

Regarding the presumption of innocence, with specific relevance to pre-trial detention, although pre-trial detention requires a certain degree of suspicion, a suspect or defendant must not be seen as guilty while under investigation. Therefore, innocence should be presumed even if the person has been convicted in the past. To this end, article 278 of the CCP prescribes that recidivism may not be taken into account, when deciding whether to adopt pre-trial detention.[71]

When opting for a precautionary measure, the judge should determine whether each of the available measures is appropriate, having regard to the nature and severity of the danger to be faced in the particular case (art. 275§ 1). Pre-trial detention should thus be appropriate and may in no case be disproportional to the seriousness of the offence and the likely sentence to be imposed (art. 275 § 2). Consequently, the judge may not impose pre-trial detention, if it is likely that the defendant could be granted a suspended sentence (art. 275).

Because of its severity, the law prescribes that pre-trial detention should remain a measure of last resort, to be ordered only when other lighter measures prove inadequate (art. 275 § 3). Further, the rights of a suspect or defendant should be respected, even if the person is held in pre-trial detention. To this end, article 277 of the CCP prescribes that the modality of execution of pre-trial detention should safeguard the rights of prisoners, unless these rights are incompatible with the grounds for detention.[72]

2.3.2. The right of a defendant to be tried in his/her presence

In Italy, the accused can be tried in his/her absence. At the beginning of the preliminary hearing, in case of absence of the defendant, the judge must formally ascertain if this is due to some impediment, or to the fact that the defendant was not duly notified of the hearing. If a factual impediment is ascertained, or in case of doubt, the judge must adjourn the hearing and seek the advice of the parties. In the opinion of the Court of Cassation and most scholars, the defence is not under the burden to prove the facts, while it is up to the judge to conduct the necessary actions to ascertain the cause of the defendant's absence.

---

[71]   On this issue, see *infra* § 2.3.3.
[72]   For statistical data, see *infra* § 4.2 and 5.

When neither an impediment nor a mistake in the notification of the defendant has occurred, the judge formally declares the defendant absent (*contumace*), and the proceeding can go on. If the defendant subsequently intervenes, the judge must revoke the previous formal declaration. If the defendant so requires, he/she must be interrogated, or can render spontaneous statements (arts. 420 to 420*quarter* of the CCP). If the defendant subsequently intervenes and proves that, at the beginning of the hearing, he/she cannot participate due to an impediment, the judge must renew 'the relevant acts' (in general this formula is interpreted as the acts that, in the opinion of the judge, may be crucial for the adjudication of the case). However, the previous acts are considered valid and cannot be revoked. The same conditions apply at the trial stage.

As is well known, Italy has in many cases been found in violation of its obligations by the ECtHR regarding trial *in absentia* in the criminal process. In fact, the system established by the legislature does not guarantee that the defendant was really aware of the criminal process against him/her. What specifically matters is that the judge is called upon to check only the formal requirements of the notices given to the accused by the registry. The court is not under a duty to ascertain if, in practice, the defendant knew that he/she was going to be tried.

Moreover, until 2005, the Italian rules required a defendant who appeared after the final conviction, to prove that it had been impossible for him/her to participate at the trial. If such proof was not provided, the case could not be re-opened. In addition, impossibility to intervene was not considered as sufficient, in cases where the defendant had been negligent. In other words, the law required that, to re-open a case, the defendant must prove that it was objectively impossible for him/her to attend the trial, and that he/she was not negligent (he/she did not provoke on purpose, or negligently, the cause of impossibility).

After many violations found by the ECtHR,[73] which expressly asked Italy to change its system concerning trial *in absentia*, Italy modified article 175 of the CCP in 2005, in order to allow the re-opening of the criminal process – if conducted *in absentia* – when the convicted affirmed that he/she did not receive notice of the proceeding instituted against him/her. Under the new rules, a person convicted in a criminal trial can appeal the final conviction – and in so doing, re-open the case – when he/she asserts that he/she was not aware of the proceeding against him/her. The appeal must be presented within 30 days from the date when the person was informed about the conviction. The defendant is not under any burden to prove his/her unawareness, and it is up to the Court of Appeal to check the assertion.

The ECtHR has declared the new system as not being incompatible with article 6 of the ECHR.[74] However, Italian scholars have pointed out that the reform appears far from satisfactory. The main criticism is that the defendant enjoys a mere right to appeal, which means that the trial must not be completely renewed. In Italy, all the relevant evidence is admitted at trial, at which the parties have the right to examine and cross-examine witnesses. Moreover, at trial, the parties have the right to seek

---

73   The decisive conviction was adopted in the *Sejdovic* case. See, ECtHR 10 November 2004, *Sejdovic* v. *Italy*, No. 56581/00, First Section.

74   See ECtHR 1 March 2006, *Sejdovic* v. *Italy*, No. 56581/00, Grand Chamber.

the admission of relevant evidence on their behalf. At the appeal stage, the admission of new evidence is the exception, and can be ordered by the court only when strictly necessary, or when it is new and newly discovered after the conclusion of the trial.

To recognise to a convicted person a type of enlarged right to appeal, therefore, in the opinion of many scholars, is not enough, because the defendant cannot enjoy the rights provided for by the system to persons accused in a criminal trial. In sum, the process is not completely re-opened, since what is allowed is simply the right to attack a conviction through a criticism to its motivation, as is usually the case at the appeal stage.

2.3.3. The right to be presumed innocent

The Italian Constitution recognizes the presumption of innocence in article 27 § 2, which provides that the defendant cannot be considered guilty until the final judgment of conviction.[75] This principle has found specific applications in the CCP, where it is provided that, in case of uncertainty, the defendant must be acquitted. In February 2006,[76] the 'beyond of any reasonable doubt' rule (BARD) was formally introduced in article 533 of the CCP, under which the defendant can be convicted only when his/her responsibility is proven beyond reasonable doubt. Commentators have observed that the reform has implemented a conclusion that had already been achieved in the opinion of the majority of the scholars and under Italian case law.[77] In fact, the Court of Cassation, in 2002, in its larger composition (*Sezioni Unite*), acknowledged that the BARD rule must be considered the natural consequence of the presumption of innocence provided for in the Constitution.[78]

The BARD rule does not apply to pre-trial detention, notwithstanding the opinion of some scholars.[79] According to article 273, pre-trial detention can be issued when the evidence produced by the prosecutor shows, 'grave indicia of criminal reliability'. In the view of the Court of Cassation, this does not mean that, according to the evidence presented by the prosecutor, the defendant must appear responsible beyond reasonable doubt of the crimes with which he/she is charged, but rather more simply that his criminal responsibility must appear, *rebus sic stantibus*, more probable than not.

In other words, it is not necessary that the evidence produced by the prosecutor to obtain a judicial pre-trial detention order leaves no room for anything else than a judgment of conviction; on the contrary, pre-trial detention can be issued even if the prosecution evidence could be read as not being sufficient to consider the defendant guilty at trial. What matters at the pre-trial detention stage is that the prospect of conviction appears more probable that that of acquittal.

---

[75]   Concerning the issue of when a conviction is legally final, see *infra* § 2.3.6.
[76]   Act No. 46.
[77]   See Caprioli 2007, p. 143.
[78]   Cass., Sez. un., 10 luglio 2002, Franzese, *Cass. pen.*, 2002, p. 3652. See also Illuminati *supra* note 12; Stella 2003. For the beyond any reasonable rule as 'BARD', see, among many, Goldman & Goldman 2009, p. 55-66.
[79]   See, for example, Negri 2004.

In conclusion, the presumption of innocence is not completely observed in phases apart from trial, and particularly when pre-trial detention is at stake. In addition, the law permits the trial judge to consult the pre-trial detention file at any time, including previous custodial orders issued during the proceedings and evidence collected by the prosecutor that, as such, would be inadmissible at trial because of the hearsay rule. According to the rules of evidence, hearsay elements inserted in the pre-trial detention file cannot be *used* at the trial to adjudicate the case; however, their capacity to influence trial judges *de facto* is undeniably strong. Due to the fact that judges can *consult* at any time the pre-trial detention file, the system of double-dossier, according to which, to preserve a trial judges' 'unbiased mind' at the end of the investigation, is derogated from. Elements gathered by the prosecutor should be conserved in a separate file that is not accessible by the trial judges.[80]

The reason for giving trial judges the possibility to consult the pre-trial detention file is that the trial judge could, at any moment of the process, amend the pre-trial detention order, or even release the defendant, if he/she thinks that there are no grounds to justify his provisional custody. In practice, however, this results in the establishment of two different levels of applying the presumption of innocence. At the first level, the presumption is respected in the most complete way when pre-trial detention was not ordered and there is no need for the trial judge to consult the pre-trial detention file. The second level, in which the principle appears under attack, applies when, before the trial, the defendant has been placed in pre-trial detention.

2.3.4. The right to silence

A person involved in a criminal proceeding, either as a suspect or a defendant, must fully enjoy the right to silence, recognised in article 24 § 2 of the Italian Constitution, under which the right to a defence is inviolable at every phase and stage of the legal proceedings (both civil and criminal). As a consequence, the suspect and the accused have the right to remain silent, as well to give unsworn statements. A suspect/accused's lies are not sanctioned as such under the CCP, as opposed to what happens for the witness. Moreover, the suspect /accused must be warned of the risks and consequences related to the choice to give statements in a criminal proceeding.

When suspects are summoned, either by the police, prosecutor or judge, in order to be questioned or interrogated, they have the duty to present themselves, and to give their personal data to the relevant investigating authority. Before questioning the suspect, the police, prosecutor or judge must warn the suspect of the right to remain silent and of the fact that, if a statement is made regarding other persons, the suspect may become a witness in relation to those facts: in these cases, the defendant loses the right to silence regarding reported facts relating to others.

---

[80] See *supra* § 1.3 and *infra* 2.4.3. On the problem represented by the possibility – for trial judges – to consult the pre-trial detention file, see Todaro 2009, p. 1743-1776. See moreover Camon 1995, p. 166-180.

However, as explained in § 2.1.2, even in this case, the defendant can maintain the right to remain silent in relation to the charges brought against them (art. 64 § 3).[81]

The rationale of these rights is that people must be able to decide their own attitude towards the authority, when under suspicion in a criminal proceeding. As noted in § 2.1.2, the failure to give the warnings requested by law makes the statements gathered inadmissible as evidence.[82] This is the reason why the Court of Cassation has sometimes declared inadmissible as evidence statements gathered by undercover police operations.[83] Following the same arguments, the Court of Cassation has also refused to admit police testimony on the declarations given by a suspect to undercover police officers.[84]

The decision to remain silent can be taken into account when deciding a case, both regarding pre-trial detention as well as at the trial. Until 1995, there were many decisions asserting that the silence of the accused could be considered as proof of his intention to tamper with the evidence. In 1995, the Parliament intervened to prohibit such a practice. However, it is not unusual to find decisions that order pre-trial detention observing that the silence of the accused shows how he/she is not yet conscious of the harm caused, and other similar issues. At trial, the judge may explain the conviction of the accused by basing his/her decision on the accused's silence, if this is confirmed by some other positive evidence of his criminal responsibility.

2.3.5. The right to a reasoned judgment

An important feature surviving from the traditional system is that the judge's decisions must incorporate written reasons. This feature first appeared in the 18th century. The rationale for such a duty is manifold, and exists to ensure judicial accountability. It grants greater control throughout the course of the criminal process, because it strengthens the control of the appellate judge. In addition, it enhances the democratic aspects of the criminal justice system, by making the reasons for a decision available to every citizen. Most of all, the duty to justify decisions assures that the decision making process follows a rational path: if the judge has to explain why he/she has decided in favour of one party, this should

[81] See note 53.
[82] On the other hand, the CCP also provides that, when a person questioned as a witness gives self-incriminating statements, the police, prosecutor or judge must stop the interview and inform the person that investigations might be initiated against them. See *supra* § 2.1.2 and 2.2.2.
[83] Cass., 31 March 1998, Parreca, *Cassazione penale*, 2000, p. 965.
[84] It must be said that, on the defendant's statements given in the course of the proceeding, any testimony is forbidden (art. 62 of the CCP). This means that no one can testify on the statements of the suspects. The statements given by the suspect may be produced only via the written record, which may sometimes be audio or video recorded, signed by the officers who took part. The record must specify if the questioning was interrupted, at what time, and the time at which it was re-opened. To be clearer, admissions or confessions given by the suspect in an informal situation, for example at the coffee machine in the police station, are absolutely not admissible as evidence, either at trial or in the previous phases. See *supra* at the preceding note.

force him/her to make his/her decisions by reference to rational arguments. The judge must be able to persuade the reader that the decisions made were the best under the given circumstances, and not based on improper bias or resulting from corruption.[85]

2.3.6. The right to appeal

Another remaining traditional feature is the provision granting broad rights of appeal. Both convictions and acquittals may be appealed, either by the defence or the prosecutor, before the Court of Appeals (if the case was tried before the trial court), or before the Court of Assize of Appeal (if the case was tried before the Court of Assize). For cases tried before a Justice of Peace, the appeal is conducted by the trial court comprising one judge. The appeal is not a remedy provided for in the Italian Constitution; however, its tradition dates back centuries, and is unlikely to be abolished, even if many scholars and practitioners do not consider it to be consistent with the accusatorial model. The Court of Appeal may reverse the trial judgment, from conviction to an acquittal or, vice versa in case of appeal by the prosecutor. Moreover, under certain conditions, the Court of Appeal can declare the trial judgment null, ordering a new trial (or even a new prosecution, if the conditions provided for in art. 604 CCP are met).

Regardless of whether or not a decision has been appealed, it can always be submitted to the Court of Cassation, which ensures that the relevant law has been correctly applied and guarantees the uniformity of interpretation of the law. The appeal in Cassation constitutes a remedy recognised by the Constitution in article 111 § 7 and cannot be abolished without amending the Constitution. Prior to the completion of all possible remedies, the judgment reached at trial cannot be considered as final. Therefore, the sentence imposed by trial judges in case of conviction cannot be carried out if one of the parties appeals, or it is submitted to the Court of Cassation. Only after the end of the appeal and Cassation stage – or, quite unusually, if no appeals at all are presented – does the judgment become final and the sentence must be served.[86]

With Act No. 46 of 20 February 2006, the Italian Parliament abolished the right of the prosecutor and the defence to appeal against acquittal in criminal proceedings. Even if formally designed as a reform limiting the right of appeal of both parties, it was clearly a modification that involved mainly – and almost exclusively – the prosecutor. In fact, the prosecutor has the strongest interest to appeal against an acquittal, while the defendant is, in practice, much less interested in amending the trial judgment; it may happen, albeit not often, that a defendant appeals to obtain a modification of the acquittal formula (for example, to change the acquittal based on lack of *mens rea* to an acquittal for not having committed the material fact charged in the indictment).

---

[85] See Panzavolta, *supra* note 11, at p. 591-592; Illuminati *supra* note 11, at p. 567.
[86] Before the judgment has become final, a person can be kept in prison only if pre-trial custody is applied, according to the rules examined in § 2.3.1.

The Constitutional Court has since nullified this reform, declaring as a violation of the Constitution the prohibition to appeal against an acquittal for both the prosecutor and the defendant. In particular, with its decision No. 26 of 6 February 2007, the prohibition for the prosecutor to appeal against acquittals was nullified. The Constitutional Court based its reasoning on the equality of arms principle. In practice, the prosecutor would have been treated in an unreasonably unequal manner, because of the ban to appeal against acquittal, while the defendant maintained the right to appeal against convictions.

Subsequently, with its decision No. 85 of 4 April 2008, the Constitutional Court abolished the prohibition for the defendant to appeal against acquittal, asserting that this should considered to be in violation of both the equality of arms principle and the right to defence, as acknowledged in article 24 §2 of the Constitution.

There is no statistical data concerning the number of cases in which a trial judgment is amended or reversed at the appeal stage. However, it is commonly thought among lawyers that, in general, it is not difficult to obtain at least a slight reduction of the sentence at the appeal. Between 1983-2002, roughly one fourth of trial judgments (between 23-24%) were amended at the appeal stage.[87]

2.4. Rights relating to effective defence

2.4.1. The right to investigate the case

In 2000, the Parliament approved the Act of 7 December 2000, No. 397, which provided for comprehensive and detailed regulation of private investigations conducted by the defendant's, and victim's counsel. As a consequence, counsels are now allowed to seek evidence, including *inter alia* interview prospective witness, obtain expert evidence, have access to places not open to the public and ask public institutions to supply relevant documents.

Regarding the interview with persons who can provide information about facts, counsel may document the interview, using the specific forms provided for by Act No. 397/2000. The statement can be produced before the prosecutor or judge and have the same value as those produced by the prosecutor (with some slight distinction that fall outside the scope of this report).

Where a potential witness does not intend to give statements, counsel has two possibilities. First, he/she can ask the prosecutor to summon the witness. In this case, counsel has the right to be present at the witness interrogation, and is the first to ask him/her questions. Secondly, counsel can ask the judge to summon the witness for a deposition, in which case he/she will be examined and cross-examined before the judge by the prosecutor, the defendant and the victim's counsel.

In addition, counsel may obtain a warrant from the judge to enter private places, when the persons concerned do not give their consent.

Despite the undeniable improvement of defence prerogatives in criminal proceedings, the reform introduced with Act No. 397/2000 presented some

---

[87]   See Davigo & Mannozzi 2007, p. 136-138.

problems. The Court of Cassation has stated that a counsel who reports unfaithfully the statements rendered by the potential witness – for example, omitting some answers or directly falsifying a declaration of the witness – must be considered as a public officer who falsifies a public document, and consequently punished (up to six years imprisonment).[88]

The power of counsel to conduct investigations is the same, whether the defendant is in custody or not. They do not vary depending on the charges (the real discriminating factor is money, because of the features of the Italian legal aid system).

In theory, the powers to conduct private investigations are the same, regardless of the financial resources of the defendant. The legal aid provisions, in fact, cover private investigations. If the defendant is permitted to use legal aid, his/her counsel can appoint a private investigator, as well as an expert witness. However, budget limitations tend to restrict *de facto* the power of the defendant. Taking into account that the average remuneration of counsel acting under legal aid was, in 2007, slightly less than 900 Euro, it is easy to understand how problematic it is to conduct effective private investigations under the legal aid program.

The code of professional conduct for lawyers regulates the conduct of counsel in performing private investigations. Misbehaviour may be prosecuted and sanctioned under the relevant provisions.

An increasingly problematic issue relates to remedies, when the judge or prosecutor erroneously denies an application to conduct a private investigation. It is not unusual, in fact, for a specific application by counsel to be is denied, when it should be granted, according to the law. For example, article 391*bis* of the CCP provides that, in the case of a lawyer's formal request, the prosecutor is obliged to summon a person who refuses to render statements to counsel. However, it is not rare that the counsel request is not granted by the prosecutor, despite these provisions.

The Court of Cassation has stated that there is no remedy in such a case, because there is no way to overcome the discretionary powers of the prosecutor. The position is the same when the judge denies the lawyer's request to call a witness for a deposition, where he/she refused to give statements privately to the counsel. The Court of Cassation decided that the judge's denial could not be appealed. The only remedy, in such cases, should be at the disciplinary level.

In other words, the prosecutors or judges who contravened their duty should be sanctioned. In practice, this is a remote possibility, unless some other consequences are related to the illegitimate denial (for example, the defendant remained in custody and, if the evidence had been gathered, should have been released).

---

[88]   Cass., S. U., 27 June 2006, n. 32009, Schera, *Cass. pen.*, 2006, p. 3986.

2.4.2. The right to adequate time and facilities for the preparation of the defence

The Italian CCP provides for a minimum period of time that must necessarily elapse between important hearings, such as the preliminary hearing and first trial hearing,[89] and notification of them to the defendant. In particular, the defendant must be notified of the preliminary hearing at least 10 days prior (art. 419 CPP), and at least 20 days prior to the commencement of the trial (art. 429 CPP). For cases of minor gravity, where a preliminary hearing is not provided for, the defendant must be notified of the indictment and of the date of trial, at least 60 days before the start of the trial.

Access to the prosecutor's file is permitted at the end of the investigation, when the suspect must be informed of the conclusion of the investigation (art. 415*bis* CPP).[90] In addition, the suspect must be reminded of his right to have access to the prosecutor's file and to make a copy. From that moment, the prosecutor's file is freely accessible to the defendant, as well as to victims, at all times throughout the criminal process. Moreover, access to the pre-trial detention file, which contains all actions, documents and evidence related to custodial issues leading to the proceedings, is always permitted. In particular, after the end of pre-trial detention – or after notification of a milder measure limiting personal freedom – the defendant may, at any time, consult the actions and evidence upon which the judge decided to order the restriction.

After the conclusion of the preliminary hearing, if the judge decides that there is sufficient evidence to go to trial, the parties have free access to the judges' file, which, as noted earlier, contains only a small part of the actions and evidence collected by the prosecutor during the investigation.

Finally, at least seven days before the commencement of the trial, the parties must present to the judge a written list of the witnesses they intend to call to testify at trial (art. 468 CPP). The list must contain the name and whereabouts of the witnesses, as well as the facts upon which the requiring party intends to examine him/her at trial.

2.4.3. The right to equality of arms in examining witnesses

The Italian CCP now provides that only evidence produced in a public trial, and tested through cross-examination, may be used as a basis for the judge's decision. Save for exceptional cases, the judge is not able to use evidence that was not collected at trial.[91] The assessment of facts is considered to be reliable only if it is obtained after challenge by the parties, each one attempting to persuade the judge of its own viewpoint. In other words, the fact that both parties are merely heard at the trial is not enough: what matters is that, in principle, only evidence produced at

---

89 In Italy, the trial usually takes the form of several hearings. See on this issue *infra* § 4.1.
90 See, for more details on this matter, *supra* § 2.1.
91 See, on this matter, the issue concerning the pre-trial detention file, *supra* § 2.2.3.

trial and tested by examination in chief and cross-examination can be used to asses the facts of the case.

In fact, if the discussion relates to evidence acquired out of court, without cross-examination by any counterpart, its function would be limited to a critical review of evidentiary outcomes not obtained at trial. On the contrary, the parties must be given the right to participate, and to actively challenge, when the evidence to be used for the decision is being formulated, as provided by article 111§ 4 of the Constitution.

The 1988 CCP (based on the Anglo-American model) adopts the cross-examination technique to which article 111 of the Constitution indirectly refers. Paragraph 3 of article 111 grants the accused 'the right to examine or have examined witnesses against him'.

However, the most typical aspect of the accusatorial process, strictly linked to the principle of adversarial hearing – is the orality of the trial. This refers not only to the examination of witnesses, but primarily to the fact that evidence shall be developed in front of the trial judge (orality-immediacy). In other words, there must be a direct relationship between the judge called to decide the case and the sources of evidence: the trial judge shall have a personal perception of the statements to be evaluated, rather than just by means of the records drawn up by others.

The separation between the phases finds a visible example in the previously noted separation of the dossiers. The records of the investigation are not submitted to the judge and remain in the public prosecutor's dossier, at the disposal of the parties only. Before the judge, investigative records may only be used to challenge witnesses' statements during the trial examination, to point out a contradiction or a variation with what has previously been stated by the witness during the investigative stage. The judge may take into account previous statements only to evaluate the witness's reliability, but he/she may not use in evidence what has been stated out of trial, even if he/she has subsequently gained knowledge of it (art. 500 CPP).

However, separation between the phases is not applied too strictly, because it would imply losing in many circumstances the possibility to prove the facts, particularly if we consider that the trial normally takes place long after the investigation. In order to prevent the dispersion of evidence, it is inevitable to collect it during the course of the investigation –observing the possibility of the parties' challenge – whenever obtaining it at trial is not possible. This is the case of the *incidente probatorio* (depositions), in which, during the investigation, the judge, at the request of the prosecutor or defence, may order a hearing to take the testimony of a witness, with a view to the trial.

Furthermore, the reading and consequent substantive use of investigative records are permitted any time where some evidence cannot be reproduced at trial for compelling and unexpected reasons, albeit being obtained without cross-examination (art. 512, 513 and 514 CPP). Similarly, if it emerges that a witness called to testify in trial was subjected to unlawful pressure to prevent him/her from answering, or to oblige him/her to make a false declaration, prior statements used to challenge the deposition can be used as evidence (art. 500 § 4-5). Such exceptions to the principle of parties' challenge in the collection of the evidence are permitted by article 111 § 5of the Constitution, in case of 'absolute impossibility of obtaining evidence at trial' and of 'proven illicit conduct on the witness' (for example, the witness was threatened or coerced).

2.4.4. The right to free interpretation of documents and translation

Article 143 of the CCP provides for the right of the free assistance of an interpreter for the suspect/accused. This right is recognised from the first moment that the suspect asserts not to speak or understand Italian. In that case, the judge or, during the investigation, the prosecutor, must appoint an interpreter to assist the accused. Failure to do so results in the nullity of the subsequent acts by the prosecutor or judge, more specifically, an 'intermediate nullity'.[92]

However, in practice, the right to an interpreter is sometimes disregarded. In fact, the Court of Cassation has affirmed that the judge or prosecutor has the power to ascertain if the concerned person does not speak or understand Italian. In other words, the simple assertion by the defendant is not sufficient for the appointment of the interpreter, because the judge or prosecutor must verify if he/she cannot understand Italian. This leads to a paradox; to enjoy the right to an interpreter, the defendant must prove that he/she does not to speak or understand Italian. This proof often – if not always – is quite problematic. As a consequence, the 'right' to have an interpreter formally proclaimed by the law often results in a concession left to the discretion of the magistrate. It sometimes happens that the judge, in an authoritative and severe way, may ask the defendant if he/she speaks, or at least understands, Italian, and the defendant answers affirmatively, being concerned not to upset the judge (whose question he did not perfectly understand).

Moreover, in the view of the Court of Cassation, the right to the assistance of an interpreter does not mean that the interpreter must be able to speak the language of the defendant, but only that the interpreter must speak a language that the defendant understands (for a northern African, it could be sufficient in practice that the interpreter speaks French, if no interpreter who speaks Arab is available).

The right recognised by article 143 includes the free translation of the process documents. However, the Court of Cassation has stated that not all documents must be translated under article 143, but only those destined specifically for the

---

[92]   The most typical sanction provided for by the Italian CCP, in accordance with the civil law tradition, is nullity. In general, when an act is declared null by the law, it means that it must be considered void, and for this reason must be struck out from the criminal proceeding. If one or more acts are based on one that is declared null, they are affected by the same form of invalidity. In other words, they are all void and must be repeated, if possible. There are three grades of nullity, depending on the gravity of the violation. The most severe is 'absolute nullity' (art. 179 CCP), which cannot be remedied. An objection concerning an act affected by absolute nullity can be raised by a party at any time. Absolute nullity, however, can also be recognised *proprio motu* by the judge until the end of the criminal process. At the second level, there is 'intermediate nullity' (art. 180), which must be objected by the party or recognised *proprio motu* by the judge within a certain lapse of time (in general, the conclusion of the phase, subsequent to that in which nullified act was performed), after which the act can be considered as if it was correctly formed. Finally, there is 'relative nullity', whose existence must be objected in a motion by the interested party within a short time, otherwise the act is considered correct and valid. It cannot be recognised *proprio motu* by the judge.

defendant. As a consequence, the judgment does not have to be translated, because it is not destined only for the defendant, being adopted in the name of the Italian people and for all the parties (prosecutor, *parte civile*, defendant).[93] The main actions that must be translated concern the indictment and advices relating to the preliminary hearing and trial, the prosecutor's order to serve the sentence applied to the convicted person, the warrant of arrest and the judge's decisions imposing pre-trial custody. The duty to provide a translation applies also to the letters of rights referred to in § 2.1.1.

Finally, the interpreter must give guarantees of competence and independence. He/she can be appointed from a list maintained by the trial court registry. He/she must comply with some prerequisites, without which his/her involvement is sanctioned by nullity under the CCP (art. 144). To be appointed as an interpreter, a person must not have been suspended from public office, or from private practice, as a consequence of a criminal conviction; moreover, he/she cannot be under a safety measure as a consequence of a criminal conviction. A person called to trial to render testimony cannot be appointed as an interpreter in the same proceeding.

Lastly, a person married to the defendant cannot be appointed as an interpreter, unless the defendant is deaf, mute, or both. An interpreter can be disqualified at the request of the parties, in cases provided for under article 144, or when other grave reasons occur. At the time of appointment before the judge or prosecutor, the interpreter is cautioned with regard to his/her duties, and asked if there exist any reason for disqualification p article 144.

3. The professional culture of defence lawyers

Counsels practising in criminal law tend to perceive themselves as a counterpart to the 'system', including both the prosecutor and judges. In other words, they tend to conceive their work as giving to their client the best possible defence, and are not keen to cooperate with prosecutors or judges, unless this is, at the same time, in the interests of their client.

If we look at the quality of criminal defence services, the main problems seem to be related to the legal aid system, and to counselling when appointed by the court. Regarding the latter, it may happen that lawyers appointed *ex officio* lack the necessary training and experience to prepare a good defence. Since 2001, the law has required the local bar associations to organise and control the training of lawyers who are eligible to be appointed *ex officio*. However, the services of counsel appointed *ex officio* only partially reach the same standard of quality of those carried out by hired counsel.

It is possible to say that sometimes the same practitioner works in a different manner, when engaged by a client, than when appointed by the court. As far as concerns the legal aid system, we already pointed out the reasons for this related to

---

[93]   Cass., Sez. VI, 22 October 2008, C.e.d., n. 242227. At least 15 other decisions of the Court of Cassation, dating back to 1997, confirm this.

the inefficiency of the system.[94] This involves – or may involve– some unsuitable consequences. In particular, in cases with indigent clients, counsel is not as motivated as he/she should be in representing the interests of the defendant. We do not assert that this is the rule: there are many cases of lawyers working at their best regardless of their remuneration,[95] but of course, with such structural inefficiencies in the system, there remains the risk that counsels are not adequately motivated.

Another feature that may bear consequences on the quality of service is the low number of large firms that are used to dealing with a case from multiple points of view (criminal, fiscal, corporate).These firms are concentrated only in Rome and Milan, and even then, they represent a small number even when compared to the overall number of lawyers in those cities.

According to recent research promoted by the Penal Chamber of Milan, and undertaken by AASTER, an Italian company working in the field of social sciences,[96] it emerged that lawyers tend to affirm that their corporation is in a period of crisis.[97] Notwithstanding their large number,[98] or perhaps because of it, the interviewed lawyers perceive as a critical problem the difficulty to create large firms, where work on single cases can be handled together with other colleagues. It must be observed that, in the criminal law field in Italy, co-management of the case is not readily practicable, due to the typical claim of the client, who usually does not accept the his/her case is managed by more than one or two lawyers at the same firm.

The large number of lawyers, as well as the necessity to work individually on single cases, has led to a myriad of small firms that are sometimes over specialised and lacking the ability to give adequate services on the multifaceted specific aspects of legal practice (civil, criminal, administrative, fiscal). In addition, the number of lawyers means that in some areas, practitioners are not able to earn enough to maintain a high standard of service.[99] The difficulty of earning an adequate salary

---

[94] The right to mandatory legal assistance and to free legal assistance works differently in juvenile criminal proceedings: the law actually provides that the counsel appointed by the court is automatically remunerated by the State in any case. The State may recover the expenses sustained by the person assisted if they are able to afford them – if the annual income of the family unit is over the limit mentioned: see Caianiello & Illuminati *supra* note 11, at p. 143-144.

[95] When interviewed on the point, more than one counsel asserted that they do not care if the legal aid system remuneration is inadequate, or if they will receive any remuneration at all. When they have a case, they do their best, because 'our task is to undermine the case of the prosecutor and the police, making our best at this aim'.

[96] The online site is <www.aaster.it>.

[97] Guastella 2009, p. 10-11. See on the same matter Caianiello & Illuminati *supra* note 11, at p. 147-149.

[98] In Italy, there are more than 213,000 practicing lawyers, representing 36.8 lawyers per 10,000 inhabitants (the third in Europe after Liechtestein and Spain). See Guastella *supra* note 99. Regarding low number of large firms that are used to dealing with a case from multiple points of view, see Malatesta M., 'Le transformazioni dell'avvocatura italiana', online at <www.nelmerito.com>, 26 February 2010.

[99] From the interviews conducted, it emerged that 68% would favour severe restrictions to access to the legal practice, while 65% would approve the *numerus clausus* policy in the Law Faculty of the State. Some 63% would promote a system of external checks and certifications

→

for their work constitutes a factor that, at least indirectly, could undermine counsel independence. In fact, a traditional prerogative of the Italian legal profession – the discretion of counsel to refuse or accept cases for potential clients – could be drastically weakened if the main concern of practicing counsel was to find sufficient financial resources to reach a dignified standard of life.

4. Political commitments to effective criminal defence

4.1. Perception of criminal justice system

In general, confidence in criminal justice system has been decreasing in Italy over the last 10 years. During the 1990s, confidence in criminal justice reached a high point, due to the famous national inquiry into political and business corruption known as 'Cleaned Hands'. After that time, trust gradually lessened, due probably to disillusion provoked by the lack of change in the political system. Moreover, the rise of Silvio Berlusconi, as a protagonist of the Italian political life, lead to a conflict between justice and Government, due to the numerous criminal proceedings pending against Berlusconi. At least seven *ad hoc* Acts were adopted by the Parliament to interfere with cases involving the Prime Minister;[100] in addition, the Prime Minister and the political forces in his alliance have raised strong polemics against those judges and prosecutors responsible for initiating a criminal process against him: sometimes it appeared that the fight moved by the right coalition involved the judiciary as a whole.

---

for the standards of services provided by legal firms. Among them, 23.6% consider such checks necessary to protect the clients from the risks due to incompetent colleagues.

[100] The first was the reforms enabling the transfer of criminal proceedings to another district, where there is the risk that all the judges of the trial court before which the case is pending lack of the necessary impartiality (Act. No. 248, 7 November 2002). Secondly, the law reducing the time necessary for the efficacy of the statute of limitations (Act. No. 251, 5 December 2005). Thirdly, the law prohibiting proceedings against the five most important charges of the Italian State: the President of the Republic, the President of the Council of Ministries, the Presidents of the two Parliament Chambers, the President of the Constitutional Court (Act. No. 140, 20 June 2003). Fourthly, the law prohibiting the prosecutor to appeal against an acquittal (Act. No. 46, 20 February 2006). It is interesting to observe that these four Acts were declared, in whole or in part, unconstitutional by the Italian Constitutional Court. Finally, Act. No. 124, 22 July 2008 – one of the first Acts of the new Parliament, elected the previous May – restored the stay of proceedings initiated against the most important charges of the Italian State, because the analogous provisions of Act. No. 140, 20 June 2003 had in the meantime been nullified by the Italian Constitutional Court. On 7 October 2009, with decision No. 262, the Constitutional Court nullified Act No. 124, 22 July 2008, because it violated the equality of citizens before the Law, provided for by art. 3 of the Italian Constitution and representing one of its most fundamental principles. To those Acts must be added Act No. 367, 5 October 2001, approved with the declared intent to interfere with the criminal process involving, among others, Cesare Previti, Berlusconi's former counsel and at the time Senator of the Italian Republic. The Act had the intent to impede to the prosecutor from producing as evidence numerous documents obtained via rogatory from the Swiss judicial authorities. Moreover, the Legislative Decree No. 61, 11 April 2002 amended the crimes *financial or accounting fraud*, so causing the acquittal of Silvio Berlusconi in the criminal process for charges including such conduct.

Above all, the first reason for the lack of confidence is the significantly unreasonable length of proceedings. The average length of a criminal process in Italy is 1589 days. In the period between 1 July 2001 – 30 June 2002, it amounted to 1,457 days.[101] The average length of a trial is 139 days for a case tried before a single professional judge (*Tribunale in composizione monocratica*), and 117 days for those tried before a panel of three professional judges (*Tribunale in composizione collegiale*).[102] The average time elapsing from the beginning of an investigation to the start of the trial is roughly three years:[103] this period must be added to the length of the criminal process. In sum, the average length of the Italian criminal proceeding as a whole, from the start of the investigation to the end of the process, amounts to roughly seven or eight years.

In addition, at trial, several months may elapse between one hearing and the next. The CCP prescribes at article 477 that, if the trial cannot be finished in one hearing, the judge must adjourn the case to the following day and, in any case, to fix the new hearing not later than 10 days later.[104] However, this provision is mostly – if not always – disregarded, because of the busy hearing schedules, and no sanction is usually imposed for its violation.[105]

From Eurispes Research it emerged that, at trial, the main reasons to adjourn the hearing are the impossibility for the accused or for his/her counsel to attend the trial (14.2%), the request of the defence to better prepare the case (6.6%), logistical problems (6.8%), double booking of the hearing (3.1%), error in notifying to the accused of the hearing (9.4%), error in informing prosecution witnesses to attend trial to testifying (9.2%), the unjustified absence of prosecution witnesses (39.9%). Italy is at seventh place in the list of the Countries found by the ECtHR to be in violation due to the unreasonable length of the proceedings.

The excessive length of the criminal process – as well as civil, whose situation is perhaps even worse – dates back for decades. As an example, at the entry into force of the 1989 CCP, it was said by the political world that the new model of criminal process would favour the solution of the 'traditional problem' of the

---

[101] Data from the Official Site of the Italian Ministry of Justice <http://www.giustizia.it/ministro/uffstampa/articolo_cerrato.htm>. Of course, the outlined times are not all employed in hearings. Actually, it is quite the opposite. On average, a criminal trial does not take more that four -five hearings at the trial stage, one or two at the appeal and just one (two in exceptional cases) before the Court of Cassation. This means that, of the 1,589 days, the most part is spent waiting between one hearing and the other, or, what takes the most part of time, between the trial and the appeal stage.

[102] EURISPES, *Rapporto sul processo penale. Sintesi*, September 2008, online at <http://www.astrid-online.it/--giustizi/Documenti/index.htm>, p. 2. In general, from one hearing to the next one pass various months, on average 2-3 months (but, in big forum as Rome, 6-7 months).

[103] EURISPES, *Rapporto*, cit. *supra* note 31, p. 2.

[104] An analogous provision was present in the previous Code of criminal procedure.

[105] If ever prosecuted for the violation of art. 477 CPP, a judge could easily object that it is impossible to observe the mentioned provision, and that the violation was not voluntarily committed. Moreover, he could prove that the disregard for art. 477 CPP was due to his far overbooked schedule hearings, and that the overbooking dates back decades because of the huge amount of pending cases waiting to be decided (which is true for the most part of trial courts).

unreasonable duration of the proceedings.[106] Scandals sometimes arise. In January 2008, officers of the Minister of Justice, during an inquiry involving the Office of the Prosecutor of the trial court of Bologna, found a closet with more than 2000 files apparently forgotten, and for this reason destined to be sent to the archives due to the statute of limitations.[107]

Therefore, it is not surprising that 53.7% of the interviewees, in a recent inquiry, said they were not confident in the criminal justice administration (while, in 2004, 52.4% declared to have confidence),[108] and that 62.3% of them claimed that the main problem of Italian justice is its excessive length.[109]

It is interesting to note that, while among the judiciary – judges and prosecutors – the view is that those most responsible for the delays in the administration of justice are on the Bar side, in the opinion of the latter it is just the opposite. It is probable that both opinions are in part true. On one side, Italy has an overwhelming number at the Bar, slightly greater then 213,000. This may give rise to some abuse[110] of the procedural provisions, and in general may lead to a growth of the level of litigation in the society. Moreover, it may lead to an excessive use of the appeal tools that represent, for the judiciary, one of the major reasons for the unreasonable length of the process.[111]

On the other hand, from the data mentioned above, it is possible to calculate that roughly 68% of hearing adjournments are due to inefficiencies imputable to bad administration by the public officers delegated to follow the process, rather then the lawyers.

It should be noted that general amount of professional and non professional judges in Italy is not particularly low.[112]

The length of the proceedings is at the basis of the high number of acquittals in Italy, due to the statute of limitations rules. According to recent research on the trial

---

[106] A group of Italian researchers dedicated two years to this issue. See on this subject Kostoris 2005.

[107] DINO M., *Fascicoli dimenticati, scontro fra magistrati*, <http://archiviostorico.corriere.it/2000 /gennaio/08/Fascicoli_dimenticati_scontro_fra_magistrati_co_0_0001082806.shtmli>.

[108] EURISPES, *Rapporto Italia 2009*, <http://www.scribd.com/doc/11570329/Sintesi-Rapporto-Italia-Eurispes-2009>, p. 2-3.

[109] EURISPES, *Rapporto Italia 2009, supra* at the preceding note, p. 63-64.

[110] In this sense the Report of the General Prosecutor toward the Court of Cassation, 2009, online at <http://www.astrid-online.it/--giustizi/Documenti/Inaugurazi2/index.htm>, p. 40-45.

[111] See Nunziata 2004.

[112] In Italy there are 9037 professional judges and 8937 non professional judges (judges of peace, honorary prosecutor and judges. The last two categories are appointed by the Ministry of Justice, on application of the interested persons. Honorary prosecutors and judges are allowed respectively to prosecute and adjudicate cases of minor importance, concerning crimes punished up to 4 years of imprisonment). Data from the site of the Minister of Justice <http://www.giustizia.it/ministro/uffstampa/articolo_cerrato.htm>. The annual expenses for justice in Italy amount to 752,593,326,137 Euro that means 127 Euro per inhabitant. The sum represent the 1.0% of the Italian National budget (from the Report of the General Prosecutor toward the Court of Cassation, 2009, p. 35. The report is freely downloadable <http://www.astrid-online.it/--giustizi/Documenti/Inaugurazi2/index.htm >).

stage in criminal proceedings,[113] at the national level, at the end of the trial, in 6.7% of cases, the accused is released because of the expiry of the statute of limitations. The data does not take into account the hypotheses where the case is dismissed at the end of the investigation, because of the statute of limitations, and at the appeal stage, in which release is permitted.

To understand the problem, it is necessary to realise that the Italian system of statute of limitations is quite peculiar. According to the rules provided for in the CCP, there is no distinction between the period of time *before* the start of the prosecution, and the period *after* the prosecution commences until the end of the process. In other words, the statute of limitations accrues from the date of the commission of the crime, and do not stop at the initiation of the prosecution, nor after the trial judgment. In a summary, the terms concerning the statute of limitations continue throughout all of the criminal process subject to an extension by one quarter. As example, if a crime was committed in 2000, and the law provides an expiry after of 10 years, if the prosecution starts in 2004, there are only six years to reach a final judgment on the merits (four years under the ordinary statute of limitation term, plus two years due to the commencement of the prosecution). However, this is not much, considering the traditional length of the Italian process.

Finally, a managerial approach in the administration of justice is considered controversial, even if scholars have more recently endorsed this as a solution at the legislative level to prosecute and try criminal cases.[114]

4.2.   *Political commitment to criminal justice*

If we look at the reforms introduced in the field of criminal justice in Italy during the last 18 years, we see a fragmented and contradictory picture. Taking into account that any generalisation implies at least some mistakes, due to a subjective interpretation of a complex phenomenon, we can divide into three phases the political interventions in the field of criminal justice. At first, there was, at the beginning of the 1990s (1992-1997), a shift toward a more efficient fight against some traditional forms of crime, such as organised crime and corruption: this led to the diminution of some relevant safeguards for the defence. In particular, the so-called 'Martelli Decree' (decree No. 306 of 8 June 992, approved by the Parliament with Act. No. 356/1992), as well as some decisions of the Italian Constitutional Court, notably restricted the defendant's right to confrontation, by permitting the use of out of court statements collected during the investigation by police and the prosecutor.[115]

It is worth noting that, in those years, Italy was racked by two facts: on one hand, the famous inquiry started in Milan called 'Clean Hands', which led to the fall of the traditional political parties, such as the Christian Democrats and the Socialist Party (and the rise of new political leaders, the most famous of which is the current

---

113   EURISPES, *Rapporto sul processo penale. Sintesi*, September 2008, online at <http://www.astrid-online.it/--giustizi/Document/index.htm>, p. 4.

114   See *supra* § 1.2.

115   See Panzavolta *supra* note 11, at p. 595-600; Illuminati *supra* note 11, at p. 573-576; Pizzi & Montagna *supra* note 11, at p. 449-460.

Prime Minister, Silvio Berlusconi); on the other, by the assassination – through two terrible bombing attacks – of famous judges involved in the fight against organised crime, Giovanni Falcone and Paolo Borsellino, and their respective escorts.[116]

In a second period (1999-2001), the Parliament re-introduced some safeguards considered fundamental for the accusatorial system: in particular, the Italian Constitution was amended to assure at the highest level the right to confrontation in criminal processes, and the prohibition of the use of statements collected unilaterally out of court prior to trial. Moreover, a new Act concerning private investigations in criminal proceedings by defendants and victim's counsel entered into force. Other new Acts were also approved, improving both the legal aid system and the duty counselling.[117]

Finally, it is possible to categorise a third period (2001-2009), characterised for its 'unequal approach' in the field of criminal justice. On one hand, since 2001, numerous Acts were introduced to improve defence safeguards (mostly to intervene in criminal processes involving relevant political leaders);[118] on the other, new reforms were approved to strengthen the fight against particular crimes, such as street crimes/blue collar crimes and immigration, considered at the basis of the growing sense of insecurity among the Italian population.[119]

The policy followed by the political forces and the Government in recent years led to a distinction among the crimes. For some criminal conduct, the Government showed an intention to be tough, while for others it appeared not to favour – or at least to speed up – their prosecution. In particular, in 2008, a recent reform promoted by the Government and approved by the Parliament, named 'Security Pack' (*Pacchetto Sicurezza*),[120] introduced new provisions directing the judges to give priority to proceedings started with the arrest of the suspect,[121] and to proceedings in which pre-trial detention is applied.

Moreover, when arrest is applied, the prosecutor is now obliged to file an indictment against the arrested person within 30 days from the arrest; finally, even in the absence of an arrest, but when pre-trial detention has been applied and not revoked by the Tribunal of freedom, or by the Court of Cassation, a preliminary hearing must be dispersed with, no matter how serious is the crime charged, and the case is to go directly to trial. The reforms approved in 2008 had the effect of

[116]   In the Capaci killings – in addition to Giovanni Falcone, three police officers and Falcone's wife, Francesca Morvillo, at the time a justice at Palermo's trial court, also lost their lives. In the D'Amelio Drive bombing, together with judge Paolo Borsellino, five police officers, who worked as his police escort, were assassinated.

[117]   Duty counselling was partially reformed by Act No. 60, 6 March 2001; legal aid was improved by Act No. 134, 29 March 2001.

[118]   See in this sense the Acts mentioned *supra* at note 100.

[119]   As noted above, despite the fact that the total number of crimes has not significantly increased in the last 10 years, the fear of crime has increased among Italian population. See *supra* § 1.4.

[120]   The 2008 Act named 'security Pack' is Act No. 125, 24 July 2008.

[121]   Or where the suspect is in custody. The reform was introduced with Act No. 125, 24 July 2008. See, on this subject, Valentini E., 'La poliedrica attività del nuovo giudizio immediato'; Allegrezza S., 'La nuova fisionomia del giudizio direttissimo'; Illuminati G. & Vicoli D., 'Criteri di priorità e meccanismi sospensivi: un difficile connubio in tema di accelerazione dei tempi processuali' direttissimo'. All the contributions are published in Mazza & Viganò 2008.

improving the enforcement of provisions against street crime, for which arrest and pre-trial detention are traditionally most common, and of immigration crimes, being the new area of concern for the political forces. With this aim, since 2002, with Act No. 189, 30 July 2002, new forms of crime concerning immigration have been introduced, all of which are punished with severe penalties, and permitting the police to arrest the suspect caught in the act of committing them.

Requiring the judges to give precedence to cases in which arrest took place or, at any rate, a pre-trial detention order is in force, the 2008 reforms had the effect – among others – of improving the enforcement of criminal provisions concerning immigration. Finally, in July 2009, with an Act again named 'Security Pack',[122] a new offence was approved by the Parliament criminalising the mere status of being an illegal immigrant. Notwithstanding the mild penalty provided for by the law (a fine from 5,000 Euro up to 10,000 Euro), a special proceeding was introduced, so as to permit to the judges of peace – who have jurisdiction over the new crime – to deal with cases involving illegal immigration in priority to other proceedings.

With respect to other crimes, such as corruption or general white collar crimes – for which arrest or pre-trial detention is much more unusual – political forces did not show the same determination. Of course, in theory, the fight against corruption and organised crime continues to represent a priority: in the 2009 Security Pack, Act No. 94, 15 July, 2009, some provisions concerning organised crime were introduced. However, by overburdening the schedules of Italian trial courts with street crimes and immigration crimes, which must be dealt with in advance of other crimes, means that *de facto* other forms of crime will only be treated later, with a higher risk of acquittal due to the statute of limitations.[123]

With such an approach, there is not much room for concern regarding effective criminal defence, particularly in relation to the traditional problems (counsel appointed *ex officio* system, legal aid, length of the proceedings). In particular, there is clearly no intention to intervene with reforms that could advantage, among other things, extra EU foreign indigent defendants.

5.   Conclusions

The framework emerging from the considerations discussed above is far from coherent and, for this reason, far from satisfactory. On one hand, the Italian system has improved its safeguards in the field of the effective criminal defence in many respects. In particular, the protections recognised to the defendant at the investigation phases, during questioning before the police, the prosecutor and the judge, can be considered as positive aspects. Notwithstanding some exceptions, it is possible to affirm that the suspect called to give statements by criminal law enforcement agencies is usually aware of his/her rights and of the risks of his/her choices at that stage. The mandatory attendance of counsel during police questioning (as well as judge interrogation according to art. 294), the mandatory

---

[122]   The 2009 Act named 'security Pack' is Act No. 94, 15 July 2009.

[123]   This appears particularly true for corruption and financial crimes, which are not expressly mentioned in the new 2008 priority criteria provided for by Act No. 125/2008.

notice to counsel in cases of prosecutor interrogation, the necessity in all these cases to appoint a counsel *ex officio*, if the defendant has not chosen one, make it more unlikely that he/she might be subject to a trick or *escamotages* to undermine his right to silence.

In addition, there is the letters of rights that the prosecutor must give to the defendant during the investigation phase improve his/her level of awareness of the criminal proceedings. Moreover, access to the file is effectively assured (the problem often being the opposite: how to protect the right to privacy of the persons involved in a criminal processes); surprises or unexpected moves by the prosecutor at trial are quite rare.

Finally, right to confrontation is effectively applied in Italian courts, as well as the prohibition against using investigative statements unilaterally made by one of the parties. This assures equality of arms among the litigants (this conclusion is strengthened if we look at the possibility for the defendant to conduct private investigations).

On the other hand, the Italian system does not show due regard to other fundamental features. Among them, the legal aid system is highly unsatisfactory, for at least two reasons. It is open only to persons with a very low annual income, and not appealing for the counsel, who are remunerated significantly less than when paid by the client. This renders unlikely, in general, the possibility to conduct private investigations for defendants admitted to legal aid.

Another feature that should be reconsidered is the right to an interpreter and the translation of documents, which is too frequently disregarded in practice by the case law, whose interpretation of the CCP is far from being consistent with the ECtHR standards in the same field. In too many cases, the interpreter is not appointed when he/she should be, and the translation of documents is not ordered. The minimum basis for an effective criminal defence thus seems irrevocably undermined.

Finally, the peculiarities of pre-trial detention, and of the recent reforms called 'Security Pack' in 2008 and 2009, make it clear that, when pre-trial detention is applied, equality of arms is far more difficult to achieve: in other words, the case of the prosecution has many more chances to win than that of the defence. The picture is probably more worrying if we consider that, often, most of the negative aspects outlined in this report are present at the same time: for example, when the defendant is a street criminal with previous convictions, with no salary (or a very low one); or when the defendant is an illegal immigrant, charged with crimes concerning immigration. In such cases, the chance that those defendants can enjoy an effective criminal defence does not seem very high.

Finally, not enough attention is paid to on the empirical aspects involved in the reforms introduced by the legislature in the field of criminal process. We have seen that, in general, there is a lack of official statistics on many aspects that deserve some monitoring. Moreover, it is very rare that any proposal for reform concerning criminal justice presented to the Parliament is accompanied with a study on the practical impacts it might have on the system (persons involved, costs, length of the proceeding).

In other words, reforms are conceived at an abstract and ideal level (or are used as a means for propaganda, as in the case of the crime of illegal immigration), but rarely accompanied with a field study regarding the practical consequences they could imply. Once again, this is not suitable for a system, such as the Italian one, which is not functioning well in practice (in which the outcome of the process may be formally correct, but substantially unfair).

6. Bibliography

Books

Barbagli 2007
Barbagli, M., *Immigrazione e criminalità in Italia*, Bologna: Il Mulino, 2007.

Caianiello 2003
Caianiello, M., *Poteri dei privati nell'esercizio dell'azione penale*, Torino: Giappichelli, 2003.

Conso & Grevi 2005
Conso, G. & Grevi, V. (eds.), *Commentario breve al codice di procedura penale*, Padova: Cedam, 2005.

Conso & Grevi 2008
Conso, G. & Grevi, V. (eds.), *Compendio di procedura penale*, Padova: Cedam, 2008.

Cordere 1966
Cordero, F., *Ideologie del processo penale*, Milano: Giuffrè, 1966.

Cordero 2006
Cordero, F., *Procedura Penale*, Milano: Giuffrè, 2006.

Davigo & Mannozzi 2007
Davigo, P. & Mannozzi, G., *La corruzione in Italia. Percezione sociale e controllo penale*, Bari: Laterza, 2007.

Di Bitonto 2004
Di Bitonto, M.L., *Profili dispositivi dell'accertamento penale*, Torino: Giappichelli, 2004.

Iacoviello 1997
Iacoviello, F.M., *La motivazione della sentenza penale e il suo controllo in cassazione*, Milano: Giuffrè, 1997.

Illuminati 1979
Illuminati, G., *La presunzione d'innocenza dell'imputato*, Bologna: Zanichelli, 1979.

Lozzi 2008
Lozzi, G., *Lineamenti di procedura penale*, Torino: Giappichelli, 2008.

Negri 2004

Negri, D., *Fumus commissi delicti. La prova per le fattispecie cautelari*, Torino: Giappichelli, 2004.

Nobili 2005

Nobili, M., *Il principio del libero convincimento del giudice*, Milano: Giuffrè, 1974.

Siracusano 2004

Siracusano, D. et al. (eds.), *Diritto processuale penale*, Milano: Giuffrè, 2004.

Chapters in Compilations

Caianiello & Illuminati 2007

Caianiello, M. & Illuminati, G., 'The Investigative Stage of the Criminal process in Italy', in: E. Cape, J. Hodgson, T. Prakken and T. Spronken, *Suspects in Europe. Procedural Rights at the Investigative Stage of the Criminal Process in the European Union*, Antwerp–Oxford: Intersentia, 2007, p. 129-154.

Articles in Journals

Amodio & Selvaggi 1989

Amodio, E. & Selvaggi, E., 'An Accusatorial System in a Civil Law Country: The 1988 Italian Code of Criminal Procedure', *Temple Law Review*, 1989, p. 1211-1240.

Grande 2000

Grande, E., 'Italian Criminal Justice: Borrowing and Resistance', *American Journal of Comparative Law*, 2000, p. 228-260.

Illuminati 2005

Illuminati, G., 'The Frustrated Turn to Adversarial Procedure in Italy (Italian Criminal Procedure Code of 1988)', *Washington Universal. Global Studies Law Review*, 2005, p. 567-581.

Panzavolta 2005

Panzavolta, M., 'Reforms and Counter-Reforms in the Italian Struggle for an Accusatorial Criminal Law System', *North Carolina Journal of International Law and Commercial Regulation*, 2005, p. 577-622.

Pizzi & Montagna 2004

Pizzi, W.T. & Montagna, M., 'The Battle to Establish an Adversarial Trial System in Italy', *Michigan Journal of International Law*, 2004, p. 429-466.

Statistical and Bibliographical References

Major statistical and research resources
Data on both criminal and civil justice may be found at the Italian Ministry of Justice site, <www.giustizia.it>, under the link *dati statistici* (statistical data). Some of the data was supplied through a specific application used for this research, and is not freely accessible online.

See the online site <http://www.astrid-online.it/>, a site dedicate to Italian juridical issues (many in administrative law). In particular, see under the link *Diritti e giustizia* (Rights and Justice).

See the reports of the Italian Centre for Social Sciences, Eurispes. In particular, the report regarding the length of the criminal processes in Italy may be consulted at the online site of the *Camere penali* (Penal Chambers), the Italian private association of criminal counsels (<www.camerepenali.it>), at the link *Rapporto sul processo penale* (Report on the Italian Criminal Process).

See also the issue No. 3 of the Review 'Studi sulla questione criminale. Nuova serie di', *Dei delitti e delle pene*, 3, 2008 entirely dedicated to the highly disputed relation between immigration and crime, edited by Dario Melossi, with subtitle 'Subordinazione informale e criminalizzazione dei migranti', p. 9-125.

Dorris de Vocht

CHAPTER 10 POLAND[*]

1.   Introduction

1.1.   General information

Poland is a parliamentary democratic republic located in the centre of Europe covering a territory of just over 312,000 km2 and with a population of approximately 38.5 million people.[1]

The political system is laid down in the Polish Constitution which defines Poland as a 'democratic state ruled by law and implementing the principles of social justice'.[2] The executive power is exercised by the government led by the Prime Minister. Legislative power is vested in both the government and a parliament consisting of two chambers (the *Sejm* and the Senate). The president has the power to veto legislation passed by parliament.

The territory is divided into 16 administrative provinces (voivodships). Poland's largest city and capital is Warsaw, with a population of approximately 1.7 million people.

The ethnic diversity of Polish society was severely reduced by the events of World War II and the migrations that followed it: the number of Jews, Germans, Ukrainians, Belarusians and Lithuanians in Polish society dropped drastically.

A large majority of the population belongs to the Roman Catholic Church making Poland one of the most devoutly religious countries in Europe.[3] The Roma people are far less numerous and less controversial in Poland than in most other

---

[*]   This country report has been reviewed by Małgorzata Wąsek-Wiaderek, associate professor at the John Paul II Catholic University of Lublin.

[1]   For extensive demographic information, see the Demographic Yearbook of Poland 2008 available at <http://www.stat.gov.pl/gus/5840_3697_ENG_HTML.htm>.

[2]   Art. 2 Constitution of Poland of 1997.

[3]   Different surveys show different rates of religious observance, but in general the number of Poles belonging to the Catholic Church fluctuates between 90 and 95% of the country's population: see <http://en.wikipedia.org/wiki/Roman_Catholicism_in_Poland>.

East European countries. Estimates of the Roma population in Poland range from 15,000 to 50,000.[4]

1.2. Outline of the legal system

1.2.1. History

The Polish legal system is based on the continental legal system (civil law tradition) with predominantly German influences. The history of the law and legal system of Poland is undoubtedly influenced by its lively political history. Poland regained independence at the end of World War I, after having been divided between the neighbouring countries of Austria, Prussia and Russia for over a century. Shortly afterwards however, its independence was again lost – this time to the Soviet Union.

In 1989, Poland was the first country of the Eastern Bloc to overthrow the communist regime and start the transformation into a democratic country based on the rule of law. Although Poland managed to keep a considerable amount of autonomy during communism, this transition required fundamental economic, social and legal reforms. Shortly after the start of this transition process, Poland joined the Council of Europe and ratified the European Convention on Human Rights. On 1 May 2004, Poland joined the European Union.

1.2.2. Sources of law

The Constitution of 1997 defines several sources of universally binding Polish law: the Constitution, statutes (*ustawa*), ratified international agreements and regulations (*rozporządzenie*).[5] The Constitution forms the supreme law of the Polish Republic.[6] Statutes are basic acts of universally binding law in Poland and are issued by the Sejm. In order to come into force, acts must be published in the Journal of Laws of the Republic of Poland (*Dziennik Ustaw*).

There are also acts of internal law, such as resolutions (*uchwała*) adopted by the Sejm, Senate and the Council of Ministers, as well as orders (*zarządzenie*) issued by the President of the Republic of Poland or by a minister. Regulations (*rozporządzenie*) are issued only by those organs that are expressly referred to in the Constitution and must be issued on the basis of specific authorization contained in the statute.[7]

---

[4]   <http://www.mongabay.com/reference/country_studies/poland/SOCIETY.html>.
[5]   Art. 87 § 1 Constitution.
[6]   An English version of the Polish Constitution is available at the website of the Sejm (lower house of Polish parliament): <http://www.sejm.gov.pl/prawo/konst/angielski/kon1.htm>.
[7]   See Rakowski & Rybicki. The competent organs to issue regulations are the President of the Republic of Poland, the Council of Ministers, the National Broadcasting Council, the Chairman of the Committee who is a member of the Council of Ministers, and the minister who manages the relevant area of public administration.

1.2.3. Court system

There are three types of courts in Poland: general, administrative and military courts.[8] General courts operate at three levels: the District Court (*Sąd Rejonowy*), the Provincial Court (*Sąd Okręgowy*) and the Court of Appeal (*Sąd Apelacyjny*). The common courts are competent to hear criminal and civil law cases, cases concerning family and custody law, as well as labour law and social insurance cases. The Supreme Court (*Sąd Najwyższy*) is the highest central judicial organ and is located in Warsaw.[9]

The Constitutional Court has exclusive power to express opinions on the Constitution. Legal acts that are not in conformity with the Constitution may be annulled by this Court. Citizens have the possibility to file a complaint with the Court that relates to the Constitution. It is also possible for common courts to ask the Constitutional Court to answer a legal question on the conformity of a legal act with the Constitution.[10]

1.2.4. Role of European Convention on Human Rights

According to the Constitution of 1997, ratified international agreements possess the force of law.[11] Once an agreement has been published, it becomes part of the domestic legal system and may be applied directly.

The ECHR, which entered into force in Poland in 1993, has had a considerable influence on post-communist legal reform. Several changes in criminal (procedure) law have been inspired by article 5, 6 and 8 of the ECHR, as well as by the case law of the European Court of Human Rights.[12]

From the very beginning, Poles have been very active in filing complaints to the Strasbourg institutions. Poland has often been in the top three countries in terms of the number of complaints. The Code of Criminal Procedure provides for the possibility to re-open criminal proceedings, following a judgement of the European Court of Human Rights.[13]

---

[8]   Art. 175 Constitution.
[9]   Information in English on the Polish Supreme Court is available at its official website: <http://www.sn.pl/english/index.html>.
[10] See art. 188-197 of the Constitution. A translation into English of the Act on the Constitutional Tribunal is available at the website of the Polish Constitutional Tribunal: <http://www.trybunal.gov.pl/eng/index.htm>.
[11] Art. 91 Constitution.
[12] An important example concerns the power to decide on the application of pre-trial detention. During communism this power was vested in the prosecutor, but – since he cannot be considered to be a 'judicial officer' within the meaning of art. 5 § 3 of the Convention – this decision is now to be made by the court. See, for example, ECtHR 4 July 2000, *Niedbała* v. *Poland*, No. 27915/95. It should be stressed that, by the time of the judgement in the Niedbała case, Polish criminal procedure law had already been changed accordingly.
[13] Art. 540 § 3 CCP 1997 states: 'The proceedings shall be re-opened for the benefit of the defendant, when such a need results from a decision of an international authority acting under the provisions of an international agreement which has been ratified by the Republic of Poland.'

The provisions of the ECHR are directly applicable before national courts. In practice, provisions of the ECHR are most often applied by the higher courts (Supreme Court and Constitutional Court). In particular, the Constitutional Court plays an important role in implementing Strasbourg principles into Polish law. For lower courts, it is far less common that provisions of the ECHR are directly applied.

1.3. Outline of the criminal justice system

1.3.1. General information

The most important acts are the Criminal Code of 1997 and the Code of Criminal Procedure of 1997 (CC and CCP respectively), which replaced the socialist criminal codes of 1969. The main objectives of the post-communist reform of criminal procedure were to:

-    enlarge judicial control over the pre-trial investigation and to reach a better balance between the pre-trial stage and judicial proceedings;
-    strengthen the adversarial character of the judicial proceedings;
-    improve the position of the suspect/defendant and the victim in criminal proceedings.

Immediately after they entered into force, the new criminal codes came under strong criticism both from the media and from some politicians. The codes were criticised for being too liberal and lenient at a time of rising crime.[14] The new CCP has been amended numerous times since it entered into force on 1 September 1998, with the most important amendments being implemented in January 2003 (entering into force on 1 July 2003), which affected nearly one-third of the Code.

A criminal offence (*przestępstwo*) can take the form of a *zbrodnia* or a *występek*.[15] The first category is more severe and concerns criminal acts that are punishable by at least three years deprivation of liberty. The latter category concerns offences that are punishable by a fine of a certain amount or a penalty of limitation or deprivation of liberty of at least one month.[16] These categories of criminal offences (*zbrodnia* and *występek*) should be distinguished from *wykroczenia*, which are petty or administrative offences regulated by a separate substantive and procedural code. *Wykroczenia* are not considered to be criminal offences.

Criminal cases are initially heard by a district court (*Sąd Rejonowy*) or, in more serious cases, a provincial court (*Sąd Okręgowy*). Within the district courts, there are also so-called 'branch courts' (*Sąd Grodzki*), which are competent to hear cases of petty/administrative offences and some other minor cases. A decision of the district

---

[14]   Krajewski 2004, p. 401-402. See also Zielinski 2003, p. 118: '(...) there is a view that the tendency to establish extended systems of procedural safeguards for the accused has violated the principle of equality before the law so that the law protects those who are in conflict with the law instead of protecting the victims of unlawful acts'.

[15]   Art. 7 CC 1997.

[16]   Also, a *zbrodnia* can only be committed intentionally while – in cases described by law – a *występek* can also be committed without intent. See arts. 7, 8 and 9 CC 1997.

court may be appealed to the provincial court. Decisions delivered in first instance by the provincial court can be reviewed by one of the appellate courts. Cassation is reviewed only by the Supreme Court.[17] The execution of sentences is regulated by a separate Code on the Execution of Sentences, which also dates from 1997.

1.3.2. Phases of criminal proceedings

Criminal proceedings consist of three phases: pre-trial proceedings, the judicial phase (proceedings at the trial court) and proceedings after the final judgement has become valid (execution phase). Polish criminal procedure may be considered as a mixed system, in the sense that pre-trial proceedings are mainly inquisitorial, whereas the trial phase is characterised by more adversarial elements.

Pre-trial proceedings are instituted when there are reasonable grounds to believe that a crime has been committed. They are conducted by the police or the prosecutor, but always under the supervision of the latter. Pre-trial proceedings may take the form of an inquiry (*dochodzenie*), or an investigation (*śledztwo*).[18] Although the differences between these have gradually diminished over the last few years, traditionally the former is carried out by the police in less complicated cases and the latter is reserved for more complex cases requiring greater involvement by the prosecutor.

When concluding the investigation, the prosecutor decides whether or not to bring the case to court. If he decides to do so, an indictment should be filed with the court within fourteen days after the close of the investigation.[19]

In the preparatory phase before the actual trial, two kinds of actions (may) take place: first, the preliminary examination of the indictment and, secondly, the preparation of the trial. Particularly in the first phase, important decisions affecting the position of the defence can be taken: for example, when the prosecutor has asked the court to sentence the suspects without conducting a trial,[20] the president of the court will organize a court session to consider this request.[21] It should be noted that, nowadays, there are more possibilities for the defence to participate in hearings during the preparatory proceedings than under the former CCP of 1969.

Court hearings are conducted orally and are generally open to the public.[22] As a rule, the defendant has to be present at the first instance court hearing. However,

---

[17] Murzynowski 2005, p. 386.

[18] Murzynowski 2005, p. 395.

[19] In case of an inquiry (*dochodzenie*) the indictment is prepared by the police and subsequently approved by the prosecutor: art. 331 § 1 CCP 1997. If the suspect is in pre-trial detention the indictment should be filed within 7 days: art. 331 § 3 CCP 1997.

[20] This possibility is set out in art. 335 CCP and will be discussed later.

[21] Art. 339 CCP §1 under 3.

[22] In exceptional circumstances, the court may decide to exclude the public from the trial. This is possible when, for example, at least one of the defendants is a minor, or when the public nature of the trial could lead to a disturbance of public order, offend decency, or disclose circumstances that, due to significant State interests, should remain secret. See arts. 359 and 360 CCP 1997.

there are several exceptions to this rule that allow the court to (continue to) proceed the trial in the absence of the defendant.[23]

A leading principle of Polish criminal procedure is that the court should rely on evidence obtained at the trial hearing (principle of immediacy). There are, however, important exceptions to this rule that make it possible for the court to use records of statements made during pre-trial investigation as evidence. For example, the record of a witness testimony may be used when the witness refuses to make a statement at the court hearing, or when the witness states that he can no longer remember the facts. Generally, evidence obtained at the investigative stage has full evidentiary value in the court proceedings and may constitute the basis of the verdict, provided it is disclosed (read out aloud) at the trial.[24]

1.3.3. Participants in the proceedings

The most important participants in the criminal proceedings are: the prosecutor (and other investigating authorities such as the police), the suspect/defendant, the defence lawyer and the judge. There is no investigating judge in the Polish criminal justice system. This position was abolished shortly after World War II and has never been reintroduced. Judicial control over pre-trial proceedings is carried out by common courts.[25]

The State Public Prosecution (*Prokuratura Krajowa*) forms part of the Ministry of Justice. The Minister of Justice (taking the position of general prosecutor) heads the prosecution service. After the breakdown of communism, it was felt that appointing the Minister of Justice as the prosecutor with the highest rank would safeguard against any abuses and mistakes that could occur during the transition towards democracy. However, the plurality of functions of the Minister poses several problems, such as the risk of political pressure on the public prosecution when exercising his/her criminal competency. This issue was the subject of criticism by the European Union during Poland's accession process and is also criticised within Poland.[26] Several attempts to improve the situation have been undertaken, but these were not successful thus far.[27]

Trying criminal cases is not reserved to professional judges: in several instances, the judicial panel is composed of both professional and lay judges. However, since 2007, the participation of lay judges in Polish criminal procedure has been considerably restricted.[28]

---

[23] On the right of the defendant to be tried in his presence, see § 2.3.2.
[24] Kruszyński 2007, p. 198.
[25] For example, common courts have the power to hear certain witnesses during pre-trial proceedings. Certain investigating methods – such as the control and transcription of telephone calls – require judicial authorisation.
[26] The debate on this issue was started by Waltoś, a leading scholar in Polish criminal law: Waltoś 2002a.
[27] Marguery 2008, p. 185-189.
[28] Since an amendment of the CCP in July 2007, cases dealt with in first instance by a district court or a provincial court are, as a rule, heard by one professional judge. Before this amendment, the general rule was that criminal cases at first instance were generally heard by →

Another way in which citizens can take part in criminal proceedings is through a private indictment to the court (private prosecution). This is only allowed with respect to a few offences defined in the criminal code (such as insult and other offences against dignity). Subsidiary prosecution – which should be distinguished from private prosecution – means that, in all cases investigated *ex officio*, a victim may support the accusation brought by the prosecutor. A victim may also act as a subsidiary prosecutor instead of the public prosecutor, but only when the latter refuses to prosecute the case.

1.3.4. Consensual and special proceedings

Polish criminal procedure provides for several alternative settlement mechanisms resembling guilty plea proceedings. In short, there are three categories: issuing a judgement without trial on request of the prosecutor (art. 335 CCP), issuing a conviction without evidentiary proceedings (art. 387 CCP) and taking evidence only in part with the consent of the parties (art. 388 CCP). These three proceedings are only conducted with the consent of the suspect. In case of conviction without evidentiary proceedings, the initiative to embark on such proceedings must be taken by the suspect.[29]

In Polish literature, it is argued that defence rights might be breached in the proceedings of article 387 CCP in circumstances were the defendant confesses to a crime in the expectation of an alternative settlement, but the prosecutor subsequently withdraws his consent to the article 387 CCP procedure. If the case is then dealt with in an ordinary procedure, the prosecutor may use the confession of the defendant. The fact that there are no guarantees for the defendant that the prosecutor will not withdraw his consent at a certain stage of the procedure is a serious point of concern from the perspective of the rights of the defendant.[30]

The three settlement procedures mentioned above are used quite often in practice. For example, in 2008, more than 9% of convictions were issued without evidentiary proceedings (art. 387 CCP), and over 34% of cases that resulted in a conviction constituted a judgement without trial at the request of the prosecutor (art. 335 CCP).[31]

Generally, the proceedings under article 335 CCP will lead to a lower sentence than in case of a 'full trial'. The request of the prosecutor is dealt with by the court in the preparatory stage of the trial proceedings. The defendant and his defence lawyer have the right to be present at this hearing.

---

a panel of one professional and two lay judges. Now, such a panel of three judges is reserved for cases dealing with more severe offences *(zbrodnia)*.

[29] Such a request can only be granted when the prosecutor – and, if relevant, the victim – agree to it.

[30] A similar risk seems to exist in the art. 335 procedure. See on this matter: Kulesza 2007, p. 32.

[31] Proceedings under art. 335 CCP have, in particular, gained considerable importance over the last few years. In 2004, this kind of settlement was used in only 9% of all convictions. See data retrieved from statistical information on the functioning of the criminal justice system available at the website of the Ministry of Justice: <http://www.ms.gov.pl/statystyki/prokur_dzial_1_pol_2008.pdf>.

Legal assistance is of major importance in consensual proceedings: the lawyer is able to inform the defendant of the consequences of the alternative proceedings and to make an estimation as to whether it is better than having a 'full trial'. Nevertheless, according to Polish criminal procedure, participation of a defence lawyer in these proceedings is not obligatory: only when the suspect requests the issuing of a judgement without evidentiary proceedings the court *may* appoint a defence lawyer at the request of the defendant.[32] Since consensual proceedings could still lead to considerable sanctions (for example proceedings under art. 335 CCP can be undertaken in the case of criminal acts punishable by a maximum of ten years imprisonment), it would be better if (free) legal assistance would be guaranteed on a larger scale.

There are also three types of special proceedings – summary proceedings (*postępowanie uproszczone*), penal order proceedings (*postępowanie nakazowe*) and 'speedy' proceedings (*postępowanie przyspieszone*) – which play an important role in the Polish criminal law system. A substantial part of all criminal proceedings is dealt with through one of these special judicial proceedings. For example, in 2008, penal order proceedings were used in 8% of all convictions.[33] Since this report focuses on defence rights in ordinary criminal procedure, these special types of proceedings will not be dealt with *in extenso*. However, within the context of defence rights, special reference should be made to the 'speedy' proceedings, which were introduced in 2007. In this kind of proceedings, defendants can be brought to trial immediately and must always be represented by a defence lawyer. Nevertheless, the defence lawyer often has very limited time to prepare the defence. This is one of the reasons why such proceedings are widely criticized for their adverse effects on the rights of the defence and for being ineffective. Currently, a draft law introducing considerable changes to the 'speedy' proceedings is being prepared by Polish parliament.[34]

1.3.5. Legal aid system

There is no unified system of legal aid applying to the different legal fields. In criminal cases, the decision to grant legal aid is always taken by a judge. There is no separate group of lawyers acting in legal aid cases: the judge appoints a lawyer from a list provided by the local bar associations. As a rule, all lawyers are obliged

---

[32] Art. 387 § 1 CCP. In all other situations, the defendant may ask for the appointment of a defence lawyer free of charge under the regular scheme of art. 78 CCP. On the provision of legal aid, see § 2.2.2.

[33] There has been, however, a decrease in the use of this kind of proceedings: in 2004 it was still 19%. See <http://www.ms.gov.pl/statystyki/prokur_dzial_1_pol_2008.pdf>.

[34] Information provided by M. Wąsek-Wiaderek (country reviewer Poland), August 2009.

to provide legal assistance free of charge for the defendant.[35] Remuneration – which is covered by the State – is regulated by Ministerial decree.[36]

Legal assistance free of charge in criminal cases is one of the aspects of the Polish criminal justice system that needs immediate improvement. During the last few years, there have been several attempts – for example, by the Polish Helsinki Foundation for Human Rights (HFHR) – to raise political awareness of the problems that exist in this respect.[37] A coalition of NGO's, supported by the National Ombudsman, has been urging the Ministry of Justice to realise the need for reform of the legal aid system. Draft legislation has been prepared but, until now, these efforts have not resulted in actual (legal) reform of the organisation of free legal assistance in criminal cases.

As mentioned by Bojarski in the Monitoring Report on Access to Legal Aid in Poland, there is no separate budget for legal aid in Poland. Costs of legal aid are covered by the state, through the budgets of particular courts, within a general paragraph headed 'costs of proceedings before courts and public prosecutor's'.[38] This means that the decision of a judge whether or not to award legal aid could be influenced by the financial limitations of the court budget.[39]

Lack of reliable statistical information in this respect makes it difficult to estimate and evaluate the functioning of the legal aid system. For the purposes of this report, the Ministry of Justice was asked about the annual amount spent on legal aid in criminal cases: the answer was that this kind of information is not available. There exists some data on state expenditure for free legal aid (in general), but statistical data on, for example, issues such as which part of the funds relates to legal aid in criminal cases as opposed to civil and other cases; the number of cases in which parties were granted legal aid; in which cases legal aid was granted and for which reasons; is not systematically collected by the courts, nor by the Ministry of Justice.[40]

---

[35] However, lawyers fulfilling a function within one of the organs of the bar may be released from this obligation. For more information on the appointment of legal assistance free of charge in cases of obligatory defence, and at the request of the suspect; see § 2.2.2.

[36] Decree by the Minister of Justice of 28 September 2002 on costs of free legal assistance paid by the state (*Rozporządzenie Ministra Sprawiedliwości w sprawie opłat za czynności adwokackie oraz ponoszenia przez Skarb Państwa kosztów nieopłaconej prawnej udzielonej z urzędu*).

[37] The Polish Helsinki Foundation has been cooperating with the Public Interest Law Initiative and several other non-governmental organizations in a project called *Promoting Access to Justice in Central and Eastern Europe* focusing on the need for reform of legal aid systems in Central and Eastern European countries. Within this project a country report on the provision and availability of free legal assistance in Poland was written. The Polish country report which was published in 2002 is available at: <www.pili.org/>. In 2003 the country report was republished in a more extensive form by the Polish Helsinki Foundation: Bojarski 2003a.

[38] Bojarski 2003a, p. 38 and 45.

[39] See hereafter § 2.2.2.

[40] Bojarski 2003a, p. 46.

1.3.6. Political and public perceptions of crime

In general, it is believed that Polish citizens tend to be rather punitive in their outlook. The post-communist period has been characterized by profound changes in crime patterns in both quantitive and in qualitive terms. As a result, more liberal penal law reforms were confronted with a growing fear of crime and new populist politics of law and order. In short, over the last few years, two contradictory tendencies can be detected: on the one hand a trend towards liberal criminal law reform, and on the other a tendency for recourse to punitive crime control policies. Initially, criminal justice policy and (the predominantly liberal) criminal law reform were mainly dominated by experts. However, after 1998, it has been increasingly dominated by politicians from conservative parties such as the Law and Justice party (*Prawo i Sprawiedlowość*).[41]

1.4. Statistics on the criminal justice system

Quite detailed data is published by the Ministry of Justice.[42] These concern *inter alia* the number of criminal cases dealt with per year, the number of pre-trial investigations, the application of pre-trial detention and the number of acquittals and convictions. However, these statistics do not cover any defence-related subjects (such as the number of criminal cases in which the suspect/defendant is assisted by a defence lawyer), nor legal aid matters (such as the number of cases in which legal assistance free of charge is awarded).

Prison overcrowding was one of the main problems of the Polish criminal justice system during communism and to a certain extent it still is. The Government has made the reduction of the prison population a priority, but it is a complex problem. There is a growing number of cases before the national courts, as well as before the ECtHR, where applicants allege inhuman or degrading conditions of detention (art. 3 ECHR) in Polish prisons, in particular because of the excessive crowding of prison cells.[43] Currently, over 85,000 people are incarcerated, including almost 10,000 detainees in pre-trial detention.[44]

---

[41] Krajewski 2004, p. 377-407.
[42] <http://www.ms.gov.pl/statystyki/statystyki.php>.
[43] Memorandum to the Polish Government, Assessment of the progress made in implementing the 2002 recommendations of the Council of Europe Commissioner for Human Rights, Strasbourg, June 20th 2007, CommDH(2007)13, available at: <https://wcd.coe.int/ViewDoc.jsp?id=1155005&Site=COE#P195_19268>. It should be noted that art. 248 of the Code of Execution of Sentences *(Kodeks Karny Wykonawczy)* allows prison governors 'in particularly justified cases' to place detainees in cells below the statutory size (3 square metres) for an indefinite period. However, this provision was declared unconstitutional by the Constitutional Court in its landmark decision of 26 May 2008 (SK 25/07) and it will therefore lose force as from 6 December 2009.
[44] Official statistical data from 31 August 2009, available on the website of the General Administration of Penitentiary Services: <http://www.sw.gov.pl/images/1242925436.pdf> and <http://www.sw.gov.pl/images/1253000444.pdf>.

Poland has one of the highest prison population rates of the countries of Central and Eastern Europe.[45]

The Polish prison population rate per 100,000 of the national population is 221. Despite the fact that the prison population rate is still high, statistics show a decrease in the prison population over the last few years, as well as a decrease in pre-trial detention. Since 2003, the absolute numbers of pre-trial detainees are as follows: 2003: 37,207, 2004: 34,475, 2005: 35,142, 2006: 34,291, 2007: 31,722 and 2008: 24,848.[46] The statistics also reveal a growth in the use of alternative measures (particularly bail).

Finally, it should be noted that, according to the statistical information provided by the Ministry of Justice, the overall conviction rate in Polish criminal procedure is very high. The percentage of acquittals fluctuates between 2 and 3%.

2.   Legal rights and their implementation

2.1.   The right to information

2.1.1. Information on the nature and cause of the accusation

With respect to the right of suspects to information, it is important to note that, in Polish criminal procedure, a distinction is made between the 'suspected person' (*osoba poderjzana*) and the 'suspect' (*podejrzany*).

A suspected person may be arrested and detained by the police for a maximum of 48 hours and certain secret methods of investigation may be used against him.[47] When a request for pre-trial detention is filed with the court within the first 48 hours, the detention may be prolonged for another 24 hours, which means that the deprivation of liberty before pre-trial detention may be up to a maximum of 72 hours.[48] Arresting a suspected person is possible when there is good reason to believe that he has committed an offence, and it is feared that such a person may go into hiding, destroy the evidence of his offence, or if his identity cannot be established.[49]

A person is considered a suspect (*podejrzany*) if a written order about presenting the charges to him (*postanowienie o przedstawieniu zarzutów*) has been drawn up, or if the charges have been presented to the person directly (without the order) in relation to interrogating him as a suspect.[50]

---

[45]   Belarus (468), Ukraine (323) and Moldova (227): Walmsley 2009.
[46]   <http://www.ms.gov.pl/statystyki/prokur_dzial_2008.pdf>.
[47]   Such as observation, or interception of communication.
[48]   Kruszyński 2007, p. 184.
[49]   Art. 244 § 1 CCP.
[50]   Art. 71 § 1 CCP. The difference between these two ways of formally 'charging' the suspect will be discussed later.

Information provided to the suspected person and the suspect

The arrested person should immediately be informed both of the reasons for his arrest and his rights.[51] This information is provided *both orally and in writing*. Pursuant to article 244 § 3 CCP, the cause of arrest should be indicated in the record of arrest. A copy of this record must be given to the arrested person. The CCP does not stipulate the specific rights of which the suspected person should be informed. However, since an amendment to the CCP in January 2009, it is expressly specified in article 244 § 2 that the arrested person should be informed of his right to be assisted by a lawyer.

Generally, it is agreed that the suspected person should also be informed of the right to contact a lawyer, to have the lawfulness of his detention examined by a judicial authority, to inform a next of kin of his arrest and to contact a consulate (where applicable). It is important to stress that there is *no* legal obligation to inform the suspected person of his right to silence. This obligation only applies to the suspect.[52]

Until he is formally charged, the suspected person may not be interrogated.[53] Nevertheless, immediately after his arrest, the police should inform the suspected person that he has the right to make a statement (explanation).[54] Such statements – which are taken down in the record of the arrest – may not be used as evidence in court.[55] However, the record of the arrest is an official document and some Polish authors are of the opinion that it may be read out at the trial,[56] a view disputed by other authors.[57] Either way, it should be stressed that the record of the arrest can never be read out in order to compare what the suspect is saying at the trial with what he said during his arrest. However, it might be of certain value in assessing the credibility of explanations given by the defendant during trial.

The fact that there is no legal obligation to inform the suspected person of the right to silence can be criticised for several reasons. First of all, it is clear that an arrested person who provides 'an explanation' in which a confession is made, might feel compelled to repeat this statement at the first formal interrogation. Thus, even though the first informal confession may not be used as evidence in court, it can affect the position of the arrested person and limit his possibilities to embark upon a

[51]   Art. 244 § 2 CCP. The lack of information about the reasons for the arrest may be invoked as a ground for appeal *(zażalenie)* against an arrest. Pursuant to art. 246 CCP, in such an appeal, a suspected person may file a complaint with the court about the legality, reasonableness or lack of appropriateness of the arrest. Undoubtedly, these grounds also cover the lack of adequate information about the reasons for the arrest. There is also another possibility: an arrested person may bring an appeal against the manner of execution of arrest by the police to the public prosecutor under art. 15 § 7 of the Act on the Police *(Ustawa o Policji)*.

[52]   Art. 300 in conjunction with art. 175 CCP.

[53]   Pursuant to art. 389 § 1 CCP *(argumentum a contrario)*, the witness testimony of a person subsequently charged with a criminal offence cannot be read out at the trial and cannot be used as evidence.

[54]   Art. 244 § 2 CCP.

[55]   The statement is neither a witness testimony, nor is it taken in the form of an interrogation. See art. 389 CCP.

[56]   See, for example; Klejnowska 2004, p. 227-228.

[57]   See, for example; Kmiecik 2000, p. 21.

specific defence strategy later on in the proceedings. Furthermore, according to a recent report drawn up by representatives of the bar, the judiciary and the prosecution services, in practice police officers are heard as witnesses in court in relation to statements made by a suspected person upon his arrest.[58]

As noted above, the formal charge 'transforming' the suspected person into a suspect can take two forms: the suspected person can be subject to a written charge, which is to be served on the suspect (*postanowienie o przedstawieniu zarzutów*), or the charges can be presented to him orally as a way of subsequently interrogating him as a suspect. In short, filing a written charge is a more formal way of charging the suspect. There are, however, several situations in which the authorities may orally present the suspect with the charges at the beginning of his initial interrogation, without first handing over a written order: for example when, an inquiry (*dochodzenie*) is carried out, or when the case is dealt with in 'speedy' proceedings (*postępowanie przyspieszone*).[59] Filing a written order on presenting the charges is always obligatory when pre-trial detention is applied.[60]

Furthermore, when the suspect is formally charged, he (or his defence lawyer) may request verbal information on the basis of the charge and request that a justification (statement of reasons) for the charge is provided in writing. The suspect should be instructed of his right to make such a request.[61] Although it is difficult to assess how often suspects ask for such a written statement of reasons, there is some criticism in Polish literature on the actual value of the justification.[62]

Information provided to the defendant

Any person against whom an indictment has been filed, as well as any person in relation to whom the state prosecutor has filed a request to the court for conditional discontinuance of the proceedings, shall be considered a defendant.[63] The defendant is informed of the nature and cause of the accusation against him through the

---

[58]   Daniuk et al. 2006, p. 30-31.

[59]   Art. 517b § 3 and 325g § 1 CCP. Also, in cases not amenable to delay during an investigation (*śledztwo*), a person suspected of committing an offence may be examined as a suspect prior to the issuance of an order on the presentation of charges, if there are grounds for the issuance of such an order (for example, when delay of the interrogation might result in the loss or distortion of evidence): art. 308 § 2 CCP.

[60]   During an investigation (*śledztwo*), the written charge may be drawn exclusively by the prosecutor. As noted above, during an inquiry (*dochodzenie*), filing a written charge is not required: it may be issued by the police, but, in practice, they will choose to orally present the charges to the suspect at the beginning of his first interrogation.

[61]   The written justification should, in particular, indicate which facts and evidence were accepted as the basis of the charge and should be served on the suspect and his lawyer within 14 days: art. 313 § 3 and 4 CCP. See Kruszyński 2007, p. 195-196.

[62]   According to Kulesza (a leading scholar on Polish criminal law and a practicing defence lawyer), 'as a rule written reasons for the charge are laconic, general and even misleading as to their evidentiary basis', Kulesza 2007, p. 15. See also: Kulesza 2005, p. 420-421. Also, according to a practising defence lawyer in Poznań, the justification usually contains only a few sentences, and often many weeks transpire before the defence receives it. Information provided by practising defence lawyer from Poznań, August 2009.

[63]   Art. 71 § 2 CCP.

indictment (act of accusation; *akt oskarżenia*), which is filed by the prosecutor to the court at the end of the investigative stage.[64] The indictment should contain at least a detailed description of the act imputed to the defendant, whether the defendant is considered to be a repeat offender, an indication of the criminal statute under which the imputed acts are classifiable and a statement of reasons. The statement of reasons should include all the facts and evidence upon which the accusation is founded and, if necessary, should indicate the legal grounds for the charge and the circumstances relied on by the defendant in his defence.[65]

2.1.2. Information concerning the relevant evidence/material available to the authorities

Access to relevant evidence/material: before closing of the investigation

Inspection of the case file (as well as making copies and the issuance of certified copies for a fee) during the investigation by the suspect and/or his defence lawyer requires the permission of the person conducting the preparatory proceedings (police or prosecutor). Until recently, this was specified in article 156 § 5 CCP.[66] The suspected person (*osoba poderjzana*) is not considered to be a party to the pre-trial proceedings. However, he may ask the prosecutor or the court to have access to the case file.

In practice, the defence is often denied access to the case file during the investigation. In more complex cases in particular, denying access until the end of the investigation seems to be the rule instead of the exception. For that reason, the article 156 § 5 CCP, as well as the practice based on it, have been widely criticized in Polish legal literature. The main points of criticism concerned the fact that: the legal provisions did not stipulate that denying access should be the exception; the legal provisions did not formulate any (specific) grounds on which the decision to deny access should be based; there was no judicial control or effective remedy open to the defence when access to the case file was denied; and there were no special arrangements for suspects held in pre-trial detention.[67]

With respect to the last point of criticism, it is important to note that, in 2008, article 156 § 5 was declared unconstitutional by the Constitutional Court, with particular reference to suspects held in detention and their right – as guaranteed by article 5 and 6 of the ECHR – to effectively challenge their detention.[68] According to the Constitutional Court, the challenged provision disregards the principle of

---

64   Art. 331 § 1 CCP.
65   Art. 332 CCP.
66   Art. 156 § 5 CCP: 'Unless provided otherwise by law, the inspection of files of the preparatory proceedings in progress, the making of copies and photocopies of the same by parties, defence counsels, legal representatives and statutory agents, and the issuance of certified copies or photocopies, for a fee, shall require permission by the person conducting the preparatory proceedings (…)'.
67   See *inter alia* Kruszyński 1998, p. 148, Wąsek-Wiaderek 2003a, p. 65 and Wąsek-Wiaderek 2003b, p. 260.
68   Decision of 3 June 2008, K 42/07, summary in English available at: <www.trybunal.gov.pl/eng/>.

proportionality, since it allows for an excessive limitation of the rights of the individual, including the right to a defence. In addition, according to the Court, the provision does not fulfil the principle of subsidiarity, since the effectiveness of preliminary proceedings could be ensured using other methods that would be less burdensome for the citizen.

That article 156 § 5 CCP, and its application in practice, could raise problems with respect to the guarantees specified in article 5 § 4 of the ECHR had already been stressed by the ECtHR prior to the judgement of the Constitutional Court.[69] Referring to the Strasbourg case law, the Constitutional Court decided that the right to a defence should be the decisive factor in deciding which parts of the case records should be made accessible to the detainee and his defence lawyer, and that materials from the pre-trial investigation justifying the motion of a public prosecutor should be freely accessible.

As a result, since the publication of this judgement in the Journal of Laws (*Dziennik Ustaw*) public prosecutors have been obliged to apply article 156 § 5 in accordance with the ruling of the Constitutional Court. In the meantime, this part of the provision has been changed. On 28 August 2009, a new § 5a was added to article 156 CCP, stating that, at the pre-trial stage of the proceedings, a suspect and his defence lawyer must be granted access to the evidence indicated in the motion for (prolongation of) detention.

However, the public prosecutor still has the right to refuse access to certain evidence, if there are justified grounds to believe that access to the case file 1) would endanger the life and health of a victim or another participant to the proceedings; 2) could cause the destruction or falsification of evidence; 3) could prevent the arrest of co-suspects, or other persons suspected of having committed other offences discovered during the proceedings; 4) would reveal conducted police operations or; 5) could jeopardize the due course of the pre-trial proceedings in another illegal manner.

The refusal to provide access to the case file in pre-trial proceedings is subject to interlocutory appeal, which is dealt with by the prosecutor. Access to several categories of documents cannot be denied.[70] If a detained suspect is allowed to consult the case file the document will be send to the detention centre. There the suspect may make written notes from the case file. The same applies to suspects remaining at liberty; they may consult the case file with the consent of the prosecutor and make notes in writing at the prosecutor's office.

---

[69] See, for example, ECtHR 6 November 2007, *Chruśhiński* v. *Poland*, No. 22755-04 and ECtHR 15 January, *Łaszkiewicz* v. *Poland*, No. 28481-03. It is well established in the case law of the European Court on Human Rights that a suspect held in pre-trial detention should, as a rule, at least have access to those documents necessary to challenge the legitimacy and lawfulness of the detention.

[70] The defence may not be refused permission to copy a record of a procedural action in which it participated or had the right to participate, as well as a document obtained from such a party or prepared with the participation of the same: art. 157 § 3 CCP.

Access to relevant evidence/material: final stage of the pre-trial investigation

At the end of the investigation, the defence has two more possibilities to inspect the case file:

- to be presented with the contents of the case file by the investigative authority; and
- to examine the files (by themselves) before the presentation mentioned under 1.[71]

The difference between 1 and 2 is that the first activity is carried out by the investigative authorities (the suspect and his defence lawyer are presented with the material by the authorities), while the second activity concerns the right of the defence to personally examine the material before the presentation by the authorities.

In practice, when presenting the defence with the contents of the case file, the authorities verbally inform the suspect and his defence lawyer about the most important parts of the file. This may involve reading out particular items of evidence, or providing a summary of them.

During the presentation, the suspect and his defence lawyer may comment on the material presented and submit statements or explanations. In practice, this activity can take up to a few hours, but no longer than a day. Often, the defence lawyer will read the files earlier and use the time set for final examination to familiarise his client with the most important materials. The examination takes place in the office of the police or prosecutor or, when the suspect is detained, at the place of detention.[72]

The defence should file an express request for a final examination of the case file.[73] The suspect is informed of his right to file the request at the beginning of the first interrogation.[74] The authorities should set an 'appropriate time' for the defence to inspect the material.[75] This has been required since 2003, when the provision was amended; before then, the authorities were obliged to invite the defence *ex officio* to make use of its right to examine the case file, before closing the investigation. If the request is not filed, the investigation is closed without a final examination. In practice, defence lawyers use the possibility to inspect the case file at this stage of the proceedings only in the most complex cases.[76]

---

[71] Both possibilities are regulated by art. 321 CCP.
[72] Daniuk et al. 2006, p. 45-51.
[73] Art. 321 § 1 CCP.
[74] This is specified in the written information provided to the suspect before commencement of the first interrogation: art. 300 CCP.
[75] Art. 321 § 1 and 2 CCP. See § 2.4.2 below.
[76] Information provided by a practising defence lawyer from Poznań, August 2009.

Access to relevant evidence/material: after closing the investigation

After the investigation is closed, the rights of the defence to have access to the case file can no longer be restricted. The suspect and his defence lawyer have the right to examine and copy the files pertaining to the case. Upon a motion from the defendant or his lawyer, photocopies of the documents of the case shall be provided, but at their expense. The president of the court may, on justifiable grounds, order certified copies made from the files of the case to be provided at a cost. If there is a danger of revealing a state secret, inspection of files, or making certified copies and photocopies shall be undertaken, under conditions imposed by the (president of the) court. Certified copies shall not be released unless provided otherwise by law.[77] Furthermore, according to article 157 § 1 CCP, a defendant may obtain a certified copy of every decision issued in his case, free of any costs.

The state prosecutor may inspect the files of the case at every stage of the proceedings and require them to be sent to him for that purpose. Nevertheless, this is not allowed where it would limit access to the files by other participants in the proceedings, particularly the defendant and his lawyer. When files are sent to the state prosecutor, he is under the obligation to provide access thereto for the defendant and his lawyer.[78]

Although the defence has an unrestricted right of access to the case file after the investigation is closed, some lawyers are of the opinion that it is much easier for the prosecution to have access to the file during the trial than for the defence.[79] The scope of this problem, however, is not clear.

2.1.3. Information on rights (letter of rights)

According to the CCP, a suspect should be advised of certain rights and obligations prior to the first examination.[80] The information is handed over to the suspect by the person conducting the interrogation (a member of the police or prosecution) in a written, standardized form. Although the CCP does not use the term 'letter of rights', this written information might be considered as such. The rights contained in this document are *inter alia*: the right to silence, the right to submit motions for evidentiary actions, the right to have the assistance of a defence lawyer, the right to acquaint oneself with the materials of the proceedings and the right to have a defence lawyer present during questioning.[81]

The CCP prescribes that the suspect should sign the form, after reading it, as a confirmation of receipt. Although this is considered to be proof of the fact that the suspect was indeed informed of his rights, the signature is, of course, no guarantee that the suspect has understood the rights and obligations mentioned in the form.

---

[77] See art. 156 § 1, 2, 3 and 4 CCP.

[78] See art. 158 CCP. However, according to some lawyers; in practice it is difficult to have access to the case file when it is sent to the prosecutor's office: information provided by practising defence lawyer from Poznań, August 2009.

[79] Jurkiewicz 2001.

[80] Art. 300 CCP.

[81] See annex I for the contents of this document.

There is no express obligation for the interrogating official to verify whether the suspect has understood the meaning of the rights. In fact, there is no legal obligation to provide any oral explanation or clarification with respect to the information mentioned in the form.[82]

According to a report drawn up by the Polish Bar Association, the rules noted above are generally complied with in practice. The interrogator always asks the suspect if he has understood the wording of the information served on him. Furthermore, if doubts are raised, the interrogator will, according to the report, provide an additional, precise explanation concerning the suspect's rights.[83]

Nevertheless, it is noted (for example, by the HFHR) that the wording of the form is too difficult and formal and that explanation on how the rights mentioned in the form could be effectuated is lacking. For example, the form mentions the right to make use of the assistance of a defence lawyer, but there is no information on what the suspect could or should do to bring this right into effect. Accordingly, the actual effect of the written information will often depend on whether, and to what extent, additional information is provided by the interrogating authority. There is also some criticism in Polish literature (by practising defence lawyers) that, for example, states that there is a lack of adequate time to read the letter of rights before the first interrogation.[84]

There is no legal obligation to provide a suspect with a written translation of the information about his rights. However, since he will be provided with the presence of a translator during the first interrogation (see § 2.4.4 below), he should be able to obtain an oral translation of this document. Also, it should be noted that, according to the latest visit of the Committee for the Prevention of Torture (CPT), the delegation noted at most police and Border Guard establishments that were visited the presence of apprehension protocols (containing *inter alia* information on the detained person's rights to notify a third party of the fact of his detention, contact a lawyer and be examined by a doctor) in a range of foreign languages.

However, the 2006 Report of the CPT also notes that a small number of detained persons have alleged that they had not been informed of their rights and/or did not understand them. Admittedly, detainees were asked to sign the part concerning their rights in the apprehension protocol and received a copy of the protocol; however, the delegation gained the impression that this was done more as a bureaucratic procedure rather than as a way of ensuring that a detained person is in a position to understand his rights fully and therefore to exercise them effectively.[85]

---

[82]   In this respect, reference should be made to a recent judgement of the ECtHR involving Poland, in which the Court stressed that, in the circumstances of that case, the assertion in the letter of rights that the applicant had been reminded of her right to remain silent, or to be assisted by a lawyer, could not be considered reliable, in the sense that the signing of the form and the fact that the applicant had not requested a lawyer could not be considered as a clear and unequivocal waiver of the applicant's right to the guarantees of a fair trial: ECtHR 31 March 2009, *Płonka* v. *Poland*, No. 20310/02, § 37.

[83]   Daniuk et al. 2006, p. 20-22.

[84]   Lewandowski 2008, p. 61.

[85]   See Report to the Polish Government on the visit to Poland carried out by the European Committee for the Prevention of Torture and Inhuman or Degrading Treatment or

→

In addition to the information provided in the letter of rights, a suspect should be informed about his right to remain silent before every interrogation in the course of the investigation.[86]

2.2. The right to defend oneself

2.2.1. The right of a suspect/defendant to defend themselves

The suspect/defendant has the right to conduct his own defence.[87] There is no express legal obligation for the authorities to inform the suspect of this right, which covers both the investigative and the trial stages.[88]

The CCP also stipulates that the participation of a defence lawyer in the proceedings does not preclude the personal participation of the defendant. A suspect/defendant who is assisted by a mandatory defence lawyer (see § 2.2.2 under 'mandatory defence') has the right to defend himself.[89]

Although the right of the suspect to defend himself covers all phases of the criminal proceedings (including the appeal and cassation stages), it should be noted that the presence of the detained defendant at the appeal hearing is not guaranteed.[90] Accordingly, the right of the defendant to defend himself can be restricted at that stage.

Punishment (CPT) from 4 to 15 October 2004, available at: <www.cpt.coe.int/documents/pol/2006-11-inf-eng.pdf., p. 16-17>.

[86] Art. 175 § 1 CCP. There is an express provision regulating the obligation of the trial judge to inform the defendant of his right to silence: art. 386 § 2 CCP.

[87] Art. 6 CCP. See also art. 42 § 2 of the Polish Constitution: 'anyone against whom criminal proceedings have been brought shall have the right to defence *at all stages of such proceedings*. He may, in particular, choose counsel or avail himself – in accordance with principles specified by statute – of counsel appointed by the court' (emphasis added).

[88] Nevertheless, the 'letter of rights' handed to the suspect at the beginning of the first interrogation mentions the right of the suspect to refuse to give answers, or to provide explanations, as well as the right to submit motions for actions in inquiry or investigation.

[89] Art. 86 § 2 CCP.

[90] A defendant in detention may request to be brought to the appellate trial, but this request can be denied if the appellate court considers the presence of the defence lawyer sufficient. When the court decides not to bring the defendant to the trial and the defendant does not have a defence lawyer, one will be appointed by the court (art. 451 CCP). See on this matter: Wąsek-Wiaderek 2000. Recent Strasbourg case law shows that the provision currently laid down in art. 451 CCP can, despite previous changes after judgements by the ECtHR, in practice still lead to a breach of art. 6 § 1 ECHR. See ECtHR 9 June 2009, *Sobolewski* v. *Poland (no. 2)*, No. 19847/07 where the Court decided that '(...) where the scope of a particular appeal filed with such a court [the appeal court] is not confined to pure questions of law, Article 6 requires, in the absence of compelling reasons to the contrary, that the accused be allowed to be present at the hearing of his appeal and that he be notified in advance in clear terms of his right to do so' (§ 41). Although the case law of the Supreme Court concerning the interpretation of art. 451 CCP is completely consistent with the Strasbourg case law (in several judgements the Supreme Court has stressed that detained defendants should be brought to the appeal hearing if the appeal court is asked to decide on questions of evidence and the factual circumstances of the case), it still happens in practice that some appeal courts wrongly apply the provision and consider the presence of the defence lawyer sufficient. Usually, such incorrect application of art. 451 CCP will be successfully raised in the cassation appeal.

With respect to cassation proceedings, it is important to note that cassation can only be filed by a (defence) lawyer or a legal advisor.[91] The appointed attorney is not obliged to file cassation, but if he declines to do so, he must inform both the court and the client about this decision. According to the HFHR, appointed lawyers often refuse to file cassation, arguing that there are no grounds for it.[92]

In recent case law, the Supreme Court has stressed the importance of the right of the defendant to file cassation. In 2008, the Supreme Court ruled that the information provided by an appointed defence lawyer to the court stating that there are no grounds for filing cassation should take the form of a legal opinion rather than a one sentence statement.[93] In addition, according to the case law of the Supreme Court, the time limit of 30 days for submitting a cassation appeal starts on the day on which the defendant obtains information that an *ex officio* defence lawyer does not intend to submit cassation.[94] Moreover, there are some decisions confirming that the court should appoint a second defence lawyer if the first is not diligent in exercising his duties.[95]

Unfortunately, these rules as laid down in the case law of the Supreme Court are not always respected in practice. It still happens that defence lawyers refuse to bring a cassation appeal (which could be successful), depriving the defendant of his right to bring a case to the Supreme Court.[96] Recently, the ECtHR has found a violation in two cases where the national (appeal) courts failed to inform the defendant that he had a new time limit for lodging a cassation appeal after his legal aid lawyer had refused to assist him.[97]

As rightly pointed out by the two dissenting opinions attached to these judgements, it is a pity that the ECtHR based its finding of a violation only on the fact that the applicant was not informed of the new time limit. After all, the real problem for the indigent defendant is the fact that, according to Polish law, the

---

[91]   Art. 526 § 2 CCP.
[92]   Bojarski 2003a, p. 96.
[93]   Decision of 10 September 2008 (II KZ 43/08). This judgement of the Supreme Court has been criticised in Polish literature. One of the reasons for this is the fact that the express reasons why the defence lawyer does not see a justification for filing cassation is a matter between the defendant and his lawyer and that, therefore, the defence lawyer is only obliged to inform the court of the (mere) fact that he does not see grounds for cassation. See, for example; Bojańczyk 2009.
[94]   Decision of 6 May 2008 (II KZ 16/08).
[95]   See: decisions of 12 March 2008 (II KZ 1/08), 10 September 2008 (II KZ 43/08) and 21 October 2008 (IV KZ 68/08). Information provided by M. Wąsek-Wiaderek, February 2009.
[96]   See, for example, three cases of the ECtHR where the Court held that, due to the refusal of the legal aid lawyer to file cassation, the applicant could not be blamed for not exhausting domestic remedies: ECtHR 9 June 2009, *Sobolewski v. Poland (no. 2)*, No. 19847/07, ECtHR 9 June 2009, *Strzałkowski v. Poland*, No. 31509/02 and ECtHR 21 July 2009, *Seliwiak v. Poland*, No. 3818/04.
[97]   ECtHR 19 March 2009, *Kulikowski v. Poland*, No. 18353/03 and ECtHR 19 March 2009, *Antonicelli v. Poland*, No. 2815/05.

defence lawyer can still, quite easily, deprive the defendant of the right to have his case dealt with by the Supreme Court, by refusing to prepare a cassation appeal.[98]

2.2.2. The right to legal advice and/or representation

The suspect/defendant has the right to be assisted by a lawyer. This covers all phases of the proceedings.[99] Before the first interrogation, the suspect is informed of several rights, among which is the right to have the assistance of a defence lawyer.[100] The right to be assisted by a lawyer also applies to an arrested (suspected) person who does not yet have the status of a suspect: he has the right to contact a lawyer and talk to him directly.[101] The police should inform the suspected person of the right to contact a lawyer and to talk to him, immediately upon arrest.[102] It should be noted that the confidentiality of this conversation is not guaranteed, since the person who made the arrest may reserve the right to be present at the meeting.

In practice, it rarely happens that defence lawyers are involved in this early stage of the proceedings.[103] This is as a result of several circumstances. First of all, there is no right to legal assistance free of charge in the first phase of the proceedings immediately after arrest. This means that effectuation of the right to contact a lawyer after arrest is only possible for suspects who are able to pay for the lawyer themselves. Even when this is the case, realising the right to legal assistance at this stage is not easy. In this respect, it is problematic in practice that arrested persons are often informed that they have the right to one phone call – in which case they may prefer to contact a family member or a friend.

Furthermore, the arrested person should be able to state at least the (sur)name of a lawyer. The police are in no way legally obliged to be of any assistance in this regard and, as a rule, there are no lists of lawyers' names available at the police station. In addition, it is not guaranteed that a lawyer who is contacted by the arrested person will be available to come to the police station at short notice. With respect to ordinary criminal proceedings, the Polish criminal justice system does not provide for any kind of on call duty system guaranteeing that legal assistance is available for arrested persons outside office hours (weekends, evenings). However, since assistance of a defence lawyer is obligatory in 'speedy' proceedings (*postępowanie przyspieszone*), members of the bar are obliged to be on call, in order to offer legal assistance in such cases.[104]

[98] See the dissenting opinions of Judges Bonello and Mijović attached to the judgement of 19 March 2009.

[99] Art. 6 CCP and art. 42 § 2 of the Constitution.

[100] Art. 300 CCP. See also the letter of rights mentioned under 2.6.

[101] Art. 245 § 1CCP.

[102] As noted earlier, this obligation was, until recently, not expressly mentioned in criminal procedure law (it was only specified that the arrested person should be informed of his rights, without stipulating which rights), but, since the amendment of the law of 15 January 2009, art. 244 § 2 CCP now states that the arrested person 'should immediately be informed of his rights *including his right to use the assistance of a lawyer*' (emphasis added).

[103] See Daniuk et al. 2006, p. 24-33.

[104] In Polish literature, it is argued that there is a discrepancy in the protection of interests of defendants: while in ordinary proceedings, legal assistance is not obligatory even in serious

→

The lawyer (*adwokat*) providing legal assistance to an arrested person will only be considered a 'defence lawyer' (*obrońca*) after his client has officially been charged. Before that, the lawyer can assist the suspected person as a plenipotentiary (*pełnomocnik*). Since the CCP grants several procedural rights and possibilities only to the 'defence lawyer', it is important that the lawyer is qualified as such.

Mandatory defence

In some cases, the assistance of a defence lawyer is mandatory. A distinction can be made between personal circumstances affecting the possibility of the suspect to conduct his own defence, and circumstances connected to the severity and/or the complexity of the case.

With respect to the first category, the suspect must have a defence lawyer if he is (1) a minor; (2) deaf, dumb or blind; (3) there is good reason to doubt his sanity; or (4) when the court deems it necessary, due to circumstances impeding the defence.[105]

Furthermore, the accused must have a defence lawyer in proceedings before a provincial court (*Sąd Okręgowy*) as a court of first instance, if he is accused of a serious offence punishable by at least three years imprisonment (*zbrodnia*), or deprived of his liberty.[106] As noted above, in 'speedy' proceedings (*postępowanie przyspieszone*), there is also an obligatory defence.

If, in the abovementioned circumstances, the suspect/defendant does not have a defence lawyer of his own choosing, the president of the court having jurisdiction shall appoint a defence lawyer *ex officio*.[107] Current Polish criminal procedure does not require the (mandatory) attendance of a defence lawyer at any of the individual procedural actions in the investigative stage: the presence of the defence lawyer is only mandatory at the trial stage of the proceedings.[108]

Apart from the cases of mandatory defence for the entire proceedings, there are also circumstances in which the suspect/defendant needs the assistance of a defence lawyer to conduct certain procedural actions (*ad hoc* mandatory assistance: *przymus adwokacki*). This obligation exists, for example, when a suspect/defendant wants to file cassation, or appeal against a verdict of a higher court (*Sąd Okręgowy*).

---

cases, in the course of 'speedy' proceedings, it is available for persons suspected of less severe offences (mostly driving under the influence of alcohol). See, for example; Arciuch 2008. On 'speedy' proceedings; see § 1.3.4.

[105] In these circumstances, the participation of the defence lawyer in the trial is mandatory, as well as in those sessions where the presence of the accused is mandatory: art. 79 CCP.

[106] It is also so at the appellate and cassation hearing, if the (president of the) court finds it necessary: art. 80 CCP. This provision does not apply to the investigative stage of the proceedings, but is only applicable after the case is sent for trial. See the resolution of the Supreme Court 20 January 2004 (III KK 226/03).

[107] In such a case, the participation of the defence lawyer at the main trial is mandatory: art. 81 § 1 CCP.

[108] This was different before amendment to the CCP in July 2003: before this change, the presence of the defence lawyer in cases of obligatory defence was mandatory at the final examination of the case file: art. 321 CCP (old).

Legal assistance of indigent suspects/defendants

There are two categories of cases in which indigent suspects/defendants can be provided with legal assistance free of charge. First there are cases of mandatory defence (see above) and secondly, where the suspect/defendant is appointed a defence lawyer since he is unable to pay for the costs himself.

The principle underlying the first category is that, in the interests of justice, a defence lawyer should participate in the procedure in all cases where the defendant is 'vulnerable' for some reason, and therefore restricted in his ability to defend himself. As a rule, the financial situation of the suspect/defendant is not taken into account in these cases of mandatory defence: when the suspect is not assisted by a defence lawyer of his own choosing, legal assistance free of charge will be appointed to him, irrespective of his financial situation. In theory, the court may charge the defendant with the costs of mandatory legal assistance in case of conviction. According to research conducted by the HFHR, this rarely happens in practice.[109]

The legal framework for providing indigent suspects/defendants with legal assistance free of charge – the second category – is found in article 78 § 1 CCP. A defendant[110] who has not retained a defence lawyer, may demand that a lawyer be appointed to him *if he can prove that he is unable to pay the defence costs without prejudice to his and his family's necessary support and maintenance*.[111] When free legal assistance is granted, the suspect/defendant generally does not have to make a contribution: the costs are borne by the State Treasury.[112]

There is no express legal obligation for the judicial authorities to inform the suspect/defendant of his right to request to have appointed a defence lawyer free of charge. In addition, the right laid down in article 78 § 1 CCP is not mentioned in the letter of rights that is handed over to the suspect at the beginning of the first interrogation. However, if the prosecutor forms an opinion that a person cannot bear the costs of proceedings, he is obliged to instruct that person about the right to demand the appointment of a lawyer.[113] This arrangement is criticised, because it means that it is at the prosecutor's discretion to decide when a suspect will – or will not – be informed about the conditions, procedure, and right to avail oneself of the opportunity to request free legal assistance.[114]

---

[109] However, the actual scope of the phenomenon is not known: Bojarski 2003a, p. 102.

[110] The article only mentions the accused, but is also applicable to the suspect (since, as noted earlier, whenever the term 'defendant' is used generally in the CCP, such provisions apply to the suspect as well).

[111] The court may withdraw the appointment of a defence lawyer *ex officio* if it subsequently comes to light that the circumstances leading to the appointment do not exist: art. 78 § 2 CCP.

[112] Although there is a possibility in the CCP for recovery of the costs of legal assistance, in practice, all poor defendants are exempted from court fees.

[113] This obligation is laid down in art. 138 § 1 of a Decree by the Minister of Justice of August 2007 regulating the functioning of the prosecution's office (*Rozporządzenie Ministra Sprawiedliwości regulamin wewnętrznego urzędowania powszechnych jednostek organizacyjnych prokuratury*).

[114] Bojarski 2003a, p. 102-103.

The decision regarding the entitlement to free legal assistance is, at all stages of the criminal proceedings, taken by a judge: he decides whether the request for free legal assistance should be granted, given the financial circumstances of the suspect/defendant, and, if so, which lawyer should be appointed.[115] Lawyers are appointed following the order of a list provided to the court by the (local) bar association, without paying attention to the specialisation and/or the availability of the lawyer. This means that lawyers who have little or no experience in criminal law may also be appointed in a complex criminal trial. Formally, the judge is not obliged to take into account the preference of the suspect/defendant. However, this does not mean that it may not happen in practice. The appointed lawyer will usually be informed of his appointment in writing.

One of the weakest features of the Polish legal aid system is the fact that the judge has a wide discretionary power when deciding on a request for legal aid. There is no clear means test. The only (financial) criterion for assessing whether a suspect/defendant should be granted free legal assistance is article 78 § 1 CCP, which is a rather vague provision.[116] There are no clear guidelines as to which information should be provided[117] by the applicant, and/or objective criteria upon which to decide whether or not a request should be granted. As a result, the practice is unclear and divided. For example, according to research conducted by the HFHR, some judges also tend to take into account past financial circumstances, the fact that other relatives could be able to pay the defence costs and other factors.[118] Furthermore, it sometimes happens that appeal courts refuse to appoint an *ex officio* defence lawyer under article 78 CCP to bring a cassation appeal (or a motion for re-opening of the proceedings), taking into account not only the financial situation of the defendant, but also the prospects of success of such a legal remedy in the given case. Obviously, this is contrary to the wording of article 78 CCP. Fortunately, such decisions are rather exceptional.[119]

Also important is the fact that the court has to pay the costs for free legal assistance out of its own – in many cases rather limited – budget.[120] Often, judges

---

[115]   According to art. 81 § 1 CCP, the competent judge in this respect is the president of the court having jurisdiction in the case. However, in practice, it is often the head of the criminal department of the court, or the trial judge, who decides on a request for free legal assistance: Bojarski 2003a, p. 101.

[116]   'A defendant who has not retained a defence lawyer may demand that a defence lawyer be appointed to him *ex officio*, if he can duly prove that he is unable to pay the defence costs without prejudice to his and his family's necessary support and maintenance'.

[117]   Generally, they should at least be able to provide documents confirming that they are in receipt of an allowance, or a tax certificate confirming their income. See Kruszyński 2007, p. 194.

[118]   Bojarski 2003a, p. 100-108.

[119]   Information provided by M. Wąsek-Wiaderek, July 2009. See, for example, the decision of the Supreme Court of 12 June 2007, V KZ 36/07, published in: Lex No. 475341; see also *mutatis mutandis* the decision of the Supreme Court of 28 June 2007, II KK 36/07. The ruling of the Supreme Court allowing for such a practice has been strongly criticised in Polish literature: Stefański 2008, s. 142-146.

[120]   Bojarski 2003a, p.45.

have to deny requests because of the financial limitations of the court budget.[121] The decision on the request for free legal assistance cannot be appealed.

Although only members of the bar may be appointed as a legal aid lawyer, in Poland, university legal clinics also play an important role in this respect. At these clinics, students provide legal advice to indigent citizens *inter alia* in criminal cases. For example, at the Legal Clinic of the University of Lublin, students visit detention centres once a month. They speak with detainees and provide legal advice, after approval of their supervisors from the University.[122]

Legal assistance free of charge during the preliminary investigation

In theory, the right to legal assistance free of charge covers all phases of the proceedings. In most cases, the existence of any of the personal circumstances justifying (or demanding) mandatory legal assistance will already be identifiable during the preliminary investigation. In that case, the prosecutor is obliged to request the court to appoint a defence lawyer immediately. However, even if the prosecutor files this request at an early stage of the proceedings, in practice, the appointment will, at the earliest, occur after the court hearing that decides on the application of pre-trial detention (which has to take place within 72 hours after arrest).[123]

As noted earlier, participation of the defence lawyer is, at no point of the preliminary investigation, obligatory in cases of mandatory defence. This means that, although the defence lawyer might have been appointed at an early stage of the proceedings, until the commencement of the main trial, there are no specific procedural actions at which his attendance is mandatory.

Furthermore, it is important to note that legal assistance free of charge at the request of the indigent suspect/defendant does not cover the first stage after arrest. As is the case with the appointment in cases of mandatory defence, in practice, appointment of a defence lawyer free of charge at the request of the suspect will

---

[121]   Interview with a judge from the District Court of Puławy (Lublin region, 2004), conducted by the author of this report within the framework of PhD research on the right to legal assistance in Polish criminal procedure. Within the framework of this research, which was finalized in July 2009, several judges, academics and 13 criminal defence lawyers in Poznań, Lublin and Warsaw were interviewed during various visits to Poland in 2003, 2004 and 2007. Also, in 2004, the researcher spent several weeks at law firms in Poznań and Lublin following the daily practice of two defence lawyers. The results of this research have been published in: De Vocht 2009. See, on the financial limitations of the court budget when it comes to legal aid, also Bojarski 2003b: 'In the present financial situation of the administration of justice, when deciding about granting legal aid, courts when forced to make savings may be led by considerations not related to the merits but rather of a financial nature' and Rekosh 2002: 'Finances play a large role. The justice systems are generally resource-poor, aggravated by the tendency to lump legal aid funding together in the same budgetary pool with court administration. As one Polish judge put it starkly in a survey conducted by the Polish Helsinki Foundation for Human Rights, the president of his court gave the judges a choice: decrease legal aid or wear their coats in the courtroom in the coming winter'.

[122]   Information provided by M. Wąsek-Wiaderek, August 2009. For more information on legal clinics in Poland, see: <http://www.fupp.org.pl/index_eng.php>.

[123]   Daniuk et al. 2006, p. 34-36.

generally not be realised before the first hearing of the court, which decides on pre-trial detention. The lack of possibilities to have legal assistance appointed in the first phase of police interrogations has been criticised by the CPT.[124]

The choice of lawyer

The suspect/defendant has the right to choose his own lawyer if he is able to pay for the legal assistance himself.[125] When a lawyer is appointed by the court – in case of mandatory defence or at the request of the suspect/defendant – there is no (absolute) right to choose.[126]

All members of the bar (*adwokatura*) have the obligation to provide legal assistance free of charge.[127] However, the actual number of *adwokats* providing free legal assistance is not known, since the bar does not keep this kind of data.

There are no limitations in the CCP, other than the rule that only persons entitled to defend cases pursuant to the Law on the Bar may be engaged as a defence lawyer.[128] However, there is a limitation to the number of defence lawyers a suspect/defendant may appoint: according to the CCP, the accused may not have more than three defence lawyers at any one time.[129]

---

[124] 'For as long as there is not an effective system of free legal aid for indigent persons at the stage of police custody, any right of access to a lawyer will remain, in most cases, purely theoretical': Report to the Polish Government on the visit to Poland carried out by the European Committee for the Prevention of Torture and Inhuman or Degrading Treatment or Punishment (CPT) from 4 to 15 October 2004, available at: <www.cpt.coe.int/documents/pol/2006-11-inf-eng.pdf>. Therefore, one of the recommendations of the CPT was: 'a fully fledged and properly funded system of legal aid for persons in police custody who are not in a position to pay for a lawyer to be developed *as a matter of urgency*, and to be applicable from the very outset of police custody. If necessary, the relevant legislation should be amended' (p. 62) (emphasis added).

[125] According to art. 83 § 1 CCP, it is primarily the right of the defendant to retain the defence lawyer. However, before an accused deprived of liberty retains a defence lawyer, one may be retained by another person. The detainee should immediately be informed of such appointment, which is in any case only temporary: the appointment becomes final when the suspect/defendant approves it. Nevertheless, until this happens, the defence lawyer has the possibility to act in the furtherance of the suspect/defendant, for example, by filing an appeal against the pre-trial detention order. See Grzegorczyk 2004, p. 293. Appointment by another person is also possible in case of a minor or an incompetent person: then the legal representative, or the person in whose custody the suspect/defendant is, may undertake to act in his favour in the proceedings and, in particular, appoint a defence lawyer (art. 76 CCP).

[126] According to art. 81 § 2 CCP, the president of the court having jurisdiction in the case may appoint a new defence lawyer, in place of the acting lawyer, upon a justified motion of the accused or his defence lawyer. The fact that the request appointing a new defence lawyer should be well motivated, is also stipulated in the case law of the Supreme Court: Decision of the Supreme Court (SN) 20 March 1986, I KR/86, OSPiKA 1987, No. 7-8. See also: Wiliński 2006, p. 321-322.

[127] Only a small number of lawyers who fulfil certain positions within the (organs of the) bar are exempted from this obligation.

[128] Art. 82 CCP. See § 3.1 below.

[129] Art. 77 CCP.

Remuneration of lawyers

The fees for acting as an appointed defence lawyer are regulated by ministerial Decree.[130] Although this Decree specifies only minimum amounts, in practice, it is not likely that a judge will grant more than the minimum. Several minimum amounts are awarded for different stages and different court proceedings. For example, there is a fixed minimum amount for acting in the preliminary investigation, irrespective of the amount of work that is actually done.[131]

It is hard to say in general how these fixed fees relate to commercial rates. However, generally speaking, remuneration in legal aid cases is usually much lower than remuneration for privately funded cases.

It should be noted that not all lawyers are happy with the duty to provide free legal assistance. This is not only due to the extra work (on top of the already heavy workload connected to the relatively small population of Polish lawyers), but also because the specialisation of the lawyer is generally not taken into account when the judge decides on the appointment. This means that, for example, a lawyer specialising in civil law could be asked to act as a defence lawyer in a complex criminal case. Nevertheless, there is also a number of (especially younger) lawyers just starting a private law office who are willing to do a lot of *ex officio* cases, because it provides an important part of their income.

Quality of legal assistance free of charge

There are indications that the quality of legal assistance is sometimes lower in cases of free legal assistance, as compared to privately funded defence work. The HFHR receives many complaints from clients who are not satisfied with the legal assistance provided by their officially appointed lawyer.[132] Most often, these complaints involve the lack of action by of the lawyer (not informing the client, not visiting detained clients, not responding to phone calls and letters).

A small scale interview conducted by the HFHR among lawyers shows that more than half of the respondents 'admitted' that, generally, they would visit 'paying' clients more often than clients in appointed cases.[133] About 25% also stated that the quality of legal assistance is lower in general.[134] According to the research conducted by the HFHR among clients in criminal and civil cases, there is also a noticeable difference between the reasons for satisfaction with a retained lawyer versus an appointed one.[135]

---

[130] Decree of 28 September 2002 on the costs of free legal assistance paid by the state (*Rozporządzenie Ministra Sprawiedliwości w sprawie opłat za czynności adwokackie oraz ponoszenia przez Skarb Państwa kosztów nieopłaconej prawnej udzielonej z urzędu*).
[131] For providing legal assistance to a suspect in the preliminary investigation: approximately 48 Euro (PLN 180) when it is *dochodzenie* and 80 Euro (PLN 300) when it is *śledztwo*; art. 14 § 1 Decree on the costs of free legal assistance paid by the state.
[132] Bojarski 1999, p. 52-62. See also Daniuk et al. 2006, p. 51.
[133] Bojarski 2003a, p. 78.
[134] Bojarski 2003a, p. 78.
[135] Bojarski 2003a, p. 126. The three most cited reasons for satisfaction with a hired lawyer were: 'Tries hard / shows commitment'; 'Is well acquainted with my case and the case file'; 'Tells

→

Nevertheless, there are also lawyers who state that they do not differentiate between appointed and privately funded cases in everyday practice.[136]

There are no separate or specific rules of professional ethics for acting as a defence lawyer in legal aid cases. It should be noted that, in general, the disciplinary supervision of the Bar has, over the last few years, been criticised for being ineffective.[137]

Consultation and communication in private

The suspect(ed person) who is detained at the police station has the right to contact a lawyer and to talk to him directly.[138] As noted earlier, confidentiality is not guaranteed, since the person who made the arrest may reserve the right to be present when such a conversation takes place. In practice, this kind of supervision only has limited meaning, since it rarely happens that defence lawyers are involved in this early stage of the proceedings.[139]

During pre-trial detention, communication (orally and through correspondence) is, as a rule, confidential: this is laid down in the Code of Execution of Sentences[140] and in the CCP.[141] The only limitation to the right to private consultation provided for in the CCP concerns the first 14 days of pre-trial detention: in these first two weeks, the prosecutor who gives permission for such a conversation may, 'where particularly justified', demand that he or a person authorized by him shall be present at such a meeting.[142] After the first 14 days of pre-trial detention, it is no longer possible to supervise the meetings between the detainee and his client (nor to impose any other limitations on the right to private consultation).

> me what is going on in the case'. The three most often cited reasons for satisfaction with an appointed lawyer were: 'Comes to hearings'; 'Is nice/polite', 'Is well acquainted with my case and the case file'. According to the author of the Monitoring Report (Bojarski), the results of this research raise the question as to whether clients have different expectations of the appointed lawyer if 'the very fact of the *ex officio*'s attorney's presence at hearings is worthy of praise'.
>
> [136] Interviews conducted with defence lawyers within the framework of PhD research (see footnote 121). Some of the lawyers interviewed claimed to give legal aid cases and paid cases an equal amount of attention. Others, however, admitted to spending less time on legal aid cases and not giving priority to the latter in case of clashing obligations.
> [137] See § 3.2 below.
> [138] Art. 245 § 1 CCP.
> [139] Daniuk et al. 2006, p. 24-33. See § 2.2.2 on the reasons for the absence of defence lawyers in the first phase after arrest.
> [140] *Kodeks Karny Wykonawczy.* The relevant provisions of this code are art. 215 with respect to persons held in pre-trial detention and art. 8 § 3, which deals with prisoners serving a sentence.
> [141] Art. 73 § 1 CCP.
> [142] Art. 73 § 2 CCP. The CCP does not specify those grounds that may justify an infringement of the right to confidential communication, and there is no judicial supervision on this decision of the prosecutor (no possibility of appeal). During the first 14 days of detention, the prosecutor also has the power to control the correspondence of the detainee (art. 73 § 3 CCP). As a rule, reading the contents of privileged correspondence (such as letters to and from a lawyer) is not allowed.

In practice, this supervision does not happen very often: it is mostly restricted to complex cases of organized crime and corruption. However, this does not mean that it cannot affect the possibilities of the defence. Since the supervision is generally carried out within hearing of the detainee and his lawyer,[143] some lawyers tend to postpone the first visit to their client, or choose to discuss only the required minimum, without going into the details of the case.[144] Clearly, this will affect the possibilities of the suspect to have practical and effective legal assistance at a vital phase of the proceedings – the first 14 days of the detention, during which the most important interrogations will take place.

Nevertheless, it seems that, generally, most lawyers do not consider this form of supervision to be a major threat to effective criminal defence. This is not only because it only happens in certain criminal cases, but also because the impression exists that the supervisor does not actually listen to the conversation.[145]

The question however, is whether this is relevant for the breach of confidentiality: as stressed by the ECtHR, an interference with the lawyer-client privilege does not require an actual interception or eaves-dropping to have taken place.[146] Furthermore, the rather mild opinion of the Polish Bar on this aspect of criminal procedure is probably influenced by the fact that many Polish lawyers are still used to remaining passive during these early stages of the criminal process. This could explain why it is considered acceptable to postpone the first, in depth, conversation with the detained client until after the first 14 days of pre-trial detention.[147]

In 2004, the Polish Constitutional Court held that the form of supervision mentioned above is compatible with the constitutional right to a defence.[148] However, it is not clear whether the supervision within hearing as foreseen and carried out in Polish criminal procedure constitutes a breach of article 6 of the ECHR.[149] Generally, the defendant's right to communicate with his legal representative out of the hearing of a third person is considered part of the basic requirements of a fair trial in a democratic society. The ECtHR has, on many occasions, stressed the importance of confidentiality in meetings between the defendant and his lawyer. The Strasbourg case law shows that supervision is only

---

[143]   As noted earlier, this kind of supervision is also possible in the first hours after arrest (according to art. 245 § 1 second sentence CCP).

[144]   Interviews with defence lawyers conducted within the framework of PhD (see footnote 121).

[145]   Ibidem.

[146]   'A genuine believe held on reasonable grounds that their conversation was being listened to might be sufficient, in the Court's view, to limit the effectiveness of the assistance which the lawyer could provide': ECtHR 13 March 2007, *Castravet* v. *Moldova*, No. 23393/05, § 51.

[147]   Interviews with defence lawyers conducted within the framework of PhD (see footnote 121).

[148]   Decision of 17 February 2004 (SK 39/02).

[149]   According to some Polish authors, the supervision is in breach of art. 6 ECHR. See, for example, Kruszyński: 'Even though this [supervision of art. 73 CCP] contravenes ECtHR jurisprudence, it constitutes Polish law and it cannot be appealed': Kruszyński 2007, p. 195.

allowed when there are 'very weighty reasons' for it and that supervision within hearing should always be *ultimum remedium*.[150]

There is no ECtHR decision against Poland on the supervision under the current article 73 CCP. There is, however, a recent judgement on the supervision as carried out under the old Polish code of criminal procedure. In that case, the Court decided that the supervision, which lasted for over five months, constituted a breach of article 6 § 3 (c), taken in conjunction with article 6 § 1 ECHR.[151] The Court noted in this connection that, in the supervision order, the prosecutor merely referred to the relevant legal provisions, with no reference being made to the grounds on which this decision was made. The Court further noted that, not only were the supervisors present in the same room, but they also listened to the conversations between the applicant and the lawyer. According to the Court, the fact that the authorities were actively preparing the bill of indictment against Rybacki, taken together with the considerable length of that period, strengthened the conclusion that the absence of unhindered contact with his lawyer throughout that period negatively affected the effective exercise of his defence rights.[152] As noted earlier, the decision in the *Rybacki* case concerned a situation prior to the current CCP, when supervision of the meetings between the lawyer and his detained client were possible for almost the entire stage of the pre-trial proceedings.[153] Whether the (general) considerations of the Strasbourg Court, that Rybacki's contact with his lawyer did not allow for an effective exercise of his defence rights given the fact that the police officers in the case were present in the same room and listened to the conversations, might still be relevant for the current situation, remains to be seen. To a large extent, this will depend on whether the authorities are able to prove that there were sufficient ('very weighty') grounds showing that this kind of supervision was necessary and justified in the given circumstances.

The right to private consultation during trial is not expressly specified in the CCP. Usually, the defendant and his lawyer do not sit next to each other in the courtroom.[154] As a rule, the defence lawyer sits on a bench in front of his client. Private communication during trial is more difficult where defendants are deemed dangerous and/or are accused of very severe criminal acts. They are often placed in a special 'cage' in the courtroom at a certain distance from their lawyers. However, the defence lawyer, or his client, may always ask the presiding judge for a break in the hearing for consultations.

---

[150] See *inter alia*: ECtHR 28 November 1991, *S. v. Switzerland*, No. 12629/87 and 13965/88, ECtHR 1 January 2001, *Lanz v. Austria*, No. 24430/94 and ECtHR 12 March 2003, *Öcalan v. Turkey*, No. 46221/99.

[151] ECtHR 13 January 2009, *Rybacki v. Poland*, No. 52479/99.

[152] See § 57 onwards of the judgement.

[153] The old code of criminal procedure also enabled the prosecutor to disallow meetings between the lawyer and his detained client.

[154] Except for less complex cases held in small courtrooms.

2.3. Procedural rights

2.3.1. The right to release from custody pending trial

The decision to apply pre-trial detention is taken by the court. Until the final judgement at first instance, pre-trial detention cannot exceed the two year limit.[155] Application of pre-trial detention requires a general ground[156] and a specific ground. The following specific grounds are mentioned in the CCP:

There is good reason to fear that the suspect may take flight or go into hiding, particularly if he has no permanent residence in Poland, or when his identity cannot be established;

- There is good reason to fear that the suspect would induce other persons to give false testimony, or attempt to obstruct the criminal proceedings in some other manner;
- The need to apply pre-trial detention in order to secure the proper conduct of proceedings may be justified by the potential severe penalty, if the defendant has been charged with a serious offence (*zbrodnia*) or with a *występek*[157] carrying the statutory maximum penalty of deprivation of liberty of a minimum of 8 years, or if the court of first instance sentenced him to a penalty of deprivation of liberty of no less than 3 years.
- In exceptional cases, pre-trial detention may also occur when there is good reason to fear that the defendant charged with a severe offence (*zbrodnia*), or an intentional *występek*, would commit an offence against life, health or public safety, particularly if he threatened to commit such an offence.[158]

Furthermore, pre-trial detention may only be applied if the evidence collected indicates a high probability that the suspect has committed an offence. It should not be applied when other preventive measures are sufficient.[159] The other preventive measures (*środki zapobiegawcze*) that can be applied in Polish criminal procedure are, for example: bail, police supervision,[160] a ban on driving certain vehicles, a ban on practising a certain profession, or a ban on leaving the country. Non-isolatory preventive measures, such as bail, are ordered by the public prosecutor (during the investigation), or by the court (during the judicial proceedings).

In applying pre-trial detention, the court may require that the measure be amended when an agreed bail is posted with the court within the prescribed time-

---

[155] Except for certain specific circumstances specified in art. 263 CCP.
[156] It may be applied in order to secure the proper conduct of the proceedings and, exceptionally, to prevent a new serious offence from being committed by the suspect: art. 249 § 1 CCP.
[157] See § 1.3.1 for the distinction between *zbrodnia* and *występek*.
[158] Art. 258 §1, 2 and 3 CCP.
[159] Art. 249 § 1, art. 257 § 1 and art. 259 § 1, 2 and 3 CCP.
[160] Police supervision (*dozór Policji*) means that the suspect has to follow the rules set by the prosecutor; for example he can be required to report to the police station at set times (art. 275 CCP).

limit.[161] There are two versions of bail: individual bail (*poręczenie majątkowe*) and communal bail (*poręczenie społeczne*). In the first case a financial deposit is required. The amount, kind and conditions of the bail, and particularly the time-limit for making the deposit, shall be specified in the order. The property or sum of money constituting bail shall be transferred or paid to the State Treasury. If bail ceases to be necessary, the property and sum of money pledged shall be released; if, however, the accused is sentenced to a deprivation of liberty, bail shall be withdrawn only after he has begun serving his sentence.

In case of communal bail, a third person – for example the employer of the suspect – will be required to state that the accused will appear whenever summoned and will not unlawfully obstruct the course of the proceedings. A guarantee to this effect may also be accepted from any trustworthy person.[162] If the defendant subsequently fails to appear in court, the guarantor may face a disciplinary penalty (a fine).[163]

The suspect and his defence lawyer may request release under bail at any time.[164] Such a request is examined by the public prosecutor in the course of the investigation and by the court, at the judicial stage of the proceedings. A request for bail, and a concrete proposal for a sum of money, may also be contained in every appeal against the decision concerning detention on remand.

With respect to practice, it should be noted that pre-trial detention is quite often still applied. The legal assumption that pre-trial detention should only be applied when other preventive measures are not sufficient (*ultimum remedium*) is not reflected by everyday practice. Many complaints filed with the ECtHR concern the duration and the (lack of) relevant and sufficient grounds for pre-trial detention. The Strasbourg case law shows that these complaints are often well-founded.[165]

However, it should be stressed that the practice has improved, compared to the situation before 1989, when pre-trial detention, which could be ordered by the prosecutor, was one of the weakest features of the Polish criminal justice system. As mentioned in § 1.4, the relevant statistics show a considerable decrease in the application of pre-trial detention over the last few years, as well as a growth in the use of alternative measures (particularly bail).

In general, defence lawyers often do challenge the application of pre-trial detention and make use of the legal remedies Polish criminal procedure has to offer in this respect. Nevertheless, it follows from empirical research conducted by Izydorczyk, that it is quite rare that a defence lawyer is present at the first hearing, when the court decides on the application of pre-trial detention. According to

---

[161] Art. 257 § 2 CCP.

[162] See art. 266-275 CCP.

[163] Art. 285 in conjunction with art. 287 § 1 CCP.

[164] Pursuant to art. 254 CCP, an accused may request the quashing of the detention order, or replace it with a less severe preventive measure at any time.

[165] See for example: ECtHR 28 July 2005, *Czarnecki* v. *Poland*, No. 75112/01, ECtHR 25 May 2006, *Gołek* v. *Poland*, No. 31330/02, ECtHR 4 May 2006, *Celejewski* v. *Poland*, No. 17584/04, ECtHR 20 June 2006, *Drabek* v. *Poland*, No. 5270/04, ECtHR 6 July 2006, *Telecki* v. *Poland*, No. 56552/00, ECtHR 8 January 2008, *Marczuk* v. *Poland*, No. 4646/02. In most cases, a violation of art. 5 ECHR is based on the lack of 'relevant and sufficient grounds' justifying the continuation of the deprivation of liberty.

Izydorczyk, one of the main reasons for this is connected to the strict time limits within which the court has to decide, as well as the fact that, at this early stage of the proceedings a defence lawyer has often not yet been assigned to the case.

In addition, he asserts that lawyers sometimes stay away from these hearings, because they fear that their presence might be interpreted as some sort of admission of guilt by the defendant, which might harm his defence later on in the proceedings. Court hearings where decisions are taken on the prolongation of pre-trial detention are more often held in the presence of a defence lawyer.[166]

2.3.2. The right of a defendant to be tried in his/her presence

One of the principles of Polish criminal procedure is that the defendant not only has the right, but also has the obligation, to be present at the main trial.[167] As a result, there is no trial *in absentia* in Poland in the original sense of this concept. There is only a possibility to examine the case without the presence of the defendant in certain special proceedings.[168] The judgement must be quashed if the hearing was held in the absence of the defendant in circumstances where his presence was obligatory.[169]

However, there are several exceptions to the mandatory presence of the defendant, allowing the court to conduct or continue the trial partially in his absence. These exceptions concern the following situations:

- the defendant, who has already given evidence to the court, leaves the courtroom without the permission of the presiding judge;
- the defendant, who has already given evidence to the court and has been notified of the date of the adjourned or interrupted hearing, has not come to that hearing or justified his non-appearance;
- a co-defendant, who provided justification, has not appeared at the adjourned or interrupted hearing (the court may then continue the hearing to the extent that it does not directly concern the absentee, provided that this does not limit his right of defence);
- the defendant, through his own fault, works himself into a state where he is unfit to participate in a hearing or session where his presence is deemed mandatory (the court may then continue the hearing, even if he has not yet given his explanations);
- the defendant, notified of the date of hearing, states that he will not participate in the hearing, or prevents himself being brought to the hearing;

[166] Izydorczyk 2002, p. 135-172. Although, the empirical research discussed in this work was conducted almost 10 years ago (1998-2001), Izydorczyk believes the current practice to be quite similar: Izydorcyzk 2008, p. 36.

[167] The presiding judge may issue a ruling in order to render it impossible for the defendant to leave the court before the conclusion of the hearing. Furthermore, he may demand that a defendant who does not appear should immediately be arrested and brought to the trial.

[168] Summary proceedings and penal order proceedings: there is a right to bring a 'protest' (*sprzeciw*) against judgements issued by default, with the result that the trial will be conducted again in the presence of defendant.

[169] Art. 439 § 1 under 11 CCP.

or having been personally notified of the hearing does not appear in person without a good cause (the court may then continue the proceedings without his presence, unless it finds the presence of the accused indispensable).[170]

Most of these exceptions are new in the Code of 1997, with the result that the principle of mandatory presence of the accused has lost much of its meaning. A judgement issued in the circumstances described above is not considered as a judgement by default.

The defence lawyer may act on behalf of his absent client, without having to fulfil any formal requirements. As noted above, in cases of mandatory defence, participation of the defence lawyer at the main trial is obligatory.

2.3.3. The right to be presumed innocent

The right to be presumed innocent is guaranteed both by the Constitution[171] and the CCP.[172] The suspect/defendant must be regarded as innocent until his guilt is established by a valid judgement. When conducting an investigation, the judicial authorities are bound by the principle of objectivity, which means that they are obliged to inquire into, and duly consider, the circumstances both in favour and to the prejudice of the defendant.[173] During the investigation or court proceedings, disclosure to the media of any material relating to personal details of the suspect, or the circumstances of the case, is forbidden, unless the relevant person consents.[174]

In general, there are no indications that the presumption of innocence principle is not being complied with in practice. More specifically, the low acquittal rate that is characteristic of the Polish criminal justice system cannot be considered as evidence of a factual presumption of guilt, but is probably mainly the result of the fact that only strong cases are taken to court. However, there is some Strasbourg case law against Poland in the context of pre-trial detention and the presumption of innocence. In a few cases, a breach of article 5 § 3 and/or article 6 § 2 ECHR has been based on the fact that Polish courts justified the application or prolongation of pre-trial detention by stating that the suspect had not confessed, or that the evidence against the defendant indicated that he had committed the offence with which he had been charged.[175]

---

[170]   These exceptions are specified in arts. 376 and 377 CCP.
[171]   Art. 42 § 3 Constitution.
[172]   Art. 5 CCP.
[173]   Art. 4 CCP.
[174]   Only if there is a wider public interest, the prosecutor or the court may disclose the personal data or an image of the suspect: Kruszyński 2007, p. 193.
[175]   ECtHR 4 October 2005, *Górski* v. *Poland*, No. 28904/02, ECtHR 7 March 2006, *Leszczak* v. *Poland*, No. 36576/03, ECtHR 6 February 2007, *Garycki* v. *Poland*, No. 14348/02, ECtHR 9 December 2008, *Wojciechowski* v. *Poland*, No. 5422/04 and ECtHR 3 February 2009, *Kauczor* v. *Poland*, No. 45219/06.

2.3.4. The right to silence

The right to silence is specified in the CCP.[176] According to the relevant provision, a suspect/defendant has the right to make statements, but he may refuse to respond to particular questions, or to make any statements in general. The suspect should be informed of his right to silence. According to criminal procedure law, this should happen at least twice during the proceedings:

- before the interrogation; and
- at the main trial, after the indictment has been read.

Before the first interrogation this information, is provided in written form: the rights laid down in article 175 § 1 CCP are part of the standardized document (letter of rights) that is given to the suspect at the commencement of the first interrogation.

There are no indications that, in practice, the information on the right to silence is not provided in compliance with the relevant legal provisions. Obviously, the confession of the suspect plays an important role in the proceedings. For example, the confession is necessary to follow alternative consensual proceedings (such as issuing a judgement without trial at the request of the prosecutor: see § 1.3.4), or to obtain the status of crown witness (świadek koronny). As noted above, there are a few Strasbourg cases against Poland in which the national courts, in their decision on pre-trial detention, relied on the fact that the suspect had not confessed his guilt.[177] Clearly, this is in breach of the presumption of innocence.

There is no legal obligation to inform the suspected person (as opposed to a suspect) of his right to silence (see § 2.1.1).

According to case law of the Supreme Court, the fact that the suspect/defendant makes use of his right to silence may not be deemed as incriminating.[178] Thus, exercising the right to silence may not affect the penalty imposed.[179] This is also the case where a suspect gives a false explanation when interviewed.

The defendant has no obligation to prove his innocence, or to adduce evidence to his own detriment.[180] There is, however, no express legal obligation on the authorities to inform the suspect/defendant of the right not to incriminate himself.[181]

---

[176]   Art. 175 § 1 CCP.
[177]   See § 2.3.3.
[178]   Decision of the Supreme Court (SN) 4 November 1977 (V KR 176/177, OSNKW 1/1987, item 7).
[179]   Kruszyński 2007, p. 193.
[180]   Art. 74 § 1 CCP.
[181]   However, the obligation to yield to certain investigatory acts (such as psychological and psychiatric tests) mentioned in art. 74 § 2 CCP, as an exception to the rule that the suspect/defendant is not obliged to prove his innocence or to adduce evidence to his own detriment, is specified in written form (letter of rights) that is handed over to the suspect at the commencement of the first interrogation.

2.3.5. The right to reasoned decisions

In Polish criminal procedure, several different types of decisions may be given:

- Instructions (*zarządzenia*): when the law does not require a judgement or an order. Depending on the stage of the proceedings, decisions in the form of instructions may be taken by a judge, a public prosecutor or the police.
- Judicial decisions (*orzeczenia*): procedural decisions on legal matters, which can take two forms. First, the form of an order (*postanowienia*), when the law does not require a judgement. The CCP prescribes whether an order is to be taken by a judge, a public prosecutor or by the police. Secondly, judicial decisions can take the form of a judgement (*wyrok*).[182]

The right to reasoned decisions is not expressly specified in the Constitution, but can be derived from certain provisions of the CCP. For example, the obligation to give reasons for an order (*postanowienia*) is specified in the CCP.[183] Furthermore, there is a provision that prescribes what should be included in the statement of reasons for a judgement (*wyrok*).[184] Decisions on preventive measures, such as pre-trial detention, also require specific reasoning.[185]

Insufficient or incoherent reasoning of a first instance judgement may be invoked as a ground for appeal. Moreover, very frequently, a complaint regarding the lack of adequate and complete reasoning of second instance judgements is raised in cassation appeals.

With regard to some decisions, in practice authorities simply copy the contents of the applicable legal provision, without specifying the relevant circumstances of the case. For example, the decision of the prosecutor to supervise the meeting between a lawyer and his detained client (see § 2.2.2) requires justification. The prosecutor must explain why supervision is necessary, given the legal requirement that it is only allowed in 'particularly justified cases'.

In practice, however, the reasoning is often of a rather general nature: many prosecutors only refer to the content of the relevant legal provision, and to a standard formula that supervision is necessary given the interest of the investigation. Obviously, the general and vague wording of the relevant legal provision (what is a 'particularly justified case'?) does not encourage the authorities to be overly specific in this respect.

---

[182] Art. 93 § 1 CCP. See Marguery 2008, p. 184-185.
[183] Art. 94 CCP.
[184] Art. 424 CCP.
[185] According to art. 251 § 1 CCP, the justification for an order on the application of a preventive measure (such as pre-trial detention) shall 'present evidence demonstrating that the accused committed an offence, and refer to the facts indicating the existence of grounds necessitating the application of a preventive measure. In case of pre-trial detention it should be further explained why applying other preventive measures has been regarded as insufficient'.

2.3.6. The right to appeal

A distinction should be made between an interlocutory appeal (*zażalenie*) and an appeal (*apelacja*). The first appellate measure can be filed against certain decisions and acts that are not final judgements. Interlocutory appeals may be brought against orders of a court that preclude the rendering of a judgement, orders with respect to precautionary measures, and other orders in cases prescribed by law.

The right to file an interlocutory appeal is vested in the parties, as well as persons directly concerned by the order, unless otherwise provided by law.[186] Depending on the situation (for example, the type of decision), an interlocutory appeal should be filed with the court or the prosecutor. It should be stressed that, for certain important decisions taken during pre-trial investigation (affecting the position of the defence), judicial review is not possible. For example, in relation to a decision of the prosecutor to deny the defence access to the case file, an interlocutory appeal can only be filed with a higher prosecutor.[187] Furthermore, the decision of the prosecutor to supervise conversations between the lawyer and the client during the first 14 days of detention cannot be appealed.[188]

An appeal (*apelacja*) may be filed against all judgements of first instance courts. The time limit for filing such an appeal is 14 days. In some instances, the appeal can only be filed by a lawyer.[189] Although the appeal covers both factual findings and legal issues, the appeal court may only conduct evidentiary proceedings to a limited extent. It is bound by certain limitations with respect to altering the judgement of first instance. For example, it is not possible to convict a defendant who has been acquitted at the first instance proceedings.[190] As noted earlier, it is not always guaranteed that the detained defendant will be brought to the appellate hearing: the appellate court may deny a request to be brought to trial when it deems the presence of the defence lawyer to be sufficient.[191]

2.4. *Rights relating to effective defence*

2.4.1. The right to investigate the case

Equality of arms (including the right to be present at investigative acts)

As in most continental legal systems, the possibilities of the defence to influence the (course and outcome of the) proceedings, are in several ways, more limited during pre-trial investigation than during judicial proceedings.

However, it should be stressed that, at least on paper, equality of arms between defence and prosecution has undoubtedly improved since the entering into

---

[186] Art. 459 § 1 and 2 CCP.

[187] See § 2.1.2.

[188] See § 2.2.2.

[189] Art. 446 § 1 CCP: 'An appeal from a judgement rendered by a provincial court, but not originating with the state prosecutor (…) should be prepared and signed by a lawyer'.

[190] Art. 454 CCP.

[191] See § 2.2.1.

force of the new CCP. For example, according to current criminal procedural law, the defence lawyer has the right to be present during the interrogation of his client.[192] Also important is the fact that the possibilities of the defence to challenge pre-trial detention have been improved. During the communist regime, decisions on the application for or the extension of, pre-trial detention were, as a rule, taken in the presence of the prosecutor, but in the absence of the suspect and his defence lawyer. Under the new CCP, this inequality has been largely removed, by providing the defence lawyer with the right to be present at all court hearings at which decisions on pre-trial detention are taken.[193]

Although these and other legal changes have undoubtedly strengthened the adversarial character of pre-trial investigation, there remain strong indications that the enhanced rights have not (yet) resulted in a noticeable change of practice. In general, Polish defence lawyers tend to remain rather passive in the pre-trial phase. For example, the possibilities to take part in fact-finding activities, or to be present at interrogations, are not often utilised.[194]

There are several reasons to explain this passive approach. First of all, there are important remaining procedural difficulties limiting the possibilities of the defence prior to trial. By far the most important of these flows from the fact that access to the case file is still limited in many cases.[195] Obviously, the fact that the defence cannot have access to the case file will affect the possibility to make use of other procedural rights, such as the possibility to file a request for investigatory actions and to (effectively) challenge pre-trial detention.

Secondly, there are practical reasons for the lack of active defence lawyers during the pre-trial investigation. Most importantly is the fact that the right to legal assistance free of charge is only available to the suspect (not the suspected person). Furthermore, in practice, it is not likely that a (free) defence lawyer will be appointed before the first hearing of the court deciding on the application of pre-trial detention.[196]

Even when defence lawyers are appointed during the pre-trial investigation, this mostly concerns cases of mandatory defence: appointment of legal assistance free of charge at the request of the suspect (due to his financial situation) generally takes place at a later stage of the proceedings. Consequently, for suspects who are not able to pay for legal assistance themselves, it is not likely that a defence lawyer will be appointed at an early stage of the proceedings.

Finally, considerations of a traditional or a strategic nature have a strong influence on the role of the defence lawyer during the pre-trial investigation. Polish defence lawyers are used to being passive in this phase of the proceedings since,

---

[192]   Art. 301 CCP. This right was not expressly provided for in the former CCP of 1969.
[193]   For an extensive analysis of the principle of equality of arms in Polish criminal procedure; see Wąsek-Wiaderek 2003b.
[194]   On the subject of interrogating suspects in the presence of a lawyer; see Kruszyński 2007, p. 195: 'During the interview a lawyer may be present if the suspect so requires. In practice, a request for a lawyer to advise at this stage is made, most frequently, by suspects who are able to pay privately. In other cases, it is unusual for a lawyer to attend the interview'.
[195]   See § 2.1.2.
[196]   See § 2.2.2.

during the communist regime, active participation in pre-trial investigation was in most cases impossible. Despite the more recent legal changes in favour of the defence, many lawyers still believe that remaining passive during the investigation is often the best strategy: first of all not to 'annoy' the prosecutor (which could harm the case) and, secondly, to prevent the prosecution from gaining insight into the defence strategy at an early stage of the proceedings, destroying the element of surprise at the trial.[197]

Obviously, this defence strategy does not take into account the fact that the results of the investigation phase are of great importance to the case and, thus, if the defence does not make use of its possibilities to influence this stage of the proceedings, it will not always be possible to properly compensate for this lack of activity during the trial.

The right to seek evidence, investigate facts and interview prospective witnesses

During the preliminary investigation, the suspect and his lawyer have the right to file motions for certain investigatory actions to be performed. Such a request must be filed with the prosecutor or the police (depending on who is conducting the investigation). All evidentiary motions are decided on the basis of a provision of the CCP that contains five (exhaustive) grounds for refusal.[198]

The suspect and his defence lawyer may not be denied admission to participate in actions that are carried out at their initiative.[199] The right to file motions also includes the right to request the police to hear prospective witnesses. As with every evidentiary motion, such a request may be refused.[200]

Furthermore, a defence lawyer is entitled to take part in all activities that cannot be repeated during the trial (the so-called *czynności niepowtarzalne*) such as the inspection of the crime scene.[201] In certain circumstances, it is also possible for the defence to ask the court to hear a witness during the preliminary investigation.[202]

---

[197] Interviews with defence lawyers conducted within the framework of PhD (see footnote 121). On the passivity of defence lawyers during pre-trial proceedings; see Kulesza 2005, p. 419-422 and Kulesza 2007.

[198] Art. 170 § 1 sub 1-5 CCP: '§ 1. An evidentiary motion shall be denied when: (1) the taking of such evidence is inadmissible, (2) the fact to be proven is either irrelevant to the resolution of the case, or has already been proven consistently with the allegations of the moving party, (3) the evidence would be irrelevant to the establishment of the fact in question, (4) it is impossible to take the evidence, or, (5) the evidentiary motion aims, in an obvious manner, to slow down the proceedings.'

[199] However, the appearance of a suspect deprived of liberty shall not be procured, if this were to involve 'serious difficulties': art. 315 in conjunction with art. 318 second sentence CCP.

[200] Under art. 170 CCP.

[201] Art. 316 § 1 and 2 CCP.

[202] When there is a danger that the witness cannot be heard at the hearing (for example, because he will leave the country or is seriously ill), the suspect or his defence lawyer may submit a motion demanding that the witness be heard by the court: art. 316 § 3 CCP.

After the final examination of the case file, the suspect and his lawyer have the right to file motions to supplement the investigation. Such a request should be filed within three days after the final examination.[203]

Apart from the right to ask for additional investigation, the defence also has the right to participate in investigatory activities carried out of the initiative of the authorities (police/prosecution). A request to be present at such activities can only be denied 'in particularly justified cases' and 'if the interest of the investigation so require'.[204] Obviously, these are rather vague terms, allowing much discretionary power to the authorities.

After the close of the preliminary investigation, the defendant and his lawyer have the right to file requests to take evidence at the trial stage. When the defendant receives the details of the charges he is asked to file evidentiary motions within seven days.[205] After this period, the defence also has the right to file evidentiary motions during the trial. The presiding judge decides on whether to grant or rejecting the evidentiary motions, as well as on the order of the evidentiary acts. As noted earlier, evidentiary motions can only be denied on certain (exhaustive) grounds.[206]

It is worth mentioning that the order in which witnesses (and experts) are heard at the trial was changed in the new CCP of 1997. Under the old Code of 1969, parties were only allowed to ask questions after the judge(s). This was changed to enhance the activity of parties in the proceedings: nowadays, the general rule is that, after a witness has expressed himself freely, other persons may ask questions in the following order as called upon by the presiding judge: the state prosecutor, subsidiary prosecutor, attorney of the subsidiary prosecutor, private prosecutor, civil plaintiff, attorney of the civil plaintiff, expert, the entity referred to in article 416 CCP (the entity that acquired the material benefits of the criminal act), *defence lawyer, the defendant* and, finally; members of the panel of judges.[207] Therefore, when a witness is called at the request of the defence, the defendant and his defence lawyer should have the first opportunity to ask questions.

However, the general impression is that, until now, changing the legal order of the questioning has not lead to significant changes in practice.[208] The examination of witnesses and experts is still, as a rule, dominated by the presiding judge.

Although, in theory these rights equally apply to all defendants, for obvious reasons, it will often be more difficult for a suspect/defendant who is not assisted by a defence lawyer to adequately exercise the right to file requests to perform certain investigative acts. Effectuating these rights might be more difficult for indigent defendants.

---

[203]   Art. 321 § 5 CCP.

[204]   Also, the request of a suspect who is deprived of his liberty may be denied, if his transport to the place of the activities would involve serious difficulties. See art. 317 CCP.

[205]   Art. 338 § 1 CCP.

[206]   Art. 170 § 1 CCP formulates five grounds; see 4.1.

[207]   However, the members of the panel of judges may, when necessary, ask additional questions, out of sequence. A party on whose motion the witness was admitted puts its questions before the remaining parties: art. 370 § 1, 2 and 3 CCP.

[208]   Interview with a judge of the District Court of Poznań, conducted within the framework of PhD (see footnote 121).

There is little empirical data on the use of these rights of the defence in practice. However, it is known that, generally, evidentiary motions are very rarely filed by the defence during the preliminary investigation. As noted earlier, Polish defence lawyers prefer to wait for the trial. Research conducted by Gwirdoyń shows that, when defence lawyers do file a request for an evidentiary action to be performed, it is not likely that the lawyer will be present when it is actually carried out.[209]

During the trial, the attitude of the Polish lawyer towards fact finding is also rather passive. More specifically, he will not easily conduct a 'private' investigation on his own. Traditionally, investigation in criminal cases is considered to be the prerogative of the judicial authorities. Interestingly enough, the research by Gwirdoyń shows that the majority of the questioned lawyers were of the opinion that a 'private investigation' is not allowed, although there is no provision in the CCP, or in the rules of professional ethics, stating that this kind of research is forbidden.

The right to obtain expert evidence

During the preliminary investigation, expert opinions are usually obtained at the initiative of the prosecution. The defence has certain rights in this respect: if evidence based on an opinion issued by experts, a scientific institute, or a specialised establishment is admitted, the suspect and his defence lawyer shall be served with the order on the admission of this evidence, permitted to participate in the examination of the expert and permitted to acquaint themselves with the (written) opinion of the expert.[210]

When the defence wants to have an expert appointed, it must file a request with the prosecutor (during the preliminary investigation), or with the court (during the trial). There are no specific provisions regulating such requests.[211] If the court admits the request of the defence to appoint an expert, it will appoint a so-called 'court expert' from the list of experts present in every provincial court (*Sąd Okręgowy*), or another person having appropriate expertise. There is no private expert opinion in Polish criminal procedure: an expert opinion prepared at the request of the defence by an expert who is not appointed by the court will not be admitted as 'expert opinion'.

Although, in theory this right applies equally to all suspects/defendants, to adequately exercise the right to file requests to obtain expert evidence will often be more difficult for a suspect/defendant who is not assisted by a defence lawyer. Furthermore, the costs of the expert opinion will only be paid by the state if the expert is eventually officially appointed by the judge. Since the chances that this

---

[209]   Gwirdoyń 2004, p. 18-19. The main reasons formulated for this practice were: (1) the lack of time; (2) the fact that there is no possibility to influence the action carried out; and (3) the defence strategy.

[210]   Again, the appearance of a suspect deprived of liberty shall not be procured, if this were to involve serious difficulties: art. 318 CCP.

[211]   The general evidentiary motions are regulated in art. 315 CCP (preliminary investigation) and art. 170 § 1 CCP (trial).

will happen are limited, suspects are often reluctant to spend money on expert opinions. Of course, this is even more relevant when the suspect is indigent.

2.4.2. The right to adequate time and facilities for the preparation of the defence

Summons and notifications

The general rule is that the suspect and his defence lawyer, who are authorised to participate in a procedural action, should be notified of the time and place thereof.[212]

If the authorised person fails to appear, such action shall not be carried out if there is no evidence that he has been (duly) notified, or if there is good reason to suppose that the failure to appear was due to a natural disaster or other extraordinary circumstances, or if the person properly explained the failure to appear and requested that no procedural action be taken in his absence.[213]

The time limit in which such notifications should be sent out is not specified and is therefore, in many cases, left to the discretion of the authorities. In a few cases, the legislator has been more specific. For example, it is expressly provided that at least seven days should elapse between the service of notice of the first instance hearing and the day on which this hearing is to be held.[214] Of course, the defence can ask the court for an adjournment, if it feels that more time is required to prepare the case. Whether such a request will be granted is up to the presiding judge.

With respect to some procedural actions, it is expressly stated in the CCP that the authorities are not obliged to wait for the defence lawyer to appear. For example, with respect to the right of the suspect to be interrogated in the presence of his defence lawyer, the absence of the lawyer 'shall not prevent the examination from being conducted'.[215]

In (at least) one instance, it is expressly stated that the authorities are not obliged to inform the defence lawyer. This relates to the (first) hearing on the application of pre-trial detention, where the defence lawyer should be admitted if he appears, but there is no obligation to notify him of the hearing.[216] Since the prosecutor is always informed of this hearing, this regulation creates (unnecessary) inequality between prosecution and defence. Although it is beyond doubt that

---

[212]   Unless otherwise provided by law: art. 117 § 1 CCP. Examples of procedural actions in which the defence has a right to participate can be found in art. 315-318 CCP, concerning investigatory actions carried out during the pre-trial investigation.

[213]   Unless otherwise provided by law: art. 117 § 2 CCP.

[214]   If this time limit is not observed, the hearing shall be adjourned on the motion of the defendant or his defence lawyer, filed before the commencement of judicial proceedings: art. 353 CCP.

[215]   Art. 301 CCP. According to some lawyers, it is common practice that the authorities will not wait for the arrival of the defence lawyer and will start the interrogation in his absence: information provided by practising defence lawyer from Poznań, August 2009.

[216]   Such an obligation only exists when the suspects requests this and notification does not render the action difficult: art. 249 § 3 CCP.

hearings on the application of pre-trial detention are bound by strict time limits, in most cases it should be possible to call the defence lawyer and inform him of the hearing.

Limited access to the case file

As noted above the lack of access to the case file is considered to be one of the most important obstacles for effective defence during the pre-trial investigation.[217]

With respect to examination of the case file at the end of the investigation, it is provided in the CCP that the authorities should set an 'appropriate time' for the defence to inspect the material.[218] This should be in accordance with the importance and the complexity of the case, and there should be at least seven days between the date of service of the notice to the suspect and his defence lawyer and the date of inspection.[219]

2.4.3. The right to equality of arms in examining witnesses

Right to secure the attendance of the witness

The suspect/defendant and his defence lawyer have the right to file evidentiary motions (including calling and hearing certain witnesses) during all phases of the proceedings.[220] During pre-trial investigations, such a request has to be filed with the police or the prosecutor, and during the trial with the trial judge. As noted earlier, all evidentiary motions are decided on the basis of a general provision in the CCP containing five grounds for refusal which are exhaustive but also quite broad.[221]

As a rule, during the pre-trial investigation, witnesses will be heard by the police or the prosecutor. However, in certain circumstances it is also possible for the defence to request that a witness is heard by the court during the preliminary investigation.[222]

There is no possibility to file an (interlocutory) appeal when a request to call (and hear) a certain witness is denied. Nevertheless, the defence may submit the same evidentiary motion for a second time, if the first one was dismissed.[223] It is also possible to invoke the refusal to conduct certain investigatory actions as a ground

---

[217]   See § 2.1.2.

[218]   Art. 321 § 2.

[219]   Art. 321 § 1 and 2 CCP. According to the Supreme Court, when setting a date, the authorities should at least take into account 'the size of the evidential material, its legibility and the individual perceptual abilities of the suspect'. Decision of the Supreme Court (SN) 22 September 1995 (I KZP 31/95 OSNKW 1995/11-12).

[220]   See § 2.4.1.

[221]   Art. 170 § 1 sub 1-5. The third ground, in particular, is broad. It states that a request may be denied when the evidence would be irrelevant to the establishment of the fact in question.

[222]   See § 2.4.1.

[223]   Art. 170 § 4 CCP.

for appeal with the court of second instance.[224] In practice, the defence often relies on this ground.

As noted above, immediacy is a leading principle of Polish criminal procedure, but there are important exceptions to this that make it possible for the court to use as evidence records of statements made during the pre-trial investigation.[225] It follows from the case law of the ECtHR that denying the request of the defence to hear the witness at the trial, and the subsequent use of the witness testimony given at the pre-trial stage, might result in a breach of the rights of the defence as specified in article 6 ECHR.[226]

Right to examine the witness

During the pre-trial investigation, the suspect and his defence lawyer have the right to be present at the interrogation of a witness being heard at their request.[227] However, the presence of the suspect who is deprived of his liberty may be denied if his attendance would cause 'serious difficulties'.[228] When the witness is not heard at the motion of the defence, the suspect or his defence lawyer may file a request to be present at the hearing, but such a request can be denied if the interests of the investigation so require.[229] In all cases, the presence of the defence implies that active participation (for example, asking questions, making remarks) is allowed.

During the trial, the right of the defence to examine witnesses is, as a rule, absolute. As noted earlier, the order in which persons are examined at trial is such that the suspect and his defence lawyer have the right to ask questions before the judge(s).[230] The right to examine a witness face to face at trial may, however, be limited when it concerns an anonymous witness. In that situation, examination will have to be carried out under such conditions as to prevent disclosure of the witness identity.[231]

2.4.4. The right to free interpretation of documents and to translation

Interpretation

The right to an interpreter is regulated in the CCP. According to the relevant provision, which was introduced into the code in 2003, the suspect/defendant has the right to be assisted by an interpreter free of charge 'when he does not have

---

[224] A mistake of fact may justify quashing the first instance judgement, if it could have influence on the outcome of the case: art. 438 point 3 CCP.
[225] See § 1.3.2.
[226] See ECtHR 4 November 2008, *Demski v. Poland*, No. 22695/03. Currently, there are also two cases pending against Poland with regard to this matter: *Jakubczyk v. Poland*, No. 17354/04 and *Chmura v. Poland*, No. 18475/05.
[227] Art. 315 § 2 CCP.
[228] Art. 318 § 2 CCP.
[229] Art. 317 § 2 CCP.
[230] See § 2.4.1.
[231] Art. 184 CCP.

sufficient command of the Polish language'.[232] The need for an interpreter is assessed by the police or the prosecutor during the pre-trial stage, and by the court at the trial stage. The interpreter should be appointed by the authorities: it is not possible for the defendant to bring his own interpreter.[233]

The interpreter should be called in 'for the actions in which the defendant participates', including consultations between the defendant and his lawyer.[234] In practice, according to practising interpreters, courts and prosecutors are quite diligent in this matter: the procedure of calling in an interpreter is followed automatically in every case in which the person (the defendant, a witness) is a foreigner, or a person of foreign origin.[235] Because the procedure is so automatic, it often happens that an interpreter is also called in when the person is a foreigner with a residence permit in Poland and speaks Polish quite fluently.[236]

The costs of the interpretation are born by the State Treasury. If the right to interpretation is breached, it could be invoked during appeal as a procedural shortcoming that had an influence on the outcome of the case.[237]

Translation of documents

According to the provision on the right to interpretation, the suspect/defendant should obtain a translation of the most important decisions. The accused has the right to translated copies of the charge(s), any amendments of the charge(s), the indictment and the final judgement.[238] In practice, other documents are also translated – those deemed important to the course of the proceedings (such as, for example, the notice of the hearing at which the court will decide on the application of preliminary detention). According to the personal experience of some translators, sometimes literally everything is translated, even including trivial letters.

Again, the necessity of translation is determined by the organ that is conducting the procedural act (police, prosecutor or court). The costs of translation are born by the State Treasury. If the right to translation is breached, it could be

---

232 Art. 72 CCP.
233 In practice, whenever a translator is needed, a secretary in the court/prosecutor's office takes the register of sworn translators in the given language and makes phone calls to see which translator is available on the given date. Some courts have established close relations with some interpreters, whom they believe to be better than others, and call them more often.
234 Kruszyński 2007, p. 193. See Grzegorczyk 2004, p. 262.
235 Information on practice incorporated in this paragraph was kindly provided by J. Miler-Cassino and Z. Rybińska (sworn translators practicing in Warsaw), in cooperation with D. Kierzkowska (president of the Polish Society of Sworn and Specialized Translators, TEPIS), October 2009.
236 In this case, the interpreter will just sit in the court, in case his/her assistance might be required, while the foreigner speaks directly to the court. It seems that this practice of automatic appointment also provides some sort of safeguard for the judge, to prevent the possibility that the final ruling may be challenged on formal grounds, for example, by claiming miscommunication due to absence of an interpreter, or that the defendant did not have access to an interpreter and his/her rights were therefore violated.
237 This ground for appeal is specified in art. 438 CCP.
238 Art. 72 § 3 CCP. Kruszyński 2007, p. 193.

invoked during appeal as a procedural shortcoming that had an influence on the outcome of the case.[239]

Competence and independence of interpreters and translators

The legal and professional status of sworn translators in Poland is regulated in legislation of 25 November 2004 (*Ustawa o zawodzie tłumacza przysięgłego*). Under this new act, only persons who pass a specialist examination before the so-called State Examination Commission will be authorized to practise this profession.[240]

Before a person is allowed to pursue this profession, it will be necessary for him to take an oath and be entered into the register of sworn translators. The register is kept by the Minister of Justice and is published annually in the official gazette of the Ministry of Justice. According to the new act, the translator has no right to refuse a request on the part of the court, prosecutor, police or a public administration body, to interpret or translate, unless 'particularly important' reasons arise. Moreover, the translator must justify any such refusal.

The activities of sworn translators are subject to control by *voivodes* (Polish regions). Any allegations of default or inappropriate fulfilment of the translator's duties shall be examined by the so called Professional Accountability Commission.[241] The variety of penalties available under the act to discipline translators and interpreters include: admonition, reprimand, suspension of the right to practise the profession and, ultimately, termination of such right. The rates of remuneration are fixed by the Minister of Justice and apply only to translations commissioned by the court, prosecutors, the police and public administration bodies.[242]

There is a general opinion among sworn translators that the rates of remuneration are inadequate.[243] They are much lower than the rates for 'commercial' translation. As a result, many sworn translators prefer to work for companies or natural persons, and some even avoid assignments from criminal justice authorities. This may influence the availability of interpretation and translation.

---

[239] This ground for appeal is specified in art. 438 CCP.
[240] The State Examination Commission is appointed by the Minister of Justice. Its members compromise four persons designated by the Minister of National Education, three by the Minister of Justice, one by the Minister of Labour and three by translators' organisations.
[241] There is quite a comprehensive Code of Ethics prepared by the independent association of court and specialized translators (TEPIS, <www.tepis.org.pl>) in cooperation with the Polish Ministry of Justice.
[242] The information mentioned under the heading 'Competence and independence of interpreters and translators' is taken from: <www.agisproject.com/>.
[243] The rates are fixed, based on a per page amount (1125 characters). For example, the rate per page of sworn translation from English into Polish is approximately 5.5 Euro (PLN 23), and the rate per page from Polish into English is approximately 7 Euro (PLN 30). The rates for every commenced hour of interpreting are the rates as for translation increased by 30%. Recently, the Minister of Justice prepared amendments to the legal framework concerning the rates for translation but these changes have been adjourned due to the current financial crisis.

Pursuant to the CCP, rules concerning experts apply also to translators.[244] This means that a translator, like an expert, may be challenged for lack of impartiality.[245] The impartiality of an interpreter may be challenged by both parties (defence and prosecution). Complaints concerning the quality of interpretation should be addressed to the organ before which the proceedings are pending. The procedural organ is also able to replace the translator on the request of the parties to the proceedings. In practice, there could be concerns regarding impartiality on both sides: sworn translators may be considered partial by the defendant, since they are appointed by the authorities. On the other hand, it sometimes happens that there are concerns, or even suspicions, on the part of the authorities that a sworn translator (a foreign national and, at the same time, a Polish citizen) instructs a suspect of the same foreign nationality.

3. Professional culture of defence lawyers

3.1. Professional organisation

The legal profession in Poland is organised into two separate Bar associations: the Bar of *adwokats* (*adwokatura*) and the bar of legal advisors (*radca prawny*). Historically, legal advisors were mostly in-house company lawyers, but with the passing of time, their powers and possibilities have been extended to also providing legal assistance to private persons. However, in criminal cases, the role of the legal advisor is still rather limited: he can only represent a victim (civil party), or other party to the proceedings not being the defendant. During the pre-trial stage, the legal advisor might give legal advice to a suspect (at his request), but he cannot be appointed as a legal aid lawyer. Only in cases of petty/administrative offences (*wykroczenia*) is the legal advisor allowed to act as a defence lawyer.[246]

The Polish Bar is an independent and autonomous professional organisation[247] consisting of a national organisation (The Polish Bar Council: *Nazcelna Rada Adwokacka*) and local Bar associations. The governing bodies of the Bar are also independent and have the right to self-regulation. Nevertheless, there is some state administrative control, since the Minister of Justice has certain supervisory powers over the Bar.[248] Over the past few years, there has been a strong tendency to bring the Bar under closer supervision by the Government. This was particularly the case under the Government led by *Prawo i Sprawiedlowość* and led to strong opposition by the Bar.[249]

---

[244] Art. 204 § 3 CCP.

[245] See art. 196 CCP with reference to experts.

[246] Art. 24 § 1 Code of Procedure for Petty Offences (*Kodeks Postępowenia w sprawach o wykroczenia*).

[247] Art. 1 § 2 Law on the Bar: 'The Bar is organised as a self-governing body'.

[248] For example, the Minister of Justice has the right to veto a lawyer who has been nominated to enter the Bar and may request the Supreme Court to repeal resolutions of the Bar's governing bodies that are contrary to the law.

[249] In 2007, this situation – the continuing 'campaign' of the Polish Government to gain control over the bar and other legal professions – received international attention by the CCBE (Council of Bars and Law Societies of Europe) and IBAHRI (International Bar Association's

→

There is no specialist section or organisation for criminal defence lawyers. Historically, there is no strong tradition of specialisation among Polish lawyers, but this seems to be changing. All members of the Bar are permitted to act in criminal cases (although there are certain restrictions for trainee lawyers to act before courts). Because specialization is generally not taken into account when the judge appoints a lawyer to provide legal assistance free of charge, all members of the Bar may occasionally be involved in a criminal case.

According to the CCP only a person entitled to defend cases pursuant to the Law on the Bar may be engaged as a defence lawyer (*obrońca*).[250] According to the Law on the Bar, an individual may be entered on the list of advocates if he:

- is of unblemished character and by his conduct to date warrants that he shall properly practise the profession of an advocate;
- enjoys full public rights and has full capacity to enter into legal transactions;
- holds a degree in law in Poland, and has obtained a Masters degree in law, or has completed foreign law studies recognized in Poland; and
- completed his advocacy training in Poland and passed the advocates' final examination.[251]

In practice, at least until recently, it was not easy to become a member of the Polish Bar. The examination procedures were highly competitive. There was (and still is) a growing number of law graduates, but only a limited number of available traineeships at law offices. In this respect, the Polish Bar Association has faced substantial criticism over the last few years. One widely criticised aspect of the legal profession concerned the examination and admission of new members: examination procedures were not transparent and there were frequent allegations of nepotism. Furthermore, the Bar has been accused of deliberately keeping the number of its members as low as possible, in order to control competition.

Eventually, as a result of growing political pressure and a judgement by the Constitutional Court, the Law on the Bar was changed in 2005 to introduce a more uniform admission procedure, also weakening the discretionary power of the Bar to deny access to the profession. Recently, there has been another substantial amendment to the Law on the Bar following several judgements of the Constitutional Tribunal. As a result of these latest changes, the power of the

---

Human Rights Institute). These organisations published a report in which the attitude of the Polish Government and the legislative amendments resulting from it, were severely criticised as constituting a threat to the rule of law in the Polish justice system: Justice under Siege: a report on the rule of law in Poland – An International Bar Association Human Rights Institute/Council of Bars and Law Societies of Europe Report, November 2007, available at: <www.ccbe.eu/fileadmin/user_upload/NTCdocument/11_2007_Nov06_Report1_119434486 0.pdf>.

250   Art. 82 CCP.
251   Art. 65 Law on the Bar.

Minister of Justice in the admission procedure, and the possibilities to enter the Bar without prior completion of the advocates' training, have *inter alia* been changed.[252]

It is still difficult to determine whether the situation is (considered to be) different under the new examination procedures. However, it should be noted that the number of advocates seems to be growing. Currently, there are 9,236 *adwokats* in Poland, of which 7,260 are in active practice.[253] This means that a substantial number (1,976) does not practice at the moment, perhaps, for example, due to age, or other professional activities. Those who do practice mainly do so either in individual offices (*kancelaria indywidualna*) (6,453) and in a group office (*zespoły adwokackie*) (168). The remainder (639) work as lawyers in companies.

The role of the Bar organisation in criminal proceedings is mainly twofold. First, it plays a rather limited role in the provision of free legal assistance: the regional Bar associations have the responsibility to provide the courts with lists of lawyers who can be appointed in legal aid cases. Secondly, the Bar should supervise the quality of legal assistance provided by its members and, more specifically, consider any disciplinary complaints filed against them.

3.2. *Professional ethics*

3.2.1. Organisation of the disciplinary procedures

The Polish Bar association has exclusive responsibility in disciplining its members. Disciplinary courts exist at two levels: within the chambers of the Bar association (*sąd dyscyplinarny izby adwokackiej*) and at a national level (Higher Disciplinary Court: *Wyższy Sąd Dyscyplinarny*). Both courts are solely comprised of lawyers.[254]

Professional disciplinary proceedings are governed by the Law on the Bar. Cases are brought to the disciplinary court by a disciplinary prosecutor (*rzecznik dyscyplinarny*, a member of the bar). Complaints against advocates may be brought by dissatisfied clients, and also by procedural organs (the court or the prosecutor), when they are of the opinion that a defence lawyer has shirked his duties during the pre-trial investigation, or during the trial stage.[255] In addition, the Minister of Justice may order that disciplinary proceedings are brought by the disciplinary prosecutor.[256] The following disciplinary penalties exist: admonition, reprimand,

---

[252]   Law of 20 February 2009, published in the Journal of Laws *(Dziennik Ustaw)* of 2009, No. 37, poz. 286.

[253]   Data available for 31 December 2008. To compare: in the years between 1995 and 2004, the total number of members fluctuated between 7,277 and 7,795 (active members: between 4,409 and 5,733).

[254]   A regular cassation appeal may be filed against a disciplinary decision taken by the Higher Disciplinary Court at second instance. This cassation appeal is – as in ordinary court proceedings – dealt with by the Supreme Court.

[255]   Art. 20 § 1 CCP. Also, since an amendment of the CCP of 2007, there is a possibility for the court to impose a fine (of up to approximately 2,700 Euro/PLN 10,000) on a defence lawyer who, without justification, does not show up at the trial, or leaves early without the permission of the judge. This sanction is specified in art. 285 § 1a CCP.

[256]   In such a case, the Minister of Justice has the status of a party to the proceedings.

fine, suspension from practise (from three months to five years), or expulsion from the Bar.

There is only limited statistical data available on how the complaint mechanism works in practice. There is no centralised registration system of the amount of complaints that the organs of the Bar receive every year, and in how many cases this leads to an official investigation and/or procedure.[257]

The efficiency of the disciplinary proceedings has been severely criticised over the last few years. For example, the bar has been accused of using delaying tactics and of not responding to complaints.[258] One of the results of this criticism is that, in 2007, the CCP was amended to introduce the possibility for the judge to impose a fine of approximately 2,700 Euro (PLN 10.000) when the Dean of the Bar does not respond to a complaint within 30 days.[259]

3.2.2. Rules of professional ethics

The obligations of (defence) lawyers towards their clients are primarily described in, and regulated by three regulations:

- the Law on the Bar of 1982;
- the lawyer's Code of Conduct of 1998; and
- the Code of Criminal Procedure of 1997.

The rules contained in the Code of Conduct are of a rather general nature. It is a characteristic of the Polish rules of professional ethics that there are many references to 'the dignity of the profession', and similar vague concepts relating to the honour of the profession of lawyer, such as reliability and conscientiousness. There is also a heavy emphasis on lawyers' independence from their clients. Furthermore, there are no specific rules for acting as a defence lawyer in criminal cases.[260]

Since the post-communist changes in criminal procedure constitute new challenges for defence lawyers, the creation of specific professional rules for acting

[257] The only source available in this respect is the publication provided by the bar every four years (*Sprawozdania Organów Adwokatury*). This document contains only a limited amount of information.
[258] 'All responsibility lies with professional bodies, which have been widely criticized as not fulfilling this task properly. The state, though legally capable of doing so, does not use its power in this respect. (...) The Helsinki Foundation for Human Rights often receives complaints after the complaint [about different kinds of attorney conduct, with most clients complaining about *ex officio* lawyers] was lodged with the disciplinary board but then was insufficiently explained or even ignored, the applicant believes; in some instances the complaint receives no answer at all. As follows from the experiences of the HFHR the quality of legal services and the oversight of the profession constitute a subject that hardly enjoys any interest at all. No surveys are conducted in this area. The professional corporation may settle disciplinary cases at their absolute discretion, which sometimes leads to overlooking the unprofessional conduct of the lawyers': Bojarski 2003a, p. 123.
[259] Art. 20 § 2 CCP, as amended in 2007.
[260] The only rule in the Code of Conduct that is limited to legal assistance in criminal cases is art. 29, in which it is stated that 'during visits to incarcerated persons, an advocate should endeavour to maintain the solemnity and dignity of the profession'.

as a defence lawyer, and the formulation of explicit criteria for realizing an effective defence, is recommended.

The CCP contains several provisions that describe the obligations of the defence lawyer towards his client. By far the most important provision in this respect is the rule stating that the defence lawyer may act in the proceedings only in the furtherance of the interests of the accused.[261]

3.3. Perception of defence lawyers and their relationship with other legal professions

3.3.1. General comments

Although it is difficult to make statements in general on the profession of *adwokat* – obviously lawyers are all individuals with their own professional qualities and personal characteristics – it could be said that, traditionally, the profession is of a rather elitist and conservative nature. In particular, the older members of the Bar consider it to be an *officium nobile* requiring certain qualities that not all lawyers possess. As noted above, at least until 2005, the examination procedures for entering the Bar were highly competitive.

The dignity of the profession is a central theme in the regulation of professional ethics and the Law on the Bar. The profession is considered to be the most prestigious and (financially) lucrative of the legal professions, and therefore the most popular career choice among young law graduates. However, many new *adwokats* prefer to work in fields such as commercial and business law: criminal law is – particularly from a financial point of view – not the most attractive field of work.

3.3.2. Quality (assurance) of free and retained legal assistance

As noted earlier, the provision of legal assistance in criminal cases is not limited to qualified (specialized) criminal defence lawyers. Since there are many differences between individual lawyers, it is difficult to formulate general opinions. However, there are indications that the quality of legal assistance provided in appointed cases is lower than in retained cases.[262]

There are probably many different reasons for the (presumably) low(er) level of quality of legal services in appointed cases. One is that these cases are appointed to all members of the Bar, irrespective of their field of expertise and/or availability.

---

[261] Art. 86 § 1 CCP. According to the HFHR, there is a need for specific and concrete rules describing the professional obligations of defence lawyers providing legal assistance free of charge 'It seems that it would be sensible to develop more detailed standards of *ex officio* legal aid: the list of duties of a lawyer hired by the State for an indigent person. The existing principles of professional ethics are too general and refer to reliability, conscientiousness, but not, for example, directly to the duty to contact the client before the trial, or the duty to keep case files for each client.(...) The Polish state "hires" an *ex officio* lawyer, pays him or her remuneration and does not control the quality of service in any way': Bojarski 2003a, p. 129.

[262] § 2.2.2.

Many lawyers feel burdened by the duty to act in appointed cases dealing with legal matters with which they are not (very) familiar. Sometimes, lawyers even 'sell off' their legal aid cases to a more qualified colleague.[263]

Also important is the lack of an effective mechanism for quality control or assurance. As pointed out by Bojarski in the Monitoring Report of the HFHR, there are no studies or data related to the quality of legal aid, nor is there a system of evaluation of the legal aid system. Furthermore, there are no special mechanisms to determine the quality of legal representation in appointed cases and there is no system of quality control. All responsibility (for disciplinary procedures) lies with professional bodies, which have been criticized over the last few years for being ineffective.[264]

3.3.3. Perceptions on the role of the defence lawyer

The political transition of 1989 has not resulted in any fundamental changes in the (academic) perceptions on the role of the defence lawyer.[265] The main reason for this is that the perception of the role of the defence lawyer was not considerably affected by the communist regime: pre-1989 Polish literature on the subject is not fundamentally different from contemporary legal writing.

Under the communist rule, criminal law was mainly regarded as a political instrument: a useful tool to fight the enemies of the communist regime and, thus, to help achieve the government's objectives. Obviously, this idea of criminal law and criminal procedure made the defence lawyer's task to defend the personal interests of his client very difficult. The complexity of this matter can be illustrated on the basis of Soviet literature, in which the role of the defence lawyer, and the limits of this role in the criminal process, was discussed extensively.[266] Although there was much debate about these matters, the prevailing opinion in Soviet literature was

---

[263]   During the 'Legal Aid Forum' held in June 2002 in the context of the Access to Justice project, mention of this practice was made by a lawyer from Poznań: 'I have been specializing in civil law, including commercial law, for 30 years and my experience will obviously influence the nature of my speech. [...] My biggest concern is caused by the fact that the majority of *ex officio* cases relate to criminal law. Every time, a new *ex officio* case is received, and in my case there are several every month, I have a huge dilemma since I am not a specialist in criminal law. I cannot responsibly take such a case since, as I have mentioned, for 30 years I have been specializing in civil law. Therefore, I look for one of my colleagues who would like to replace me in this duty, I enter into an agreement, of course against payment, and pay for the service; every year, this amounts to about 15 thousand PLN – these are expenses I incur for my substitution for *ex officio* cases, I receive a reimbursement from substitution of 2-3 thousand per year, the rest is my cost': Bojarski 2003a, p. 85-86.

[264]   Bojarski 2003a, p. 123. See § 3.2.1.

[265]   'There has been little change in the perceived role of the defence lawyer in criminal proceedings in Poland since the decline of Communism, either in theory or in practice': Kruszyński 2007, p. 199.

[266]   Important questions were *inter alia*: is the defence lawyer allowed to continue his activities when he is convinced that his client is guilty?; are there circumstances in which the defence lawyer is obliged to actively contribute to the conviction of his client?; are there exceptions to the rule of professional privilege when the disclosure of confidential information is in the public interest?

that defence lawyer's public duty superseded his responsibility as (a partial) defender of the personal interests of his clients. A closer look at Polish legal literature on the subject shows that the public duty of the defence lawyer was propagated not nearly as strongly as was the case in the Soviet Union. The most drastic opinion in this respect – the idea of the defence lawyer as an assistant to the court (*pomocnik sądu*) – was expressed only by a limited number of authors during the early years of Polish communism.[267]

Another perception is that, generally, the Polish defence lawyer is considered to be *dominus litis*. As noted earlier, he may only conduct actions that are in the client's interest. Since the lawyer has a responsibility in this respect, it is up to him to assess whether a certain defence strategy is in the interest of the client: in exceptional circumstances this could even be an action of which the client does not approve. Although, obviously, such situations should be avoided as much as possible (given the mutual trust that should exist between lawyer and client), it is not forbidden for the Polish defence lawyer to act against the will of his client: the general opinion in Polish legal literature is that such a defence is allowed.[268] This view is a remarkable feature of Polish criminal defence ethics, which is at variance with the professional rules of other countries, where the will of the client is paramount.

Generally, the 'public view' of defence lawyers seems to have changed over the last few decades. There is much criticism of the functioning of lawyers expressed by the media, by politicians and by the public. According to some defence lawyers, this was different during communism, when the profession was well respected for its devotion to the protection of human rights.[269]

With respect to the defence lawyer's relationships with other actors in the criminal process, it should be noted that some defence lawyers seem to be reluctant to act 'against' the prosecutor during the pre-trial investigation. The prosecutor is considered to be the 'master' of the proceedings, and to act against his will could damage the case for the defence. Some defence lawyers raise this as one of the (formal/strategic) reasons for their passivity during the pre-trial investigation.[270]

In the Polish criminal justice system, there are many young professional judges active at the lower courts. Some members of the bar are of the opinion that young judges are (too) easily convinced and/or influenced by the prosecution. In addition, some defence lawyers criticise the fact that members of the prosecution and the judiciary are already in the courtroom when the defence enters, and that they stay in the courtroom in between sessions. According to some lawyers, this could give the impression to their client that his case is being discussed in the

---

[267]   The most important is L. Schaff. See: Schaff 1953.

[268]   See for example Kruszyński: '(...) the defence lawyer must act independently in determining the defence strategy; they must act in such a way that their participation in the proceedings does not prevent the accused from acting independently and vice versa. However, the defence lawyer may take actions which are contrary to their clients will, provided that they are to the clients benefit': Kruszyński 2007, p. 200. This point of view is shared by several other authors such as T. Grzegorczyk, S. Waltoś and H. Gajewska-Kraczkowska: see Grzegorczyk 1988, p. 31, Waltoś 2002b, p. 303 and Gajewska-Kraczkowska 1992, p. 1138-1139.

[269]   Interview with defence lawyers conducted within the framework of Phd (see footnote 121).

[270]   Ibidem.

absence of the defence.[271] Whether this assumption is realistic or not, the fact is that this practice may reflect – or at least give the impression of – a legal culture in which the prosecution is favoured compared to the defence.

4. Political commitment to effective criminal defence

4.1. Public perception of crime

It is undisputed that criminality in Poland has changed both in quantitative and qualitative terms since the breakdown of communism. For example, several categories of crime that were relatively unknown under communism – such as drug related offences – have become increasingly common during the last decade. Furthermore, organised and financial crime flourished during the transitional period.[272] As a result, over the last few years, combating crime has become one of the main topics in national politics and has received an increasing amount of media attention. As noted earlier, the Polish public is generally believed to be rather punitive.[273] However, given the effect that the political and media attention may have on society, it is disputed whether the public perceptions and fear of crime are genuinely realistic.[274]

According to a survey conducted by a European consortium among inhabitants of the European Union, about their experiences with crime and law enforcement, it seems that the Polish population is very afraid of crime.[275] However, it is interesting that this high level of fear of crime does not correlate with the actual victimisation rate: the survey also illustrates that Poland shows a clear and consistent downward trend in the level of common crime since 1990. From a European perspective, Poland has turned from a high crime into a medium crime country. For example, rates of burglaries, robberies and pick-pocketing have decreased significantly over the last few years. There also seems to be a remarkable decrease in sexual crime compared to previous years. Levels of consumer fraud and bribery of officials (corruption), however, are relatively high in Poland. The level of drug related crime is extensive, which seems to correlate with the significant level of fear of crime. Although feelings of unsafety are still widespread, there seems to be a downward trend moving towards the European average. According to the survey, the Polish population is very critical of the performance of the Police in controlling crime.[276]

---

[271] Ibidem.
[272] Krajewski 2004, p. 379. On the emergence of business crime in post communist Poland; see Bojarski & van Dijck 2007, p. 257-282.
[273] Krajewski 2004, p. 392. In this article, reference is made to several sociological writings – dating already from the 1960s – supporting this claim (p. 392-395).
[274] See, for example, the 'moral panic' disseminated by the Polish media on the magnitude of Poland's drug problems: Krajewski 2003, p. 279.
[275] According to the survey, Poland is one of the two European Countries with the greatest fear of crime. See van Dijk et al. 2005.
[276] For the results mentioned above; see van Dijk et al. 2005.

It is important to note that the results of the 2005 survey are partly undermined by the results of a more recent study published by the Institute of Justice. First of all, this study shows that since 2004 the general level of fear of crime has decreased and the trust in the police has significantly increased.[277] Furthermore, according to the autumn 2008 Eurobarometer,[278] Poles do not consider crime as one of the most important issues facing the country. Compared to other European countries, crime is cited much less often by Polish citizens when asked about the most important national problems. The main problems mentioned instead are of a financial/economic nature.[279]

4.2. Changes in criminal policy

Since the breakdown of communism, Polish criminal policy has undergone several phases. In a nutshell, two main phases can be distinguished: first, the years until the entering into force of the new criminal codes (1997) and secondly, the period since then. Until 1997, Polish criminal law politics were mainly liberal and dominated by experts who were able to convince the various political coalitions that it was necessary to strengthen the legal protection of suspects/defendants in criminal procedure. Soon after the criminal codes of 1997 entered into force, it was found that, due to *inter alia* the rise in crime and increasing caseloads, a newly established balance between legal protection and effective criminal control had to be adapted.[280] Several more recent developments in criminal procedure aimed at an acceleration of the criminal process – most of them introduced through a large scale amendment of the CCP in 2003 – can be explained on the basis of this new trend. These include:

- an increase in the number of exceptions to the principle of immediacy – for example, the use of witness statements made before trial;
- an increase in the categories of cases in which the trial hearing may be conducted in the absence of the accused;
- a broadening of the possibilities for alternative settlement procedures (*porozumienia karnoprocesowe*); and
- the introduction of anonymous witnesses (*świadek anonimowy*) and 'crown witnesses' (*świadek koronny*) to combat organised crime.

The rise of the phenomenon of 'abuse of procedural rights by the defence' (*nadużycia prawa do obrony*) might also be considered typical of this increased focus on efficiency in Polish criminal politics. Until recently, this was a relatively

---

[277]   Siemaszko et al. 2009, p. 243-244.
[278]   Eurobarometer is a series of surveys regularly performed on behalf of the European Commission. Each survey consists of approximately 1,000 interviews per Member State. The results of these interviews are incorporated in reports on public opinion of certain issues relating to the European Union.
[279]   Over 40% of the population consider the healthcare system as one of the two most important problems facing their country. In second place, respondents cite rising prices/inflation (36%).
[280]   Krajewski 2004, p. 401-402.

unknown phenomenon in Polish legislation, legal literature and case law. Over the past few years, several amendments have been made to criminal procedure law with the aim of preventing abuse of procedural rights. An example is the introduction of a provision stating that an evidentiary motion (of the defence) shall be denied when it aims – in an obvious manner – to slow down the proceedings.[281]

The developments mentioned above show that, during the past few years, the focus of the legislator has shifted more towards the instrumentalist function of criminal law – efficient crime fighting. *Prawo i Sprawiedlowość*, the former political party of the current president of the Polish Republic, known for its rather repressive criminal law policy, has had a substantial influence over the last few years. This has decreased considerably since October 2007, when the liberal Civic Platform (*Platforma Obywatelska*) became the leading party in Polish politics. It is important to note that, since the breakdown of communism, there have been 18 different Ministers of Justice, which illustrates a lack of stability in this area of national politics.

Of course, it cannot be said that a greater focus on efficiency in the criminal process will automatically have adverse implications for the defendant and his right to defence. Generally, dealing with a criminal case in an efficient manner and within a reasonable time will also be in the interest of the defendant. Whether specific efficiency mechanisms may interfere with the rights of the defendant will obviously depend on the way they are carried out in practice. An important example in this respect may be found in the 'speedy' proceedings (*postępowanie przyspieszone*) introduced in 2007, which are widely criticised for their adverse effects on defence rights.[282]

5.   Conclusions

Over the last two decades, the Polish criminal justice system has undergone many changes. Under communist rule, the possibilities to effectively exercise defence rights were severely limited in several respects. These limitations were not only the result of shortcomings in procedural rights and privileges afforded to the defence, but were also interrelated with the organisation of criminal proceedings and the imbalance in the distribution of powers between the prosecution and the judiciary.

With the entering into force of the current CCP, many new procedural safeguards were introduced that improved the ability of suspects/defendants to conduct an effective defence in criminal procedure. Examples of new provisions improving the legal protection of suspects are *inter alia*: the explicit right to contact and consult a lawyer after arrest, to be informed on certain procedural rights before questioning and to have a lawyer present during questioning.[283] Although there is hardly any recent statistical data or empirical research on the participation and/or performance of Polish defence lawyers in contemporary criminal proceedings, it is

---

[281]   Art. 170 § 1 under 5 CCP.
[282]   See § 1.3.4.
[283]   Arts. 245, 300 and 301 CCP.

clear that, in practice, certain difficulties still remain. The most important points of concern identified in this report are the following:

- *Legal assistance free of charge.* Until now, post-communist legal reforms have not (substantially) affected the Polish legal aid system in criminal cases. The system shows many deficiencies, such as the lack of clear criteria for awarding legal aid (there is no clear means test nor a clear merits test), the too great discretionary power for the judge deciding on legal aid, the lack of a separate budget for legal aid and the lack of reliable statistical information to evaluate the functioning of the legal aid system. In addition, it is not guaranteed that free legal assistance is available at an early stage of the proceedings (immediately after arrest).284 Furthermore, the obligation to have legal assistance in the proceedings before the Supreme Court, and the fact that, in practice, legal aid lawyers can – quite easily – refuse to prepare and file a cassation appeal, may deprive indigent defendants of their right to have their case examined by the Supreme Court. Finally, the lack of an effective mechanism for quality control or assurance is important. There is no available data related to the quality of legal aid and no adequate system of evaluation of the legal aid system. These problems seriously affect the possibility of indigent suspects/defendants to realize an effective defence and they therefore require immediate attention and change.
- *Lack of information.* Realizing an effective defence is only possible when the suspect is well informed of his rights. The suspect, as well as his defence lawyer should, as early as possible, have access to the relevant material in the case file. In both of these areas, Polish criminal procedure shows deficiencies. Although the suspect is informed of certain important procedural rights (letter of rights), there is no legal obligation on the authorities to inform the suspect of how he can enforce these rights (for example, the letter of rights mentions the right to legal assistance, but not the right to have a lawyer appointed free of charge). Also important is the fact that suspected persons are not informed of the right to silence. It is true that they may not be interrogated in the capacity of a suspect and that their statements may not be used as evidence in court, but if a suspected person chooses to make a statement it could, obviously, limit his possibilities to choose a defence strategy later on in the proceedings. Finally, (limited) access to the case file is one of the most important limitations facing the defence in the pre-trial investigation. Before trial, inspection of the case file requires the permission of the prosecutor, who has a wide discretionary power in this respect. At least until recently, it quite often happened that the defence would be denied access to the case file during much of the pre-trial investigation. The Constitutional Court declared the relevant provision of the CCP unconstitutional and, as a result, it was amended in August

---

284 This is an aspect of the Polish legal aid system that has been criticised by the CPT: see reference in footnote 122.

2009. Although this amendment has only been in force for one month, and there is no large scale information as yet available as to its practical consequences, according to some lawyers, access to the case file during the pre-trial investigation remains limited.285

- *Confidentiality.* After arrest and during the first 14 days of pre-trial detention, communication between the lawyer and the client can be supervised. There is relatively little concern about this lack of confidentiality among members of the bar. This is mainly because the supervision is not carried out on a large scale and it is not considered problematic to postpone the first in-depth consultation with the client until after the first 14 days have passed. Nevertheless, from the point of view of effective criminal defence, as a matter of principle it is important that, in practice, the supervision is carried out within the hearing of the authorities and during a vital stage of the proceedings. As a rule, during these first 14 days of detention, the most important interrogations will take place. Therefore, private consultation is essential for realizing an effective defence.
- *Legal culture.* Although there is no recent empirical data available on this subject, there are indications that the opinion (still) prevails within the bar that remaining passive during the pre-trial investigation is often considered the best defence strategy. Obviously, this has a significant impact on the implementation of defence rights and, as a result, the new improved legal options open to the defence during the pre-trial investigation remain largely theoretical. This requires further empirical research, not only in relation to the actual performance/activities of defence lawyers in the pre-trial investigation, but also into the question whether, and if so, to what extent, this passive attitude actually has consequences for the effectiveness of the defence. It is also important to note that, over the last decade, there has been little development in professional ethics. Despite changes in criminal procedure and new procedural options open to the defence, there are (still) no specific rules in relation to acting as a defence lawyer and for providing an effective defence in criminal cases.

6.   Bibliography

Books

De Vocht 2009
De Vocht, D., *Defence in Transition. Legal Assistance in Criminal Cases in post-Communist Poland* (Verdediging in transitie. Rechtsbijstand in strafzaken in postcommunistisch Polen), Nijmegen: Wolf Legal Publishers, 2009.

---

285   Information provided by practising defence lawyer from Poznań, August 2009.

Grzegorczyk 1988
Grzegorczyk, T., *The defence lawyer in pre-trial investigation* (Obrońca w postępowaniu przygotowawczym), Wydawnictwo Uniwersytetu Łódzkiego, 1988.

Grzegorcyzk 2004
Grzegorczyk, T., *Code of Criminal Procedure. Commentary* (Kodeks Postępowanie Karnego. Kommentarz Zakamycza), Krakow: Zakamycze, 2004.

Grzegorcyzk 2008
Grzegorczyk, T., *The Code of Criminal Procedure and the Law on the Crown Witness. Commentary* (Kodeks postępowania karnego oraz ustawa o świadku koronnym. Komentarz), Warsaw: Wolters Kluwer, 2008.

Gwirdoyń 2004
Gwirdoyń, P., *A compendium of criminalistic defence tactics* (Zarys kriminalistycznej taktyki obrony), Krakow: Zakamycze, 2004.

Izydorczyk 2002
Izydorczyk, J., *Application of pre-trial detention in practice* (Praktyka stosowania tymczasowego aresztowania), Łódź: Wydawnictwo Uniwersytetu Łódźkiego, 2002.

Klejnowska 2004
Klejnowska, M., *The suspect as a source of information on the criminal act* (Oskarżony jako osobowe źródło informacji o przestępstwie), Kraków: Zakamycze, 2004.

Kulesza 2005
Kulesza, C., *The effectivity of the participation of the defence lawyer in criminal procedure – in a comparative perspective* (Efektywność udziału obrońcy w procesie karnym – w perspektywie prawnoporównawczej), Kraków: Zakamycze, 2005.

Marguery 2008
Marguery, T.P., *Unity and Diversity of the Public Prosecution Services in Europe. A study of the Czech, Dutch, French and Polish systems*, dissertation University of Groningen, 2008.

Schaff 1953
Schaff, L., *Criminal Procedure in the Polish People's Republic – a Discussion of General Principles* (Proces Karny Polski Ludowej – Wyklad Zasad Ogólnych), Warsaw: Wydawnictwo Prawnicze, 1953.

Siemaszko et al. 2009
Siemaszko, A., Gruszczyńska, B. & Marczewski, M., *An atlas on crime in Poland (4)* (Atlas przestępczości w Polsce (4)), Warsaw: Oficyna Naukowa, 2009.

Waltoś 2002b
Waltoś, S., *Criminal Procedure – an Overview of the System* (Proces Karny – Zarys Systemu), Warsaw: Wydawnictwo Prawnicze, 2002.

Wąsek-Wiaderek 2000
Wąsek-Wiaderek, M., *The Principle of 'Equality of Arms' in Criminal Procedure under Article 6 of the European Convention of Human Rights and its Functions in Criminal Justice of Selected European Countries*, Leuven Law Series, Leuven: Leuven University Press, 2000.

Wąsek-Wiaderek 2003b
Wąsek-Wiaderek, M., *The principle of equality of arms in Polish criminal procedure from a comparative perspective* (Zasady równości stron w Polskim procesie karnym w perspektywie prawnoporównawczej), Krakow: Zakamycze, 2003.

Wiliński 2006
Wiliński, P., *The right to defence in Polish criminal procedure* (Zasada prawa do obrony w Polskim procesie karnym), Krakow: Zakamycze, 2006.

Chapters in Compilations

Izydorczyk 2008
Izydorczyk, J., 'Application of pre-trial detentention in the context of Habeas Corpus, the right to defence' ('Stosowanie tymczasowego arestowania w kontekście instytucji Habeas Corpus, prawo do obrony'), in: P. Wiliński et al. (ed.), *Stosowanie tymczasowego aresztowania w Polsce – analiza i rekomendacje*, Lublin: Rule of Law Foundation, 2008, p. 33-42.

Kruszyński 1998
Kruszyński, P., 'The right of the suspect to defence in the new code of criminal procedure' ('Prawo podejrzanego do obrony w nowym k.p.k.'), in: E. Skrętowicz (ed.), *Nowy kodeks postępowania karnego. Zagadnienia węzłowe*, Krakow: Zakamycze, 1998, p. 141-152.

Kruszyński 2007
Kruszyński, P., 'The Investigative Stage of the Criminal Process in Poland', in: E. Cape et al. (ed.), *Suspects in Europe – Procedural Rights at the Investigative Stage of the Criminal Process in the European Union*, Antwerp: Intersentia, 2007, p. 181-206.

Kulesza 2004
Kulesza, C., 'The defence lawyer in pre-trial investigation – several aspects' ('Obrońca w postępowaniu przygotowawczym – wybrane aspekty'), in: A. Marek (ed.), *Wspólczesne problemy procesu karnego i jego efektywności – księga pamiątkowa profesora Andrzeja Bulsiewicza*, Toruń: Tnoik, 2004, p. 201-215.

Lewandowski 2008

Lewandowski, Ł., 'The practice of applying pretrial detention in Poland' ('Praktyka stosowania instytucji tymczasowego aresztowania w Polsce') in: P. Wiliński, J. Izydorczyk, D.R. Swenson, D. Raczkiewicz, Ł. Lewandowski, M. Wasylczuk & M. Gilewicz, *Stosowanie tymczasowego aresztowania w Polsce. Analiza i rekomendacje*, Lublin (etc.), 2008, p. 61-64.

Murzynowski 2005

Murzynowski, A., 'Criminal Procedure', in: S. Frankowski (ed.), *Introduction to Polish Law*, The Hague: Kluwer Law International, 2005, p. 377-407.

Zielinski 2003

Zielinski, A., 'Changes in Court Decision-Making in Poland since 1989', in: J. Přibáň et al. (ed.), *Systems of Justice in Transition – Central European Experiences since 1989*, Aldershot: Ashgate, 2003, p. 109-120.

Articles in Journals

Arciuch 2008

Arciuch, M., 'Exercising the right to defence in the speedy proceedings' ('Realizacja prawa do obrony w trybie przyspieszonym'), *Palestra*, 5/6, 2008, p. 67-80.

Bojańczyk 2009

Bojańczyk, A., 'On the procedural obligations of a court appointed defence lawyer to file an extraordinary review motion in criminal proceedings (part I)' ('W sprawie obowiązków procesowych obrońcy wyznaczonego z urzędu do sporządzenia nadzwyczajnego środka zaskarżenia (cz. 1)'), *Palestra*, 5/6, 2009, p. 50-55.

Bojarski 1999

Bojarski, Ł., 'Does the appointment of *ex officio* counsel need to be changed?' ('Czy instytucja obrony z urzędu wymaga zmian?'), *Palestra*, 5/6, 1999, p. 52-62.

Bojarski & Van Dijck 2007

Bojarski, J. & van Dijck, M., 'Combating Business Crime in Poland', *Tilburg Foreign Law Review*, 3, 2007, p. 257-282.

Gajewska-Kraczkowska 1992

Gajewska-Kraczkowska, H., 'The Bar in Poland: Professional Ethics and the Legal Position of the Defense Counsel in Criminal Cases', *Capital University Law Review*, 1992, p. 1125-1144.

Jurkiewicz 2001

Jurkiewicz, G., 'A larger power. Courts discriminate lawyers in allowing access to the case file' ('Większa siła. Sądy dyskryminują adwokatów w udostępnianiu akt'), *Rzeczpospolita*, 5-3-2001.

Kmiecik 2000
Kmiecik, R., 'The right to silence of the suspected arrested person – in light of the nemo tenetur principle' ('Prawo do milczenia zatrzymanej osoby podejrzanej – w świetle reguły nemo tenetur'), *Prokuratura i Prawo*, 7/8, 2000, p. 17-22.

Krajewski 2003
Krajewski, K., 'Drugs, Markets and Criminal Justice in Poland', *Crime, Law and Social Change*, 40, 2003, p. 273-293.

Krajewski 2004
Krajewski, K., 'Crime and Criminal Justice in Poland', *European Journal of Criminology*, 1, 2004, p. 377-407.

Kulesza 2007
Kulesza, C., 'Effective defence in the pretrial proceedings and a favor procuratori' ('Efektywna obrona w postępowaniu przygotowawczym a favor procuratori'), *Prokuratora i Prawo*, 4, 2007, p. 5-33.

Stefański 2008
Stefański, R.A., 'Commentary to the decision of June 28th 2007 ('Glosa do postanowienia z 28 VI 2007, II KK 36/07'), *Państwo i Prawo*, 5, 2008, p. 142-146.

Waltoś 2002a
Waltoś, S., 'Public Prosecution Service – its place in the structure of public organs, organizations and functions' ('Prokuratura – jej miejsce wśród organów władzy, struktura I funckje'), *Państwo i Prawo*, 4, 2002, p. 5-18.

Wąsek-Wiaderek 2003a
Wąsek-Wiaderek, M., 'Access to the case file for the detained suspect and his defence lawyer – the European standard and Polish law' ('Dostęp do akt sprawy oskarżonego tymczasowo aresztowanego i jego obrońcy w postępowaniu przygotowawczym – standard europejski a prawo polskie'), *Palestra*, 3/4, 2003, p. 55-71.

Other Sources

Bojarski 2003a
Bojarski, Ł., *Access to Legal Aid in Poland: Monitoring Report*, Warsaw, 2003, available at: <http://lib.ohchr.org/HRBodies/UPR/Documents/Session1/PL/HFHR_POL_UPR_S1_2008anx_AccesstoLegalAidinPoland.pdf>.

Bojarski 2003b
Bojarski, Ł. 'Access to Legal Aid: Information about the Project', in: *Access to Justice in Central and Eastern Europe: A Source Book*, Public Interest Law Initiative, INTERIGHTS, Bulgarian Helsinki Committee and Polish Helsinki Foundation for

Human Rights, Hungary, 2003, available at: <www.pili.org/en/content/view/55/53/>.

Daniuk et al. 2006

Daniuk, B., Daniuk, B., Derezińska, M., Hermeliński, W., Kładoczny, P. & Sędek, A., *The right to defence in preliminary investigation* (Prawo do obrony w postępowaniu przygotowawczym na tle dostępu do pomocy prawnej w postępowaniu karnym), Report by the Polish Bar Association, Warsaw: NRA, 2006.

Rakowski & Rybicki 2000

Rakowski, P. & Rybicki, R., *Features – An Overview of Polish Law*, 2000, available at <http://www.llrx.com/features/polish.htm>.

Rekosh 2002

Rekosh, E., *Still No Justice for All*, 2002, available at: <www.pili.org/en/content/view/121/26/>.

Van Dijk et al. 2005

van Dijk, J., Manchin, R., van Kesteren, J. & Hideg, G., *The Burden of Crime in the EU. Research Report: a Comparative Analysis of the European Survey of Crime and Safety (EU ICS)* 2005, available at: <http://www.unicri.it/wwd/analysis/icvs/pdf_files/EUICS%20-%20The%20Burden%20of%20Crime%20in%20the%20EU.pdf>.

Walmsley 2009

Walmsley, R., *World Prison Population List*, 8th edition, January 2009, available at: <http://www.kcl.ac.uk/schools/law/research/icps>.

7.   Annex Contents 'letter of rights'

Instructions for the suspect concerning his/her rights and duties

The suspect has the right to:

- submit explanations (art. 300 k.p.k).
- refrain from submitting explanations or answering questions (art. 300 k.p.k.).
- apply for permission to voluntary accept the responsibility (art. 142 k.k.s).
- apply for performing acts of inquiry or investigation and being present at hearing of evidence (art. 300 k.p.k.).
- use the assistance of the defense counsel (art. 300 k.p.k.).
- final acquaintance with procedure materials (art. 300 k.p.k.).
- demand to be cross-examined with the participation of appointed counsel whose absence does not hinder the hearing (art. 301 k.p.k.).
- apply for or express agreement to the aggrieved party's petition to send the case to the institution or trustworthy person for mediatory proceedings (art. 23a § 1 k.p.k.).

- use the free services of an interpretor, in case he/she does not have a sufficient command of the Polish language (art 72 § 1 k.p.k.).
- take advantage of being sentenced without trial if the circumstances defined in art. 335 § 1 k.p.k. exist.

The suspect is obliged to yield to:

- external examination of the body and other examinations not connected with violation of body integrity, it is also legal to take prints and photographs and show the suspect to other people for identification purposes (art 74 § 2 sub 1 k.p.k.).
- psychological and psychiatric tests and examinations involving operations on the body, with the exception of surgical ones, on condition that they are performed by a qualified health service employee conforming with the indications of medical knowledge, they do not threaten the suspect's health, when carrying out these examinations is indispensable; in particular the suspect is obliged, keeping the above mentioned conditions in mind, to yield to blood, hair sampling or organism secretions (art. 74 § 2 sub 2 k.p.k.).
- taking by the police officer of the cheek mucosa swab if this is indispensable and there is no fear of putting in danger the health of the suspect or other people (art 74 § 2 sub 3 k.p.k.).

The suspect remaining at large:

- is obliged to turn up at each call during the penal proceedings and to notify the organ conducting the proceedings about each change of residence or sojourn in excess of 7 days; in case the suspect fails to turn up without justified reason, he/she can be detained and forcibly fetched (art 75 § 1 and 2 k.p.k.).
- in case the suspect stays abroad it is his/her duty to indicate the accommodation address for correspondence, otherwise the letter sent to the last known address in the country, or if such address does not exist, the letter attached to the records of the proceedings shall be regarded as delivered (art. 138 k.p.k.).
- if the suspect, fails to give a new address, changes the place of residence, or does not live at the indicated address, the letter sent to this address during the proceedings is regarded as delivered (art 139 of k.p.k.).

Hereby I acknowledge the receipt of the instructions concerning my rights and duties before the first interrogation.

....   place/day/month/year   ....
(signature suspect)

Idil Elveris

CHAPTER 11 TURKEY*

1.   Introduction

1.1.   Basic demographic information

Turkey is a republic established in 1923 from the remnants of the Ottoman Empire. It is located in a peninsula straddling from the eastern Balkans to the Caucasian mountains in an East-West direction and from the Black Sea in the north to the Mediterranean Sea, Syria and Iraq in the south. The vastness of its territory is illustrated by the fact that its area is the size of both France and UK. Since 1950, parliamentary democracy has persisted, despite three regime breakdowns in 1960, 1971 and 1980,[1] and a short lived military rule.

Turkey has been a member of the Council of Europe since 1949, a member of NATO since 1952 and has involved itself in European integration by becoming an associate member in 1963.[2] It has had a customs union arrangement with the European Union (EU) since 1995. The possibility of full membership was offered to Turkey in 1999 by EU Council's decision in Helsinki. In December 2004, Turkey was found to have met the Copenhagen criteria and membership negotiations began on 3 October 2005.

The latest census in Turkey was held on 31 December 2007, showing a population just over 70 million, with slightly more males than females.[3] Almost one in every five persons lives in Istanbul and the population is concentrated in the coastal areas of the West and Northwest of the country, as well as the Aegean and Mediterranean coasts. The median age of the population is 28.3. It is estimated that about 17% of the population is Kurdish, representing the largest ethnic minority. There are smaller Arabic, Assyrian, Roma, Christian and Jewish populations.

---

*   This country report has been reviewed by Asuman Aytekin İnceoğlu, assistant professor at İstanbul Bilgi University Faculty of Law.
    The report was written with substantial contributions from Asuman Aytekin Inceoğlu and Barış Erman members of the Faculty of the Istanbul Bilgi University School of Law.
[1]   Keyman & Onis 2007, p. 15.
[2]   Keyman & Onis 2007, p. 61.
[3]   <http://www.tuik.gov.tr/PreHaberBultenleri.do?id=3894>.

1.2. The nature of the criminal justice system

The Turkish criminal justice system is inquisitorial in nature. It has to a large degree been influenced by continental European models. In fact, the Penal Code and Code of Criminal Procedure (CCP) which were in place until 2005 were taken from Italy[4] and Germany respectively. The main principles of the criminal justice system are as follows: no prosecution without trial;[5] the search for the factual truth;[6] the principle of immediacy;[7] compulsory prosecution;[8] the free evaluation of evidence;[9] and *in dubio pro reo*.

In 2005, both the Penal Code and the CCP were replaced *in toto*. While various criminal law systems and domestic needs were evaluated during the preparation of both the new Criminal Code and new CCP, the German influence is still strong, particularly in terms of the latter. The main goals of the changes made to the CCP were to achieve a speedy trial, to strengthen the rights of the accused and the defence, and to introduce new investigative methods in order to establish a balance between freedom and security. To achieve these goals, the following reforms were introduced: intermediary appellate courts were re-established, compensation claims arising from private law disputes are to be heard in civil courts, parties may address witnesses directly and ask them questions without the intervention of the presiding

[4]   The law was adopted with some changes, including the Ottoman Penal Code, while Italians also changed their code in 1930. Any changes in the law followed the 'new' Italian Code, called the 'Rocco Code'. For further information on this, see Centel, Zafer & Cakmut, 2008, p. 35.

[5]   Öztürk, Tezcan, Erdem, Sırma, Saygılar & Alan 2009, p. 139-140. Art. 225 of the CCP also provides that judgment can be rendered only on the defendant and the actions mentioned in the indictment.

[6]   As the goal is to reach the truth, the judge can look for evidence on his/her own and add this to the process. However, the evidence must be obtained by lawful means, since looking for the truth is not a goal *per se*, Öztürk, Tezcan, Erdem, Sırma, Saygılar & Alan 2009, p.137-139. This point was confirmed in an interview with attorney 1. A total of eight interviews were conducted in order to draft this report between 23 August and 7 September 2009. All interviews were held in Istanbul, two of which were with police officers, two with prosecutors and four with criminal defense attorneys. A breakdown of the interviews can be found at the end of this report in the appendix. In that regard, the claims and defence of the parties are also not binding on the judge. The judge is not even bound by the admissions of the defendant; art. 225/2 CCP (Öztürk, Tezcan, Erdem, Sırma, Saygılar & Alan 2009, p.137-139).

[7]   Art. 217/1 and 188/3 CCP. As a result of this principle, except in cases provided for by law, the judge cannot merely read previous witness statements in the hearing, since witnesses must be heard in person by him/her; art. 210 CCP. Recently, particularly in cases involving the fight against organized crime, resort to the use of secret investigators, hearsay evidence concerning witnesses and anonymous witnesses has caused some debate (Öztürk, Tezcan, Erdem, Sırma, Saygılar & Alan 2009, s.140-141).

[8]   This principle sets out the prompt initiation of the investigation upon receipt of information that an offence has been committed (art. 160/1 CCP), and the filing of an indictment and continuing the prosecution when the suspicion is strong and the conditions for filing a case are fulfilled.

[9]   This principle sets out that everything can be used as evidence that is going to help resolve the dispute and will assist the judge to form an opinion, unless the evidence is unlawfully obtained; art. 217/1 CCP.

judge, victim-offender mediation has been adopted in the criminal justice system, new investigative methods and precautionary measures have been introduced, including judicial control and interception of telecommunications, and special types of search and seizure.

Both laws have been hailed as significant reforms within the EU accession process, but criticism has been common.[10] It has been argued that concepts were taken from different countries and systems, giving rise to a lack of coherence in the Codes. Further, both Codes were prepared in seven months and did not allow ample opportunity for discussion.[11] For instance, victim-offender mediation was presented solely as a diversion mechanism – a time saver – rather than an idea based on restorative justice. Hence, it was not properly understood by practitioners. Neither was the necessary infrastructure to make it work thought about,[12] or its use promoted to the public. It is no wonder that it has not served its intended purpose.[13]

Likewise, the mandatory rights to counsel and probation have not fulfilled their expected benefits. For crimes committed prior to 2005, the old Criminal Code continues to apply, creating confusion. Further, the retroactivity in the *bonam partem* principle is applied to include revision of judgments that are already being executed, thus creating extra work for courts.

Promulgation of both Codes was accompanied by seminars for judges, but these did not necessarily address all of the judges' needs.[14] The police also reacted to the introduction of the new Codes. Some even claimed that, with all the rights that defendants now had, it was no longer possible to catch anybody.[15] For instance, the police had to take all apprehended persons directly to the prosecutor. Neither did the police want to do that nor – given their workload – did prosecutors wanted to interrogate everyone, in order to determine whether to seek detention or release.[16] The media reported the views of the police, including claims that their authority was being compromised.[17] Partly to address these concerns, the law was changed, obliging the police to inform the prosecutor and take instructions from him/her.[18]

The police are now obliged to immediately inform the prosecutor about any person apprehended and all other appropriate circumstances. Thereafter, the prosecutor may order the police to detain or release the person. Accordingly, the detainee will be taken to the prosecutor only in the exceptional case of this being

---

[10]   Attorney interviews, as well as academic resources, point out to this fact. An attorney has described the crime control model adopted in the Code as outdated and unsatisfactory for the needs of the society, (interview with attorney 1).

[11]   Centel & Zafer, 2005, p. 40. Interviews with attorney 1 and attorney 2.

[12]   Kalem 2008, p. 88, 107.

[13]   Inceoglu, Aytekin & Karan 2008, p. 45.

[14]   'I am the only brave one to escape the seminar because they are talking about the theory of crime. Do you know how many years I have been a judge? Don't you tell me about the theory of crime!'; 'We go to seminars but they do not really help! The Education Division [of the Ministry of Justice] just puts what ever is in the Official Gazette into fliers. Nothing is being done by experts'; comments of judges and from the unpublished part of the author's research notes taken in the course of the research concerning criminal legal aid.

[15]   <http://www.tumgazeteler.com/?a=1792621>.

[16]   Interview with attorney 3.

[17]   Interview with attorney 4.

[18]   Art. 90/5 CCP.

ordered by the prosecutor.[19] However, apprehended minors must be brought before a specialized prosecutor, who will conduct the investigation personally.[20]

Turkey is a signatory to the European Convention on Human Rights (ECHR) and the jurisprudence of the European Court of Human Rights (ECtHR) affects Turkish legislation, as well as practice.[21] In 2004, an amendment made to the Turkish Constitution elevated the ECHR (along with other international agreements that concern fundamental rights) to the level of directly applicable law. Further, the Constitution specifically provides that, if there is a conflict between international agreements concerning fundamental rights and freedoms duly put into effect and domestic laws, the provisions of the former shall prevail. In addition, judgments of the ECtHR on criminal matters will constitute a ground for renewal review of criminal proceedings, if the ECtHR has found that the judgment of a local court convicting a defendant has been rendered in violation of the ECHR. In that case, the applicant is entitled to a retrial within one year.[22]

While these regulations are important, further changes in the laws may be necessary.[23] The number of applications against Turkey before the ECtHR is very high. Further, Turkey is mostly found to be in violation of the right to a fair trial.[24] Between 1998 and 2008, Turkey was found to have violated the right to a fair trial 528 times,[25] followed by violations concerning protection of property (453); the right to liberty and security (340); the length of proceedings (258); and the right to an effective remedy (180).[26] The high number of applications and violations suggest serious problems with the justice system and access to justice, prompting the

---

[19] Öztürk, Tezcan, Erdem, Sırma, Saygılar & Alan 2009, p. 394.

[20] Art. 15 of the Law on the Protection of Children.

[21] When the army had a free rein in the 1990s in the Southeast of Turkey, this led to widespread human rights abuses, which were brought before the ECtHR. The government lost cases that related to extra judicial killings, the right to life, torture and inhuman treatment, to name but a few. Today, with the changing atmosphere following the capture of the PKK leaders, life in the region has been normalised, and martial law has been lifted, although sporadic attacks continue.

[22] Code of Civil Procedure, art. 311.1 (f) and 2. In addition, the decision of the ECtHR must have been rendered after 4 February 2003, and must be final.

[23] Possible remedies sought in relation to irregularities by governmental authorities and the police are described in 2.1.4.

[24] Prime Ministry Human Rights Report 2008, see <http://www.siviltoplumakademisi.org.tr/haberler/son-haberler/446-2008-nsan-haklar-raporu-ackland>, <http://www.zaman.com.tr/haber.do?haberno=869531>, <http://www.tumgazeteler.com/?a=4290961>.

[25] Annual Report 2008 of the European Court of Human Rights, Council of Europe, p.139.

[26] The remainder of the cases concern the freedom of expression (169); inhuman or degrading treatment (144); lack of effective investigation (116); the right to life/deprivation of life (64); lack of effective investigation (48); the right to respect for privacy and family life (44), see <http://www.echr.coe.int/NR/rdonlyres/D5B2847D-640D-4A09-A70A-7A1BE66563BB/0/ANNUAL_REPORT_2008.pdf>. One can note that some of these concern the right to an effective defence. Freedom of assembly and association (28); other articles of the ECHR (27); prohibition of torture (20); the right to free elections (5); no punishment without law (4); the right to education (3); the prohibition of discrimination (2); the freedom of thought conscience and religion (1).

government to consider introducing the right for individuals to apply directly to the Constitutional Court.[27]

It is difficult to conclude that the new Criminal Code and CCP have meant that the system favours the defendant.[28] Critical problems remain, such as backlog and delay, particularly effecting detained defendants. The time between detention and the first hearing sometimes lasts for months.[29] It is common that 3-4 months pass between hearings. Overcrowding in prisons has grown. The media and human rights organizations continue to report police violence.

Further, it is difficult to say that the EU harmonization process has made the police more accountable. The number of policemen found guilty for torture and bad treatment is minimal, and deaths in police custody,[30] by not obeying 'stop' orders by the police,[31] or in prison,[32] still occur. At the same time, a policeman who shot and killed a cyclist for not obeying the 'stop' order was sentenced to 16 years pending appeal, the highest ever sentence for such an offence.[33]

Nevertheless, in order to start criminal action against public servants, the permission of their superiors should be sought. While permission is increasingly given, obtaining it makes the process longer, as it adds another hurdle in the already long path to seek justice.[34] The fact that the Minister of Justice has, for the first time, apologized for the death of an inmate, also shows that the improvement is more visible in prisons than in the police.[35]

Wide use of phone tapping as part of the interception of communications, and disproportionate grounds for search and seizures continue. Decisions of the Court of Cassation address substantive criminal law issues much more than criminal procedure, and therefore do not focus on irregularities.[36] Recently, the government changed the regulations on interception of communications in order to counter allegations of unlawfulness.[37] However, the worries did not subside and, in fact,

---

[27]   <http://www.frmtr.com/hukuk/2677962-anayasa-mahkemesi-aihm-gibi-calisacak.html>.
      Even the President of the Court has suggested the same: see <http://yenisafak.com.tr/Politika
      /Default.aspx?t=13.12.2007&i=87242>.

[28]   Attorneys interviewed think that some changes have been goodand some bad.

[29]   This caught public attention, due to a famous singer being detained pending the first hearing
      218 days thus far; <http://www.sabah.com.tr/Gundem/2009/08/19/
      deniz_seki_aihme_basvurdu>.

[30]   <http://bianet.org/konu/festus-okeyin-oldurulmesi>.

[31]   <http://www.haberturk.com/haber.asp?id=147935&cat=200&dt=2009/05/20>. Similarly, a
      father and son of 13 years were killed by the police in southeastern Turkey; see the report of a
      human rights advocacy group: <http://www.ihd.org.tr/index.php?option=com_content&
      view=article&catid=34:el-raporlar&id=132:ahmet-kaymaz-ve-ur-kaymazin-yam-hakkinin-lal-
      edddlarini-arairma-celeme-raporu>. The policemen were acquitted.

[32]   <http://www.ntvmsnbc.com/id/24938906>.

[33]   <http://www.sabah.com.tr/Gundem/2009/08/21/polise_16_yil_hapis>.

[34]   Interview with attorney 1.

[35]   However, prisons have again made the headlines with the non-release of two gravely ill
      inmates, on the basis of reports by the Institute of Forensic Medicine that considered their
      condition 'fit'. The Institute has been the subject of fierce criticism lately, and when one of the
      inmates later died, the President ordered an auditing of the Institute; see:
      <http://www.hurriyet.com.tr/gundem/12109809.asp?top=1>.

[36]   Interview with attorney 3.

[37]   See <http://www.mevzuatlar.com/sy/resmiGazete/rga/09/08/07080901.htm>.

Istanbul's head prosecutor has recently discovered that his calls were being recorded, and some 55 other judges and prosecutors were being tapped under orders from the Justice Ministry.[38] In 2009, the number of judgments involving phone tapping was 23,852.[39]

For 2009, the total amount of the criminal legal aid budget is approximately 5.546.827 Euro,[40] while the funds allocated for the police in 2007 and 2008 was slightly over 3 billion Euro.[41] In other words, the funds available for legal aid do not even amount to one per cent of the police budget. Attorneys providing legal aid get paid months late, triggering protests and, in the Istanbul Bar's case, a strike since June 2009 to date.

Turkey is highly centralized and the police constitute part of the Ministry of Internal Affairs. In that sense, it operates under the auspices of the General Directorate of Security, which has authority over the national police. However, in rural areas, the Gendarmerie is in charge, although some suburban districts of Istanbul also fall within their jurisdiction. While geographically the Gendarmerie seems to cover more areas, the areas under police control have a far greater population. Investigations conducted by the Gendarmerie and the police are said to be different, with the latter acting more in conformity with the law, as it is more educated, organized and confident.[42] Recently, calls have been made for abolition of the Gendarmerie.[43] In addition, the Gendarmerie is a military unit, while administratively it is under the control of the Ministry of Internal Affairs, leading to conflicts in terms of accountability.

1.3.   The structure and the processes of criminal justice system

The first stage of the criminal justice process is the investigation stage and the person who is subject of the inquiry is called a suspect. Criminal proceedings may be initiated following the complaint of the person who has been the victim of a crime, or who has been affected by the crime (for example, if the victim is dead his/her family), or *ex officio* by the prosecutor. If the victim chooses to first go to the

[38]   'Turkey's phone-tapping scandal, Who's on the phone?', *The Economist*, 21 November 2009, vol. 393, No. 8658, p. 34.
[39]   'Sizi Dinledik! Sesinizi Çok Beğendik...', Güncel Hukuk, Aralık 2009/12-72, p. 26-31.
[40]   The amount is 11,093,654.20 Turkish liras; see table at <http://www.barobirlik.org.tr/calisma/duyuru/pdf/2009_cmk_cari_gider.pdf>. The government funds allocated for criminal legal aid have seen an almost four fold increase in 2006 as compared to 2005, reaching almost 66,700,000 Euro. This was due to the vast expansion of the scope of the mandatory legal aid. However, as the funds ran out, the scope of mandatory legal aid was limited. This will be discussed in detail in 1.5.
[41]   Emniyet Genel Müdürlüğü 2008 Faaliyet Raporu, p. 71 and Emniyet Genel Müdürlüğü 2007 Faaliyet Raporu, p. 98.
[42]   Interview with attorney 1. The same attorney explains that, in the Gendarmerie, while officers are educated, they are not conducting the investigation. Sergeants are in charge, and they try to have their own legal rules in an order-command structure.
[43]   Almanac Turkey 2006-2008: Security Sector and Democratic Oversight released by the Turkish Economic and Social Studies Foundation (TESEV), p. 217, 228. For the pdf version, see <http://www.tesev.org.tr/UD_OBJS/PDF/DEMP/almanak2008_02_07_09.WEB%20icin.pdf>.

police, the police inform the prosecutor of the crime. If, however, the victim chooses to first go to the prosecutor, he/she directs the inquiry to the respective division of the police, be it narcotics, murder or otherwise.[44] Prosecutors have stated that police officers working for specialized divisions were more professional (and easier to work with) than the regular police officers located in neighbourhoods.[45]

Citizens make their complaints mostly by going to the police. A much smaller proportion first goes to the prosecutor.[46] In large towns, the 'prosecutor of initial complaints' refers the complaints to investigating prosecutors, while in smaller places, one prosecutor performs both functions. One prosecutor mentioned that, in cases of crimes such as forgery or threat, the police direct victims to go through the prosecutor.[47] Felonies (such as murder, drugs) should be directly investigated by the prosecutor but, even in those cases, the assistance of the police is sought.[48] It should be noted here that the prosecutor does not have his/her own staff to undertake the investigation, but instead rely on the police. In matters other than criminal investigations, the police report to their superiors and not to the prosecutor.[49]

Therefore, the prosecutor only has limited control of the police, because the judicial police cannot remain on duty for a prolonged time, due to new assignments from their superiors. Nevertheless, when the police conduct an investigation, the prosecutor must get involved, since the police must act according to the instructions of the prosecutor.[50] Indeed, the prosecutor asks the police to carry out various actions. For instance, the police are asked to take the statement (interview) of the victim, witness and the suspect, or obtain the final medical report (if there is bodily harm).[51] One prosecutor added that he often reminds the police to immediately contact him, should they need an order for search and seizure.[52]

The police in Turkey have two functions. The first is administrative, in the sense of crime prevention and law enforcement, while the other is judicial. In other words, the primary function of the police is proactive, while the secondary function is reactive (after the commission of crimes). Indeed, the difference is also reflected in two core pieces of legislation: The Law on the Responsibilities and Jurisdiction of the Police (of 1934), as well as the CCP. While the former is more about the administrative function of the police (when to use a gun, or what actions it is authorized to do in general), the latter deals more with what it can do at what stage in the performance of the judicial function.[53]

---

[44] Interview with police officer 1.
[45] Interviews with prosecutor 1 and prosecutor 2. Working with the specialist divisions of the police seems to allow prosecutors to develop a face-to-face and day-to-day interaction with the police, and hence direct the investigation, whereas if police from the police stations are involved, this is mostly done over the phone.
[46] Interview with prosecutor 1. In the courts, citizens apply to the so called prosecutor of initial complaints (müracaat savcısı).
[47] Interview with prosecutor 2.
[48] Interview with prosecutor 1.
[49] Art. 164/3 CCP.
[50] Interview with prosecutor 2.
[51] Art.13(G) of the Act on the Responsibility and Jurisdiction of the Police.
[52] Interview with prosecutor 1.
[53] Interview with police officer 1.

This duality means that the police have different superiors depending on the function it performs. The prosecutor is the head of investigation in Turkey and therefore, when performing judicial functions, the police (as well as the Gendarmerie, Customs Control and Coast Guard) are to follow the order and instructions of the prosecutor when carrying out an investigation. It has been asserted that these units sometimes conduct investigations that are 'rubber stamped' by the prosecutor.

Administratively, these units are not subject to the oversight of the prosecutor. They remain employees of their respective organisations. Nevertheless, for crimes involving longer processes, such as tapping and similar, the police work closely with the prosecutor.[54]

While the law says the opposite,[55] in practice, when evaluating the success of a police officer, the good performance of judicial functions does not seem to be taken into account.[56] Further, although there is a regulation on the judicial police, there is in fact no separate judicial police as an entity that works under the authority of the prosecutor. In other words, the prosecutor has no say in deciding who will be working under him/her. This is instead determined by the hierarchy within the police force. In fact, the establishment of the judicial police has long been debated in Turkey. According to one attorney, the police do not want its establishment as this would mean loss of power for them.[57] The current structure allows them to have a role in every investigation, and they want judges and prosecutors to continue to rely on them.

The police have apprehension powers without a warrant if the person is caught *in flagrante delicti* and, in addition, is considered likely to abscond, or his/her identity cannot be instantly determined. In 2007, there were a total of 444,587 arrests made by the police for crimes against property and person.[58] This does *not* include arrests made for organized crime (6,191), narcotics (38,454), cyber crimes (1,287), terror (2,256) and other crimes (6,879). The police must inform the prosecutor when they detain a person. The prosecutor can order the police to release him/her. A person who is not released within 24 hours must be brought before the judge for interrogation. This period may be extended up to 36 hours to allow time for travelling.[59]

---

[54] Interview with police officer 1.
[55] Art. 11 of the Regulation on Judicial Police.
[56] In other words, the prosecutor writes an evaluative report that is not even sent to the direct superiors of the officer; Arslan, p. 8. One prosecutor refered to this as a problem, interview with prosecutor 2.
[57] Interview with attorney 4.
[58] Emniyet Genel Müdürlüğü 2007, Faaliyet Raporu, p. 135.
[59] An exception to this rule is art. 251/5 CCP, which provides that the period of detention for offences listed under art. 250 (offences under the competence of Specialized Aggravated Felony Courts) is 48 hours, with a possible extension up to 60 hours due to time for travelling. In both cases, these periods are subject to an additional extension, where the crime is allegedly committed by more than two offenders. This additional period can be ordered by the prosecutor for 24 hours at a time, and may not be longer than 4 days in total (art. 91/3 CCP).

If a warrant for apprehension is issued by a court, but the suspect is detained within the jurisdictional boundaries of another court, the latter may arrest him/her temporarily, prior to the suspect being sent to the court issuing the warrant. The detainee must be brought before the court within a maximum of 24 hours following the apprehension.[60] However, a problem arises from the application of this rule. The arrest is based on the warrant issued by another court, and the judge in whose geographical boundaries the suspect is found does not have access to the case file in order to evaluate the conditions for a lawful arrest. In addition, the maximum period of time for the accused to be brought before the court issuing the warrant has not been defined by law.[61]

As a result, the accused may be deprived of his/her liberty for an extended period, without having precise information about the contents of the charges against him/her.[62] Indeed, one of the interviewed attorneys pointed out that the judge dealing with the actual arrest has no information or documents, other than a one page warrant, thereby effectively depriving him/her of the possibility of evaluating the release, even if the suspect defends him/herself by saying that he/she was abroad at the time and can demonstrate this by showing his/her passport.[63]

The prosecutor decides whether or not to issue an indictment based on the evidence collected, including the statement of the accused. If he/she finds that the evidence collected is not sufficient, or that no trial may be conducted due to other legal restrictions, no indictment will be filed, and the detainee, if still under custody, must be released. This decision is subject to revision by the presiding judge of the nearest aggravated felony court.[64]

If, after the interrogation, the prosecutor has a strong suspicion that a crime has been committed, he/she will refer the suspect to the judge with a request for pre-trial arrest. In that sense, arrest is a precautionary measure rendered by the judge during the investigation, or by the court of first instance during prosecution (after the approval of the indictment). Pre-trial arrest can be ordered when there is a strong suspicion that a crime has been committed and there is a reason for arrest.[65] Reasons for arrest are as follows: if the suspect or defendant is likely to abscond, hide, or there are circumstances creating that suspicion; if the suspect or defendant's actions create strong suspicion that he/she will destroy, hide or change evidence, or attempt to pressure witnesses, victims or others.

Further, the law provides a catalogue of crimes, where a reason for arrest 'may be presumed'. This is a widely criticised provision. It has been claimed that judges, without looking for strong suspicion, automatically decide to detain when the crime

[60] Art. 94 CCP.
[61] Nuhoğlu 2009, p. 186.
[62] Öztürk, Tezcan, Erdem, Sırma, Saygılar & Alan 2009, p. 400, note 74.
[63] Interview with attorney 3.
[64] Art. 172 CCP. An amendment to the CCP gave the prosecutor the power to postpone the filing of the prosecution under certain conditions.
[65] Art. 100 CCP.

falls within the 'catalogue'. These crimes include murder, production and trade of drugs and sexual offences.[66]

Alternatively, there may be sufficient evidence to file an indictment, but no need for pre-trial arrest. This is usually the case where the crime for which the suspect is to be charged does not fall within the catalogue, such as petty theft or property damage.

In any case, the judge or court will order the arrest following a hearing, where the defendant is present.[67] In addition, the law provides for mandatory defence counsel for the arrest hearing.[68] However, an attorney stated that the mandatory counsel provided serves mostly as an 'alibi' proving that the suspect has not been subject to inhuman treatment, rather than engage in a proper defence since there is no real possibility to communicate with the suspect in the infrastructure at the court house.[69]

At the end of the investigation, if the prosecutor decides that there is sufficient evidence to press charges, he/she prepares an indictment and submits it to the court. It should be noted that the legal determination for filing an indictment is less stringent (a sufficient level of suspicion),[70] than the one required for an arrest (strong suspicion).[71] The court may reject the indictment, but this must be done within 15 days of its presentation.[72] If rejected, the prosecutor may correct the indictment and present it again, or file an objection.[73] It is important to mention that no hearing takes place during the approval or the rejection of the indictment. As a result, the charge is not determined following a three party hearing, and the defendant or the defence lawyer will have no opportunity to question the indictment before the court.[74] When the indictment is accepted by the court, the person is no longer called a suspect, but rather is a criminal defendant.

The pre-trial period is reserved for the preparation of the trial. This period extends from the approval of the indictment by the court until the beginning of the first hearing, the date of which is determined by the court, according to its own schedule.[75] The prosecutor formally notifies the defendant of the indictment and the date for the first hearing.[76] During this period, no witnesses or experts will be heard, except in cases where these persons are not likely to be able to appear before the court during the trial – for example, where the witness is terminally ill.[77] In addition, evidence gathering procedures may be completed or repeated, if need be.[78]

---

66   Art. 100/2 CCP.
67   Art. 101 CCP.
68   Art. 101/3 CCP, Nuhoğlu 2009, p. 182.
69   Interview with attorney 3.
70   Art. 170 CCP.
71   Art. 100 CCP.
72   Art. 174/3 CCP.
73   Art. 174/4-5 CCP.
74   Yenisey 2009b, p. 248.
75   Art. 175 CCP.
76   Art. 176 CCP.
77   Art. 180, 181 CCP.
78   Art. 181/2 CCP.

The hearing can only begin when all required persons (the judges, prosecutor,[79] clerk, and, in cases where counsel is mandatory, the defence lawyer) are present.[80] As a rule, the defendant must also be present during all hearings. The defendant may, however, be excused, if he/she has already provided a statement, if his/her attorney makes a request to that effect,[81] or if the defendant is transferred to a prison facility outside the province of the court due to necessity or health or disciplinary reasons.[82] In any of these cases, the proceedings may commence, but shall not be concluded, unless the defendant has been interrogated by the court, or the court can acquit the defendant based on evidence in the file,[83] except in situations where the sentence to be given consists of seizure of property and/or a fine, in which case the trial may be conducted and the sentence given *in absentia*.[84]

The law provides that statements obtained by the police in the absence of a lawyer cannot be accepted as a basis for conviction, unless it is confirmed by the suspect or criminal defendant before a judge or the court.[85] It must be noted that no indication of duress is needed for this provision to be applied, and a simple statement by the defendant before the judge would suffice to negate the evidence obtained from a police interrogation in the absence of a lawyer. In this case the evidence will be considered unlawful, and will be declared inadmissible.[86]

In fact, police abuse has, over time, established a pattern of confessing at the police station and denial in court.[87] Therefore, the introduction of this provision through the new CCP of 2005 was one of the measures taken by the legislature to restrict possible unlawful interference by the police.[88] After the entry into force of the new CCP, the Turkish Court of Cassation no longer requires a positive indication of duress, even when this constitutes a reason for the defendant to retract his/her previous statement at the police (10th Chamber for Penal Affairs of the Court of Cassation., 23 January 2006, E. 2005/1716, K. 2006/19).

It must be noted, however, that the judgment of ECtHR of *Salduz* v. *Turkey*[89] refers to the provisions of the previous CCP. The current law has abolished most of the points of concern in that case, rendering inadmissible any statement made before the police if not given with the presence of a lawyer. Attorney interviews have raised problems with the way these rights are used in practice. These are explained in 2.2.2.

---

[79]   Except before a 'court of peace', according to art. 188/2 CCP.
[80]   Art. 188/1 CCP.
[81]   Art. 196/1 CCP.
[82]   This may particularly be the case where the defendant has been transferred to another prison due to illness or as a disciplinary measure. In this case, he/she is accused by judicial notice, according to art. 196/5 CCP.
[83]   Art. 193/2 CCP.
[84]   Art. 195 CCP.
[85]   Art. 148/4 CCP.
[86]   Art. 148 CCP expressly states that the evidence 'will not be a basis for conviction', meaning that it is inadmissible.
[87]   See Kunter, Yenisey & Nuhoğlu 2008, p. 1067.
[88]   See Öztürk, Tezcan, Erdem, Sırma, Saygılar & Alan 2009, p. 368-370.
[89]   ECtHR 27 November 2008, *Salduz* v. *Turkey,* No. 36391\02.

Precautionary measures, such as search, seizure and the interception of (tele)communications,[90] can be utilised during the investigation phase.[91] The latter has been very controversial, due to recent events in Turkey (described in 1.2), and is possible by way of listening to communications, recording, determination and evaluation of signals.[92]

In order to intervene in communications, there must already be an investigation or prosecution for a crime specified by the law.[93] Secondly, there must be a strong suspicion that one of those crimes has been committed.[94] Thirdly, it must not be possible to obtain any evidence in any other way. Lastly, the decision to do so shall be taken by the judge or, in urgent matters, by the prosecutor.[95] In the latter case, the prosecutor must submit the decision to intercept (tele)communications for the judge's approval and the judge must make his/her decision within 24 hours. The judgment can be issued for a maximum of three months and can be extended once for a further three months.[96]

The fact that, in urgent situations, the prosecutor can also order precautionary measures, makes the prosecutor's role in the criminal justice process somewhat awkward. It has been said that this has made the prosecutor 'judge like'.[97] Considering the close relationship between prosecutors and judges in Turkey (to be discussed in section 3), the danger is that is that the judge may be seen as an extension of the prosecutor. In that sense, it is disappointing that the reform strategy developed by the Ministry of Justice continues to group judges and prosecutors together and does not envision any separation.[98]

The Criminal Code refers to three different types of suspicion. Yet, the Court of Cassation has not rendered a decision discussing the differences among these.[99] *Reasonable* suspicion is required for conducting a search and seizure;[100] *sufficient* evidence for filing an indictment;[101] and *strong* suspicion for most precautionary measures, such as the intervention of communications, arrest, seizure of real property rights and appointment of secret agents.[102]

---

[90] Art. 135 CCP. Before the new Code, interceptions were regulated under a different law relating to the fight against organized crime and could be undertaken for those crimes.

[91] Art. 116 CCP and the subsequent art.

[92] These are defined in a regulation, but some issues still remain unclear, such as whether the provision includes the reading of SMS and emails; İnceoğlu Aytekin A, Türk Hukukunda Adli Amaçlı İletişimin Denetlenmesi, in Prof. Dr. Uğur Alacakaptan'a Armağan, Cilt 1, p. 110.

[93] These crimes are serious and necessitate such intervention due to their nature.

[94] Art. 135/6 CCP.

[95] Art. 119 CCP.

[96] If the crime involves organized groups, the judge can extend the period as many times as is necessary for periods not to exceed one month.

[97] Interview with attorney 1.

[98] The Judicial Reform Strategy, which talks about 'judges and prosecutors', see: <http://www.sgb.adalet.gov.tr/yrs.html>.

[99] In Turkey, not all decisions of the Court of Cassation are published. It is up to the Court itself to publish important decisions in its journal. Therefore, there may be decisions that have not been published, but which discuss the different types of suspicion.

[100] Art. 116 CCP.

[101] Art. 170 CCP.

[102] Arts. 100, 128, 135, 139 CCP.

According to one prosecutor, 'in practice one does not see any of the criteria [applied by judges or prosecutors]'.[103] Prosecutors explained that they want the police to be specific and undertake additional investigation, before coming to them with requests for precautionary measures: 'This is abstract! I cannot tell who is reporting the crime. I could be living in that house'.[104] Similarly: 'I tell them do not come to me with just a record (*tutanak*). Test the suspicion'.[105]

Some prosecutors do not turn down the police, particularly in popular investigations. For example, intercepted phone conversations irrelevant for the proof of the alleged crimes have been leaked to the media and used to create an image of guilt. This not only violates the personal rights of the suspect and the presumption of innocence, but also constitutes pressure on the judge. It has also been pointed out that interception was not the issue in such cases, but keeping the personal data and preventing leakage was a real problem.[106]

Indeed, allegations concerning irregularities about the application of precautionary measures and their proportionality have been widely discussed by the public, particularly in the case of *Ergenekon*.[107] The case involved over a hundred suspects charged with 'membership of an armed organization', 'attempting to eliminate the government by force and violence, or to prevent it from doing its job either partially or completely' and 'provoking an armed rebellion against the government'. The indictments accuse the suspects of creating internal conflict, chaos and terror, in an attempt to set the grounds for a military intervention. Suspects include famous journalists, university professors, intellectuals, party officials, activists, presidents of universities, academics and generals in the military. The investigation began on 3 October 2008 and involved search warrants issued for the police involving several houses, NGOs, and offices.[108]

---

[103] Interview with prosecutor 2.
[104] Interview with prosecutor 1.
[105] Interview with prosecutor 2.
[106] Interview with prosecutor 2.
[107] 'Ergenekon Case, A chance for Turkey to face its recent past' EU Commissioner <http://www.aa.com.tr/en/ergenekon-case-a-chance-for-turkey-to-face-its-recent-past-eu-commissioner.html>.
[108] The house of Prof. Türkan Saylan, a doctor specialising in leprosy and co-founder and long-time president of the Association for the Support of Contemporary Living which is known for her support of girls' education, was raided by the police for 7 hours. At the end of the investigation, documents and hard-discs of computers were seized by the police. As Saylan said later, the documents and computers included the scholarship information of the girls who were supported by the Association and the database of the recipients was destroyed by the police. Thus, 9,074 students could not get their scholarship stipends due to the lack of the necessary documents. This was done while she was struggling with highly advanced breast cancer and undergoing chemotherapy treatment over the last five years. The actions of the police were considered disproportionate, as she could not abscond due to her health problems. Prof. Dr. Saylan died on 18 May 2009. Another example is the journalist, columnist and editor of the newspaper Cumhuriyet (*the Republic*), Ilhan Selcuk, who was also apprehended in the Ergenekon case. He was questioned for 11.5 hours and, approximately 40 hours later, was released with the *prohibition of leaving the country*. His detention was also subject to protests, as he was 84 years old and his detention was harmful to his health. As subsequently decided, 'prohibition of leaving the country' would have been a sufficient

→

All of this is worrying when one considers that the mechanisms for excluding evidence obtained illegally or unfairly are not strong. The very court that hears the case on the merits is expected to decide whether the evidence was obtained illegally. In fact, the law provides that the judgment should discuss evidence, including illegally obtained evidence present in the file, and explain why it was not taken into consideration.[109] These provisions presuppose that any unlawful evidence will be in the case file from the beginning of the investigation until the conclusion of the trial,[110] but fail to appreciate that, once in the file, evidence, no matter whether it has been illegally obtained, would be difficult to ignore by the court.

Indeed, attorneys have expressed concern that the judge is a human being who can be tempted to take the illegally obtained evidence into consideration.[111] Therefore, illegally obtained evidence should, ideally, be taken out of the court file and deposited elsewhere.[112] Further, the current IT system used by judges allows them to see all information about suspects, including all other pending trials against him/her,[113] creating possible bias against the suspect.

There are three kinds of criminal courts in Turkey all of which are courts of first instance. The Courts of Peace hear offences with a maximum of two years imprisonment as the prescribed sentence and related monetary fines. These courts are the only criminal courts that do not work with prosecutors. Cases are initiated on the basis of citizen complaints. In these courts, a single judge conducts the hearings and is responsible for all judicial decisions.

Aggravated Felony Courts[114] have jurisdiction over crimes with prison sentences of life or over 10 years. In these courts, hearings are conducted, and decisions are made, by three-judge panels, with one presiding judge.

Finally, General Criminal Courts have jurisdiction over all other types of cases that are otherwise not within the jurisdiction of either the Court of Peace or the Aggravated Felony Court. Similar to Courts of Peace, a single judge presides in these courts.[115]

---

precautionary measure to protect his health; see <http://todayszaman.com/tz-web/detaylar.do?load=detay&link=184216>.

[109] Art. 230/1/b CCP. Interestingly, when writing to the prosecutor, the police must mention which evidence that it obtained was unlawful; art. 6/6 of the Regulation on the Judicial Police.

[110] Öztürk, Tezcan, Erdem, Sırma, Saygılar & Alan 2009, p. 373. These authors defend this choice of the legislature, although the majority of the doctrine is criticized; Ünver 1998, p. 185-187; Şen 1998, p. 209-212; Yıldız 2002, p. 203-205; Erman 1998, p. 79.

[111] Interview with attorney 1. This point was made by attorneys 3 and 4 as well.

[112] Interview with attorney 2.

[113] Informal discussion of the authors with a judge in the Criminal Court of General Jurisdiction in the course of conducting other research.

[114] Some authors use 'Court of Assize';, see Turkish Criminal Procedure Code (Ceza Muhakemesi Kanunu) Yenisey F. (co-ed), Istanbul 2009.

[115] With regard to geographical jurisdiction, Courts of Peace and General Criminal Courts have jurisdiction in cases that originate within district boundaries, while Aggravated Felony Courts are competent in cases that originate within the province boundaries. Accordingly, each district has at least one Court of Peace and General Criminal Court, and each province has at least one Aggravated Felony Court. Existing courts may have multiple chambers, so that they can deal with the workload effectively.

With regard to appellate courts, the Court of Cassation in Ankara is the highest and only appellate court.[116] The new Criminal Code introduced intermediate appellate courts, but these are yet to be established.[117] In Turkey, there is no plea bargaining system (guilty plea procedure), nor are there expedited proceedings.

1.4. Levels of crime and the prison population

In recent years, the media has 'discovered' crime as an interesting and popular issue. It can therefore be said that, due to increased media coverage, crime has become more visible. This has led to arguments that crime has 'exploded' in Turkey.[118] Possibly feeling under pressure, the police claim that, in 2008, crime levels were down, particularly concerning crimes against property, such as bag snatching, which showed the highest reduction with 41%.[119] There is no specific data that could be used to defend these claims. Police statistics only reflect crimes reported to the police, and the accuracy of that data is questionable. There are also no systematic victimization surveys held in Turkey that would show clear trends. However, considering the worldwide reduction of crime rates over the past decade, without more sound data, it would be difficult to argue that the situation in Turkey is different.[120]

Turkey has not participated in the International Crime Victims Surveys as a whole, but in 2005, the study was done on a smaller scale for Istanbul households.[121] The study found that, when compared with other major European cities, Istanbul had lower victimization rates when it comes to 'contact offences' (such as robbery, theft) than most European capitals, while the rates for 'non-contact offences' (such

---

[116] Ten of its 30 chambers are responsible for appellate review of criminal cases, and the workload between chambers is determined according to subject matter. Thus, for example, the First Chamber is responsible for reviewing cases of murder and related offences, and the Sixth Chamber for some white collar crimes. Each chamber has five judges, one of them being the presiding judge. The decision of the Court in a criminal case is final and binding (since there is no second level appellate court) and sets a precedent for other cases by example only. However, en banc decisions of the Court of Cassation are binding.

[117] Decisions rendered at first instance by courts can be reversed or approved, but the court of first instance can insist on its ruling, in which case the matter is reviewed by the General Assembly of the Court of Cassation, which will be then issue a decision that is final.

[118] <http://www.radikal.com.tr/haber.php?haberno=213770>. The article quotes police statistics and states that, in 2006, crime increased by 61%. Further, the article states that, in 2006, the police apprehended 186,316 people, while in 2005 the number was 168,076 and in 2004 238,727. The article also states that the fact that the number of apprehended increased by only 11% while crime increased by 61% could be read as a sign of passive resistance by the police against the EU harmonization legislation. Similarly, the media has quoted the Ankara Chamber of Commerce research, stating that crime increased dramatically by 35.5%. <http://www.tumgazeteler.com/?a=977087>, or the President of the Court of Cassation talking about the crime explosion: <http://www.gencturkhaber.com/video/Hasan-Gerceker--Suc-patlamasi-var.html,015930>.

[119] Emniyet Genel Müdürlüğü 2008, Faaliyet Raporu, p. 28.

[120] Jahic & Akdas, 2007.

[121] Jahic & Akdas, 2007.

as car theft, burglary) were higher. However, the fear of crime was found to be among the highest in Europe.

It can be argued that the 'discovery' of crime by the media has contributed to this high fear. In fact, the media has often portrayed street children who sniff paint thinner as violent and cold-blooded thugs. Also, bag snatching and other robberies prevalent in big towns have been demonized in the media.[122] While these figures cannot be used to describe crime in the whole country, it must be remembered that Istanbul is the largest city in Turkey.

Foreigners in Turkey are viewed as a security threat but, rather than imputing criminality on them, there is a tendency to deport them. Some foreigners awaiting deportation are held in prison-like facilities in appalling conditions,[123] but the public does not see them responsible for crime. Foreigners of African descent are a new phenomenon in Turkey and are stereotyped as drug dealers, although they make their living by street vending. Refugee advocacy groups report that the African community in Istanbul is discriminated against and ill-treated and harassed by the police.[124] The case of *Festus Okey*, a Nigerian refugee suspected of drug dealing, became famous when he died at the Beyoglu Police Station in Istanbul.[125]

Further, when it comes to sex workers from the Commonwealth of Independent States, Russian or Eastern European countries, the public has a bad impression. This is often the case, even if they are victims of trafficking. They are regarded as 'hot passionate, blond bombshells' willing and available for any sexual acts required of them. For most people in Turkish society, women from the Soviet Bloc countries have become equated with the term 'prostitute' regardless of whether they are sex workers or not, and have been given a special name 'Natasha'.[126] Because of these prejudices, regardless of their visas or status, foreign woman with blonde hair become subject to harassment by locals and the police. A public survey

---

[122]   <http://www.milliyet.com.tr/default.aspx?aType=SonDakika&ArticleID=1013111>.

[123]   <http://www.radikal.com.tr/haber.php?haberno=252036>.

[124]   United States Committee for Refugees and Immigrants, *World Refugee Survey 2008 – Turkey*, 19 June 2008, available at <http://www.unhcr.org/refworld/docid/485f50d776.html> [accessed 5 November 2009]. According to the report of Refugee Advocacy and Support Program by the Helsinki Citizens Assembly, police officers demand money from asylum seekers of African backgrounds when checking their ID and during home raids. If the asylum seekers refuse to give money, the police threaten to accuse them of possessing drugs.

[125]   Police Cover Up in Okey's Death <http://bianet.org/english/english/101739-police-cover-up-in-okeys-death>. According to the information of the Helsinki Citizens Assembly, on the 20 August 2007, Festus Okey was stopped by police officers in Beyoglu. At the time Mr. Okey had another friend with him. Both of them were searched by the police and asked to show their IDs. The friend of Mr. Okey stated that the police officer searching Festus Okey started to hit him in the street. Both of them were taken to the police station, on the grounds that they did not have their identity cards on them and the friend said that he lost sight of Festus while being taken to the station. While he was giving his statement at the ground floor of the Beyoglu Police Department, he heard a gun shot.

[126]   Gülçür L, İlkkaracan P. 'The Natasha Experience': Migrant Sex Workers from the Former Soviet Union and Eastern Europe in Turkey: Women's Studies International Forum vol. 25 (411-21) Copyright Elsevier 2002 <http://www.scribd.com/doc/7343044/NATASHA-Experience>.

on xenophobia and racism[127] found that 18% of Turkish people would not like foreigners as their neighbour,[128] while over 50% do not want non-Muslims to have jobs in public places.

One of the major issues has been the overcrowding of prisons. The prison population has doubled since 2000.[129] Ethnic data is not gathered in Turkey, so any number as to the ethnic profiles of the prison population would only be an estimate. In the past, overcrowding has been addressed by frequent amnesties, but the building of new prisons (with EU funds) has dispensed with that option. It has also been argued that frequent amnesties, or parole laws, were undermining efforts to fight crime. According to the Ministry of Justice, as of 31 October 2009, the total number of persons in prison was 116,690 and rising, with a capacity of only 85,000 beds. (During the course of the writing of this report alone, the number went up by 3,197. On 31 August 2009, the number was 113,493,[130] while on 29 March 2009, it was 109,162).[131]

This number includes those in pre-trial detention, detainees that are currently being tried, detainees pending the outcome of their appeal and convicts. Half the figure consists of detainees who are held together with convicts, as there are few facilities separately designed for detainees. Further, conviction rates in Turkey are low and only one of every two persons are found guilty.[132]

Worse, attorney interviews indicate worrying trends: the decision to continue detention is automatic and made on the file, without an appearance in court, despite the principle of immediacy;[133] to continue with detention until the defendant provides a statement, for fear that, once released, he/she may not be found again;[134] and detention decisions without proper reasoning.[135]

1.5. Legal aid for persons suspected or accused of a crime

As indicated earlier, for a country of 70 million people, expenditure for legal aid is very low by international standards, amounting to less than 1 Euro per person.[136] Criminal legal aid is available without a means test for anyone who requests it, from

[127]   The Frekans Research Field and Data Processing Co. conducted the survey, as part of a project to promote the Turkish Jewish community and culture, with the sponsorship of the European Commission and the Beyoğlu Rabbi's Office Foundation. A total of 1,108 people around the country were questioned between 18 May and 18 June 2009.
[128]   <http://www.kanalahaber.com/icimizdeki-irkcilik-urkutuyor...-haberi-32360.htm>.
[129]   <http://www.cte.adalet.gov.tr/#>.
[130]   <http://www.cte.adalet.gov.tr/>.
[131]   <http://www.cte.adalet.gov.tr/kaynaklar/istatistikler/yas_cins_ogrenim/genel.htm>.
[132]   The latest figures are from 2007, which shows that of the total 2,189,082 cases heard before the courts, only 48.7% ended with conviction, 20% with acquittal and the rest with other decisions: see <http://www.adli-sicil.gov.tr/istatistik_2007/ceza%20mahkemeleri/ceza2-2007.pdf>.
[133]   Interviews with attorneys 3 and 4.
[134]   Interview with attorney 1.
[135]   Interview with attorney 3.
[136]   Figures of 2006 of the European Commission for the Efficiency of Justice (CEPEJ) were about the same; see <http://www.coe.int/t/dghl/cooperation/cepej/evaluation/2006/Turkey.PDF>.

the moment of detention until appeal. When the criminal defendant is disabled (to the extent that this disability effects his/her capacity to give a defence), or a minor, he/she must have counsel appointed as a matter of law (mandatory criminal legal aid).[137] For crimes that carry a sentence of a minimum of five years,[138] counsel is also mandatory.[139] Mandatory counsel is required when the suspect is before the investigative judge for detention. In other words, the system operates 'on request' unless mandated by law.

Research in the Istanbul criminal courts has found that less than three per cent of all criminal defendants had access to a government paid lawyer. The same research found that just over half of defendants had five years of schooling or less.[140] Similarly, research conducted in the Umraniye and Bayrampasa prisons among detainees and convicts found that 76.2% of them had eight years of schooling or less.[141]

Given the widespread poverty in Turkey, with average monthly income per household being approximately 600 Euro,[142] legal aid carries great importance, particularly when one considers that criminal defendants have such a profile. These are groups who often cannot afford to hire a private attorney, and the existence and easy accessibility of legal aid therefore becomes crucial for their access to justice. In fact, research shows that only 18.5% of the urban population in Turkey has ever made use of the services of an attorney, with the second most common reason being that it was expensive.[143]

The government has delegated provision of the criminal legal aid service to local bar associations. Yet, there is no department at the Ministry of Justice that oversees the provision of these services. Many local bar associations have established Criminal Procedure Practice Units/Centers, which administer the service with funds provided by the government. Accordingly, there is no institution that is responsible for the delivery of legal aid as a matter of policy and monitoring. There are also no quality assurance mechanisms or monitoring of the delivery of the

[137] One police officer explained that, if the suspect is illiterate, they also ask the Bar for an attorney; interview with police officer 2.
[138] Representation by a lawyer is not mandatory, even for some rather serious offences such as manslaughter, sexual assault, or other serious assault cases, because the minimum prison sentence for these crimes is two years and not five.
[139] For a discussion of the changes in the law concerning mandatory representation, see Elveris, Jahic & Kalem 2007, p. 161, 243-252.
[140] Elveris, Jahic & Kalem 2007, p. 182.
[141] İstanbul'da Şiddet ve Şiddetin Sosyolojik Arka Planı Araştırma Raporu, Istanbul 2008, p. 125.
[142] Derived from 2007 statistics reported in Turkish Statistical Institute. (2008); *Turkey in Statistics 2008.* Ankara: Turkish Statistical Institute, p. 38. See <http://www.tuik.gov.tr/IcerikGetir.do?istab_id=5>. Approximately one fifth of the population lives below the poverty line; see <http://www.radikal.com.tr/haber.php?haberno=242747>. In 2008, one of every seven families was receiving economic assistance, either from the government or family; see <http://www.radikal.com.tr/Radikal.aspx?aType=RadikalDetay&ArticleID=932340&CategoryID=80>.
[143] Kalem, Jahic & Elveris 2008, p. 19.

services.[144] The responsibility of the lawyer in providing legal aid services is dealt with via the internal disciplinary mechanisms of the bar associations.

It was asserted that, when there are complaints filed against an attorney by judges for failing to appear in court without reason, or the attorney submits too many excuses for non-appearance in court, the Bar appoints a Board member to determine whether the situation requires an investigation. The matter is usually not taken further than this although, in the past, there have been attorneys who have been punished.[145] One can therefore conclude that the proper workings of the internal disciplinary mechanism of the Bar depend to a large degree on the sensitivity of the Bar organizations' own administration.

The current legal aid system operates under an appointment system. Any suspect or defendant who wishes to benefit qualifies, regardless of their financial status or the seriousness of crime in question.[146] When a criminal defendant requests a lawyer, this is relayed to the Bar by the police, prosecutor, judge or the court. In any case, if they comply with the request, the police ask the Bar to send a lawyer. However, the Istanbul Bar has been operating a boycott on such services for months,[147] due to the delayed payment of legal fees to CCP lawyers. Therefore, in Istanbul, even in cases where the presence of an attorney is mandatory, no counsel is being appointed. The suspect or his/her relatives can no longer directly apply to the Bar to request a legal aid lawyer.

Legal aid is provided by attorneys who sign up to do so with the Bar. There are not many organizational requirements for attorneys to work for the CCP service. Some bars request attorneys to attend courses concerning criminal legal aid delivery, but this is not standard practice. There are no restrictions stating which lawyers qualify to provide the service. Any lawyer with a license to practice can do so. The regulation on legal aid states that, as long as there is no conflict of interest among co-defendants, the same lawyer can represent more than one criminal defendant. A suspect or defendant has the right to benefit from an attorney at all stages of the investigation and prosecution, which includes any appeal.[148]

The suspect/defendant must be reminded that he/she has the right to legal assistance, may request collection of exculpatory evidence and is to be given the opportunity to invalidate the existing grounds of suspicion against him/her and

---

144   Another study conducted in an urban poor part of Istanbul to assess whether people could understand the language used to remind them of their rights found that 65% of people could not do so. Results of this research were presented at the Annual Conference of the Law and Society Association in July 2006, in Baltimore, USA. The presentation was by Galma Jahic and Idil Elveris, and was titled 'Pilot study of Legal Problems and Legal Needs of the Urban Poor in Istanbul.'

145   Interview with attorney 4. The same attorney said that it was difficult to monitor attorney performance only on the basis of the file, but if there was an intention to do so, a system could be easily set up. However, in his opinion, the current Bar was not willing to undertake this.

146   Whether the defendant has no attorney because he/she is indigent, or because he/she does not wish to retain one for any other reason, is irrelevant.

147   Very recently, some disctricts in the city have lifted the boycott.

148   Art. 149/1 CCP.

put forward issues in his/her favour.[149] This provision, along with all others, refers directly to the right of the suspect/defendant to defend him/herself.

There is no public defender service and lawyers are paid on a case-by-case basis in respect of action taken by them, according to a criminal legal aid fee tariff. The tariff specifies tasks and the corresponding fees, depending on the court hearing in the case, or the stage the action is taken (investigative or prosecutorial). In other words, there is a flat fee for each type of work. Lawyers often complain that the tariff is lower than the minimum fee tariff of the Bar while travel allowances are minimal.

For instance, for work that is done during the investigative phase (without further specification as to what this may be), an attorney is entitled to 69 Euro; for cases tried in Courts of Peace, 107 Euro; for cases in Courts of General Jurisdiction 118 Euro; for cases in Courts of Aggravated Felonies 215 Euro.[150] The travel allowance is 0.70 Euro.[151]

Further, the fees typically are paid late, are subject to tax and must be approved by the prosecutor.[152] The latter issue is said to undermine the independence of the legal profession.[153]

Interviews conducted among judges, prosecutors and attorneys found that members of all three professional groups thought that the CCP service was not operating efficiently. However, the reasons they saw and solutions they offered, differed. Judges gave waiting time as a concern and attributed this to the Bars and attorneys themselves.[154] Similarly, prosecutors also gave waiting time for the arrival of an attorney as a problem, but they also complained about attorneys not taking their job seriously, by engaging 'in show' rather than proper defence, or repeating useless statements instead of developing a proper defence, and by not dedicating themselves to the service they are providing.

They also expressed dissatisfaction with the Bar concerning the inefficiency of the appointment system, lack of control of the quality of the provided service and the change of lawyers during the legal process.[155] These statements should be read with caution, as the time that the interviews were conducted coincides with the wide application of mandatory criminal legal aid (between June 2005 and December 2006). At that time, the law required that, in almost every case in General Jurisdiction and Aggravated Felony Courts, a counsel be appointed for the criminal defendant. As the system could not cope with these demands, there were long

---

[149] Art. 147 CCP. There is a similar provision under art. 23 of the Regulation on arrest, custody and provision of statement, number 25832.

[150] These amounts are in Turkish lira as follows: 146 Turkish liras; 226 Turkish liras; 248 Turkish liras; 452 Turkish liras.

[151] This amount is the equivalent of 1.5 Turkish liras.

[152] The attorneys must show a proof of the work done, by either taking the hearing record (if appointed after the filing of the indictment), or by police interview documents (if appointed in the investigative stage), to the prosecutor's office to have its authenticity approved. To have this process expedited, sometimes the Bar is said to assign people to the prosecutor's office on a temporary basis.

[153] Herkese Adalet ve Özgürlük İçin CMK Platformu, 4 July 2009.

[154] Elveris, Jahic & Kalem 2007, p. 229.

[155] Elveris, Jahic & Kalem 2007, p. 230.

waiting times for courts and consequent delays. This was one of the reasons why the law was subsequently changed so as to apply to a much more narrowly defined list of circumstances.

On the other hand, the majority of lawyers stated that there were problems such as the lack of experience of CCP lawyers, absence or poor communication/contact with defendants, lawyers mainly trying to show off in court rather than conduct competent work, poor pay and tardy financial compensation for expenses, delays due to the assignment system, lack of quality monitoring, large workloads and a general lack of motivation.[156] As can be seen, this research somehow showed that the criminal justice actors were aware of the lack of oversight over the system exercised by the bar, or other relevant authority, leading to quality related problems in legal aid delivery.

Indeed, the study found a direct correlation between being represented by a criminal legal aid attorney and being convicted.[157] Further, it demonstrated that training, motivation and fees are all interrelated matters. However, the government has thus far not done anything to address these concerns.

2. Legal rights and their implementation

2.1. The right to information

2.1.1. Apprehension

Individuals apprehended or detained[158] are to be promptly notified, *in writing*, or when that is not possible, orally, of the grounds of their apprehension and the charges against them.[159] This right is triggered at the time of apprehension, or as

---

[156]   Elveris, Jahic & Kalem 2007, p. 231. When asked about what should be done to improve the situation, almost half of judges saw an on-duty CCP lawyer at the court as a possible solution, particularly in relation to the problem of delays. Prosecutors, on the other hand, believed that the most important thing would be to increase the motivation of the CCP lawyers, by increased payments and improved training. The majority of lawyers have stated that, to increase the motivation of the CCP lawyers would improve things significantly, and efforts should be made to make the services more attractive and interesting for experienced lawyers. Many lawyers have also stressed the importance of training, and that meetings, which would allow them to share their practices and support each others' work, would also be of great benefit. More awareness raising activities, and the promotion of the service among the general population, were also mentioned as necessary for overall improvement.

[157]   Elveris, Jahic & Kalem 2007, p. 215.

[158]   It should be noted that the arrest takes place on the initiative of the police, while detention is by order of the prosecutor.

[159]   Art. 19(4) of the Constitution; arts. 90(4), 98 (4), 141(1)(g), 147(1)(b)(f), 170(3)(h), 176 (1), 191(3)(b) CCP; arts. 6(4) Regulation on Arrest, Detention and Provision of Statement (police interview) of the Ministry of Justice; arts. 6(7) and 23 of the Regulation on Arrest, Detention and Provision of Statement (police interview) of the Ministry of Justice. For the regulation see: Official Gazette date 6 January 2005, No. 25832. Similarly, see Circular no: 3 issued by Ministry of Justice, on the application of the law on arrest, provision of statements and custody, Official Gazette date 1 January 2006. The requirement for 'charges' to be notified to the apprehended person includes 'information about the grounds for apprehension',

→

soon as practicable thereafter. In practice, there is a difference between an apprehension made spontaneously and detention orders.[160] The former is more of an after-thought, as the police try to first control the situation and, for example, remove any weapons. They must then indicate the nature of the suspicion.

In terms of detention orders, the police must explain to the suspect that he/she is sought for instance for a murder charge, or that an apprehension order is pending against him/her. For example, if the crime involves drugs, the police should state whether it is for import, export or just use.[161]

In practice, the police are said to be in the habit of taking a suspect without any explanation, or by merely saying 'the prosecutor wants you'.[162] Sometimes, a notice arrives in the mail saying 'please contact police station x', without stating whether as a witness or suspect.[163] It is said that the amount of information given by the police varies according to the level of education, financial situation and social status of the suspect. The more one knows about their rights, or the lesser seriousness of a crime one is accused of, the more open the police are said to become.[164]

However, if someone is charged with organized crime, narcotics, murder or money laundering or is subject to hot pursuit and his/her house has been surrounded very early in the morning, one cannot obtain the same information.[165] In other words, in these type of situations one cannot know the extent to which detained persons are informed of their rights. One attorney said that the information that comes from the prosecutor (to the police or defendant) is sometimes not sufficiently clear.[166]

The information can be given orally, but must eventually be recorded. At this stage, the suspect must be informed only of the character and source of the accusation brought against him/her. This includes a description of the alleged offence and the circumstances surrounding it. The police shall also inform the suspect promptly prior to the first interrogation about his/her legal rights, after taking measures to prevent him/her from escaping, and harming him/herself and others.[167]

An Apprehension and Detention Record, Suspect and Defendant Form[168] must be filled out, and a signed copy provided to the suspect. This form includes the

---

according to art. 13 of the Law on Duties and Authority of the Police, and art. 6 (4) of the Regulation on Apprehension, Detention and Provision of Statement.

[160] Interview with police officer 1.

[161] Interview with attorney 3.

[162] Interview with attorney 1.

[163] Interview with attorney 3.

[164] Interview with attorney 1.

[165] Interview with attorney 1. 'They search your house the whole day and you learn the charge only in the late afternoon. Once attorneys are involved, you are more likely to learn your rights. The attitudes and manners can change with our arrival'.

[166] Interview with attorney 3.

[167] Art. 90(4)CCP; art. 6 of the Regulation on Arrest. According to art. 147 CCP, this information will be repeated at the beginning of the first interrogation.

[168] A copy of this form is attached to the Regulation on Arrest, detention and provision of statement, Official Gazette No. 25832.

following information: personal data of the defendant, the place, date and time of apprehension, apprehending officer and crime leading to apprehension, prosecutor notified of the apprehension, or prosecutor ordering the detention. The form states that the defendant must provide information about his/her identity in a truthful way and notes that giving false or no personal information constitutes a crime.[169] The form then lists the rights of the defendant as follows:

- Right to silence.
- Right to inform a person of the suspect's own choosing that he or she has been apprehended.
- Right to put forward issues in his/her own defence in order to rebut suspicions about him/her.
- Right to an attorney.
- Right to ask for release from the judge of peace.

The defendant must sign this form, saying that he/she has been read these rights and understood them. It is possible that, in some cases, suspects/defendants end up signing the form without really reading it, since there are no guarantees that the police actually inform the suspects of their rights verbally.

There used to be two separate documents, one recording the apprehension and/or detention and a separate defendant rights form. This new version combines the two forms, although they serve separate purposes. This could be seen as a weakness, since the personal data of the suspect and the crime may make it appear as an internal police document. In a sense, the form could be seen as a 'letter of rights'. It should be noted that the form is written in surprisingly plain Turkish.[170] In practice, the police are said to formulate the question as 'do you know your legal rights', without explaining them one by one.[171]

There are some further formalities that must to be completed by the police. For instance, the police keep a book recording the reason of apprehension, hour and the name of the person who was informed that the suspect was been apprehended,[172] even if the suspect does not want anyone to know about it. In cases where the person is apprehended by force, his/her detention is ordered by the prosecutor, and he/she is sent for medical examination to a state hospital, or to the Institute of Forensic Medicine, by the order of the prosecutor.[173] The medical examination will be repeated if the suspect is released, transferred or brought before other judicial authorities, or if the duration of detention is prolonged.[174]

The suspect can be questioned only after this formality. While the medical examination was introduced to prevent inhuman treatment and torture, one attorney mentioned that some doctors were insensitive about the issue and the

---

[169] See 2.3.4 on the right to silence.
[170] Unfortunately the text in the CCP remains difficult to understand.
[171] Interview with attorney 2.
[172] Art. 13(G) of the Act on the Responsibility and Jurisdiction of the Police.
[173] Art. 9/1 of the Regulation on Arrest Detention and Provision of Statement.
[174] Art. 9/2 of the Regulation on Arrest Detention and Provision of Statement. If the person is wounded he/she is sent to the Institute of Forensic Medicine; interview with police officer 1.

examination was not conducted thoroughly but simply by asking the suspect whether he/she had any complaints. In addition, the suspect was taken to the doctor by the police officer who apprehended him/her, rather than and not by a separate officer. Worse, the officer may be present when the suspect is examined by the doctor, making it more difficult – if at all possible – to talk about any possible inhuman treatment.[175]

When a suspect is taken into custody, the police must inform the prosecutor and await his/her instructions.[176] This is mostly true for serious crimes, such as murder causing bodily harm, or crimes that create public reaction (for example, sexual abuse of children of murder). One police officer said that, for lesser crimes, prosecutors do not always want to be contacted.[177] This was confirmed by a prosecutor, who said that, for cases involving unidentified suspects (whose name and address has not been determined), there was no point in contacting them.[178] When contacted, the prosecutor can order one of the three things: he may want to interview the suspect; he/she may tell the police to interview the suspect and then have him/her released; or he/she may instruct the police to take the suspect into detention for him/she to later question the suspect.[179]

2.1.2. Police interview

There are two possibilities for a police interview to take place. First, after the apprehension, if the release of the suspect is not ordered by the prosecutor. Secondly, the person is detained by the order of the prosecutor. In both cases, the suspect is in detention and the charges against him/her are explained to him/her before questioning. This information must be supplied both verbally and in writing. Each record must be read and signed by the suspect. The suspect has the right to have an attorney present while being interviewed by the police. Research involving cases filed in 2000 and 2001 indicated that only 8.7% of defendants had an attorney at this stage. It is unknown if and to what extent the new CCP has affected representation levels at the police interview, but the same research quotes lawyers who claim that police officers do not inform suspects of the right to a lawyer, and sometimes discourage suspects from requesting lawyers. While the researchers indicated that they did not have information on how widespread these negative practices were, they should still raise concerns.[180] This point was repeated in attorney interviews (see 2.2.2).

Lawyers have further reported that they sometimes face difficulties in having a confidential conversation with their clients[181] in police stations, and that the police

---

[175]   Interview with attorney 4.
[176]   Art. 90/5 CCP.
[177]   Interview with police officer 1.
[178]   Interview with police officer 2. Prosecutors also let the police know in advance what the police need to do, depending on the crime investigated.
[179]   Interview with police officer 1.
[180]   Elveris, Jahic & Kalem 2007, p. 195.
[181]   Interview with attorney 2. This attorney has mentioned that, due to security concerns, the gendarmerie was in the room.

are not always accommodating in that sense. Another attorney explained that keeping attorneys waiting, or not letting them inside the police station, was a police tactic.[182] In fact, one attorney described an instance two years ago, where the police has threatened to record even the gaze of the suspect to his attorney, but more recently at the same station, he was given a list of questions by the police that they were going to ask to the suspect and was even allowed to make a copy thereof.[183] This can be read as a sign of changing attitudes.

As noted above, the police may interrogate the suspect[184] under certain circumstances (for example, the prosecutor does not wish to do so him/herself, or the suspect is not a minor). The statement given before the police can be used at trial as evidence, as long as it is taken in the presence of an attorney, or is confirmed by the suspect before a judge or the court (see 1.3). If there is an inconsistency between the statement at the trial and previous statements of the defendant, the police interrogation may be read at the trial, if (and only if) his attorney was present at the police interrogation, so that the criminal defendant will have opportunity to explain this inconsistency.[185]

While giving a statement, or during interrogation, a defendant/suspect shall be reminded not only of the charges against him/her, but also that he/she may request the collection of exculpatory evidence. He/she and shall be given the opportunity to invalidate the existing grounds of suspicion and to put forward issues in his/her favour.[186] If detained, the suspect must be furnished with the legal and factual grounds and reasons, and the contents of the decision shall be explained orally. Additionally, a written copy of the decision shall be given to him/her.[187]

This right can be seriously limited when the prosecutor issues a decision requiring secrecy, an issue which will be discussed in 2.4.1. Nevertheless, when the suspect wants to offer evidence, such as site visits that could give rise to further evidence (for example, the place where he/she obtained the drugs), this is done by notifying the prosecutor[188] and obtaining an order for search and seizure.

The regulation on arrest states that these duties shall be performed by trained police who are experienced, patient, calm, and smart, and who understand the psychology of criminals and have passed a psycho-technical test.[189] One police officer interviewed said that he was conducting 10-15 interviews per day and explained that it took him six months to learn how to conduct an interview. He confirmed that one must control himself and protect himself against provocations, since the suspect may say anything he/she wants.[190] It is important to note that the ECtHR has declared Turkey to be in violation of the ECHR in a considerable

---

[182]   Interview with attorney 4.
[183]   Interview with attorney 2.
[184]   Art. 161/2 CCP.
[185]   Art. 213 CCP. In addition, the police may not repeat the interrogation of the suspect. If any need arises to do so, it must be done by the prosecutor; art. 148/5 CCP.
[186]   Art. 147 (1)(f) CCP; also see a similar provision in art. 23(1)(g) of the Regulation on Arrest Detention and Provision of Statement.
[187]   Art. 101 (2) CCP.
[188]   Interview with police officer 2.
[189]   Arts. 30 and 31 of the Regulation on Arrest Detention and Provision of Statement.
[190]   Interview with police officer 2.

number of cases involving police behaviour. Although it has been alleged that the police no longer resort to violence, human rights group claim that, in the last three years, 31 people have died in police custody.[191]

Apart from the obligation to remind the suspect/defendant of his/her rights at certain stages, and getting him/her to sign the related records, there are no further obligations to verify whether he/she has properly understood the information on his/her rights. Research has shown that, while judges and prosecutors believe that the suspects/defendants understand their rights, the majority of attorneys believe that they do not. Further, attorneys point out to serious deficiencies in the way suspects are reminded of their rights. Some attorneys have reported that, at the investigation phase, police officers do not inform the suspects of their rights, and sometimes even discourage suspects from requesting an attorney.[192]

2.1.3. Charge

A person who is not released within 24 hours, or who is detained by the order of the prosecutor shall be brought before the prosecutor for interrogation. During this interrogation, the prosecutor shall also inform the defendant of the charges against him/her. At this time, the prosecutor questions the suspect, in order to understand whether there is sufficient evidence to issue an indictment, or whether there is strong evidence justifying pre-trial arrest.

As can be seen, the right to information must be complied with at almost every stage of the investigation (on apprehension, when giving a statement, during interrogation) and later, at the trial stage, when the indictment is notified to the suspect before trial and subsequently read before him/her during trial. Thus, any amendments to the charge(s) against him/her will also be communicated to the suspect as the investigation develops.

2.1.4. Pre-trial stage and trial

The indictment must contain evidence of the offence and explain the events that comprise the charges, as well as providing the relationship between the charge and the evidence.[193] The indictment and notification shall be provided to the suspect at least one week prior to the first hearing day (see 1.3).[194] However, in practice, prosecutors may not send copies of the indictment, as they seem to think that the attorney can go to the court and obtain a copy.[195] While this may be true for persons who have an attorney, people without counsel would not even think to do this. The attorney can be present in all sessions of the hearing, even if the accused is not

---

191   English version of the article is not available. For Turkish; see M.Utku Şentürk, 'Ne bu şiddet bu celal?', 25/11/2009, quoting Human Rights Watch. See <http://www.radikal.com.tr/ Radikal.aspx?aType=RadikalDetay&ArticleID=966116&Date=26.11.2009&CategoryID=77>.
192   Elveris, Jahic & Kalem 2007, p. 195, 229.
193   Art. 170 CCP.
194   Art. 176 (4) CCP.
195   Interview with attorney 1.

present at trial.[196] The suspect must be informed beforehand of any changes in the nature of the crime charged.[197]

Individuals who had not been given written documentation of the grounds of apprehension, or of pre-trial arrest and the charges against him/her or who have not been provided with an oral explanation of the grounds, may claim material and emotional losses from the State.[198] It was claimed, however that the jurisprudence of the Court of Cassation made it very difficult to actually do this, requiring the claimant to be absolutely innocent.[199] While the number of applications is not high, compensation amounts have been growing.[200] At the same time, it was pointed out that the court hearing these cases is a criminal court, not well versed in compensation cases.[201] Further, it was pointed out that, without exhausting this domestic remedy, people cannot apply to the ECHR.[202] Yet., the process was very long (and had complications such as officers no longer serving in the same post, or witnesses dying).

The failure of public authorities to carry out their duties also gives rise to criminal liability,[203] but it has been said that most cases get dropped. When asked about the frequency of attorneys using these measures, two attorneys replied that once clients considered themselves 'saved', they did not want to resort to administrative, disciplinary or criminal measures.[204] Nevertheless, these cases have become more frequent as judges and attorneys have become more conscientious about the issue.[205] It has also been indicated that disciplinary and administrative investigations against the police or other authorities have been more effective in preventing repetition of unlawful practices, than have filing compensation claims. In addition, the Parliament's Commission on Human Rights has explained that the highest number of complaints it received from citizens concerned the judiciary, but due to principles of separation of powers and judicial independence, it could not act on these, thus barring a possible avenue for addressing citizens' complaints.[206]

---

[196] Provided that he/she is interrogated.

[197] Art. 226 CCP.

[198] Art. 141(1)(g) CCP.

[199] Interview with attorney 3. The Court of Cassation held that 'it is not to be determined whether the arrest was proper but whether the plaintiff (the suspect in the original trial) could be held liable in any way for the measures taken against him, such as confessing to the crime or attempting to escape, led to the arrest', Yargıtay Ceza Genel Kurulu, 1986/5-5 E. 1986/79 K. 3.11.1986.

[200] Interview with attorney 1.

[201] Interview with attorney 3.

[202] Article 35 §1 ECHR 'The Court may only deal with the matter after all domestic remedies have been exhausted, according to the generally recognised rules of international law, and within a period of six months from the date on which the final decision was taken.'

[203] Art. 257 CCP.

[204] Interview with attorney 1 and attorney 2.

[205] Interview with attorney 1.

[206] <http://www.tbmm.gov.tr/komisyon/insanhak/insanhaklari.htm>.

2.2. The right to defend oneself

2.2.1. The right of a person to defend him/herself

Both the ECHR and the Turkish Constitution[207] expressly state that everyone (either a suspect or defendant) has the right to defend him/herself in person or through legal assistance. While some articles of the CCP expressly refer to this right, it exists without a doubt throughout the whole criminal process (starting from the very beginning of the investigation phase). In fact, most of the procedural rules and 'subsidiary' rights in the CCP are for the effective use of this right (these have been already explained under section 1.5).

While a person can always say that he/she does not want an attorney, this is not an irrevocable waiver. In other words, even if the suspect states that he/she does not want an attorney at the investigation stage, he/she can change his/her mind at a later stage. In general, the suspect/defendant, after being reminded of his/her right to an attorney, either chooses an attorney, or one is appointed at his/her request.

2.2.2. The right to legal advice at the investigation stage

The right of the attorney to consult with the suspect (or defendant), to be present during the provision of the statement or interrogation, and to provide legal assistance, shall not be prevented/restricted at any stage of the investigation and prosecution process.[208] If the suspect requests an attorney, then the attorney must be contacted before proceeding with the statement or interrogation. In other words, if the suspect/defendant has requested legal assistance, he/she cannot be questioned further.[209]

Whether the police actually suspend the interview if the suspect asks for counsel is a different matter. When specifically asked about this, most attorneys have answered 'the police should'. One attorney explained that the prosecutor should be notified about this.[210] Another said that some stop, while others say 'you should have said this before, I have now started'. This attorney explained that it very much depended on the attitude in the city or the director of the police in the district.[211] One attorney stated that it also depended on the socio-economic status of the suspect. If he/she is unemployed and does not appear to have a family, then the police are inclined to act according to a social hierarchy.[212] Another one said that everything was possible,[213] while one prosecutor simply said 'I stop'.[214]

---

[207]   Art. 6 of the ECHR and art. 36 of the Constitution.
[208]   Art. 149(3) CCP.
[209]   Even at the investigation stage in terrorist cases, where access to an attorney may be delayed by the judge for up to 24 hours pursuant to art. 10 of Law, No. 3713, provision of statement/interrogation is delayed until the arrival of the attorney.
[210]   Interview with attorney 1.
[211]   Interview with attorney 3.
[212]   Interview with attorney 4.
[213]   Interview with attorney 1.

It is of course difficult to assess what happens in reality, but attorneys also mentioned a worrying practice called 'oral interview'.[215] Although the police must remind the suspect of his/her rights, take him/her for a medical check and ensure that he/she has an attorney, this is not always done. Instead, the police meet and introduce themselves to the suspect; make the suspect trust them, scare him/her or, depending on the crime, try to patronize the suspect. Policemen abound in the station: one apprehends the suspect, one searches him/her; one prepares him/her for the interview; one scares him/her and one speaks to him/her to obtain information before the attorney arrives. Upon arrival, attorneys feel that the suspect has been 'broken down', the scene has been already set up and the 'informal' interview has taken its course.

When confronted by attorneys about this practice, the police retort that 'it is not a crime to chat someone up'.[216] One attorney described incidents where the attorney arrived, only to find that the interview had already taken place and the suspect had signed the form. The only missing signature was the attorney's. When the attorney refused to sign, or only signed with reservation, the police requested another attorney from the Bar, saying that the previous attorney did not arrive.

On another occasion, the police pressure the suspect to sign a record issued against the advice of the attorney. The attorney explained this by the fact that the police want attorneys that suit them.[217] Other police tactics undermining the right to an attorney and the right to silence are discussed in length under 2.3.4.

Indeed, research measuring access to criminal legal aid lawyers at different stages of the criminal justice process found that representation levels in police stations was only 7.3%.[218] In order to measure this, records of statements given to the police were examined. These records had boxes indicating whether the defendant wanted to provide a statement. In some cases, the 'no' box was checked, however, there still was a statement. One possible answer to this seems to be confirmed by the above explanation. Even if the suspect tries to remain silent or requests an attorney, the police may try to talk them slowly into providing a statement. At the same time, one police officer explained that suspects do not want an attorney, because they also know that they will only receive a fine (for possession of drugs).[219]

It has been suggested that this police practice may have developed due to the text of the reminder of the right to silence.[220] It does not mention what happens when someone chooses to speak after he/she has been warned. In other words, it does not specify, like the 'Miranda' warning, that 'everything you say can and will be used against you'. The police seem to use the information obtained through

---

[214] Interview with prosecutor 2. Research evidence shows that access to criminal legal aid is the highest at the prosecution stage, where 23.7% of people had a lawyer, Elveris, Kalem & Jahic 2007, p. 188.

[215] Interview with attorney 1.

[216] Interview with attorney 1.

[217] Interview with attorney 4.

[218] Elveris, Jahic & Kalem 2007, p. 187.

[219] Interview with police officer 2.

[220] Interview with attorney 1. Unfortunately for defendants, this statement is not true, since possession of drugs, even for personal use carries a 1-3 year sentence.

informal means when corresponding with the prosecutor. Judges are said to be aware of this police practice, but do not confront the police for resorting to these illegal methods. Instead, some question the defendant about statements obtained. One attorney[221] stated that sometimes a judge takes into account unlawfully obtained evidence, knowing it is unlawful, only because the judge is curious why the defendant committed the crime. Under such circumstances, the attorney interviewed reminds the judge of the fact that curiosity may not be the reason to hear unlawful evidence.

Concerning investigation of terrorism cases, access to an attorney may be delayed by the judge for up to 24 hours. However, the suspect cannot be interrogated during this time.[222] Further, if there is evidence showing that the attorney is aiding communication among members of a terrorist organisation, the judge may decide that correspondence can be provided only under the supervision of an official, and documents handed over or exchanged may be reviewed by the judge. The judge then decides whether the whole or part of the documents is to be returned, thus compromising attorney-client privilege.

Juveniles[223] above the age of fifteen who have been charged with a terrorism offence, shall be tried not in juvenile courts, but like adults in felony courts. This is in direct violation of the UN Convention on the Protection of the Rights of the Child.[224] For people charged with terrorism, alternatives to imprisonment, postponement of the sentence, as well as parole are inapplicable.[225] In other words, when it comes to terrorism cases, there appears to be a separate procedure for investigation and trial, which is different from other criminal cases.

2.2.3. The right to legal representation at the trial stage

If the suspect is detained, he/she can have up to three attorneys. Nevertheless, the design of the court room does not allow the defendant to sit together with his/her attorney. One attorney said: 'You communicate from a distance. This is desperation!'.[226] Further, research conducted before the Istanbul Courts has shown that, in 90.4% of cases, the criminal defendant had no attorney.[227] The research also

---

[221]   Interview with attorney 1.

[222]   Art. 10 of the Act on Fighting Terror No. 3713, published in the Official Gazette on 12 April 1991.

[223]   Juvenile justice and courts appear to be a problem in itself. Juveniles below the age of 15 should be delievered to juvenile police as soon as they are apprehended, but this seems to be the case only in Istanbul. One attorney said that, outside Istanbul, juvenile police operate as a transfer station taking the child to the court. All other actions are taken by the terror police.

[224]   Art. 40.3 of the Convention on the Protection of the Rights of the Child: 'States Parties shall seek to promote the establishment of laws, procedures, authorities and institutions specifically applicable to children alleged as, accused of, or recognized as having infringed the penal law'. Pursuant to art. 9 of the Act on Fighting Terror, children of 15 and above are prosecuted by Specialized Aggravated Felony Courts. This thus constitutes a breach of the Convention.

[225]   Art. 13 of the Act on Fighting Terror.

[226]   Interview with attorney 3.

[227]   Of those who were represented by an attorney, 7.2% were represented by private attorneys while 1.9% were represented by CCP lawyers.

found that representation by counsel was different according to the type of court – 4.5% for Courts of Peace, 10.3% for Courts of General Jurisdiction and 42.1 percent for superior courts.[228] The latter number is still less than half, in a court that hears the gravest crimes and where defendants are usually detained and sentenced to long prison terms.

In fact, the same research showed that 74.2% of offenders who receive a prison sentence do so without ever being represented by a lawyer.[229] At the same time, attorneys appointed under the criminal legal aid system may not be dismissed by the suspect/defendant.[230] This can be seen as a problem, as it is common practice that most of the legal aid attorneys do not visit their clients in jail.

However, in cases where the appointed attorney does not appear at the hearing, or fails to fulfil his/her duties, then *the judge or the court* must take the necessary steps to immediately appoint another attorney.[231] In such cases, the suspect/defendant may draw the attention of the judge/court to this issue and ask for a replacement. At the same time, the suspect/defendant may always choose an attorney of their own from outside the legal aid scheme, therefore ending the duties of the appointed attorney.

2.2.4. Independence and competence of defence lawyers

There is no separate criminal defence bar in Turkey, although some lawyers never take any criminal defence work, some take only criminal work, and some do both. It is understood that young lawyers who try to develop a clientele and expertise often undertake criminal legal aid work. Legal aid work is not, however, highly regarded. As soon as the attorney believes that he/she has developed expertise, they move away from the system. One often hears that the criminal legal aid service is of low quality. Indeed, the research conducted before the Istanbul courts found a correlation between being represented by a criminal legal aid attorney and being convicted.[232] While we do not know how many attorneys in Turkey take legal aid cases, the number in Istanbul is 3,167 out of 23,884 attorneys registered with the Bar.[233]

There is no bar exam or any similar qualifying scheme necessary to either practice law before getting a licence, or to maintain it. The fact that the legal aid service is being delivered by a professional organisation that has been established to

---

[228] Elveris, Jahic & Kalem 2007, p. 190-191.
[229] Elveris, Jahic & Kalem 2007, p. 216.
[230] Art. 7(2) of the Regulation, Official Gazette of 3 February 2007, No. 26450.
[231] Art. 151/1 CCP. It is said that the Court of Cassation insists on the proper application of this rule. The court must adjourn the hearing in order to provide the defendant with a lawyer, giving the lawyer sufficient time to examine the case and to prepare a defence (see Öztürk, Tezcan, Erdem, Sırma, Saygılar & Alan 2009, p. 239; Ünver & Hakeri 2009, p. 208). According to case law, it will be unlawful for the court to give a sentence in a hearing where the (mandatory) attorney is absent (10.CD. 26. 12.2005 t., E. 2005/24359, K. 2005/19605, Ünver & Hakeri 2009, p. 208).
[232] Elveris, Jahic & Kalem 2007, p. 215.
[233] See <http://www.istanbulbarosu.org.tr/Document.asp?Konu=301&DocumentIndex=cmuk/tanitim.htm>.

further the interests of a profession, rather than to protect clients, is a matter of concern. This is suggested by the fact that the Bar brings up the issues concerning criminal legal aid solely in terms of late or no payment of the attorneys' fees. Whether the service is of good quality and whether the suspects' rights to defence are observed is never discussed. The current boycott by the Istanbul Bar only goes to emphasize this point.

Research has shown that the CCP Units do not function properly. A majority of judges and prosecutors interviewed believe that the Units have some problems related directly to their management.[234] For them, delays in appointment and the arrival of attorneys seem to be the most important problems. Judges have stated that the Bar fulfils its main tasks, but it is not able to accomplish them on time. Hence, the court often has to wait for the attorney to arrive.

Legal aid lawyers, on the other hand, believe that the Unit also does not function well, but for the following reasons: lack of experience of the CCP Unit attorneys, absence or poor communication/contact with the suspects/defendants, poor pay and tardy financial compensation for their expenses, delays due to the assignment system, lack of quality monitoring, large workload and a lack of motivation.[235] This issue will be dealt further under section 3.

The Bar has been reluctant to establish requirements for lawyers to attend courses to participate in legal aid, undermining the quality of the service. If attorneys fail to provide quality service, the matter can be referred to disciplinary proceedings, but a glance at the 2008 Report of the European Commission for the Efficiency of Justice (CEPEJ) shows that Turkey has a very low number of disciplinary proceedings per 1000 lawyers.[236] Once an attorney is assigned to a case by the CCP unit, he/she is subject to professional rules just like a private matter. In other words, he/she must exercise the same duty of care. An attorney may refuse the assignment/abstain from performing the duty on reasonable grounds.[237]

2.3. Procedural Rights

2.3.1. The right to release from custody pending trial

This right is not expressly stated in Turkish law. While this could be seen as a weakness in terms of defendants' rights, the right can nevertheless be inferred from the direct application of the ECHR in terms of human rights matters, or the Constitution provisions concerning the right to personal freedom and security.

---

[234]   Both groups have also expressed concern with regard to the quality of the service provided by the attorneys, including their lack of interest and inexperience and the superficial way in which they handle cases.

[235]   Elveris, Jahic & Kalem 2007, p. 231.

[236]   European Judicial Systems, Edition 2008: Efficiency and Quality of Justice, CEPEJ, p. 218.

[237]   Art. 6 of the Regulation on Arrest Detention and Provision of Statement and the CCP Unit Directive of the Istanbul Bar. Date of entry into force 17 April 2008; for the text, see <http://www.istanbulbarosu.org.tr/Document.asp?Konu=302&DocumentIndex=cmuk/icy onetmelik.htm>. Art. 6 of the Regulation on Arrest Detention and Provision of Statement and the CCP Unit Directive of the Istanbul Bar.

As indicated in 1.4, prison overcrowding is a significant problem. Particularly in large towns, prisoners take shifts to sleep in beds, while prisons in the Black Sea region operate at half their capacity. In the last five years, there has been extensive reform in the prison system, with considerable improvements in some prisons. Further, new prisons have been built, increasing capacity of the system; however, the figure is still 30,000 short. The government should also question whether spending 476 Euro[238] per month for each person in jail is a good investment, given the literacy and poverty rates in the country, as well as the low funding of legal aid.

Indeed, the total prison population and incarceration rates have been increasing, and have more than doubled since 2000.[239] At that time, over 50% of all the prison population consisted of detainees,[240] who may not be found guilty at the end of their trials. In 2007, of the 1,920,862 total cases, only 1,065,953 ended with a guilty verdict,[241] of which 767,868 resulted in custodial sentences. This amounts to 72.1% of all convictions. It should be noted that custodial sentences include prison sentences converted to fines, security measures (for example, to be prohibited from going to particular places or from practicing a particular occupation) and suspended sentences.[242] Given all of this, the high detention rates are worrisome.

One of the reasons for overcrowding is that the sentences prescribed for crimes are still lengthy when compared with other European countries.[243] Further, the time served to qualify for parole has been lengthened. Under the new law on Corrections, a person must spend two thirds of his/her sentence behind bars before being eligible to be released on parole. Up until 2005, this period was half of the sentence. In addition, courts rarely resort to issuing bail, limiting its use.[244] The high detention may also be read as a sign of a serious problem with the legal aid system, despite the current rule of mandatory representation in detention hearing.

Data concerning the average length of time spent in custody awaiting trial (or pending trial) is not published. However, considering the average length of prosecution in Turkey (246 days in all criminal courts),[245] and the rather high percentage of detentions, it is fair to assume that suspects/defendants may be kept in custody for a long time. Where the crime is not within the jurisdiction of the Aggravated Felony Court, the maximum period of detention is one year.[246] If deemed necessary, this may be extended for a further six months. Where the crime is under the jurisdiction of the Aggravated Felony Courts, the maximum detention period is two years and any extension granted shall not exceed three years.[247]

---

[238] This amount equals to 1,000 Turkish liras.
[239] <http://www.cte.adalet.gov.tr/>. See also the table in footnote 1. The trend is clearly visible.
[240] Source: <http://www.cte.adalet.gov.tr/#>.
[241] Statistics 2007 announced by the General Directorate of Criminal Records and Statistics, see <http://www.adli-sicil.gov.tr/istatistik_2007/ceza%20mahkemeleri/ceza11-2007.pdf>.
[242] See <http://www.adli-sicil.gov.tr/istatistik_2007/ceza%20mahkemeleri/ceza11-2007.pdf>.
[243] Centel, Zafer & Cakmut 2008, p. 545.
[244] See art. 109 and 113 of CPC.
[245] Statistics 2007 announced by the General Directorate of Criminal Records and Statistics, see <http://www.adli-sicil.gov.tr/istatistik_2007/ceza%20mahkemeleri/ceza1-2007.pdf>.
[246] CCP art. 102.
[247] Pursuant to art. 12 of Law numbered 5320, the periods stated under art. 102 of the CCP will enter into force on 31 January 2010. Until then, the periods stated under art. 110 of the former

→

It should also be said that there are alternatives to detention, such as judicial control,[248] but attorneys explain that this is not used by judges very much.[249] This alternative can be used when the reasons for detention are present (strong doubt that a suspect committed a crime, is likely to abscond or destroy evidence). Further, the maximum sentence of the crime should be three years or less.[250]

An attorney described a worrying practice concerning detained defendants.[251] Sometimes, detainees make it to court but their attorney does not appear. In this case, the judge simply decides that the suspect cannot be questioned and detention should continue.[252] Other times, the attorney appears in court, but the detainee does not, due, for example, to a breakdown of the prison car. In this case, particularly when the detainee is yet to be interrogated, the judge would not release him/her, despite indications pointing out that detention may have been inappropriate.[253]

Further, in the investigation stage, the failure of the courts to remain open after 5 pm means that some suspects spend the night at the police station, particularly if they have been apprehended by the police after 3 pm,[254] because the completion of paper work takes approximately 2 hours. Those suspects apprehended 'after hours' are taken into custody, to be taken to the prosecutor the next day. This indicates the need for a night court.[255]

2.3.2. The right of a defendant to be tried in his/her presence

In general, a trial cannot be held regarding a defendant who fails to appear.[256] However, there are many exceptions to this rule. For example, if the collected evidence is sufficient to render a judgment other than a conviction, the trial may be concluded in the absence of the defendant, even if he/she has not been interrogated concerning the merits of the case. If the defendant escapes, or does not appear at the hearing, following an interrogation about the case, and his/her presence is considered no longer necessary by the court, then the hearing may be conducted in his/her absence.

CCP apply. It is nevertheless unclear what the maximum years of detention may be under the new CCP as well as the former CCP.
[248] Arts. 109 and 110 of the CCP on judicial control.
[249] Interviews with attorneys 1 and 4.
[250] Judicial control can include the following measures: prohibition from leaving the country; to be present at a certain time and place as determined by the judge; to attend courses and invitations determined by the judge; to refrain from driving certain vehicles; to undergo drugs or alcohol treatment; to provide security for payment of compensation to be later determined for the victim, or other costs, or child support; to refrain from carrying a weapon. If the person under judicial control acts contrary to the judicial control order, he/she can be immediately detained, irrespective of the sentence he/she faces.
[251] Interview with attorney 1.
[252] As the attorney put it 'Your attorney is not here. We cannot interrogate you. Detention is to continue. Back to prison, off you go!'.
[253] The attorney has explained that judges think that, while the suspect is under their control, they should complete all formalities before the suspect disappears; interview with attorney 1.
[254] Interview with police officer 2.
[255] Interview with attorney 1.
[256] Art. 193(1) CCP.

Further, if the alleged crime prescribes a judicial fine or confiscation of assets as the sole punishment, then the hearing can be conducted, even if the defendant fails to appear.[257] In addition, if the court deems the presence of the defendant unnecessary after considering his/her right of defence, it shall continue to conduct the hearing and conclude the case in the absence of the defendant. However, if the defendant has no attorney, the court shall ask the Bar to appoint an attorney for him/her. If the defendant is allowed back into the courtroom, the proceedings conducted in his/her absence shall be explained to him/her. No doubt these provisions have been drafted to expedite proceedings, but their broad application may have serious consequences for defendants.

With respect to organized crime cases,[258] where the number of the defendants are large and, in some hearings actions will be taken that do not concern all of them, the court may decide to conduct sessions in their absence.[259] If the hearing had been conducted in the absence of the defendant, the defendant, if supported by justifiable reasons, may claim the reinstatement of the decisions and interactions of the court within one week after he/she has been notified.[260] However, if the defendant was not present because he/she was excused upon his/her own request, or if he/she had been represented by an attorney, he/she does not have this right.

2.3.3. The right to be presumed innocent

The Constitution states that, until proven guilty, a person shall be deemed innocent. The attorney interviews we have conducted concerning this right have exposed some myths about this presumption: one attorney said that, although he does not think it is completely violated, it is the defendant who must attempt to prove that he/she did not commit the crime.[261] Another attorney stated that general community did not believe in the concept,[262] and only when people themselves experience an injustice, do they understand its importance.[263] One prosecutor pointed out that, in a society where there is a saying 'where there is smoke, there must be fire', there can be no talk of the presumption of innocence.[264] He pointed out that the system was trying the defendant and not the evidence.

---

[257] Art. 195 CCP.

[258] For example, producing and trading narcotic or stimulative substances committed within the activities of a criminal organization, crimes committed by using coercion and threats within an organization formed in order to obtain unjust economic gain, crimes as defined by the second book, section 4, chapters 4-5-6-7 8 of the Criminal Code (except for arts. 305, 318, 319, 323, 324, 325 and 332).

[259] However, if during the sessions conducted in their absence, a circumstance is revealed that affects them, these shall be notified to them in the following session; art. 252(1)(b) CCP.

[260] Art. 198 CCP.

[261] Interview with attorney 2. He noted that, in his opinion, judges tried to be fair, not always trying to convict. Another attorney expressed the opposite view; judges were very accustomed to crime and criminals and prone to punishment; interview with attorney 1.

[262] 'We have not internalized the concept. If the police have brought him in, he must have done something. If Forensics says so, it should be provocation. If the attorney says he is innocent, he must be guilty', Attorney interview 1.

[263] Interview with attorney 1.

[264] Interview with prosecutor 2.

While governmental figures and courts refer to suspects and use careful language in public, attorneys indicated that the way the media portrays suspects undermines the right to be presumed innocent. Even if the person is acquitted, in the eyes of the public, he/she often remains guilty.[265] One attorney said that investigations are made which involve use of the media, and people are shown on television with handcuffs. In fact, as the hearings get closer, news about the matter increases, creating possible bias in judges as well.[266] One prosecutor said that telephone conversations are leaked to newspapers, leading the suspect to become 'suspicious' in the eyes of the public, and thus creating pressure on judges.[267]

One attorney has stated that the legal requirement of the deletion of criminal records after the legally prescribed period is often overlooked. When the person needs to provide a criminal record (for example, to apply for a job), prior convictions come up, which cause further prejudice.[268]

These statements indicate concerns about the actual application of the presumption of innocence, particularly when one bears in mind the high number of detainees and the high acquittal rates, as described in 1.4. Indeed, detained people, even if they are subsequently released, carry a social stigma that is already attached to them. One attorney mentioned the famous case of an alleged sex offender, who turned out not to be the offender. He later had difficulty buying bread or going to the mosque.[269] In fact, the crime of 'attempting to influence fair prosecution' was created,[270] in order to prevent this, but the effect of this provision is unclear.

2.3.4. The right to silence

The right to silence is also implicitly recognized in the Constitution. No one can be forced to provide a statement or evidence that would incriminate him/herself or his/her relatives (specified in the law). Further, both the Constitution and the CCP expressly state that the suspect has a right to silence.[271] However, as discussed in section 2.2.2, it is no secret that people have been forced by the police to confess.[272] Perhaps this is why the law now provides that, if the statement was taken without a lawyer being present, then that confession or statement cannot be used to convict someone, if it is subsequently retracted in court before a judge.

Interviews with criminal justice professionals have shown conflicting points of view as to the extent of the use of the right. One police officer said that suspects use their right to silence because they think that the police are being unfair to them, and

---

[265] Interview with attorney 4.
[266] Interview with attorney 3.
[267] Interview with prosecutor 2.
[268] Interview with attorney 4.
[269] Interview with attorney 3.
[270] Art. 288 CCP.
[271] Art. 38 Constitution, art. 147 CCP.
[272] As recently, in 2009, the Commission on Human Rights, operating under the Turkish Parliament, has detected partial human rights abuses in the form of degrading treatment amounting to torture; see the Report of the Commission dated 9 June 2009, <http://www.tbmm.gov.tr/komisyon/insanhaklari/belge/Beyoglu_Ilce_Emniyet_Müdürlü gü_inceleme_Raporu.pdf>.

[in protest], want to only talk to the prosecutor.[273] One prosecutor explained that the police sometimes record that the suspect wants to use the right to silence, because they cannot be bothered taking a statement, issuing the form and writing down the interview. In that case, it is easier for them to say that the suspect will not talk to them and refer the matter to the prosecutor.[274] This prosecutor suggested that this is why, on paper, it looked like there were many people who used the right to silence. However, this did not reflect the truth. He also said that Turkish people were inclined to talk by swearing to god that they did not commit the crime.[275]

The same point was also made by an attorney. He said that, unlike in the United States, it was very common for suspects to talk, whether or not in the presence of an attorney. In hearings, suspects also usually wanted to talk, and would not accept advice that they be silent.[276] Nevertheless, he said that it was not correct that the right is not exercised at all, although depending on the place of the investigation, there might be some resistance.

Most of the attorneys, however, pointed out that the police try to talk the suspects out of using the right, by resorting to various tactics. This could be done through 'sticks' – either by threatening to include the family of the suspect in the investigation,[277] or to blame the suspect for other unresolved matters. Sometimes 'carrots' were offered too, such as saying that the suspect would be released if he talked, or that the provision of a statement would constitute a mitigating circumstance.[278] This latter point apparently creates problems in building trust between the client and the attorney, particularly when the client obtains conflicting information from the police and the attorney. However, case law points out that, the fact that a suspect makes use of the right to silence, cannot be used as a ground either for rejection or as a mitigating circumstance at sentencing before the court.[279]

At law, a person cannot be convicted solely based on his confession. The Court of Cassation has held that, for a confession to be accepted as grounds for conviction, other corroborative evidence is required.[280] When asked why the police preferred that suspects talk, it was explained that, when corroborated with other evidence, such as phone tapping,[281] or witness statements,[282] the confession can lead to a

---

273 Interview with police officer 2.

274 Interview with prosecutor 2.

275 Interview with prosecutor 2.

276 Interview with attorney 3.

277 Interview with attorney 4.

278 Interview with attorney 3.

279 4.CD., 1.5.1997, 1070/2947, see: <http://yargitay.gov.tr/Mevzuat/emsal/971070_4c.txt>.

280 According to the Court of Cassation, the confession must be made before a judge, in an overt and definitive way, must be reasonable and possible and not be withdrawn. In addition, there must be corroborative evidence present in the case (CGK, 7.3.1983, 3/104, see: Savaş & Mollamahmutoğlu 1995, p. 767). Further, the confession must be based on the persons' free will. No confession will be accepted for conviction if scientific evidence is inconsistent with it, and no other corroborative evidence is found (CGK, 2.12.1991, 1-301/334, YKD July 1992, vol. 18, p. 1108).

281 Interview with attorney 2. It has been suggested that more recently, investigations increasingly begin with intercepted phone conversations.

282 Interview with attorney 1.

conviction. Further, it has been indicated that the police sees itself as a party in the matter, and feels that it must justify the apprehension of a suspect.

Reducing the number of unresolved matters also contributed to the pressure to obtain a confession.[283] This was also confirmed by one police officer,[284] although he said there was no such thing as pressure. On the other hand, one prosecutor noted that they received too many unresolved cases from the police.[285] This could be the reason why the police are reluctant for defendants to use this right.

Meanwhile, it should be noted that suspects must answer questions concerning their identity in a truthful fashion, which can perhaps be considered to undermine the right to silence, since revealing an identity might trigger the finding of previous criminal records. Indeed, the police use the ID cards of persons it apprehends to ascertain their identity. If they do not carry one, this is obtained from the internet (census records) and if not, a finger print is used.[286] Without ascertaining the identity, no statement is taken. Further, the law provides that information concerning the economic and social status of the suspect shall be obtained.[287] According to one attorney, whether this information can be considered information relevant to the substance of the crime, or solely as a matter of identity, is of debate, but the police view it more like the latter and do not accept that a suspect would remain silent about this information. However, this may lead to further questions about the crime, further undermining the right to silence.[288]

2.3.5. The right to a reasoned judgment

The right to a reasoned judgment is enshrined in the Constitution, as well as the CCP, and covers all judgments, including minority opinions.[289] Further, the judgment must state not only the reasons, but also any legal remedies against the judgment, as well as the time period within which any documents must to be filed and where.[290] It has been suggested that judges have a tendency to 'cut and paste' the allegations of the prosecutor and defence arguments put forward, and write the judgment accordingly.[291] Others sometimes repeat the grounds mentioned in the Code,[292] and then add 'for the above explained reasons' as a standard sentence. Similarly, the Court of Cassation had a tendency to write 'approved, for the judgment is in line with substance and procedure'.[293] However, it has found that a judgment based on insufficient reason, such as cases where the reasons only include expressions like 'based on the discretion of the court', were contrary to the law.[294]

283 Interview with attorney 3.
284 Interview with police officer 2.
285 Interview with prosecutor 2.
286 Interview with police officer 2.
287 Art. 147 CCP.
288 Interview with attorney 3.
289 Art. 34 and 230 CCP.
290 Art. 40/2 Constitution, art. 232/6 CCP.
291 Interview with attorney 3.
292 Interview with attorney 2.
293 Interview with attorney 3.
294 4.CD., 18.5.1994, 1437/4605, Centel & Zafer 2005, p. 674.

When it comes to decisions concerning detention, judges are said to use vague language deliberately in an attempt to refrain from appearing to provide their opinion on the merits, particularly if it is them who will subsequently hear the case. They therefore use standard formulations, such as 'according to evidence in the file'.[295] One attorney said that, while this was a fair concern, perhaps the system should be changed so that decisions of this kind would be made by a 'judge of liberties'.[296] Another attorney has said that judges repeat the conditions as stated in the law, such as the way the crime was committed, or the situation of the victim, without providing an explanation as to exactly what these actually were.[297] This violates the jurisprudence of the ECtHR, which states that a justification that simply recites the legal provisions as a ground does not constitute a 'reason'.

Yet another attorney said that judges were getting better in writing opinions, but they were still far below the standard of the ECtHR.[298] In fact, one attorney went as far as to say that in Turkey decisions concerning detention, as well as release from detention, contained the same wording.[299]

While the high workload of the first instance and appellate courts might be a contributing factor in the writing of opinions in this manner, one must also remember that, in Turkey, decisions of the courts of first instance are not available online. The Court of Cassation has a journal, but this contains decisions selected by the court itself. It may be that, once all court judgments will be available online, as is to the current proposal, this might force judges to write better opinions and justifications.

2.3.6. The right to appeal

Either party can appeal the judgment, whether it is a conviction or an acquittal. If only the prosecution files an application for appeal, then the principle of *reformatio in peius* is triggered. The defendant should thus not be placed in a worse position as a result of the appeal of the prosecution. A judgment can be appealed only if it is against the law. If the law that should be applied is not applied or is misapplied, this constitutes a violation of the law.[300] The right to appeal must be exercised within seven days either from the verbal announcement of the decision to the criminal defendant, or to his/her lawyer. If neither was present at the final hearing, then the period of appeal starts with the service of the judgment. Usually, decisions are first announced orally and the reasoned judgment is written later (sometimes months later). During this time, lawyers file a pleading to reserve the right to appeal. When the reasoned judgment is served, then a detailed appeal submission is made explaining the law and the reasons for appeal.

---

[295] Informal discussion of the author with a judge in the Criminal Court of General Jurisdiction.
[296] Interview with attorney 3. This judge of liberties would be a seperate cour that only hears matters concerning detention. It does not exist under Turkish law but the attorney points out that it is needed.
[297] Interview with attorney 2.
[298] Interview with attorney 1.
[299] Interview with attorney 3.
[300] Art. 288 CCP.

It is questionable that all persons involved in the proceedings know about this right. In their case, appeals without proper grounds may not have much merit. While the law provides safeguards, such as automatic appeal (*ex officio*) for decisions that carry a sentence of 15 years or higher, or re-directing to the proper venue where the appellant files the appeal at the wrong place, overall the right to appeal is not easy for those proceeding *pro se* to exercise effectively. Indeed, research shows that people who had private counsel were more likely to appeal a judgment than those who proceed with a criminal legal aid lawyer, or someone acting *pro se*. The ratios were 41.3%, 51% and 14% respectively.[301] This may mean that defendants (particularly first time offenders) who do not have a lawyer are not aware of the fact that they have a right to appeal, or perhaps do not know how to do it. On the other hand, these results also indicate that, even among those who do have a lawyer, the right to appeal is not always exercised.

Appeals are made to the Court of Cassation in Ankara. As a rule, an appellate review is conducted over the file. Only in certain situations, such as a judgment sentencing the defendant a to minimum of ten years, or upon request of the defendant, or *ex officio*, will there be a hearing.[302] The Court of Cassation is the only venue of appeals, and its workload has grown enormously over recent years. In 2007, there were in total 323,738 pending appellate cases of which 182,733 were filed in that year alone.[303] In other words, 141,005 of pending cases were filed before 2007 and still awaited appellate review. Of the 323,378 cases, only 129,420 were reviewed in 2007, leaving almost one third of the total number for the following year.

This pattern of incoming applications exceeding outgoing decisions has remained unchanged over the years and further contributes to delays. Even back in 1997, there were a total of 136,129 cases pending appeal, of which 7,770 were applications from previous years.[304] The numbers grow exponentially year by year and it was recently decided that intermediary courts of appeal should be established, but this law is still to be operational. Yet, one prosecutor said that this would not be a solution,[305] while one attorney questioned the wisdom of only using it to address the heavy case load.[306] It has been also said that there are not enough judges in Turkey to staff these courts, while the government continues to require that judges retire at 65.

The imbalance between the number of incoming and outgoing cases extends to the waiting times for appellate review. In 2007, 391 days (over a year) were needed for a file to be reviewed by the Court of Cassation. In 1997, the same figure was 28 days while, as late as 2001, the figure was 77 days, jumping to 139 days in 2002.[307] If one remembers that the first instance process is also long, these delays in appeal

---

[301] Elveris, Jahic & Kalem 2007, p. 218.

[302] Art. 299 CCP.

[303] See   <http://www.adli-sicil.gov.tr/istatistik_2007/yarg%C4%B1tay/yarg%C4%B13-2007.pdf>.

[304] See   <http://www.adli-sicil.gov.tr/istatistik_2007/yarg%C4%B1tay/yarg%C4%B13-2007.pdf>.

[305] Interview with prosecutor 2.

[306] Interview with attorney 1.

[307] See   <http://www.adli-sicil.gov.tr/istatistik_2007/yarg%C4%B1tay/yarg%C4%B18-2007.pdf>.

also effect the prison population, since one fifth of them consists of people who are awaiting the outcome of their appeal.

Attorneys have said that the heavy workload of the Court of Cassation causes files to not be properly reviewed,[308] or even read at all.[309] In 2007, the reversal rate in criminal cases was 31.9%, while the affirmation rate was 39.5%.[310] The remaining decisions involved partial reversal, denial of appeal and the application of the time bar. It should be noted that the ratio of time barred cases has also been increasing, reaching 7.1% in 2007, suggesting that the time bar is slowly becoming a mechanism to cope with the serious case load in the appellate process. In addition, when a ground for appeal is rejected by the Court of Cassation, the wording used for the purpose is merely 'rejection of the appeal', with no further justification as to the reasons.[311]

On the other hand, two attorneys interviewed expressed concerns about a practice that has developed, following the case law of the Court of Cassation, regarding suspension of the judgment.[312] Suspension of the judgment[313] is a new mechanism where the court refrains from issuing/declaring a final judgment. In one sense, it is an alternative to the execution of a prison sentence of two years or less. In other words, instead of issuing a judgment and not executing the prison sentence, the court does not issue a judgment, but refers the defendant to a period of probation. If the defendant commits another intentional offence within five years following the suspension of the judgment, or if he/she does not comply with the requirements of the probation, the suspension will be withdrawn and the judgment will be announced. Otherwise, the case will be dropped.

The decision to suspend the judgment is not subject to appeal, as there is no judgment to appeal against. The only remedy is to file an objection to a higher court than the one rendering the judgment.[314] The Court of Cassation has held that the decision on suspension cannot be reviewed on the merits, but solely on whether or not the conditions to declare it in fact exist.[315] Suspension of the judgment deprives the defendant from the right to be acquitted. Further, it puts the person on probation for up to five years. While the person is subject to probation, the judicial record shows a suspended judgment. While most commentators are critical of this, the judges of the Court of Cassation defend their point of view.[316]

---

[308] One attorney asserted that the length of attention per file could be 2 minutes, while another said this was 6 minutes; interviews with attorney 3 and 4.

[309] Interviews with attorney 2 and 3.

[310] <http://www.adli-sicil.gov.tr/istatistik_2007/yarg%C4%B1tay/yarg%C4%B15-2007.pdf>.

[311] Interview with attorney 2.

[312] Interviews with attorney 1 and 4.

[313] Art. 231/5 CCP.

[314] Art. 231/12 CCP.

[315] CGK 25.9.2007, 183-190.; 8. CD., 25.10.2007, E. 2007/8653, K. 2007/7249, 8. CD., 13.7.2006, E. 2006/5860, K. 2006/6504. Also see Interview with attorney 3. CGK 25.9.2007, 183-190.

[316] For a paper of a judge of the Court of Cassation criticizing the view of commentators, see Erel 2009, p. 34-36.

2.4. Rights relating to effective defence

2.4.1. The right to investigate the case

In the investigation stage, procedural actions are carried out secretly, unless specified otherwise by the law, without prejudice to the right of defence.[317] However, a decision requiring secrecy can be issued by the prosecutor after taking into consideration two things. First, it should be determined whether a lack of secrecy endangers the goal of the investigation, and secondly, whether this would ensure a fair trial.

As the law uses such broad terms, it can be said that the right to investigate the case may be limited at will. Indeed, one attorney described an incident in which a secrecy decision was rendered, due to the high number of attorneys who went to court to review the file, thus giving the prosecutor no opportunity to work on it.[318] He explained that the first consideration (lack of secrecy endangering the goal of investigation) usually prevails over the latter.[319]

It has been suggested that secrecy decisions are often rendered in organized crime cases.[320] This is done by automatically grouping accomplices into a 'gang', and extending detention times (which can be more than 24 hours). When there is secrecy, not only reviewing but also the taking copies of the documents in the investigation file, without paying court dues, can be problematic. While the suspect has the right to have his attorney present, irrespective of whether it is a search, seizure or provision of a statement, it can sometimes lead to situations such as described by one attorney: 'We did not know what the accusation was. We got into a room. The client looks at me and I am looking at the client'.[321]

The law allows the suspect to request the collection of evidence and be given the opportunity to challenge the existing grounds of suspicion against him/her, and to put forward issues in his/her favour.[322] However, this right appears to be seriously undermined, even when there is no secrecy. A request for the court to write to various authorities asking for responses, or to explore a premise, or simply have a witness heard, are often met with resistance.[323] Witnesses may be brought together with the suspect and with each other at this stage, only if irreparable harm shall result from not doing so, or for identification purposes.[324]

One would think that the latter option should be easier, as it does not really require the judge or prosecutor to engage in any extra effort. However, judges apparently believe that the investigation should be done on the file and that they therefore should not engage in the collection of evidence at this stage, but rather, at

---

[317] Art. 157 CCP.
[318] Interview with attorney 3.
[319] Interview with attorney 3.
[320] Interview with attorney 3.
[321] Interview with attorney 2.
[322] Art. 147 CCP.
[323] Interview with attorney 3.
[324] Art. 52(2) CCP.

the trial stage. This limits the right, despite the fact that it is a mandatory provision. In other words, the judge has no discretion.[325]

The situation is even more problematic when the investigation involves secret witnesses, as there is no opportunity for the defence either to see what he/she has said or to question him/her. In fact, one may not even know whether the secret witness exists. The practice of anonymous witnesses is said to undermine the equality of arms principle.

2.4.2. The right to adequate time and facilities for the preparation of the defence

Article 6 §3.b of the ECHR provides that everyone charged with a criminal offence has the right to have adequate time and facilities for the preparation of his/her defence. In terms of a specific amount of time, the law states that there must be at least one week between the service of the indictment and the hearing day.[326] Further, if this period is not adhered to, the defendant shall be reminded of his/her right to request a postponement of the hearing.[327] However, as noted in section 2.1.2, it does not seem customary to send a copy of the indictment to the defendant. Further, the law provides that, if the nature of the crime changes, the defendant cannot be convicted of another provision, unless he/she had been informed prior to this change and had been given the opportunity to provide a defence.[328] Where an additional defence is necessary, the defendant shall be given time upon his/her request.

In practice, when it becomes apparent during the trial that the defendant should have been charged with a provision requiring a higher sentence, the defendant is asked whether he/she will submit additional defence.[329] This means that the judge is seriously considering resorting to the higher sentence but he/she does not explain this to the defendant in a clear way. If the defendant has no counsel, he/she will not understand what this amounts to and he/she can easily end up with a higher sentence without having the opportunity to prepare a proper defence. By doing this, the judge makes sure that the record reflects the opportunity of the defendant to provide an additional defence. This guarantees that the verdict cannot be reversed on that ground. While this may look correct on paper, in substance this is anything but correct.

A lack of time was highlighted as a problem in the investigation phase. For instance, a prosecutor may be working on the file for over six months, leading to dozens of files of evidence. However, when it comes to the available time for the attorney before the statement of the suspect is taken, this might only be half an hour, leaving no time for any defence.[330] During the trial, if the attorney changes, the court may adjourn the hearing to a later date. If the new attorney maintains that

---

[325] Interview with attorney 3.
[326] Art. 176 (4) CCP.
[327] Art. 190 CCP.
[328] Art. 226 CCP.
[329] Interview with attorney 2.
[330] Interview with attorney 3.

he/she has not been given sufficient time to prepare a defence, then the hearing must be adjourned.

2.4.3. The right to equality of arms in examining witnesses

Article 6§3.d of the ECHR states that everyone charged with a criminal offence has the right to examine, or have witnesses against him examined. The CCP does not regulate the rights of the suspect or his/her attorney to take statements from prospective witnesses. The statement of a witness may be taken only by the prosecutor, judge or court. However, it is not clear whether the decision to take the statement of the witness can be made by their own initiative, or upon request of the suspect/defendant and his/her attorney. At the prosecution stage, however, the attorney may ask direct questions to the defendant, the intervening party, the witnesses, experts, and other summoned individuals.[331] The defendant may also direct questions with the help of/via the judge.

In practice, however, lawyers complain that judges do not let them ask questions directly. In the words of one attorney, nine out of 10 judges would not allow it.[332] He continued:

> 'When you ask why, the judge replies that he applies the law that way. When you insist that this is what the law says, the judge responds that this is the way he applies the law. I will ask [the questions]. My practice, the practice of this court is like this. But if there is anything called the law, it should not be this way. (…) But he did not internalize it [the law]. So he resists'.

Another attorney says:[333]

> 'The courtroom is not designed for that! How can I question someone whose face I do not see? When I tell the witness to turn to me, then I am told not to engage in a show. But I have to communicate with the witness! Do not do this, do not do that! They see us like slaves or people they rule over from the bench. There is no infrastructure, no recording, no stenography! In a system where it is the judge who dictates the hearing record, you have no right to ask questions. I always waive this right and imply with my petitions to the judge the kind of questions I want asked [to the defendant] and he asks. This is my solution'.

Where the defendant requests the witness or expert to appear before the court, or requests evidence to be collected, he/she must submit a written application to that effect to the judge or the court, indicating the events they are related to, at least five days prior to the day of the hearing.[334] In cases where the application is denied, the defendant may bring these individuals along to the hearing, in which case, they must be heard.[335] However, one attorney indicated that he knows of cases where

---

[331]   Art. 201 CCP.
[332]   Interview with attorney 3.
[333]   Interview with attorney 1.
[334]   Art. 177 CCP.
[335]   This rule has been criticised, since its absolute implementation may give rise to manipulation/abuse, such as the delay of the proceedings.

this request has been denied.[336] The presentation of evidence must be denied if it is unlawfully obtained, if the evidence is irrelevant and if the request is made only to delay the proceedings. One attorney said that, if he has made 50 requests for the collection of evidence, only two have been granted so far.[337]

When special or technical knowledge is required for the solution of a case, the judge may decide to obtain the opinion of an expert on its own initiative, upon request of the prosecutor, or of a party.[338] The expert is entitled to ask questions to the suspect/defendant, in order to collect information to write a report. After this, the parties are given time to either asking for a new expert opinion, or to submit comments concerning the expert report. In practice, however, expert opinions particularly if they concern forensic matters or psychological fitness reports, are sent to the government established Forensic Medicine Institute. This institution has been controversial for years, and recently has been embroiled in scandalous decisions,[339] to the point that the President has tasked the State Auditing Authority to conduct a review of every aspect of its actions over the past three years.[340]

2.4.4. The right to free interpretation of documents and to translation

Article 6 §3.e of the ECHR states that everyone charged with a criminal offence has the right to have the free assistance of an interpreter, if he cannot understand or speak the language used in court. In conformity with the ECHR, the law prescribes that, if the defendant does not speak enough Turkish to express himself, the essential parts of the accusation and defence shall be translated by an interpreter appointed by the court.[341] This also applies in the investigation phase for the suspect, victim and witnesses. The interpreter, at this stage, is appointed by the judge or prosecutor. The fact that a suspect has this right in the investigation stage can be inferred from the record of custody, which requires officers to indicate whether an interpreter has been provided.[342] In addition, during consultation with an attorney, the detainee has the right to benefit from the assistance of an interpreter.[343]

At least in Istanbul, there is a roster of translators, but their proficiency has not been determined. Nor are they salaried staff.[344] It is usually up to the parties to find an interpreter and bring him/her along. Their fees are minimal. This can be

---

[336] Interview with attorney 4.
[337] Interview with attorney 3.
[338] Art. 63 CCP.
[339] These include the contamination of sperm from an autopsy of a young woman's body; the release of a Mafia convict on the grounds of sickness, while refusing to do the same for terror convicts who were on the verge of death due to cancer; mixing up blood samples and writing the report with the wrong sample; rendering a medical report claiming that a 14 year old girl who was sexually harassed was not emotionally stressed due to the incident.
[340] <http://www.hurriyet.com.tr/gundem/12109809.asp>.
[341] Art. 202 CCP.
[342] Art. 12 of Regulation, No. 25832.
[343] Art. 41 of the Regulation on the visit of detainees, *Official Gazette* No. 25848, 17 June 2005.
[344] Interview with attorney 2.

problematic when the job concerns the whole day, or involves going to the prison.[345] Attorneys have said that court staff get involved in translation when it comes to Kurdish, while for Western languages, greater efforts are made.[346] One prosecutor explained that use was also made of police resources, although, the police seem no more resourceful than the courts. To arrange for translation, they seem to contact consulates, resort to tourists and, worse, to asylum seekers, who are held in detention (to be deported) by the Foreigners Police.[347]

Defence attorneys said that they did not want to use those translators found by the police, since they feel that the relationship between the police and the translators is ongoing.[348]

3.   The professional culture of defence lawyers

'The profession was born in Turkey as a bourgeois profession without precedent'.[349] This quote captures perfectly the fact that, unlike in the Western world, there was no such thing as an attorney in Ottoman courts until the 19th century. Disputes were heard in Shariah courts sitting only with a judge (*kadı*) and the parties. There was neither any appeal nor defence.[350] While there were persons who specialized in drafting petitions to authorities (*arzuhalci*) on behalf of the people, they did not appear in court. They can be considered as the core of the profession.[351] Since there were no local attorneys, the first bar organization in Turkey was established in Istanbul in 1870 by foreign nationals.[352]

The Westernisation/Modernisation movements in the 19th century and the growing trade relations with the West, led to the establishment of Western style courts in Turkey. With the establishment of modern Turkey in 1923, Sharia law and courts were abolished. In the first years of the Republic, criminal law, civil law, commercial law, procedural laws were all translated and taken from Western countries *in toto*. In that sense, the Turkish revolution-modernization project is very much based on the idea of law as a tool of social change. Indeed, in 1924, the Parliament passed the Law on Attorneys, making it a profession in Turkey for the first time.[353] In 1939, the number of attorneys was only 1,631.[354] Today, the profession numbers 63,487.[355]

---

345   Interview with attorney 3.
346   Interview with attorney 1.
347   Interview with police officer 2.
348   Interview with attorney 4.
349   Inanici 2000, p. 135.
350   Inanici 2000, p. 135.
351   Yilmaz 1995, p. 196.
352   Battal & Erdem 1985, p. 678. The first Ottoman Bar had to wait for eight more years to become established in Istanbul.
353   Yilmaz 1995, p. 197. In 1938, a new law was adopted. Finally, the current law was enacted in 1969.
354   Ozkent 1948, p. 647.
355   <http://www.barobirlik.org.tr/tbb/avukat_sayilari/2008.aspx>. About a third of the profession is female.

At the same time, the reception of new laws did not mean that attorneys who were educated in the Sharia law tradition were happy to apply them. This led to confrontations between the government in Ankara and the Istanbul Bar.[356] It was clear to the government that a new breed of lawyers, who would take a strong stance in defending the values of the Republic, was necessary. In 1933, the University of Istanbul was 'reformed' through the retirement of old law school teachers.[357] Further, a new law school was established in Ankara to rival Istanbul, in order to inculcate the ideas of the Republic into the legal profession. There are speeches of the then Minister of Justice, who puts the responsibility for safeguarding the revolution on the shoulders of the prosecutors and judges.[358] However, attorneys remained suspicious.[359] While this led to very strict controls of the profession, such as the purging of bar members, it also led to a close relationship between the state and the profession, since the Bar owed its powers to state regulation. The profession obtained its independence in 1969. However, arguments about the control and monitoring exercised by the Ministry over the Bar continue even today.

Given this historical background, attorneys feel that judges and prosecutors do not see them as equals.[360] In fact, in terms of courtroom architecture, the prosecutor and judge sit next to each other at the bench, while the defence lawyer sits lower and away from his/her client, preventing consultation during hearings. Similarly, when the court takes a break for discussion of whether to release a detained criminal defendant, the prosecutor does not retire like everybody else, but remains in the courtroom along with the judges.[361] Prosecutors' close social relationship with judges starts when they are candidate judges and prosecutors during their internship, and continues throughout their career.

Although their functions are separate, prosecutors and judges are regulated by the same law; they reside in the same buildings (provided by the government); they commute to work together (in shuttles provided by the government); they holiday in the same place; they marry each other and work in the same building next to each other. Not surprisingly, this leads attorneys to feel sidelined.

In fact, the attorneys who we interviewed complained about not being given an opportunity to talk in court, or being given time, but asked to 'do it in two minutes'.[362] Sometimes, the words are put into their mouths, implying an attitude of 'I know what you will be saying'.[363] At the same time, an attorney has said that

---

[356]   Attorneys of the Istanbul Bar resisted the new government, by electing eight times as its president Fikri Lutfi, a man known for his preference for the sultan, Ozman 2000, p. 169.

[357]   Ozman 2000, p. 171.

[358]   Akzambak 2005, p. 171-172.

[359]   Ozman 2000, p. 173. Commissions were established, which purged 374 out of 805 attorneys of the Istanbul Bar. Inanici reports that the number was 473 out of 960, Inanici 2000, p. 138.

[360]   69.4% of lawyers agree with the statement that the prosecutor is treated as being superior than lawyers; Cirhinlioglu 1997, p. 81.

[361]   This issue has been pointed out in the EU Commission's reports; see Björnberg & Cranston 2005, p. 20-22. To what extent, and whether this practice has changed, should be separately investigated.

[362]   Interview with attorney 3.

[363]   Interview with attorney 3.

judges are under time pressure due to their heavy work load,[364] as well as the burden of dictating the hearing record.[365] Lawyers themselves were also not doing their part.[366] One attorney indicated that attorneys should not just wait for the indictment to be prepared by the prosecutor, but should work with the prosecutor during the investigation so as to understand the point of view of the prosecutor, as well as to ensure that the prosecutor views facts from the view point of the defence.[367]

One attorney said that some attorneys were providing a defence only at the last hearing.[368] This suggests a tendency of attorneys to have a collaborative or passive role vis-à-vis the prosecutor. One attorney specifically referred to judges as acting like a *kadi* setting his/her own rules in disregard of the law, or seeing him/herself as a *kadi*.[369]

On the other hand, research conducted in the Istanbul criminal courts found that a majority of judges made positive comments about the role of the defence lawyer in the criminal justice process, by allowing easier communication between the judge and the defendant, and helping the process to function properly.[370] For judges, they were seen as a mediator or a 'double check', to make sure that he/she does not miss anything. Some judges mentioned that lawyers were an important guarantee that the legal rights of the defendant will not be violated.

Prosecutors, on the other hand, were more suspicious, and only half of them made positive comments.[371] In their opinion, the impact of the lawyer depended on the lawyer him/herself and his/her qualities.

In the same research, lawyers also saw their contribution in positive terms, again pointing out similar views as judges. Interestingly, there is no separate criminal defence Bar in Turkey, but in the professional discourse, one often sees references to the profession of 'defence'.[372] This groups all attorneys into the category of 'defence', as if attorneys do nothing else apart from criminal work. In fact, some lawyers never undertake any such activities.

The finding that only one in five persons makes use of the services of an attorney was mentioned in 1.5. The first common reason for not using attorneys was that respondents thought they could represent themselves.[373] This suggests that many people may not understand the function and benefits of having an attorney. It was also explained (in 2.3.4) that many suspects do not use the right to silence.

364 Interview with attorney 2.
365 It should also be noted that, in Turkey, there is no recording of the hearings. In order to find out what happens in the hearings, one must read the hearing records. However, these records do not always reflect what transpires in court in reality, as they are dictated by the judge to a court reporter. The judge, of course, filters whatever transpires in the hearing.
366 Interviews with attorney 1 and 2.
367 Interview with attorney 1.
368 Interview with attorney 4.
369 Interview with attorney 1.
370 Elveris, Jahic & Kalem 2007, p. 234.
371 Elveris, Jahic & Kalem 2007, p. 235.
372 Inanici 2000, p. 141.
373 Elveris, Jahic & Kalem 2008, p. 21.

When asked why this would be the case, one attorney[374] explained: 'The culture of going to a lawyer is not established. The fact that it is new, plays a role in this. People think it will not make them credible. Since he hired an attorney he must have some things that he cannot answer for. Maybe it is better if I do my own defence'.

The accessibility study concerning criminal courts asked judges for their assessment as to why defendants did not request criminal legal aid lawyers. Most of them replied that this was because they did not believe they needed a lawyer.[375] In marked contrast to judges (and prosecutors), the majority of lawyers stated that *ignorance* and *lack of rights consciousness* among defendants were the main reasons for defendants not requesting an attorney. Some lawyers also responded in terms of the 'failure of law enforcement agencies to remind the defendants of their rights' and/or the 'absence of campaigns, activities, materials promoting this service'.

While it is clear that the culture of retaining an attorney is not well developed in Turkey, many factors may be contributing to this. Attorney interviews imply a resistant culture among judges towards attorneys rendering an active defence. One attorney said that even some colleagues state that they do not take criminal cases, because there is not much for an attorney to do in a criminal case.[376] The existing culture of the defence bar, and the regulations prohibiting the promotion of legal services, may be also contributing to this.

Interviewed attorneys described defence lawyers as passive and not brave.[377] One attorney said that attorneys were not doing their homework well.[378] Another said that attorneys considered defence work as something to be done only in court, and in an oral and written fashion.[379] Another lawyer said that, in general, attorneys have been passive.[380]

Indeed, research at the Istanbul criminal courts found a correlation between conviction rates and the type of representation. In both the General and Aggravated Felony courts, defendants who were not represented by a lawyer at all had the lowest conviction rates. Defendants represented by CCP lawyers in Aggravated Felony courts had the highest conviction rates, and in General courts, rates were similar to those represented by private lawyers.[381] While the results do not explain the reasons, it is nevertheless disappointing since, without seeing the benefits, people may be inclined never to retain a lawyer.

Worse, attorneys underline the independence of the profession much more than the public service side of it. This is also obvious in the discourse surrounding

---

[374] Interview with attorney 3.
[375] Elveris, Jahic & Kalem 2007, p. 225. Judges explained that defendants trust the judge or the court to defend them, are ignorant/indifferent, do not want to deal with the service, distrust lawyers, do not believe that the lawyer can make a difference in their cases, or believe in their own capacity to defend themselves.
[376] Interview with attorney 2. In his view: 'It is in fact quite the opposite. If an attorney is going to help anyone, this is in criminal cases'.
[377] Interview with attorney 1.
[378] Interview with attorney 2.
[379] Interview with attorney 3.
[380] Interview with attorney 4.
[381] Elveris, Jahic & Kalem 2007, p. 215.

legal aid, where the issue is discussed from the point of unpaid legal fees rather than the quality of the service provided.

At the same time, the criminal legal aid study contained some data about the way attorneys perceive themselves when they provide defence: 'Defence does not mean changing the truth; it means submitting evidence that also raises things that are beneficial for the criminal defendant. This does not mean changing the direction of the judiciary. There is a misconception that the lawyers present guilty people as innocent during the legal process. But no! We are not judges, we are lawyers. We undertake the defence of a particular side and make sure that the evidence to their advantage is presented'.[382] One prosecutor said that due to the inquisitorial system, the prosecution does not only collects evidence to convict the defendant, but also exculpatory evidence that may lead to his/her release. It therefore seems that the prosecutor acts like a defence counsel. Although the police do not directly work under the prosecutor, the police expect the prosecutor to be chief of the police. This all may lead to confusion and contradictory functions for actors. In order for everybody to do their job, the system had to decide which model to adopt.[383]

Not only do they seem to have ethical dilemmas about their role, but attorneys also feel conflicted when doing their job. It has been indicated that legal representation during the police stage is complex, involving trying to understand the facts and the legal basis of the case, preventing the illegalities of the police and reaching the truth by fair and just ways.[384] Attorneys also feel torn between fighting illegalities and not harming their clients. While a lawyer has to act in the interest of his/her client, 74.8% of lawyers do not think that their colleagues act according to ethical standards.[385]

In view of all this, it is difficult to make conclusions. One thing that appears clear is that criminal justice actors, as well as society, have question marks about the role of a defence lawyer. While attitudes may be changing, particularly in places where there is a lower case load and younger judges,[386] this is not happening very quickly.

4.   Political commitment to effective defence

While this report indicates that, without a doubt, there have been many developments concerning defence rights in the last five years, it is difficult to

---

[382]   Elveris, Jahic & Kalem 2007, p. 236. To further illustrate the confusion surrounding this matter, an incident in the training for criminal legal aid lawyers undertaken by Idil Elveris can be described. In the training, role plays were assigned to participating lawyers. One person was asked to play the role of a defendant who was detained for stealing a car. The lawyer was visiting him in jail to discuss his release. The defendant was in a dire financial situation and desperate to get out of jail to take care of his family. He described the events leading to his arrest at length, but his attorney interrupted him to say: 'Do as I tell you. It didn't happen at night. The dawn was breaking when all this happened. You will get a lesser sentence when you say so'.

[383]   Interview with prosecutor 2.
[384]   Interview with attorney 1.
[385]   Cirhinlioglu 1997, p. 94.
[386]   Interview with attorney 2.

interpret this as a political commitment to effective defence. While they were relatively small in number and in no way representative of the whole country, let alone of Istanbul, our interviews still show the different attitudes and values among the criminal justice actors, making the job of an attorney very difficult. The police, judges and prosecutors should be trained to make the use of the defendants' rights more effective.

An unacceptable number of people are still not represented in court. Even if they are represented, the service is of low quality and the government does not even seem to care, as is evidenced by its indifference to the boycott by the Istanbul Bar. When mandatory legal counselling rules proved to be expensive, the government preferred to limit the right, rather than considering a new model. The difference in resources allocated for the police (3 billion Euro) and legal aid (5 million Euro) make the government's priorities very clear. The media's 'discovery' of crime is contributing to public fears about crime, and encourage tougher sentencing polices, which then directly affects the prison population.

All of this makes it very difficult to conclude that the government cares about effective defence. Although laws change, and many reforms have been made in the past five years, the critical problems of the criminal justice system remain, and attitudes concerning limiting of the right to defence prevail. It is, of course, difficult to know the precise extent of these attitudes, and further research is required. However, it cannot be said that the government demonstrates sufficient political will and commitment to provide effective defence.

5. Conclusions

The key problems identified in this report may be summarised as follows:

- a slow criminal justice process from first instance[387] to appeal (one fifth of the prison population consists of people awaiting the outcome of their appeal), which therefore undermines the process of justice;
- prison overcrowding, due to longer times served under new criminal laws and the disproportionate application of detention, as well as inadequate provision for pre-trial release/bail;
- lack of lawyer involvement throughout the criminal justice system, which appears to result from a number of factors, including the failure to inform suspects and defendants in an effective way of their right to a lawyer, and a general lack of public knowledge concerning people's rights;
- lack of institutional framework for *effective* management, monitoring and policymaking for legal aid, as well as inadequate legal aid provisions and mechanisms for ensuring the availability of lawyers;
- low rates of pay for legal aid lawyers;

---

[387] The CEPEJ report of 2008 indicates 311 days for robbery cases, while 333 days for intentional homicide. CEPEJ, Scheme for Evaluating Judicial Systems 2007, Country: Turkey, p. 28.

- a culture of passivity amongst defence lawyers particularly at the investigation stage, as well as a general negative attitude towards legal aid cases;
- a professional culture amongst judges and prosecutors that diminishes the potential impact of defence lawyers;
- lack of implementation of ECtHR judgments against Turkey, which have set higher standards in defence rights.

6.   Bibliography

Books

Akzambak 2005
Akzambak, M., *Atatürk'ün Devrimci Adalet Bakanı Mahmut Esat Bozkurt*, Itanbul: Zafer, 2005.

Ansay 1996
Ansay, T., *Introduction to Turkish Law*, The Hague-London-Boston: Kluwer, 1996.

Björnberg & Cranston 2005
Björnberg, K. & Cranston, R., *The Functioning of the Judicial System in the Republic of Turkey*, Report of an Advisory Visit, 2005.

Centel & Zafer 2005
Centel, N. & Zafer, H., *Ceza Muhakemesi Hukuku*, Istanbul:Beta, 2005.

Centel, Zafer & Cakmut 2008
Centel, N., Zafer, H. & Cakmut, O., *Türk Ceza Hukukuna Giriş*, Istanbul: Beta, 2008.

Cirhinlioglu 1997
Cirhinlioglu, Z., *Türkiye'de Hukuk Mesleği*, Ankara: Şafak, 1997.

Elveris & Jahic 2006
Elveris, I. & Jahic, G., *Pilot study of Legal Problems and Legal Needs of the Urban Poor in Istanbul*, 2006.

Elveris, Jahic & Kalem 2007
Elveris, I., Jahic, G. & Kalem, S., *Alone in the Courtroom: Accessibility and Impact of Criminal Legal Aid*, Istanbul: Istanbul Bilgi University Publications, 2007.

Jahic 2008
Jahic, G., *European Sourcebook of Crime and Criminal Justice Statistics 2008, Questionnaire covering the years of 2003-2007*, 2008.

Kalem, Jahic & Elveris 2008
Kalem, S., Jahic, G. & Elveris, I., *Justice Barometer: Public Opinion On Courts in Turkey*, Istanbul: Istanbul Bilgi University Publications, 2008.

Keyman & Onis 2007
Keyman, F. & Onis, Z., *Turkish politics in a changing world, Global Dynamics and Domestic Formations*, Istanbul: Istanbul Bilgi University Press, 2007.

Kunter, Yenisey & Nuhoğlu 2008
Kunter, N., Yenisey, F. & Nuhoğlu, A., *Muhakeme Hukuku Dalı Olarak Ceza Muhakemesi Hukuku*, Istanbul:Beta, 2008.

Öztürk, Tezcan, Erdem, Sırma, Saygılar & Alan 2009
Öztürk, B., Tezcan, D., Erdem, M.R., Sırma, Ö., Saygılar, Y.F. & Alan, E., *Nazari ve Uygulamalı Ceza Muhakemesi Hukuku*, Ankara:Seçkin, 2009.

Savaş & Mollamahmutoğlu 1995
Savaş, V. & Mollamahmutoğlu, S., *Ceza Muhakemeleri Usulü Kanununun Yorumu*, Vol. 1, Ankara: Seçkin, 1995.

Sen 1998
Şen, E., *Türk Ceza Yargılamasında Hukuka Aykırı Deliller Sorunu*, Istanbul: Beta, 1998.

Ünver & Hakeri 2009
Ünver, Y. & Hakeri, H., *Ceza Muhakemesi Hukuku, Cilt 1*, Ankara: Seçkin, 2009.

Yenisey 2009a
Yenisey, F., *Turkish Criminal Procedure Code - Ceza Muhakemesi Kanunu*, Istanbul: Beta, 2009.

Yildiz 2002
Yıldız, A., *Ceza Muhakemesinde İspat ve Delillerin Değerlendirilmesi*, diss. Istanbul, 2002.

Articles in Journals

Battal & Erdem 1985
Battal, S. & Erdem, N., 'Avukatlık Mesleğinin Türkiye'deki Tarihçesi', *Ankara Barosu Dergisi*, 5-6 1985, p. 675-685.

Inanici 2000
Inanici, H., 'Turkiye'de Avukatlık Ideolojisi', *Toplum ve Bilim*, 87 Winter 2000-2001, p.135-163.

Ozkent 1948

Ozkent, H., 'Dünün ve Bugünün Türk Avukatlığına ve Barolarına Kısa Bir Bakış', *İstanbul Barosu Dergisi*, 22, 10, 1948, p. 643-651.

Ozman 2000

Ozman, A., 'Siyaset, hukuk, ideoloji ekseninde hukukçu kimliğinin yeniden tanımlanması: Erken Cumhuriyet dönemi üzerine bir inceleme', *Toplum ve Bilim*, 87 Winter 2000-2001, p. 164-177.

Yilmaz 1995

Yilmaz, E., Bir meslek olarak dünden yarına avukatlık, AHFD, s. 1-4, 1995.

Chapters in Compilations

Elveris 2009

Elveris, I., 'Adalet Hizmeti? Istanbul Adliyelerinde Gozlemler', in: S. Kalem (ed.), *Adalet Gözet: Yargı Sistemi Üzerine Bir İnceleme*, 2009, p. 71-104.

Erel 2009

Erel, K., 'Yargıtay Kararları Işığında Hükmün Açıklanmasının Geri Bırakılması, Türk Ceza Hukuku Derneği Yayını', in: *Ceza Muhakemesi Kanununun* 3 Yılı, TCHD yay., Istanbul, 2009, p. 329-348.

Erman 1998

Erman, S., 'Sentez Raporu', İstanbul Üniversitesi Hukuk Fakültesi Eğitim Öğretim ve Yardımlaşma Vakfı Yayını, in: *Prof. Dr. Nurullah Kunter'e Armağan*, Istanbul: Beta, 1998, p. 75-83.

Gülçür & İlkkaracan 2002

Gülçür, L., İlkkaracan, P., 'The Natasha Experience': Migrant Sex Workers from the Former Soviet Union and Eastern Europe in Turkey: Women's Studies International Forum, vol. 25 (411-21), Copyright Elsevier 2002, <http://www.scribd.com/doc/7343044/NATASHA-Experience>.

Inceoğlu & Aytekin 2008

İnceoğlu Aytekin A, Türk Hukukunda Adli Amaçlı İletişimin Denetlenmesi, in *Prof. Dr. Uğur Alacakaptan'a Armağan*, Vol. 1, Istanbul, 2008, p. 103-126.

Inceoglu, Aytekin & Karan 2008

Inceoglu Aytekin, A. & Karan, U., 'Türkiye'de Ceza Davalarında Uzlaşma Uygulamaları: hukuki çerçevenin değerlendirilmesi', in, Jahic, G. and Yesiladalı, B. (eds), *Onarıcı Adalet: Mağdur-Fail Arabuluculuğu ve Uzlaşma Uygulamaları: Türkiye ve Avrupa Bakışı*, Istanbul Bilgi Üniversitesi Yayınları, 2008, p. 45-81.

Kalem 2008
Kalem, S., 'Ceza Davalarında Uzlaşma: Uygulayıcı Görüşü', in: Jahic, G. and Yesiladalı, B. (eds), *Onarıcı Adalet: Mağdur-Fail Arabuluculuğu ve Uzlaşma Uygulamaları: Türkiye ve Avrupa Bakışı*, Istanbul: Istanbul Bilgi Universitesi Yayınları, 2008, p. 88-107.

Mahmutoğlu 2009
Mahmutoğlu, F., 'Kamu Davasının Açılmasının Ertelenmesi ve Hükmün Açıklanmasının Geri Bırakılması', Türk Ceza Hukuku Derneği Yayını *in: Ceza Muhakemesi Kanununun 3 Yılı,.*, Istanbul, 2009, p. 349-368.

Nuhoğlu 2009
Nuhoğlu, A., 'Koruma Tedbiri Olarak Tutuklama', Türk Ceza Hukuku Derneği Yayını, in: *Ceza Muhakemesi Kanununun* 3 Yılı, Türk Ceza Hukuku Derneği Yayını, Istanbul 2009, p. 175-191.

Ünver 1998
Ünver, Y., 'Ceza Hukukunda Objektif Sorumluluk', İÜHF Ceza ve Ceza Usul Hukuku Anabilim Dalı, in: *Ceza Hukuku Günleri – 70. Yılında Türk Ceza Kanunu Genel Hükümler,* Istanbul: Beta, 1998, p. 109-195.

Yenisey 2009 (b)
Yenisey, F., 'Kamu Davasının Açılması ve İddianamenin İadesi', Türk Ceza Hukuku Derneği Yayını *in: Ceza Muhakemesi Kanununun 3 Yılı*, , Istanbul, 2009, p. 232-251.

Other Sources

Almanac Turkey 2006-2008: Security Sector and Democratic Oversight released by Turkish Economic and Social Studies Foundation (TESEV), see <http://www.tesev.org.tr/UD_OBJS/PDF/DEMP/almanak2008_02_07_09.WEB%20icin. pdf>.

Arslan F., *Türkiye'de ve Avrupa'da Kolluk Adalet İlişkisi* <http://www.caginpolisi.com.tr/48/10-11-12-13-14-15.htm>.

Commission for the Efficiency of Justice (CEPEJ), Scheme for Evaluating Judicial Systems 2007, Country: Turkey, European Judicial Systems, Edition 2008: Efficiency and Quality of Justice, CEPEJ.

Emniyet Genel Müdürlüğü 2007 Faaliyet Raporu, (Activity report for 2007, General Directorate of Security), see: <http://www.egm.gov.tr/Duyurular2008/2007_EGM_Faaliyet_Raporu.zip>.

Emniyet Genel Müdürlüğü 2008 Faaliyet Raporu, (Activity report for 2008, General Directorate of Security), see: <http://www.egm.gov.tr/Duyurular2009/Faaliyet_Raporu.pdf>.

İstanbul Ticaret Odası, İstanbul'da Şiddet ve Şiddetin Sosyolojik Arka Planı Araştırma Raporu, Yayın No: 2008-11, Istanbul 2008

Jahic & Akdas 2007

Jahic, G. & Akdaş, A., *Uluslararası suç mağdurları araştırması: İstanbul hane halkında suç mağduriyeti*, Ankara: TÜBİTAK project no: 104K100. Final report available through ULAKBİM, at <http://www.ulakbim.gov.tr/>.

<http://www.cte.adalet.gov.tr/>.

<http://www.tuik.gov.tr/PreHaberBultenleri.do?id=3894>.

Ministry of Justice, Judicial Reform Strategy, Ankara 2009, see: <http://www.sgb.adalet.gov.tr/yrs.html>.

7.   Annex

TITLE	EXPERIENCE	PLACE AND DATE OF INTERVIEW
A1 Attorney (Female)	20 years experience	Istanbul, 25/8/2009
A2 Attorney (Male)	8 years experience	Istanbul, 26/8/2009
A3 Attorney (Male)	4 years experience	Istanbul, 28/8/2009
A4 Attorney (Male)	4 years experience	Istanbul, 28/8/2009
Pr1 Prosecutor (Male)	16 years experience	Istanbul, 2/9/2009
Pr2 Prosecutor (Male)	15 years experience	Istanbul, 7/9/2009
Po1 Police officer (Male)	12 years experience	Istanbul, 23/8/2009 (Over Skype)
Po2 Police officer (Male)	2 years experience	Istanbul, 5/9/2009

PART III

ANALYSIS AND CONCLUSIONS

Ed Cape
Zaza Namoradze
Roger Smith
Taru Spronken

CHAPTER 12 THE STATE OF THE NATIONS: COMPLIANCE WITH THE ECHR

1.   Introduction

This chapter compares the key findings from the nine country reports (chapters 3 – 11) with the standards derived from the European Convention on Human Rights (ECHR) and relevant jurisprudence of the European Court of Human Rights (ECtHR) as discussed in chapter 2. Together, the country reports provide a representative account of the diverse experience and history of Europe – bound by much that is common in their history and culture, whilst divided by much that is different. As we demonstrated in chapter 2, in respect of some aspects of effective criminal defence the ECtHR jurisprudence is quite clear, making evaluation relatively straightforward. However, some of the relevant case law is less clear, and in respect of some aspects of effective defence either the ECHR is silent or the ECtHR is, for a variety of reasons, reluctant to become engaged, or has not been engaged because of the absence of complaints. These factors, together with the difficulties in collecting and collating data from such a varied collection of jurisdictions, means that analysis by reference to ECHR standards is a challenging enterprise.

2.   National contexts

The nine countries in the study are geographically very different. Three – Italy, France and Turkey – border the Mediterranean. Two – Poland and Hungary – lie on the eastern border of the European Union and emerged from domination by the Soviet Union only in the early 1990s. By contrast, three of the countries – France, Germany and Belgium – sit firmly at the centre of Europe, both geographically and culturally. Two – Finland and England and Wales – rest on the northern periphery of Europe. All nine countries have a complex and intertwined past. All have been affected, and in many cases scarred, by great imperialist ambitions – their own and others. The influence of conquests by Rome and Napoleon are still to be seen in the civil law traditions of the countries of mainland Europe. Eight of the countries are members of the European Union. Turkey, which we take for this study to be unequivocally part of Europe, is a candidate country for membership. England and Wales is notorious for its scepticism of a Union of which it has been a grumbling member for thirty years.

The countries are of varying size. Five are large, having populations of over 50 million – Germany, Turkey, England and Wales, France and Italy – with Germany significantly larger than the others. By comparison, Poland is middle-sized, with a population of just under 40 million. Belgium and Hungary are relatively small, at around 10 million each. Finland has a population of just over 5 million. Size might not immediately seem relevant to a country's ability to provide effective defence for those suspected or accused of crime. However, size and composition of the population does influence crime rates, the organisation of the legal profession, the justice system and legal cultures, which in turn influence access to effective criminal defence.

Each country in the study contains significant ethnic minorities, though of different origins and of varied degrees of integration. Belgium, Finland and England and Wales have entrenched and long-established minorities whose language and other rights are recognised in their legal systems. Belgium accommodates three regions, each with its own official language – Dutch, French (Walloon) and bilingual Brussels. Finland has two official languages – Finnish and Swedish, and also recognises Sami, the language of the Laps. Welsh is an official language on a par with English within Wales. Turkey and Hungary have long-established minorities which not only feel themselves to be marginalised, but which are also likely to be disproportionately represented amongst suspects and defendants; Turkey's Kurds constituting around 17% of its population, and Hungary's Roma perhaps as high as five per cent. Conversely, other countries have minorities as the result of recent migration. Around eight per cent of the population of England and Wales describes itself as non-white. For most mainland European states, major immigration from outside Europe occurred only after the Second World War. Turks constitute two per cent of the German population. Italy and France have large and growing minority populations from North Africa and eastern Europe. Minority populations can easily find themselves demonised as more prone to crime than indigenous groups, and are frequently disproportionately represented as suspects and defendants.

Many of the countries face, or have faced, major threats from terrorism. Statistically, crimes involving terrorism amount to a minute proportion of individual cases but consume significant resources within the criminal justice systems of a number of countries – at the present time, particularly Turkey and England and Wales. The threat of terrorism has also been used to justify the restriction of rights of a particular range of suspects and defendants. Though worthy of further study, we have concentrated on the position of the majority of criminal suspects and defendants in this report; that is, those who are suspected or accused of non-terrorist crime.

In general, the nine jurisdictions in the study fall within the three traditions identified in chapter 1[1] as inquisitorial, adversarial and post-state socialist.

---

[1]   Chapter 1 § 3.

However, in practice, the contemporary operation of criminal procedure in the respective jurisdictions may be less dissimilar than the classification suggest. Inquisitorial systems are increasingly acknowledging adversarial elements. The classic role of the instructing judge is diminishing. Belgium has retained control by a magistrate, the *juge d'instruction*, during the investigative stage in around 10% of cases.[2] In France, the role has been maintained only in about half that percentage of cases and it has recently come under political attack.[3] In Germany, another civil law country, all investigation is in the hands of prosecutors and only intrusive investigative measures require a judicial warrant from an investigative judge.[4] All criminal justice systems, however classified, acknowledge the adversarial nature of the trial. As a civil law country, Italy provides the clearest symbolic break in procedure from the investigative stage with its 'double dossier' system whereby the inquisitorially obtained pre-trial dossier is not seen by the trial judge.[5] One difference between civil and common law systems is that the former often include the victim within the proceedings as a 'civil party'.[6] Finland probably recognises this to the greatest extent by incorporating a mediation element between defendant and victim in its criminal procedures.[7] On the other hand, the adversarial commitment of the criminal justice system in England and Wales has not prevented the growth of various diversionary mechanisms designed to keep offenders out of courts.[8]

All nine countries have one firm common commitment. They are all members of the Council of Europe and signatories to the European Convention on Human Rights (ECHR). Between them, they have given effect to the ECHR in three stages. Turkey, Belgium, Germany, Italy and the United Kingdom (of which England and Wales is part) brought it into effect in the 1950s. (West) Germany joined in the 1970s. Finland, Poland and Hungary brought it into effect in the 1990s after the fall of the Soviet Union. In fact, the domestic impact of signing and ratifying the Convention has intensified for many countries over the last couple of decades. The UK's Human Rights Act 1998 only incorporated the Convention into domestic law from October 2000. This has had an enormous influence on its legal system. In the same year, France introduced reforms to the code of criminal procedure that incorporated defences directly derived by the ECHR; its Cassation Court now applies ECtHR decisions.[9] Italy incorporated the fair trial principles of article 6 ECHR in 1999, and in 2007 its Constitutional Court declared the ECHR superior to domestic law.[10] The move by signatories to give the Convention more authority paralleled the drive by the ECtHR to develop the jurisdiction of article 6. Most relevant for this development has been the court's increasing willingness to require

---

[2]   Chapter 3 § 2.1.1.
[3]   Chapter 6 § 1.3.
[4]   Chapter 7 § 1.4.1.
[5]   Chapter 9 § 1.3.2.
[6]   See for instance Belgium, Chapter 3 § 1.2.2.
[7]   Chapter 5 § 1.3.
[8]   Chapter 4 § 1.3.
[9]   Chapter 6 § 1.2.
[10]   Chapter 9 § 1.2.

legal representation during the investigative stage of the criminal process – the development of the 'Salduz doctrine'.[11]

Europe's diversity is manifest within the country studies. The degree of information and range of statistics available in different countries varies widely – between those that routinely catalogue official statistics and sources (for example, England and Wales) and countries with less data to draw upon (for example, Belgium and Turkey). The countries also vary in their experience of sociological and academic examination of the operation of law and legal system actors. Such examination has been less a part of the civil law than the common law world, influenced as it has been by legal sociology undertaken in the United States of America. In addition, the federal nature of a country like Germany has made it difficult to find reliable country-wide statistical and other information on matters such as the total expenditure on legal aid. Thus, our national experts have had varying degrees of assistance from previous studies and established traditions of research.

3.   Compliance with ECHR standards

The following analysis examines the application in the jurisdictions in the study of the principles and standards derived from the ECHR as set out in chapter 2. The analysis is not intended to be comprehensive; a full analysis for each country would be very extensive and is beyond the scope of this study. The purpose of the analysis here is to point to some of the most significant concerns about compliance with ECHR standards in respect of access to effective criminal defence.

3.1.   Procedural rights relating to fair trial in general

In one country, Italy, there appears to be a systematic breach of article 6 § 1 ECHR. For decades it has faced serious questions about whether it meets the requirement to hold a trial within a reasonable time, and it has frequently been criticised for delay by the ECtHR. Nevertheless, the average length of a case from the decision to prosecute is still around five years, and seven from the start of the investigation.[12] As a further inducement to delay, a significant number of cases, seemingly around seven per cent, are caught by the statute of limitations for which time runs generally from the commission of the crime. Thus, the criminal justice system enters a vicious circle in which endemic delay caused by inefficiencies attributable to poor administration by public officials and frequent hearing adjournments, are exacerbated by deliberate attempts by the defence to invoke the statutes of limitation. Another effect of lengthy proceedings is that suspects are held for long periods of time in pre-trial detention, with seriously implications for the presumption of innocence.[13]

---

[11]   Chapter 2 § 4.3.
[12]   Chapter 9 § 4.1.
[13]   Chapter 9 § 2.3.3.

There are a number of general issues concerning the position of Turkey. Chapter 11 records that the ECtHR has found it to be in violation of the right to fair trial no less than 528 times in the decade between 1998 and 2008, mostly in respect of police conduct. It seems that the telephones of Istanbul's top prosecutor and 55 other judges and prosecutors were recently tapped by their own Ministry of Justice, indicating a lack of respect for judicial and prosecutorial independence.[14] However, the chapter does record improvements. Although accountability has been variable, the police are reported to have improved their conduct. Judges have become more willing to be conscientious in the protection of rights. Further, disciplinary and administrative investigations against the police appear to have had a degree of effectiveness. Nevertheless, the Parliamentary Commission on Human Rights has reported that the judiciary are its greatest single cause for complaint, this trend persisting even though the Commission has no powers to investigate judicial misconduct.[15]

3.2. The presumption of innocence and the right to silence

The presumption of innocence is a key element of fair trial, protected by article 6 § 2 ECHR. The state must prove its case against the defendant. The presumption of innocence implies the right of a defendant to remain silent. The ECtHR has stressed that article 6 and the privilege against self-incrimination come into play as soon as a person's situation has been substantially affected, which means that all defence rights that derive from article 6, such as being informed of the right to silence and to legal assistance, can arise even before a person has been arrested.[16] Italy is an example of a jurisdiction where the right to silence is safeguarded throughout the investigation by the mandatory attendance of a lawyer during police questioning, the provision of a letter of rights, and the exclusion of evidence of statements where these safeguards have not been respected.[17]

However, the implications of ECtHR jurisprudence on the presumption of innocence are not recognised in practice in all jurisdictions in our research. In France the investigation judge has the duty to caution the suspect on his right to silence, but there is no duty for the police to do so before interrogation. Defence lawyers are considered to be the appropriate conduit for informing suspects on their right to silence during the *Garde à Vue*. However, lawyers are not allowed to be present during police interrogation, and earlier research has demonstrated that in practice remaining silent during the *Garde à Vue* is difficult given the significant psychological pressure to speak exerted by the police, and the fact that in practice, if not in law, silence is often taken as an indication of guilt.[18] Reforms in recent years in England and Wales allow courts to draw inferences from 'silence', and the police caution given to suspects on arrest and on being interviewed draws this to their

---

[14]   Chapter 11 § 1.2.
[15]   Chapter 11 § 2.1.4.
[16]   Chapter 2 § 2.2.
[17]   Chapter 9 § 2.1.1 and 2.3.4.
[18]   Chapter 6 § 2.3.4.

attention. Moreover, linked reforms have allowed greater reference to be made at trial to previous misconduct of a defendant.[19]

Our research has also found practices that circumvent the duty to caution the suspect. In Poland there is a distinction between a 'suspected person', being a person deprived of their liberty by the police who is not yet formally charged, and a 'suspect'. The police are under no duty to inform a 'suspected person' of their right to silence. Although statements that a 'suspected person' makes to the police may not be used in evidence, it is difficult for a suspect to understand the difference between statements made as a 'suspected person' and those made as a 'suspect'. In Hungary, the police are reported to circumvent the requirement to tell a suspect of his right of silence by the use of certain ploys. Essentially, the suspect may be interviewed as a witness, prior to the formal commencement of proceedings. As a consequence, people who are *de facto* suspects may be interviewed without any caution, even though their statements may subsequently be used in evidence.[20] In Italy police may question a suspect at the point of arrest, but the answers may not be used as evidence and can only be used for the purposes of the investigation. This can, nevertheless, result in the police obtaining incriminating evidence from a suspect without them being cautioned.[21]

Other practices that indirectly interfere with the presumption of innocence were reported in respect of various jurisdictions. Media coverage of cases prior to the trial was reported, for both France and Turkey, as sometimes being such that it was potentially prejudicial to the defendant's presumption of innocence.[22] In most jurisdictions in the study, apart from England and Wales, trial and sentence are dealt with together, requiring defendants to prepare for sentence even whilst maintaining their innocence.

3.3. Bail and pre-trial detention

Although the ECtHR has formulated strict criteria for the application of pre-trial detention – requiring specific indications of a genuine requirement of public interest, regular review, that alternative measures should be seriously considered and that the presumption should always be in favour of release[23] – our study reveals that the use of pre-trial detention varies greatly between jurisdictions. In England and Wales, it is estimated that 28% of all defendants are remanded in custody at some stage of the proceedings.[24] In Hungary, the equivalent percentage appears to be well over 95.[25] This seems to indicate that pre-trial detention is ordered routinely without reference to individual circumstances and, indeed, defence lawyers reported that pre-trial custody is used to obtain confessions.

---

[19]   Chapter 3 § 2.2.2. Although it should be noted that the ECtHR has not found the relevant legislation to be in breach of art. 6 in this respect.
[20]   Chapter 8 § 2.1.1
[21]   Chapter 9 § 2.1.2.
[22]   Chapter 6 § 2.3.3, Chapter 11 § 2.3.3.
[23]   Chapter 2 § 2.3.
[24]   Chapter 4 § 2.3.1.
[25]   Chapter 8 § 2.3.1.

Similarly, in Germany, defence lawyers reported that preventive detention was used as a way of 'motivating' confessions.[26] Around half of the prison population in Turkey and more than half in Italy are on remand and defendants often find that custody, once ordered, is routinely renewed.[27] The over-use of prison is also reported for Poland, with lawyers rarely being present at pre-trial detention hearings – sometimes deliberately due to a fear that their presence will be regarded as an indication of guilt.[28]

Most countries draw distinctions between various stages of pre-trial custody. Although the concepts vary from country to country, there is typically a progression from police arrest, to detention as a suspect, and then to detention following judicial order. The conditions of detention in police custody can be unsatisfactory. Understandably, perhaps, the police often have wide discretion as to short periods of detention immediately after arrest. The exercise of this power may be badly documented and all kinds of prejudice and pressure to confess may, thereby, be concealed. There are suggestions, for example, in the report for England and Wales of a possible bias in relation to ethnicity.[29] Provisional detention, *Garde à Vue*, is widely used in France.[30] There is little information on informal grants of bail by the police where conditions may be imposed on a suspect, noted even as a problem in England and Wales which generally has well documented procedures. Hungary provides an example of how the right to silence may be implicitly subverted by the indiscriminate use of pre-trial custody, which can last up to three years. Although other actors in the criminal justice system disagreed, defence counsel were unanimous in their view that pre-trial detention was used to put pressure on a defendant to plead guilty. Hungary also persists in delaying trials, despite frequently being found in violation of article 5 ECHR, which requires 'trial within a reasonable time or release pending trial'.[31]

3.4. Equality of arms and adversarial hearing

The concept of fairness has been expanded in the jurisprudence of the ECtHR to encompass the general principle of the equality of arms – the defence must not be at a disadvantage compared to the prosecution.[32] More precise aspects of the equality of arms principle are interwoven with other rights such as access to the file, and examination of witnesses, which are dealt with under the separate headings below.

The chapters in Part II show subtle indications that at least the appearance of even-handed justice may be affected by local custom, even if there is no proof of actual prejudice. Defence lawyers in Belgium reported that judges often start the hearing of cases without waiting for the defence lawyer to arrive, and that they are

---

[26]   Chapter 7 § 2.1.2.
[27]   Chapter 9 § 1.4; Chapter 11 § 1.4.
[28]   Chapter 10 § 1.4.
[29]   Chapter 4 § 2.3.1.
[30]   Chapter 6 § 1.3.
[31]   Chapter 8 § 2.3.1.
[32]   Chapter 2 § 2.4.

more disposed to grant adjournments to the prosecution than to the defence.[33] In a number of civil law countries, and in particular in France and Italy, there are active debates about the role of the prosecutor and whether they should belong to the independent judiciary or should be separated.[34]

Whatever the origin of the legal tradition, in all countries the trial is adversarial in the sense that each party is afforded an opportunity to present his case at trial.[35] In most inquisitorial jurisdictions, however, the judge leads the trial, decides on guilt, and on sentence in the event of a conviction. In the civil law jurisdictions in the study the inquisitorial tradition is still strong in the pre-trial phase, where the suspect is not considered a party but an object of investigation. As most case law of the ECtHR addresses the equality of arms requirements during the trial phase there is much less jurisprudence regarding the pre-trial phase, although more recently the increasing importance of this phase has been acknowledged.[36] The rule in England and Wales, that a suspect cannot normally be interrogated after charge,[37] is not recognised in the civil law tradition, and neither is the immediacy principle in the sense that evidence must be presented in its most original form at trial (that is, normally by oral evidence given by the witness). In most civil law countries in the study the evidence is gathered in the pre-trial phase, including by the interrogation of witnesses. After having finalised the inquiry the court decides on the evidence in the file and rarely questions witnesses in open court. Germany and Finland provide exceptions to this, where the immediacy principle is in principle adhered to and all evidence is normally assessed in open court.[38] Italy is also exceptional, having introduced an adversarial criminal procedure in which the defence is afforded extensive rights to investigate pre-trial and where there is a strict separation between the investigation phase and the trial phase; the information collected during the preliminary investigation is not admitted or used as evidence at trial.[39]

The guilty plea procedure is well established in England and Wales,[40] but many other jurisdictions have introduced various forms of expedited proceedings, often predicated on an acceptance of guilt by the accused. Such procedures may advantage defendants by increasing the speed of process and by providing discounted sentences, but they have a number of potential disadvantages, such as subjecting defendants to disproportionate pressure to plead guilty. Finland provides a notable example of the increased use of a fast-track disposal procedure. A written procedure introduced in 2006 now disposes of around 30% of all cases without a hearing, even though it can apply to cases where the maximum sentence is up to two years imprisonment.[41] A foreseeable consequence of this sort of

---

[33]   Chapter 3 § 3.2.
[34]   Chapter 6 § 1.3; Chapter 9 § 1.2.
[35]   Chapter 2 § 2.4.
[36]   Chapter 2 § 2.4.
[37]   Chapter 4 § 2.3.4.
[38]   Chapter 7 § 2.4.3; see also Ed Cape et al. 2007, p. 95; Chapter 5 § 1.3.
[39]   Chapter 9 § 1.3.
[40]   Chapter 4 § 1.2.
[41]   Chapter 5 § 1.3.

approach was reported in relation to Germany, where judges and courts appear to have become used to dealing with cases by agreement and have come to regard defence initiatives, such as motions to introduce new evidence, as time-consuming and unnecessary.[42] There is also concern in some jurisdictions, such as France, that expedited procedures leave insufficient time for preparation by the defence.[43]

3.5. Right to information on the nature and cause of the accusation and access to the file

ECtHR jurisprudence on the right to information on the nature and cause of the accusation is strongly dependant on the nature and complexity of the case. There is a positive duty on member states to inform the suspect of the nature and cause of the accusation, but although the preference is that such information should be provided in writing, it is accepted that it may be provided orally.[44] Jurisdictions vary on the extent to which suspects are entitled to be informed of significant details of the case against them whilst the police or prosecution are still conducting the investigation.

England and Wales probably has the most detailed system regarding information to be provided at the investigative stage, with duties set out in a statutory code.[45] The code requires information to be provided both as to the reasons for arrest and as to the suspect's rights. Confirmation that the requisite information has been given must be recorded in the custody record, which is required to be kept in respect of all arrested persons detained at a police station, and a written notice of rights must be provided to the suspect. By contrast, in France and Belgium there is no requirement to inform a suspect of the nature of the allegation against them once arrested; being a clear breach of ECHR requirements.[46] The Belgium Supreme Court has ruled that the article 6 right to know the nature and cause of the accusation does not apply during the stage of criminal investigation by the police. In some circumstances, where a judge is conducting the investigation, there is a requirement to inform the suspect that there are 'serious indications of guilt.' Such notification may, however, be delayed, for example, until after a search has been conducted. It is reported that in the majority of cases where the police interview a suspect who may be the target of a prosecution, the suspect is not informed of the nature and cause of the accusation until they are charged with an offence.[47] The practice in other countries is to provide information to those involved in a criminal case much earlier in the process.

Practitioners report that there are sometimes problems with the provision of adequate information to suspects. In Italy, a suspect has the right to information about the charge against him and any amendments to it. However, the ECtHR criticised Italy in a case where the judge failed to alert the suspect when he had

---

42	Chapter 7 § 1.4.1.
43	Chapter 6 § 2.4.2.
44	Chapter 2 § 3.1.
45	Chapter 4 § 2.1.1.
46	Chapter 6 § 2.1; Chapter 3 § 2.1.1.
47	Chapter 3 § 2.1.1.

altered the legal definition of the case against him.[48] In Poland, a 'suspected person' is entitled to information on the reasons for arrest and their subsequent rights. However, though referring to the right to a lawyer, these do not include the right to silence.[49] Turkey is an example of a country where the law is strong but practice is weak. Someone arrested or detained in Turkey is entitled to prompt notice in writing or, if this is not possible, orally of the grounds of arrest and the charges against them. However, in practice this principle is reportedly honoured more in the breach than the observance, particularly in relation to poorer suspects.[50]

3.6. Rights to information on defence rights

According to recent ECtHR case law the judicial authorities have to take positive measures in order to ensure effective compliance with article 6 ECHR and to inform suspects of their right to legal aid and to legal assistance. The Court held that it is not sufficient for this information to be given in writing, for instance by a letter of rights, but that authorities must take all necessary steps to ensure that the suspect is fully aware of his defence rights, and that he understands the implications of his conduct under questioning.[51] Most jurisdictions in this study have rules concerning the provision of information to the suspect as to his rights, orally or in writing. England and Wales has detailed rules on what kind of information should be given to the suspect orally, and has a clear letter of rights.[52] Germany introduced a requirement for a letter of rights in January 2010.[53] Finland requires information to be given orally, although there is a debate about whether it should be written.[54] In Poland, a suspect is entitled to a written notice of rights prior to examination. However, the form of notice has been criticised as being too complicated and lacking practical information, such as how the suspect can actually obtain legal assistance.[55]

There are, however, jurisdictions that do not meet the ECtHR standards in this respect. In France, a suspect under investigation (*Garde à Vue*) is informed of his right to legal assistance orally, which must be noted in the record of interrogation, but not of his right to silence.[56] Belgium has no rule that obliges the police or judiciary to inform suspects of their rights to remain silent or to be legally represented.[57]

---

[48] Chapter 9 § 2.1.3.
[49] Chapter 10 § 2.3.4.
[50] Chapter 11 § 2.1.1.
[51] Chaper 2 § 3.2.
[52] Chapter 4 § 2.2.1.
[53] Chapter 7 § 2.1.1.
[54] Chapter 5 § 2.3.1.
[55] Chapter 10 § 2.1.3.
[56] Chapter 6 § 2.1.
[57] Chapter 3 § 2.1.1.

3.7.   Disclosure of the evidence and access to the case file

A major issue arises over the precise point at which an accused is entitled to know the evidence against them. Clearly, they must be told before trial,[58] but at what earlier stage? There is no specific case law under article 6 ECHR clarifying at what point in the investigative phase material evidence should be disclosed. In the context of article 5 § 4 ECHR there is case law stipulating that the principle of equality of arms requires defence access to those documents in the investigation file which are essential in order to effectively challenge the lawfulness of pre-trial detention. So there is no clear guidance to be drawn from Strasbourg case law on the minimum requirements during the pre-trial phase. From our study it appears that law and practice is somewhat variable. Many countries effectively follow the example of Belgium.[59] There, a suspect may ask to see the file while under investigation, but such a request is usually denied until after the investigation is closed. Once charged, defendants may see and copy the file on payment of the appropriate costs. Copies are free for defendants in the Assise Court, others may apply for exemption. Otherwise, they have to pay.

In England and Wales, there is no right to disclosure of the case against a suspect at the investigative stage, although the police are encouraged in training to consider what information to divulge.[60] There is, however, no right to read witness statements or the investigator's file and, thus, no way the defence can monitor disclosure. There is a statutory scheme for disclosure prior to trial. Despite its codification, recent research by the Crown Prosecution Service (CPS) Inspectorate found significant non-compliance by both police and the CPS.[61] In Poland, on charge, a person is entitled to information about the case against them but actually obtaining access to the case file prior to trial may be difficult as it depends upon the discretion of the judge. The Constitutional Court has recently required defence access to the case file during the investigation phase. Previously, this was generally not allowed. The Criminal Procedure Code has since been amended, but wide grounds for refusal remain.[62] In Finland, evidence should be disclosed to a suspect at the investigative stage unless doing so will hinder investigation of the crime.[63] Practitioners report that this exception to disclosure is applied rather more often than it should be, particularly early in an investigation. By contrast, the defence in Hungary is entitled to very little disclosure until the close of the investigation. They are guaranteed access only to expert reports and minutes of a limited range investigative procedures.[64] Significantly, this is reported to hinder applications for pre-trial release from custody. A similar issue arises in Turkey; a suspect has a right

[58]   Chapter 2 § 3.3.
[59]   France, Chapter 6 § 2.2.1, Germany, Chapter 7 § 2.1.2, Hungary, Chapter 8 § 2.1.2.
[60]   Chapter 4 § 2.1.2
[61]   Chapter 4 § 2.1.4.
[62]   Chapter 10 § 2.1.2.
[63]   Chapter 5 § 2.3.1.
[64]   Chapter 8 § 2.1.2.

to request the collection of evidence during the investigative phase but judges often prove resistant in practice.[65]

3.8.   Right to self-representation

The ECtHR has ruled that the right to self-representation is not absolute and that member states enjoy a wide margin of appreciation and may require compulsory legal representation if the interests of justice so require.[66] Many jurisdictions in our study require mandatory legal representation in a number of circumstances dependent on the severity of the crime or where a suspect or defendant is considered vulnerable. This seems to be in accordance with the Strasbourg case law. The law in Italy, where assistance of counsel is mandatory in each and every criminal prosecution regardless of the seriousness of the offence, is questionable. Mandatory representation cannot be derogated from, nor be waived.[67] As we have argued in Chapter 2 it is very doubtful whether forcing a lawyer upon an unwilling client can be considered to be in compliance with a right to fair trial. Although the strict rule of mandatory representation in criminal proceedings in Italy seems to be justified by reference to the interests of the accused, we argue that the absence of a right to waive legal assistance is in violation of the basic right of an accused to defend himself if he wishes to do so.[68]

3.9.   Right to legal assistance and to legal aid

The right to legal assistance is inextricably bound up with the right to legal aid. Unfortunately, the jurisdictions in the study do not publish information on legal aid in a form which allows easy comparison between them. A key indicator of a legal aid scheme's effectiveness is, unavoidably, the level of expenditure. However, some countries are so remiss in relation to statistics that they provide no published information whatsoever on the overall cost of legal aid, with some combining legal aid expenditure with other spending, such as that on courts. Where available, the figures for legal aid expenditure per case provide a further indication of the degree of service expected from lawyers acting under legal aid. Traditionally, the legal aid scheme England and Wales is regarded as both the most expensive and the most extensive in Europe. However, Finland has what appears to be a well-managed scheme which may rival it. All other jurisdictions in the study appear to have inadequate legal aid provision.

Recent Strasbourg case law has confirmed the importance of legal assistance for a proper defence in all its aspects, and that the right to legal assistance arises immediately upon arrest. Especially in the early stages of the criminal investigation it is the task of the lawyer, amongst other things, to ensure respect for the right of the accused not to incriminate himself. The ECtHR has also stressed that the principle of equality of arms requires that a suspect, from the time of the first police

[65]   Chapter 11 § 2.4.1.
[66]   Chapter 2 § 4.1.
[67]   Chapter 9 § 2.2.1.
[68]   Chapter 2 § 4.1.

interrogation, must be afforded the whole range of interventions that are inherent to legal advice such as discussion of the case, instructions by the accused, the investigation of facts and search for favourable evidence, preparation for interrogation, support of the suspect and control of the conditions under which a suspect is detained.[69] The ECtHR has even set standards for sanctioning breaches of the right to legal assistance by ruling that incriminating statements obtained from suspects who did not have access to a lawyer may not be used in evidence.

Legal assistance is such an important defence right that it is worth summarising the various schemes in some detail. This overview includes remarks, where appropriate, on the right to private consultation with a lawyer.[70]

3.9.1. Belgium

In Belgium there is a constitutional right to legal assistance.[71] However, there are only limited rights to legal assistance during interrogation by the police or by an investigating judge, seemingly in breach of the *Salduz* doctrine. As a rule, such interviews are not currently even audio-recorded. The police are currently permitted to interrogate during the 24 hours following arrest, and there is discussion as to whether this should be extended to 48 hours. During this period, a person cannot consult with their lawyer.

There is a system of 'first' and 'second' line legal aid. First line legal aid is advice from a 'house of justice'. Second line assistance is obtained from a Legal Aid Bureau. All trainee lawyers are required to do some work for the bureaux. There is a means test and a merits test. A single person is eligible for free legal aid if they have a monthly net income below 865 Euro and, subject to a contribution, up to 1,112 Euro. Remuneration is low and slow, being made retrospectively on the basis of points per element of a case. Thus, the average remuneration per case for the Flemish bar appears to be as low as 367 Euro. Payment is made late, often more than a year after the case has finished. There are also anomalies in how the points system values different types of cases. There is a lack of research into the roles played by Belgian lawyers and other criminal justice actors. The majority of defence lawyers appear to adequately represent their clients. However, there also seems to be a minority who are not specialised in this field and whom judges deem ignorant and incompetent. This may be because there are no minimum quality requirements and trainee lawyers are widely used. As noted in chapter 3, there is also concern as to a lack of empathy between some defence lawyers and their clients.

3.9.2. England and Wales

In England and Wales there is a statutory right to consult a lawyer privately at any time during detention at a police station.[72] Around half of detainees are thought to ask for it and the majority receive it. Legal assistance at the police station is

---

[69]   Chapter 2 § 4.3.
[70]   As set out in Chapter 2 § 4.5.
[71]   Chapter 3 § 2.2.2.
[72]   Chapter 4 § 2.2.2.

provided free of charge regardless of the financial circumstances of the suspect. Recent changes have been made to this scheme and there is a concern that the government may be intending to restrict its availability. Access to a lawyer can be delayed in specified circumstances for up to 36 hours, but in practice this is rare. There are practical problems with the operation of the police station legal advice scheme in relation to the lack of private telephone facilities in police stations. There can also be difficulties over privacy in relation to consultations in prisons or at courts, due to inadequate facilities.

Legal aid for magistrates' court proceedings is available free for defendants with a gross annual income of under 14,160 Euro and on a contributory basis under 25,340 Euro. It is likely that around a third of defendants in magistrates' courts and a significantly higher proportion in the higher courts (for example, 95% of those facing trial in the Crown Court) receive legal aid. Annual expenditure on criminal legal aid was £ 1.4bn in 2007/8. Expenditure peaked in 2006 but has been falling since then. It appears likely that something like six per cent of all solicitors and 40% of all barristers undertake criminal work (there is a split legal profession). The level of remuneration for legal aid work is controversial and is of particular concern to solicitors and more junior barristers.

3.9.3. Finland

In Finland a suspect or defendant has a right to representation, which need not be by a lawyer.[73] Legal aid is guaranteed by the Finnish constitution and international human rights conventions. Legal aid has a 'dual nature' – it is provided through public legal aid offices and private attorneys, who may or may not be members of the Finnish Bar. The fact that a lawyer need not be a member of the Bar Association raises issues about the quality of what are sometimes graphically described as 'wild lawyers.' Eligibility for legal aid is set at a net income of less than 1,500 Euro per month for a single person. Eighty per cent of the population are estimated to be eligible. Assistance from a publicly funded private practitioner may be available in all serious cases but not in more straightforward ones, such as 'drunk driving'. The court may appoint a public defender without applying a means test in certain types of cases, even against the wishes of the suspect. A criminal suspect or defendant in custody is entitled to legal representation free of charge. A public defender is free, whereas a private lawyer's services are means-tested. Suspects tend to choose private lawyers. Indeed, private lawyers constituted around two thirds of all appointments in 2007. Basic remuneration is 100 Euro per hour, with a basic maximum from the end of 2009 of 80 hours, down from the former limit of up to 100 hours, although an extension of another 30 hours may be available in difficult cases. A lawyer may be appointed to oversee certain types of surveillance, but he may not have contact with the suspect. This is somewhat akin to the 'special advocate' procedure used in England and Wales.

---

[73]   Chapter 5 § 2.1.

3.9.4. France

In France, when a suspect is held 'Garde a Vue' there is a right to consultation with a lawyer for an arbitrary period of 30 minutes prior to the initial police interview.[74] The role of the defence lawyer has been dismissively described as that of a 'tourist' or 'social worker'.[75] Legal aid is organised through the local Bar and utilises predominantly inexperienced lawyers or trainees. Problems of confidential consultation between lawyers and their clients persist through the instruction stage, with little opportunity for private consultation. Criminal legal aid expenditure in 2006 was just over 100 Euro per case. Eligibility for free legal aid for someone with no dependants is set at a net income of below 911 Euro a month. This is just below the level of the minimum wage. Remuneration is significantly below private rates. Interestingly, some disrespect for legal aid lawyers was reported by defendants themselves because of the low status and remuneration of legal aid lawyers.

3.9.5. Germany

In Germany, there is mandatory legal representation in some serious cases. In less serious cases there may also be discretionary legal representation.[76] In the case of mandatory representation, the lawyer is appointed by the court, although it will often take note of the defendant's preference. The state scheme guarantees payment to counsel on the basis of recouping the cost from the defendant. The scheme is geared to representation at the trial stage. Eligibility for legal aid is set at just under 1,000 Euro a month for a single person. The state does not seek to recover the legal aid costs if the defendant is acquitted, or if the defendant's income is below the minimum. In exceptional cases requiring mandatory representation, the court may appoint a lawyer even where the defendant has himself appointed one. This can happen when judges suspect that retained counsel may 'drop out' or because the appointed lawyer 'ideologically' sides with the defendant or delays the proceedings. State authorities are bound to assist a defendant with their choice of counsel. Assistance means more than simply providing a list of lawyers, but extends to providing guidance. There are privately organised regional networks of lawyers who operate emergency schemes to provide assistance, sometimes with the support of the regional bar association. There is no information about overall expenditure on criminal legal aid.

3.9.6. Hungary

Hungary also has a system of mandatory legal representation in a range of circumstances including, where it applies, during the investigative stage and at trial.[77] Representation is mandatory during certain special procedures, such as

[74]   Chapter 6 § 2.2.2.
[75]   Chapter 6 § 2.2.2.
[76]   Chapter 7 § 2.2.
[77]   Chapter 8 § 2.2.1.

expedited and *in absentia* hearings. As a result, in 2006 and 2007, over 70% of defendants were represented by a lawyer. If defendants have no pre-existing lawyer the prosecution will often not wait while one is identified but will proceed with the investigation in their absence. Defence counsel must be appointed before the first interrogation, but evidence suggests that attendance at such interrogations is variable over the country and only occurs in around a third of cases nationally. This appears to reflect the very short period– in one district, an average of only 30 minutes – between notification to the lawyer and the start of the interrogation. Notification to the defence lawyer is often made by fax rather than telephone, and the police interview may commence without direct contact with the lawyer. A crucial systemic problem in this scheme is that defence lawyers are chosen by the investigating authorities. This has resulted in an overly close relationship between some defence lawyers and those who give them work.

There is credible evidence of low levels of quality of appointed lawyers, whose approach is reportedly less thorough than those lawyers retained directly by their clients. In fact, this was the finding of a survey by the Hungarian Helsinki Committee in 2003. If the appointed lawyer does not attend trial in a relatively straightforward case, the judge will appoint a lawyer on the spot. To anticipate this, the Budapest Bar Association operates a scheme under which trainees – with law degrees but not having passed the Bar exam – take turns in being on duty to pick up such cases. Some judges have questioned the quality of representation thus provided. The maximum time that a representative has to study the file in such circumstances is half an hour. Trainees also provide defence in local courts, although theoretically under the professional supervision of their supervisor. Thus, trainees undertake a considerable proportion of assistance and representation during the interrogation stage and in local courts. Questions arise as to the quality of such representation since neither the Ministry of Justice nor the Bar Associations monitor quality. A 1999 study, for example, suggested inadequate standards of representation by lawyers appointed to act for juveniles. Payment of defence lawyers in legal aid cases is made for different stages of the case by the investigating authority, the prosecution and the court. This payment scheme fragments any overall accountability for the good working of the system as a whole.

Where defendants are in detention there are practical restrictions on contact between them and their lawyer: telephone calls are limited, and prisons can be a long way from the lawyer's office, impeding access in person. Some prisons have only one interview room. As a consequence, busy lawyers cannot always see their client, even when they do attempt to visit them in prison.

3.9.7. Italy

In Italy, a suspect generally cannot be questioned by the police in the absence of a lawyer, regardless of the gravity of the case.[78] Legal assistance is mandatory in all cases. The police must appoint a lawyer if the suspect does not have one. *Ex officio* lawyers are appointed by the Bar Association from a pool of lawyers who have

---

[78]   Chapter 9 § 2.2.2.

attended a specified course. The appointment is made using a computer-based system that matches competence with the requirements of the case. The suspect or defendant is required to meet the costs of the lawyer except where their annual income is below 9,300 Euro. There are no 'taper' arrangements to mitigate the effect for those suspects or defendants who are just over the financial limit. Moreover, a lawyer must pursue the debt vigorously against the client in order to secure state payment of the fee in the case of default. This can affect lawyer-client confidence. Legal aid fees are low, the average being between 1,000-1,500 Euro per case, which is around a quarter of the private rate. There is, however, a practice in less serious cases or where the lawyer is appointed at trial, of lawyers acting for free, either for political or ethical reasons.

The number of grants, and the cost, of legal aid has grown rapidly in recent years. In the decade from 1996, the cost of legal aid rose from 4 million Euro to 70 million Euro. The choice of lawyer can be made in writing or orally, but if made orally it must be confirmed in writing in the records of the police or prosecutor. Attendance by the lawyer can be waived but in practice, with the exception of attendance at searches and inspections, it is usual for the lawyer to attend interviews. Legal representation is required at trial, the judge appointing a lawyer *ex officio* if the defendant has not done so. Culturally, Italian defence lawyers act adversarially. Lawyers must be members of the Bar Association, which requires successful completion of the Bar examination. There is a voluntary association of criminal practitioners, the Penal Chamber, which is organised nationally and locally. A compulsory national Bar Association code is supplemented by a voluntary code of professional conduct drafted by the Penal Chamber.

3.9.8. Poland

In Poland, responsibility for granting legal aid rests with the judge and there is concern that judges may be influenced by budgetary considerations.[79] There is no separate legal aid budget, and there is a lack of statistical information on legal aid. There is, in principle, a right to be represented by a lawyer at all stages of criminal proceedings, and a suspect must be informed of this. However, legal aid does not cover the period prior to the first court hearing concerning pre-trial detention. Thus, police interviews may be conducted in the absence of legal representation. Moreover, the courts frequently employ expedited proceedings, in which legal representation is not required. Communication between the lawyer and their client can be supervised during the first 14 days of pre-trial detention. The legality of this practice has been upheld by the Constitutional Court, but there is doubt as to whether the ECtHR would come to the same conclusion.[80] There is, apparently, relatively little concern amongst members of the bar about this lack of confidentiality. This is mainly because such supervision is not carried out on a large scale and lawyers do not consider postponing the first in-depth consultation with the client until after the first 14 days have passed to be problematic.

---

[79]   Chapter 10 § 2.2.2.
[80]   Chapter 2 § 4.5.

Representation during the period immediately following arrest is rare and, as noted, is not funded by legal aid. The court may order mandatory defence in some circumstances, for example, where the accused is a minor. In practice, legal assistance in these circumstances is free of charge to the accused. Otherwise, representation may be free if the suspect or defendant is unable to pay, but there is no clear means test. Thus, in practice, defence representation often depends upon the prosecutor's ability to identify whether the accused is eligible for legal aid. This has been criticised as giving the prosecutor too much discretion.

Lawyers are appointed from a Bar Association list, without regard to specialisation, and there is no appeal against the appointment decision. This can mean that an inexperienced lawyer is appointed to represent a client in a complex case. Only qualified lawyers can represent defendants in court, but law clinics are used for advice, for example, in detention centres. Mandatory appointment of a lawyer does not mean that their attendance at hearings prior to the main trial is mandatory, and thus representation may be lacking at procedural hearings prior to trial. All members of the bar have a duty to provide legal representation, but the numbers that actually do are unknown. Minimum fees are regulated by ministerial decree for separate elements of cases, and remuneration levels are less than for private cases. There are indications, supported by research, that the quality of legal assistance is low. Reform of the legal aid system has been contemplated, but is currently stalled.

3.9.9. Turkey

In Turkey there is a right to representation at hearings following arrest.[81] However, such hearings have been criticised as being more about providing a safeguard against ill-treatment than anything else.[82] A further safeguard against abuse is provided by a rule that a statement by the defendant in the absence of a lawyer cannot be accepted as the basis for conviction unless confirmed to the court. There was some suggestion in interviews conducted for the research that the police circumvent the requirement of legal representation through a series of strategies designed to elicit information from the suspect before the formal interview conducted in the presence of lawyer. There are often practical problems in finding a room in which a confidential consultation between a lawyer and their client can be conducted. There are even reports that some police officers are deliberately obstructive. Research in Istanbul suggested that there was legal representation in only 10% of cases for courts of general jurisdiction, although this rose to just over 40% of cases in the superior courts. Around three-quarters of those sentenced to imprisonment were not represented at trial.

Legal aid is available without a means test from the time of first detention through to appeal, but expenditure on criminal legal aid is less than 1 Euro per capita. This low level of expenditure suggests, *inter alia*, low levels of remuneration. Indeed, the fee for an aggravated felony, for example, is only 215 Euro. Legal aid is

---

81   Chapter 11 § 1.3.
82   Chapter 11 § 1.3.

managed by local Bar associations, without any supervision by the Ministry of Justice. Both judges and prosecutors have expressed dissatisfaction with the quality of defence representation. To an extent, this concern is shared by lawyers themselves who admit, at least collectively, to failings such as delays and low motivation. Ordinary professional disciplinary proceedings provide the only form of quality control. In legal aid cases the accused has no right to dismiss the lawyer. Furthermore, the Istanbul bar is currently boycotting the legal aid scheme because of late payment, and as a result legally-aided representation in Istanbul is not currently available at all.

3.9.10. Standards of representation, roles and independence

Whilst ECtHR jurisprudence regarding the right to legal assistance is clear,[83] it is less clear as to the circumstances in which right to free legal aid applies. Although the ECtHR has set standards for a merits test – when the interests of justice require free legal aid – the margin of appreciation for member states to choose a system for making free legal assistance available is very broad, and case law on when an accused person is considered not to be able to pay for legal assistance is completely lacking.[84] The same is also true in respect of the role and standards of lawyers. The ECtHR has been reluctant to hold states liable for the failures of lawyers to provide effective legal assistance, and it has required states to intervene only if a failure to provide effective representation is manifest or sufficiently brought to their attention.[85] This means that the mechanisms for delivering legal aid and for securing quality standards is to a large extent left to member states and national bars, with the consequence that in many jurisdictions such issues are not given any priority.

In most of the jurisdictions in the study legal aid work is poorly remunerated and is often undertaken by young and inexperienced lawyers or trainees. Not all countries require legal assistance to be provided by members of the bar.[86] Unsurprisingly, in view of its relatively high expenditure on criminal legal aid, England and Wales has developed the most sophisticated quality assurance mechanisms. Legal aid is provided by lawyers working in solicitors' firms that must have a contract with the Legal Services Commission (LSC).[87] The LSC has sought to improve the quality of provision using a number of mechanisms. All criminal solicitors and paralegals providing advice in police stations must pass an accreditation test, and the LSC has recently piloted a quality assurance scheme for court advocacy covering both solicitors and barristers.[88] There is also a system of 'peer review' relating to the quality of solicitors' work, although there are some

---

[83]   See § 3.9.

[84]   Chapter 2 § 4.4.

[85]   Chapter 2 § 4.6.

[86]   See for instance Finland Chapter 5 § 3.

[87]   Legal aid services in the higher courts are generally provided by barristers, who are not covered by the contract arrangements, but they must be instructed by a contracted firm of solicitors.

[88]   Devereux et al. 2010.

questions about its efficacy. However, recent procedural reforms have put pressure on the role of defence lawyers, notably by increasing disclosure obligations on the accused and their lawyers prior to trial. The position may also have been adversely affected by the widespread introduction of fixed fees for legal aid work which, in effect, place limits on the amount of work that can be done in defending a client. There is a paucity of recent empirical evidence on the quality of criminal defence work, and there are fears that the approach of the LSC to administering legal aid may have encouraged an overly managerialist approach to practice.

Nevertheless, no other jurisdiction in the study demonstrates this degree of concern with the quality of criminal defence lawyers. In Belgium, lawyers acting in legal aid cases are not seen as sufficiently experienced, and there is particular criticism of the defence of mentally vulnerable people.[89] In Finland, there is some question whether lawyers are sufficiently proactive. Further, there is some difficulty reported regarding the adversarial role of defence lawyers.[90] In Germany, membership of the Bar is compulsory. No specialist qualification is required to practice criminal law, but specialism is recognised through a particular title acquired through meeting rules on theoretical understanding, practical skills and expertise. A total of 2,276 lawyers have obtained this title. There are no specific compulsory professional development (CPD) requirements for qualified lawyers, although there is a legal obligation for lawyers to continue their studies. This failure to require CPD has been criticised by some representatives of the bar. There are reports of varying quality – sometimes claimed to be the result of inadequate remuneration for legal aid work. Indeed, state fees do appear to be lower than private fees.[91] In France, there are specialisation requirements for criminal defence work, but in practice legally-aided criminal defence is largely carried out by inexperienced or trainee lawyers.[92]

In Hungary, legal aid remuneration rates are very low and much lower than those charged to private clients. Even though the President of the Hungarian Bar estimated in 2005 that the fee needed to be at least 20 Euro an hour to attract lawyers to undertake the work, the usual hourly rate is currently only 12 Euro an hour. It seems likely that the low remuneration levels affect the quality of work undertaken.[93] In Italy, low rates of remuneration are also a problem. There are a considerable number of lawyers who undertake legal aid work in small firms, and such firms may be too small to allow work to be shared when this would be appropriate.[94] Income from legal aid work tends to be too low to maintain a high standard of service, particularly for *ex officio* work.

In Poland, lawyers tend to be rather passive, particularly in the pre-trial phase, but even during the trial phase. For example, lawyers seldom engage in investigation on behalf of the defence. In part, this appears to be due to the continuing influence of the culture of legal practice during the communist era, and

89   Chapter 3 § 3.4.
90   Chapter 5 § 3.
91   Chapter 7 § 3.4.
92   Chapter 6 § 2.2.2.
93   Chapter 8 § 2.2.3.
94   Chapter 9 § 3.

the lawyer continues to determine what is in the interest of his client and may, in the extreme, act contrary to the client's express wishes.[95] Poland has a bar that is divided between advocates and legal advisers, the latter having limited representation rights in criminal cases. There is no tradition of specialisation and all lawyers may undertake some criminal work. There has been criticism of the effectiveness of the bar's disciplinary mechanisms, and there is no active monitoring of quality.

In Turkey, legal aid work is not highly regarded. It tends to attract young lawyers who quickly move on to more lucrative areas of work when they have gained experience. Research has found a positive correlation between legal representation and conviction, a finding to be treated with caution but also concern. Criminal advocates feel that they are seen as very junior partners in the criminal process. Indeed, spacially, the prosecutor sits with the judge and the advocate is down in the well of the court. Moreover, the emphasis in Sharia law on justice without lawyers has persisted, and many defendants believe that they can represent themselves and do not need a lawyer. Additionally, lawyers do not appear to have a strong collective self-image. In fact, around three-quarters of lawyers surveyed thought that their colleagues had inadequate ethical standards.[96]

3.10. Right to investigate

As explained in chapter 2, article 6 ECHR does not contain any explicit provision giving the defence the right to seek evidence, investigate facts or to interview prospective witnesses. The ability of the accused to carry out these kinds of activities during the preliminary investigation stage varies widely across the jurisdictions in the study. Although the common law system in England and Wales provides the most robust example of cross-examination rights, the accused has no right to require the police to pursue particular lines of enquiry, nor to apply to a judge to review any refusal to do so. In most civil law jurisdictions, the accused has a right to conduct investigations, but judges, prosecutors and the police are reluctant to allow the defence to influence the investigation of the case. This puts the accused at a considerable disadvantage, especially in those systems where evidence gathering, including the questioning of witnesses, is carried out during the pre-trial phase. In Finland, suspects have the right to request the police to seek evidence on their behalf, although such a request can be turned down if it is believed that the investigation would thereby be jeopardised.[97] In Germany, the accused and their counsel can be present during examinations undertaken during the investigation stage. The accused has the right to pursue their own investigation but not to require the prosecution to do so. As a matter of practice, it seems that the defence in Germany rarely pursues its own investigation.[98]

In Hungary, although there is some dispute with prosecutors and judges, defence counsel report that most requests for pre-trial evidentiary motions are

---

[95]   Chapter 10 § 3.3.3.
[96]   Chapter 11 § 3.
[97]   Chapter 5 § 2.3.2.
[98]   Chapter 7 § 2.4.1.

refused. Low rates of legal aid remuneration hinder the preparation of the defence by appointed defence lawyers. Some defence lawyers argue that the defence should be allowed to appoint its own expert to give evidence where the court has appointed one. In Italy, the suspect has right to gather evidence with the consent of prosecutor or judge, although there is a problem of the cost for those on legal aid. There is no remedy if the judge refuses to grant an application to gather and submit evidence, something that is reported as being 'not rare'. Italy operates a 'double dossier' system in which the investigative file is closed and another opened for the purposes of the trial. The judge can refer to the investigative file to test credibility, but not for the purposes of direct evidence.[99] In Turkey, lawyers complain that judges often do not allow them to question witnesses at trial. There is a particular problem with forensic evidence which is often sought from the government-established Forensic Medicine Institute. The Institute has a reputation for incompetence and is subject to a review by the State Auditing Authority on the instruction of the President.[100]

3.11. Right to be tried in one's presence and to participate

Although in principle the accused has the right to be present at hearings and to participate in the process, the ECtHR has ruled that a trial in absentia is not in itself incompatible with article 6 ECHR as long as the accused may subsequently obtain a fresh determination of the merits of the charge where it has not been established that the defendant waived his right to be present.[101] So a waiver to attend trial does not interfere with the fair trial requirement provided the accused has been duly summoned.

In Finland 20% of cases are tried in the absence of the accused, and nearly one third of district court cases are dealt with by a written procedure. Although this is done only if the defendant has confessed and consented to the case being decided without a hearing, the country researchers acknowledge that this procedural method is contrary to the principle of orality and immediacy that are the key principles of Finnish criminal proceedings.[102] Many other countries have summary proceedings that can be conducted in the absence of the defendant, although often confined to cases where no prison sentence is imposed.[103] Normally, lawyers can represent their absent clients in court, as is the case in France, Belgium and Poland.[104] In Poland, in principle, trial in absentia is not permitted, but there are many exceptions to this rule with the result that the rule regarding mandatory presence of the defendant has lost much of its meaning. The same may also be said of Germany, although the circumstances in which there may be a trial in absentia are more limited.[105]

---

[99]   Chapter 8 § 2.4.1.
[100]   Chapter 11 § 2.4.3.
[101]   Chapter 2 § 5.2 and § 8.5.2.
[102]   Chapter 5 § 2.2.2.
[103]   England and Wales § 2.3.2; Turkey § 2.3.2; Hungary § 1.3.
[104]   Chapter 6 § 2.3.2; Chapter 10 § 2.3.2.; Chapter 3 § 2.2.2.
[105]   Chapter 7 § 2.3.2.

Problems have arisen in Italy, where the system did not guarantee that the defendant was made aware of criminal process against him. However, following a number of adverse judgements of the ECtHR, it is now possible for the accused to appeal where they were ignorant of the proceedings against them.

3.12. *Adequate time and facilities to prepare the defence*

The right to adequate time and facilities to prepare the defence includes the right to be informed of the accusation and the right of access to the file, which are dealt with under separate headings above. Here we address the facilities that should be available to the defence. Although the ECtHR has placed emphasis on the duty of the authorities to ensure that rights guaranteed by article 6 ECHR are practical and effective, the Court has not particularised how this has to be done.[106]

The country reports show that in nearly all jurisdictions in the study problems arise with regard to short periods of notification prior to investigative acts that may be attended by the defence or prior to court appearances, the lack of opportunity or facilities for defence lawyers to communicate with (detained) clients, and strict time limits relating to inspection of the case file or having no right to pre-trial to the case file at all.[107] In Poland, time limits for notification of the defence of certain investigative acts are not specified, and thus left to the discretion of the authorities who do not have to wait for the lawyer to be present in order to proceed.[108] In Belgium there is no opportunity in the pre-trial stage for the defence to take a copy of the investigative file, and because there is only a limited amount of time available for inspection, and files are increasingly extensive, the system is completely inefficient. Lawyers are obliged to gather at the registry in order to take notes from the file in stressful circumstances, described by some as 'prehistoric'. In Turkey there are complaints that the defence does not even receive a copy of the indictment.[109] In Hungary and Italy, in the trial phase lawyers are appointed 'on the spot' without being able to properly prepare the defence or even to become acquainted with the defendant.[110] In France there is pressure on lawyers not to request adjournments for the preparation of the defence because this will hinder the trial process.[111] Positive practice is reported in respect of Germany, where hearings are set and postponed in consultation with the defence, and summonses include a trial plan delineating which piece of evidence, and especially which witness, is to be examined during any particular trial session.[112] Germany is also the only civil law country in this study where the police may not proceed with interviewing before

---

[106] Chapter 2 § 5.3 and § 8.5.3.
[107] Poland, Chapter 10 § 2.4.2; France, Chapter 6 § 2.4.2; Belgium, Chapter 3 § 2.4.2; Turkey Chapter 11 § 2.4.2; England and Wales, Chapter 4 § 2.4.2.
[108] Chapter 10 § 2.4.2.
[109] Chapter 11 § 2.1.2.
[110] Chapter 8 § 2.4.2; Chapter 9 § 1.5.
[111] Chapter 6 § 2.4.2.
[112] Chapter 7 § 2.4.2.

the lawyer has arrived where a suspect has indicated that he wants a lawyer to be present.[113]

3.13. *Right to free interpretation and translation*

Article 6 ECHR provides for free interpretation if the suspect does not understand the relevant language. According to case law the scope of this right is not limited to oral statements but also covers documentary material and pre-trial proceedings. However, the ECtHR has determined that not every document has to be translated in written form, and that oral translation suffices in many cases.[114]

This study has identified a variety of problems. For example, a number of jurisdictions, among them England and Wales, have no clear statutory right to interpretation and translation. In Belgium, interpreters are appointed only in the higher, Assize, court and not in the lower courts. There is, in any event, an arbitrary limit of three hours' assistance in respect of the consultation between the lawyer and their client.[115] There are widespread problems in terms of the quality of interpretation and translation, and few countries regulate quality very well. There are a variety of projects, such as the one in the Antwerp Court of First Instance, that are designed to improve the position. The practice in England and Wales is to encourage the use of translators and interpreters who are registered with the appropriate professional bodies.[116] However, it seems that the standard of interpretation and translation is low in a number of countries, of which Hungary is an example.[117] Remuneration is pretty uniformly regarded as low across the jurisdictions, and is particularly as a problem in Turkey.[118]

There are difficulties over the extent of the interpretation and translation that is required. A number of jurisdictions regard the final judgement as a public document and, therefore, not one which requires translation for the defendant. This is the case in Italy and Germany, in the latter case because it is expected that the defendant's lawyer will explain it.[119] Even more problematically, some countries will not provide interpreters at state expense to cover consultations between lawyers and their clients – for example, Hungary.[120] In France, some registered interpreters refuse to take cases because of the low level of payment.[121]

4.   Conclusion

In this Chapter we have attempted to establish to what extent there is compliance across the jurisdictions in the study with ECHR standards as analysed in chapter 2.

---

[113]   Chapter 7 § 2.2.3.
[114]   Chapter 2 § 6.
[115]   Chapter 3 § 2.4.4.
[116]   Chapter 4 § 2.4.4.
[117]   Chapter 8 § 2.4.4.
[118]   Chapter 11 § 2.4.4.
[119]   Chapter 9 § 2.4.4; Chapter 7 § 2.4.4.
[120]   Chapter 8 § 2.4.4.
[121]   Chapter 6 § 2.4.4.

These standards vary in clarity and precision, which is inherent to the reactive nature of the ECHR complaint mechanism. With regard to the right to silence and prohibition on self-incrimination, the right to be released pending trial, information on the cause and nature of the accusation and the right to legal assistance, the ECtHR has developed a rather clear minimum baseline that allows conclusions to be drawn regarding compliance. In respect of other aspects of effective criminal defence, such as access to the case file, information on rights, legal aid and assistance, free interpretation and translation, and adequate time and facilities to prepare the defence, the jurisprudence provides less clear guidance on how they should be regulated in order for them to be 'practical and effective'. The country studies demonstrate that problems of access to effective criminal defence arise especially in relation to such rights. Earlier studies have provided evidence for the proposition that although the basic requirements of fair trial in the ECHR appear to be, more or less, guaranteed in the criminal justice systems of the EU, a more in-depth examination of the implementation of these rights raises doubts as to whether everyday practice is in line with the Strasbourg standard in all member states.[122]

We divide our concluding remarks on this analysis into three parts. Firstly, there are some evident specific discrepancies between ECHR fair trial standards and practice in particular countries in the study. Secondly, there are aspects of effective criminal defence where Strasbourg standards are relatively clear but in respect of which there are problems common to many jurisdictions in the study. Thirdly, however, the majority of deficiencies in access to effective criminal defence relate to elements where ECtHR case law is less clear or insufficiently detailed to provide adequate guidelines or where there is a lack of relevant case law.

In the first category, the following conclusions may be drawn. In Italy the persisting violation of the reasonable time requirement has a paralysing effect on the administration of criminal justice, including on the possibility for suspects to effectively use their defence rights. In addition, mandatory legal assistance in all criminal cases breaches the right of suspects to defend themselves. In Turkey, the cultures of all professional participants in the criminal justice system, that is, the police, lawyers, prosecutors and judges, appear to inhibit the meeting of ECHR standards. In Poland, the power to restrict confidential communications between lawyers and their clients during the first two weeks of pre-trial detention is clearly a violation of Strasbourg requirements. In Belgium and France there is no requirement for the authorities to inform suspects upon arrest of the nature of the suspected offence, nor is there a duty to inform the suspect of his right to silence.

In the second category, there are concerns that are common in many jurisdictions relating to the right to silence, the (conditional) right to be released during trial, the right to information on the charge, and the right to legal assistance. Problems with regard to the right to silence arise where practices are applied that circumvent the duty to caution the suspect, or where silence can lead to adverse consequences for the accused. The use and length of pre-trial detention in the majority of jurisdictions in the study raise serious concerns as to whether the requirements of article 5 ECHR are applied in practice. In many jurisdictions the

---

122 Spronken & Attinger 2005; Spronken et al. 2009: see also Cape et al. 2007.

571

right of suspects to effective legal assistance during the police interrogation stage is not ensured. This results from a variety of factors; for example, because this is not permitted according to national law, because legal aid is not effectively provided for at this stage, because there is no emergency scheme for providing a lawyer, because lawyers are not available or because even if available, they remain passive.

In relation to the third category, a principle concern relates to the quality of legal assistance. The ECtHR has always been reluctant to establish standards; for various reasons, but primarily because of the importance of the independence of the legal profession. As stated in chapter 2, the Strasbourg enforcement mechanism is not designed for the ECtHR to prescribe detailed rules as to how member states should adhere to fair trial requirements;[123] in those areas where ECtHR judgments are more specific, it is more likely that the requirements will be complied with, but where guidance from the ECtHR is lacking compliance is more problematic. It appears from the analysis in this chapter that the latter is the case with regard to access to the case file, information on rights, rights to investigate, free interpretation and translation, and adequate time and facilities to prepare a defence in general. A common cause of the problems described is that national regulations lack detail on practical implementation and on the precise moment that the rights arise. For those who cannot afford legal assistance, effective use of their defence rights is largely impossible without an effective legal aid system and lawyers that are willing and able provide competent legal assistance. The analysis in § 3.9 shows that legal aid mechanisms, and quality assurance for lawyers providing free legal assistance, is a major problem in almost every jurisdiction.

5.   Bibliography

Cape et al. 2007
Cape, E., Hodgson, J., Prakken, T. & Spronken, T., *Suspects in Europe*, Antwerp: Intersentia, 2007.

Devereux et al. 2010
Devereux, A., Tucker, J., Moorhead, R. & Cape, E., *Quality Assurance for Advocates, London: Legal Services Commission*, 2010, available at <http://www.legalservices.gov.uk/docs/cds_main/Annex_Ci_QAAFinalReportNovember2009.pdf>.

Spronken & Attinger 2005
Spronken, T. & Attinger, M., *Procedural Rights in Criminal Proceedings: Existing Level of Safeguards in the European Union*, 2005, available at <http://arno.unimaas.nl/show.cgi?fid=3891>.

Spronken et al. 2009
Spronken, T., Vermeulen, G., de Vocht, D. & van Puyenbroek, L., *EU Procedural Rights in Criminal Proceedings*, Antwerp: Maklu, 2009.

[123]   Chapter 2 § 8.1.

Ed Cape
Zaza Namoradze
Roger Smith
Taru Spronken

CHAPTER 13 THE EFFECTIVE CRIMINAL DEFENCE TRIANGLE: COMPARING PATTERNS

1.   A model for analysis

One of the major challenges of this research is not only to define the common features of the content and scope of the right to effective defence,[1] but also to evaluate the extent to which defence rights are actually available in a jurisdiction, in particular in the nine European jurisdictions that are the subject of this study. Chapter 12 provides an analysis of the country reports by reference to the principles of effective criminal defence and compliance with ECtHR jurisprudence as described in chapter 2. In this chapter we adopt a more systemic approach that deals with the interrelated nature of the various aspects of criminal defence. The assumption is that all rights and guarantees that we have identified as playing a part in criminal defence are linked and that there must be a balance between all of these elements in order to provide a framework in which criminal defence can be effective. This means that not only the statutory framework or regulations that are inherent to a fair trial are in place, but also that this framework is sufficiently precise and practical so that defence rights work in real terms.[2] In order to visualise the interrelationship between the various rights we have developed a model: 'the effective criminal defence triangle'. In the first part of this chapter we will describe this model, and in the second part we will apply the model in order to analyse five themes that arise from our study of the nine jurisdictions: the right to legal assistance; legal aid; the right to interpretation and translation; adequate time and facilities to prepare the defence (including access to information); and the use of pre-trial detention. Before explaining the effective criminal defence triangle we recall how we have defined the content and scope of effective defence for the purposes of our research.[3]

---

[1]   See chapter 1 § 1 and chapter 2.
[2]   See chapter 1 § 1.
[3]   See further chapter 1 § 1.

2. The content and scope of effective criminal defence

With regard to the content and scope of the right to effective criminal defence we look beyond the right to legal representation. We adopt a more holistic approach in which the right to legal advice and representation is based on, and arises out of, the right of an accused person to defend themselves. As explained in chapter 1 we place the suspect or defendant at the centre of our inquiries. It is therefore necessary to approach the assessment of access to effective criminal defence in any particular jurisdiction at three levels:

-   Whether there exists a constitutional and legislative structure that adequately provides for criminal defence rights taking ECtHR jurisprudence, where it is available, as establishing a minimum standard.
-   Whether regulations and practices are in place which enable those rights to be 'practical and effective'.
-   Whether there exists a consistent level of competence amongst criminal defence lawyers, underpinned by a professional culture that recognises that effective defence is concerned with processes as well as outcomes, and in respect of which the perceptions and experiences of suspects and defendants are central.

Therefore we place the lawyer's contribution within the wider context of other defence rights such as the facilities to prepare a case and to examine witnesses demanded by article 6 of the ECHR. This approach raises broader questions about the effectiveness of criminal defence as a whole than when it is looked at only from the perspective of lawyers themselves or of the bodies and governments that might be funding them to provide criminal legal aid. The right to legal assistance is in our opinion not the legal foundation of defence rights 'but a *prerequisite* for the effective exercise of (other) defence rights'.[4]

Of course, an accused person is concerned with the quality and performance of their lawyer; but the accused needs reassurance not only that the lawyer has done the best possible with the resources available but also that the criminal justice system as a whole has provided for equality of arms, effective representation and effective participation. The normative framework that contributes to this aim can be found in a range of principles and rights deriving from the ECHR that in our view are essential components of effective criminal defence. In chapter 2 we have examined the Convention jurisprudence with regard to the presumption of innocence, the right to silence, equality of arms and adversarial trial and the right to bail, as elements that have an overall impact on the position of the defence. We did the same with the more specific defence rights such as the right to information and the rights that promote effective participation, such as the right to investigate and seek exculpatory evidence, to have adequate time and facilities to prepare a defence, to be present at hearings and to question witnesses. In addition we analysed the ECtHR jurisprudence on the right to interpretation and translation, that are

---

[4]   Spronken 2003, p. 53.

essential for a suspect who does not understand or speak the language to effectively conduct a defence, as well as the right to reasoned decisions and appeal.

Chapter 2 provides an overview of the ECtHR jurisprudence on these rights, broadly following the order and structure in which they appear in the Convention. The analysis in chapter 2 demonstrates that the various elements that can be found in the fair trial requirements are often interwoven (for an overview see the frame below). The general principles of equality of arms and adversarial trial, the presumption of innocence, and the right to silence have an overall impact on other more specific defence rights such as the right to legal assistance and access to the case file. However, there is also a relationship of interdependence between the more specific defence rights. For example, effective legal assistance for indigent suspects is closely linked with the regulation of the legal aid system, and the ability of the lawyer to give legal advice and assistance will be less effective to the extent that there is no right to information to the case file. Nevertheless, we attempted in chapter 2 to unravel, in as detailed a way as possible for each right, what the baseline requirements are according to ECtHR case law. With regard to some rights these requirements are quite clear, but we also identified areas where the jurisprudence is less clear, and areas where there are gaps in the jurisprudence. For example, the case law of the ECtHR is ambiguous as to the time in the criminal proceedings that certain rights crystallise, such as the moment at which access to prosecution material should be provided. Jurisprudence on how suspects should be informed of their rights is still fragmentary, as are the guidelines on what powers the defence should have in the investigative phase.

Summary of the rights analysed in chapter 2

- o Procedural rights relating to fair trial in general
  - Presumption of innocence
  - Right to silence and prohibition of self incrimination
  - Equality of arms
  - Right to adversarial hearing
  - Bail or the right to be released pending trial
- o The right to information
  - On the nature and cause of the accusation
  - On defence rights
  - On material evidence/access to case file
- o Right to defence
  - Right to self representation
  - Right to legal advice and representation
    - Moment at which the right arises
    - Choice and provision of lawyer for indigent suspects
    - Private consultation
    - Lawyers role and independence
- o Procedural rights relating to effective defence
  - Rights to investigate the case
  - Seek evidence and interview prospect witnesses
  - Right to be tried in presence and participate in process
  - Adequate time and facilities for preparation of defence
  - Right to call and question witnesses
  - Free interpretation and translation
  - Right to reasoned decisions
  - Right to appeal

3. The effective criminal defence triangle

In order to demonstrate the ways in which the various rights and elements we have explored in chapter 2 are related and influence each other we have rearranged them in a model we call 'The Effective Criminal Defence Triangle'.

Effective Criminal Defence Triangle

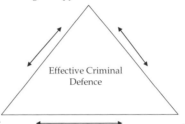

- Presumption of innocence
- Right to silence
- Equality of arms
- Adversarial trial
- Right to defend oneself
- Right to be present and participate at hearings
- Right to information (accusation, file)
- Right to call and question witnesses/experts
- Right to appeal

Effective Criminal Defence

- Information on rights
- Caution of the right to silence
- Bail
- Adequate time and facilities to prepare defence
- Right to investigate
- Right to reasoned decisions
- Procedural enforcement mechanisms (exclusionary rule, nullity)

- Interpretation
- Translation
- Legal assistance
- Defence culture
- Quality control
- Legal aid system

The basic purpose of the triangle is to classify the procedural rights and safeguards that form the core normative framework of our analysis, and to demonstrate how they are connected.

Top of the triangle

At the top of the triangle are the rights that are of paramount importance in ensuring effective criminal defence and which have an overall impact on the way in which criminal proceedings should be conducted: the presumption of innocence, the right to silence, equality of arms, and adversarial trial. These rights and principles set standards for procedural and evidential rules and regulate the fundamental roles and positions of the participants in the criminal investigation and trial. The rights to defend oneself, to be present at hearings, to information on the accusation and the file, to call and question witnesses and experts, and to appeal are more specific rights that relate to criminal defence. Together these rights could be called substantive procedural rights, indispensable in guaranteeing a fair trial and ensuring effective defence.

Left corner of the triangle

On the left corner of the triangle are the provisions that support the rights and principles that are placed at the apex. Some of them are mentioned in the ECHR, such as the right to bail in article 5 § 4 ECHR, and the right to have adequate time and facilities to prepare a defence in article 6 § 3b ECHR. Others are elaborated to a certain extent in Strasbourg jurisprudence, as is the right to reasoned decisions, and to information on rights, and the enforcement mechanisms that should be available when rights are violated or not duly respected. To a large extent, however, regulation of these aspects is left to member states. As we have seen in the country reports the practical implementation of these supportive rights is highly dependant on the character of the particular criminal justice system.

Right corner of the triangle

Rights to interpretation and translation, and to legal assistance, which are necessary for the accused to effectively understand – and to actually be able to participate in – criminal proceedings, are placed at the right corner of the triangle. The rationale for separating the right to legal assistance (including the right to legal aid) and the right to interpretation and translation, from the other rights placed at the top of the triangle is to acknowledge that these rights have a different function. They are distinguished from other procedural safeguards such as the right to be informed, examine witnesses – in short the entire catalogue of procedural rights laid down in international treaties – in that they are pre-conditions or supportive rights enabling the suspect to defend themselves effectively and make use of the other safeguards afforded to him. This does not mean that the rights to interpretation and translation, and to legal assistance, are not core rights or principles; but they are core rights of a different nature.

3.1. The rationale for the triangle

For a suspect or accused to have access to effective criminal defence in any particular jurisdiction, elements in all three corners of the triangle must be present in a satisfactory form. In order for these essential principles to be effective they need to be expressed in sufficient detail, supported by appropriate enforcement mechanisms and judicial cultures, and supplemented by rights which ensure transparency and utility. Since we are concerned with effective criminal defence, our model pays attention not just to whether there is a right to legal assistance, but also to issues such as when the right to legal assistance arises, whether the proceedings can continue without legal assistance where a suspect of accused wishes to have such assistance, and mechanisms for delivering legal assistance. Whilst the ECtHR has emphasised legal assistance as constituting an essential element of the right to fair trial, in principle it does not deal with the quality of legal assistance regarding it as primarily an issue between the lawyer and their client.[5]

---

[5]   See chapter 2 § 4.6.

Our model requires that we pay attention to mechanisms that secure the quality of legal assistance. Similar issues also arise in respect of the right to interpretation and translation. Finally, since in all jurisdictions many, if not most, suspects and defendants are poor, in relative or absolute terms, an essential element of the right corner of the triangle is the right to legal aid (or other forms of financial assistance for the costs of defence) and the right to *free* interpretation and translation, and the structures and mechanisms for delivering it. Effective criminal defence should not only be available to those that can afford it, but should be available to all.

We emphasise that there is a relationship between the corners of the triangle, and that rights in each corner have to be regulated in sufficient detail for effective criminal defence to be realised. The effective criminal defence triangle functions like an organism. The rights and principles at the apex are the heart of a fair trial and effective defence. Without oxygen, blood and veins, the right and left corner rights, the heart cannot function. However, that is not the only feature of an organism; the various components also have to be in balance and act symbiotically, requiring appropriate timing, in order to be practical and effective. Without legal assistance defence is possible, but unlikely to be effective other than in simple, straightforward, cases. Without interpretation and translation it is hard to imagine how a defendant could actually participate in the proceedings. The right to silence cannot protect the suspect from making incriminating statements when he is not made aware of this right before an interrogation, and it is difficult for most suspects to exercise their right to silence during police interrogations without proper advice before the interrogation starts and without having a lawyer present during the interrogation.

We have to keep in mind that deficits at any corner of the triangle could lead to the conclusion that the fair trial requirements are not met as a whole. A clear example of how this works can be found in the *Salduz* judgment of the ECtHR:[6] the Court found a violation of article 6 ECHR, not because the right to a lawyer was not provided for in Turkish criminal proceedings, and not because the suspect was not duly cautioned as to his right to silence, but because there was no timely assistance of counsel before and during police interrogation.

3.2. *An aspirational model*

Finally, we should stress that effective criminal defence is not a concept that can be measured in absolute terms. The model, and the rights that are involved, have an aspirational value; there is probably no jurisdiction that perfectly meets one requirement, let alone all requirements. As with the earlier comparison with an organism, it is possible that deficits in one part may be compensated by rights or processes in other parts, because other components take over the function of the damaged one. It can also work the other way around. A sophisticated regulation of legal assistance can be ruled out as contributing to effective defence if procedures become so lengthy that there is no opportunity for a decision to be made within a

---

[6]   ECtHR, Grand Chamber, 27 November 2008, *Salduz* v. *Turkey*, No. 36391/02.

reasonable time.[7] So it will always be a matter of balance and the overall picture will always be a relative one: there is no system that is perfect. However, our analytical model enables strengths and weaknesses to be identified, and enables an assessment to be made of the levels to which safeguards are in place and of what is needed to improve the effectiveness of criminal defence.

3.3. A worked example

The *Salduz* case, and the discussions that arose from the judgment in countries such as Belgium and France which, until now,[8] have not provided for an effective right to legal assistance at the investigative phase of the criminal process, can be used to illustrate how the triangle analysis works and how the corners interrelate.

In both Belgium and France the suspect can invoke his right to silence (apex right); but in our model it is equally important to have detailed regulations in place in order to ensure that a suspect will be effectively protected against possible involuntary self-incrimination. This means that the suspect should be cautioned (left corner right). However, cautioning the suspect is not enough, in itself, to realise effective defence. In order to be able to defend himself the equality of arms principle (apex right) must be respected and therefore the suspect requires legal assistance (right corner right).

Issues that relate to the left corner of the effective criminal defence triangle are:

- Is there a requirement for the suspect to be cautioned?
- What is the exact text of the caution?
- Does the right to legal assistance imply assistance during police interrogation or only the right to consult a lawyer prior to the interrogation?
- How must the suspect be informed of his right to have a lawyer present?
- Should this right apply in all cases, including for minor offences?
- Can the suspect wave this right and if so what safeguards should be in place?
- What kind of information is given by the police before questioning?

The right corner of the triangle deals with the following issues:

- How long do the police have to wait for the lawyer to come to the police station?
- How much time is there to consult a lawyer before the first interrogation?
- May legal advice be provided by telephone?
- How can an indigent suspect get timely legal assistance?
- Is there an emergency scheme for providing legal assistance, and if so is this provided at no cost to the suspect?

---

[7] A situation that is found in Italy for example. See chapter 9 § 1.5.
[8] It should be noted that as the text of this book is being finalised, legislative changes are in progress in Belgium and France in order to comply with the *Salduz* judgment.

- What is the role of the lawyer during the interrogation, can he intervene, and is it possible to have a private consultation during the interrogation?
- What is the capacity of the Bar to meet the need for legal assistance during police interrogation?
- Must lawyers be specifically trained to provide legal assistance during police interrogation?
- Is it possible to have an interpreter present during the lawyer/client consultation?

4.   Five central issues

4.1.   Introduction

In this section we use the triangle model to analyse five themes arising from the country reports: legal assistance; legal aid; interpretation and translation; time and facilities to prepare a defence; and pre-trial detention. The themes were identified by applying the triangle analysis to the data obtained in respect of each of the nine jurisdictions in the study. In doing so we were able to identify across the jurisdictions the most common deficiencies, in law and/or in practice, by reference to each corner of the triangle. Here, we analyse those deficiencies by examining the interrelationships to assess whether the deficiencies are compensated for, or exacerbated, by elements in the various corners of the triangle, and vice versa.

4.2.   Legal assistance

We have identified legal assistance, which includes legal advice *and* representation, as 'a *prerequisite* for the effective exercise of [other] defence rights'[9] and, indeed, as an important element of fair trial. Before proceeding further, an example of a real case illustrates the importance of competent legal assistance, and its relationship with other features of our effective criminal defence triangle. The case occurred in England and Wales, but it could have occurred in a very similar way in any jurisdiction in our study. It concerns deficient legal assistance at the investigative stage, but it has implications for effective criminal defence at any stage of the criminal process.

4.2.1. Deficient legal assistance: an example

A woman, Ms X, stabbed her partner, Ms Y, in the neck and Ms Y died almost immediately. Both were alcoholics, and had been drinking heavily and, it appeared, had become involved in an argument. Ms X ran out of the apartment shouting that she had stabbed her partner. She was arrested shortly afterwards on suspicion of murder, and taken to the local police station. She asked for legal advice, and a couple of hours later she was seen by the duty lawyer. The lawyer spent only five minutes with her before the police interviewed her. The lawyer was present during

---

[9]   Spronken 2003, p. 53.

the interview, and Ms X answered police questions. She was subsequently charged with murder.

Under English law, the circumstances give rise to a number of possibilities. Ms X could be guilty of murder if she stabbed Ms Y intending to kill her or to do her grievous bodily harm. She could be guilty of manslaughter, which is classified as either 'voluntary' or 'involuntary'. The former applies if, *inter alia*, she was suffering from diminished responsibility or satisfied the test for the defence of provocation. The latter applies if she killed Ms Y without the requisite intention, for example, if they were engaging in a drunken fight in which Ms X had intended no serious harm, or was too drunk to form an intention. Murder carries a mandatory sentence of life imprisonment whereas for manslaughter, whilst life imprisonment is possible, the sentence is within the discretion of the judge. If Ms X was acting in self-defence, she would have a complete defence to any criminal charge.

At trial the prosecution sought to make use of what Ms X said in the police interview as evidence of her culpability for murder. Her (new) defence lawyer sought to have this evidence excluded on the grounds that, having regard to the circumstances in which it was obtained, admitting it as evidence would have an adverse effect on the fairness of the proceedings; whilst she exercised her right to legal advice, that advice could not have been adequate given that, having regard to the complexity of her legal situation, a consultation of five minutes was wholly inadequate. Given the seriousness of the alleged offence, the lawyer should have spent time taking careful instructions from Ms X, advising her on whether she should answer questions in the police interview, and considering whether in view of her alcoholism she should be examined by a doctor before the interview. The judge refused to exclude the evidence, and Ms X was subsequently convicted of murder following a jury trial. She later appealed on the basis that the judge should have excluded the evidence on the grounds put forward at trial, and because at the time of the police interview she was still under the influence of alcohol. Her appeal was unsuccessful. The appeal court determined that the trial judge was within his rights not to exclude evidence of the police interview and, in relation to the second ground for appeal, that had Ms X really been under the influence of alcohol, the court was sure that the defence lawyer would have brought this to the attention of the police.

This case provides a useful illustration of the dynamic relationship between legal assistance and the other elements of the effective criminal defence model. Ms X's culpability, from a legal perspective, was heavily dependent on evidence as to the precise sequence of events and her mental state at the time of the stabbing. There were no eye-witnesses to those events, and the forensic evidence did not point with any degree of certainty to one or other of the possible offences or defences. Therefore, the determination of Ms X's criminal liability relied heavily upon her explanations. Whether or not she was still under the influence of alcohol at the time of the police interview, she is likely to have been highly traumatised by the events that had occurred only a few hours before, and her lawyer could not possibly have had time to have advised Ms X so that she was fully aware of the implications of what she said in interview.

The law in England and Wales provides for a right to legal assistance, available without cost to the suspect, and the police acted properly in bringing that to Ms X's attention and giving effect to her request for advice. Thus the supportive rights and structures (in the right hand corner of the evaluative triangle) were satisfied other than in relation to the quality control of the legal assistance. This deficiency could not have been compensated for by other features identified in the effective criminal defence triangle. Ms X had a right to silence at the police interview,[10] and notification of that right would have been given to her in the form of the caution given on arrest and at the beginning of the police interview. Whether it was given in a form which she could understand or whether, given her alcoholism, she was capable of understanding it, is not known but unlikely. Otherwise, all of the principles of fair trial were present, except that it is difficult to argue that Ms X benefited from the principle of equality of arms in circumstances where her legal adviser did not meet minimum quality standards. With regard to the left corner of the triangle, apart from the question of notification of her right to silence, most of the relevant factors were satisfied except, arguably, the mechanisms for enforcement of effective criminal defence. Since the components of effective criminal defence were not in equilibrium, it is difficult to conclude that Ms X had access to effective criminal defence or, therefore, that her trial was fair.

4.2.2. Legal assistance and the ECtHR

As was demonstrated in chapter 2, whilst the ECtHR has treated legal assistance as being an essential element of the right to fair trial, for a variety of reasons various aspects of its precise scope and characteristics have been relatively unexplored by the court. Article 6 § 3c ECHR provides that a person charged with a criminal offence has the right, *inter alia*, to defend himself 'through legal assistance of his own choosing…', and the jurisprudence is now clear that fair trial requires access to legal assistance by a person deprived of their liberty from the time of first police interrogation. If a suspect makes incriminating statements during such interrogation, without having had access to legal assistance, these statements may not be used as evidence to justify a conviction.[11] The jurisprudence is less clear regarding the role of lawyers acting for people suspected of or accused of crime and, except in relation to professional privilege, regarding the facilities that should be accorded to defence lawyers. Whilst the right of a person to choose their lawyer is clear for those who can pay for legal assistance themselves, the position is ambiguous where legal assistance is paid for by the state. The jurisprudence does not address the mechanisms by which legal assistance should be provided and, broadly, the ECtHR has only dealt with the outer limits of the standard and quality of criminal defence work.

---

[10]   Although as noted in chapter 4 § 2.3.4, this is subject to significant restriction.
[11]   See Chapter 2 § 4.3.

4.2.3. Access to legal assistance

All of the jurisdictions in the study subscribe to the right to legal assistance, at least following the initial stages of the criminal process; inevitably since they are all signatories to the ECHR. However, as we have demonstrated in chapter 12, the position is much less clear when the right to legal assistance is broken down into its component parts, and when considered in practice. This is particularly true of access to legal assistance at the investigative stage, especially where investigation and interrogation is conducted by the police. The legal position regarding access to legal assistance for people detained and interrogated by the police is changing rapidly across Europe as a result of the *Salduz* decision of the ECtHR,[12] and a number of jurisdictions are introducing a clear legal right to legal assistance at this stage; although there are varying degrees of resistance to recognising that the right extends to having a lawyer present *during* police interrogations.

Even where there is a right to legal assistance at the investigative stage, access to a lawyer is often limited, in practice, in a variety of ways. In a number of jurisdictions, such as Belgium, the police are under no duty to inform a suspect of the right, which is exacerbated by the fact that a person who is the subject of investigation does not have to be told that they are, in fact, a suspect.[13] Similarly, in Turkey, whilst the police are under such an obligation, there is evidence that in practice they often fail to provide this information.[14] In Finland, although there is a right of access to legal assistance from the outset of pre-trial investigations it would appear, at least from legal aid statistics, that lawyers almost never get involved at this stage.[15]

It is evident in a number of jurisdictions where there is a right to legal advice at the investigative stage that a variety of mechanisms limit or deter the involvement of lawyers. Research evidence established that this was the case in England and Wales in the period following the introduction, in the mid 1980s, of a statutory right to legal advice at the police station. It was found, for example, that the police would inform suspects of their right to legal advice in a way that was incomprehensible, tell them that waiting for a lawyer to arrive would extend the period of their detention, or encourage them to defer their decision.[16] Whilst there is little recent research evidence, an official report in 2009 expressed concern that only half of suspects held in custody by the police have legal advice, and it recommended that the Legal Services Commission (the body responsible for administering legal aid) conduct research into 'the reasons for the low level of take-up in police stations'.[17]

---

[12]   ECtHR, Grand Chamber, 27 November 2008, *Salduz* v. *Turkey*, No. 36391 02. And see Chapter 2 § 4.3.

[13]   See Chapter 3 § 2.1.1 and § 2.1.3.

[14]   Chapter 11 § 2.1.1.

[15]   Chapter 5 § 1.3 and § 2.1.

[16]   Sanders and Bridges 1990.

[17]   National Audit Office 2009, p. 9. Interestingly it also recommended that the research should examine 'the consequences of suspects moving through the criminal justice system without representation'.

The experience in England and Wales is mirrored in a number of jurisdictions in our study. In Poland, until recently, the police were able to take advantage of a distinction between 'a suspect' and 'a suspected person' to achieve a similar result. A suspected person may be detained by the police for up to 48 hours without being formally arrested. Whilst they cannot be interrogated during this period they must be told that they can make a statement, and it would seem that the police officer who takes such a statement can give evidence of it at trial. It was only in January 2009 that the law was changed requiring a suspected person to be informed of their rights, including the right to a lawyer, although it appears that there are still significant impediments to exercising this right.[18] Similarly, in Hungary prospective suspects are sometimes interrogated as 'witnesses', and suspects may be placed in short-term detention and informally questioned by police. In either case, although the record of the interview may be referred to in court, the person does not have to be informed of their procedural rights including access to a lawyer.[19] In Italy, where the police are prohibited from questioning a suspect in the absence of a lawyer, this prohibition may be avoided if the questioning takes place at the time of arrest, or during a search, although the product of such questioning cannot be directly be used as evidence.[20] In Turkey, although a suspect has a right to have a lawyer present during a police interview, it appears that the police often informally interview suspects before the arrival of the lawyer.[21]

4.2.4. Timeliness

Another major impediment to legal assistance, especially at the early stages of the criminal process, is a lack of adequate mechanisms for ensuring its availability in a timely fashion. This is especially true where the suspect cannot afford to pay for a lawyer privately. There are two problems here: first, the failure to establish structures and procedures to ensure that lawyers may be contacted, and are available, at all times; and second, legal aid decision-making processes that do not enable quick decisions to be made about eligibility. The system in England and Wales provides an example of a jurisdiction where these problems have been largely solved. Lawyers who provide legal advice at police stations are required by the terms of their contract with the Legal Services Commission to have established procedures by which they are available at any time of day or night, and for those suspects who do not have a lawyer or whose lawyer cannot be contacted, a duty lawyer scheme ensures that a lawyer is always available to provide advice to suspects held in custody by the police. This is bolstered by a non-means tested legal aid scheme under which all suspects held in custody are entitled to legal aid automatically. However, this is unusual in the jurisdictions in the study. In Belgium, for example, there is no system for ensuring the availability of a lawyer and access to a duty lawyer is not possible until after a person has been detained for 24 hours.[22]

[18] See Chapter 10 § 2.2.2.
[19] See Chapter 8 § 2.1.1.
[20] See Chapter 9 § 2.1.2.
[21] See Chapter 11 § 2.2.2.
[22] Chapter 3 § 2.2.2.

Similarly, in Turkey, there is no scheme to ensure the availability of a lawyer at the investigative stage.[23] In Hungary, suspects who cannot provide the police with contact details for a lawyer normally will not be able to obtain access to legal advice promptly.[24] In Poland, the decision to grant legal aid is made by a judge and thus a decision will not normally be made until, at the earliest, the court hearing that determines pre-trial detention; and in any event, legal aid does not cover the initial stage following arrest.[25]

4.2.5. Choice of lawyer

Problems with access to legal assistance are not limited to the investigative stage, although it is at this stage where in many jurisdictions the difficulties are at their most acute. There are significant limitations on the choice of lawyer where the suspect or accused is not able to pay privately. In some jurisdictions, such as England and Wales, the choice of lawyer is largely preserved in legal aid cases, although there are limitations.[26] For example, only lawyers whose firms have a contract with the Legal Services Commission can provide legal assistance in legal aid cases, and the number of such firms has been significantly reduced since the turn of the century. However, in many jurisdictions there is no choice where the lawyer is appointed by the court, and/or legal representation is mandatory (for example, Germany and Hungary), or in legal aid cases (for example, France, Italy, Poland and Turkey). In a number of jurisdictions (for example, Germany[27] and Hungary[28]) there are concerns, in such cases, that there is an unhealthy relationship between lawyers and those who appoint them, leading to concerns about both independence and quality. Choice can also be limited by court listing practices. For example, in France, a hearing may proceed without a defendant, who wishes to be represented, from being represented by their own lawyer, or by a lawyer at all.[29]

4.2.6. Compensation for lack of access to legal assistance?

It is sometimes argued that access to legal assistance at the investigative stage is of less significance, in terms of fair trial rights, in jurisdictions with an inquisitorial tradition because of the role that prosecutors and/or the judiciary play in the investigative process (and the relationship between the investigation and trial stages). This is a particular example of a wider argument that absence of a right to competent legal assistance does not necessarily interfere with fair trial rights if it is compensated for by other principles or mechanisms.[30] It was demonstrated in an earlier study, *Suspects in Europe*, that in most jurisdictions the notion that absence of

23 Chapter 11 § 2.2.2.
24 Chapter 8 § 2.2.2.
25 Chapter 10 § 2.2.2.
26 Chapter 4 § 1.5 and § 2.2.2.
27 Chapter 7 § 3.4.
28 Chapter 8 § 2.2.3.
29 Chapter 6 § 2.2.3.
30 And see the discussion of the '*Salduz* principle' in Chapter 2 § 4.3.

legal assistance is compensated for by the role of the prosecutor and/or judge 'is wholly at odds with practice, with the majority of cases being dealt with exclusively by the police, either on their own initiative or [only] under the broad supervision of a judge or prosecutor'.[31] This is supported by the findings of the current study, but we also found that suspects and defendants who are not represented may be subject to particular disadvantage in a variety of ways. In a number of jurisdictions there is no obligation on the investigative body to inform those who are treated as suspects, whether or not formally designated as such, of their procedural rights (for example, Belgium,[32] and Poland in the case of a suspected person[33]) or, in particular, their right to silence (for example, Finland[34] and Belgium[35]). In other jurisdictions, whilst there may be an obligation to inform a suspect of their rights, such information is provided in a technical language unlikely to be understood by many suspects (for example, Hungary[36]) or only in written form without oral explanation (for example, Poland[37] and Turkey[38]). Whilst in most jurisdictions there are severe limits on access to the investigative file prior to the commencement of formal legal proceedings in some, such as Germany[39] and France,[40] the suspect who is not in receipt of legal assistance is at a particular disadvantage because they have no right personally to inspect the file.

The unrepresented accused may also be at a disadvantage in later stages of the criminal process even if one accepts the classic account of the inquisitorial role of the judge. Many jurisdictions have rules concerning compulsory representation in certain circumstances, meaning that an accused cannot personally defend themselves in such cases. For example, in Poland, an appellant has no right to be present at an appeal hearing, and no right personally to file cassation, although representation is mandatory.[41] In Belgium the court can, in certain circumstances, prevent the accused from submitting arguments in person even in cases where representation is not compulsory.[42]

4.2.7. Procedural and evidential rules

As illustrated by the case at the beginning of this section, even if a suspect or accused does have a right to legal assistance, this does not in itself guarantee access to effective criminal defence. There are, of course, procedural and evidential rules that, it may be argued, interfere with fair trial rights irrespective of the assistance of a lawyer. We have already noted the lack of a right to information that is in the

[31] Cape et al. 2007, p. 19.
[32] Chapter 3 § 2.1.3.
[33] Chapter 10 § 2.1.1.
[34] Chapter 5 § 2.2.3.
[35] Chapter 3 § 2.1.3.
[36] Chapter 8 § 2.1.3.
[37] Chapter 10 § 2.1.3.
[38] Chapter 11 § 2.1.1.
[39] Chapter 7 § 2.1.5.
[40] Chapter 6 § 2.1.
[41] Chapter 10 § 2.2.1.
[42] Chapter 3 § 2.2.1.

hands of the police or prosecutor at the investigative stage, and we might include here legal or practical limitations on the right to silence, and the various concerns with guilty plea and expedited hearing procedures that are considered further in § 4.5. However, our research also demonstrates that there are a variety of legal and cultural factors that may inhibit the effectiveness of lawyers acting for the defence, and systemic factors that can result in poor levels of performance by defence lawyers.

4.2.8. The professional and inter-professional context

We noted earlier that in some jurisdictions there is concern about the impact of the system of appointment of lawyers for the defence on both independence and quality. Seen from the perspective of the accused, laws or professional rules that treat lawyers as officers of the court (for example, in Germany,[43] and England and Wales[44]), or which mean that lawyers do not have to act on their clients' (lawful) instructions (for example, in Poland[45]) mean that they may be deprived of effective criminal defence at least as defined by the accused themselves. There is also widespread concern that structural and cultural factors favour the prosecution and disadvantage defence lawyers. Whilst the police and prosecutors often work closely together, and share information, resources, and, to an extent, organisational objectives, defence lawyers are often perceived as outsiders who impede the administration of justice. In many jurisdictions, prosecutors and judges share a common training that sets them apart from lawyers acting for the defence and procedural, and even physical, factors (such as the layout of the courtroom) may favour the prosecution.

4.2.9. The quality of legal assistance

As important as the external limitations on the effectiveness of legal assistance, however, are the various factors that in most jurisdictions result, at best, in variable levels of quality on the part of lawyers acting for those suspected or accused of crime. With the notable exception of England and Wales,[46] most jurisdictions in our study do not require any special qualifications for lawyers acting for the defence, even where they are funded by the state or where representation is mandatory. This is exacerbated by the fact that in most jurisdictions there is no method of monitoring performance or assuring the quality of the work of defence lawyers. Whilst most, if not all, bar associations have professional conduct rules, few have articulated detailed standards in relation to criminal defence, and there is little evidence that professional disciplinary mechanisms are used effectively to deal with poor standards of performance.

Moreover, there is significant evidence of inadequate standards on the part of some defence lawyers in many jurisdictions, particularly those acting on

[43]   Chapter 7 § 3.3.
[44]   Chapter 4 § 2.2.4.
[45]   Chapter 10 § 2.2.1 and § 3.3.3.
[46]   Chapter 4 § 3.

appointment and/or under legal aid, and of passive defence cultures. In England and Wales non-qualified lawyers are often used to provide advice at police stations (although they do have to satisfy the standards of an accreditation scheme).[47] In Belgium[48] and Hungary[49] trainee lawyers often provide legal assistance in legal aid cases, and in France[50] such assistance is often provided by newly qualified lawyers. In Hungary[51] and Finland[52] lawyers do not attend initial interrogations in the majority of cases even though the suspect has a right to legal assistance, and in both Hungary[53] and Poland[54] they are routinely absent from early court hearings even when important decisions, such as pre-trial release or detention, are being made, and even in cases where representation is mandatory. There is an apparent reluctance by defence lawyers to use rights of cross-examination of witnesses in Poland,[55] and where clients are in pre-trial detention lawyers in jurisdictions such as Belgium are often reluctant to visit them.[56] A passive culture, particularly amongst lawyers acting in legally-aided cases, appears to be widespread in almost all of the countries in the study.

It may be argued that such deficiencies are often associated with lack of defence rights (for example, limited rights to information at the investigative stage in most jurisdictions), no or limited rights to investigate or interview prospective witnesses (in many jurisdictions), no absolute right to call or cross-examine witnesses (for example, Belgium and France), or low legal aid remuneration rates (in most jurisdictions). However, whether the deficiencies are systemic or related specifically to the culture and competence of lawyers who act for the defence, the result in practice is that access to legal assistance does not necessarily amount to access to effective criminal defence. Thus a right to legal assistance, whilst a pre-requisite to effective criminal defence, does not guarantee it.

4.3.   Legal aid

In the effective criminal defence triangle legal aid is, of course, closely linked to the right to legal assistance. However, we deal with the legal aid as a distinct aspect of effective criminal defence. We have identified legal assistance as a pre-requisite to effective criminal defence; it is fundamental for all suspects and defendants. Legal aid (which we use here as a short-hand for a variety of methods by which legal services may be provided either free of charge or at reduced cost), on the other hand, is a mechanism for ensuring that legal assistance is in principle available to all suspects and defendants. In other words, it enables the right to legal assistance to be

---

[47]   Chapter 4 § 3.
[48]   Chapter 3 § 3.4.
[49]   Chapter 8 § 2.2.3.
[50]   Chapter 6 § 1.4.
[51]   Chapter 8 § 2.2.3.
[52]   Chapter 5 § 1.3 and § 5.
[53]   Chapter 8 § 2.2.3.
[54]   Chapter 10 § 2.2.2.
[55]   Chapter 10 § 2.4.1 and § 3.3.3.
[56]   Chapter 3 § 2.2.2.

a practical and effective right for those who cannot afford to pay for legal assistance themselves.

According to article 6 § 3c ECHR indigent suspects must have access to free legal assistance, provided that the interests of justice so require.[57] The ECtHR has ruled in general that the seriousness of the offence and the severity of the potential sentence, the complexity of the case, and the social and personal situation of the defendant, must be taken into account and, more specifically, that the right to free legal aid exists whenever the deprivation of liberty is at stake. The reality in most, if not all, jurisdictions in the study is that the majority of suspects and defendants are relatively or absolutely poor or of limited financial means. It is obvious, therefore, that a system to make legal aid available in accordance with the criteria of the ECtHR to indigent suspects is crucial. Without an adequate legal aid scheme, legal assistance will simply be blocked for the majority of suspects and defendants and thus access to effective criminal defence, and thus their right to a fair trial, will be violated.

4.3.1. Complicated, unclear and slow application methods

The Strasbourg case law requires member states to actively inform suspects of their right to apply for legal aid, but detailed arrangements on how to make legal aid available come within the margin of appreciation of the member states.[58] Although guidance can be found in the Strasbourg case law as to the circumstances in which the interests of justice require legal aid, the question of when suspects and defendants are to be considered as not being able to pay for legal assistance themselves remains largely unanswered.

Except for Finland, and England and Wales at the investigative stage, where in most cases those accused of crime are entitled to legal aid regardless of their financial circumstances,[59] in all other jurisdictions in the study the legal aid system proves to be the weakest point in safeguarding a fair trial for indigent defendants. In the majority of the jurisdictions there are complicated means and merits tests that make it difficult to determine quickly whether a suspect is eligible for legal aid.[60] In some jurisdictions legal aid is provided free of charge regardless the financial situation of the defendant in cases of mandatory defence,[61] although in many of these jurisdictions costs for legal aid must be repaid if the defendant is found guilty. In Belgium, France and Poland there is no legal obligation to inform suspects of their right to legal aid. In Poland the means test is very vague, with the result that suspects and defendants are at the mercy of the determining authorities in terms of

---

[57]   See Chapter 2 § 4.4.
[58]   See Chapter 2 § 4.4.
[59]   In England and Wales means-testing, having been abolished in 2001, has been re-introduced for magistrates' court proceedings and is being re-introduced for Crown Court proceedings.
[60]   Chapter 3, § 1.4; Chapter 6, § 1.5; Chapter 7, § 1.6: Chapter 8, § 1.5 and § 2.2.6; Chapter 9, § 1.5; Chapter 10, § 1.3.5 and § 2.2.2; Chapter 11, § 1.5.
[61]   Chapter 3, § 1.4; Chapter 5, § 1.6; Chapter 7, § 1.6; Chapter 8, § 2.2.6; Chapter 9, § 1.5; Chapter 10 § 2.2.2; Chapter 11, § 1.5.

whether or not they have access to free legal assistance.[62] The manner in which suspects are required to provide information on their financial circumstances is often complicated, raising the question of how, in particular, suspects who are deprived of their liberty are able to provide the required information.

It is often not clear at what point free legal assistance is available, or within what time limit suspects can expect a decision on legal aid to be made. The thresholds for eligibility for free legal aid are often very high,[63] and in many jurisdictions the costs incurred have to be paid back on conviction, a fact of which they are often warned in advance. Complicated and bureaucratic procedures for providing legal aid and high eligibility thresholds not only hamper access to legal aid but also function as impediments to receiving legal aid in sufficient time. In jurisdictions that have a means test and which do not have an emergency scheme to provide legal assistance upon arrest regardless of the financial situation of the suspect, it is highly questionable whether it is possible for an indigent suspect to receive legal assistance before the first police interrogation, as required by the *Salduz* jurisprudence.

An example of the tension between the right to legal assistance during criminal proceedings and the legal aid system is provided by Italy. In Italy, legal assistance is mandatory in all criminal proceedings, irrespective of the seriousness of the offence. If a suspect or defendant has not instructed a defence lawyer, a duty lawyer will be appointed, even against his will. However, the duty lawyer is not paid for by the State, and the suspect or defendant is obliged to pay the duty lawyer. Only if the suspect is indigent is the lawyer paid for by the state. In order to be eligible for state financial assistance, the annual income of the suspect must be below 9.296 Euro, which means that only a small percentage of suspects and defendants are eligible.

4.3.2. Availability, quality and independence of criminal defence lawyer in legal aid cases

The legal aid system affects not only the suspect or defendant's access to a lawyer and adequate legal advice, but also the availability, quality and independence of the lawyer. In most jurisdictions in the study, again with the exception of England and Wales and Finland, remuneration for legal aid work is extremely low compared to the 'normal' fees charged by lawyers and, in some cases, is hardly remunerated at all.[64] This inevitably has an impact on the availability of lawyers for legal aid work

---

[62]   Chapter 10 § 2.2.2.

[63]   See for instance Chapter 8, § 2.2.6; Chapter 6, § 1.5; Chapter 7, § 1.6.2; Chapter 9, § 1.5.

[64]   In Belgium, Chapter 3, § 1.4, the average remuneration per case is between 367 Euro and 401 Euro per case. In Turkey, Chapter 11 § 1.5, for legal aid the investigative phase an attorney is entitled to 69 Euro; for cases tried in courts of peace 107 Euro; for cases in courts of general jurisdiction 118 Euro; for cases in courts of aggravated felonies 215 Euro, in addition fees are paid late or not at all. In France, Chapter 6, § 1.5, the average fee for a more complex case is between 190 Euro and 400 Euro and the average remuneration in a misdemeanour case is 129 Euro. In Poland, Chapter 10, § 2.2.2, the payment for legal aid during preliminary investigation is between 40 Euro and 80 Euro. In Italy, Chapter 9, § 1.5, there has been a long practice that for less serious cases lawyers ar not remunerated at all.

and for the quality of their work, especially where better remunerated work is available. Low remuneration rates and fixed fee schemes do not encourage defence lawyers to participate in legal aid work, or to invest more than minimal time and effort in a criminal case. This often means that suspects and defendants in custody are rarely visited by their lawyers, are often not kept informed of the ongoing criminal proceedings, and that lawyers only attend hearings where they are obliged to be present and do little on behalf of their clients even when they do attend hearings. If legal assistance is not adequately paid for, it can hardly be expected that lawyers will put time and effort into case preparation, will seek exculpatory evidence, or make effective applications for bail or release from pre-trial custody.

In some jurisdictions the result of inadequate remuneration is that legal assistance for indigent defendants is provided by trainees or young and inexperienced lawyers. In other jurisdictions the provision of legal assistance to indigent suspects and defendants (without adequate remuneration) is considered to be a deontological duty, with the result that indigent suspects are at the mercy of the lawyer who happens to be appointed. Another approach in some jurisdictions is the compulsory appointment of lawyers in cases where legal assistance is considered to be absolutely necessary, lawyers then being obliged to provide their services at very low cost. It seems that in most jurisdictions free legal assistance is provided, to a large extent, at the cost of the lawyers.

Legal aid mechanisms can also threaten the independence of lawyers. There is evidence, for example in Hungary and Germany, that the way that legal aid lawyers are appointed creates a relationship of dependency on those who appoint them, with the result that they may be hesitant to zealously defend their clients' interests. However, threats to independence can also arise in jurisdictions that have a sophisticated legal aid system. In England and Wales, for example, there is concern that the independence of lawyers may be infringed by contractual requirements imposed by the Legal Services Commission, particularly where standards that were originally created as minimum requirements are transformed, often as a result of budgetary considerations, into maximum requirements.[65]

4.4. *Interpretation and translation*

4.4.1. The significance of interpretation and translation

In our model, as with legal assistance, interpretation and translation is regarded as a pre-condition for effective criminal defence. For those who do not understand the language in which investigations and proceedings are conducted, it is impossible for them to participate and to exercise other rights and make use of other safeguards without interpretation and translation.[66] Our approach embodies a simple, straightforward, proposition. If a suspect or accused person cannot understand what is said to them or what is written in any relevant document, or if what they

---

[65] Bridges & Cape 2008, *passim*.
[66] We concentrate here on suspects and defendants who do not speak and understand the language in which the investigation or proceedings are conducted, but many of the issues also concern those who have hearing or speech impediments.

say or write cannot be understood by those investigating or judging them, they do not have access to effective criminal defence and cannot have a fair trial. The significance of this becomes even more apparent when it is remembered that, leaving aside issues associated with evidence as to guilt (for example, whether it is disputed, is largely circumstantial, complex, unlawfully obtained, etc.), whether a person is, and should be found, guilty of an offence frequently does not simply depend upon a factual state of affairs, but on the interpretation of a complex array of facts, and on the relationship between observable facts, facts determined by inference, and mental states and attitudes that themselves may be complex and nuanced. The differences, for example, between statements such as 'I intended to injure her', 'I wanted to injure her', 'I thought she might be injured', and 'I thought she might have been injured', may be critical in a particular case, requiring a significant level of cognitive ability to differentiate meanings which may easily be lost in the absence of sufficiently competent interpretation or translation.

Access to competent interpretation and translation by those who need it presupposes that a number of legal provisions and practical mechanisms are in place covering identification of those who require interpretation or translation, access to interpretation or translation of relevant verbal encounters and documents in a timely fashion, and quality and independence of that interpretation and translation. With regard to identification, the ECHR simply refers to a right to the assistance of an interpreter for those who 'cannot understand or speak the language of the court' (art. 6 § 3e).[67] Jurisprudence of the ECtHR shows that the onus is on the judicial authorities to show that the person does speak the relevant language, but it is not clear as to how that is to be determined. As noted in chapter 2,[68] it is clear that the right is not limited to oral statements made during the course of trial, but covers documentary material including during pre-trial proceedings.

It is evident that failure to establish clear lines of responsibility, and procedures, for identifying the need for interpretation or translation at all stages of the criminal process is likely to result in some suspects and defendants who require interpretation or translation not receiving it. A person who does not speak the relevant language will not, of course, be able to communicate with their lawyer if they have one (unless the lawyer happens to speak their language) and thus they will be denied the other pre-requisite of effective criminal defence. In addition, many of the principles of fair trial will not be satisfied. It could not be said that there is equality of arms if the accused cannot understand the accusation, evidence or procedure. The trial would not, in any meaningful sense, be adversarial, and the person could not take advantage of any right to call or examine witnesses. They would hardly be in a position to defend themselves and whilst, of course, they may be present at hearings, they would not be able to participate in any real sense. Appeal would be difficult if they had not understood the basis of their conviction or sentence. With regard to supplementary rights, they would not be in a position to understand information given to them as to their rights, or any caution regarding

---

[67]   Similarly, art. 5 § 2 ECHR, provides that a person who is arrested must be promptly informed 'in a language which he understands' of the reasons for arrest and any charge against him.

[68]   Chapter 2 § 6.

their right to silence. Whilst there may be adequate time to prepare their defence, they would not have the facilities to do so in a practical and effective way. Any right to investigate would be meaningless, as would any right to reasoned decisions since they would not understand any reasons given.

4.4.2. Identification of the need for interpretation and translation

All this may seem obvious. Yet the law and procedures for identifying those suspects and accused who cannot understand the language of the investigator or court, and for providing competent interpretation or translation, in many of the jurisdictions in our study mean that it is likely that numerous suspects and defendants are precisely in this position. In a number of the jurisdictions the law provides that a person who does not understand the language has a 'right' to interpretation or translation. A 'right' implies something that may be exercised at the instance of the person concerned. However, whether or not the law is expressed in this way, it is often the case that determination of whether a suspect or defendant understands the relevant language rests with the investigator or judge rather than with the suspect or defendant himself (for example, in Poland, Germany, France, and England and Wales).[69] This involves a paradox that is identified in chapter 9 on Italy. How does a person who does not understand the relevant language establish that they do not do so? It may be relatively straightforward (although this is not necessarily the case) if the suspect or defendant knows virtually nothing of the relevant language; but how does a person who knows something of the language demonstrate that they do not understand the language to the level of sophistication necessary for the proceedings in hand?[70] Further, whilst there may be incentives for the investigator or judge to err on the side of caution in making the decision,[71] there may also be pressures in the other direction if, for example, an interpreter is not readily available (which may particularly be the case at the investigative stage or in relation to a minority language), or where the cost of the interpreter or translator has to be paid out of the budget of the decision-maker.

---

[69]   See § 2.4.4 in the respective chapters. Unless otherwise noted, for all references to law and practice concerning interpretation and translation in countries in the study see § 2.4.4 of the relevant country chapter.

[70]   Arts. 2 § 1 and 3 § 1 of the proposed directive on interpretation and translation requires member states to ensure that suspects or accused persons who do not understand and speak the relevant language are provided with interpretation and translation. Further, art. 2 § 3 provides that states shall ensure that a procedure is in place to ascertain whether they speak or understand the relevant language, although member states are left to determine what that procedure shall be. However, arts. 2 § 4, and 3 § 4 provide that states must ensure that suspects and accused persons have a right to challenge a decision that there is no need for interpretation or translation. See generally *Proposal for a Directive of the European Parliament and of the Council on the right to interpretation and translation in criminal proceedings* (the proposed directive on interpretation and translation), Brussels, 9.3.2010 COM (2010) 82 final.

[71]   And that is what the ECtHR jurisprudence requires of them. See chapter 7 § 2.7.

4.4.3. Accessibility of interpretation and translation

The next requirement is the accessibility of interpretation and translation, and this involves questions concerning the extent of the interpretation and translation requirement, whether mechanisms exist to ensure that it is available in a timely fashion, and whether it is available free (or, at least, at a cost that the suspect or defendant can afford). In terms of access to effective criminal defence the starting point should be that a person who does not understand the language to the required level should be put in a position that is no different from a person who does have a full understanding of the language. This would mean that all oral communications at which the suspect or defendant is present should be interpreted, and all written documents that would be available to any suspect or defendant are translated, and that this should be done free of charge. As noted in chapter 2[72] the ECtHR has not gone this far and, in particular, has not determined whether the state should be under an obligation to provide free translation of lawyer/client communications, but has determined that it is not required that all documents be translated.[73]

In some jurisdictions, such as France, England and Wales and Turkey, there is a right to translation of lawyer/client communications, funded by the state. However, in other jurisdictions, such as Hungary, there is no such right. The consequence, as is observed in chapter 8 on Hungary, is that unless the accused is able to afford to pay for an interpreter himself, he is not only forced to rely on a state appointed interpreter, but has to wait until he or she is available, normally immediately before the relevant procedural act. As a result, there is a direct negative impact on other rights such as that of adequate time and facilities for preparation of the defence.

4.4.4. Which documents are to be translated?

With regard to translation of documents there is a wide range of practices in the jurisdictions in the study but many, in line with the jurisprudence of the ECtHR, do

---

[72] Chapter 2 § 6.

[73] In the proposed directive on interpretation and translation, art. 2 § 1 provides that interpretation is to be provided 'during those proceedings before investigative and judicial authorities, including during police questioning, during all necessary meetings between the suspect and his lawyer, during all court hearings and during any necessary interim hearings'. Art. 2 § 2 further provides that 'where necessary, legal advice received throughout the criminal proceedings is interpreted for the suspect'. Art. 3 § 1 and § 2 provides for interpretation of 'all essential documents' which shall include 'the detention order depriving the person of his liberty, the charge/indictment, essential documentary evidence and the judgement'. This gives member states a large degree of discretion in determining which documents have to be translated, and falls short of putting the person who requires translation in the same position as a person who does not. However, art. 3 § 3 does provide that a suspect or accused, or their lawyer, must be permitted to make a reasoned request for translation of further documents, and art. 3 § 4 requires that they be given a right to challenge a decision that translation is not necessary. Where there is an obligation to ensure interpretation or translation, art. 4 states that the cost must be covered by the member state irrespective of the outcome of the proceedings.

not provide for translation of all relevant documents. For example, in Hungary the indictment is translated, as are court decisions and judgements, but not the minutes of the procedural actions nor the records of court hearings. In Italy only documents specifically directed at the accused have to be translated, so that court judgements are not. In Germany it is for the court to determine which documents are to be translated, but there is no right to have the reasons for court judgements translated. In Belgium it would seem that whilst there is an extensive right to translation from one of the official languages into another (although apparently limited to defendants who do not speak another language), this is not the case in respect of translation into another language. These deficiencies are, of course, exacerbated if communication between an accused and their lawyer is inhibited by lack of interpretation rights.

4.4.5. Quality and independence

The issue of timeliness presents a particular problem at the investigative stage of the criminal process where processes have to be conducted and decisions made without delay. The problems are compounded where the accused only understands a language that is less common in that particular jurisdiction, and there are implications for both the quality and independence of interpretation and translation.[74] Questions of quality and independence are largely beyond the scope of the ECHR and, therefore, the jurisprudence of the ECtHR, in a similar way as applies to defence lawyers.[75] Before examining the position in the jurisdictions in the study it is worth briefly exploring the consequences of interpretation or translation that is not independent or of sufficient quality to enable access to effective criminal defence. Lack of independence may, of course, mean that the interpreter or translator has an interest in acting contrary to the interests of the suspect or accused. Concerns about this are raised in the chapter on Hungary, where both lawyers and judges reported that a limited number of interpreters may be routinely appointed by the investigating authorities, raising questions about whether they were dependent on those authorities.[76] Although the possible implications are not spelt out, they are obvious. The importance of interpretation and translation being of sufficient quality is illustrated by the example given at the beginning of this section. If the interpreter or translator cannot accurately convey the precise sentiment being expressed, then rather than providing an exculpatory account, the translated words may be understood as an admission of culpability (or, indeed, vice versa). Thus an incompetent interpreter or translator may actually have

---

[74] Art. 5 § 1 of the proposed directive on interpretation and translation requires that interpretation and translation be provided 'in such a way as to ensure that the suspect or accused person is fully able to exercise his rights'.

[75] Arts. 2 § 1 and 3 § 1 of the proposed directive on interpretation and translation require that interpretation and translation be of 'a quality sufficient to safeguard the fairness of the criminal proceedings', so that member states would clearly have a large degree of discretion as to how this is to he achieved, and how it is to be monitored.

[76] It may well be that there are similar concerns in other states, but we did not obtain evidence of this.

an adverse effect on access to effective criminal defence, and on the chances of a fair trial. This is equally true where inadequate quality of interpretation or translation means that the suspect or accused does not understand, for example, the evidence against them or the reasons for a judgement.

In some jurisdictions there are very specific requirements regarding interpreters and translators. For example, in Italy the Code of Criminal Procedure provides, *inter alia*, that an interpreter or translator must not have been suspended from office as a result of a criminal conviction, must not otherwise be involved in the proceedings and, normally, must not be married to the accused. However, such rules are designed to ensure propriety and independence, but not competence. In some jurisdictions there have been attempts to deal with competence. For example, in Poland translators must pass a specialist examination and be registered with the Ministry of Justice, and are subject to a disciplinary mechanism. This is the most comprehensive attempt to ensure quality in the jurisdictions examined in this study. The downside, however, is that there is concern that inadequate remuneration leads some interpreters and translators to avoid assignments from the criminal justice authorities. The concerted attempt in Poland to establish a compulsory quality assurance system is, however, unusual. In England and Wales, whilst there are professional associations responsible, *inter alia*, for quality and for the professional discipline of their members, membership is not mandatory and criminal justice agencies and defence lawyers, whilst encouraged to use interpreters and translators who are members of such associations, are not required to do so. Similarly, in France and Finland there is no requirement that criminal justice agencies or lawyers use interpreters or translators with any specific qualification or who are members of a professional body. In Turkey there is no national quality assurance mechanism, and there is anecdotal evidence that courts resort to using court staff, or even people such as university students who happen to be in court, to interpret.

4.5. Adequate time and facilities

The right to adequate time and facilities to prepare a defence is guaranteed by article 6 § 3b of the ECHR, and is a supplementary right in our effective criminal defence model. As indicated in chapter 2[77] the right to adequate time and facilities is closely related to other article 6 rights, and is necessary in order to ensure that those rights are 'practical and effective', and not merely 'theoretical and illusory'. The meaning of 'adequate time and facilities' is clearly highly dependant on the context and, in particular, the stage of criminal proceedings in question, and this leaves member states with a significant degree of leeway in terms of legal regulation and practice. Space does not permit a full analysis of all aspects of the right, but some of its major features and, and, relationships to other aspects of effective criminal defence, will be explored.

One of the significant features of criminal investigations and proceedings is that they are largely conducted according to the needs, interests and timetables, not of the suspect or accused, but of the investigative and judicial authorities. Although,

---

[77]   Chapter 2 § 5.3.

in a sense, those who commit crime invite investigation and prosecution, suspects and defendants generally (which, of course, includes people who are innocent of any crime) do not determine whether or when they are arrested or investigated, and do not determine the subsequent course, or speed, of events. If equality of arms, the presumption of innocence, and the right of a person to defend themselves, are to have any meaning in practice, then those who are investigated or prosecuted must be accorded adequate time and facilities to prepare their defence. Furthermore, lack of adequate time and facilities will make a mockery of any formal right to adversarial trial, and any formal right to call and/or examine witnesses.

Our research demonstrates that across the jurisdictions in our study, suspects and defendants are denied adequate time and facilities to defend themselves in a variety of ways, at various stages of the criminal process, and that this has consequences for, and is interrelated with, other aspects of the right to effective criminal defence. For our purposes, we can divide the analysis into three parts: the initial stages of investigation; preparation for bail and trial hearings; and expedited procedures.

4.5.1. Preparation at the initial stages of the investigation

The jurisprudence of the ECtHR has concentrated mainly on time and facilities in relation to the 'trial', that is, the hearing(s) at which guilt or innocence is determined. However, in practice it is the case in all of the jurisdictions in the study that what is said or done at the investigative stage can have a determinative effect on the eventual outcome of the case. This has been recognised by the ECtHR in relation to the right to legal assistance in respect of which the Court has held that where '[n]ational laws ... attach consequences to the attitude of an accused at the initial stages of police interrogation which are decisive for the prospects of the defence in any subsequent criminal proceedings... Article 6 will normally require that the accused be allowed to benefit from the assistance of a lawyer already at the initial stages of police interrogation'.[78] Equally, it may be argued that in such circumstances, the suspect should also have adequate time and facilities to prepare their defence.

It was noted in § 4.2 that in a number of jurisdictions, and for a variety of reasons, a person who is *de facto* a suspect may not be designated as such (for example, Poland and Hungary). In other jurisdictions, a person who is a suspect does not have to be told that they are (for example, Belgium[79]), or does not have to be given information about the nature of the allegation (for example, Belgium[80] and France[81]). Our research, and previous research[82] shows that in many jurisdictions there is no obligation to give a letter of rights to the suspect, or there is lack of clarity as to the precise moment a letter of rights should be given. Clearly, if a

---

[78]   ECtHR, Grand Chamber, 27 November 2008, *Salduz v. Turkey*, No. 36391 02, § 52; and see generally chapter 2 § 4.3.
[79]   Chapter 3 § 2.1.1.
[80]   *Ibidem.*
[81]   Chapter 6 § 2.1.
[82]   Spronken et al. 2009.

person is not aware that they are a suspect, or does not know why they are suspected, they cannot begin to prepare their defence. However, the fact that the status of a person as a suspect has been made clear to them does not necessarily mean that they are then in a position to begin preparation of their defence. Leaving aside the question of whether the suspect has access to legal assistance, for a person to begin to prepare their defence they must have access to the information that implicates them in the suspected offence. It was noted in § 4.2 that in most jurisdictions in the study there are severe limits on the suspect's access to the investigative file prior to commencement of formal legal proceedings. Whilst access to the investigative file at the early stage of the process is a sensitive and complex issue,[83] the question of whether this amounts to a limitation on the suspect's right to adequate facilities requires serious consideration.

It could be argued that the fact that a suspect has a right to silence means that they do not have to begin to prepare their defence at the investigative stage. If they do not have access to information regarding the suspected offence, they can simply remain silent. However, there are a number of problems with this argument, rendering it an inadequate justification for breach of the right to adequate time and facilities to prepare a defence. First, it assumes that the suspect is aware that they can remain silent, and the evidence suggests that in a number of jurisdictions a suspect either does not have to be told of this right or may not in practice be so informed (for example, Finland,[84] France,[85] and Belgium[86]), or may not understand a caution that is administered.[87] Second, whilst the ECtHR is of the view that the right to silence 'lies at the heart of the notion of a fair procedure under article 6',[88] it has held in a number of cases that it is not an absolute right.[89] Thus in England and Wales the law is such that a suspect who does not tell the police of the facts on which they rely in their defence at trial is at risk of that being used, in effect, as evidence against them, and the ECtHR has held that this does not breach the right to fair trial.[90] Third, there is evidence that some suspects, even if they are aware of the right, either have difficulty in maintaining silence in the face of questioning,[91] or fear that it will have adverse consequences for them,[92] and in a number of jurisdictions it would seem that such fears are warranted.[93]

---

[83] The presumption of innocence, and the burden of proof, would indicate that a suspect should not have to respond to an allegation that they have committed a criminal offence without first being given information about that allegation. On the other hand, it is argued that giving such information to a suspect before they are interviewed would enable a guilty suspect to adjust their response in order to demonstrate their innocence.
[84] Chapter 5 § 2.2.3.
[85] Chapter 6 § 2.3.4.
[86] Chapter 3 § 2.3.4.
[87] Noted in respect of Germany. See chapter 7 § 2.3.4.
[88] ECtHR 20 April 2010, *Adetoro* v. *UK*, No. 46834/06, at § 47.
[89] *Ibidem*, at § 47, and see the cases cited in chapter 2 § 2.2.
[90] Chapter 4 § 2.3.4.
[91] This is noted in the chapter on France, for example. See chapter 6 § 2.3.4.
[92] Noted in respect of Germany, for example. See chapter 7 § 2.3.4.
[93] For example, in Belgium it may affect decisions about pre-trial detention (chapter 3 § 2.3.4), and this is also the case in Hungary (chapter 8 § 2.3.4), and in Italy (chapter 9 § 2.3.4). 'Silence'

4.5.2. Preparation for pre-trial detention hearings and trial

Time to prepare an application for pre-trial release is often limited, at least in relation to the initial hearing, because of the summary nature of the process. As indicated in § 4.6, in many jurisdictions, such as England and Wales, and Hungary, the ability of the accused, and their lawyer if they have one, to prepare for pre-trial detention hearings is further inhibited by the lack of a right of access to information regarding the material which forms the basis of the allegation or charge, and/or the material upon which an application for pre-trial detention is to be made.

Subject to what is said below about the various forms of expedited hearing, adequate time for preparation for the trial hearing is not normally problematic, although there is a particular concern in relation to Italy that time for preparation will in practice be limited in cases where a judge modifies the indictment without giving notice to the accused.[94] There are also concerns in England and Wales that adjournments are often so short that adequate preparation is not possible.[95] However, the study does reveal a number of practical and procedural limitations in terms of the facilities afforded to the accused at the trial-preparation stage. Whilst in most jurisdictions the material on which the prosecution relies is made available to the accused after proceedings have formally commenced, there are limitations on this in some jurisdictions. In England and Wales the prosecution are required to supply the accused with material that it intends to use at trial,[96] but there is a complex procedure concerning disclosure of other material gathered during the investigation which can result in potentially exculpatory material not being disclosed. In Belgium the accused, or their lawyer, has a right to view the file, but they have to pay in order for copies of it,[97] and the position is similar in Germany,[98] and Hungary.[99] In France, the accused's right to the file is dependant upon them having a lawyer, and there is evidence to suggest that some judges delay inserting evidence in the file in order to keep it from the defence lawyer.[100]

There is ECtHR authority for the proposition that the accused should have an independent right to investigate the accusation, as expressed in the *Dayanan* case,[101] where the ECtHR stated that a suspect, already at the police interrogation stage must be afforded the complete range of interventions that are inherent to legal advice, such as the investigation of facts and search for favourable evidence and the

---

at the investigative stage may also affect sentence. This is noted in respect of Hungary (chapter 8 § 2.3.4), and in England and Wales 'silence' at the investigative stage may limit any sentence discount for a guilty plea under the Criminal Justice Act 2003, s. 144.

[94] Chapter 9 § 2.1.2.
[95] Chapter 4 § 2.4.2.
[96] Although in less serious cases (i.e., summary cases tried in magistrates' courts), the prosecution may choose to serve a summary of the evidence rather than witness statements (see chapter 4 § 2.1.4).
[97] Chapter 3 § 2.1.2.
[98] Chapter 7 § 2.1.5.
[99] Chapter 8 §2.1.2.
[100] Chapter 6 § 2.1.
[101] ECtHR 13 October 2009, *Dayanan v. Turkey*, No. 7377/03, § 32.

preparation of interrogations.[102] So it may be argued that adequate facilities to prepare a defence includes a right to investigate. In most jurisdictions the accused is, in practice, limited to asking the police or prosecutor to pursue a particular line of enquiry or to interview witnesses, and in some jurisdictions there is a formal process for doing so.[103] In Italy there is comprehensive and detailed regulation of investigation by the defence,[104] but this is unusual. In England and Wales the accused does have an unfettered right to investigate, but they have limited powers to do so, and the legal aid fee structure is such that it is largely discouraged. Whilst the accused may request the police to pursue a particular line of enquiry there is no such thing as an evidential motion.[105] Similarly, In Hungary, the defence is entitled to investigate and to interview prospective witnesses, although such witnesses are under no obligation to co-operate.[106] However, even if investigation by the accused is permitted, in practice the cost of doing so will normally mean that a legally-aided accused will not be able to afford to do so, as is clearly the case in Italy. In France, the investigating authority may be requested to interview particular witnesses, but whether they act on that request is for them to decide. Interviewing of witnesses by the accused (or, more likely, their lawyer), or the use of private investigators, is often viewed with suspicion.[107] The position is similar in Belgium where, moreover, professional rules prevent defence lawyers from interviewing prospective witnesses.[108] Thus the general picture is that the ability of the accused to either initiate or conduct investigation of the case is severely limited.

4.5.3. Preparation for expedited hearings

In England and Wales, the only common law jurisdiction in the study, the guilty plea procedure is a central feature of the criminal process, with the vast majority of defendants being dealt with by way of a guilty plea.[109] Whilst traditionally the inquisitorial approach does not recognise such a procedure, many jurisdictions in the study have adopted procedures that either resemble the guilty plea, or which expedite the trial process in some other way. The issue of relevance here is whether such procedures allow for adequate time and facilities for preparation of the defence. The lack of preparation time for the defence in 'speedy' proceedings appears to have been recognised in Poland where legislation is planned in order to deal with the problem. However, there is concern in England and Wales, particularly in respect of cases dealt with in magistrates' courts, that the guilty plea procedure, coupled with managerial devices such as efficiency targets, means that there is pressure on defendants to indicate whether they are pleading guilty or not

---

[102]   Chapter 2 § 2.4.
[103]   For example, Poland (see chapter 10 § 2.4.1)
[104]   Chapter 9 § 2.4.1.
[105]   Chapter 4 § 2.4.1.
[106]   Chapter 8 § 2.4.1.
[107]   Chapter 6 § 2.4.1.
[108]   Chapter 3 § 2.4.1.
[109]   Chapter 4 § 1.2.

guilty without having had adequate time to consider the prosecution evidence.[110] A similar concern is expressed in respect of the expedited hearing procedure in France. Whilst the prosecutor has 24 or 48 hours to prepare such a case, the defence lawyer only has a few hours to read the papers and prepare the defence.[111]

4.6. Pre-trial detention

The right to release pending trial is, in our model, a supplementary right on the left corner of the triangle. Viewed in terms of outcomes it is possible for an accused person to have a fair trial, and indeed to have benefited from an effective criminal defence, if they are detained pending determination of guilt. However, this is not necessarily the case. As will be explored further below, detention in itself may prevent access to effective criminal defence if, for example, it interferes with access to legal representation or prevents adequate preparation of the defence. When considered in terms of process, and in particular the process from the perspective of the accused, fair trial and access to effective criminal defence may be denied if the accused is unnecessarily detained pending trial, particularly if the detention is lengthy. A person who is acquitted after a lengthy period of pre-trial detention is unlikely to regard their treatment as fair, and they are unlikely to believe that their defence has been effective. Apart from the direct effects of incarceration (and conditions for pre-trial detainees are often worse than for sentenced prisoners), they may have lost their employment, or contact with their family, suffered ill-health, or suffered more generally from the perception that they are guilty by virtue of being in custody. Even if the accused is convicted, their defence will not have been effective if they do not receive a custodial sentence, or the sentence is less than the period for which they have been detained pre-trial, or if the period of pre-trial detention does not count as part of their sentence.

Under the ECHR release pending trial is not, of course, an absolute right. Indeed, it is not regarded as an aspect of the right to fair trial, but is governed by article 5, which provides that everyone arrested or detained on suspicion of a criminal offence is 'entitled to trial within a reasonable time or to release pending trial', and that any release may be 'conditioned by guarantees to appear for trial' (art. 5 § 3). As demonstrated in chapter 2,[112] the case-law of the ECtHR shows that in considering pre-trial detention the judicial authorities must examine whether there is a genuine public interest justifying deprivation of liberty, where pre-trial detention is ordered it must not exceed a reasonable time, and decisions must be reasoned. After a certain lapse of time, reasonable suspicion that the accused has committed an offence no longer suffices to justify detention, and continued detention is only permitted if it is justified on other grounds such as the risk of absconding, re-offending, or interference with the investigation or evidence, having due regard to the right to liberty and the presumption of innocence. Alternatives to detention, such as conditional release must be considered, and any conditions

---

[110]   Chapter 4 § 1.3 and § 2.4.2.
[111]   Chapter 6 § 2.4.2.
[112]   Chapter 2 § 2.3.

imposed must be relevant to a legitimate objective such as ensuring the accused's appearance at trial or preventing them from interfering with the evidence.

Compliance with the ECHR, and ECtHR jurisprudence, requires a member state to have in place clear legal provisions: regulating the circumstances in which an accused person can be kept in pre-trial detention; establishing a fair process by which the decision is to be made; imposing limits on the length of such detention; containing provisions for review of that detention; which set out the circumstances in which a person may be subjected to conditional release; and which require the reasons for decisions to be articulated. Furthermore, the judicial authorities must consider each case having regard to its particular circumstances, including those relating to the suspected offence, and its investigation, and to the circumstances of the accused. Automatic decisions to detain based on particular factors, such as the seriousness of the suspected offence, are not permitted, and neither are conditions that are not directed at legitimate objectives. Arguably, conditions that do not take account of the circumstances of the accused (for example, money bail that the accused cannot afford) are also not permitted.

4.6.1. The implications of pre-trial detention

Having regard to our model of effective criminal defence, pre-trial detention amounts to a fundamental challenge to the presumption of innocence. The ECtHR accepts that in some circumstances the presumption can, in effect, be overridden by the public interest but only in carefully prescribed circumstances. Pre-trial detention also challenges the equality of arms principle, and this is particularly so if as a result of their detention the accused is denied the facilities and resources to effectively defend themselves. Thus it is necessary to consider what disadvantages a person in pre-trial detention may suffer. These may relate to the pre-trial detention hearing itself. If the decision is made at a time when the accused has not had access to the material on which the accusation is based, or on which the application for pre-trial detention is based, then they cannot fully participate in that hearing and are denied the opportunity to make effective representations for their release. This is exacerbated if, as a result of their detention, they are not able to instruct a lawyer or to consult with a lawyer in conditions that enable that consultation to be effective. Furthermore, even if they are able to instruct a lawyer, effective criminal defence relies on the lawyer being willing and able to represent them on a similar basis to a person who is not in detention. At subsequent hearings, the fact of detention may interfere with their ability to investigate the accusation and prepare their defence.

4.6.2. Recognition of a right to pre-trial release in practice

With the exception of Turkey,[113] where pre-trial release is not expressly governed by domestic law, most jurisdictions in the study have laws in place that regulate pre-trial detention and release in compliance with the ECHR. However, in many of

---

[113]   Chapter 11 § 2.3.1. With the exception of the chapter on Finland, the law and practice on pre-trial detention is dealt with in § 2.3.1 of the respective chapters.

those jurisdictions the proportion of defendants who are held in pre-trial custody, and the proportion of the prison population who are in pre-trial detention, is relatively high. In some jurisdictions this is a result, in part at least, of the fact that conditional release or release on bail, whilst available, is often not used in practice. In Turkey there is no system of bail. In Poland, although the situation has improved in the last decade, there is concern that courts impose pre-trial detention without sufficient regard to the requirement that it be ordered only if other preventive measures are not sufficient, and it has been the subject of a number of adverse decisions of the ECtHR in this respect. Similarly, in Hungary there is evidence that courts resort to pre-trial detention without sufficient regard to the individual circumstances of the case, and it too has been the subject of a number of adverse ECtHR decisions. In France, although the office of the liberty and security judge was introduced in 2000, there is evidence that pre-trial detention hearings may in practice be little more than a procedural formality, with concern centred on overly close relationships between prosecutors and the judges, and on inappropriate weight being placed on the perceived guilt of the accused. In some jurisdictions, such as Hungary and France, there is a perception that pre-trial detention, or the threat of it, is used to encourage suspects to confess.

4.6.3. Effective participation in pre-trial detention hearings

If an accused is to participate effectively in the hearing that determines whether they are to be subjected to pre-trial detention they must have a right to be present, to some disclosure of information regarding the accusation and regarding the grounds that are said to justify their detention, and to effective representation by a lawyer. In many jurisdictions in the study access to information concerning the alleged offence is limited at this early stage of the criminal process. In England and Wales, for example, the accused has no right to information at the first court hearing when pre-trial detention is considered, beyond the fact of the criminal charge itself. In Hungary the position is similar.[114] This is particularly important if the seriousness of the alleged offence, or the perceived likelihood of guilt, is used as a basis for denying pre-trial release, or for determining the conditions to be imposed on pre-trial release.

4.6.4. Legal assistance and pre-trial detention

With regard to legal representation, this is clearly important not only as a mechanism for seeking to ensure that the court only takes into account legitimate factors in determining whether to order pre-trial detention, but also because a competent lawyer can explore with the accused factors relevant to conditional release, such as their financial circumstances, whether (if relevant) other accommodation is available for them to live in, whether support might be available from an employer etc., or whether suitable facilities (such as a bail hostel, or drug unit) are available. In some jurisdictions, such as Poland, indigent defendants are

---

[114] See further § 4.5 of the chapter.

particularly disadvantaged in this respect because the legal aid decision is not taken until the pre-trial detention hearing.[115] In other jurisdictions, even if a lawyer has been instructed, and even in cases of mandatory representation, lawyers frequently do not attend (at least) the initial pre-trial detention hearing. This is reported to be the case in Turkey, and in Poland where empirical research has found that (in addition to the problems of legal aid) some defence lawyers are reluctant to attend such hearings because of a fear that their presence may be interpreted by the judge as an indication of the accused's guilt. Effective defence at this stage of the process also requires that lawyers are not only well-versed in the relevant law, but that they are also well informed about the practical options available that may facilitate conditional release. In Belgium it is reported that lawyers often do not appear to be aware of such facilities, and that judges often have to make suggestions to lawyers regarding them, rather than lawyers actively securing such information in order to argue for the conditional release of their clients.

4.6.5. The impact of being in pre-trial detention

As noted above, once an accused is in pre-trial detention this may, in practice, limit or negate their access to effective criminal defence by limiting their ability to participate, to prepare their defence and to be legally represented. In England and Wales, defence lawyers often complain that it is difficult to hold timely and adequate consultations with clients in pre-trial detention, which is compounded by the fact that courts often have inadequate facilities for lawyer/client consultations.[116] In fact access by lawyers to their clients in prison is reported to be difficult, particularly for indigent defendants, in a number of the jurisdictions, including Belgium,[117] and Hungary.[118]

5.   Conclusions

In respect of the five central themes analysed in this chapter, we draw the following broad conclusions as to the action that is necessary to ensure that suspects and defendants have access to effective criminal defence.

5.1.   *Legal assistance*

The analysis demonstrates that in many jurisdictions in the study a variety of factors prevent access to competent legal assistance at all stages of the criminal process. In any particular jurisdiction the law establishing the right to legal assistance needs to be sufficiently clear and precise to ensure that those who are *de facto* suspects, and those accused of crime, are covered by the right. It requires transparent mechanisms for making suspects and defendants aware of their rights,

---

[115]   Chapter 10 § 2.2.2.
[116]   Chapter 4 § 2.2.3.
[117]   Chapter 3 § 2.2.2.
[118]   Chapter 8 § 2.2.4.

and which ensure that those whose function it is to notify suspects and defendants of their rights are accountable for doing so in a way that may be understood by the recipient. Procedures need to be established for facilitating timely access to legal assistance, and this includes those cases where a decision has to be made about eligibility for public funding. Such procedures need to be supported by structures that ensure that legal assistance can be delivered in a timely fashion (such as duty lawyer schemes) and which, in principle, enable the accused to exercise choice. Enforcement mechanisms (whether disciplinary and/or evidential and procedural) need to be in place to ensure that the right to legal assistance is a real and effective right. Procedural and professional rules are required to enable and require the lawyer to provide effective advice and assistance so that legal assistance does not simply provide a due process gloss on what may otherwise be an unfair investigative and trial process. In particular, this requires bar associations to take a pro-active approach to establishing and embedding appropriate professional standards, and methods for assuring that those standards are routinely met.

5.2.   *Legal aid*

Our analysis demonstrates that in most jurisdictions in the study, legal aid provision is inadequate. The objective of a legal aid system should be to put suspects and defendants who cannot afford legal assistance in the same position as those who can. This requires: clear, and workable, mechanisms for ensuring that suspects and defendants are informed of the availability of legal aid; where legal aid is not available to all suspects and defendants, a merits test that clearly identifies the circumstances in which a person is eligible in accordance with an interests of justice requirement, and a means test that is transparent and which ensures that those who cannot afford to pay for legal assistance secure financial assistance; mechanisms for ensuring that legal aid is available at short notice; and remuneration that is sufficient to ensure that competent and suitably experienced lawyers are willing and able to carry out the work that is necessary to effectively defend their clients. This, of course, has significant financial implications and we are fully aware of the competing calls on government budgets. However, effective criminal defence is just as essential to a fair criminal justice system as effective police investigation and effective prosecution. One way of approaching this is for governments to take a 'whole cost' approach to criminal justice policies. Policing, crime investigation and prosecution are rarely simply reactive, and all governments develop priorities and strategies in determining what is to be regarded as criminal, how it is to be policed, and how it is to be investigated and prosecuted, or otherwise dealt with. What we are suggesting here is that in so doing, account should be taken of the costs to be incurred in providing effective criminal defence, so that the full costs of any particular policy or strategy are known.[119] With this knowledge, governments

---

[119]   In England and Wales, the government introduced a legal aid impact test (LAIT) according to which, in proposing new crimes, the relevant government department has to incorporate projections as to the legal aid costs. The LAIT is too limited, and should be expanded to wider criminal policy decisions, and it has been criticised in a recent official report as being not

→

would be in a better position to determine whether criminalisation is the most appropriate, and affordable, course of action in respect of any particular social problem.

5.3. Interpretation and translation

It is clear from our analysis that interpretation and translation for those suspects and accused who do not have a sufficient knowledge of the relevant language is critical to the question of whether they have access to effective criminal defence, not only as a discrete right, but also in terms of whether most of the other elements of effective criminal defence are satisfied. This has, in effect, been recognised in the Stockholm Programme that was adopted by the European Council of 10-11 December 2009, and the Roadmap under which interpretation and translation has been given priority for action. Yet we see that in many of the jurisdictions we have examined, interpretation and translation is not, from the perspective of the suspect or accused, an unfettered right. At best, it is a conditional right that depends upon the judgement of others as to whether it may be exercised. Where it is accepted that interpretation or translation is necessary, in many jurisdictions significant limitations are placed on the extent to which interpretation or translation is to take place, at least in so far as it is to be paid for by the state. Furthermore, in many jurisdictions the selection and regulation of interpreters and translators is such that independence and competence cannot be guaranteed. The overall result is that many suspects and accused who do not speak or understand the relevant language are not put in the same position as those who do. To the extent that they are not, they do not have access to effective criminal defence.

In our view the proposed draft directive on interpretation and translation,[120] if adopted, will contribute significantly to dealing with a number of the problems that we have identified in the jurisdictions in the study. Whilst states are left to determine what procedures should be adopted for identifying those who do not speak or understand the relevant language, a key aspect of the draft proposal is that suspects and defendants must have a right to challenge a decision that there is no need for interpretation or translation. The proposal regarding which documents are to be translated gives member states a large degree of discretion in determining this, and falls short of putting the person who requires translation in the same position as a person who does not. However, it does propose that a suspect or accused, or their lawyer, be permitted to make a reasoned request for translation of further documents, and that any decision be subject to challenge. The provision on quality of interpretation and translation also leaves member states with a large degree of discretion in terms of determining minimum quality standards, and says nothing

---

sufficiently effective (see Magee 2010, p. 59). However, we suggest that the principal provides a sound basis for developing a 'whole cost' approach.

[120] Proposal for a Directive of the European Parliament and of the Council on the right to interpretation and translation in criminal proceedings (the proposed directive on interpretation and translation), Brussels, 9.3.2010 COM (2010) 82 final, and see the footnote to § 4.4.3.

about how quality is to be assured, and this is an area where the relevant professional bodies will have a key role to play.

5.4. *Adequate time and facilities*

The analysis identified three particular stages of the criminal process where there are significant deficiencies, both in terms of time and facilities for preparation of the defence, across jurisdictions: the investigative stage; pre-trial detention hearings; and expedited trial procedures. The right to adequate time and facilities to prepare a defence, guaranteed by article 6 § 3b ECHR, is inevitably broadly articulated since, in particular, it is highly context specific. The time and facilities required by the defence at the investigative stage will be different as compared to that needed for trial preparation, and will differ even at the investigative stage depending upon factors such as the seriousness and complexity of the suspected offence, the approach taken by the police and prosecutor, and the intellectual capacity of the suspect. The right to adequate time and facilities is probably incapable of being made subject to close, prescriptive, regulation at the EU level, or even at the national level. We suggest that, as a general principle, the time and facilities available to the defence should be no less than that applicable to the police and prosecution. That is not to argue that the defence be given the same time, powers and resources as the police and prosecution, but that to the extent that they differ, there need to be compensating mechanisms.

The first requirement is that a person be given clear notice of their status in any particular investigation or prosecution. If a person is, in fact, suspected of a criminal offence in respect of which investigative actions, such as interview or search, are to be conducted, they cannot begin to prepare their defence unless they are aware of this. At this point they should be informed of their rights which follow from being a suspect and be given a letter of rights setting out details in a form a suspect can understand. There are circumstances, such as where covert surveillance is being conducted, where to put the suspect on notice would defeat the purpose of the investigative action, but these can be catered for by specific exceptions to a general rule. At the same time, the person should also be notified of their procedural rights (the 'letter of rights'). Similarly, as a general rule, the suspect or accused should have timely access to all information, inculpatory and exculpatory, and without cost, that is in the hands of the police or prosecutor. Again, there may need to be exceptions to this rule, particularly at the investigative stage. However, even at that stage, it should be recognised that a suspect is severely inhibited from preparing their defence if they do not have access to such information. Even if there are valid arguments for withholding such information during the investigation, by the time that an application is made for pre-trial detention, it should be clear that an accused cannot adequately prepare for such an application if they are not given access to the material on which the application is based.

Our analysis demonstrates that in many jurisdictions the time and facilities available for lawyer/client consultations, and for preparation, are severely limited. Investigations are largely conducted according to the timescale of the investigating authority, and pre-trial detention and expedited procedures are governed by similar imperatives. These often ignore the needs of the suspect or accused in terms of preparation, and it is important that those needs are built into the various processes where the problems are most acute.

Finally, it is clear that in all jurisdictions the ability, in practice, of the suspect or accused to investigate the accusation is extremely limited. In some jurisdictions the defence is prevented from interviewing prospective witnesses, and in others defence lawyers are unclear about their investigative powers. However, even in those jurisdictions where the accused is clearly permitted to carry out investigations, they are in practice limited by lack of powers and resources. That, of course, places a great deal of responsibility on the investigation and prosecution authorities to act fairly, and to be mindful of the need to gather exculpatory as well as inculpatory evidence. Such a responsibility is capable of being regulated. In many jurisdictions the suspect or accused can make an application for evidence to be gathered or witnesses to be interviewed, although in many there is no formal procedure for doing so, and in no jurisdiction can the suspect or accused insist on such investigations. What is necessary in order to ensure that the right to adequate facilities to prepare a defence is fully recognised is a formalised procedure whereby such requests can be made, with the possibility of judicial review where such an application is refused.

5.5. Pre-trial detention

Pre-trial detention presents a challenge to the presumption of innocence and, as such, should only be used where this is necessary for a legitimate purpose prescribed by article 5 ECHR and the relevant jurisprudence. The evidence from our study shows that not only does unwarranted detention prior to conviction and sentence amount to a denial of effective criminal defence in itself, but also that those who are kept in detention pre-trial are often denied other rights of effective criminal defence. In particular, those in detention frequently do not have the facilities that would enable them to prepare their defence, and often either face obstructions in attempting to find and instruct a lawyer or, in practice, face difficulties in consulting with their lawyer.

Since a person in pre-trial detention is, by definition, legally innocent release prior to trial should be a prima facie right. In other words, release from custody should be the default position. Evidence from our study shows that in many jurisdictions this is not the case. In some jurisdictions this is because the law itself is deficient. In others, whilst the law may be relatively satisfactory, judges do not apply the law to the specific circumstances of the case, so that the *de facto* default position is that the accused is kept in custody whilst waiting for the trial. In some jurisdictions conditional release is inhibited because the facilities are either not available to support it, or judges and/or lawyers are not sufficiently informed of the facilities available. These problems are exacerbated by the fact that, in many jurisdictions, the material on which applications for detention are based is not disclosed to the accused, legal aid is not in practice available at this stage, and if it is, lawyers are reluctant to attend pre-trial detention hearings and argue the case for release on behalf of their clients. The result, in a number of jurisdictions, is that the remand population is high, at great cost both to the individuals involved and to state budgets.

A pre-condition for a fair, consistent, and accountable system of pre-trial detention and release is clear legal regulation giving defendants a prima facie right to pre-trial release, which can only be displaced on grounds that accord with the requirements of the ECHR. The law should also clearly provide for conditional release, setting out the circumstances in which, and the purposes for which, conditions can be imposed. Given the tendency of judges, and prosecutors, in some jurisdictions to apply blanket rules that ignore specific circumstances, there should be a requirement for decisions to detain, or to impose conditions, to be justified in writing, to be time-limited, and to be subject to review by a higher court. Sufficient time, facilities and disclosure should be given to enable the accused to fully prepare and participate in pre-trial detention hearings, and legal aid mechanisms should be designed to ensure that defence lawyers can, and are encouraged to, attend such hearings. Pre-trial detention hearings should observe the same adversarial principles as apply to trials. Finally, facilities are necessary to support conditional release and to make it a viable alternative to detention for those accused in respect of whom there are particular concerns, such as drug addiction or the lack of settled accommodation.

6. Towards effective criminal defence – the interrelationship between principles, laws, practices and cultures

We have set out here a normative, aspirational, model of effective criminal defence. Whether, in any particular jurisdiction, a person who is suspected or accused of having committed a crime has access to effective criminal defence does not simply depend upon whether they have access to legal assistance. However competent the lawyer is, access to effective criminal defence relies on the presence of, and interrelationship between, a range of principles, laws, practices and cultures. The significance of the ECHR and the jurisprudence that flows from it has been, and continues to be, critical in establishing standards in relation to effective criminal defence. However, as was argued in chapter 2,[121] there are important limitations. Some of them are practical, such as the back-log of cases waiting to be heard. Others are systemic; the *ex post* nature of the application process, the weak mechanisms for ensuring compliance with ECtHR decisions, and the reservation of rules of evidence to member states. Furthermore, in relation to certain factors that we identify as crucial elements of effective criminal defence, in particular the standards of criminal defence lawyers, the ECtHR has largely, and rightly, been reluctant to go beyond broad requirements. Whilst we do not accept that standards are simply a matter between a lawyer and their client, the importance of the independence of lawyers and the legal profession means that the role and standards of criminal defence lawyers, and the policing of those standards, should largely be left to the legal professions albeit with appropriate encouragement from the EU and national governments.

---

[121]   At § 8.1. See also, for example, Vermeulen & van Puyenbroeck 2010, p. 49.

National governments clearly have an important role to play in establishing the legislative context within which effective criminal defence is possible. As we have demonstrated, evidential and procedural rules, and effective enforcement mechanisms, which are properly the subject of legislation, play a key part in ensuring access to effective criminal defence. Similarly, national governments have a key role to play in establishing structures, and making resources available, to ensure that legal assistance, and interpretation and translation, are available in a timely fashion to those who could not otherwise afford them. However, as with the ECHR, there are areas where, whilst national governments have a role in encouraging and facilitating effective criminal defence rights, they should hesitate before becoming too involved. Again, we would point in particular to the role and standards of criminal defence lawyers.

There are other aspects of the constituent elements of the right to effective criminal defence that are largely beyond the reach of legislation, or which are so entrenched in a criminal justice system that legislation is either not appropriate, or is not sufficient, to create the necessary conditions for effective criminal defence. Our analysis shows, in particular, that there are cultural attitudes and practices that will require considerable effort over time in order for them to change. We have seen, for example a variety of ways in which the prosecution is privileged over the accused, and their lawyers, including common training for prosecutors and judges, access to information, and even the physical layout of courtrooms. What is necessary is for there to be a commitment, at all levels and in all sectors of the criminal justice system, to working towards the entrenchment of effective criminal defence.

7. Bibliography

Bridges & Cape 2008
Bridges, L. & Cape, E., *CDS Direct: Flying in the face of the evidence*, London: Centre for Crime and Justice Studies, King's College, 2008.

Cape et al. 2007
Cape, E., Hodgson, J., Prakken, T. & Spronken, T., *Suspects in Europe: Procedural Rights at the Investigative Stage of the Criminal Process in the European Union*, Antwerp: Intersentia, 2007.

Magee 2010
Magee, I., *Review of legal aid delivery and governance*, London: Ministry of Justice, 2010.

National Audit Office 2009
National Audit Office, *The Procurement of Criminal Legal Aid in England and Wales by the Legal Services Commission*, London: The Stationery Office, 2009.

Spronken 2003
Spronken, T., *A Place of Greater Safety*, Leiden: Kluwer, 2003.

Spronken et al. 2009

Spronken, T., Vermeulen, G., de Vocht, D. & van Puyenbroek, L., *EU Procedural Rights in Criminal Proceedings*, Antwerp: Maklu, 2009.

Chapters in Compilations

Vermeulen & van Puyenbroeck 2010

Vermeulen, G. & van Puyenbroeck, L., 'Approximation and mutual recognition of procedural safeguards of suspects and defendants in criminal proceedings throughout the European Union', in: M. Cools, B. De Ruyver, M. Easton, L. Pauwels, P. Ponsaers, G. Vande Walle, T. Vander Beken, F. Vander Laenen, G. Vermeulen and G. Vynckier (eds.), *EU and International Crime Control*, Antwerp: Maklu, 2010, p. 43-62.

Articles in Journals

Sanders & Bridges 1990

Sanders, A. & Bridges, L., 'Access to legal advice and police malpractice', *Criminal Law Review*, 1990, p. 494-509.

Ed Cape
Zaza Namoradze
Roger Smith
Taru Spronken

EFFECTIVE CRIMINAL DEFENCE IN EUROPE
EXECUTIVE SUMMARY AND RECOMMENDATIONS

1.   Introduction

This executive summary provides an overview of the results of a research project 'Effective defence rights in the EU and access to justice: investigating and promoting best practice', which was conducted over a three year period commencing in September 2007. The project partners are Maastricht University, JUSTICE, the University of the West of England and the Open Society Justice Initiative. The project was funded by the European Community and the Open Society Institute. The complete results of the research project and a full account of the analysis and conclusions are published in a book, E. Cape, Z. Namoradze, R. Smith and T. Spronken, *Effective Criminal Defence in Europe*, Antwerpen-Oxford: Intersentia, 2010.

Every year, millions of people across Europe – innocent and guilty – are arrested and detained by the police. For some, their cases go no further than the police station, but many others eventually appear before a court. Many will spend time in custody both before and following trial. Initial attempts by the European Union (EU) to establish minimum procedural rights for suspects and defendants failed in 2007 in the face of opposition by a number of member states who argued that the ECHR rendered EU regulation unnecessary. In this context the aim of the research project was to explore and compare access to effective defence in criminal proceedings across nine European jurisdictions. The project team also set out to contribute to implementation of the right of suspects and defendants to a real and effective defence, especially for those who lack the means to pay for legal assistance themselves. The jurisdictions examined were Belgium, England & Wales, Finland, France, Germany, Hungary, Italy, Poland and Turkey. The reason for choosing these jurisdictions was that they constitute examples of the three major legal traditions in Europe – inquisitorial, adversarial and post-state socialist.

The European Convention on Human Rights (ECHR) protects defence rights principally through article 5 (right to liberty) and article 6 (the right to a fair trial). In addition to the general fair trial rights, such as the presumption of innocence, the right to silence, equality of arms, and the (conditional) right to release pending trial, the rights protected include: the right to information; the right of an arrested person to defend themselves in person or through a lawyer of their choice, to be paid for by the state if they cannot afford to pay for legal assistance where this is in the interests of justice; and a number of procedural rights such as the right to adequate time and facilities to prepare a defence, participation rights, the right to free interpretation and translation, and the right to reasoned decisions and to appeal. The study includes an analysis of the baseline requirements that, according to European Court of Human Rights (ECtHR) case law, have an impact on the position of the accused and also an analysis of how the rights inter-relate.

The project examines not only how the rights are framed in domestic legislation, and whether standards set by the ECHR are met, but also how these rights are implemented in practice and whether or not structures and systems exist to enable individuals to effectively exercise these rights. For instance, domestic legislation may provide for the right to a lawyer immediately on arrest but if there is no system by which a lawyer can be contacted on a 24 hour basis then the arrested person may not be in position to exercise their right to counsel effectively. In addition, the project explores legal and professional cultures since they also have an impact on effective criminal defence. For instance, the law may provide for a right to cross-examine witnesses or to call evidence, but without lawyers who actively use these rights on behalf of defendants, they will not be available in practice.

In order to conduct the research and to come to meaningful conclusions the project team initially defined the scope of the right to effective defence in order to create a basis for data collection and analysis. A set of monitoring indicators was developed to assess how the rights are implemented in practice. A desk review of available data and research was conducted in each of the nine countries supplemented, for most jurisdictions, by interviews with various criminal justice actors. Country reports were produced for each jurisdiction from this research, complemented by other studies. All of the data and conclusions were reviewed by highly respected experts in each jurisdiction.

The executive summary provides:

- a short guide to the main issues concerning criminal defence rights for each jurisdiction in the study
- in light of these findings, recommendations designed to improve access to effective criminal defence in practice for each jurisdiction
- overall conclusions, and recommendations for EU legislation and other supportive measures.

2.   Issues and recommendations concerning individual jurisdictions

2.1.   Belgium

Major issues

The Belgian criminal justice system has undergone a number of changes in the last ten years which have helped further defence rights, but there remain significant impediments to effective criminal defence.

614

One of the major concerns is the rights of suspects before trial. There is currently a distinction between persons officially accused and those who are merely the target of investigations. The latter do not have to be informed of the nature of the allegations against them until they are formally indicted. There is, in any event, no obligation to inform suspects of their procedural rights in writing, including the right to remain silent. Although lawyers for accused persons have a right of access the file at the end of the investigation, the content of the file has to be copied in writing at the court building.

Anyone involved in criminal proceedings is entitled to legal aid if they cannot afford a lawyer. However, there is no obligation to inform suspects of this right. In addition, it does not include the right to be represented during interrogation by an investigative judge or the police. There is no right of access to a lawyer in the 24 hours between arrest and remand in pre-trial custody by a judge. There are no quality control mechanisms for lawyers providing legally-aided criminal defence and there is no requirement that they be specialised in this field. Remuneration is low for legal aid work, and payment is often delayed by up to a year and a half. Generally, in practice there are different standards of representation for those who can afford to pay private lawyers compared to that for indigent defendants who have to rely on legal aid lawyers.

The right to interpretation and translation is not fully recognised. There are three official languages in Belgium and anyone who understands one of those languages is entitled to a translation of case documents into one of the other official languages. However, anyone whose first language is not one of the three official languages is not entitled to a translation of the documents into one of the three official languages or into his own native language. Legally-aided suspects in pre-trial detention are only entitled to free access to an interpreter for a maximum of three hours. Evidence suggests that the quality of interpreters and translators is often low, there being no selection criteria or quality control mechanisms.

Recommendations

1. Ensure that all people who are made aware by the authorities that their situation may be substantially affected by criminal proceedings (and no later than when they are deprived of their liberty) receive a letter of rights and information about the nature of the allegations against them, whether or not they are formally accused.
2. Give effect to the right to legal assistance by allowing access to a lawyer as soon as a person is deprived of their liberty, including during the first 24 hours of detention, and establish an emergency police station scheme to ensure that anyone who is arrested can effectively exercise that right.
3. Introduce a clear right to interpretation and translation for suspects and accused persons at all stages of the criminal process, accompanied by an appropriate quality assurance mechanism.

2.2. England and Wales

Major issues

The legislative framework of England and Wales is comprehensive and guarantees most fair trial rights, apart from translation and interpretation. There are, however, a number of substantive and policy factors that curtail those rights in practice.

Whilst legal regulation of the investigative stage commands widespread respect and the right to legal advice at the investigative stage is well established, suspects' rights are restricted during this stage of the criminal process in a number of ways. Suspects have no right to information about the nature of the allegations against them, beyond the grounds for arrest, before police interviews. This, combined with the fact that 'silence' during a police interview may be taken as indicative of guilt at the trial stage, can lead to violation of the procedural rights of the accused. Suspects have no right to require the police to follow lines of inquiry or interview particular witnesses. Although there is no legal impediment to suspects making their own enquiries, in practice this is limited particularly for those reliant on legal aid.

A number of changes to evidential and procedural rules have eroded the adversarial nature of the criminal justice system and the presumption of innocence. For instance, defendants are effectively required to disclose the nature of their defence both at the investigative stage and before trial. In addition, defendants' previous misconduct, whether or not resulting in a criminal conviction, can be used at trial to show their propensity to commit offences and to undermine their credibility as witnesses.

Although expenditure on legal aid is very high in comparison to other countries, a series of attempts has been made by the government to cap spending and reduce eligibility and remuneration. For instance, fixed fees for police station and court work restrict the amount of work that defence lawyers can do, which has an adverse impact on equality of arms. In addition, appeal rights are limited in practice by legal aid restrictions, and this is particularly important in more serious cases.

Finally, a significant proportion of defendants who are kept in custody pending the outcome of their trial or sentence are eventually acquitted or given non-custodial sentences, raising the question whether defendants are unnecessarily refused bail.

Recommendations

1. Introduce greater participation rights for suspects and defendants, and their lawyers, require fuller disclosure by the police and prosecution at the investigative stage and before plea is taken, and introduce more effective judicial oversight of arrest and bail decisions.
2. Ensure that access to effective defence is not compromised by reductions in legal aid eligibility and remuneration, and increase the availability of legal aid for appeals.

3. Review the disclosure obligations of suspects and defendants to ensure that either adversarial rights are not undermined or, to the extent that they are compromised, are adequately compensated for by appropriate protective mechanisms that ensure equality of arms and respect for the presumption of innocence.

2.3. Finland

Major issues

Finland's current legal framework has many safeguards to guarantee the right to a fair trial, although recent law reforms has clawed back some of these safeguards.

On arrest, there is no obligation to provide suspects with a letter of rights, including information on the right to silence. In recent years, police investigative powers have continued to expand at the expense of rights of suspects. The increased use of covert methods of investigation, such as surveillance, and the use of private informants and undercover police officers, raises serious concerns about the use of illegally obtained evidence at trial, as it is not automatically deemed inadmissible by the court.

Defendants can be tried in absentia, and without a lawyer, if their presence is deemed unnecessary because they have previously confessed to the crime, or because their case is considered routine. Defendants do not need to agree to be tried in their absence, and the court is not required to determine why the defendant did not appear. Defendants tried in their absence may be sentenced to up to three months imprisonment and have no right to a retrial 30 days after conviction. Twenty per cent of all cases are dealt with in this way.

In addition, significant numbers of defendants waive their right to trial without the advice of a lawyer. In 2008, approximately 30% of defendants pled guilty and agreed to have their case judged through a written procedure, rather than in a full hearing. Although judges are required to obtain the consent of the accused to proceed with a written procedure, it is unclear that defendants' consent is fully informed, given that they are rarely represented by a lawyer.

Lawyers who act for defendants are not required to have any criminal defence experience or undergo any specific training. As a result, the quality of defence work, including in legal aid cases, varies considerably. The position is exacerbated by the fact that lawyers are not required to be members of the Finnish Bar Association, and those who are not members are not subject to the supervision or discipline of the bar association.

Evidence suggests that lawyers are generally reluctant to take an active role during the pre-trial stages of criminal proceedings. Lawyers rarely independently investigate the facts of cases, or interview any witnesses, relying on the police to carry out all the investigation that is necessary. This puts the defence at a severe disadvantage, since they will seldom be in a position to meaningfully challenge evidence at trial.

Recommendations

1. Introduce a letter of rights for suspects detained at police stations.
2. Promote access to lawyers by establishing an emergency legal aid scheme to facilitate the provision of advice and assistance at police stations 24 hours a day.
3. Encourage a more pro-active role for lawyers at the investigative stage, and establish effective quality control mechanisms and monitoring for lawyers providing criminal defence services.

2.4.   France

Major issues

In the last twenty years, criminal procedure and defence rights have undergone a number of changes in response to both condemnations by the ECtHR and perceived threats to security. There remain a number of shortcomings which prevent the effective exercise of defence rights.

The *Garde à Vue* procedure (used when someone is arrested and detained by the police) is still not compliant with ECHR standards. Most notably, access to a lawyer is not guaranteed on arrest and is limited to a 30 minute consultation. Lawyers can be excluded from the interrogation and are not given access to the case file. The police at this stage are not required to inform suspects of their right to remain silent.

Investigations are conducted by the police either under the supervision of a prosecutor or of an investigation judge. However, in most cases, the police are not adequately supervised by either, and are free to conduct the investigation as they see fit. Prosecutors and judges often simply check the case file to ensure that 'on paper' the police have complied with all their duties. Since defence lawyers are often not involved at this stage, this is likely to have a negative impact on the outcome of the case for suspects because prosecutors and judges rely heavily on the police file at court. If suspects have not been able to put their case forward, or to request that information favourable to them be obtained, this information will not form part of the file. As expedited trial procedures are increasingly routinely used, there is often no time for the defence to put forward alternative evidence, and no judicial evaluation of the facts.

French legal culture creates a professional divide between prosecutors and judges, who are members of the *Magistrature*, and defence lawyers. Prosecutors and judges share a common training and view their role as dominant and necessary to protect the public interest. Defence lawyers are viewed with suspicion. The legal tradition does not recognise a role for strong, pro-active, defence lawyers. Instead, the defence lawyer's role is premised on dialogue and compromise, which discourages lawyers from engaging in active and zealous defence. Furthermore, most legally-aided criminal defence work is carried out by young lawyers as part of their training, who are unlikely to have the confidence or skills to stand up to a corps of more experienced judges and prosecutors, raising concerns about equality of arms.

Recommendations

1. Review Garde à Vue procedures to ensure that suspects are provided with a letter of rights on detention, and with prompt access to lawyers prior to and during any interrogation, irrespective of the offence under investigation.
2. Ensure that prosecutors and judges adequately supervise investigative acts conducted by police officers.
3. Introduce measures designed to improve the status and quality of criminal defence lawyers, and to ensure adequate time, resources and facilities for preparation of the defence in all cases.

2.5. *Germany*

Major issues

Although Germany's existing legal framework guarantees, to a large extent, the right to a fair trial a number of problems remain.

During the investigative phase, the investigation authority has the power to classify persons as either 'suspects' or 'accused'. Suspects do not have the same rights as accused persons, such as the right to legal assistance or the right to information. Although accused persons have the right to legal advice prior to interrogation, there is no systematic mechanism to enable accused persons to consult with a lawyer, and police officers sometimes try to persuade accused persons that it is not necessary for them to do so. As a result, accused persons are routinely interrogated and held in custody for long periods without receiving the assistance of a lawyer. Lawyers are often denied access to an accused person's case file during the pre-trial investigation and unrepresented accused are only given excerpts from the case file and only then if, in the view of the investigating authority, the interests of the investigation or of witnesses are not jeopardised.

Legal aid is available in limited circumstances, based on the seriousness of the offence and the vulnerability of the accused, and not on financial need. The defendant's indigence is only relevant in determining whether or not they must reimburse the costs of their representation. The process by which indigence is determined is complicated and places undue burden on the accused. Funding for legal aid is inadequate, especially during the pre-trial phase. Many services, such as the costs of investigation by the defence, are not covered, discouraging lawyers from engaging in these activities. Further, payments to lawyers are not promptly made. Appointed counsel are not required to have any criminal defence experience; there are few specific practice standards, and lawyers often disregard continuing professional training requirements. As a result, the quality of defence work in legal aid cases varies considerably.

An active defence culture is not encouraged by the various criminal justice actors. Defence lawyers are sometimes not seen as independent as some rely on the courts for regular appointments. Judges and prosecutors tend to be critical, sceptical, and distrustful of the results of defence investigations, assuming witnesses were unduly influenced by the defence. As a result, defence lawyers rarely engage in independent investigations of their clients' cases. Evidence suggests that judges, moved by considerations of efficiency, often deny defence motions to gather, produce, and introduce evidence, regarding them as unco-operative acts intended to delay proceedings. It appears that this perception has influenced the behaviour of defence lawyers, who hesitate to stand up to the court and file such motions.

Recommendations

1. Ensure that all people who are made aware by the authorities that their situation may be substantially affected by criminal proceedings (and no later than when they are deprived of their liberty), whether or not they are formally designated as a 'suspect' or 'accused', are afforded the same rights, are clearly informed of those rights, and that those rights may be exercised in a practical and effective way.
2. Introduce a simple means and merits test for legal aid to facilitate access to legal aid for all indigent defendants at all stages of the criminal process.
3. In order to raise the standards of criminal defence lawyers, develop effective training requirements and quality assurance mechanisms for them, and ensure adequate remuneration for legal aid work, particularly at the pre-trial stage, which is paid in a timely manner.

2.6.   Hungary

Major issues

The legal framework which guarantees defence rights is well-established, but implementation poses a number of problems in practice.

Evidence suggests that the police routinely circumvent the right to silence during the investigation, informally hearing prospective suspects as witnesses, or questioning them during administrative short-term arrest without informing them of their procedural rights, including the right to remain silent. Whilst statements made in such circumstances cannot be introduced as direct evidence at trial, they may remain part of the case file and may be referred to in court. In addition, official suspects have very limited access to the case file during pre-trial investigations.

Although access to legal assistance at the investigative stage is guaranteed by law, for a variety of reasons suspects rarely, in practice, have access to a lawyer. There is no duty lawyer scheme, and even if the police notify defence lawyers, they do not have to wait for the lawyer to arrive before interrogating suspects. Even in mandatory defence cases, lawyers do not normally attend police interrogations. Where lawyers do attend the police station they are unlikely to be allowed more than 30 minutes for consultation with their clients before the interrogation.

Furthermore, the state is not bound to provide, or fund, an interpreter for lawyer-client consultations, putting indigent suspects who do not speak Hungarian at a particular disadvantage.

In principle, legal aid is available for all indigent defendants at all stages of the criminal process, and in certain mandatory defence cases. There is, however, no institution with responsibility for managing legal aid services or monitoring quality. Responsibility for appointing legal aid lawyers and paying them rests with the relevant investigating authority. This raises obvious concerns about the independence of lawyers providing these services. Evidence suggests that the quality of work done by such lawyers is often inadequate, that they are often absent from hearings, and are passive when they do attend. Appointed counsel are not required to have experience or training in criminal defence. Legal aid remuneration is considered to be inadequate.

The overuse of pre-trial detention is widespread, and can last for up to three years. From 2003 to 2007 alternatives to pre-trial detention were only used in two per cent of cases. Defendants are not given access to the material that forms the basis for detention, thereby breaching the equality of arms principle and preventing them from meaningfully contesting their detention. In light of the potential length of pre-trial detention, research has shown that the threat of pre-trial detention is often used to induce confessions.

Recommendations

1. Ensure that all people who are made aware by the authorities that their situation may be substantially affected by criminal proceedings (and no later than when they are deprived of their liberty), are provided with adequate time and facilities to meet with their lawyers, and with interpreters, funded by the state where necessary.
2. Give practical effect to the right to legal assistance by establishing a national authority to administer legal aid and monitor the quality of services provided by legal aid lawyers, including the creation of a scheme to ensure prompt appointment of lawyers that does not rely on the investigating authority, and by introducing adequate remuneration for legal aid work.
3. Introduce measures to encourage the use of alternatives to pre-trial detention, and allow defendants access to the material that forms the basis for their detention prior to trial.

2.7. *Italy*

Major issues

Whilst Italian law generally guarantees those rights essential to a fair trial, there remain obstacles that prevent defendants and suspects from exercising their right to an effective defence.

There are insufficient procedural safeguards in place to ensure that the accused can exercise their defence rights. Although suspects are given a letter of rights that includes the legal definition of the crime alleged, there is no requirement that suspects be informed of any modification to the crime charged in the indictment. The right to counsel following arrest can be delayed for up to 48 hours on the authority of a prosecutor and five days on the authority of a judge. This denies suspects the opportunity to consult with counsel prior to their interrogation. Additionally, prosecutors can deny suspects access to the case file during the investigative stage. Suspects and defendants who do not understand Italian face additional challenges, since those who have even limited knowledge of Italian are often denied an interpreter, or are provided with an interpreter who do not speak their native language.

Systemic deficiencies in Italy's legal aid system result in a high proportion of poor defendants being denied competent legal services. Whilst all accused persons must be represented by counsel, the low threshold for legal aid eligibility requires many poor defendants to go into debt to pay for their lawyer. Those who do qualify for legal aid are often unaware that they can apply. In 2006, only just over six per cent of defendants – not including juveniles – received legal aid. The lack of adequate funding for legal aid services results in remuneration that is so low that many lawyers refuse appointment. Often, those who do accept appointment provide the accused with inadequate representation as they lack the funds to conduct even the most basic investigation of the case.

Finally, the overuse of pre-trial detention, and the unreasonable length of proceedings, limit the accused's access to a fair trial. Whilst the law provides that pre-trial detention should be a measure of last resort, more than half of Italy's prison population is in pre-trial detention or awaiting final sentence. The average length of a criminal case is over four years.

Recommendations

1. To promote access to legal assistance, raise the eligibility threshold to allow more suspects and defendants access to legal aid, and ensure that remuneration is sufficient to encourage and facilitate competent legal assistance.
2. Ensure that pre-trial detention is, in practice, used as a measure of last resort by establishing practical alternatives to pre-trial detention, and introduce measures to speed up the criminal process.
3. Introduce measures to ensure that all suspects and defendants who do not have a sufficient understanding of the Italian language have access to competent interpretation and translation.

2.8. Poland

Major issues

Although the Polish criminal justice system has undergone a positive transformation since the end of communism, a number of problems remain that inhibit access by defendants and suspects to effective criminal defence.

At the investigative stage, a distinction is made between 'suspected persons', who have not yet been officially charged, and 'suspects', who have been officially charged. Suspected persons are not entitled to the same protections as suspects and yet can be detained for up to 48 hours. Suspected persons do not have to be given a letter of rights or be informed of their right to remain silent. Although suspected persons may not be interrogated until they are formally charged, in practice the police inform them that they have the right to make a statement. Such a statement forms part of the arrest record and whilst not formally amounting to evidence, in practice police officers may give evidence of its contents to the court.

The rights of those who are formally treated as suspects are frequently not effective in practice. For instance, the rights specified in the letter of rights are often not understood by suspects, and the letter of rights does not explain how the rights, such as the right to consult a lawyer, are to be exercised. The right to information is also not absolute and prosecutors can deny access to the file during the investigative stage. Furthermore, in certain cases prosecutors can supervise the consultation between a lawyer and a suspect during the first 14 days of detention. There is no judicial review of a prosecutor's decision either to deny access to the file or to supervise lawyer-client consultations. The lack of procedural rights, combined with a culture which does not encourage an active defence during the pre-trial stage, means that defence rights at this stage are largely theoretical.

Despite the fact that accused persons are entitled to a lawyer at all stages of criminal proceedings, in practice legal aid is generally not available at the investigative stage or at early hearings such as those at which a decision is made regarding pre-trial detention. The decision to grant legal aid is made by judges, who must pay for it out of their individual court budget. In addition, there is no clear means or merits test and judges, therefore, have a wide discretion to deny legal aid except in certain mandatory cases. Legal aid remuneration rates are relatively low and there is evidence that the quality of representation is often poor.

Recommendations

1. Ensure that all people who are made aware by the authorities that their situation may be substantially affected by criminal proceedings (and no later than when they are deprived of their liberty) are afforded the same rights, whether or not they are formally designated as a 'suspect' or a 'suspected person', are clearly informed of those rights, and ensure that those rights may be exercised in a practical and effective way.
2. Ensure the effective implementation of the right to legal assistance by creating an independent agency to administer the criminal legal aid system, with responsibility for ensuring the provision of advice and representation at all stages of the criminal process without regard to local court budgets, and subject to clear criteria regarding means and merits.
3. Introduce measures designed to improve the status and quality of criminal defence lawyers, in particular, to ensure that they act in a more pro-active manner including by being present to advise and assist at the early stages of the criminal process.

2.9.   Turkey

Major issues

The legal framework for the protection of suspects' and defendants' rights in Turkey is extensive. However, in practice, these legal safeguards are often not applied, leading to violations of defence rights.

Substantive rights at the police station and during the investigative phase are often not respected. Although the right to information is recognised, in practice people are often apprehended or summonsed by the police without being given reasons. Similarly, there is a requirement that a letter of rights be provided to suspects before the first interrogation, but this is more of a formality than an opportunity for suspects to effectively exercise their rights. Suspects have the right to request that certain evidence be gathered at the investigative stage. However, prosecutors can issue secrecy decisions on very broad grounds which prevent suspects or their lawyers from accessing any information about the investigation. This in turn prevents suspects from knowing the grounds on which they are held and from being able to meaningfully challenge their status as suspects. The number of people in custody has increased since the introduction of the new criminal code. Pre-trial release is not commonly used, but a majority of defendants detained pending trial are either acquitted or given a non-custodial sentence.

In theory, anyone may be represented free of charge under the criminal legal aid system, both at the police station and during any phase of the trial. However, the police and other justice system actors often fail to inform suspects of this right in a manner understandable to them or discourage them from requesting a lawyer. Overall, the number of people who are able to exercise their right to free legal assistance is strikingly low. There is no central independent agency responsible for assessing the need for legal aid or for managing and monitoring the delivery of legal aid. These functions have been delegated to local bar associations. There are no quality control mechanisms for the provision of legal assistance in criminal cases.

Legal and professional cultures have an adverse impact on equality of arms and the right to an adversarial trial process. Defence lawyers are often passive both during the investigative phase and at trial. This is partly due to inadequate remuneration for defence work, and to the lack of quality assurance mechanisms concerning the work of defence lawyers. In addition, prosecutors and judges often share a common training, making judges more receptive to prosecution arguments. Judges are also resistant to pro-active defence lawyers, often preventing them from speaking in court or from cross-examining witnesses, or denying their requests for the production of evidence.

Recommendations

1.   Ensure that the legal rights of pre-trial detainees are respected, including an effective right to challenge the grounds of detention, and by giving them access to information concerning the allegations against them. Introduce a letter of rights that enables suspects and accused persons to understand their defence rights.

2. Improve the current legal aid system to ensure that the right to legal assistance is available in practice by creating an independent agency to administer criminal legal aid, with responsibility for ensuring the provision of advice and representation at all stages of the criminal process, and for assuring the quality of defence lawyers.
3. Foster mutual respect between all criminal justice actors to ensure mutual understanding of roles, and in order to facilitate a pro-active role for criminal defence lawyers.

3.   Overall conclusions and recommendations

Effective criminal defence is an essential component of the right to fair trial. Whether, in any particular jurisdiction, a person who is suspected or accused of having committed a crime has access to effective criminal defence does not simply depend upon whether they have access to the assistance of a lawyer. Competent legal assistance, whilst necessary, is not sufficient. For criminal defence to be effective there must exist a constitutional and legislative structure that provides for the rights set out in the ECHR, institutions and processes that enable them to be practical and effective, and legal and professional cultures that facilitate them.

The ECHR, and the case law of the ECtHR, play a critical role in establishing standards in respect of effective criminal defence. However, there are both practical and systemic limitations on their ability to provide detailed standards for, and to ensure full compliance with, all of the essential components of effective criminal defence. Our research demonstrates that whilst, of course, there is significant variation across the nine jurisdictions in the study, there are important limitations on access to effective criminal defence in all countries that we have examined. In addition to the consequences for the individuals caught up in criminal justice processes, this has significant implications for the European Union (EU) policy of mutual trust and recognition.

Responsibility for compliance with ECHR standards principally rests on the governments of member states. We have made specific recommendations concerning each jurisdiction that in our view, if followed, would significantly improve compliance and the prospects of citizens having access to effective criminal defence. The EU also has responsibility, particularly because it has set itself the objective of maintaining and developing an area of freedom, security and justice and, since ratification of the Lisbon Treaty, the ECHR has become an integral part of EU law. Furthermore, article 82 § 2 of the Treaty of the European Union provides for the establishment of minimum rules in respect of, *inter alia*, the rights of individuals in criminal matters. The EU has commenced this process with the adoption of the Stockholm Programme and the accompanying Roadmap for fostering protection of suspected and accused persons in criminal proceedings. However, responsibility does not end there. Our research and analysis shows that criminal justice professionals, including lawyers who advise and assist suspects and defendants, do not always respect the rights of those suspected or accused of crime, and there is much to be done, beyond the reach of legislation and procedural rules, to realise a real commitment to effective criminal defence rights as an essential element of the right to fair trial.

The EU programme of action in respect of the rights of individuals in criminal proceedings has already begun with the publication of a draft Directive on translation and interpretation. This is to be followed by legislative proposals on: information on rights and on charges; legal advice and legal aid; communication with relatives, employers and consular authorities; and special safeguards for vulnerable suspects and accused persons. The programme also includes plans for a Green Paper on whether other minimum procedural rights need to be addressed. We hope that our findings, analysis and conclusions will contribute to the effective realisation of this programme of action, and we make recommendations for consideration in this process below.

3.1.   General recommendations

We make the following general recommendations for action by the EU, national governments, and criminal justice professionals.

- The EU should include in its legislative programme all of the specific areas for action that we identify below in order to establish minimum requirements that would contribute to, and enhance access to, effective criminal defence in all member states. Such legislation should include mechanisms for monitoring implementation to ensure that, over time, member states meet those minimum requirements.

- Working with member states and professional organisations, the EU should establish mechanisms for identifying and disseminating good practices which contribute to enhancing access to effective criminal defence including, specifically, a 'whole cost' approach to criminal justice policies.

- Working with member states, the EU should encourage and support the routine collection and publication of statistical evidence, and relevant research, in order to render criminal procedures and practices transparent, and to enhance accountability.

- Working with relevant professional organisations, the EU and member states should encourage and support suitable training for criminal justice professionals (the judiciary, prosecutors, police, lawyers, and interpreters and translators) to assist in entrenching practices and attitudes directed to facilitating effective criminal defence.

- The EU should encourage and support bar associations to articulate standards of good practice, and to take responsibility for disseminating and enforcing such standards, in order to improve both the status and professional standards of criminal defence lawyers, including those who are funded by the state.

- The EU should encourage member states to develop organised, systematic and purposeful responses to the need to provide free and effective legal assistance to all indigent criminal defendants, including by the establishment of independent executive agencies to administer legal aid. Such agencies would be responsible for formulating and implementing the government's legal aid policy and budget, monitoring its performance, determining legal aid needs and finding cost-effective solutions for legal aid delivery

3.2. Specific proposals

We make the following specific recommendations for legislation by the EU, although we recommend that the governments of member states take appropriate action as soon as is practicable.

3.2.1. Information on rights and charges

A Directive should include –

With regard to information rights –

- A requirement that a Letter of Rights be given to a person when they are made aware by the authorities that their situation may be substantially affected by criminal proceedings (and in any event no later than the when they are factually deprived of their liberty).

- An obligation to takes steps to ensure that a person served with a Letter of Rights understands it, including the provision of a translation of the Letter of Rights where the recipient does not understand the relevant language or is unable to read or comprehend it.

- Minimum requirements as to the rights to be referred to in the Letter of Rights, including legal assistance, legal aid, the right to silence, the right to information as to the grounds for arrest or detention, and additional rights for vulnerable suspects and defendants.

- An obligation to establish effective enforcement mechanisms designed to ensure that the Letter of Rights requirements are complied with, including an obligation to obtain written confirmation of receipt from the suspect or accused, and appropriate evidential mechanisms.

With regard to information as to detention and the suspected offence –

- An obligation to inform the person concerned of their status in a criminal investigation and, in particular, whether they are a suspect or a witness.

- An obligation to inform a person who has been arrested or detained of the grounds for their arrest or detention.

- An obligation to provide, before the first interrogation by police or a prosecutor, information as to the material on which the suspicion or accusation is based or, if such information is not provided, a prohibition on any adverse consequences resulting from failure or refusal to answer questions, or failure or refusal to provide information that may subsequently be relied upon in the person's defence.

3.2.2. Legal assistance and legal aid

A Directive should include –

- A requirement that a right to legal assistance arises no later than the point when a person is made aware by the authorities that their situation may be substantially affected by criminal proceedings (and in any event no later than the when they are deprived of their liberty), and which applies throughout the criminal proceedings.

- An obligation on the investigative or prosecution authorities to bring the right to legal assistance, and to legal aid, to the attention of the person concerned in a form that they can understand, both in writing by means of a letter of rights, and orally, and an obligation on the judiciary at the first available opportunity to verify that the accused understands the implications of not being legally represented.

- An obligation to establish mechanisms that ensure that legal assistance is available without delay at all stages of the criminal process, including for those who cannot afford to pay for legal assistance themselves.

- An obligation to establish effective enforcement mechanisms that apply where access to legal assistance is delayed or denied, which may include prohibition on conducting procedural actions, the exclusion of evidence, and/or judicial review.

- Minimum requirements regarding eligibility for legal aid, including a merits test that ensures that vulnerable suspects and defendants and those who are at risk of a custodial sentence are eligible, and a means test that ensures that those who cannot afford to pay for legal assistance are eligible. Further, there should be a requirement that procedures for determining eligibility do not interfere with access to legal assistance at the time that it is required.

- Requiring that member states, in cooperation with the respective bar associations, develop and implement minimum quality criteria for criminal legal aid and quality assurance mechanisms, and establish minimum requirements regarding remuneration for lawyers providing legal assistance paid for by the state that ensure that sufficient competent lawyers are willing and able to provide legal assistance when it is required.

3.2.3. Interpretation and translation

- A draft directive has been published by the EU (*Proposal for a Directive of the European Parliament and of the Council on the right to interpretation and translation in criminal proceedings*, Brussels, 9.3.2010 COM (2010) 83 final). The need for such a directive has been established by this research.

- The draft directive does not prescribe a procedure by which the need for interpretation or translation is required, but we note that it does require that an accused person be given the right to challenge a decision that there is no need for interpretation or translation. Our research supports the need for such a requirement.

- The draft directive prescribes in wide terms the circumstances in which interpretation is to be provided. Our research supports the need for such prescription. We recommend that consideration be given to requiring either that interpretation of lawyer-client consultations be provided by a different interpreter than an interpreter appointed for conversations where the police or prosecutor are present, or that interpretation of lawyer-client consultations be covered by the equivalent of legal professional privilege.

- The draft directive provides for translation of 'all essential documents', which falls short of a requirement that all prosecution material be translated. We note, however, that a suspect or accused must be permitted to make a reasoned request for translation of further documents, and that they be given the right to challenge a decision that translation is not necessary. We recommend that authorities be required to consider such requests, or such challenges, by reference to the right to fair trial and not by reference to the potential cost.

- The draft directive requires that interpretation and translation be of 'a sufficient quality to safeguard the fairness of the criminal proceedings'. We recommend that this be extended to include an obligation that it be provided in such a way that is sufficiently independent of the appointing authority and that, where possible, it be provided by an interpreter or translator who is a member of a professional body that has responsibilities for quality and professional discipline.

3.2.4. Access to the case-file, and time and facilities to prepare the defence

We recommend that there should be a Directive concerning access to the case file, and time and facilities for preparation of the defence that includes, or that one of the other proposed directives should include –

- An obligation to provide the accused with access to the case file, or prosecution material, in such a form and at such a time that is sufficient to enable a suspect or accused person to effectively prepare their defence, and to enable them to prepare for any particular hearing.

- A requirement that the obligation normally be satisfied by making available copies of original documents (or electronic versions thereof) unless this is contrary to the interests of justice, the safety of witnesses, or security.

- An obligation to provide for a procedure during the pre-trial phase that enables an accused person be given the right to challenge a decision not to provide access to the (complete) case file.

- An obligation to provide such information free of charge to the accused.

- An obligation to establish mechanisms enabling suspects or accused persons to make application for witnesses to be interviewed or material to be gathered, with the possibility of judicial review where an application is refused by the investigative or prosecution authorities.

3.2.5. Pre-trial detention

The green paper should include consideration of –

- A requirement that an accused person has a prima facie right to pre-trial release, which may only be displaced where there are substantial grounds for believing that the accused will abscond, commit further imprisonable offences, or interfere with the course of the investigation or justice, or where it is in the accused's own interests to be kept in pre-trial detention.

- A requirement that if unconditional pre-trial release is not appropriate for the reasons listed above, then the suitability of conditional release must be considered, and that conditions may only be imposed for the purposes of ensuring that the accused will attend court, will not re-offend, or will not interfere with the course of justice, or for their own protection. Also, a requirement that any money bail condition be set at a level that takes into account the financial circumstances of the accused and is proportionate to the specified risk.

- A requirement that member states ensure that alternatives to pre-trial detention are available together with practical mechanisms facilitating their use, and that suitable facilities are available for accused persons in particular circumstances, for example, bail hostels, drug units, etc.

- A requirement that pre-trial detention hearings observe, as far as possible, the same adversarial principles as apply to trials, and that accused persons are given access to material on which an application for pre-trial detention is based in sufficient time to enable them to make an effective application for pre-trial release.

- A requirement that pre-trial detention may only be ordered by a judicial authority, that the determining authority should be required to give written reasons for their decision, that detention be reviewed at established regular intervals in order to determine whether it continues to be necessary, that decisions be subject to review by a higher court.

Maastricht, May 2010

ANNEX 1 DESK REVIEW PRO-FORMA

This pro-forma sets out the information to be obtained in the Desk Review phase of the research. Although the order in which the information is collected does not matter, it is important that report of the desk review sets out the data in the same order as in this pro-forma, referring to the question number as appropriate. Where appropriate, for example, to provide important contextual information, or to indicate recent or prospective changes, the information requested should be accompanied by narrative. Also, where appropriate, the in-country researcher should include proposals and recommendations, e.g., regarding the need for routine data collection as to legal aid expenditure, etc.

Sources of data will include: laws (constitution, statutes, codes and case-law, as relevant); professional rules; statistics (both official and statistics collected by non-government bodies); existing research. In each case, the source of the data should be specified. Where the question concerns whether there is a right, regulation, exception, etc., specify the source with as much precision as possible: e.g., the Police and Criminal Evidence Act 1984, s 58; the Criminal Procedure Code, art. 3(1); Constitutional Court, Decision No. 82/94, 1 December 1994; the Law Society's Code of Conduct 2007, rule 1.01. Referencing should follow the style used in the sample chapter from *Suspects in Europe*.

If data requested in this pro-forma is not available, this fact should be noted – the fact that data is not routinely collected, or is not made publicly available, is an important research finding in itself. For example, if no statistics are routinely collected (or are collected but are not made available) on the proportion of defendants who are represented at court, it would be difficult for a country to demonstrate whether, and the extent to which, it is in compliance with article 6(3)(c).

Some questions specifically ask whether a rule or practice differs depending upon whether a suspect or defendant is able to pay privately and/or is in receipt of legal aid. In gathering the data, consider whether there are, or are likely to be, any differences in principle of in practice depending upon whether the suspect/defendant –

> (d) is able to pay for legal services at a full commercial rate, or
> (e) pays privately, but a lower than commercial rate, or

(f) is in receipt of, or is entitled to, legal aid (or other forms of state assistance, such as legal provision by a public defender service).

There is no word limit for the desk review. The desk review and the critical account will form the basis of the country report, which has a word limit of 15,000.

1.   General statistical and other information

(Generally, statistics should be for the most recent year available, although an indication should be given if there are significant changes from year to year. If there is relevant data on ethnicity relating to any of the following categories of data, this should also be included.)

(1) Legal aid and state expenditure
    (a) Absolute and per capita expenditure on criminal legal aid –
        (i) at investigative stage
        (ii) at later stages
    (b) Proportion of the population who are eligible for legal aid
    (c) Proportion of suspects/defendants who have legal advice and/or representation –
        (i) at investigative stage
        (ii) at later stages
    (d) Proportion of suspects/defendants in receipt of legal aid –
        (i) at investigative stage
        (ii) at later stages
    (e) Proportion of suspects/defendants who make a financial contribution or against whom a contribution order is made on conviction, and figures on amounts of contributions/orders.
    (f) Average remuneration per case (i.e. amounts paid to lawyers).
    (g) Legal aid expenditure by type of work (e.g. profit costs, travelling/waiting, experts, etc.).
    (h) Number of cases and expenditure on interpretation/translation.

(2) Criminal justice system
    (a) Number of arrests
    (b) Proportion of those arrested who are then proceeded against
    (c) Proportion of those proceeded against who are kept in custody pending trial, including any data on average length of time spent in custody awaiting trial, or who are subject to conditional release pending trial.
    (d) Proportion of those proceeded against who are convicted/found guilty.
    (e) Proportion of those who are convicted/found guilty who are given a custodial sentence.
    (f) Proportions of those in (b), (c), (d) and (e) who are legally represented.
    (g) Where there is a guilty plea or expedited hearing procedure, in what proportion of cases is there a guilty plea or expedited hearing.

(3) The legal profession

    (a) Number of lawyers belonging to bar associations.

    (b) If it is possible to practice without belonging to a bar association) Proportion of lawyers belonging/not belonging to bar associations.

    (c) Number and proportion of practising lawyers who engage in criminal defence work.

    (d) Number and proportion of lawyers who receive legal aid for (i) and work, and (ii) criminal defence work.

    (e) Number and proportion of lawyers working for public defender services.

    (f) Number of complaints about lawyers, and outcomes of any complaints/disciplinary procedures.

2.   Right to information concerning the accusation

(1) Is there a legal obligation requiring –

(i) a suspect (i.e. person being questioned by police or prosecutor in circumstances where there are grounds to suspect that they have committed an offence), and/or
(ii) a defendant (i.e. person against whom criminal proceedings have commenced),

to be informed of the nature and cause of the accusation against him/her?

If so –

    (a) What is the source of that obligation?

    (b) When does the duty arise?

    (c) Is the right absolute or conditional?

    (d) What is the extent of the information that has to be supplied?

    (e) In what form does the information have to be supplied (e.g. verbal, writing, summary or in full)?

    (f) Is there a continuing obligation to provide information as the investigation/case develops?

    (g) Is there any existing evidence as to whether and how this obligation is complied with?

    (h) Are there any sanctions or remedies if the obligation is not complied with?

(2) Is there a legal obligation requiring –

    (i) a suspect (i.e. person being questioned by police or prosecutor in circumstances where there are grounds to suspect that they have committed an offence), and/or
    (ii) a defendant (i.e. person against whom criminal proceedings have commenced),

to be informed in detail of the accusation against him/her (i.e. information about the investigation and evidence obtained), including material that is not put/to be put before the court?

If so –

  (a) What is the source of that obligation?
  (b) When does the duty arise?
  (c) Is the right absolute or conditional?
  (d) What is the extent of the information that has to be supplied?
  (e) In what form does the information have to be supplied (e.g. verbal, writing, summary or in full)?
  (f) Are there any time limits for the provision of information?
  (g) Is there a continuing obligation to provide information as the investigation/case develops?
  (h) Is there any existing evidence as to whether and how this obligation is complied with?
  (i) Are there any sanctions or remedies if the obligation is not complied with?

(3) Is there a legal obligation to provide the information referred to in (1) and (4) to the suspect or defendant in a language which s/he understands?

If so –

  (a) What is the source of that obligation?
  (b) Is there any existing evidence as to whether and how this obligation is complied with?
  (c) Are there any sanctions or remedies if the obligation is not complied with?

(4) Is there any difference between poor or legally-aided suspects and defendants and those who are well able to pay privately –

  (a) in law?
  (b) in practice?

(5) Is there any obligation to give a suspect or defendant a 'letter of rights' informing them of their rights?

If so –

  (a) What is the source of that obligation?
  (b) Who has to provide the 'letter of rights'
  (c) At what stage does the letter of rights have to be provided?
  (d) Is there an obligation to provide the 'letter of rights' in a language that the suspect/defendant understands?

636

(e) Is there an obligation to verify whether the suspect/defendant understood the rights included in the 'letter of rights'?

(f) Is there any existing evidence as to whether and how this obligation is complied with?

(g) Are there any sanctions or remedies if the obligation is not complied with?

3. The right to defence

(1) Does the suspect/defendant have the right to defend themselves –

(i) at the investigative stage?
(ii) at the trial stage?
(iii) is there any difference between the first instance and appeal or cassation stage?

If the suspect/defendant does have the right to defend themselves –

(a) What is the source of that right?
(b) When does the right arise?
(c) How is the suspect/defendant to be informed of the right?
(d) Does the right differ depending on the financial resources of the suspect/defendant and/or whether they are legally aided?
(e) Is there any existing evidence as to whether and how this right is exercised?

(2) Does a suspect/defendant have the right to the assistance of a lawyer?

If so –

(a) What is the source of that right?
(b) When does the right arise? (e.g., on arrest, only on being brought before a court, etc.)
(c) How is the suspect/defendant to be informed of the right?
(d) How is a request for a lawyer recorded?
(e) Does the right differ depending on the financial resources of the suspect/defendant and/or whether they are legally aided?
(f) Are there circumstances where legal assistance is mandatory?
(g) Are there any circumstances where legal assistance is not permitted (e.g., during interrogation, at an appearance before a prosecutor, at a hearing before an examining magistrate)?
(h) Is there provision for a right or obligation to a lawyer to be waived by the suspect/defendant?

(3) Does a suspect/defendant have a right to choose his/her lawyer?

If so –

(a) What is the source of that right?

(b) Is the right absolute?

(c) Does the right differ depending on the financial resources of the suspect/defendant

(d) If choice is restricted, does the suspect/defendant have a right to ask for a replacement (e.g., if they do not trust an appointed lawyer)?

(e) Is there any existing evidence as to the exercise of this right?

(4) What are the arrangements for contacting and/or appointing a lawyer?

(a) Are these arrangements contained in law, procedural rules, protocols, etc?

(b) Do they differ depending on the financial resources of the suspect/defendant and/or whether they are legally aided?

(c) How do the arrangements differ if the suspect/defendant is in custody?

(d) Is there any existing evidence as to how these arrangements work in practice? (e.g. the proportion of requests that result in legal assistance being received, delay in contacting lawyers, facilities for legal consultations and whether they are in private, etc.).

(e) Where a suspect/defendant requests a lawyer, are there any restrictions on what the police/prosecutor/court may do before legal assistance is procured?

(5) What provision is there, if any, for indigent suspects/defendants to be provided with legal advice and/or representation free or at reduced cost –

(i) at the investigative stage?
(ii) at the trial stage?
(iii) is there any difference between the first instance and appeal or cassation stage?

If there is such provision –

(a) What is the legal framework for it?

(b) How are suspects/defendants informed of the provision?

(c) Are there any legal or professional obligations on lawyers to provide legal advice and/or representation?

(6) Who makes the decision regarding entitlement to free or subsidised legal advice and/or representation –

(i) at the investigative stage?
(ii) at the trial stage?
(iii) is there any difference between the first instance and appeal or cassation stage?

(d) How is this regulated? (e.g. by law, procedural rules, professional conduct rules, etc.)

    (e) Is there any existing evidence about how the decision-making and appointment process works?

(7) Is there a means test for free or subsidised legal advice and/or representation?

If so –

    (a) What is the legal framework for the means test?
    (b) How is the means test defined?
    (c) Does the means test differ depending on the stage of the proceedings?
    (d) How do eligibility levels relate to possible comparators, e.g. minimum wage?
    (e) Who applies the means test?
    (f) What information has to be supplied by the applicant?
    (g) Are there provisions for the suspect/defendant to make a contribution, and/or for recovery of costs from them (e.g. on conviction)?
    (h) Is there existing evidence about the means test, how it is applied, how long it takes for a decision to be made, what impact it has (if any) on the proceedings (e.g. are proceedings adjourned whilst a decision is made, what length of delays are typical, etc.)?

(8) Is there a merits test for free or subsidised legal advice and/or representation?

If so –

    (a) What is the legal framework for the merits test?
    (b) How is the merits test defined?
    (c) Does the merits test differ depending on the stage of the proceedings?
    (d) Who applies the merits test?
    (e) What information has to be supplied by the applicant?
    (f) Is there existing evidence about the merits test, how it is applied, how long it takes for a decision to be made, and what impact it has (if any) on the proceedings (e.g. are proceedings adjourned whilst a decision is made, what length of delays are typical, etc.)?

(9) Are there any special restrictions on the availability of legal aid, legal advice or representation, choice of lawyer, etc. in terrorist cases?

If so –

    (a) What is the source of the restrictions?
    (b) How are terrorist cases defined?
    (c) Is there existing evidence of the application of the restrictions?

(10) What types of work does legal aid cover, and does this differ depending on the stage of proceedings?

(a) Are there restrictions on the amount of work that can be done/will be paid for?
(b) Does legal aid cover –

- tracing and/or interviewing witnesses?
- carrying out other investigations?
- instructing experts?

(11) Are there any consequences for the accused, or the police/prosecutor, for the admission or use of evidence or for the final decision (sentence), if a suspect/defendant–

(a) Does not have legal advice/representation?
(b) Is not informed about their right to a lawyer or about their right to legal aid?
(c) Who wants a lawyer is denied access to a lawyer or when access to a lawyer is delayed (certain procedural actions (e.g. interview) are carried out in the absence of a lawyer)?
(d) Is denied the right to have a lawyer of his/her own choice, or to have his/her lawyer replaced?

(12) What are the arrangements for the remuneration of lawyers in legal aid cases?

(a) What is the legal framework for remuneration?
(b) Does it differ depending upon the type of case, stage of proceedings, etc.
(c) How do levels of remuneration compare with remuneration for privately funded cases?
(d) Is there any existing evidence on how the system of remuneration works in practice?

4.   Facilitating effective defence

(1) What rights and/or powers do the suspect/defendant and/or their lawyer have to –

(i) Seek evidence?
(ii) Investigate facts?
(iii) Interview prospective witnesses (or require the police/prosecutor to do so)?
(iv) Obtain expert evidence?

In relation to any such right or power –

(a) What is the source of that right?
(b) Is it absolute or conditional?

    (c) Does the exercise of any such right depend on the financial resources of the suspect/defendant or on whether they are in receipt of legal aid?

    (d) Does the exercise of any such right differ for a suspect/defendant who is in custody?

    (e) Are their any professional limitations on a lawyer carrying out any of these activities?

    (f) Is there existing evidence as to whether and how such rights are exercised?

    (g) Are there any sanctions or remedies if a right/power is denied?

(2) What right does the suspect/defendant (personally or by their lawyer) have to apply for bail (i.e., release from custody, whether or not involving a financial obligation) –

(i) during the period following initial (provisional) arrest?
(ii) pending the outcome of the investigation?
(iii) pending final determination of the case?

In relation to any right to apply for bail –

    (a) What is the source of the right?
    (b) Who makes the decision regarding bail?
    (c) Is release on bail dependant on payment of money?
    (d) What conditions, if any, can be imposed when a person is released on bail?
    (e) Does the exercise of the right depend upon the financial resources of the suspect/defendant?
    (f) Is there any existing evidence as to the practical implementation of any right to apply for bail?

(3) What period of notification to the defence is required before any appearance before a prosecutor, judge or court and what provision is there for any hearing to be delayed/adjourned in order to give the accused and/or their lawyer time to prepare?

    (a) What is the source of any period of notification?
    (b) Is there any existing evidence as to how this works in practice?
    (c) Is there any sanction or remedy if the period of notification is not complied with?

(4) With regard to evidence put before a trial court, and witnesses giving oral evidence at court –

(i) Who decides what evidence is to be produced, and which witnesses are to be called to give oral evidence?

(ii) If these decisions are not made by the accused or their lawyer, does the accused or their lawyer have a right to demand that evidence be produced and/or that witnesses be called to give oral evidence?

(iii) What right does the accused or their lawyer have to examine or cross-examine witnesses?

(iv) Is there any provision for evidence obtained illegally or unfairly to be excluded at trial?

In relation to these issues –

(a) What is the legal source of the procedures and rights (if there are such rights)?

(b) Does exercise of any rights depend upon the financial resources of the accused?

(c) Is there any existing evidence as to how the processes work in practice?

(5) Is there a guilty plea and/or expedited hearing procedure (in which the court does not hear and/or review the evidence)?

(a) What is the legal source of such procedures?

(b) How does any guilty plea procedure and/or expedited hearing procedure operate?

(c) What are the formal (legal) incentives for a defendant of entering into a guilty plea/expedited hearing procedure: e.g. sentence discount, bail, etc?

(d) Is there any existing evidence as to how this process works in practice: incentives (formal and informal), plea bargaining, etc.

(6) Does a suspect/defendant have a right to a private consultation with their lawyer –

(i) at the investigative stage, and
(ii) at the trial stage?

(a) What is the source of any such right?

(b) Are there any sanctions or remedies if the right is breached?

If there is a right to a consultation in private –

(a) Are there any limitations on the right?

(b) What is the legal source of the limitations?

(c) Who decides whether a consultation is not to be held in private?

(d) Does it make any difference if the suspect/defendant is in custody?

(e) Is there any existing evidence as to the extent to which the power to limit private consultations is used?

(f) Are there any sanctions or remedies if the right is breached?

(7) Does a lawyer acting for a suspect/defendant have a right to communicate in private with third parties (e.g., witnesses, experts, etc.)?

    (a) What is the source of any such right?
    (b) Are there any limitations on exercising the right?
    (c) Who decides whether any such right is to be interfered with?
    (d) Is there any existing evidence as to the extent to which any such right is interfered with?
    (e) Are there any sanctions or remedies if the right is breached?

(8) Are lawyers subject to any other form of interference with their ability to act in the best interests of their clients?

If yes –

    (a) What interference is permissible, and in what circumstances?
    (b) What is the legal source of any form of interference?
    (c) Does it make any difference if the client is in custody?
    (d) Does it make any difference if the lawyer is funded by legal aid or is a public defender?
    (e) Is there any existing evidence as to the use of such power?
    (f) Are there any sanctions or remedies if there is such an interference?

(9) Is there a bar association?

If yes –

    (a) Is the bar association independent of government and government institutions?
    (b) What is the legal entity of the association?
    (c) Do practicing lawyers have to belong to the bar association?
    (d) Are there any restrictions on membership of the bar association by qualified lawyers?
    (e) Does the bar association have exclusive responsibility for discipline of the legal profession? How does the disciplinary process work?
    (f) Does the bar association have a specialist section for criminal defence lawyers and/or is there a specialist organisation for criminal defence lawyers?
    (g) What are the functions of such specialist section/organisation?

(10) How are the obligations of lawyers to their clients –

(i) Described, and
(ii) Regulated?

(a) Are there any differences in respect of criminal defence lawyers?
(b) Is there a complaints mechanism for clients dissatisfied with the service provided by their lawyer?
(c) Is there any existing evidence as to how the regulation and complaints mechanisms work, especially in relation to criminal defence lawyers?
(d) Are the results of complaints and/or disciplinary proceedings published?

(11) In relation to criminal defence work –

(i) Is the provision of legal services limited to qualified lawyers?
(ii) Are there any minimum quality of service requirements placed on lawyers doing criminal defence work?

If yes to (ii) –

(a) Who are the requirements imposed by?
(b) What are the requirements?
(c) How are they regulated and enforced?
(d) Is there any existing evidence as to how the quality of service requirements operate in practice?

5.   The right to interpretation and translation

(1) Does a suspect or defendant have a right to free assistance of an interpreter if s/he cannot understand or speak the language of their lawyer, the investigator or the court?

If yes –

(a) What is the source of any such right?
(b) How is the need for an interpreter determined?
(c) Who has responsibility for determining it?
(d) Who pays for it?
(e) Is there any existing evidence as to how it works?
(f) Is there any remedy or sanction if the right is breached?

(2) Does a suspect or defendant have a right to free translation of documents, evidence, etc. if s/he cannot understand the language in which they are written?

If yes –

(a) What is the source of any such right?
(b) How is the need for translation determined?
(c) Who has responsibility for determining it?
(d) Who pays for it?
(e) Is there any existing evidence as to how it works?

(f) Is there any remedy or sanction if the right is breached?

(3) Is there any regulation of the competence and independence of interpreters and translators?

(a) What is the source of any such regulation?
(b) How does it work?
(c) Is there any remedy or sanction available to the suspect/defendant if an interpreter or translator is not competent or independent?

6.   Additional guarantees for vulnerable groups

(1) Are there any special provisions concerning –

(i) the right to legal assistance,
(ii) bail, or
(iii) proceedings

for juvenile suspects and defendants?

If yes –

(a) What is the source of any such special provisions?
(b) How is 'juvenile' defined?
(c) What are the special provisions?
(d) Is there any existing evidence as to the use and application of the special provisions?
(e) Is there any remedy or sanction if the special provisions are not provided?

(2) Are there any special provisions concerning –

(i) the right to legal assistance,
(ii) bail, or
(iii) proceedings

for mentally vulnerable suspects and defendants?

If yes –

(a) What is the source of any such special provision?
(b) How is 'mentally vulnerable' defined?
(c) What are the special provisions?
(d) Is there any existing evidence as to the use and application of the special provisions?

(e) Is there any remedy or sanction if the special provisions are not provided?

7.   Guarantees for trials in absentia

(1) Can the accused be tried in his/her absence?

If yes –

  (a) What protection or guarantees exist?
  (b) What is the source of any such protection or guarantee?
  (c) Is there any existing evidence as to the number and proportion of trials conducted in the absence of the accused, and as to how such trial work?
  (d) Is there any remedy or sanction if any such protection or guarantee is breached?

ANNEX 2 CRITICAL ACCOUNT OF THE CRIMINAL JUSTICE SYSTEM PRO-FORMA

Purpose of the critical account

The purpose of the critical account of the criminal justice system in each jurisdiction included in the research study is to provide a critical, dynamic account of the system and processes using existing sources of information in order to provide a context against which data collected during the research study may be understood. Together with the Desk Review, it will provide a basis for determining whether further research is required for the purposes of the country report, and much of the information gathered for both the critical account and the desk review will be used when writing the country report. Where relevant you may cross-refer to information in the Desk Review rather than repeat information.

The overarching goal of the project is to contribute to effective implementation of indigent defendants' rights to real and effective defence, as part of a process of advancing observance of, and respect for, the rule of law and human rights. The specific research objectives are set out in the paper entitled *Research Questions, Data Sources and Methodology*. As noted in that paper, effective criminal defence has three dimensions: the contextual dimension; the procedural dimension; and the outcomes dimension. The critical account will be the principal source of information on the contextual and outcomes dimensions, but may also provide some information on the procedural dimension in so far as this data is available.

The guideline length for the critical account is 8,000 words, although you may feel it necessary to exceed this, and it should broadly follow the structure set out below. Since criminal justice systems in most jurisdictions are, to a greater or lesser extent, changing rapidly the account should be dynamic in the sense of conveying the primary characteristics of those changes and the 'direction of travel'. Where available, reference should be made to existing data, statistics, and other existing research evidence. Referencing should follow the style in the sample chapter from *Suspects in Europe*.

1.   Introduction

A brief introduction to the criminal justice system and processes, describing its typical characteristics, the significant areas of change in the past 10 years, the application of the European Convention on Human Rights (ECHR), major recent or current issues (e.g. terrorism, prison overcrowding, immigrants and crime, etc.).

2.   Crime in its social and political context

    (a) Brief geo-political information, e.g., population, concentrations of populations, ethnicities.

(b) Crime levels, whether they increasing/declining/static, how crime is measured, incarceration rates (both for sentenced and non-sentenced prisoners), ethnic profiles of suspect/defendant and imprisoned populations.

(c) The public and political perceptions of crime – whether crime is a major consideration for the public and in the media, the place of crime in political debate, fear of crime, statistics on and perceptions of whether crime is largely committed by e.g., poor people, 'outsiders' (egg ethnic minorities), organised gangs, etc.

(d) Attitudes to dealing with suspects and defendants, and whether these are changing, e.g., can attitudes be described as liberal, are they becoming more or less punitive, are punitive measure popular, perceptions of human rights norms as they relate to crime and those accused of crime.

(e) Political and public perceptions of criminal justice professionals and institutions – lawyers, police, prosecutors, judges and the courts.

(f) Political and public perceptions of and attitudes to state expenditure on the criminal justice system, and to expenditure on legal aid/assistance to suspects/defendants.

(g) Political and public perceptions of justice and access to justice, especially in the case of poor suspects/defendants.

(h) Perceptions and awareness of rights within the criminal justice system.

3.   **The structure and processes of the criminal justice system**

(a) The basic tradition and characteristics of the criminal justice system e.g. inquisitorial/adversarial.

(b) Relevant stages of the criminal process and the relevant nomenclature (e.g., in England and Wales there are essentially three stages: (1) Pre-charge or investigative stage when the subject of the enquiry is known as the suspect; (2) From charge to trial, when the person is known as the defendant or accused; (3) Post-conviction, when the person is known as the convicted person or criminal, or appellant if they are appealing against conviction and/or sentence).

(c) Classification of offences.

(d) The structure and functions of the criminal courts, first instance and appellate.

(e) How criminal proceedings are initiated and processed, including the basic stages (e.g. arrest, charge, plea), and whether guilty pleas or expedited proceedings are possible (and the extent of use of such procedures).

(f) Whether there are mechanisms for dealing with criminal conduct by administrative means (and the extent of use of such mechanisms).

(g) The relationship between the investigative stage and the trial stage – the principle of immediacy in theory and practice, the use of pre-trial statements of the accused and witnesses as evidence at trial, mechanisms for excluding illegally or unfairly obtained evidence.

(h) Who decides what material is to go before the trial court, and which witnesses are to be called to give oral evidence.

4.   Criminal justice professionals and institutions

(a) The role of the police, prosecutors and judges, the structures and institutions within which they operate, and their relationships with each other.
(b) The role of criminal defence lawyers and the structures within which they operate (egg public defenders, private practice, the extent of specialisation, etc.).
(c) Perceptions of criminal defence work within the legal profession.
(d) The relationship between criminal defence lawyers and other criminal justice professions and institutions.

5.   The organisation of legal aid

A description of the legal aid system and other mechanisms for providing legal services to poor and relatively poor suspects and defendants, including:

(a) whether there is an institution that has overall responsibility for legal aid, and a description of its status and functions;
(b) how legally-aided legal services are delivered, e.g. through the private bar, through a public defender service, etc.
(c) if legally-aided services are provided through the private bar, the organisational arrangements, e.g., restrictions on which lawyers/firms can provide legal aid services;
(d) financial arrangements relating to legal aid, e.g., whether lawyers are paid on a per case basis, whether they are paid for time spent or a fixed fee, etc.

6.   Rights and freedoms

Whether, and/or how, the following are given effect, in theory and in practice:

(a) the presumption of innocence
(b) the 'right to silence'
(c) the burden of proof
(d) the right to a reasoned judgement
(e) the right to appeal

7.   Conclusions

The major issues and challenges for the criminal justice system over the next few years, including the major issues arising from the desk review and major prospective changes to the criminal justice system and/or processes.

8.   Selected bibliography

The major books, research reports and other sources on the criminal justice system and processes (both those in English and those in the language of the relevant jurisdiction).

ANNEX 3 GUIDANCE FOR COUNTRY REPORTS

1.   Purpose of the country reports

The country reports serve two primary purposes. First, they provide the major source of information (in addition to the desk review and critical account) in respect of the nine countries in the study on which the research team will base its analysis, conclusions and recommendations. Second, they will form discrete chapters of the book that will be published out of the research.

2.   The need to be analytical and critical

Before writing the country report you will have feedback from the country reviewer and the research team. It is important that the country reports are both analytical and critical. There are normally significant differences between what the law states and what actually happens in practice, and as far as possible a person reading your report should be left with an understanding of what those differences are and how important they are. We will circulate the England and Wales country report as soon as it is completed as an example of what we mean by 'analytical and critical'.

We recognise that in all jurisdictions there is a lack of data and empirical research on the criminal justice system and processes. Lack of data is, in itself, an important finding. Lack of empirical research should not prevent you from using the best available evidence in order to analyse, and draw conclusions about, the aspects of the criminal justice system and processes in which this research project is interested.

3.   Word limit

The maximum total number of words (excluding footnotes) is 15,000. It is important that, as far as possible, you comply with this as there are limits on the total size of the book of which the country reports will form a part. However, we recognise that this is a difficult task and that your report may be a couple of thousand more words than this.

4.   Writing guidelines

In addition to this document, you will be supplied with *Authors instructions*. Please make sure that you look at them and follow them as far as possible. In addition, please note the following:

> (a) You report must follow the structure of the country report guidelines set out below.

(b) You must use no more than three levels of headings, following the numbering system below. In order to ensure that all country reports are consistently structured, all headings that are numbered in the structure below (e.g. 2, 2.3, 2.3.1 – but not a), b)) must be used in the same way and in the same order, using the same words for the heading. Level 2 or 3 headings that are not specified below (e.g. 1.1, 2.1.1) are within your discretion. You should not use numbered headings beyond Level 3 (e.g., you should not have a heading numbered 2.1.1.1 or 2.1.1.2).

(c) In order to make the reports readable for a non-lawyer readership, the precise reference to code and legislative provisions should be put in a footnote rather than in the text. For example, in the text you may write 'The Criminal Code provides that...', with the relevant provision or paragraph number being placed in a footnote.

(d) All monetary values should be expressed in Euros, with the local currency equivalent being put in a footnote.

(e) Where interviews, or other forms of field work, have been conducted for the purpose of writing the country report, this should briefly be explained, either in the introduction section or in a footnote when the research is first referred to. If the research includes interviews, a brief indication should be given of the status of the interviewees should be given (e.g. five judges, three prosecutors and six lawyers who undertake criminal defence work) together with the period over which the interview were conducted (e.g., Interviews were conducted between 1 May 2009 and 15 June 2009 in three cities including London.).

5. Structure of the country report

As noted above, the country report must follow this structure.

5.1. *Introduction (up to five pages)*

This should set the scene for understanding the report and its findings. Researchers can decide what information to include [e.g., specificities of criminal justice systems; country information; poverty levels, discrimination and other major social and political issues if relevant, etc.]. There should be some reference to size of population and other basic demographic information so that a reader unfamiliar with the country has some understanding of it.

The introduction must include a section on the organisation of legal aid:

- spending on criminal legal aid;
- organisational responsibility for administering it;
- methods of delivering legal aid services (e.g. private lawyers, public defenders, duty solicitor schemes, etc);
- eligibility;

- methods of application for and/or appointment of lawyers funded by the state; and
- stages of the criminal process at which it is available.

5.2. *Legal rights and their implementation:*

5.2.1. The right to information

Including –

- the nature and cause of the accusation
- detailed information (right of access to, or copies of the file) concerning the relevant evidence/material available to the police/prosecutor/examining magistrate
- letter of rights (information on rights)

5.2.2. The right to defend oneself

Including –

- the right of a suspect/defendant to defend themselves
- the right to legal advice and/or representation

This section should include:

(a) the point at which the right arises
(b) choice of lawyer,
(c) provision for the lawyer to be provided free if they cannot afford a lawyer and the interests of justice so require,
(d) arrangements for access to lawyers,
(e) whether there is right to consult, and communicate in private, with the lawyer,
(f) how the right to an independent and competent lawyer who is professionally required to act in the best interests of their client is given effect,
(g) any special provisions for vulnerable suspects/defendants.
(h) existence of legal aid schemes
(i) remuneration of lawyers

5.2.3. Procedural rights

5.2.3.1. The right to release from custody pending trial

5.2.3.2. The right of a defendant to be tried in their presence

5.2.3.3. The right to be presumed innocent

5.2.3.4. The right to silence

5.2.3.5. The right to reasoned decisions

5.2.3.6. The right to appeal

Analysis of each of the procedural rights listed above should include:

    (a) Legal recognition (of the right in general terms)
    (b) Procedural protection (procedural mechanisms designed to ensure that the right can be effectively realized)
    (c) Evidence about how the right is implemented in practice
    (d) Analysis/evidence of how it works for poor defendants
    (e) Analysis/evidence of how it works for ethnic minorities, where relevant (i.e. when: 1. laws and procedures discriminate against minorities on their face, or operate to have a disproportionate impact; 2. there is evidence of discrimination against minorities in granting access to certain rights as established in prior research)

Researchers are encouraged to refer to ECtHR judgments against their country where relevant.

5.2.4. Rights relating to effective defence

5.2.4.1. The right to investigate the case

Including rights to –

    - equality of arms (including the right to be *present* at investigative acts such as identification line-ups or search)
    - seek evidence
    - investigate facts
    - interview prospective witnesses
    - obtain expert evidence

5.2.4.2. *The right to adequate time and facilities for preparation of defence*

5.2.4.3. *The right to equality of arms in examining witnesses*

(This refers to the right to secure the attendance of witnesses, and to examine or to have examined witnesses, favourable to the defendant on the same conditions as those against them.)

5.2.4.4. *The right to free interpretation of documents and translation*

(i.e., during interrogation/hearings/communication with counsel for suspects/defendants who cannot understand or speak the language.)

5.3. *Professional culture of defence lawyers*

Lawyers' role in criminal proceedings and their duty to the client as reflected in ethical rules and standards, and as perceived by lawyers and other actors; the existence (or otherwise) of unified professional body(ies) and their role/perceptions of their role; the extent to which the legal profession(s) take responsibility for legal aid, and other related issues.

5.4. *Political commitment to effective criminal defence*

Analysis of government policies in the areas of criminal defence and legal aid, and in related fields – e.g. crime and criminal justice policy, minorities, poverty – if they affect the realisation of effective criminal defence rights.

5.5. *Conclusions*

Analysis of the position of poor defendants in criminal proceedings in light of the findings set out in the country report

ANNEX 4 THE ROLE OF THE COUNTRY REVIEWER

The role of the country reviewer is essentially to review the Country Report for their respective country in order to 'validate' it. This is particularly important because (a) in most countries there is a lack of empirical evidence as to how the criminal justice system 'works', and (b) it is very important for the success of the project that the country reports are regarded as fair and valid accounts.

The in-country researcher for each country will, as a first stage, have worked on a Desk Review and a Critical Account. The Country Report is based on this work together with any further research conducted following consultation with the research project team, and should be written in compliance with a structure supplied to the in-country researcher (a copy of which is supplied to the country reviewer). The country reviewer need only read the Country Report, and does not need to read the Desk Review or the Critical Account.

In reviewing the Country Report the country reviewer should:

- correct any factual errors;
- make appropriate suggestions regarding the clarity of the report, taking into account the requirement that it be readily understood by readers from other jurisdictions;
- consider the validity of any conclusions drawn from the available evidence and make any appropriate suggestions.

This should be provided in a written report that is given to, and discussed with, the in-country research, and also sent to the research project team.

A peer-reviewed book series in which the common foundations of the legal systems of the Member States of the European Community are the central focus.

The *Ius Commune Europaeum* series includes horizontal comparative legal studies as well as studies on the effect of treaties within the national legal systems. All the classic fields of law are covered. The books are published in various European languages under the auspices of METRO, the Institute for Transnational Legal Research at the Maastricht University.

Recently published:

Volume 76: *European Cooperation between Financial Supervisory Authorities, Tax Authorities and Judicial Authorities*, M. Luchtman
Volume 77: *Access to Justice and the Judiciary: Towards New European Standards of Affordability, Quality and Efficiency of Civil Adjudication*, A. Uzelac and C.H. van Rhee (eds.)
Volume 78: *The European Private Company (SPE): A Critical Analysis of the EU Draft Statute*, D.F.M.M. Zaman, C.A. Schwarz, M.L. Lennarts, H.-J. de Kluiver and A.F.M. Dorresteijn (eds.)
Volume 79: *Constitutions Compared. An Introduction to Comparative Constitutional Law* (2nd edition), A.W. Heringa and Ph. Kiiver
Volume 80: *Rechtsbescherming en overheidsovereenkomsten*, K. Wauters
Volume 81: *Derden in het contractenrecht*, I. Samoy
Volume 82: *The Right to Specific Performance. The Historical Development*, J.H. Dondorp and J.J. Hallebeek (eds.)
Volume 83: *Financial Supervision in a Comparative Perspective*, M. Poto
Volume 84: *Enforcement and Enforceability – Tradition and Reform*, C.H. van Rhee and A. Uzelac (eds.)
Volume 85: *Fact-Finding in Civil Litigation. A Comparative Perspective*, R. Verkerk
Volume 86: *The Making of Chinese Condominium Law. A Comparative Perspective with American and South African Condominium Laws*, L. Chen
Volume 87: *Effective Criminal Defence in Europe*, E. Cape, Z. Namoradze, R. Smith and T. Spronken